VERNACULAR ELOQUENCE

D1262447

VERNACULAR ELOQUENCE

What Speech Can Bring to Writing

Peter Elbow

OXFORD
UNIVERSITY PRESS

OXFORD

UNIVERSITY PRESS

Oxford University Press, Inc., publishes works that further
Oxford University's objective of excellence
in research, scholarship, and education.

Oxford New York

Auckland   Cape Town   Dar es Salaam   Hong Kong   Karachi
Kuala Lumpur   Madrid   Melbourne   Mexico City   Nairobi
New Delhi   Shanghai   Taipei   Toronto

With offices in

Argentina   Austria   Brazil   Chile   Czech Republic   France   Greece
Guatemala   Hungary   Italy   Japan   Poland   Portugal   Singapore
South Korea   Switzerland   Thailand   Turkey   Ukraine   Vietnam

Published by Oxford University Press, Inc.
198 Madison Avenue, New York, NY 10016

www.oup.com

Oxford is a registered trademark of Oxford University Press

Library of Congress Cataloging-in-Publication Data
Elbow, Peter.
Vernacular eloquence : what speech can bring to writing / Peter Elbow.
p.   cm.
ISBN 978-0-19-978250-5 (cloth : alk. paper)—ISBN 978-0-19-978251-2 (pbk. : alk. paper)
1. Language and languages—Style. 2. Narration (Rhetoric) 3. Rhetoric. I. Title.
P301.E48   2011
808—dc22   2011011432

Two cartoons from Michael Leunig's *Goatperson and Other Tales* (1999)
reproduced with permission by Penguin Group (Australia).

1 3 5 7 9 8 6 4 2

Printed in the United States of America
on acid-free paper

To my wife Cami, with my deepest love and appreciation.
And she "has grammar and spelling for two." (W. S. Gilbert)

The lexis, grammar, and larger structures of oral and written language may become alike, with the norm being a writing that is largely indistinguishable from speech.
(Horowitz and Samuels, "Comprehending Oral and Written Language" 1)

I am inclined to think the written language of the future will go back (or rather forward) to being more processlike . . . the traditional objectlike nature of written discourse is itself changing . . .
(Halliday, "Spoken and Written Modes of Meaning" 79)

When writers are able to talk their text into a computer, speech errors may suddenly appear in writing. But other things may also happen. Writing, as some linguists and computer experts suggest, may change form and become more speechlike, more like a talking text than we now know, but yet not "speech writ down." There is also the possibility that what will emerge will be a "friendlier" text than could or would be produced by the pen or typewriter.
(Horowitz and Samuels, "Comprehending Oral and Written Language" 26)

I feel sorrow for those students whom education has made tone deaf. . . . Books henceforth shall be seen and [no longer] heard.
(Ivan Illich, "Vernacular Values" 46 and 36)

From *Goatperson and Other Tales*, by Michael Leunig.

Contents

Acknowledgments

I'm indebted to far more people than I can name here. For these eight years, whenever I've chatted with anyone—at a conference or at a party or on a train—the topic of speech and writing always seemed to come up. I've picked every brain I could find. I'll name a few people here and hope that I'm not forgetting or repressing those who gave me especially good help.

Most important to me have been Don Jones and Irene Papoulis, my precious writing group.

I got especially rich, helpful, and engaged responses from Helen Fox, Pat Schneider, John Trimbur, and Craig Hancock.

These are some of the people who have helped my thinking about speech and writing or seen parts of drafts at various stages and given me useful responses: Janet Bean, Pat Belanoff, Sheridan Blau, Maria Jose Botelho, Kathy Cassity, Wallace Chafe, Jane Danielewicz, John Dawkins, Christiane Donahue, Rosalia Dutra, Robert Eddy, Ed Finegan, David Fleming, Lisa Green, A. R. Gurney, Jr., Jim Hartley, Anne Herrington, Rosalind Horowitz, Asao Inoue, Suzie and Ricky Jacobs, Dick Johnson, Steve Katz, Eileen Kennedy, Stephanie Kerschbaum, Carmen Kynard, Catherine Madsen, Paul Matsuda, Rebecca de Wind Mattingly, Charlie Moran, Tom Newkirk, Arthur Palacas, Tony Papirio, Edward J. Pelz, Brian Street, Tom Roeper, Hephzibah Roskelly, Haj Ross, Deb Rossenkill, Erika Scheurer, Mary Scott, Peggy Speas, BJ Tomlinson, Camilla Vasquez, Ruth and Lloyd Weinreb, Wini Wood, John Wright. Many thanks to the DGG for early help and support.

I was able to teach a couple of graduate seminars on speech and writing and I'm grateful for what I've learned from the students.

For a number of years, the topic at the UMass Symposium for the Study of Writing and Teaching Writing has hovered around issues of speech and writing. I thank the faculty members who've attended for what I've learned from them.

I'm particularly fortunate for the generous help from people at Oxford University Press: Patterson Lamb, Shannon McLachlan, Brendan O'Neill, and Rick Stinson.

With this much help, the book should be perfect! Unfortunately I wasn't smart enough to benefit from all the good things that people sent my way.

VERNACULAR ELOQUENCE

Introduction to the Book

THE OBSESSION THAT has kept me energized for the eight years of writing this book takes the form of both anger and excitement. I've long been angry at how our present culture of "proper literacy" tells us that we are not supposed to do our serious writing in the mother tongue we know best and possess in our bones—but rather only in the prestige, correct, edited version of standardized English or what I will sometimes call "correct writing." This helps explain a lot that we see about serious writing in the world. Many people have learned to *manage* or *handle* adequately "correct English," but in doing so, they muffle or clog their thoughts into language that's far less clear and interesting than they could have used in the language of their talking. Many other people don't even feel that writing is an option for them and feel excluded—yet they speak smart, eloquent, interesting things. And finally, even many of those who can write well are often reluctant to write, and they are continually distracted as they write by nagging critical voices.

I can't change our culture's more or less single standard for the language of serious literate writing (though I'll discuss in the last two chapters a radical change that's coming faster than most of us realize). But I can show how speakers of all the many versions of English can not only *use* their mother tongue (or whatever language comes most easily to mind and mouth) for serious writing, but in fact *improve* their serious writing by doing so.

More recent than my anger is my excitement. For most of my career, I've known how useful it is to invite *wrong* writing on the way to right writing. I've been a champion of freewriting. Like many others, I've known that freewritten language tends to be lively and even clear (though often not usable as it comes out). What's new for me is a much richer understanding of the myriad linguistic and rhetorical virtues in unplanned spoken language—virtues that most people can't find when they are engaged in serious writing.

Two Worlds of Writing

There's a newish world of writing where lots of people are busy all hours of the day and night emailing, tweeting, and blogging on the internet. Students startle their professors by sending chatty emails using the slang they write to buddies on Facebook. Much writing in this new world is a kind of "speaking onto the screen"; indeed, plenty of people, especially "literate people," don't consider this writing to *be* writing. *"Email? That's not writing!"* Actually, people have been writing in everyday vernacular spoken language for centuries in diaries, informal personal letters, grocery lists, and exploratory musings to figure out their feelings or thoughts. (The central terms here, "speech" and "writing," are slippery. I'll do some careful defining in the Introductions to Parts One and Two.)

But writing online and in diaries does not destroy a second world of "literate" writing—*"real"* writing—the serious writing that people have to do for school, college, workplace, and the "literate" media: all kinds of essays, articles, reports, studies, and memos. Think of job and college applications and how much the language matters. Most magazine and book writing is supposed to be literate—along with most newspaper writing and even letters to the editor. I'm trying to write literate or correct writing in this book—more or less. "Literate" implies Edited Written English (EWE)—where "edited" means "correct"—which means standardized English ("standard" or prestige). Shorthand: "no mistakes." Students are constantly warned not to confuse their everyday speech with "serious" writing. EWE or standardized written English is a dialect or language that differs in grammar and register from everyday speech. The distance between everyday speech and literate writing is most obvious in the case of speech that people often call "bad": nonprestige versions of English like Black or Latino or working-class English. But even I, growing up White, comfortable middle class, middle Atlantic—growing into a version of English called "standard" and even "good"—even I am not supposed to use my everyday unmonitored talk-language for serious writing. In short, *"correct writing" is no one's mother tongue.*

So in one world of writing, people feel free to speak onto the screen or page; in the other, people feel pressured to avoid speech on the page. I won't join the chorus of literate commentators who lament all the bad writing in the world of email and web. I see problems with writing in *both* worlds. I'd say that *most* writing is not very good, whether it's literate writing or "e-writing," and whether it comes from students, amateurs, well-educated people, or learned scholars. Considering all that's written and published, not so much is really smart, interesting, and worth reading—not so much of it gives "delight and instruction" (to use Horace's formulation). My goal in this book is to show how to improve *careful literate* writing, though what I say will also help people tweet better.

Here are two arguments I'm *not* making: First, *Let's just use everyday unplanned speech for all writing, not just for email and chat rooms.* No. Second, *If we want good writing, let's <u>avoid</u> unplanned speech.* No. I'm suggesting a third approach:

> Let's <u>welcome</u> unplanned speech for the rich resources it has, even for careful writing, but nevertheless learn ways to keep what's valuable—and ways to change what needs changing.

This is a way of relating to speech that many genuinely good writers have been using for ages. But I can help many more people learn it—getting the benefits of speech for careful writing. And with this approach to speech, I can help more people write more comfortably and better—and also help teachers teach better. In short, I'll show how even serious, formal, and "literate" writing can be even more careful and better, paradoxically enough, if it enlists the various resources of careless speech. We can find these resources in the kind of speech we don't have to think about or monitor, the kind of language that we blurt. Much of this book is an extended analysis of many unnoticed features of everyday speech that turn out to be sorely needed for good careful writing. You might say that this book represents my love affair with speech—and my conviction that (despite this metaphor) I can bring her home to live with me and my wife, writing.

The Practical and Theoretical Goals

From a practical point of view, I'll be suggesting two major concrete ways to enlist speech for writing: talking onto the page at the early stages of writing (the theme of Part Two); and reading aloud to revise at the late stages (the theme of Part Three). These two uses of the tongue can help people write better and with more enjoyment—whether they are writing school essays, workplace reports and memos, magazine articles, newspaper op eds, poems, or memoirs. (Note that I am mostly ignoring in this book the huge and necessary middle stages of *substantive revising*—the careful conscious process of trying to get our thinking and organization straight. I give two practical suggestions for revising in Chapter 10, but I don't see much role for the tongue in revising— except for the obvious value of talking things over with others.)

But if practical advice were my *only* goal, this book would be much shorter. My larger project here is to ask readers to rethink the very nature of speech and writing and how they relate to each other. Above all, I want to rethink what our culture means by *literacy*. I might as well state here my underlying claim in all its nakedness:

> Every person who has some version of English as a native language *already* knows enough to produce excellent writing in English and good enough punctuation—even if they speak a nonprestige version of English and don't read much.

I can give more force to this very large claim by spelling out some qualifications that will emerge:

- Careful substantive revising requires careful thinking. Not everyone can do that. But it doesn't take new knowledge, it takes practice.
- Much serious writing requires a final draft in "correct English." To produce this without help—to get rid of everything commonly called mistakes or bad or wrong English—requires specialized knowledge that we don't get for free with our native spoken language.
- When people want to write in certain genres about substantive topics— for example, about politics or climate change or God—they can't usually produce excellent writing without some of the substantive information and vocabulary and genre-knowledge that goes with those topics. Still, in certain genres like personal essays, creative nonfiction, or poetry, it *is* possible to write brilliantly about politics, climate change, or God—without any special knowledge.

I'm not claiming that good writing is easy. Just because we know enough to do something well doesn't make it easy. Good writing almost always takes hard work—sometimes struggle. As John Dewey insisted, the mere *possession* of knowledge or experience is not enough; we have to *reflect* on it—work with it and exploit it in ways that I explore in the book. In Part Three, for example, I emphasize the need to stop and listen and reflect on the spoken language we get for free with our native speech.

Still, I stand by the naked claim as a useful summary of the book: everyone with a native language has what it takes to write well and punctuate adequately.

Much of what I suggest here is a call for more work with the mouth and ear. Our knowledge of our native language is mostly tacit. It's kinesthetic—as though it's in the body. We don't have to think consciously to use our spoken vernacular in all its complexity. When the linguist Tom Roeper looks at how humans (especially children) speak with mastery of their native language, he notes, "The body is just an extension of the mind" (20). (See too Mark Johnson, *The Body in the Mind: The Bodily Basis of Meaning, Imagination, and Reason*.) But in order to use the tacit knowledge in our mouths and ears for good writing, we will need to engage in plenty of conscious reflection and thinking.

Nor do I run away from putting my argument in its negative form: that our culture of literacy functions as though it were a plot against the spoken voice,

I've permitted myself to speak loosely, seeming to equate "mother tongue," "home language," "vernacular," and "language that comes most easily to mind and mouth." I was first alerted to the genuine differences one day when I gave a workshop for adult college students and invited them to do a bit of private writing in their mother tongue. In the discussion afterward, a young man who grew up in the Caribbean said something like this: "Thank you; I enjoyed it; that was interesting. But it was *hard*. I haven't used that language in many years. It's much easier for me to write in the language I have to use for school papers and grant proposals." His response forced me to clarify my pragmatic priority: my main goal is to harness for writing whatever language comes quickest and easiest to mind and mouth. He helped me realize that this language might well *not* be the "mother tongue" or even the language used at home. And yet that young man from the Caribbean might well have some linguistic and cognitive riches available to him in the very language that didn't come so quickly to mind and mouth.

So I'm afraid I will persist in my imprecision and tend to lump all those terms together. More often than not, the language that comes most easily—the "untaught vernacular"—will tend to be "native" and "home." When there are differences, I'd say, go for what's quick and easy—but keep your ear out for any "vernacular" advantages you might be neglecting. My main argument is about the linguistic power and sophistication of what virtually everyone begins to possess viscerally before the age of four. I have to trust that readers careful enough to catch my lack of imprecision will remember this qualification and keep it in mind as they read. (Keith Gilyard has already called me forcefully on this imprecision in previous essays.)

the human body, vernacular language, and those without privilege. That is, our pervasive cultural assumptions about speech, writing, and literacy—especially as they are communicated through schooling—seem as though they were designed to make it harder than necessary for people to become comfortably and powerfully literate. The seeds of this book have lain dormant in my first book about writing, *Writing Without Teachers*. I now enrich my argument that teachers are not necessary for learning to write well. In fact, institutional instruction sometimes gets in the way.

> This is not far from a larger argument made by Ivan Illich in his "Vernacular Values." He's interested in even broader more pervasive economic and political "vernacular values"—and in particular the loss of them. He points out that the word
>
> > [v]ernacular comes from an Indo-Germanic root that implies "rootedness" and "abode." *Vernaculum* as a Latin word was used for whatever was homebred, homespun, homegrown, homemade as opposed to what was obtained in formal exchange. . . . Varro . . . picked the term to introduce the same distinction in language. For him, vernacular speech is made up of the words and patterns grown on the speaker's own ground, as opposed to what is grown elsewhere and then transported [through formal exchange]. And since Varro's authority was widely recognized, his definition stuck. (41)

In the last section, I'll try to show that we are moving with surprising speed toward a different culture of literacy—"vernacular literacy." We're already well into a culture that invites spoken language into correct writing—as long as it is mainstream speech ("White") and also avoids "grammar mistakes." But we're on our way, I'll argue, toward a culture of literacy in which *all* spoken vernaculars of English will be considered valid for serious writing. Writing will no longer be judged against *two* standards as it is now: correctness and quality. The only standard for both writers and readers will be the primal one: is the writing any good?

For this development, Dante provides a model. In a small book, *De Vulgari Eloquentia,* he argued that the vernacular language of children and nursemaids in his native Florence was in fact *nobler* than Latin—and he was writing in the fourteenth century when Latin was the only language considered acceptable for serious writing. I'm not claiming that the various vernacular versions of everyday spoken English are in themselves *nobler* than edited written English—merely that they contain a rich store of eloquent linguistic resources that are badly needed *even* for our most careful and formal written English.

I stole Dante's title for my book. But I didn't call it *Vulgar Eloquence* because his Latin word *vulgar* doesn't mean "vulgar" in English; it means "the common tongue or the ordinary language of the people." So my title, *Vernacular Eloquence,* is the most accurate way to translate *De Vulgari Eloquentia*. Notice, by the way, how a word that used to mean simply *ordinary* and *of the people* has slid into meaning *coarse, dirty,* or *obscene.* That linguistic change points to the theme of my book.

What Kind of Book Is This?

It's certainly not a step-by-step manual or practical handbook. My main goal is to change how everyone *thinks* about writing and literacy—to change the widespread tendency to stress the differences between speech and writing. I'll be showing all kinds of useful similarities, overlaps, and hybrids. That makes the book theoretical. Yet the theory is practical because I describe two concrete practical activities that will help people write better and with more satisfaction.

Is this a book for a broad audience or for teachers and scholars? When I wrote *Writing Without Teachers* in 1973, I didn't worry about teachers and scholars. I was trying to stand on a hilltop and shout to everyone who wants to write. But teachers and scholars eventually read my book and it affected the way many of them thought about writing and taught it. This time I'm making my job harder by trying for a more diverse audience: not just writers and potential writers, but teachers too—and also scholars and researchers. I can't pretend I've mastered the frightening array of scholarship that this book bears on. But I have explored some of it and I will occasionally describe it quickly.

Trickier still, I'm also trying to write for people in the general intellectual community who think about writing and literacy but don't care about the scholarship. I'm thinking about people who read articles and reviews about writing in *The New Yorker* and the *New York Times* by writers like Louis Menand or Adam Gopnik; or books about literacy like Sven Birkerts's *The Gutenberg Elegies,* Lynne Truss's *Eats, Shoots & Leaves,* Richard Lanham's *The Electronic Word: Democracy, Technology, and the Arts,* and Robert Darnton's *The Case for Books: Past, Present, and Future;* or books about language and thinking by writers like Steven Pinker, Oliver Sacks, and Malcolm Gladwell.

But how can I speak to scholars without clogging up the text for general readers? I won't use footnotes, but I have put bits of scholarly reference or discussion into shaded boxes—right at the spot on the page where they pertain. Readers can simply glance at a box when they enounter it and make a quick decision about whether to read it, skim it, or skip it. They won't have to turn to the end of the chapter or the book or even to the bottom of the page. I love the information, ideas, and complications in these boxes and deep down hope that everyone will read them, but I recognize that many readers will simply want to follow my main line of thinking and not be slowed down. But the material in the boxes is not usually very technical and will often interest general readers.

How does this book differ from two of my earlier books, Writing Without Teachers *and* Writing With Power? In this book I'm working out a large theory whereas in those books I was trying to be mostly practical. I'm implying here the same *writing process* that I explicitly advised in those books: a dialectical alternation between easy freewriting and drafting on the one hand, and careful conscious revising and editing on the other. But conceptually, those books were framed entirely in terms of *writing*. This one looks through the lens of speech. Till now, I didn't understand the role of speech and spoken language in writing—even in freewriting.

Overview of Sections

Part One: What's Best in Speaking and Writing?

I explore here the various advantages in both speech and writing as human ways of using language. I spend much more time exploring speech. It's new territory among most teachers and theorists of writing. It turns out that there are many virtues in unplanned careless spontaneous spoken language—virtues that we seldom notice because such language is usually unsatisfactory for serious careful writing. The goal of the book is to take all the virtues of speech and combine them with all the virtues of writing. That's not quite possible, but it's helpful to try to get as close as possible to that ideal.

Part Two: Speaking onto the Page: A Role for the Tongue in the Early Stages of Writing

We can enlist many of the virtues of unplanned speaking and spoken language during the early exploratory and drafting stages of writing by "speaking onto the page"—letting our fingers be guided by the mental process we use effortlessly in everyday speaking. Freewriting is the easiest and most obvious way to learn this process. When we revise with care, we can *retain* those virtues of easy speech—even for writing that ends up "correct" and far from speech—and get rid of what's not suitable.

Part Three: Reading Aloud to Revise: A Role for the Tongue during Late Stages of Writing

Careful reading aloud is far different from careless speaking, but it's another powerful way to use the untutored tongue for writing. We can harness this process of careful reading out loud for the late stage of revising (after substantive revising). If we read every sentence aloud carefully with full investment—and if we then fiddle and adjust our words till they feel right in the mouth and sound right in the ear—the resulting sentence will be strong and clear. It may not be correct for standardized English, and the register might be too colloquial for the genre we are using, but it will have what's most precious and hard to get in writing: clarity and strength. Problems in correctness and register can be fixed during final revising. Reading aloud is not just for sentences. It will also help us improve weaknesses in longer passages and in organization.

In contrast to the generative process of easy speaking onto the page, careful reading aloud is an editing or testing process that involves critical, self-conscious scrutiny. Where speaking onto the page accepts everything that comes to mouth, reading aloud rejects much of it. Reading aloud reshapes what is unclear and awkward. Yet both speaking and reading aloud rely entirely on the untutored tongue, indeed on the body: on the linguistic knowledge that we have somehow internalized and made tacit since toddlerhood.

Part Four: Vernacular Literacy

Our present culture of proper literacy demands what is, in a sense, a single grammatical and rhetorical standard for serious literate writing—that is, for Edited Written English. I don't defend this standard, but I assume that it will be with us for the time being—even though, as I show, its grip is loosening in certain limited ways. This restriction makes writing harder because the language differs from everyone's native spoken language. Few students or professionals can prosper unless they produce writing that is "correct." So for most of the book, I am addressing a short-term pragmatic goal: how to use our untutored tongues—our various spoken vernaculars—to make it easier to write pieces that will end up meeting that single standard of prestige nonspoken language.

But in this final section, I look first at the difficulties caused by our single standard; then I turn to a new culture of literacy in which the various versions of spoken English will finally be accepted as appropriate and valid for serious important writing. This development may sound implausible, but I explore many reasons our present culture of literacy is bringing it to birth. It took four or five hundred years for Dante's hometown spoken vernacular dialect to become the accepted standard for all serious writing in Italy, but I'd say that it's only a matter of a few scores of years before we see our new culture of vernacular literacy.

It may scare people to contemplate this new culture of vernacular literacy. It will introduce what might look at first like anarchy in literacy. But the anarchy of the world wide web is bringing rapid change to the kinds of writing that many people are willing to accept and enjoy. I explore how our culture will begin to take multiple written versions of English in stride and how this change will actually *advance* literacy in the true sense. More people will learn to write better in more ways, and more people will find excellent things to read. We'll no longer have the present situation in which potential writers get the following message:

> *First show that you can write correctly. Then we'll see whether you can write anything good.*

In the new culture of vernacular literacy, the only standard for both writers and readers will be the primal one: is the writing any good? Readers will learn better what they are already starting to learn: if they want good writing, they need to look for it in spoken versions of English—even in versions different from their own.

Literacy Stories

Between most of the chapters I have inserted very short "Literacy Stories." They sketch moments in the history of writing and literacy at different periods in history and in different places around the globe. I want to immerse readers in some of the wildly diverse ways in which humans have used written language.

I also intend these stories as entertaining interludes or changes of pace from the longer discursive chapters. ("Interludes" are little plays or entertainments that are slipped between the main events—half-time shows, as it were.

Inter = "between"; *ludus* = "play" or "game.") But cumulatively, I trust they will reinforce the larger project of the book. I want to jiggle the widespread assumption that there is some kind of best or Platonic form for writing—or that changes in writing always follow some kind of natural evolutionary process. In particular, I'm trying to show that changes in writing and literacy standards can often come suddenly and are likely to result from strong cultural and political forces.

Even more than the rest of the book, these stories call on realms of knowledge that I have not studied firsthand. So you'll see me leaning heavily and quoting extensively from other sources.

PART ONE

WHAT'S BEST IN SPEAKING AND WRITING?

Introduction: "Speech" and "Writing"

My overall project is to find what's best about speaking and then bring it to what's best about writing. So the task here in Part One is to explore advantages in both. But first I need to take some care about the meaning of the words themselves.

St. Augustine said he knew just what "time" meant—until he stopped to wonder. So too with "speaking" and "writing." They seem like simple words till we try to pin them down. In this book I want to use these words with some precision. After all, in the end, I'll be celebrating what might be called mixtures and hybrids between speaking and writing—so I can't write clearly about mixtures unless I try to be clear about the two ingredients being mixed.

Much of the confusion about speaking and writing comes from not noticing how these words operate in multiple realms or dimensions. We need to distinguish three dimensions:

1. Speaking and Writing as Different Physical Activities

We mostly don't get confused as to whether we are using our mouths or our fingers to produce words. There are some borderline perplexities—such as if we dictate to someone else who writes our words down—or if we dictate into voice recognition software. I can unperplex those activities in the Introduction to Part Two. For now the obvious everyday distinction between physical speaking and writing will do.

2. Speech and Writing as Different Physical Modalities or Media

Normal speaking produces sound, and since sounds are nothing but air molecules that are squeezed closer together than usual, spoken words decay the moment they are heard.

> She: *How could you have _said_ that to me?*
> He: *But I never _said_ that.*

They'll never know whether he said it or not. The words are gone forever—unless a recorder has been on.

Sounds also exist in the medium of *time*. It's a medium that traps us in the *now* and sweeps us implacably forward. We can't experience the past or the future—only thoughts or conceptions of past or future.

Writing, on the other hand, produces visible marks that persist through time—on the page or the screen or the billboard—as long as we want them to persist (or longer!). We can examine written words at whatever time or pace we want—looking forward to see who dunnit or back to find who the heck Stepan Arkadyich Oblonsky is. We can skim or re-read.

And visible words exist in *space*. Space is a medium of remarkable freedom, for we can look back where we came from and forward where we're headed—look left and right, up and down, often for great distances. We can compare two or three versions of a visible text almost simultaneously, whereas it's extremely difficult to compare multiple spoken discourses. (We can *record* audible words now and thus "check the audible record," yet it's very hard to compare recorded texts, and besides, we cannot hear more than a few words at a time.)

In short, the physical and sensory modalities of speech and writing are as distinctly different as the physical processes of speaking and writing. And here too we have an intriguing borderline example: sign language. It's a kind of "speaking" that is visual-and-spatial (like writing), yet temporal (like speaking).

3. Speech and Writing as Different Linguistic Products

This is where things get muddy. People commonly assume that the language that comes from people's fingers is not like the language that comes from their mouths. But linguists have shown that strictly considered, there is no real difference between them. That is, any kind of language is sometimes spoken and sometimes written. Linguists show the vast overlap by collecting huge "corpora" of millions of strings of spoken and written language. When they jumble together all the strings, they find they can't usually identify which ones were spoken and which were written. That is, when we look at spoken and written language that was produced in a full range of human contexts and purposes, the dividing line between spoken and written pretty much disappears. The linguist Douglas Biber probably has more experience and authority than anyone else on this topic, and in a 2007 survey of all the research on speech and writing, he and Camilla Vasquez conclude as follows: "[T]here are few, if any, absolute linguistic differences between the [language that is produced by the] written and spoken modes . . ." (537; see also Biber *Variation*).

People tend to assume that writing is more formal than speaking, but that's not always the case. Some writing is more informal and "speech-like" than much speech (consider the writing people put in diaries or email). And some speech is more formal and writing-like than much writing (consider certain lectures, announcements, and interviews). "Nothing consistently differentiates all varieties of speaking [spoken language] from all varieties of writing [written language]" (Chafe *Discourse* 48).

But after linguists have finished demolishing the distinction between spoken and written language, they turn around and start using it again—but in a more careful way. They recognize that it's useful to distinguish what they call "*typical speech*" and "*typical writing*." That is, they distinguish between two common *kinds* or *genres* or *registers* of language: everyday conversational *spoken language* versus careful informational or expository prose or "essayist" *written language*.

Thus, I cut Biber and Vasquez off in mid-sentence when they were saying that there's no difference between spoken and written mode. They finish their sentence as follows: "[but] there are strong and systematic linguistic differences between the registers of conversation and written informational prose—not only in English, but in other languages as well" (15). And so, interestingly, the latest and most careful analysis supports the common naive assumption that of course speech tends to be more informal than writing (as long as we add the word "typical").

Typical writing. To define this, Biber and Vasquez use the somewhat vague phrase "careful written informational prose." This makes a large umbrella that covers many kinds of writing that are called for in different fields at different educational levels and in many nonschool settings, but it's an umbrella that most people recognize. (See Olson "From Utterance" for the term "essayist prose"—which is a bit narrower since it tends to imply an argument or claim of some sort.)

Typical speech. This is what linguists mean when they use the shorthand term "spoken language." It's the language that people start speaking and internalizing from infancy. It's a language with complex and intricate grammatical rules—rules that we tend to master by around age four and usually obey without any awareness of them. This is the complex language that comes out of our mouths without planning when we have a thought or feeling to share. (But if we don't feel comfortable and safe, we may plan our words slowly and carefully and produce language that linguists would call "not typical speech.") It's also the language we usually use when we talk to ourselves inside our heads. This is the language I'll be referring to when I write about "speech" and "spoken language" throughout the book. I'll often add the terms "easy" or "unplanned" or "uncareful" to emphasize that it's casual, everyday speech. I'm distinguishing typical everyday unplanned speech from the wide range of language that *can be* spoken.

"Typical" is a matter of judgment. Biber argues that conversation is typical or "stereo-typical speech" and informational expository prose is "stereotypical writing":

> The characterization of conversation as stereotypical speaking is not controversial. All languages and cultures have conversational interactions, and it can be considered the unmarked means of spoken communication universally. ("Writing" 3)

In contrast, he calls informational expository prose "stereotypical writing" (3), but acknowledges that this is arguable. He notes that Brian Street disagrees with him and accuses intellectuals and scholars like Biber of thinking that informational prose is stereotypical only because it's the kind of writing *they* value. But Biber sticks to his guns and argues that

> [informational expository prose *is* stereotypical writing] because it maximally exploits the resources of the written mode [and] it has the opposite situational and commu-nicative characteristics from conversation: [thus] both exposition and conversation make maximal use of the communicative resources provided by their respective [physical and social] modes ("Writing" 4).

In contrast, I have an impulse to nominate *imaginative* or *literary* writing as stereo-typical writing (including poetry and memoir). These are surely the most honored forms of writing in our culture and represent the highest level of human perfor-mance in writing. In addition, interestingly, these are the kinds of writing that most people seem to *want* to do when they feel empowered to write. Given my preoc-cupation with the role of speech in good writing, I'm gratified to see Deborah Tan-nen pointing out that "[i]maginative literature has more in common with spontaneous conversation than with the typically written genre, expository prose" ("Relative Focus" 137). In literary, imaginative writing, what is *not* said is usually as important as what is spelled out, and there is often a personal element or sense of presence.

When I do writing workshops for academics, I find that even *they* often hanker to write memoirs and stories, poetry too, even though it doesn't help them in their aca-demic careers. Can it not be said that English departments in the twentieth century took on the mission to stamp out what they call amateur sentimental poetry?—and failed miserably? People *want* to write poetry and refuse to be stopped.

Here are some of the differences that linguists find between what's in casual conversation and what's typical in careful expository writing. Careful writing is claimed in general to be

1. more structurally complex and elaborate than speech, indicated by features such as longer sentences . . .
2. more explicit than speech, in that it has complete idea units . . .
3. more decontextualized, or autonomous, than speech, so that it is less dependent on shared situation or background knowledge . . .
4. less personally involved than speech, more detached and abstract and suggesting more distance . . .
5. characterized by a higher concentration of new information than speech . . .

6. more deliberately organized and planned than speech . . . (I am summarizing from Biber *Variation* 47. At the end of each item, he cites multiple research as evidence of these generalizations.)

But remember: these differences disappear once we consider the full range of language that humans speak or write.

I invite readers who are not so interested in some of these linguistic issues to skip over what follows in this long box, but I know that many other readers will appreciate it.

The Complete Overlap between Spoken and Written Language

Once we look at *all* spoken and written language and see that they cannot be distinguished in terms of whether they came from mouth or fingers, what do we get? Just an undifferentiated stew? No. We get other distinctions that trump the distinction between spoken and written language. That is, differences between speech and writing are dwarfed by *other* significant categories by which all the items in that huge pot of language *can* be meaningfully distinguished. That is, certain linguistic dimensions *override* or *trump* the difference between spoken and written words. Biber points to the following six dimensions. By "dimension" he means a particular spectrum or continuum of qualities, not a single quality. (For example, in looking at a pile of wooden blocks, we might have a dimension/spectrum of color—from black to white; a dimension/spectrum of weight—from heavy to light; a dimension/spectrum of shapes running from smooth to jagged.)

Dimension 1: Involved versus uninvolved. How much does the speaker/writer put herself into the language or keep herself out of it? We get both involved and uninvolved language from the mouth and from the fingers. For example, academics often put themselves into their *written* personal letters and often leave themselves out of their *spoken* lectures. Similarly, we can find *involved* language in both spoken conversation and written personal letters; and *uninvolved* language in both spoken press reporting and written official documents.

Deborah Tannen is among the most prominent figures in the extensive scholarship about spoken and written language, but she gradually came to argue that the very distinction itself between speech and writing is far less important and productive to investigate than the distinction between involvement and noninvolvement features of language. (See her "Oral and Literate," especially 126, "Spoken/Written," and "Relative Focus.")

Dimension 2: Narrative versus non-narrative concerns. Highly narrative stories can be either spoken or written, while telephone conversations and official documents are both non-narrative.

Dimension 3: Explicit versus implicit. How much does the language spell everything out or leave a lot implied? Note that a spoken lecture often spells out a lot, while much written literature is striking for how much it leaves implicit.

Dimension 4: Overt expression of persuasion [or not]. "[P]rofessional [written] letters and editorials are both persuasive, while [spoken] broadcasts and press reviews are not (even though the reviews are opinionated)."

Dimension 5: Abstract versus non-abstract information. "[A]cademic prose and official documents are extremely abstract, while fiction and conversations are markedly non-abstract."

Dimension 6: Evidence of "online" versus "off-line" production of words. When we produce language "online," we keep going without stopping. When we produce language "off-line," we take time to stop and plan or prepare it. Much speaking is nonstop, but some involves taking time to plan a bit. Writing too can be non-stop or carefully planned. (I'm quoting from and drawing closely on Biber's *Variation* 199–200.)

In short, these dimensions trump or cut across the distinction between speech and writing. What this analysis shows is that *context*—that is, situation, purpose, audience, genre, and so on—tell more about the language we produce than whether we use our hands or our mouths.

Exceptions: Some Small Differences between Spoken and Written Language

Biber and Vasquez did, however, find some very *small* but interesting statistical tendencies. It turns out that writing displays a somewhat wider range of different kinds of language than is found in speaking. Spoken language is somewhat constrained by the "online production conditions" where someone is listening and waiting for you to finish the sentence and so you don't have as much planning time. Certain larger grammatical complexities are harder to create on the fly and statistically rarer. The flexible "production conditions" for writers (time for pondering and revising) mean that they can and do use any kind of language they want—even language they intend to be mistaken for speech.

In this book, I'll try to do justice to the linguists' finding that, *in one sense,* speech and writing completely overlap, and *in another sense,* they are completely different. That is, on the one hand, I'll assume the libertine's credo: in the realm of language, there's nothing we can't do with our mouths and nothing we can't do with our fingers. Spoken and written language are not different if we look at the full range of human language production. This is crucial for me because I'm trying to harness more of speaking for writing.

But on the other hand, I'll spend a lot of time focusing on the differences between speech and writing in their typical forms: casual comfortable unplanned speech versus informational or essayist writing. I'm interested in casual speech *because* it's so easy—and I'll show that it has many virtues for writing that people don't notice. And I'm interested in expository or essayist writing because this is what most people find hardest, and it's what we have to do for school and work and many other purposes. It's the kind of writing that can particularly benefit from the resources of speech. (People who write poetry and fiction usually understand that speech is their friend.)

So I'll be inviting people who want to do careful expository informational writing to exploit what the tongue knows. Of course this is only a small part of the writing that people do in our culture. (Think about email, letters, newspapers, literature, diaries, blogs; see my "Spaciousness.") People probably get tricked into thinking that careful essays are typical of writing because that kind of writing made such a big dent on them when they were learning to write in school and were obliged to write in college. In our culture, carefully written essays have somehow come to be experienced as a peculiarly single doorway into adult literacy. New technologies have opened new doors into *writing*, but they haven't so much opened doors into what people feel as "genuine literacy" (much more on this in Chapter 17).

❊ ❊ ❊

To summarize:

- There's a clear and obvious difference between speech and writing *as physical processes:* the difference between using the mouth and using the hand.
- There's also a clear and obvious difference between speech and writing as *physical media or sensory modalities:* the difference between audible spoken language (existing in time) and visible written language (existing in space).
- However, when we look at speech and writing as *language* or *products,* the distinction is not so simple. They are not different if we look at the full range of spoken and written language produced in the full range of situations and contexts. But they are very different if we restrict our view to easy, conversational, casual conversation versus essayist writing. This is what people tend to have in mind when they talk about speech and writing, and it is what I'll intend when I use these words in this book (unless I specifically note otherwise).

Notice that two of these three distinctions center on the physical realm: the human body and the physical medium of transmission. The third more slippery distinction—between spoken and written *language*—is more slippery *because* it depends so much on social and cultural forces rather than the physical realm. The words we speak and write are hugely shaped by how we are trained or conditioned. But not entirely. In the following four chapters about writing and speaking, I will explore some features of spoken and written language that are not completely socially constructed, and instead depend to some degree on the physical dimension.

❊ ❊ ❊

In the Introduction to Part Two, I'll look at a fourth way of contrasting speaking and writing: as *mental processes*.

There's been a good deal of ink spilled in trying to compare *oral societies* and *literate societies* and the mentalities, ways of thinking, or identities that such societies are alleged to produce. I will ignore this topic. I have no need to enter what came to be called the "orality/literacy wars." At the end of the book, however, I will try to talk about some important characteristics of our present "culture of literacy."

1 Speaking and Writing as They are Used

The Role of Culture

SPEAKING SEEMS TO be part of human biology. All human cultures have speech. But this biology-based speech doesn't exist as pure biology; it only exists in particular cultures—indeed speech needs culture. Romulus and Remus, the legendary babies who founded Rome, were left all by themselves and suckled by a wolf. They couldn't have learned human language unless they heard humans speaking. Robinson Crusoe had language on his desert island, but it was the eighteenth-century English speech that he carried with him—along with all its values and ways of thinking.

In short, the biological gift for speech is highly flexible and it is always shaped and used in particular ways in particular cultural settings. In the first half of this chapter I will take an all too quick look at a few differences between how different cultures use speech. In the second half, I'll take a similar look at writing.

> *Culture* is a fuzzy and disputed term, but nothing here depends on a precise definition. When I speak of how speech and writing are used in cultures, I'm mostly thinking about large vaguely defined cultures like our general "modern" "Western" Anglo-American culture—in contrast, for example, with the quite different Native American culture or the early Anglo-Saxon culture; but there are smaller "cultures" with identifiable language practices—like those of bikers, scientists, bird lovers.
>
> I'm taking some pains here to emphasize the role of culture in language because I've been accused of neglecting it and emphasizing only the operation of the lone unfettered individual. I built my first book about writing (*Writing Without Teachers*, 1973) on a model of language that was heavily social and cultural. I posited there that all language use and indeed all *meanings* in language derive from a tug of war between large groups, small groups, and individuals (see 151ff).

Speaking: The Role of Culture

For most people who read this book, speaking will seem inherently easier than writing. In many spoken situations, we can just open our mouths and find words without effort. For most of us, spoken language is characteristically more casual too—most serious writing more formal. Speaking usually feels like a lower stakes use of language than writing.

But not everyone feels that way. The common feeling that speaking is easier than writing is really an accident of how we customarily use those two media in our culture. We learn how to speak from the cradle and many parents (especially middle-class literate parents) welcome their baby's every oral sound and like to imagine it as speech.

MwwawwMwwaw

He said "Mommy." What a brilliant baby!

And most of us continue to speak in the widest array of diverse contexts—from the playground to the bus to the boardroom to the bedroom.

In contrast, writing in our culture tends to be learned in school. Even if some children start to write at home by age three or four, schools almost invariably put their stamp on writing. For this reason, the job of learning to write tends to be experienced as a continual process of trying to "get it right." Email and the internet are changing this fast, but many people who didn't grow up with the internet have had the experience that everything they ever wrote was for school or work and was given to someone with authority over them for some evaluative judgment. Even when teachers are too busy to give a real response, they usually feel obliged at least to circle a few misspellings and give a grade—even if it's only a check or check plus. Besides, when we want to develop some ideas with some care, we tend to use writing. Why put it in writing if you aren't going to get it right? It's down in black and white. Of course many people don't worry about "getting it right" in email or Twitter or on Facebook, yet they often don't feel they are really writing in these settings. It's as though they feel, "This can't be writing if it isn't careful."

Yet almost everyone is terrified of speaking if it's "public speaking." Questionnaires show many people preferring to skydive than give a speech. But most people forget this terror by never considering the possibility of giving a public speech, so they continue to say, "Oh, talking is easy."

Also, many people come to our culture with a language different from English—or grow up with a stigmatized version of English such as African American English: they can feel nervous in speaking to an audience that expects standardized ("standard") English. Indeed, very "mainstream" people who find themselves in a highly "literate" or "cultured" family or subgroup are often nervous about speaking badly or wrong. Among the "cultured" classes in England—where speaking well so often counts for a great deal—stuttering is remarkably common.

Nevertheless, it's a truism in mainstream culture that speech is where we get to fool around, be loose, take chances, make a mess—at least if it's casual conversation with trusted family or friends. And it's common that people spend more time speaking with family, friends, and acquaintances than giving high-stakes speeches or navigating job interviews or engaging in guarded negotiation. We have a cultural tolerance for spoken imprecision, and if our words aren't clear we can get immediate feedback and then clarify. People often interrupt their spoken sentences in mid-course to throw in side thoughts—sometimes more than once—sometimes not even finishing the original "sentence-impulse." As we try to say what's on our mind, many of us say, "Y'know what I mean?" and add plenty of "likes" to symbolize that this is all kind of approximate. It's assumed in many informal situations that it's okay to let ourselves sort of say what we sort of mean and sort of work our way to our sort of point.

But not all cultures treat speaking so lightly. In some of them, casual speaking is scorned and ridiculed—even seen as a kind of moral lapse. (So too, many people now see careless email letters as a moral lapse). Here is Scott Momaday, writing about the Native American tradition:

> One who has only an oral tradition thinks of language in this way: my words exist at the level of my voice. If I do not speak with care, my words are wasted. If I do not listen with care, words are lost. If I do not remember carefully, the very purpose of words is frustrated. This respect for words suggests an inherent morality in man's understanding and use of language. Moreover, that moral comprehension is everywhere evident in American Indian speech. On the other hand, the written tradition tends to encourage an indifference to language. That is to say, writing produces a false security where our attitudes toward language are concerned. We take liberties with words; we become blind to their sacred aspect. (Momaday 160)

I had a firsthand chance to be surprised by this tradition. In 1970 I taught a writing class for Native American school administrators arriving at the Harvard School of Education to earn a master's degree. Things didn't go well. And it wasn't just my ineptitude. Eventually my students kindly let me in on something I'd never even conceived of. They distrusted writing itself, feeling it a flimsy, untrustworthy medium, and also the medium of lies and treachery. And this wasn't just because of all the solemn treaties Native Americans had signed in good faith with a White government that went on to break them. They had a strong sense that only speaking carried real human weight and could be trusted as a worthwhile medium of language.

In the Anglo-Saxon culture of Beowulf there was great disdain for casual, unplanned speech. The goal for virtuous men was to hold speech back and utter only sparse well-planned words—words that you scrutinize before opening your mouth. The lost and lonely speaker of "The Wanderer" says it is a "noble custom to bind

The Book of James in the New Testament speaks to the power of the tongue and the fear of this power:

> Anyone who makes no mistakes in speaking is perfect, able to keep the whole body in check with a bridle. If we put bits into the mouths of horses to make them obey us, we guide their whole bodies. . . . So also the tongue is a small member, yet it boast of great exploits. How great a forest is set ablaze by a small fire! And the tongue is a fire. The tongue is placed among our members as a world of iniquity; it stains the whole body, sets on fire the cycle of nature, and is itself set on fire by hell. For every species of beast and bird . . . can be tamed and has been tamed by the human species, but no one can tame the tongue—a restless evil, full of deadly poison. (3; 1–11)

fast his spirit chest [his mind] and his treasure-chamber [his thoughts]—think what he will." Good women were praised even more pointedly for restraining their tongues.

The very adjective for sparse careful speech—laconic—takes us to a different culture: the warlike Greek tribe from Laconia. It's as though they drank in with their mothers' milk the value of being strong and silent. Yet while loose-lipped bragging was scorned by both cultures, true boasting was admired. Beowulf boasts that he will kill Grendel's mother, and that boast keeps him fighting when he is staring death in the face and most warriors would give up. True boasting shows that you value your words more than your life. (In our present culture, we can find a trace of the warrior's boast in the technique taught by many athletic coaches: "imagining success." Try to <u>see</u> in your mind's eye how your hand goes forward and up and your shoulder follows through and the ball swishes cleanly through the basket!)

In Polynesia,

> Tuvaluan participants in conversation rarely express affect towards one another or concerning themselves. In contrast, writers of personal letters in Tuvaluan often express intimate feelings and display affect toward the recipient. (Biber *Variation* 205)

Shirley Brice Heath points out that even in the twentieth-century United States, members of an African American culture in the rural Southern Piedmont region didn't speak as much to their babies—nor constantly encourage babies and toddlers to speak—as was characteristic of the middle-class White parents who lived in the nearby town.

The ideal of taciturnity is surely not dead for males in mainstream Anglo culture. Clint Eastwood conserves his words, and the Marlboro Man saves his mouth for his cigarette. I can't resist suspecting that this "manly ideal" of taciturnity reflects a cultural connection between masculinity, war, and competition. In England it merges with understatement. I recently saw a re-run of *Foyle's War* from the BBC—and Foyle raises tightlipped understatement to a fine art. John Updike takes us to yet another manly site: "Back in New Jersey, the big men, gangsters and police chiefs and Knights of Columbus, spoke softly, forcing others to listen" ("Brother Grasshopper" 31).

Some Examples of Spoken Language from Our Culture

Writing is easy to see. You're looking at one kind of writing now. But we can't see speaking—only hear it. In fact, a rich understanding of speech had to wait till linguists could actually record everyday speech and look at transcriptions—and even at "voice prints" that diagram every acoustic detail. Here's a short example of transcribed speech from a retirement community in the Midwest of the United States. The linguist transcriber started a new line for each "intonation unit" (much more about them in Chapter 5).

NEAL
the last time we talked
you said you were a world traveler.
you've been all over the [place] [overlapping speech in brackets]

ALBERTINE

[oh yes] yes yes
that was after I married.
and we decided-
I wanted to know
the great question that was on my mind-
I'll never forget-
that's folk curiosity.
I wanted to know
what makes people tick.
and so ah . .
my husband loved to travel.
so ah . . .
the same I
so we went out to find-
what makes people tick. {chuckles}
and of all our travels
we all came back home after many many years.
that there was just one answer
everybody ticks alike. {chuckling}
There's no difference. (Saarbrücken Corpus)

Because this is mostly monologue and the transcriber didn't try to notate every pause and accent, it looks fairly normal. In contrast, here is some dinner table dialogue that's more broken as speakers interrupt each other. In addition, the transcriber records more of the audible details. He uses two dots to mark a short pause and three dots to mark what he calls a "typical pause," and he notes the duration of pause in seconds. He uses [´] for a primary speech accent and [`] for a secondary speech accent:

Speaker 1:
. . . (0.4) Have the . . ánimals
. . . (0.1) ever attacked anyone ín a car?
Speaker 2:
. . . (1.2) Well I
well Í hèard of an élephant,
. . . that sát dówn on a V̀Ẁ one time.
. . . (0.9) There's a gìr
. . . Did you éver hear thát?
Speaker 3:
. . . (0.1) No,
Speaker 2 again:
. . . (0.3) Some élephants and these
. . . (0.1) they
. . . (0.7) there
these gáls were in a Vólkswagen,
. . . (0.4) and uh,
. . . (0.3) they uh kept hónkin' the hórn,

. . . (0.2) hóotin' the hóoter,
. . . (0.6) and uh,
. . . (0.4) and the . . élephant was in frónt of em,
so he jùst procèeded to sìt dòwn on the V̀W̃.
(Chafe Discourse 61–62)

Transcriptions of actual conversation often seem to show speech as hopelessly incoherent. Speakers interrupt each other, and constantly break off in mid-syntax to start new bits. The Nixon tapes are the locus classicus for fragmented spoken language. Spoken language can look weird also because we don't get the help of sound—the intonational melodies and rhythms. (And it looks weird in a different way if we're not used to the codes that linguists use for notating some of the music of speech).

Countless journalists and researchers in various fields interview people and record their words, and when they publish transcriptions they aren't interested in the pauses and intonational melodies; they're just trying to get the spoken meaning down accurately. Here is a bit of speech transcribed from a research interview with a college student who is talking about how she experienced journal writing in a writing course:

> I wrote and wrote and wrote and wrote. The journal was better than the assignments because I really didn't care. I wrote whatever came to my mind, and there were a couple of times where I thought I can't believe I'm writing this. . . . I wasn't afraid anybody was going to read it but sometimes putting your words on paper I almost feel that it gives them a voice. They're out there somewhere and somebody's aware of them so a couple of times I had to catch myself, but I just wrote. (Paranto 236)

In this transcript, we don't see the pauses and throat-clearings: it doesn't look as messy as carefully recorded actual speech. But the researcher has kept some "spoken grammar," for example, "but sometimes putting your words on paper I almost feel that it gives them a voice." We don't usually notice the "silent editing" that journalists and researchers do in order to make their written speech more coherent. When you see a newspaper quoting someone sounding incoherent or using "bad grammar," you can assume that the reporter or editor was hostile to the figure being quoted.

I've shown only three small samples. Nothing very impressive—but speech on the hoof seldom is. We could look at the transcript of a good lecturer—someone speaking clearly but fairly spontaneously and not using a text or even following a written outline. If the lecturer is good, the transcript is remarkably coherent. It turns out that Richard Feynman—the Nobel Prize winner and well-known writer about science—had great trouble writing.

> The International Corpus of English (ICE) has spoken and written texts—a million words each—from eighteen research groups in different countries. The ICECUP (ICE Corpus Utility Programme) helps you use it and search in it. There is also COCA, the CORPUS OF CONTEMPORARY AMERICAN ENGLISH.

Most of his books were produced from transcripts of his classes and lectures.

Since the main message of my book is that we can use the resources of speaking for writing, I want to highlight the fact that humans can produce all kinds of language in speaking. Many huge "corpuses" of spoken language have been collected by linguists and many are available online. These permit you to look at lots of examples from different speaking situations.

✳   ✳   ✳

Writing: The Role of Culture

Since writing is not part of our basic biological package, it's nothing but culture. Culture is the only source of writing; most cultures have never known writing. For the rest of this chapter I will look at a few differences between how different cultures use writing.

> Gesture, drawing, and scribbling *do* seem part of the basic human package. Susan Sheridan argues that the self-modifying action of scribbling is an essential element for learning to write, and that drawing and writing are interconnected. There's a strong case to be made for drawing and writing growing out of gesture.

In our culture, as in many others, written language tends to carry more prestige and power than spoken language. When we ask someone, "Would you be willing to put that into writing?" we tend to mean, "Would you be willing to stand behind your words and take full responsibility for them?"—not "just speak" them. Writing can even seem to hold speech hostage—as though people won't take your words seriously unless you can write them. Adults who cannot read and write often feel voiceless. David Olson makes a surprising contention but cites reputable research in support: that children's first understanding of words as words is tied to their written form, not their spoken form—in our culture. (World on Paper 77).

The word "authority" derives from author, and in our culture, authority tends to require writing. "Correct speech" tends to be modeled on the rules for "correct writing" (more about this in the Introduction to Part Three and Chapter 17). Most people don't realize that we change our pronunciation to fit spelling more often than we change our spelling to fit pronunciation (Ehri 336). You can pronounce your name as you please, but to change the spelling, you need legal action.

In our culture, as in so many cultures of literacy, writing and power are linked through the idea of difficulty. Writing takes much more conscious learning than speaking, so the ability to write has been available mostly to people with more advantage, leisure, and better schools. But this "difficulty" of writing is largely a cultural artifact. It's not inherent in the task itself of writing. That is, given an alphabetic or syllabic writing system, it's extremely easy to write language that can be read later by oneself and others. Children of four and five can do it quite well—though their use of the alphabet is often idiosyncratic. (My son used an "h" to stand for both "sh" and "ch" sounds, so his writing looked peculiar at first.) But by the time children are seven or eight, most of them can spell as well as the pilgrims did—or Lewis and Clark. Here is a passage from their journal:

> The Day was ushered in by the Discharge of two Cannon, we Suffered 16 men [1] with their musick to visit the 1st Village for the purpose of Danceing, by as they Said the perticular request of the Chiefs of that village, about 11 oClock I with an inturpeter & two men walked up to the Village (my views were to alay Some little miss understanding which had taken place thro jelloucy and mortificatiion as to our treatment towards them. (1/1/1805; see Lewis and Clark)

Clark's spelling was no impediment to his soon being appointed to the U.S. Cabinet. In short, in little more than a century, we have seen a huge cultural change in our culture of literacy with regard to spelling.

The "difficulty" is not just a matter of spelling. In addition, our culture, like many others, has somehow come to insist on a dialect for correct writing that is different from anyone's mother tongue. So it's writing "correctly" that's difficult (and also, of course, writing well). So writing is not the same as writing correctly or well. As we just saw from Clark, a demand for correctness

Havelock and Goody argue that the technology of writing itself helps people think more logically and with more detachment. But scholars like Street and Gee disagree and cite research to show that the alleged cognitive effects of writing do not come from the ability to read and write in itself, but rather from how reading and writing are taught and used in a cultural social context. Scribner and Cole studied literacy among the Vai people in Africa where there are three forms of literacy: Western style schooling in English; an indigenous syllabic script that many people learn outside of school and use for letters and business purposes; and an Arabic script used for reading and reciting the Qur'an. The researchers argue that their evidence shows that *schooling* rather than literacy is the source of gains in abstract thinking: "On no task—logic, abstraction, memory, communication—did we find all nonliterates performing at a lower level than all literates" (quoted in Gee "Literacy, Discourse" 57). Scribner writes: "across a wide sample from very different cultures and culture areas, schooled literates are a more homogeneous group than are nonschooled nonliterates. Furthermore, in many ways two schooled literates in very different societies are more alike cognitively than either is like other members of the same society." (79) (See also Akinnaso.)

didn't impede writing—even in our culture. In the Western Middle Ages, the Renaissance, and up through the seventeenth century, there was no single correct form of writing. It was fine to use grammar and spelling more like we now see in seven-year-olds. Shakespeare signed his name with eleven different spellings.

In our culture, writing became deeply connected to law and legal agreements. Until the twelfth century, courts relied on spoken oaths or physical tokens like clumps of earth.

> M. T. Clancy . . . estimates that in twelfth-century England, not more than thirty thousand [written] charters were drawn up. In the period 1250–1350, by contrast, several million were made out in England alone—that amounts to almost five charters for each piece of describable property. Accompanying this change, writing materials increased ten- to twenty-fold in this period. The consumption of sealing wax at the royal chancery in England rose from three pounds per week in 1226, to thirteen pounds in 1256, and thirty-one pounds just ten years later in 1266. More sheep had to give up their skins as parchments for the purposes of documentation during a royal court hearing. At the beginning of the thirteenth century, it was a matter of a few dozen. For a perfectly ordinary session in Suffolk in 1283, over five hundred were skinned. (Illich and Sanders 36)

And yet well before the twelfth century we find this in the Qur'an: "O believers, when you contract a debt / One upon another for a stated term, / Write it down, and let a writer / Write it down between you justly" (2:282). When God spoke to most figures in early Jewish history, he spoke, but for the ten commandments he wasn't satisfied with speech: "I will give you the tablets of stone, with the law and the commandments, which I have written for their instruction" (Exodus 24:12).

We see here that the culture of writing connects with a culture's technology. When people comment on the difficulty of writing, they forget to notice how much easier it is to write now than it used to be. We don't have to prepare papyrus or kill sheep for parchment or sharpen quills. And we have email!

Magic in Both Speaking and Writing

Ever since Ferdinand de Saussure (called the father of twentieth-century linguistics), it has gone without saying that the relationship between words and things is purely arbitrary. The word "cat"—spoken or written—does not resemble in any way the furry purring thing itself. There is no inherent ontological or existential relationship between the verbal sign and the physical thing. It would be just as right to hang any of the following written signs on a cat: chat or katz or mao"—pronounced in Chinese with tone 1. In English, we could have used the word chat for cats as the French do, but for some reason we think "chat" means a cozy conversation. Words don't contain or participate in the things they represent. Socrates said that tall people contain more "tallness," but we like to say he was mistaken.

Hebrew for cat   Chinese for cat

The real reason that language so often carries magic is because humans have trouble not ascribing special power to it. Language makes so many things happen. If we say or write words in a certain way, we can make people see things that aren't there and feel things they have no reason to feel—all this with mere mouth sounds or paper marks. With words we can bring to life subtle abstractions that (as one might say) don't exist—such as "fairness" or the difference between a bed and the idea of a bed (indeed between bed as "signifier" and "signified"). So it's not surprising that so many cultures feel language as magical. When the priest says "I pronounce you man and wife," they are married (as long as they said the right words). For some people, it works when the priest says "Your sins are forgiven"—or when a husband says, "I divorce you." People fainted during many of Dickens's readings; women allegedly gave birth while watching Greek tragedies.

John's Gospel (in the King James translation) famously starts, "In the beginning was the Word." It sounds as though John is saying that the entire universe—and God too—all derive from language. What he probably meant, of course, was something much more Platonic: that in the beginning there was pure meaning or logic or rationality—logos—with no need for crude lowly things or words. Angels are said to communicate by zapping meaning back and forth—instantaneous and whole—with no need for linear, discursive language. Nevertheless, that English translation of John has powerfully infiltrated our culture with the notion of words at the heart of things.

In many cultures, spells are cast by speaking. Near the end of his Encomium on Helen, Gorgias argues that speech can act on the soul like a drug on the

> Here is David Olson:
>
> Harris has suggested that the failure to distinguish words from names produces a form of emblematic symbolism which may extend to various gods and spirits and "is often bound up in various ways with word magic and practices of name-giving. It reflects, fundamentally, a mentality for which reality is still not clearly divisible into language and nonlanguage, any more than it is divisible into the physical and the metaphysical, or into the moral and the practical." Surely a little of that word magic exists in all of us. (*The World on Paper* 71. He's quoting Roy Harris, *Origin of Writing* 131–132.)
>
> Steven Katz argues that for many Jews, especially in early eras, the very *shapes* of the letters had magical power—implying in a sense that "in the beginning was the *written* word."

Here is the French scholar, Sylvie Plane, speaking about the magic of visual signs:

> In certain cultural contexts, the bond between linguistic activity and "line"—that is, the mark or trace left by the physical gesture carried out by the writer—is consubstantial to writing. This is the case in oriental poetic creation, in particular in the calligraphic art developed in the Arabic-Muslim world, where the form of the drawn line has a figurative function that opens out the information carried by the meaning of the words while skirting around the representations forbidden by religion. It is equally the case in Japanese poetry, whose key purpose is to represent and give us ways to see what the world contains, but that we would not begin to know how to see without the help of words. Examining the way in which haiku constructs meaning, the French poet and analyst Yves Bonnefoy shows that it calls into question the arbitrariness of the signifier as has been imposed by Saussurian traditions. Specifically, he takes up a discussion developed in relation to the impressions created by the sonority of the signifier—which we know is particularly helpful in evoking mental images—and broadens it to include the graphic signifier. For him, haikus carry the trace of the figurative origins of ideograms. And they carry it more than any other written text in Japanese because the gesture itself that creates them participates in the construction of meaning, and "the signifiers are traced, after reflection, with a single stroke of the brush." (Plane 1)

body. Alcibiades called Socrates a magician with words (*Symposium* 215—c–d). T. S. Eliot argued that it's the sound of poetry—even or especially written poetry—that does the poem's work. He wrote of how the meaning of a good poem is merely the hunk of beefsteak that burglars use to distract the guard dog while they burgle the house. That is, the mere meaning of the poem serves to keep the mind busy enough so the poem can do its real work—through sound alone. If the mind weren't distracted by meaning, it wouldn't allow itself to be changed by the breaking-and-entering lawless power of audible speech (see *The Uses of Poetry and the Uses of Criticism*).

The magic of speech peeps out for most of us when someone says

I hope this plane doesn't crash.

Someone invariably replies

Don't even say that!

I've caught myself not saying "Don't say *that*"—because I tell myself I don't believe in magic!

The magic in spoken language shows itself most clearly in cursing and naming. Consider the reactions of many people to the sound of a taboo profanity—or the sound of their own name or God's name: it's as though the sound of the word still carries just a bit of juice of the thing itself. B. F. Skinner's behavioral account of language is deeply unfashionable: that the mental meaning of a word like cat consists of the tiny tiny fractional response we have toward the thing itself. But his behavioral theory has the considerable virtue of accounting for how we react to curse words and names—and sometimes to other words. It would also explain why children go in for word magic—and why students in dormitories and soldiers in the army often lose more and more of their fractional response to the sound of words like "s***" and "f***." The most powerful linguistic "magic" comes with the sound of God's name.

There are many situations that we don't associate with magic, but where speech functions to cast a spell. People with powerful personalities or strong authority can exert power over the minds of followers. Hitler comes to mind, but here's a minor example: fund-raisers on the phone fight me when I say, "Send me something by mail, I won't pledge anything over the phone." They want to use their voices, and I don't want them to have that power over me.

❊   ❊   ❊

But speech has no monopoly on magic; writing is also used for casting spells—starting millennia ago when writing was young. Here are two Greek examples:

> If you wish to appear to someone at night in dreams, say to the lamp that is in daily use, CHEAIMOPSEI ERPE BOT, let her NN whom NN bore, see me in her dreams immediately, immediately; quickly quickly (and add the usual, whatever you wish) (Betz PGM VII 407–410)
>
> If you want someone to cease being angry with you, write with myrrh [on linen] this / name of anger: "CHNEÔM." Hold it in your left [hand and] say: "I am restraining the anger of all, especially of him, NN which is CHNEÔM." (Betz PGM XII 179–181)

"Grammar" is the same word as "glamour." There are archetypal stories of persons from nonliterate cultures who see someone read from a book and afterward pick up the book and hold it to their ear—in order to hear what the book is saying. There is a mystical Jewish tradition or culture that regards letters as "essence":

> In its vision of every aspect and dimension of reality as constituted by letters, the rhetoric of Jewish mysticism appears to postulate an entirely linguistic reality. . . .
>
> The Scriptures, and the [written] words, and thus the letters themselves, are sacred because they are authored by God. (Katz 147, 49)

But nowadays, "we" (under Saussure's spell) say there is no magic in writing.

When classical Greek rhetoricians went on to develop rhetoric as a techné (a conscious "art" or science), they began to distance themselves from its magical roots—for example, running away from the use of the magical healer who was present in so many ancient texts. In her book, *Magic and Rhetoric in Ancient Greece*, Jacqueline DeRomilly argues that Gorgias sought to revise the concept of "magic" in speech:

> Sacred magic was mysterious; Gorgias's magic is technical. He wants to emulate the power of the magician by a scientific analysis of language and its influence. He is a theoretician of the magic spell of words. This is a remarkable claim—and a remarkable shifting from irrational models to rational teaching. (16)

(On ancient and Greek magic, see Greene; Wagner.)

The magic of writing lingers in certain taboos. Many literate people avoid spelling out naughty or dangerous words (as I did a few paragraphs ago). Very smart people put written prayers in the crevices of the Wailing Wall. Even among the most literate and educated of persons—writers—we see plenty of evidence of writing magic. Consider, for example, the various deeply felt ritual practices that many writers build into their writing process. They feel they can't write unless they use a certain pen or a certain computer or a certain kind of paper or a certain place or a certain pre-writing ritual, and so on. If I don't do the rain dance right, I'll get no rain—no flow, no words, no thinking.

Speaking of culture and the magic of written words, I think I see a slightly freer use of strongly vulgar words (like f*** and c***) in newspapers and magazines in England than in the United States. It could be that the trial of *Lady Chatterley's Lover* in 1965 made a big dent, at least on the cultured classes there. "The drama critic Kenneth Tynan valiantly stuttered out "f-f-f-UCK" on the BBC on 13 November 1965. The *Guardian,* around the same time sanctioned four-letter words." Penguin put *Lady Chatterley* immediately into paperback—as opposed to how *Lolita* was kept hardback for a while (Sutherland).

The most sophisticated lovers of poetry and fiction (even high literates who take Saussure as gospel) often acknowledge without embarrassment that a kind of magic is tangled up in certain kinds of language, namely, powerful poems and stories. I like Eliot's argument about the power of sound, but there's also magic in the look of a written word. (Or rather it's there for people in our culture who are willing to let it do that work.)

What follows is a long paragraph from an Updike story where he insists on the link between writing and prayer—and on the ability of written words to do God's work of bringing nonexistent things to life:

The other night I stumbled downstairs in the dark and kicked my wife's sewing basket from the halfway landing. Needles, spools, buttons, and patches scattered. In gathering the things up, I came upon my grandmother's thimble. For a second I did not know what it was; a stemless chalice of silver weighing a fraction of an ounce had come into my fingers. Then I knew, and the valves of time parted, and after an interval of years my grandmother was upon me again, and it seemed incumbent upon me, necessary and holy, to tell how once there had been a woman who now was no more, how she had been born and lived in a world that had ceased to exist, though its mementos were all about us; how her thimble had been fashioned as if in a magical grotto in the black mountain of time, by workmen dwarfed by remoteness, in a vanished workshop now no larger than the thimble itself and like it soon doomed, as if by geological pressures, to be crushed out of shape. O Lord, bless these poor paragraphs, that would do in their vile ignorance Your work of resurrection. ("The Blessed Man of Boston" 157)

Finally, I can't resist ending with one more passage of magical writing. It happens to be about writing itself:

Writing allows exactly repeatable statements to be circulated widely and preserved. It allows readers to scan a text back and forth and to study, compare, and interpret at their leisure. It allows writers to deliberate over word choice and to construct lists, tables, recipes, and indexes. It fosters an objectified sense of time, a linear conception of space. It separates the message from the author and from the context in which it was written, thereby "decontextualizing," or universalizing the meaning of, language. It allows the creation of new forms of verbal structure, like the syllogism, and of numerical structures, like the multiplication table. When writing becomes a predominant institutional and archival form it has contributed to the replacement of myth by history and the replacement of magic by skepticism and science. Writing has permitted the development of extensive bureaucracy, accounting, and legal systems organized on the basis of explicit rules and procedures. Writing has replaced face-to-face governance with written law and depersonalized administrative procedures. And, on the other hand, it has turned writers from scribes into authors and thereby contributed to the recognition of the importance of the thoughts of individuals and consequently to the development of individualism.

This doesn't look like magic, does it? But I'd claim it is. For these are words from the Encyclopaedia Britannica (see Britannica). Our culture tends to give magical credence to what is written in a highly reputable encyclopedia. The words are set out in such a way as to make us feel as if they are disembodied "truth" itself—self-authorized and valid—as though they come from God or reality. It's this kind of ritualized language that is often given the most special credence in our culture. (This passage is particularly fun because of how it does what this absent, know-it-all nonauthor is describing.)

Some of the prestige that our culture ascribes to writing must derive from its still-lingering magic. But I wager that audible speaking—with its ability to convey powerful personal presence and its music and rhythm and heightened channels of communication—does better than writing at reaching into us, touching us, and manipulating us. In any case, it takes a good deal of cultural training to keep us from feeling magic in speech and writing (see my "Writing and Magic" in *Writing With Power*).

✳   ✳   ✳

The theme of this chapter is that speaking and writing are always inflected by culture. People through time and space tend to speak and write in very different ways. In the next two chapters I'll downplay culture. I'll emphasize the uses of speaking and writing that strike me as most valuable and precious irrespective of whether certain cultures have exploited them or not. I'm no longer merely trying to describe speech and writing as they exist in cultural settings, I'm trying to argue that certain potential uses of speech and writing are particularly valuable. I'm laying the groundwork for the larger project of the book: to take what's best about speaking and add it to what's best about writing.

LITERACY STORY

Three Basic Systems for Written Language

Introduction to Literacy Stories

Between most of the chapters I have inserted very short "Literacy Stories." They sketch moments in the history of writing and literacy at different periods in history and in different places around the globe. I want to immerse readers in some of the wildly diverse ways in which humans have used written language.

I also intend these stories as entertaining interludes or changes of pace from the longer discursive chapters. ("Interludes" are little plays or entertainments that are slipped between the main events—like half-time shows. Inter = "between"; ludus = "play" or "game.") But cumulatively, of course, I hope they will reinforce the larger project of the book. I want to jiggle the widespread assumption that there is some kind of best or Platonic form for writing—or that changes in writing always follow some kind of natural evolutionary process. In particular, I'm trying to show that changes in writing and literacy standards can often come suddenly and are likely to result from strong cultural and political forces.

Even more than the rest of the book, these stories call on realms of knowledge that I have not studied firsthand. So you'll see me leaning heavily and quoting extensively from other sources.

✳   ✳   ✳

Because speech is rooted in biology, it has similar features across the wildly different languages that humans speak. "Linguistic universals" they are called. (Chomsky argues for more universals than many other linguists favor. He speaks of "universal grammar.") But because *writing* has no biological roots, it's an invented artifact, wholly a product of culture. Different cultures invented very different forms of writing. It can be close to speech or far away.

There were evidently only three occasions when humans were brilliant and creative enough to invent written language. Around 3500 BCE, the Canaanites or Semites in the Middle East came up with a kind of alphabet that was the source for our alphabet. Around 1200 BCE, the Chinese evolved their non-alphabetic "character-based" system. And around CE 200, the Mayans in Central America invented their hieroglyphic writing system. (Traditionally, the Egyptians have been credited with inventing their hieroglyphic system, but Schmandt-Besserat, in a recent review of scholarship, says that it's become clear that it was borrowed from the Mesopotamians. Some scholars speculate that there might be a few other independent inventions of writing—for example, in the Indus River region in India.)

As writing spread and evolved over the centuries from these three sources around the world, we end up with three different *kinds* of symbols for writing.

- *Alphabetic* symbols are the ones you are looking at. Compared with the other two systems, alphabetic symbols—letters—represent the *smallest* units of meaning (phonemes). For example, the letter "b" stands only for the sound or phoneme *buh*. In itself, it has no meaning; it gets meaning only when combined with other letters/phonemes (as in *bat* or *bet*).

- *Logographic* symbols—like Chinese characters or Egyptian or Mayan hieroglyphs—are at the opposite extreme. They carry the *most* meaning. They represent entire concepts; a single character/concept might be rendered in different spoken words. So characters contain no cues about the sound of spoken words. Many people don't notice that we in the West have some logographic symbols hiding, as it were, in our "Roman" alphabetic symbols. For example, our symbols "&" and all our Arabic numerals are actually logographic. They represent entire concepts and they bear no relationship at all to sound. So "2" has no relationship with the sound of the English word "two"—for it stands equally for the same concept in German (*zwei*) and French (*deux*).

- The *syllabic* system lies in the middle. Syllabic letters or symbols carry more meaning than alphabetic letters but less meaning than Chinese characters or Egyptian hieroglyphs. Being "syllabic," they obviously do relate to the sounds of the spoken language. Even in our alphabetic system, there are traces of a syllabic system, as when we use the letter "a" to mean "not" (as in the words *amoral* and *asymptomatic* and many others). If we had a single symbol for our syllable *bi*, it would mean "twoishness" (as in *bipolar*).

A written symbol that stands for a spoken *sounded* word is called *phonographic*. So alphabetic and syllabic symbols are phonographic—they give visual cues to the sound of the spoken words. A written symbol that carries meaning with no relationship to sound (like Chinese characters) is called *logographic*. (See the following page for illustrations of the three systems.)

It is common and handy to label entire writing *systems* as alphabetic, logographic, or syllabic—saying for example that we use an alphabetic writing system, that the Chinese use a logographic system, and that the Japanese use a syllabic system (for one of their systems). But it must be kept in mind that no actual writing system is wholly pure or consistent in using only one of these three kinds of symbols. Thus, I was surprised to learn in research for this book that Chinese characters and Egyptian hieroglyphs are not wholly logographic, and that *no* written language is purely phonographic or logographic—purely phonetic or semantic:

> [A]ll writing systems use a mixture of phonetic and semantic signs. What differs [from one written language to another] . . . is the *proportion* of phonetic to semantic signs. The higher the proportion [of phonetic signs], the easier it is to guess the pronunciation of a word. In English the proportion is high, in Chinese it is low. Thus English spelling represents English speech sound more accurately than Chinese characters represent Mandarin speech; but Finnish spelling represents the Finnish [spoken] language better than either of them. (Robinson 14)

In a scrupulous analysis, Florian Coulmas says that many actual writing systems are quite mixed and lack a predominant principle for the interpretation of their basic units. He puts ancient Egyptian, Akkadian, and Japanese in this category—and even English!

Robinson draws an interesting continuum of languages that run from maximum phonography to maximum logography:

Illustrating the Three Basic Systems for Writing: Alphabetic, Logographic, and Syllabic

ALPHABETIC
Obviously, alphabetic writing is the form of writing that most of us read most of the time.

LOGOGRAPHIC
Two examples of Chinese traditional characters:

狗追猫

Gǒu   zhuī   māo

Dog   chase   cat

It takes context to determine whether it means: The dog chases the cat; dogs chase cats; the dog chased [or will chase] the cat.

活也讓別人活

Huó   yě   ràng   bié   rén   huó

Live   and   let   other-people   live

Live and let live

Three Mayan Glyphs:

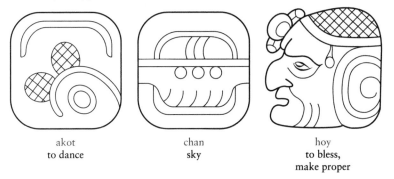

akot	chan	hoy
to dance	sky	to bless, make proper

SYLLABIC
Two Examples of Japanese Hiragana:

いぬ は と に います

Inu   ha   to   ni   imasu

The dog is at the door

しんじつ は わかりにくい です

Shinjitsu   ha   wakarinikui   desu

The truth is hard to know

■ "Pure phonography" e.g., the International Phonetic Alphabet ■ Finnish ■ French ■ English ■ Korean ■ Japanese ■ Chinese ■ "Pure logography" e.g., mathematical symbols and cryptographic codes

From Robinson

Despite the differing degrees of phonography and logography shown in this chart, Robinson insists that we must recognize that *every* writing system is linked to speech:

> Writing and reading are intimately and inextricably bound to speech, whether or not we move our lips. Chinese characters do *not* speak directly to the mind without the intervention of sound, despite centuries of claims to the contrary by the Chinese and by many western scholars. Nor do Egyptian hieroglyphs, notwithstanding the beauty of their symbols and the fact that we can recognize people, animals, objects and the natural world depicted in them. (17)

(Robinson shows examples of how the same symbol is used at one point for its visual representational meaning—as a logogram—and at another point for its sound—as a phonogram [98, 102, 104]. More about this in the Literacy Story about the Rebus after Chapter 3.)

> *Pure phonography* is represented by the International Phonetic Alphabet (IPA): a set of Roman letters supplemented with many other symbols designed to represent every sound in every language. Thus it has 107 letters for consonant and vowel sounds—and about fifty more signs to show how these sounds are made (for example, stressed or lengthened). In a few dictionaries, we see a highly simplified version of the IPA to help guide pronunciation.
>
> *Pure logography* is represented by mathematical symbols and cryptographic codes. 2 + 2 = 4 is a purely logographic "sentence."

❄   ❄   ❄

The three writing systems each have advantages and disadvantages. In our Western culture, people like to brag about how easy the alphabetic system makes literacy. Alphabetically written words derive from the sounds of spoken words, and as a result readers can sound out words *from* the page and speakers can sound out words *to* the page. The alphabetic principle works particularly well for Finns and Spaniards because they have spelling that fits consistently with speech. We English speakers are disadvantaged in this respect because of our irregular spelling. Still, alphabet users can write and read every word in the language by learning to use only twenty five to forty symbols or letters—depending on the alphabet.

Notice, then, that alphabetic and syllabic writing tends to carry an implicit *sound*; the very *form* of alphabetic and syllabic writing tickles the ear. They bridge speech and the page—a theme in this book.

In contrast, logographic writing, as with Chinese characters, bears no relationship to the sound of the spoken words (mostly). Chinese readers cannot sound out writing into speech nor speakers sound out speech into writing. Literacy in Chinese puts an immense burden on memory since it requires learning thousands of symbols or characters by rote.

Yet because written Chinese writing is independent of any spoken language, it can be read by people who don't understand each others' speech. This is a big help for speakers of the four or five mutually unintelligible forms of spoken Chinese—and for many speakers of other languages outside China. Most literate Chinese feel great pride along with a huge psychic investment in the ancient and beautiful characters. (More about Chinese in the Literacy Story following Chapter 16.)

Despite the different kinds of pride felt by Westerners and Chinese in their writing systems, the *syllabic* writing system is probably the most practical. We like to brag that in our system anyone can write anything she can say—but reading and writing are far easier with a syllabary. It may require learning a few more symbols than an alphabet (something like a couple of hundred), but once you learn them, reading and writing come much more quickly. Spanish or Finnish with regularized spelling are much better for ease and efficiency than English, but they still lose out to a syllabary. In 1820 in Arkansas, Sequoya, a Cherokee Native American man, singlehandedly invented a syllabary for the spoken Cherokee Indian language, and it was astoundingly successful at producing fast and widespread literacy. (See the Literacy Story following Chapter 11.)

Russell Bernard, a scholar of literacy, argues that a nation's rate of literacy does *not* depend on the kind of writing system its people use. "The Japanese case makes it clear . . . that the rate of literacy depends not on the nature of the writing system (phonographic versus logographic-syllabic) but rather on . . . universal schooling through grade twelve in Kanji and Kana (Bernard 24–25). Yet he concedes, "On the other hand, the Vietnamese case makes it clear that, in countries with few economic resources, rapid literacy in fewer than twelve years of schooling is more easily accomplished with romanized scripts than with Chinese characters (Bernard 25. For more about Vietnam, see the Literacy Story after Chapter 11).

2 What's Good about Writing

CULTURE WAS THE theme in Chapter 1. But cultures differ, and they also evolve. My larger goal in this book is to *change* how people in our culture see writing and engage in it. So in this chapter, I celebrate some potentialities of writing—whether or not our culture has exploited them. Indeed, my larger project is to show some important potentialities of writing that we have failed to develop. After all, in most human cultures writing was nothing *but* a potentiality. Tens of thousands of languages have been used while scarcely more than a hundred have ever been written.

> What does it mean to talk about a potentiality that a culture failed to exploit? Here's an interesting case from the realm of music:
>
>> No social history of music can succeed that does not acknowledge the partial independence of the musical language, the way it can offer abstract possibilities to the imagination irrelevant to the social and economic world of the musician, but often too tempting to turn down. . . . Bach's great Mass in B minor was never performed during his lifetime: as a Catholic Mass, it could not be played in a Protestant church, and the use of an orchestra was forbidden in Catholic churches during Bach's lifetime, although he hoped it might eventually be possible. His "Goldberg" Variations is the most successful of all his works in concert performance today, yet the kind of concert in which it can be performed did not exist for another century. (Rosen 43)

I'm looking at the many valuable potentialities of writing through three lenses:

1. Writing is spatial and visual, and this helps it do things that are hard or impossible in audible temporal speech.
2. Writing helps people step outside of their language and see it as an external object.
3. Even though writing puts language into external visible space, it also turns out to be a medium that enhances privacy.

1. Because Writing Is Spatial and Visual, It Can Do Things that Are Hard or Impossible in Audible Temporal Speech

Writing Is Great for Preserving Language and Carrying It Across Space and Time

This is the traditional reason for celebrating writing—indeed for *inventing* writing. Without durable writing, we have only memory to use in carrying thoughts to someone next door or in another land—tomorrow or one hundred years from now. The *permanence* of writing helps explain what is actually a peculiar assumption lurking in most people's minds in our literate culture: that the written word is more *real* or *authentic* than the "spoken version" of that word. This is why spelling changes pronunciation in our present culture more often than pronunciation changes spelling. (The oddity of English spelling leads people sometimes to pronounce "often" with a "t" and "calm" with an "l").

If someone gives me driving directions to her house, she often says, "It's easy; you can't get lost," but unless I write it down I usually do. Plato sees my problem differently: he says I get lost *because* of writing (*Phaedrus*). He's right, of course, that this newfangled technology of writing ruined all our memories. But we are stuck now with our disability and we need writing. And we naturally want access to more and larger stretches of language. We want to be able to buy (or download!) the *Odyssey* instead of waiting till there's a performance in town by a singer who can remember-and-recreate the whole thing.

Admittedly, with telephones and recording devices, we can also carry speech across space and time, and this is just the technology that our children call primitive. But writing is usually more convenient for anything longer than voicemail messages. People used to say that computers would obviate paper, but now we're drowning in it.

Because writing can *conserve* speech—speech that time wipes out—it tends to function as a *conservative* force—in the various senses of that word. By preserving texts, writing is usually a force for conserving culture—often a force for stability. What's old and little used tends to have prestige. We keep Roman numerals for clocks and kings. The Japanese keep old Chinese script. In most cultures that have writing, literates often assume that the *point* of writing is to resist not only linguistic change (since spoken language evolves more quickly than written language), but also to resist cultural change. And yet, paradoxically, writing can help those who *resist* tradition. "It is only in a literate culture that the past's inconsistencies have to be accounted for, a process that encourages skepticism and forces history to diverge from myth" (Crain 138—summarizing Goody and Watt).

Writing Saves Time

Because speech is so good for back-and-forth dialogue, people tend to run meetings or seminars by "having a discussion." But in discussions, only one person can talk at a time, and a few voices often dominate. Even when everyone listens and encourages, a discussion is actually a poor way to achieve one of its main goals: the maximum sharing of information and thinking from everyone. Most people who have to attend lots of meetings fret at all the wasted time.

Writing permits a much quicker sharing of more people's thinking and reactions. Many groups and organizations have learned to save time by using emails and discussion sites—even when the participants are sitting in offices near each other. People complain about the carelessness of email and the problems it can create; they sometimes forget all its advantages over spoken dialogue. Honeycutt documents a Microsoft directive that encourages email for internal communication rather than the telephone because it saves time and allows for more reflection (Crain 320). (See also the section in Chapter 7 on "inkshedding" to make meetings more effective for sharing thoughts.)

It would have been wonderful to be present when "Homer" recited his epics, but even a leisurely thoughtful silent reading of the text is much faster. Books on tape are lovely, but silent reading is faster and it permits stopping and re-reading. If I want to find out what my students have learned, it would be nice to sit down with each of them for a talk, but there isn't time. Instead I make them write their thinking in a paper or exam. I can read these quickly. And if I don't want to assess them but just hear their thinking (imagine that!—too few teachers can), I can "hear" much more if I ask for some low stakes ungraded writing—or even a letter to me.

Writing Is Good for Math and Other Calculations

We can *say* "three thousand seven hundred and forty-eight," but it was only by creatively leaping *away from speech* that humans figured out what can be done with a different and spatial representation of the number: 3,748.

> The mathematicians were the first thinkers who realized the enormous potential of writing as writing. . . . The alphabet itself was a blind alley for mathematics, as it was for music. In Greek and Roman mathematics, alphabetically based numerical systems were a hindrance rather than a help [because they treated written numerical symbols as nothing more than abbreviations for words]. (Roy Harris 135–137).
>
> If mathematics had to rely on speech as its cognitive mode, we should still be living in a primitive agricultural society. (144)
>
> [The Sumerian invention of zero as "place-holder"] represents not a development of but a complete break away from any notion that written signs should conform to or mirror the structures of spoken language. (136)
>
> [B]oth systems of Greek numerical notation (the so-called Herodianic and the alphabetic system) were retrograde moves precisely because they treated written numerical symbols as nothing more than abbreviations for words. (137)

I'm quoting Roy Harris in his larger argument that stresses the essential visual and spatial nature of writing. He inveighs against people who think of writing as merely recorded speech. He points out an important fact that we often overlook: space is not such a good medium for representing what happens in time. Note, for example, the difficulty of representing the richness of music accurately on paper. This is especially obvious when it comes to rhythm: a simple, obvious, jazzy syncopation that our body easily picks up and moves to—that same rhythm is hard to notate on paper and very hard to read. In short, it's hard to translate what we hear into something we see.

What Harris celebrates in writing is how well it represents *information*, not audible, temporal speech. The medium of space is ideal for diagrams. Harris shows how well space can represent electrical circuits, knitting diagrams, and complex logical diagrams. He focuses on things like this as paradigms for writing in order to jolt us from our habit of thinking that written-down speech is the paradigm of writing. Where Frost said that poetry is what's lost in translation, Harris says, in effect, that true writing is what we gain when we free it from time and stop thinking of it as a translation of speech. (More than one mathematician has told me about a subtle prestige or snobbism that attaches to articles in math that rely mostly on symbols and use as few words as possible.)

Mathematics and diagrams are not the only examples where writing outshines speech by stepping outside time. When people want to analyze and compare long stretches of language, they naturally resort to visible language. We need all-at-once spatial diagrams and visual schemes to see how a piece of language is working, or to make lists of agreement and disagreement among versions of a story—for example, in courtroom testimony or (classically) in the four gospel versions of Christ's life.

Insofar as writing exploits the spatial and out-of-time dimension, it is a powerful tool for examining the logic in discourse. When we speak a stretch of thinking (or when we use writing to record a linear stretch of spoken language), we often slide convincingly from one idea to the next and then to the next—till we have wandered into contradicting ourselves without realizing it. Lawyers learn to exploit the slipperiness of spoken language on purpose. But careful writing and diagrams help us see the logic (or lack of it) behind a seductive train of language. More powerful still are the formal languages that logicians have devised for analyzing complex reasoning—and these are languages that differ most from speech.

It's well to note, however, that logic pays a price for avoiding time. Logically speaking we cannot say both Yes and No. But since we live in the realm of time, there are many situations where it makes sense to say Yes on Monday and No on Tuesday. For example, it's useful to write down all the words and ideas you can think of about your topic on Monday—in effect saying nothing but Yes; but then on Tuesday cross-examine and doubt them as hard as you can—in effect trying to say No to them all. By exploiting time, we can get the benefits of both credulity and skepticism. Similarly, it can be useful to be a loose and accepting teacher or parent at certain times or for certain activities and strict for others. (For more about this see Chapter 1 of my *Writing With Power*, *Embracing Contraries*, "The Uses of Binary Thinking," and my essays about the believing game.)

I've been celebrating how visual, spatial writing evades time, while sequential speech is trapped in time. But that doesn't diminish the obvious fact that most writing *is* the representation of linear spoken language. That's why Harris has to work so hard to warn us *against* defining writing as the representation of speech.

2. Writing Helps People Step Outside Their Language and See It as an External Object

Writing Can Help Us Plan and Revise and thereby Figure Out Complex or Difficult Thinking

Whether it's a tricky professional letter, an important love letter, an intricate complex essay, or a poem, consider the arsenal of techniques that writing gives us: we can jot notes, freewrite ideas, write a draft, use an outline, revise, give a draft to others for feedback, revise some more, get more feedback, revise some more, and edit for surface features, and get someone else to copy edit. And throughout this process we can repeatedly step outside our language and our thinking—walk away, talk to others, or put it aside. I find it particularly powerful to *forget* about it for a day, a week, or a year so I can come back to it with fresh eyes and often with a different frame of mind. Most serious writers use the full arsenal. I've certainly used them all on this book. Revising is actually a dialogue with oneself (and sometimes with others) and this explains how writing helps us come up with new insights we didn't have before. Indeed, revising can serve to *free* us from what we presently think. In short, writing is an ideal medium for words that matter—for high-stakes language and thinking.

Recording equipment now lets us step outside our speech and listen to it, but anyone who tries to revise or rework spoken language with fancy splicing and dubbing equipment will quickly resort to writing.

It's hard to get complex thinking clear in speech. Over and over in my life, when I've tried to use speech to explain or argue for some important idea I cared about, I've failed utterly to make any progress in making people believe me—often even to understand me. Over and over, I had to withdraw and resort to writing before I could get anyone to listen.

Of course it's *possible* to learn to speak coherently and even eloquently for high-stakes purposes. Some people learn to draft and revise and rehearse speech in their minds—to cook their thinking internally—so that when it comes out "for the first time" it is fully developed and polished. People in nonliterate societies like Homer and Chief Seattle learned to exploit the technology of speech in a way that most people in a literate society have failed to learn.

Even in our culture of writing, some jazz musicians train themselves to improvise their best creations on the fly. So too did most classical musicians of only one or two hundred years ago. This tradition might have played at least a small part in Mozart's extraordinary ability to cook many of his incredibly rich and sophisticated pieces of music in his mind till he could finally write out the first and final draft of many symphonies, quartets, and concertos.

Still, even as the scholar of African American culture, Michael Eric Dyson, celebrates speech and the oral tradition, he goes on immediately to stress the importance of writing for greater control and the ability to rework:

> The oral form is crucial to the cultural and racial identity of the tribe, the group, and the polis, and preserves the political and ethnic imagination that grounds communal existence. On the other hand, the written form contests certain limitations of the oral

form because it situates the writer and the reader at a critical discursive juncture that encourages the articulation of conflicting memories. . . .

I think that writing per se—the capacity of people to reflect critically upon their experiences and then filter those experiences through the lens of a composed text—certainly shapes self-expression in a way different from, say, oral expression. In other words, as Ali Mazrui, the Africanist scholar, says, there is strictly speaking, something deeply conservative about the oral form because it only preserves what people remember, and more important, what they've chosen to weave into the fabric of their collective memory. . . .

It makes a big difference to have a body of writing to appeal to, and against which to contrast our self-understanding, our self-revelation, and our self-invention. It makes a huge difference to think about our ideas in relation to written words that anger us, that inspire us, that cajole us to agree or argue with what's being communicated, whether it's the writings of Ellison, or the writings of Foucault, or the writings of Baldwin, or the writings of Hurston. With writing, there's a different—and I want to stress different, not superior—moment of textual possibility than with orality, because the written narrative opens up space within its seams for the alternate reading, the alternative interpretation. (26)

Writing Encourages Explicitness, Precision, and Rhetorical Awareness

It's not just that writing *helps* or *permits* us to create complex meanings. As a physical medium and process, it actually encourages us to do so. That is, the medium of writing puts pressure on us (though of course it doesn't force us) to spell out things that we wouldn't need to spell out if we were speaking to a present listener. The pressure derives from the fact that writing can be read by people who are not present—even people we don't know. Absent readers don't share the context of our speaking—our present situation and the things in the minds of those who are with us—and as Plato noted, absent readers can't ask for clarification if we are unclear.

When we have to spell out what we leave implied in conversation, we have to work out our thinking more clearly. Our words might have *seemed* clear and convincing to live listeners, but the process of writing out our thoughts often shows us a big hole or contradiction that we didn't notice in speaking. If we want an explanation or argument to be powerful, we need to spell out assumptions—a process that sometimes shows these assumptions as dubious. Even if we want to argue for a *weak* position (like a lawyer defending a guilty client), we can do it better if we use careful revising to see the problems we need to hide. This is why people argue that literacy itself helps thinking (e.g., Havelock, *Preface*; Goody and Watt).

Writing Invites Complexity from the Reader

Just as writing gives writers time to create complex meanings in language, it also gives *readers* time to take as long as they need to re-read and work out and ponder complex meanings. Indeed, writing helps readers *surpass* writers in the complexity game. Even though speech is valuable for its "vocality"—the way it carries more meanings than silent text with its intonation—writing is valuable for its *polyvocality*. That is, readers of a text can project multiple and conflicting voices or meanings onto that one text. Where spoken intonation gloriously enriches the meaning of words by adding small nuances and large significance, it does this by suggesting a *single* intended meaning. Thus we can hear whether someone said

> I didn't think <u>he</u> stole the money
> I didn't think he <u>stole</u> the money
> I didn't think he stole the <u>money</u>

Thus, when we hear a good reading of a poem or see a good production of Shakespeare, we hear one interpretation of it. But when we read *Hamlet* in silence and know how to exploit the technology of reading, we can find myriad different and mutually conflicting interpretations of the same words.

Thus with the magic generativity of silent *written* texts, readers can see more than the writer intended or even imagined. Readers can come back again and again to the same written text and bring different mind-sets to it. ("Never trust the teller trust the tale," said D. H. Lawrence. Most literary critics have insisted that interpretation should not be limited by what the writer intended.)

> I'm not pretending that the intonation of spoken language always makes all listeners hear the same interpretation. Different viewers of a Shakespeare production may think they heard different interpretations. We filter what we hear through our own point of view.
>
> *"When she said that, she insulted my manhood."*
>
> *"Relax, she was just making a lighthearted ironic joke."*
>
> But when two listeners hear different meanings, the problem is usually too little intonation. More would have cleared up the ambiguity.

Just as writing can invite multiple interpretations, it can also invite multiple paths through a text. Centuries before the invention of hypertext, readers had already invented it: they learned to jump around as they read, browse, check the table of contents or the index, or jump to the "discussion" in a scholarly article. (This was harder when writing was on scrolls.) With writing, we can create multiple texts running down the page, and let readers *sort of* read two texts at the same time. (It's hard to *hear* two people speaking at the same time—though some mothers come close.)

Writing Helps Us Present Ourselves as We Wish

It's our speaking by which we are judged most relentlessly and savagely. I'm not just referring to raised eyebrows when we use "sloppy grammar." There's something deeper here. Speech is one of the most powerful cues by which humans most quickly and decisively decide who they approve of and who they don't. People who are completely tolerant of taboo *ideas* are often deeply prejudiced against people who use "wrong language." In truth, when people hear speech as "wrong" or "bad," it's usually something deeper than grammar they hear, and their reaction is often more visceral. What they hear is *"Alien!"—"Not from our tribe!"*

This issue is most deeply tangled up with race (more on this in Chapter 16 on Benefits). Writing can give us a voice not available to us in speaking. We can use it to communicate widely yet not reveal our race, region, or class. *Gender* is probably the identity marker that has the biggest influence on how people read a text, and women have probably been the most frequent users of anonymity or assumed names to avoid the knee-jerk reactions of prejudiced readers.

There is a long and noble tradition of people using writing to make themselves anonymous. These writers want readers to focus on *what* they said and how well—not who wrote it. Writing gives everyone access to the language of prestige or dominance. As one dog says to another in a *New Yorker* cartoon, "On the internet, they don't know you're a dog." (For a study of anonymous writing through the ages, see Mullan.)

Even when the writer's gender is not hidden, the medium of writing itself helps against sexism. Note this striking testimony from a South African woman: "[W]riting has created a free space for most women—much freer than speech. There is less interruption, less immediate and shocked reaction. . . . The book is bound, circulated, read. It retains its autonomy much more than a woman is allowed in the oral situation. Writing offers a moment of intervention" (Yvonne Vera, quoted in Mantel 29).

A research report on women academics speaks of women who "prefer the written to the spoken voice, because in this form they can project authority and influence without engaging in confrontations that raise confusing issues of appropriate response" (Aisenberg and Harrington 74).

For an interesting unexpected example of a man with a problem of "wrong speech," consider the poet James Merrill. He comes from an upper-class Connecticut family (linked to Merrill Lynch) and once remarked that he preferred giving poetry readings abroad in places like Greece because listeners there didn't have so many vexed reactions to his tight-jawed "aristocratic" accent.

Writing Helps Us See Language *as Language*

David Olson argues this point at length. We usually notice the *words*—as words—more often when we read a text than when we listen to speech. The difference is most pronounced, of course, when we are learning to read—trying to say the words one at a time and even sounding them out, letter by letter. Olson argues that we never fully lose that awareness even when we become fluent and automatic readers and think of ourselves as "not seeing the words." And when a text causes us even the slightest difficulty, we go back to consciousness of *seeing words*.

Olson insists that the visibility of words as objects

> spells the death of "word" magic or more precisely, "name" magic. Words are no longer emblems; words are now distinguished from both things and from names of things; words as linguistic entities come into consciousness.

It becomes feasible to think of the meanings of words independently from the things they designate. . . . An action on the name, as in a hex, does not affect the named because the word, unlike the name, is not a part of the thing; it is, as we say, just a word. (*World on Paper* 75–76)

As Halliday says, "when the signified is no longer a thing but has become a word, a new semiotic modality has evolved which we call writing" (*Complementarities* 140).

Olson is an enthusiast for reading. He argues that texts "permit the distinction between 'sentence meaning' and 'intended meaning' or 'interpretation'" (*World on Paper* 37). He argues that even though listeners can argue about the meaning of what someone *spoke*, readers are more likely to start finding cracks between "what does the *text* say?" "what did the *writer* mean?" and "what does it mean to *us*?"

> [T]he author loses control of the interpretation of his or her expression because of its dislocation in space and time, a conceptual gap is opened up between the meaning of an expression and the meaning that the speaker/writer had intended that the listener construct. (Olson "Orality and Literacy" 138)

I don't resist Olson's enthusiasm for reading, but I resist his nearly total neglect of writing. This blind spot leads him to neglect even better evidence for an overall claim about *text*. Readers may be more aware of language as language than listeners are, but surely it's *writers* who are even *more* aware of language as language. His claim is that *reading* helps humans understand language as language, but it seems to me that the activity of *writing* is probably more powerful in fostering the sophistication about language that he champions. Writers have to take charge of language more than readers do. (Fans of reading often neglect writing. See my "War between Reading and Writing.")

Olson's argument has a strong historical cast. He builds on a paradox. That is, he starts by acknowledging that visual writing is *impoverished* because it cannot represent more than a fraction of the rich intonational or prosodic information carried by speech. But then he celebrates this as a glorious failure.

> [T]he history of scripts is not, contrary to the common view, the history of failed attempts and partial successes towards the invention of the alphabet, but rather the by-product of attempts to use a script for a language for which it is ill-suited. (*World* 89)

Because writing is so badly equipped to represent the subtle intonational meanings in speech, he argues that the development of literacy in the West led to a host of new words that express *how* the language was uttered—words that make up for the *lack* of intonation by expressing manner and intention (illocutionary speech acts). He gives interesting historical evidence for this process. Starting with ancient Greek texts and moving onward up through Middle English to the Renaissance, he gives long lists of words and when they first show up in any written records: words like *assert, assume, contradict, deny, doubt, hypothesize, predict,* and *suggest* (108–110). Language itself becomes richer, he argues, because the medium of writing is poor: with writing, people encountered a need for interpretive words that are not so necessary in speech.

A startling idea, but I assume he is right. For I've always been struck with how often oral texts, like those from the Old Testament and other ancient poetry, tend to use naked quotation of direct speech: not indirect quotation ("He said *that* they shouldn't eat the fruit of the tree") and no interpretive words. Over and over, the writer settles for the plain word "say" and doesn't seem to give explicit indications of *how* the words were said—mood, tone, or manner. For example:

> Now the serpent was more crafty than any other wild animal that the LORD God had made. He said to the woman, "Did God say, 'You shall not eat from any tree in the garden'?" The woman said to the serpent, "We may eat of the fruit of the trees in the garden; but God said, 'You shall not eat of the fruit of the tree that is in the middle of the garden, nor shall you touch it, or you shall die.'" But the serpent said to the woman, "You will not die; for God knows that when you eat of it, your eyes will be opened, and you will be like God, knowing good and evil." (Genesis 3: 1–5)

Thus Olson writes:

> The history of literacy, in other words, is the struggle to recover what was lost in simple transcription [of speech]. The solution is to turn non-lexical properties of speech such as stress and intonation into lexical ones; one announces that the proposition expressed is to be taken as an assumption or an inference and whether it is to be taken metaphorically or literally. (Olson *World* 111)

But I cannot give up my misgivings about how Olson focuses only on readers. Surely it was *writers,* not readers, who learned to enrich language in this way. *Writers* had to say to themselves, "Let's see. My readers can't hear me recite these words. So instead of just writing "She *said* to him '. . .', I can write "She *challenged* him, '. . .'" Readers were the *beneficiaries* of an enlarged language, but writers did the heavy lifting.

I can imagine someone charging Olson with *technological determinism*: the idea that the technology of literacy all by itself changes human consciousness and thinking. When Havelock, Goody, Watt, and Ong made arguments that were vulnerable to the charge of technological determinism, their work eventually created a firestorm of resistance. Brian Street writes:

> One response to the growing role of technologies of communication in our lives is to overstate their ability to determine our social and cultural activity. This tradition has been evident in earlier approaches to literacy, where over-emphasis on the "technology" of literacy (cf., Goody, 1977) has led to assumption about the ability of literacy in itself, as an autonomous force, to have effects, such as the raising of cognitive abilities, the generation of social and economic development, and the shift to modernity. All of these features of the autonomous model were rooted in assumptions about technological determinism that the ideological model and new social practice approaches to literacy have challenged and discredited. And yet, we

now find the same array of distorting lenses being put on as we ask, what are the consequences of the present generation of "new technologies," those associated in particular with the internet and with digital forms of communication? While these forms evidently do have affordances in Kress's (2003) sense, it would be misleading and unhelpful to read from the technology into the effects without first positing the social mediating factors that give meaning to such technologies. How, then, can we take sufficient account of the technological dimension of new literacies without sliding such determinism? A range of literature from different intellectual traditions has begun to provide answers which, I suggest, if linked with the frameworks provided by New Literacy Studies and by Multimodality, may begin to help us "see" the new literacies in a fuller and more rounded way. (Street "New Literacies" 30–31)

Whether people are guilty of "technological determinism" depends a lot on differences in formulation: does a certain form of literacy *cause* a certain kind of thinking? Does it *foster* a certain kind of thinking? Does it *make available* a certain kind of thinking? I'm a cheerleader for writing—but what I'm cheering are the *potentialities* of writing as a material form. I don't say that writing in itself *causes* or even *necessarily leads to* all the good potentialities. Kress and others use the term "affordances" for what writing *makes possible* but doesn't necessarily lead to. In his *Before Writing*, Kress emphasizes how a child's activity of putting together and using the tools of writing actually does go some way toward transforming the child's consciousness. Learning to speak may involve plenty of work by babies, but the complex *materiality* of writing and its resistances can transform consciousness in new ways.

3. Even Though Writing Puts Language into External Visible Space, It's Also Good for Privacy

Writing seems the *worst* medium for privacy: once you put words on paper, there's no controlling who might read them. Think of all the children and adolescents who've had their private diaries broken into by a parent or sibling. The clever spy never puts words on paper. For private words, *thinking* is the only answer: don't say them or write them; keep them secure inside your head. If you write it, swallow the paper.

But speech is also dangerous and writing gives relief from that danger. That is, any words you speak in anyone's hearing cannot be recalled, changed, or "deleted." When the judge says "strike that from the record"—he can delete *written* words, but he can never strike the *spoken* words from the jury's ears and memories. Our most trusted loved ones and intimate friends forget many of the good things we say, but they never forget the truly bad or hurtful things we say. Most long-term relationships are stories of people who have survived words that both parties cannot forget and wish they could. (Solitary speaking is not dangerous in this way, and we tend to do it more when we are under stress or in the throes of mental illness. Humans are smart enough to look naturally for ways to use language for survival.)

If we know how to exploit the technological potential of writing, we can find that it is perfect for safe private language. We can write whatever is helpful to write and keep the words for our own eyes alone or rip up the words if the stakes are too high. When I'm confused or upset and I think inside my head about what's bothering me, the thoughts and feelings go round and round and don't usually give me relief or lead me anywhere. When I get myself to write out my thoughts and feelings—simply as they come—I usually get relief and new insights. We can tell someone to go to hell even if we love them or need them—or try out that suicide note—and all merely on paper. Of course private writing may not solve the dilemma, but it virtually always leads to progress toward clarity and perspective. At the very least, it allows me to let go of the troubled feelings enough to get some sleep—which is often impossible when the material goes round and round in my head. Of course it can be *more* helpful to speak my feelings to a trusted listener, but often enough such a person is not available—and indeed for *some* particular thoughts and feelings we don't feel we can trust anyone.

Sometimes we need to say something to a particular person—but we can't. We are too scared or it doesn't seem wise or we can't figure out how to say it. When we write out in private what we want to say, we can often figure out *whether* to say it or *how* to say it. It can lead to courage. We use paper ballots when there's a danger that voters won't or can't reveal their real opinions out loud in front of others.

I've noticed something interesting about exploratory writing on a computer. I often experience those words on the screen as less fully external or outside myself than words I print out or write on paper. I sometimes feel those pixilated words as half-inside-me and half-outside-me. It's as though a computer screen can function as a kind of "second mind" and I get to have a dialogue with it. I find two minds helpful.

But this phenomenon merely highlights something about ordinary private writing—whatever technology we use. As long as we don't give the words to anyone else, they are sort of half inside, half outside, and indeed function as a second mind.

From Brandt's extensive research:

> Many people I interviewed reported using private writing to purge feelings, primarily anger or grief. Much of this writing was never shown to anyone and was, in fact, destroyed. . . . Using writing as "a purge" or "vent" (frequently used expressions) was especially common among white and black women and among black men that I interviewed. This writing tended to occur at times of crisis: death, divorce, romantic loss, incarceration, war. (162)

She quotes one man who said that writing was, for him "an alternative to hitting people."

This helps explain, I think, that even though diaries have always been vulnerable to discovery and the CIA can now read the computer files we've deleted, nevertheless people through the ages have perennially used private diaries or journals—and still do. Diaries can function almost like a companion or second person. Diary keepers often address their diaries by name, for example, Anne Frank always began, "Dear Kitty." (See Taylor for excerpts from journals through the ages. About the concept itself of private writing—which is sometimes questioned on theoretical grounds, see my "In Defense of Private Writing.")

When I do writing workshops for teachers, I like to ask people to raise their hands if they do lots of private writing. I have a little fun by saying, "Most of you who didn't raise your hands are liars." For I can simply point out that if they do any "serious writing"—especially if it's for publication—*most* of that writing is private writing. That is, most of their exploratory writing and most of their drafts are not seen by anyone but themselves. The reason they "lied" is that they don't *feel* that writing as private. Instead they write almost as though the police (or colleagues in their field!) are about to break down the door and read these imperfect words. Even when people decide to share an unrevised draft with a friend or colleague (and it's seldom a first draft), that unchanged draft actually *was* private. That is, before they shared it, they probably read it over first and decided that it was okay to share. In effect they were consciously deciding to turn a piece of private writing into a public piece. They consciously *relinquished* the privacy that was there.

It made a big difference in my writing when I finally figured out that *most* of my "serious writing for publication" was actually private—even though my goal was a public text. *These* particular words on most of my drafts were not going to be seen by anyone but me. This made high-stakes writing easier and more adventuresome. I learned that I can try out dubious thoughts and include little comments to myself and not let anxiety infect my process of putting down words. Anxiety is unavoidable when I'm writing certain pieces for certain audiences (as with this book), but I can postpone the anxiety during most of the process of working out my thinking on paper—even letting myself write what I know will be unacceptable—and postpone the anxiety till I revise.

So there's a paradox here: language in its most dangerously permanent and public form—written rather than just thought or spoken—turns out helpful for privacy.

Thus Writing Is Ideal Not Just for High-Stakes but Also for Low-Stakes Language Use

I've just spoken of the private writing we do on the way to a high-stakes public document. But there's another kind of private writing where the goal isn't further writing: the goal is learning and understanding. The minimal case is when we write down spelling words or the conjugation of French verbs to help us learn them. But a more common form of low-stakes writing is exploited by teachers in all disciplines and has come to be known as "writing to learn" (as opposed to writing to demonstrate learning or to create good text). I've spent lots of time showing teachers in all fields how to use lots of low-stakes writing in class and for homework. We ask students to use casual easy writing to explore the ideas in their reading or lectures or class discussion. The writing is not collected—or if collected not graded at all. This helps students learn concepts and explore ideas. The goal is not a piece of writing; the goal is neural changes in the head.

I and many others in my field have been fighting against the pervasive assumption that writing in school should always be read by the teacher and evaluated. We like to point out an interesting discrepancy: teachers tend to assume that it's fine to have plenty of low-stakes academic *talk* or *discussion* in class—casual, exploratory, nongraded—but that writing always has to be high stakes and be evaluated and commented upon. (During one of my presentations, a professor objected: "But what if they write something that's *wrong* and I don't get to see it and correct it?" I wasn't quick enough to say what I thought of later: "But they *think* wrong things all the time—and *say* wrong things to their friends—and you aren't there to correct them.")

Low-stakes writing helps students learn and remember and explore their thinking, and even tends to improve their high-stakes essays. It warms up their writing and gives them fluency. And even though this low-stakes writing has all the carelessness of conversational talk or email, it actually sets a *higher* standard for clarity and liveliness in careful revised writing. That is, when I get a draft of a high-stakes paper that's completely tangled or hopelessly stiff and wooden, I can say, "When you revise, don't just straighten out your thinking and get rid of mistakes. Push for that clear lively direct voice that you've already shown me in your low-stakes writing." Yet this low-stakes writing takes no time or trouble for teachers. My mantra is that high-stakes writing needs to float on a deep wide sea of low-stakes writing.

And plenty of low-stakes writing is private in a looser sense of "privacy": not "just for me" but "just for you and me"—that is, "personal writing." So we often ask students to do low-stakes writing that they are willing to read only to a partner or small group. Or I can ask them to give it to me—but not for me to evaluate: "Tell me your thoughts about what you just read or what we just discussed in class." I can read very fast and I don't have to evaluate or respond, yet it helps my teaching enormously to hear their thinking. There's another benefit to all this low-stakes writing—subtle but powerful: it helps students experience writing as actual communication between human beings—(imagine that!)—rather than solely an exercise in writing to an authority who knows more about the topic than they do in order to be graded.

Many if not most of the personal letters we write are actually low-stakes private writing in this broader sense of the term: they are "just between you and me," and they are not trying to be good or lasting. (Some people think of email and Facebook writing as private too—till they get burned.)

Writing Can Help Us Experience Our Experience and thereby Resist Pressure

Writing can help us hang on to our own experience or thinking—hang on to ourselves—even when there are pressures from people in authority or from our culture to give it up. If I'm scared to say something to someone because of that person's authority or power over me, I might nevertheless go home and *write* what I don't dare say—even write *"to"* the person. For when I'm face to face, I often can't think clearly enough, my mind sometimes goes blank, and my voice may waver and sound completely hesitant. In my letter, I can write in a clear, strong, but nondefensive voice.

The writing might convince me not to *send* the letter—or perhaps I knew all along that I wouldn't send it. But the act of writing these words helps me hold on to my experience of what people said or how they treated me and thus to my point of view. Writing seems to give us a little more room from which to push back against the weight of expectations or authority—or if not push back, find some little path around them. Besides, the writing might even give me enough clarity of mind and courage that I *can* indeed insist on saying what I need to say—on paper or in person.

Of course plenty of people are more scared to write than to speak (and some of these scared writers have more courage than I do in speaking). But my focus here is on the *potentialities* of writing. Yes, one of the potentialities of speech is talking back when you are scared; I'd like to get better at that technology. But in the meantime, I and many others can use one of the potentialities of writing: putting private words on paper so that people or situations don't take away our agency and our ownership of how we experience things.

I noted earlier how writing can help cultures resist change. So too, it can help individuals resist culture. Of course, insofar as the culture has infiltrated our minds, private writing has no leverage for resistance. But the infiltration of a culture over an individual is never complete. Individual experiences almost always present some potential dissonance to cultural assumptions. (As a child I breathed in a culture that assumed women were the "weaker sex" and that men should do the "serious" work, and that people of color in low-status jobs should be subservient. But many of my childhood experiences violated this assumption.) So private writing can help us take our experience seriously and notice dissonance between what we think and feel and how we are supposed to think and feel. Resistance to culture depends on how well we notice and attend to our individual experiences. In short, speaking and writing are both social acts, but to different degrees. Because of the inherent potentialities of the two media, speaking tends to invite more of the social dimension and writing a bit more of the private individual dimension.

This potentiality for resisting the culture shows itself vividly in literature. Consider people like Walt Whitman, Emily Dickinson, e e cummings, Virginia Woolf, James Joyce, Mallarmé, "concrete" poets, and L=A=N=G=U=A=G=E poets. (See Roy Harris, *Signs*, on French writers exploiting spatial potentialities in writing that are unavailable in oral language.) They were all drenched in their cultures, but they used writing to push back against expectations and linguistic conventions. This "cult of originality" in writing might be peculiar to our culture; some even call it decadent or dead-end. Yet it reveals a potentiality in writing that is there to be tapped. (See Georges Bataille on literature as disruptive force.)

❊   ❊   ❊

After this chapter on the potential virtues of writing, I'll use the next three to explore the potential virtues of speech. Three to one? Writing may be the goal for this book, but the *impetus* for the book is to explore speech. We already know a lot about the virtues of writing. I think I have more news to report about the virtues of speech.

LITERACY STORY

The Development of Alphabetic Writing in the Middle East

The first thing to notice is how long it took humans to come up with writing. Our ancestors learned to put meaning into visual form 25,000 years before any of them learned to write. That is, visual art came early and it appeared in *all* cultures. Writing wasn't invented for 25,000 years and it showed up in very few cultures. Schmandt-Besserat and Erard make an interesting observation about the difference between early visual art and early writing (8). Visual art started out (and continues to be) especially good for representing what is mysterious and numinous. When writing finally comes along, it evolves from physical tokens and is used for very unspiritual and unmysterious commercial purposes like recording sheep, barrels of wine, and measures of wheat.

> The token system coincided with the Neolithic Revolution, when animals and cereals were first domesticated. About 7500 BCE probably in a Syrian village, farmers modeled counters in clay in various specific and striking shapes that were easy to recognize, remember, and duplicate. Each shape was assigned a meaning: A cone was a small measure of grain, a sphere stood for a large measure of grain. . . . This invention was simple, but it was a great invention: It was the first visual code—the first system of artifacts created for the sole purpose of communicating information. (Schmandt-Besserat and Erard 8–9. See their short essay for a useful synthesis of scholarship up to now on the "Origins and Forms of Writing.")

The token system lasted for 4,000 years. But then around 3500 BCE in Uruk (the site of Gilgamesh), temple administrators made another big breakthrough in the path to writing. They started putting these clay tokens inside clay envelopes—oversized ravioli—so no one could tamper with them. But before baking the envelopes to preserve them, they pressed these tokens into the outsides of the soft clay envelopes. Was this writing? Perhaps we don't have writing till they realized that they could skip the token so readers could just read "signs" on the *outside* of the envelope.

I love to linger over this moment. It gives us a parable for a central problem that still haunts our understanding of reading. Does a text "contain" its meaning? Is there meaning "inside" or did the maker leave it out and trick us? This story provides us a somewhat fanciful answer, but one that pleases me: meanings *used* to be inside language, but then writers stopped including them. So now our written words are empty; they don't contain what they're alleged to contain. Writers *pretend* the meaning is in there; some readers are fooled; other readers understand but agree to honor the game; others insist on focusing on the *absence*. Nevertheless, really good writers can somehow *charm* tokens back into the envelopes and thus create (seem to create?) real presence.

We get something more like writing when these Middle Easterners turned the rounded clay envelope surfaces into flat clay tablets—going from three dimensions to two.

But others date the beginning of writing with two later developments. First, folks learned to *abstract* a number. Up till then, a cone stood for a small measure of grain and a round token stood for a large measure. But then they decided they could use the round token to mean exactly *ten* small measures and the cone token for *one*. Suddenly they had the numerals *one* and *ten*. (Schmandt-Besserat and Erard 9). In a comparable move, they (always we talk about this vague "they"—but there must have been a person or small group who first figured something out) invented *syntax*. They worked out a new set of conventions whereby words can *modify* other words. Before this breakthrough, the idea of three sheep needed three symbols: "sheep, sheep, sheep." Once we get modification or syntax, the same meaning gets written with two symbols: "three" "sheep." This marks the transition out of a purely token system:

> Harris (1986) has argued that the decisive step from tokens to scripts occurs when symbols shift from *token-iterative* ["sheep sheep sheep"] to *emblem slotting* systems ["three sheep"] or what I prefer to think of as *acquiring syntax*. A system which represents three sheep by three symbols of a sheep . . . is categorically different, he suggests, from one which represents the same three sheep by two tokens, one representing sheep, the other the number. (Olson 72–73, *World on Paper*)

Harris is a semiotician with an interesting axe to grind. He is at pains to insist that writing started out recording *information*, not speech. No one says "sheep, sheep, sheep." He insists that we misunderstand the nature of writing if we give in to the pervasive assumption that writing is speech written down and that the development of writing is a triumphal story leading to the alphabet.

Harris gives a vivid example of a Native American text "written" on a skin. It's clearly a *text*; it records an expedition across the Great Lakes; it has both idiographic symbols (semi pictures) and abstract signs; it can be read with precision about what happened—with numbers and places. But *it doesn't read as words*. It

When writing begins to *constrain performance*, it enacts a process we see in music and drama. Medieval and early Renaissance music leaves an enormous amount of choice to the performer—in a real sense asking the performer to *collaborate* with the composer. Over the centuries composers came to be more and more possessive about exactly how the music should sound—how fast to go, what to stress, where to be loud and soft. So too with drama: Shakespeare invites collaboration from performers; George Bernard Shaw gives very little leeway (even spelling out what a character is probably thinking while silent).

Harris, by the way, has tough sledding in his desire to break a necessary link between writing and speech. He's fighting a long ingrained tradition (at least in the West—with our alphabet). Aristotle: "Words spoken are symbols or signs of affections or impressions of the soul; written words are the signs of words spoken." (*De Interpretatione* I. 4–6). "The sole reason for the existence of [writing] is to represent [speech]. The linguistic object is not defined by the combination of the written word and the spoken word:

> The spoken form alone constitutes the object (Saussure 1916/83)." These quotations are from Olson (66) who points also to Bloomfield, an influential figure in the development of twentieth-century linguistics: he identified speech with language itself and saw writing as "a way of recording language."

reads as a set of cues for *any* verbal performance of the meanings. Only gradually does writing start to tell readers what words to say or hear.

The Path to the Alphabet

If we want to define writing as speech written down, we get a much later date for the beginning of writing. There were a number of stages. An important step was the invention of phonograms: visual signs that stood for a sound. (More about this in the Literacy Story about the Rebus after Chapter 3.) This goes along with the cultural development of starting to use writing for purposes other than commercial transaction. Writing begins to be combined with small statues and put in tombs to ensure survival after death. Written speeches to the gods were put in the mouths of human worshippers "using sentences with subjects, verbs, and complements, bringing writing to model itself onto speech by adopting the syntax of spoken language" (Schmandt-Besserat and Erard 13). For this kind of writing, the Sumerians develop not the alphabet but cuneiform writing with wedge-shaped signs inscribed on clay by a reed stylus. Now writing begins to be used for historical, religious, legal, scholarly, and literary texts, including poetry—though cuneiform writing did not represent sounds (13).

Finally around 1700, probably in present-day Lebanon, the alphabet itself is invented—a set of symbols to represent the sounds of spoken language. The alphabet

> was invented only once—which means that all the present alphabets, from Latin, Arabic, Greek, Cyrillic, Hebrew, Ethiopian, and Tamil to Navaho derive from the same first alphabet. . . . Neither syllabic nor logographic, it owed nothing to the cuneiform; rather, it was a totally new system based on the identification of the distinctive sounds of a language and matching each with a specific sign. The first alphabet consisted of 22 letters, each standing for a phoneme—a single speech sound. The success of the alphabet was to streamline script. Compared to the some 600 cuneiform signs, the 22 letters were easy to learn allowing literacy to spread more widely. (Schmandt-Besserat and Erard 15)

This original alphabet had no vowels. But the Jews carried this alphabet one step further toward the representation of speech sounds by taking three consonants that had less work to do (aleph, yod, and hay), and using them to represent vowel sounds. When the Greeks later adapted the Semitic alphabet, they took the next step and designated true and separate vowels that had no other work to do. With these vowels

> writers could reproduce their own way of speaking to a reasonable extent, and the readers could decide the pronunciation of the author. . . . In addition

the alphabetic script was easier to learn than the earlier systems, and for that reason many more people than just a small group of professional scribes could employ written language. (Jansen 72)

Havelock launched his large career with his extended celebration and analysis of the Greek accomplishment: "At a stroke the Greeks provided a table of elements of linguistic *sound* not only manageable because of economy, but for the first time in the history of homo sapiens, also accurate" (quoted in Olson 66, *World on Paper* my emphasis).

It was the Phoenicians who carried the Hebrew alphabet to the Greeks, and it became somehow common in nineteenth-century Germanic philology to speak of the Phoenicians as *inventors* or at least propagators of the alphabet. "This is misleading. There were no Phoenicians in the Bronze Age, and so the Phoenicians did not 'invent' the alphabet" (O'Connor, in Katz 152). Katz and O'Connor suggest that it's hard not to infer scholarly antisemitism among the Germanic philologists who seemed to read the Jews out of the story. In truth, "Some of the earliest Greek texts were written right to left, showing the influence of contact with Semitic-speaking peoples, but writing left to right was established by around 500 BCE" (Bernard 23)

3 Speaking as a Process

What Can It Offer Writing?

IN THIS AND the following two chapters, I will explore the virtues in speaking and spoken language—even if some of those virtues are not exploited by all groups or cultures. For example, one of the great virtues of speaking is *ease*. And yet speaking is not so easy for people in some cultures and families and other situations. But if we identify potentialities, perhaps we can learn to exploit them.

> Speaking may not be easy if you live in a culture or even a family that keeps telling you, *Don't talk too much*, or *If you say the wrong thing you'll get in big trouble* or *What you have to say is not important*. These messages can get into the sinews. Children who are treated badly will also be hesitant to speak; if they are treated badly enough they won't speak at all. And when a whole culture treats easy speech as a danger and teaches vigilance at all costs (as I described in Chapter 1), it is failing to exploit this potentiality of speech.
>
> When I contrast the role of culture in speaking and writing versus what is potential, I can't avoid the venerable distinction between nature and nurture. Speech is particularly valuable to investigate if we want to avoid black/white either/or thinking about nature and nurture. Nature makes us genetically predisposed to speak. Yet *whether* we speak and *what* and *how* we speak is entirely dependent upon nurture or culture. Even people like Chomsky who stress linguistic universals or Universal Grammar acknowledge the many central features of speech that are dependent upon culture. Universal Grammar has to produce Chinese, English, and Inupiat.
>
> For an interesting example of nature and nurture interacting, consider this recent experiment. Monkeys traditionally fear snakes. But researchers raised lab monkeys in an environment that led them to have no fear of snakes. Yet when these monkeys saw films of normal monkeys exhibiting fear of snakes, they too developed this fear. But the researchers didn't stop there. Next they showed the monkeys films that were doctored in such a way as to show other monkeys exhibiting fear of flowers. When the lab monkeys saw these films they *didn't* come to fear flowers. In short, it appears that monkeys have a genetic *disposition* to be afraid of snakes, but they don't develop this response unless it is activated by social experience. (*National Geographic* 20–21)

In this chapter I'll focus on the *process* of speaking and explore four advantages that might be borrowed or adapted for writing. In the following two chapters I'll focus on virtues in the *product* of speaking: spoken language.

1. Speaking Is Easy

Consider the miracle of human speech. By age four or earlier, every human child who isn't brain damaged or left in the woods to be raised by wolves has mastered the essential complex structures of a native language—or two or even three.

The human capacity for speech carries the potentiality of fluent and automatic language—of easy casual communication and the exploration of thinking. In situations of comfort, most people can call on a miraculous ability to find words without trying, without looking for them, without planning. We need only open our mouths and words come out. Indeed, we sometimes open our mouths and utter words before we quite know what we are saying. There wouldn't be so many strong warnings against unplanned, unguarded speech in so many cultures if humans didn't have a propensity to blurt. We've all been burned for it. In some U.S. states, children can be ruled legally "incorrigible" and confined to an institution when they refuse to *not blurt*: it's called "talking back."

Unplanned speech can be disordered: without time to plan our thoughts and build them into coherent syntax, we sometimes create broken syntax like that we saw from Albertine in the retirement community (quoted in Chapter 1):

> and we decided—
> I wanted to know
> the great question that was on my mind-
> I'll never forget-
> that's folk curiosity.
> I wanted to know
> *what makes people tick.*

But most of what she said was fluent and connected—and this is true for most people as they get warmed up and unselfconscious in their speaking. The linguist William Labov calls attention to the *coherence* in everyday speech— even by people whose speech is often disparaged:

> Our own studies . . . of the grammaticality of everyday speech show that the great majority of utterances in all contexts are complete sentences, and most of the rest can be reduced to grammatical form by a small set of editing rules. The proportions of grammatical sentences vary with class backgrounds and styles. The highest percentage of well-formed sentences are found in casual speech, and working-class speakers use more well-formed sentences than middle-class speakers. The widespread myth that most speech is ungrammatical is no doubt based upon tapes made at learned conferences, where we obtain the maximum number of irreducibly ungrammatical sequences. (Labov 222; quoted in Shaughnessy, *Errors and Expectations* 17)

Halliday spells out this last point:

> [T]he earliest examples of spoken language that were recorded for purposes of analysis were almost always specimens of intellectual discourse —academic seminars and the like. This tends to be the most disrupted kind of speech, with lots of hesitations and changes of direction, because the speakers are having to think out what to say and are all the time listening to themselves as they go along. ["*Monitoring*" is one of Halliday's favorite words for what people tend to do when they write, but not when they talk comfortably in safety.] (*Complementarities* 132)

It usually takes a degree of safety to loosen the tongue. Yet sometimes (as with some "back talk"), when people are scared or threatened they rise to the occasion and come out with just the words they need or want to say—not carefully choosing or planning the words they speak. For a famous example, Fannie Lou Hamer is quoted with these unscripted words that had a decisive influence on the 1964 Democratic convention:

> All of this is on account we want to register, to become first-class citizens, and if the Freedom Democratic Party is not seated now, I question America. Is this America, the land of the free and the home of the brave where we have to sleep with our telephones off the hooks because our lives be threatened daily because we want to live as decent human beings—in America?

When Senator Hubert Humphrey suggested a compromise position he'd worked out with Walter Mondale, Walter Reuther, and J. Edgar Hoover, and argued that his position on the ticket was at stake, Hamer replied:

> Do you mean to tell me that your position is more important than four hundred thousand black people's lives? Senator Humphrey, I know lots of people in Mississippi who have lost their jobs trying to register to vote. I had to leave the plantation where I worked in Sunflower County. Now if you lose this job of Vice-President because you do what is right, because you help the MFDP, everything will be all right. God will take care of you. But if you take [the nomination] this way, why, you will never be able to do any good for civil rights, for poor people, for peace, or any of those things you talk about. Senator Humphrey, I'm going to pray to Jesus for you. (See Hamer)

It wasn't safety that loosened her tongue. Commitment or passion overcame danger and led her to eloquent speech without planning.

Part of the miracle of speech is *complexity*: Every human who learns a language from infancy possesses a rich, intricate, and complete native language. When any child talks without planning, his or her words obey complex rules— an intricate set of grammatical bells and whistles comparable to (though not the same as) every other human language. Steven Pinker puts it this way:

> A preschooler's tacit knowledge of grammar is more sophisticated than the thickest style manual or the most state-of-the-art computer language system. . . . The complexity of language, from the scientist's point of view, is part of our biological birthright; it is not something that parents teach

their children or something that must be elaborated in school. (*Language Instinct* 6)

As children get older they acquire further complexities of syntax and lexicon, but the essential miracle happens early.

It's not that learning to speak is easy for babies. They all put out heroic efforts in the process. But they seem to take frequent frustration in stride and look for more. Indeed, babies and toddlers seem to get pleasure from the struggle of mastering their native language.

Bill Bryson gives an example of the linguistic complexity that children naturally master early:

> . . . with certain types of verbs we use a present participle to create sentences like "I am going for a walk" but with other verbs we dispense with the present participle, which is why we say "I like you" and not "I am liking you" [a phrase that newcomers to English often use]. Very probably you have never thought about this before. The reason you have never thought about it is that it is seemingly instinctive. Most children have mastered the distinction between stative and nonstative verbs by the age of two and are never troubled by it again. (3)

By the way, it *can* happen that babies are exposed only to a *limited incomplete* language. Early U.S. slave owners often separated slaves from the same African tribes in order to impede communication. For slaves to talk to each other and to white bosses, they had to work out a "pidgin"—an incomplete language that people create when they need to communicate but don't understand each others' languages. Pidgins "have a limited vocabulary, a reduced grammatical structure, and a much narrower range of functions, compared to the languages which gave rise to them" (Crystal *Encyclopedia of Language* 334). Therefore, many of the slave babies might not have heard much of a fluent first language. Similarly in Hawai'i, imported plantation workers from various countries spoke different languages and often worked out a pidgin. Here's an example of pidgin English from China: "Tailor, my have got one piece plenty hansom silk my want you make one nice evening dress" (Wei Yun and Fei Jia 42).

But—and here's the miracle of human speech—if babies grow up hearing only an *incomplete* pidgin, they half-acquire and half-create a "creole" by virtue of the human brain's linguistic brilliance: a *full* language with all the grammatical and syntactic complexities of any other fully developed and sophisticated human language. This remarkable ability can be summarized with a simple formulation: if babies and toddlers hear only a *pidgin*, they create a *creole*.

The language commonly called "Pidgin" in Hawai'i is not a pidgin, it's a creole. So too is the language often called *patois* in the Caribbean regions. Like all creoles, these are fully developed, sophisticated languages. African American Language (or African American English) could be called a creole, though it's so well established that it tends to be called simply a language. (For an excellent short but detailed study of the history and nature of pidgins, See Sakoda and Siegel, especially Chapter 1.)

We could call English itself a creole given all the different languages it has grown from. (John McWhorter ["Pidgins and Creoles"] and R. K. Agnihotri are linguists who

---

question some of the commonly accepted ideas about pidgins and creoles that I am drawing on. Michel deGraff discusses some of the complications. Susan Romaine writes about the life cycles of pidgins and creoles.)

Arthur Palacas gives interesting examples of intricacy and complexity in Ebonics or African American Language (AAL):

> The well-known use of Ebonics "invariant be" expresses events or states that are durative, characteristic, or repeated—events that happen "all the time," and the absence of "be" means "right now." This distinction is not always made in standard English. Thus, the standard "The office is closed" is ambiguous and would be trans-lated as either "The office closed" or "The office be closed," depending on whether "The office is closed right now" or . . . "The office is closed all the time." ("Liberating Ebonics" 348)

For a bit more about African American Language or Ebonics or African American English, see Chapter 16.

But Can We Borrow the Easiness of Speaking When We Write?

Yes. This claim will sound wrong to the many people who struggle to write. But their struggle comes from the fact that our culture (like many others) assumes that "writing" means being *careful* about both content and form. They feel that their written words must always make good sense, must be clear, and must use a dialect and a grammar that differ from what they can speak with ease—not to mention getting the spelling correct. If we look past cultural assumptions and allow ourselves to write whatever language comes easily to mind or mouth and not worry over spelling, then writing is very easy.

Some people learn the potential ease of writing as they email. Some people learn it gradually in the safety of private journal writing. The quickest way to learn it is through the common exercise of freewriting or nonstop writing that is private and doesn't have to make sense. People learn that they can write words almost as easily as they can speak—and with more safety. Freewriting may allow garbage, but it leads to much that's valuable. (See Chapter 7 on freewriting.)

Many kindergartners and first graders are showing us vividly the difference between "writing" and "writing correct language." Here's a short passage from a first grader:

> 1 DAY VVAL IF THAR WAS A DAY. THAR WASSAND AND DAST AND ROK SSTONS AND SUM ATHR TYGS AND IT WAS A TUNDR CLAPS! AND APLANIT BEGAN TO RIS AN THA COD IT EARTH AND DO YOU NOW WAT IT RAND AND RAND AND RAND FOR THRITY DAYS ON THE BIG HOLS

He can read this writing back to you and so can his teacher and his parents. Here's how he would read his words:

One day, well if there was a day, there was sand and dust and rocks and stones and some other things. And it was a thunderclaps! And a planet began to rise. And they called it Earth. And do you know what? It rained and rained and rained for thirty days in the big holes.

In our culture (like many others), people are likely to think, *Everyone can talk, but not everyone can write.* Wrong. If we pay attention to the fact that we can speak onto the page and not worry about spelling and grammar, a more powerful truth emerges: *"Since everyone can talk, therefore everyone can write."* (We have to exclude the Chinese and a few other people from this happy story: they write with visual symbols that have no link at all with the sounds of their speech. More about this in the Literacy Stories following Chapters 1 and 16.)

The language we speak with ease may not be suitable for careful writing, but consider this. Uttering onto the page is an easy way to produce bad writing. That's no joke, because most people have to work very hard to produce bad writing. The linguist Chafe puts it bluntly: "Writing has to be taught, and the average person never really learns to do it very well" (44 *Discourse*). This ease in producing spoken language is a big deal—politically and psychologically. Ease goes a long way toward compensating for many of the features in spoken language that are not right for serious writing.

There are times when I have to relearn the easiness of writing—especially when I'm tangled up in the necessarily slow and painstaking process of revising. I find myself revising something important that I've worked hard to write and suddenly I see that it's tangled and even wrong. I start to rewrite— revising sentences, changing words, feeling unsure, slowing down, slowing down. I feel that I'm trying to write my way through thick molasses. This leads to growing self-doubt, anxiety, and finally—as the deadline approaches—panic. Something is tangling up my words and thoughts. It's as though my words have right-handed threads and my thoughts have left-handed threads. I can't screw my words into my thoughts—or is it that I can't screw my thoughts into my words? As long as I stay mired in frustration and anxiety, my panic grows and I get nowhere.

But over the years, I've finally learned to get myself to "wake up" and remember: "Speech! Freewriting." I can forcibly *stop* trying to "write" and strong-arm myself into radically blurted *talking onto the page*—forcing myself to write without stopping and not think so much about the words—just open my mouth and blurt. When I do this—in conditions of anxiety—the resulting language is often an odd hybrid: *more* messy and ungainly than regular talking, yet it also has a kind of blurted directness—as though someone grabbed me by the shoulders and shook me and said, *"But what the <u>hell</u> are you trying to say?"* This often gets me out of my stuckness. I've noticed that I have to keep learning this lesson over and over. For when I'm anxious and panicked, it's as though I'm in a bad dream (*writing*!) and I don't realize that I have the choice to wake up and take some control (*by talking*).

In short, here is a place where it's possible to get the best of both worlds: the ease of speaking and the safety of writing at the early stages—and then later exploit the possibilities of slow deliberate care that writing offers us.

Is it just one form of speech that's easy? For an extreme example, George Steiner convincingly claims that he has three native spoken languages. If this sounds odd, consider the argument from many scholars that if we look at all people around the globe, bilingualism is more common than monolingualism (Pratt; Illich).

And just as people vary in the number of actual languages they can speak fluently, people vary as to how many spoken *registers* or voices they can comfortably use in conversation with different audiences—and this without monitoring or planning or having to "watch their tongue." Often people develop a native fluency with a "home" register or version and also a "street" version with friends. Sometimes a more formal register can be internalized. For example, Hillary Clinton, in a free give-and-take dialogue (not a prepared speech), spoke fluently of "the issue with which I am most deeply involved." I suspect that this is not the grammar that comes most freely and naturally to her mind and mouth in a comfortable informal personal setting. Yet she had probably come to internalize this learned register so that it's also easy and even automatic in certain settings.

By the same token, some *writers* develop more than one register or style or voice in writing that they can generate in real time without having to notice or think or monitor their language. Indeed, some writers gradually learn to become comfortable and automatic in producing correct written English—learning to write as though they were "native speakers of correct writing."

For more about register, see Joos.

2. The Process of Speaking Is Good for Blurting, Gisting, and Talking Turkey

Most teachers of writing have learned to enlist this potentiality of speech. When we get a passage or a whole essay that is utterly tangled or opaque, we get hold of the student and simply ask, "What are you getting at here? I was completely lost." More often than not the student simply blurts out the point she was trying to make; it's often concise and sometimes eloquent. Sometimes it takes another try ("I still don't understand"), but the gist almost invariably pops out. "Stop" we say, "Write that down! You need those very words in your paper." (It's a big mistake for teachers to write down the words: the effectiveness of this process comes from the student writing down his or her own spoken words.)

That is, even though we often beat around the bush when we talk casually—after all, we often open our big mouths before we know what we are trying to say, and we keep trying to resay a thought that we didn't get right—nevertheless, and *after* our rambling, it turns out that speech is a remarkably powerful modality for cutting through the thicket of language to our main point. When someone after a while has the sense to say, "Peter, what are you trying to say?" it's remarkable how often I can come right to the point.

Enlisting This Blurting Knack for Writing

Freewriting, like speaking, often leads to digression; yet like speaking it also helps us gist and crunch—sum things up—especially if we ask it to take on that task. That is, after we have freewritten on a topic for a while and followed its wandering path, we can pause and stretch our limbs, take a deep breath and ask ourselves, "So what is all this about?" "I wonder what I'm really trying to say." This usually produces a piece of "crunching" or "gisting" freewriting that sums up our thinking—or rather (and this is an added advantage) it usually provides a few different summings up to help us decide among various potential main points.

At one time as I was trying to revise one of these chapters, I got confused about what I was really trying to say. So I did what I often do. I stopped and hit the CAPS LOCK key (to signal *Time out from "real" writing*) and simply blurted a freewritten response to my perplexity:

> TIME OUT. IN A WAY I'M JUST INTERESTED IN EASINESS. DOESN'T HAVE TO BE SPEECH. BUT SPEECH IS THE EASIEST LANGUAGE WE HAVE. BUT ACTUALLY I AM INTERESTED IN SPEECH. CAUSE SPEECH HAS VIRTUES I WANT TO HARNESS

This quick blurt helped me realize that I was tangled up between two different main themes, speech and easiness. The blurt helped me to see how they overlap but differ, and start to figure out how they relate to each other. It's my sense that when people have to work within the limitations of a "tweet," they call on the tongue—on the linguistic muscle for speaking—in order to condense a thought. I wonder whether tweeting leads users to more spoken language in the rest of their writing. (To find our real point, it also helps to "consult felt sense." This is a rich and complicated topic that is not central enough to this book, but that I wish every writer knew about. For more on it, see Sondra Perl's book and my "Foreword" to it—and my "Three Mysteries." See also the extensive literature on "Focusing" at a website with that title.)

In short, we can borrow for writing the gift from speech: to stop beating around the bush and hit the nail on the head.

✻   ✻   ✻

Blurted Honesty

There's a certain *kind* of blurting or gisting that involves not just directness but honesty, even when it's uncomfortable. Most people find it harder to lie when they are talking to a listener. They don't have time to plan a smooth evasion of the truth. Little children are notoriously bad at hiding their spoken lies, but a few people get good at it. Trial lawyers and presidential spokespersons get training. When most of us try to lie or tiptoe around the truth as we talk, it tends to show—or rather *sound*.

Lincoln called attention to the way people used *writing* to hide their meaning:

> In all matters but this of Slavery the framers of the Constitution used the very clearest, shortest, and most direct language. But the Constitution alludes to Slavery three times without mentioning it once! The language used becomes ambiguous, roundabout, and mystical. They speak of the "immigration of persons," and mean the importation of slaves but do not

say so. In establishing a basis of representation they say "all other persons," when they mean to say slaves—why did they not use the shortest phrase? In providing for the return of fugitives they say "persons held to service or labor." . . . Why didn't they do it [refer to slavery]? (Speech, March 6, 1860)

Imagine if the Constitution writers had been at a meeting or in a living room and someone asked them to explain what the Constitution says about who is a citizen. They would have had a hard time hiding their real meaning behind phrases like the "immigration of persons" and "all other persons" and "persons held to service or labor." In everyday talk, that kind of evasive language sticks out like a sore thumb and calls attention to how it's not saying what it's saying.

In a classic essay, Eric Havelock points to a striking example of spoken evasion that countless people heard on TV. It was the morning of January 18, 1986, and the Challenger space shuttle had just exploded right after launch. Havelock describes the sound track:

First a brief pause, perhaps to swallow, while the clouds of the explosion hovered in the air. Then the pronouncement, "A major malfunction has occurred." ("Orality, Literacy, and Star Wars" 129)

That NASA media spokesman did more than swallow. He quickly suppressed any blurt and called on his extensive training and came up with that wonderful phrase, "A major malfunction has occurred." Not even the syntax is characteristic of everyday speech. Being a "spokesman" he had training in avoiding speech.

Imagine if the spokesman had been sick that day and stayed at home and watched the explosion on TV from the living room couch. Imagine his audible gasp when the Challenger exploded. His wife calls from the kitchen "What happened, honey?" "My God, it blew up," he'd say. "They're all killed!"

Havelock points to another example. When a committee member asked the NASA spokespersons, "Was the launching considered dangerous under the circumstances?" one of them answered, "We considered the flight safety implications in the expressed area of interest." It's *possible* that those words rolled off the tongue with quick fluency; these men had good training. But it's hard not to imagine a pause while they *constructed* rather than *uttered* that sentence.

Honesty in Writing?

Havelock spent his career celebrating the way writing and literacy *separated* themselves from unplanned speaking in Greece during the sixth and fifth centuries BCE, yet he argues eloquently here that writing needs to call on the resources of speech: "When one writes, this kind of misuse [evasiveness] can be corrected by sticking as closely as possible to oral idiom" ("Orality, Literacy, and Star Wars" 129).

3. The Process of Speaking Is Good for Dialogue—Connecting with Others and Suiting Our Words to Them

The process of speaking gives us constant practice in suiting our words to an audience—and we've been getting that practice all our lives. In speaking, we usually get some immediate feedback and hear when we're unclear or when our listener is bothered or takes offense. We get a chance to clarify or even apologize. Even when we make uninterrupted monologues—giving a long explanation or set of directions or even making a formal speech—we get visual feedback. We can see from faces and bodies if listeners are involved or tuning us out. (We don't get this when we leave phone messages or talk on the radio.) When Deborah Tannen looks at the typical features of speech and writing, it's *involvement strategies* that she sees most characteristic of spoken language. These are the linguistic features that connect the speaker and listeners.

When two or more people want to work out some thinking together, what's better than speaking? They can share their ideas and spark new ones. The process is quick and easy, and it builds personal connection and intellectual energy. It can even help when people are trying to work out separate trains of thought. One of my students told me about when she and her friend were writing applications to grad school. But neither was getting anywhere. Finally they said, "Let's go to I-Hop and *talk* our ideas to each other. The listener has to take notes on what the other is saying." It worked well for them. They couldn't write till they stopping writing and started talking.

Speaking is also ideal when people want simply to *be* together—to be closer or in better communication and contact with each other. Of course, speaking isn't the only way: taking a walk, sitting in silence, or kissing are all rightly celebrated for getting close—but those avenues are not always available. Speaking is surely the most common and reliable way to turn distance into intimacy.

Bringing an almost philosophic dimension to his analysis of speech, Chafe insists on noticing what we usually ignore: that speaking is a continual attempt by people locked inside their own heads to get a meaning inside someone else's head—which they are locked out of. It turns out to be a perplexity as to how we manage this—and in fact we never quite do. There's *always* some gap between what I say and what you understand. What's interesting, though, is how close we sometimes come. Chafe looks at the details of speech to show some of the specific vocal moves and adjustments that all people naturally make because of their long history of feedback from listeners. (More on this in Chapter 5, "Intonation.")

On top of everything else, speaking conveys brute *presence*. We tend to recognize people immediately by their voices—often over a bad phone connection or when they have a cold—even after many years. "Voice prints" are evidently as reliable for identification as fingerprints. And our speaking often communicates how we're feeling. "Peter, you sound depressed," someone once said when I answered the phone with nothing but "Hi." In short, we are usually more "in" our speaking voices than in our writing (though let's not try to define "we" or "in"). Plato complained in the *Phaedrus* that writing was a bad invention because it created language with no presence. Written texts are "orphans," he said, that go around the world with no parents. He insisted that language should always create live dialogue and therefore always be accompanied by its author. (I spoke of how God used writing for the ten commandments, but more often he *spoke* to humans—no doubt to be more *with* them in the process of communicating.)

It's not that writing is wholly "dumb." Writing will almost always have some of the writer in it—at least for readers skilled at reading the "voice." But one of the benefits of writing is how it helps us *avoid* presence—helps us hide how we feel or even what we are like. Writing is ideal for anonymity—though shy literate people sometimes show themselves more in writing than speaking.

Can We Bring Any of These Dialogic Virtues into Writing?

The process of writing seems inherently handicapped for all these dialogic, audience-related jobs. When we write, we are usually alone and separate from our readers. What we write seldom goes immediately to them unless we are texting, writing email, or writing in a real-time chat room. The more serious the writing, the longer the wait till they get our words—sometimes it's years. As writers, we are often told *Remember your audience!*, but we are usually alone struggling over *meanings* and *words,* so we often forget. Besides, we often don't know our readers or even what kinds of people they might be. (Of course, one of the glories of writing as a process is that it allows us to *escape* from awareness of audience—and this can be a big help. We can work out our thinking in peace. See my "Closing My Eyes as I Speak.")

Forgetting audience is probably the main cause of weakness in student essays— a failure to create thinking and language that connect well with readers. But students are usually stuck in a difficult audience situation. The actual reader is the teacher who grades, but students are usually told not to write to the teacher but to a different audience—for example, that famous person, the "general reader."

Part of the problem here comes from the inescapable physical facts that separate writers from readers. But much of the problem is not inherent but cultural—in particular, our culture's sense that "serious writing"—especially school and academic writing—is supposed to be fairly impersonal.

In the next chapter I'll explore linguistic involvement strategies and show how serious writing can give a sense of presence or even intimacy. People notice this most when the writer adds personal elements. But it's possible to convey a subtle but effective sense of presence *without* including any explicitly personal details—without even necessarily using "I." It's a matter of using many of the fine-grained syntactic features in *spoken* language that convey a sense of presence to readers.

Recent technology has given a strong dialogic flavor to lots of writing: email, chat rooms, texting, and classrooms or meeting rooms where everyone is linked by computers. Even blogs are helping people make writing into a process with lots of almost immediate dialogue and response—not just absence and solitariness. These kinds of writing naturally lead to linguistic "involvement strategies."

I'm struck also with what seems a new cultural practice that borrows something fundamental from speaking: *literal presence.* That is, more and more people come together into each other's presence during the "solitary" process of writing. People gather in living rooms, restaurants, outdoors. Jay Parini tells of having written lots of his massive scholarly biographies of poets and writers in places like McDonalds and Burger King. He said he wanted to be around other people while he wrote solitarily. Body heat. (With laptops, we can now call up all our notes and drafts and many readings and also zap onto the web for new material.) People have always been able to gather and write in each other's company, but I've not heard much about it till recent decades. There's a fairly long tradition of writing retreats like Yaddo, but they always pride themselves on providing *solitude* for writing. Here at UMass, for nineteen years, the Center for Teaching has set up popular all-day retreats for faculty to write together in a large room or two with lunch and coffee laid on. Other colleges and universities are doing the same (see Elbow and Sorcinelli).

In exam halls or classrooms, students have traditionally been asked to write while in each other's presence, but usually this has been for testing—or classically, for punishment ("We will not talk in class. We will not talk . . .")—or when the teacher is hung over and stuck for something do. It's only since the process movement in our field that many teachers have realized that it's a positive, productive, and indeed pleasant activity to write with others.

Have these new technological and cultural practices made students, scholars, and other citizens more skilled at suiting their words to the audience when they write important high-stakes pieces? They've probably helped, but I'm struck with how much of the serious published writing I see is still audience-deaf—whether from students or scholars.

The fact remains that when we fail to suit our writing to an audience—as we commonly do—we are bypassing a well developed skill we already possess in speaking for using language to connect with an audience; we've acquired this gift naturally and easily through years of practice. So the question is how to awaken and bring that skill to the writing process.

The most natural and traditional way to awaken it is by writing a letter. Letters—even when they deal with technical or complex matters—tend to have lots of linguistic involvement strategies that increase writer-reader connection. Some teachers have learned to exploit this natural skill by saying this to students who are struggling to write or to write clearly: "Write me a *letter* with your thinking. Start off, 'Dear Peter.'" Legend has it that John McPhee begins all his writing projects with "Dear Mother." When we use this common cultural practice we write words and thoughts that connect better to readers. Experienced writers learn to revise out all the "you"s and other such features when they are inappropriate to the genre or register—while nevertheless *keeping* that valuable "flavor of address" in the words. Besides, not all genres forbid the word "you" and other slightly personal elements. I frequently find teachers and students mistakenly exaggerating the degree to which serious writing should be sanitized of any element of personal connection.

If we learn to "speak onto the page" in the ways I will explore in Part Two, we can bring to writing the language mode in which we most naturally connect with an audience. Most people have become literally conditioned to feeling an audience when they speak out loud. Try talking aloud when you are alone: you will probably sense that these words are trying to *go to someone.*

It's my argument, then, that the speech-derived practices I am suggesting in this book—speaking onto the page at the early stages of writing (the topic of Part Two) and reading aloud to revise at the late stages (the topic of Part Three)—will give us a helpful sense of addressing an audience when we write, and this will help us create language and thinking that connects better with readers.

4. Speaking Is Self-Rewarding and Helps Children Learn to Master Language

Think of babies babbling in their cribs and toddlers walking around talking nonstop to no visible listener. Linguists like to say they are practicing speech, and no doubt they are, but they are also getting sensual pleasure or having fun. The physicality of speech has this underlying potentiality of pleasure. Children like to hear themselves shout in a quiet church. People who aren't "too civilized" will sometimes let themselves shout in a cavernous hall or at the Grand Canyon: we want to feel that loud noise in our bodies and mouths and hear it come back in our ears. Most of us—having spoken or written a sentence that we particularly like—occasionally find ourselves rolling it around in our mouths later in the day.

Think of professors and politicians and others who love the sound of their own voices and can't stop talking. And young people who practice rap-speaking and go on and on: the rap cadences start to "just come" without any planning. The same thing happens to many people who work at iambic pentameter: they develop this *gear* for speaking everything in ten-syllable lines with an underlying iambic beat. These people get pleasure from just using the speaking gear and keeping it well oiled—for no other immediate purpose. The rhythm pulls language out of us. If you want to doubt this point on theoretical grounds, consider the vocal medium where self-reinforcing pleasure is universally recognized: singing. There's palpable pleasure from the interaction of creating sound by moving the mouth and the lungs—and the internal feedback that comes not just to the ears but to the face and trunk. Singers, instrumental players, and talkers—they all have the experience of "getting on a roll" and keeping going.

Can we borrow some of this pleasure and self-reinforcement for writing? Pleasure is *not* what most people feel when they write. Writing is hard work and after we struggle to finish something, we often wait months or even years to see whether we get any reward. Nevertheless, the process of writing *can* reinforce itself. A friend recently sent me something and apologized for the length. "My writing took over," she said. I've heard many people make the same comment, and it has certainly happened to me. Laurence Sterne called attention to this in his *Tristram Shandy:*

> But this is neither here nor there—why do I mention it?—Ask my pen,—it governs me,—I govern not it. (cited in Farnsworth, 100)

But why should writing sometimes "take over" and seem to proceed under its own steam—and why pleasure? At least part of the pleasure comes from the actual difficulty. I think the "taking over" and the pleasure come from our experience of *overcoming resistance*. The writing door doesn't usually open unless we push with a force we don't need for speaking. But when we get it to open we have an interesting experience of *resistance-and-no-resistance*—which suggests the phenomenon that Mihaly Csikszentmihalyi calls "flow"—and how it requires a combination of difficulty and ease.

Many writers through the ages—especially diary writers and journal keepers—have testified to the experience of starting to recount a happening or explain a thought or express a feeling—and finding that the process somehow takes over. The energy builds and they go on and on writing till they've exhausted the expressive or creative impulse and often exhausted themselves. Csikszentmihalyi and his colleagues note that this often happens to practitioners of all the expressive arts: painting, sculpture, dance, music.

Tomlinson explored testimony from dozens of fiction writers about a different way in which their writing took over. Most common was the experience of *characters* taking over a piece of fiction. The writers said things like, "I didn't *want* that character to commit suicide, but I just couldn't stop him." (But not all writers let that happen. The novelist Muriel Spark speaks for writers who won't take any nonsense from their characters: "I'm in full control. . . . Nobody in my book so far could cross the road unless I make them do it" [Mallon "Transfigured," 66]).

Perhaps the word "express" is central here—"press out": writing is ideal for helping get what is inner to become outer. Many people find writing ideal for unburdening themselves—uncovering what's hidden inside, often hidden even from themselves. Of course *speaking* is great for the same purposes, but only if we have a genuinely trusted and supportive listener. Such listeners are hard to come by. Writing is particularly valuable when we are troubled by taboo feelings or scary thoughts that we don't dare share even with close friends.

In short, if lots of people are scared or burned by writing or run away from it, this just means that they haven't learned how to use some of its inherent advantages for safety, power, and even ease. After all, writing is a technology and the current "hip techie" truism for technology applies to the technology that Plato criticized two thousand years ago: we don't get the benefit of a technology unless we learn how to exploit its potentialities. Writing down our spoken language is easy (if we forget about "correct writing"), and most people find power and pleasure in the process.

People with a strong postmodern or deconstructive cast of mind sometimes give me a hard time for talking about words and thoughts that are *inside* us versus *outside* us. *"We are socially constructed and intertextual. Everything inside us is really outside us in the culture."* What's implied in the conflict between how I talk and how they talk is really a debate between what I refer to as conflicting "lens claims" and Burke calls "terministic screens" and that Aristotle pointed to with his locution of *There's a sense in which . . .* That is, there's a *sense* in which we have nothing inside our skulls that's not outside in the culture or at least derived from it. But there's also a sense in which everything in our heads is actually different from what's outside in the culture. What we have is our own amalgamation and there's always at least a little or even a lot that could be called "unique." It's always a question of which lens is most useful in any given situation. I grant the validity of the postmodern social-construction lens; but I often find it helpful to use the other lens and notice the *differences* between the words and ideas I experience as inner and those that I find outer—or thoughts that I am able or willing to make outer. The important theoretical point is that lens claims are useful but purely theoretical: any given lens claim has no power to *refute* a conflicting lens claim; all it can do is call our attention to what the other lens fails to highlight. Conflicting lens claims are "always already true." (For more on this in the context of a particular application, see my "In Defense of Private Writing.")

❋   ❋   ❋

In this chapter I've been describing virtues in the *process* of speaking. In the next chapters (4 and 5) I'll describe virtues in the *product* of speaking, *spoken language:* the kinds of words and grammar we tend to use in easy everyday spontaneous speaking.

LITERACY STORY

The Rebus

Let's pretend we are living in the Middle East around 3500 BCE or earlier and we decide we want to invent writing—or more precisely, that form of writing which will convey spoken language. Our basic problem is daunting: how can we make a *visual representation* of an *audible sound?*—a *visual* symbol that tells readers how to make the *sound* for that symbol?

We might say

> Oh, that's easy. Folks worked that out a long time ago. We need only draw a little picture of the sun or of a tree, and those little drawings will convey to viewers the *spoken sounds* we want to convey: the sound of the spoken words "sun" and "tree." After all, way back in 7500 BCE, our forefathers made little clay tokens like monopoly pieces that stood for commodities like beer, grain, and oil. These tokens didn't even *resemble* beer, grain, and oil, but they were easy to remember and so they did the job of bringing the right sound to readers' lips with nothing but a visual cue.

But what if we want to represent the sound of words that are not so visualizable or easy to remember? How do we make a visual representation of "tomorrow," or "however" or "sometimes"? These meanings are not easy to picture with little drawings, and we can't make *tokens* for them because there are too many to remember.

It turns out that administrators of the Sumerian city state ran into exactly this problem around 3000 BCE. They wanted to make visual symbols for the *names* of individuals involved in commercial transactions: lists of who owed what to whom. It was a big problem. There were too many names to remember with visual tokens.

Whoever first solved this problem should be called a genius. He or she (it might have been a brainstorming group or even a woman) came up with one of the biggest conceptual breakthroughs in human history. We have trouble seeing the genius in it because it consists of something we associate with a simple children's game: the rebus. The rebus permits us to "write" *belief* by drawing a picture of a bee and a leaf.

> The new signs were simple, incised sketches with no concern for esthetics. They singled out things that were easy to draw that stood for the sound of the word they evoked. [For example] The drawing of a man's body stood for the sound "*lu*" and that of the mouth for "*ka*," which were the sounds of the words for *man* and *mouth* in the Sumerian language. (Schmandt-Besserat and Erard 12)

In short, they figured out that they could write a man's name, *Luka*, by putting down simple pictures of a man and a mouth. (See illustration, next page.)

There's an interesting irony or paradox here. Techniques for proto-writing up to this point had been moving away from picturing or resemblance and toward abstraction, for example, using nonrepresentational geometric shapes to stand for things like beer or wheat and using the small cone and the big ball to mean "small" and "big" measures of "grain" and eventually for the numerals *one* and *ten:* one or ten of *anything* (Schmandt-Besserat and Erard 11–12). But with the invention of the rebus, the path toward writing swerves back toward picturing even while the goal is to represent things that are not picturable:

> The stage of pictography—writing with pictures—when the technique of writing came in its form closest to visual art, was in fact the time when writing became removed from the concrete world of logography [words as images] to be formally connected with the sounds of speech by the extraordinary invention of phonograms [rebuses]. (12)

The central role of the rebus in writing is most obvious in pre-alphabetic writing and particularly in Chinese characters and Egyptian and Mayan hieroglyphs. In China, the earliest characters from the Shang dynasty were more or less just pictures—a kind of proto-writing or picture writing. These characters convey the ideas of *things* rather than spoken sounds or spoken language. Chinese characters didn't link well with spoken language until these early characters were gradually systematized much later in the Han dynasty into something very like recent Chinese characters. For that development, someone *else* had to invent the rebus. That is, even though Chinese characters and Egyptian and Mayan hieroglyphs tend to *picture a thing* (sometimes faintly or in a very stylized way), sometimes those symbols do *not* mean what they picture. Sometimes there is an added mark that says to the reader, "This little picture of a spear doesn't stand for *spear*, it stands for the initial *sound* of *spear*, that is, the sound *sp*."

Most people don't realize how pervasively this technique of the rebus is used in Chinese characters (and Egyptian hieroglyphs). Schmandt-Besserat and Erard insist that "90% of the characters consist of a graphic element that indicates pronunciation, combined with another (logographic) element that marks meaning" (16). Robinson insists that *all* writing uses sound, even Chinese. He points out that the key in deciphering the Rosetta stone came from noticing that there were only sixty-six different signs in a text with fourteen hundred signs or symbols. This meant that they had to relate to *sounds* not concepts (33).

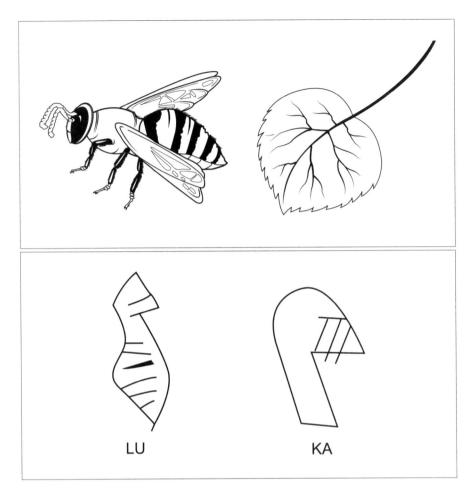

LU   KA

Two rebuses or "phongrams": signs standing for sounds. The first is the one that most people know from classic childrens games. It uses the picture of a *bee* and a *leaf* in order to "write" *belief*. The second rebus is one of the earliest known—from about 3000 BCE and produced by someone in the Sumerian city state. The first symbol is a conventional crude drawing of a man—and thus stood for the sound *lu*, meaning *man*. The second one is a conventional crude drawing of a mouth—and thus stood for the sound *ka*, meaning *mouth*. For financial record keeping, they needed to represent the name of a particular person who bought or received something. His name was *Luka*. Their problem was this: an individual name or person can't be represented with a simple picture. But someone in 3000 BCE was a genius and invented the rebus. He or she figured out for the *first* time this gateway between seeing and hearing—this method for representing an audible *sound* with visual marks. In fact, the rebus lies at the root of all writing systems. (I draw here on Schmandt-Besserat and Erard 12–13).

But in our alphabet, the role of rebuses or phonograms is not so obvious. We can't find pictures of bees, leaves, men, or mouths in our alphabet. Our letters are remarkably abstract and nonrepresentational. But the authority on writing, Ignace Gelb, insists that all writing forms derive from pictures (DeFrancis 78). In their earliest forms, Semitic letters had graphic meaning. *Aleph* means "ox" and the visual letter *aleph* derived from a minimal picture of an ox's head. But the letter came to be used to represent a *sound*—in this case the sound of the glottal stop used for saying *aleph*. *Beta* was the word for house and the letter derived from a minimal picture of a house, and it became used to represent the sound of the word for house, *beta*, that is *buh*. The Greeks kept the names of the letters and the associated sounds, but lost the representational meanings. Yet, interestingly, the Greeks added some letters that did have representational meaning: *o mikron* and *o mega* mean "small o" and "big o." Similarly, *e psilon* and *u psilon* mean "plain e" and "plain u." (This seems to be the main line of thinking here, but some "[s]cholars disagree about whether or not the letter names were based on pictographic signs" [Firmage 13].)

So once the Greeks peel away meanings from the letters of the alphabet themselves, we lose sight of how the rebus *gave* us the sounds of our letters. And now that we've lost the pictures as cues, we have to use *memory* to cross the great divide between vision and hearing—sight and sound. So too, many Chinese cannot see pictures in many of their highly stylized characters, so they need much stronger memory. The strength of the alphabet as a system is that there are only twenty-six letters for us to remember. (There are something like 80,000 Chinese characters—though one thousand of them will work for 90 percent of the writing; ten thousand will render 98 percent of the writing.)

I love the rebus because it's the conduit that permits us to get from *time* to *space*. For it strikes me that it's actually *impossible* to represent an audible event with a visual sign—*except* through the ingenious, devious, roundabout trick of the rebus.

4 Speech as a Product

Nine Virtues in Careless Unplanned Spoken Language that Can Significantly Improve Careful Writing

THERE SEEMS TO be a general prejudice against spoken language in our literate culture. I will call on Halliday to counter this bias:

> The general picture is that of written language as richly endowed, while speech is a poor man's assemblage of shreds and patches. ("Spoken and Written" 67)
>
> [P]eople confuse "spoken" with non-standard dialect, or slang, or the very informal contexts of family and peer group speech; and some linguists have added to the confusion by depicting spoken language as a disorderly mishmash of unstructured fragments, full of hesitations, false starts, unfinished clauses and mistakes, and basically a simple form of discourse, much simpler than language in its written mode. This is nonsense. It is a myth that does a great deal of harm, especially in the field of language education. . . . (*Complementarities* 132)
>
> [S]ince the study of grammar grew out of writing—it is when language comes to be written down that it becomes an object of study, not before— our grammars are grammars of the written language. . . . [W]e look at spoken language through the lens of a grammar designed for writing. Spoken discourse thus appears as a distorted variant of written discourse, and not unnaturally it is found wanting. ("Spoken and Written" 66–67)

It sounds as though Halliday is blithely overgeneralizing about true nature of speech and writing. In the Introduction to Part One, I showed how speech and writing cannot be nailed down so neatly. Halliday treats these terms in a special way. By "written language" he means language that's carefully and consciously monitored—whether actually written or spoken; by "spoken language" he means language that is spontaneously produced and not monitored—whether spoken or written. In the Introduction to Part Two, I'll take time to explore this interesting and useful way of defining the words.

And be it noted that Halliday is not defending speech at the expense of writing. He's brilliant at comparing the two kinds of language to show the complementary virtues of each. For example:

> Neither [speech nor writing] is more organized than the other, but they are organized in different ways. . . . Spoken language tends to accommodate more clauses in the syntagm (to favour greater "grammatical intricacy"), with fewer lexical items in the clause. Written language tends to accommodate more lexical items in the clause (to favour greater "lexical density"), with fewer clauses in the syntagm (71). . . . So while spoken English is marked by intricacy in the clause complex, written English is marked by complexity in the nominal group. ("Spoken and Written" 73)

My argument in this book is that linguistic and rhetorical virtues grow wild like weeds in our careless speech. That is, even though careless speaking gives us language that's wrong for careful writing, nevertheless, it is full of *valuable linguistic resources* that we need even for our most careful and formal writing. But if we want to use these virtues to improve our writing, it helps to recognize them and harvest them. Many people have learned to freewrite or write with ease—getting rough drafts that didn't cause them much anxiety and pain—but then when they revise, they rip out the good weeds with the bad. That is, they get rid of all the good language they already have in their rough writing, in their efforts to get rid of what's wrong.

1. Spoken Language Tends to Connect Better with the Audience

In the last chapter I focused on speaking as a process and noted how the very activity of speaking tends to keep us aware of audience. The listener is almost always there—in front of us or on the other end of the phone. When we write in solitude (or even in Starbucks), we often forget our audience. But if we speak onto the page, the process will help us instinctively relate our words to our audience.

Deborah Tannen was prominent among a group of linguists busily comparing speech and writing in the 1970s and 1980s. They all noticed how spontaneous conversation—a "typically spoken mode"—is relatively rich with linguistic "involvement strategies": all kinds of ways in which speakers use words that communicate their connection with the listeners and also their own connection to what they are saying. Expository writing, on the other hand—a "typically written" mode—tends to have less of that audience-oriented language and more focus only on the message. The linguist Elinor Ochs compared stories told orally and those same stories written out two days later by the same persons. She found that "the expression of social acts tends to take more discourse 'space' in the spoken versions" (72).

But before long, Tannen came to decide that the distinction between spoken and written language—or between "oral" and "literate" styles of discourse—was a red herring. She came to argue at length that the real distinction is between language with a "relative focus on interpersonal involvement" and language with "more focus on the information conveyed" ("Relative Focus" 124). For it turns out that these two different kinds of language turn up *irrespective* of whether the words were spoken or written.

Tannen has thus become widely noted for her research showing that *some* speakers use lots of involvement while other speakers do not ("Relative Focus" 132ff). And by the same token, some writers do the same thing and connect with readers, while others do not. Also, certain genres of writing lead to more involvement strategies: personal letters, emails, and freewriting. I think Tannen was the first to point out in particular that "[i]maginative literature has more in common with spontaneous conversation than with the typical written genre, expository prose" (137).

What's crucial for my purposes is to note that even though expository prose typically lacks involvement strategies, some of it is rich in these features that convey a sense of connection with the reader. So it's not an either/or matter. That is, in expository writing we can make up for the problem of absent readers and no shared context by spelling out our meanings clearly and explicitly. But that doesn't mean we have to leave out features that help create involvement with readers.

For example in a draft of this section, I started off a paragraph with this:

> *The two kinds of language turn up irrespective of whether the words were spoken or written.*

But then I found myself wanting to add a little clause at the start so as to have this:

> *The crucial point here is that the two kinds of language turn up irrespective of whether the words were spoken or written.*

In other words, when I read aloud I could feel the first sentence as a purely disembodied impersonal claim, but I wanted to communicate to readers a bit of my perspective and feeling about the importance of this point. In adding "unnecessary phrases" of this sort, I've come to realize that I sometimes clog up my prose; sometimes I have to remove some of them later in revising to make my prose "cleaner." But notice where my impulse came from: I wanted to communicate my attitude or feelings about my information ("lexicalize" them)—feelings that I would naturally have put in words if I had been speaking. I realized that I didn't want to *just* convey information.

Look: I just did it again—entirely without awareness. I wrote

> *Notice where my impulse came from.*

I didn't need "Notice where." I could have had "cleaner" prose if I'd just written this:

> *My impulse came from a desire to lexicalize . . .*

My unconscious decision was an impulse to make myself more present in my prose.

A phrase like "*Notice where . . .*" is a rather unobtrusive "involvement strategy"—a not-too-personal way of conveying a bit of presence of the writer. Needless to say, I *have* decided in this book to go further in telling my feelings or recounting experiences. Some colleagues have complained about this quality in some of my academic writing. (Still I've so far refrained from mentioning in the text when I have to get up to pee, as Jane Tompkins famously did in an academic essay.)

Another example. This section began

The last chapter focused on . . .

This is a classic locution from school and academic prose that puts "the emphasis on the message and not on the writer or reader." But I revised it to this:

In the last chapter, I focused on . . .

Let's pause for a moment over that classic academic phrase: "The last chapter focused on." It takes special training in depersonalization (training that's common in schools and universities) to lead so many of us to the fictional idea that that "the last chapter" did the focusing.

Tannen writes of how often in school writing, students are asked to strip away the linguistic features that create involvement with audience (see Michaels and Collins for powerful evidence of this in the early grades). She notes how decontextualized language—pure message focus—is often harder for a reader to connect with. "Naive" students sometimes use the second person "you" in their academic essays, but they are usually told, "In writing, we don't talk to readers." (We don't?)

But we don't need to *analyze* "involvement strategies" and "presence" as we write. They will come naturally if we speak onto the page in ways I suggest in Part Two and if we revise by reading aloud in ways I suggest in Part Three. Involvement strategies and presence will show up even when writing about allegedly "impersonal" topics. Tannen sums up the main point here: "features reflecting relative focus on involvement seem to underlie successful production and comprehension of discourse in both spoken and written modes" ("Relative Focus" 125). Ironically, her language here is strikingly depersonalized—but it's from a relatively early 1985 article—and she's subsequently moved away from this kind of language. (I've always noticed a significant lag time between when I figure out conceptually something I need to do—and when I can finally do it. I wasn't good at freewriting when I published *Writing Without Teachers*.)

2. Speaking Promotes Flexible Syntax

Yeah, right. "Flexible syntax." Why not just come out and say it: bad grammar!

Speaking does indeed promote lots of grammar that's bad for correct writing. Spoken grammar is often called bad even for speaking (*He speaks with such bad grammar.*) But that's not the whole story about grammar as it relates to speech and writing. Halliday insists on a more complicated analysis that avoids the prejudice against spoken language:

> Speech has complex sentences with simple words, while writing has complex words in simple sentences" (79 "Spoken and Written").
>
> [S]pontaneous speech . . . is not composed, cannot be revised, and when a sentence begins—or rather, a clause complex; "sentence" is a written language phenomenon—the speaker has no idea where, when (or even whether) it is going to end. (This is one of the reasons behind the myth of the formlessness of spoken language: it shifts from point to point as it goes along. But this does not mean that it is unstructured; on the contrary, speakers can, and

typically do, maintain a coherent grammatical structure over long stretches of unplanned, spontaneous speech. (*Complementarities* 149)

So even though the grammatical intricacy of speech can lead to what written grammar calls "bad," I'm insisting that the resulting grammar can nevertheless help careful writing.

For example, in unplanned speaking, we often catch ourselves in mid-sentence with an impulse to add or qualify. We just break off and start a new piece of syntax. What's interesting is that this syntactic habit *can* be very effective in writing. Look at how Halliday himself exploits this spoken flexibility in a passage I quoted near the start of this chapter:

> But since the study of grammar grew out of writing—it is when language comes to be written down that it becomes an object of study, not before— our grammars are grammars of the written language.

He interrupts himself and plops a whole new sentence into the middle of the one he is writing. Yet it works well as writing. We learn this syntactic flexibility from speech. In the passage I quoted just a few lines back, he drops in a double-phrase:

> . . . and when a sentence begins—or rather, a clause complex; "sentence" is a written language phenomenon—the speaker has no idea where . . .

Perhaps this is pushing it; the semicolon confused me at first. But he's insisting on the music of flexible speech for writing.

Here an example from Paul Krugman:

> And over time Friedman's presentations of the story grew cruder, not subtler, and eventually began to seem—there's no other way to say this— intellectually dishonest. ("Who Was Milton Friedman" 28)

Yet unskilled writers don't usually know they can do this. It is seldom taught, yet it grows wild in their everyday speaking. It can be harvested for careful writing.

Another example—from a good poet, William Stafford:

> Writers are persons who write; swimmers are (and from teaching a child I know how hard it is to persuade a reasonable person of this), swimmers are persons who relax in the water, let their heads go down, and reach out with ease and confidence. (22–23)

Notice the repetition: "swimmers are . . . swimmers are." This is characteristic of speech. We instinctively feel a need to repeat a piece of the syntactic thread we want to return to after we've strayed into one or two digressions. It's something that Henry James often does when he's inserted a digression and instinctively realizes (as we often do in talking) that readers need to be reminded of the original subway car they were riding on.

When students and insecure writers have had lots of errors red-inked by teachers, they often write defensively and play it safe with wooden Dick-and-Jane sentences. Students often don't realize they can exploit the natural gymnastic flexibility in their speech and create interesting, intricate sentences. My claim is that if we want flexibility in our written syntax, we need to do more speaking onto the page—as with freewriting. It will produce too much that is too wild. But when we revise, we can learn to use our ears and capture the best of the bravery and audaciousness of the human tongue as it leaps and jumps.

Good writers and handbooks know that it's a virtue to vary the length of sentences—notably short ones up against long ones. This is common in everyday speech. When people get practiced in *speaking* onto the page, they are quicker to exploit syntactic flexibility.

Here's an example of the kind of flexible syntax common in unplanned speech. The speaker started to use a relative clause but then instinctively changed course and used two separate clauses with no explicit grammatical connection:

> they stuck us in this crazy building—that they j—they're not even finished with it. (Ochs 69)

This example shows how speech tends to have more simple clauses (less embedding), but the connections between these simple clauses are more intricate. Halliday insists on using the term "intricate" for the kinds of connections between clauses that traditional grammar won't accept but that speakers habitually use and listeners habitually understand. In contrast, writing tends to have more intricate embedding, but the grammatical connections are more explicit. (The example is from Elinor Ochs's influential article on unplanned discourse.)

Consider this sentence that most people consider *too* flexible. *"These are the houses that we don't know what they were like inside"* (12–13). Milroy quotes it from present-day Belfast speech. He notes that English grammarians call it "hopelessly ungrammatical," but points out that it's absolutely correct in Norwegian and Danish—and was used by a U.S. presidential candidate! I hope I don't undermine my ethos by admitting that I love its lithe complexity.

---

3. Unplanned Spoken Language Is Less Bogged Down with Nominalization

When people write essays, they often come up with language like this: "*The construction of the pyramids represented the Egyptians' attempt . . .*" The same people would almost never have *said* it that way in unplanned speech—even in an academic setting. They would tend to say something more like "*When the Egyptians built the pyramids, they were trying . . .*" Something more lively and less noun-heavy. Somehow, expository or essayist writing has come to promote nominalization.

Halliday gives an example of a mild nominalization that's fairly typical even in good scientific writing:

> The conversion of hydrogen to helium in the interiors of stars is the source of energy for their immense output of light and heat. ("Spoken and Written" 79)

It's not a horrible sentence. We'd be lucky if this was the worst we had to read in textbooks or academic writing. But note how its meaning comes through more clearly and forcefully if we use the kind of language that's common in speaking—where we usually steer away from too much nominalization:

Stars convert hydrogen into helium in their cores, and that's how they get so much energy for light and heat.

OR

Stars need energy for putting out so much light and heat, and they get it by converting hydrogen into helium in their cores.

Note how the nominalized sentence is allegedly talking about *action*. But what is the verb? "*Is*." The sentence has to do with *concrete things*: hydrogen, helium, stars, light, and heat. But what is the subject? "*Conversion*." The claim of the sentence has nothing to do with things or actions; it's wholly abstract: *A conversion is a source*.

People like to say that we need nominalizations for their brevity. But when I converted that nominalized sentence into clearer, stronger spoken language, it came out shorter! This is typical. People also like to claim that we need nominalizations in order to move from "story" to "claim," but stories can be claims (my "story" version is a claim), and abstract nominalizations are often stories.

Academic and professional writers like to say they can't be precise without all their nominalizations, but that's not true. Halliday points out how nominalizations often *omit* essential meaning. Certain crucial facts are often lost when meaning is freeze-dried into an abstraction. He uses this published example, "Youth protest mounted," and calls attention to the ambiguity. Does it mean "More and more young people protested"? or "Young people protested more and more"? ("Spoken and Written" 77). "Written discourse conceals many local ambiguities of this kind, which are revealed when one attempts a more 'spoken' paraphrase . . ." (76).

Yes, nominalizations are a universal feature in language—plenty of mild ones exist in casual talk—but in academic and essayist writing, leaden nominalizations are epidemic. When academics have to produce brief abstracts for long journal articles, they usually come up with paroxysms of nominalization, embedding, and lexical density. Such abstracts often fail to give a very clear picture of what the article is actually saying. Most abstracts would be clearer, more useful, and just as short if they were blurted over a beer, "What is your article actually saying?" Bar-stool colloquialisms could easily be edited out, and the resulting abstract would be correct literate writing—and clear and brief.

> [David] McNeill argues that nominal compounds (such as "escape propulsion system" instead of "system that will propel an escape") are used in the space industry to gain a literary effect of technical expertise. Space journals even outdo the technical literature, using 200–300% more nominal compounds. The record McNeill reports is "liquid oxygen liquid hydrogen rocket powered single state to orbit reversible boost system." (Scollon 420)

Our casual speech may often be fragmented, but its verbs usually give more energy: "When the Egyptians built the pyramids," and "stars convert helium into hydrogen." We learn from years of talking to listeners that we get fewer blank stares and requests to clarify when we use concrete terms and avoid too much abstract nominalization. We come to learn what directness feels like in our mouths and ears. Halliday points out that spoken non-nominalized language tends to cast meaning as *process*—and such language tends to be truer to human experience.

But note well: I'm *not* arguing that we always speak simple crisp sentences. I'm not saying that my spoken translations about stars and hydrogen came tripping easily off my tongue. It's central to my argument to point out that I had to work hard for my translation. I had to try out at least half a dozen possibilities before finding a less nominalized version that worked. I had to use lots of conscious planning—not to mention trial and error. That is, I was trying for a *virtue of speech,* but I had to use care and deliberation and conscious choice to get it. But I knew what I was striving for because I had the feel of it in my mouth and ear.

Sadly, people who want to write "well" in our culture of literacy often try (sometimes unconsciously) to strive for certain words and phrases *because* they would not naturally come out of a mouth. Thus people write "obtain" instead of "get" or "in this way" instead of "that is how." People who believe they have a "feel for good writing" often instinctively avoid words like "get" and "in this way" in order to distinguish their writing from speech.

Look at this example of how our culture of literacy infects young minds. A student of mine had a rough draft with plenty of clarity and energy—it came naturally from his speech and freewriting. But when he revised he added heavy nominalization. Clearly he was driven by what he felt was a kind of pressure in the air to make sure his final version looked like "real writing."

> DRAFT. In the United States there is supposed to be freedom of expression, and yet there are laws against obscenity. No one can say what obscenity really is. And is obscene material really harmful? Maybe some forms of censorship are necessary, but this is just another instance of our country being called free when it is not.

> REVISED. We should admit that freedom of expression is not truly realized in the United States, since the censoring of materials which are considered obscene constitute a definite limitation of this freedom. (Elbow *Writing With Power* 289)

Everyone seems to take extreme nominalization lying down—as though there's nothing to be done about it. But we can resist. As I've learned to listen better to my tongue (and also to use the out loud techniques of Chapters 11 and 12), I find myself changing even those nominalizations that are not lethal but that nevertheless muffle meaning and make ideas harder to process. I started by writing

> This invitation to invented spelling destroys any hope that kids will learn to spell right.

But my tongue and ear led me to this simple improvement:

> If we invite kids to use invented spelling they'll never learn to spell right.

There is plenty of clear serious science writing—some of it technical— published for a wider literate audience. It's often written by high-level, award-winning scientists, but they don't run away from language with the fingerprints of speech on it.

Halliday is the master of avoiding either/or black/white thinking; his recent book about speech and writing is called *Complementarities*. He gives a cogent and interesting *defense* of nominalization. In a nutshell, he says that nominalizations have proved "good to think with"—especially in the development of scientific writing. He uses this vivid example:

> If there start to be more boys than girls, or more girls than boys, then people will certainly behave differently.

By nominalizing, he can turn that sentence into this one:

> Human behavior is certainly influenced by a change in the balance of the sexes.

This nominalized sentence has all the annoying problems we have seen—especially the retreat from experienced reality to pure abstraction. As he says, "the grammar turns these processes and qualities into pseudo-things, virtual objects like *length, motion, speed, distance, proportion*" (*Complementarities* 153)—and in this case into *behavior, change, balance, sexes*. He remarks that the growth of nominalization in the development of scientific thinking is the "story of a meaning as it travels, for example, from *move* to *motion*" (154). Pseudo-objects have their uses. While the spoken version is a story with multiple clauses, nominalization permits reducing this story to a single clause:

> Once you turn the processes and qualities into things, and turn the conjunctive relation *of . . . then* into a process . . ., it can be condensed into one quite simple clause with just two participants, *human behaviour* and *a change in the balance of the sexes*, and one process relating the one to the other. . . .
>
> [This nominalized way of saying it] suits the "crystalline," written mode of being; in particular . . . it suits the elaborated discourses of organized knowledge, because it is good to think with—it enables you to build well-ordered conceptual structures and to spin tangled skeins of reasoning. High lexical density is the price that has to be paid. (*Complementarities* 162–163)
>
> [T]he grammar of the written language tends to organize meaning around entities, or things; whereas the grammar of the spoken language organizes meaning around processes—doing and happening. . . . (*Complementarities* 165–166)

But despite this interesting and cogent argument for a virtue in nominalization, he recognizes that for *most* of our writing we don't need to use so much of it and thereby impede readers. When we get to the ninth virtue of spoken language, we'll see that Halliday has become dubious about the value of using language that turns processes into the more static "crystalline" "written mode of being."

---

4. Speaking Promotes Right-Branching Syntax—Which Is Easier to Process

Francis Christensen was notable for celebrating syntax that branches "right" rather than "left." Right-branching sentences start with the main clause and then add phrases or clauses *afterward*. If you diagram such sentences, the added bits will be to the right. In contrast, left-branching sentences "pre-add" phrases or clauses—they come *before* the main clause—and so they are to the left when the sentence is diagrammed. Notice the difference:

> (Right branching): The cumulative sentence serves the needs of both the writer and the reader, the writer by compelling him to examine his thought, the reader by letting him into the writer's thought." (*Notes* 6)

> (Left branching): Compelling the writer to examine his thought and letting the reader into his thought, the cumulative sentence serves the needs of both parties in the transaction.

My left-branching revision of Christensen's sentence is harder to process because it forces us to store the opening bits of the sentence in mind before we can process them; we have to wait before we learn what these bits are going to be *about*. This is no problem, of course, when the left branch is small or somehow very easy to process, for example, "Despite differences, speech and writing are . . ." or "Compared with writing, speech is . . ."

Left branching sentences have become a kind of syntactic cliché in journalistic writing: "Having just returned from three months in Afganistan, Phil Appleby reports that . . ." There's some kind of unspoken fear of writing, "Phil Appleby just returned from three months in Afganistan, and he reports that . . ." I'd say that the left-branching fetish reflects an assumption that good writing should avoid sounding like speech,

Christensen was interested in how right-branching syntax leads to what he calls the "cumulative sentence." He points out that it's often a "looser" sentence, but he doesn't mean that as criticism. He shows that right-branching syntax is common in good published writing but not sufficiently recognized or taught in classrooms. The linguists Horowitz and Samuels observe:

> The most readable forms of writing . . . employ right branching and keep the reader moving at a steady pace and rhythm from left to right as opposed to left branching, which is characteristic of formal prose that requires regressive movements and bottom-up reading. ("Comprehending" 32)

Right-branching syntax is common in speech because it fits how the mind comes up with language. As we are talking, it's hard to plan the left branch *before* we open our mouths. What's easier and more common is something like this: We have a thought or the germ of a thought and we want to say it; we start with the first key phrase or clause that comes to mind; it probably doesn't express the whole thought—we may not even know the whole thought yet. But as we speak, we keep adding bits. In this way, the structure *generates* thinking. Christensen calls right-branching syntax "generative rhetoric." This kind of syntax enacts the way we often enrich, refine, qualify, and double back on our first thought. And listeners and readers don't have to store the left branches while waiting for the sentence engine to arrive.

You might claim that the right-branching syntax of casual speech is bad for readers because the bits are not in the most logical or coherent sequence. This is certainly true when the randomness is extreme, yet the spoken sequence is the sequence in which a live consciousness *generated* them, and this, interestingly, is often a sequence that a live consciousness can readily follow.

The cumulative sentence is the opposite of the periodic sentence. It does not [like the periodic sentence] represent the idea as conceived, pondered over, reshaped, packaged, and delivered cold. It is dynamic rather than static, representing the mind thinking. (Christensen 6)

But I hear another skeptical response: *You and Christensen just like right-branching syntax because it lets you be lazy and careless and not think through ahead of time what you are trying to say.* Yes, speech *is* good for lazy careless unthought-through utterance. But I'm not celebrating carelessness in itself. I'm celebrating right-branching syntax as one of the *fruits* of carelessness. But to get the good fruit, we need to revise with care and make sure it works. (See Chapter 10, "The Need for Care: Easy Speaking onto the Page Is Never Enough.") When the carelessness of speaking gives right branching as a weed, we are learning a valuable syntactic *pattern* that we can exploit with care in serious writing. It is a pattern that makes language easier to process.

It might seem surprising, but Henry James (careless writer?) relies heavily on right-branching syntax. Consider this partial sentence from *The Golden Bowl*:

But she saved herself in time, conscious above all that she was in the presence of still deeper things than she had yet dared to fear, that there was "more in it" than any admission she had made represented—and she had held herself familiar with admissions . . .

But James also liked left-branching syntax. What I quoted would seem enough to make a whole sentence, but it's really only the first half. Here's the second half, and it's left branching:

so that, not to seem to understand where she couldn't accept, and not to seem to accept where she couldn't approve, and could still less with precipitation, advise, she invoked the mere appearance of casting no weight whatever into the scales of her young friend's consistency. (*Golden Bowl* 184)

I love much of James's complex syntax for the way it *enacts* the workings of a highly generative "fine" mind, but his left-branching structures are much harder to process and sometimes require too much effort for me to enjoy.

I haven't spent much time analyzing James's syntax, but as I've looked around among some of his complex sentences, I may have found a syntactic habit: "give em a right, but then hit em with a left." Here's another example of this right-and-then-left pattern. (He is celebrating the American nation and its language for the opportunities they provide to writers):

[*right branching*:] Homogeneous I call the huge American public, with a due sense of the variety of races and idioms that are more and more under contribution to build it up, [*left branching*:] for it is precisely in the great mill of the language, our predominant and triumphant English, taking so much, suffering perhaps even so much, in the process, but giving so much more, on the whole, than it has to "put up" with, that the elements are ground into unity. (James "The Question of the Opportunities" 198)

"Homogeneous I call the huge American public" is just the kind of odd impulsive motor-phrase that we are liable to blurt in speaking as we launch ourselves into a thought. (It's an example of "topic-based" syntax.)

You might say that "looser" right-branching syntax is only right for "creative" or informal personal writing. For example, here's Hemingway:

> George was coming down in the telegraph position, kneeling, one leg forward and bent, the other trailing, his sticks hanging like some insect's thick legs, kicking up puffs of snow, and finally the whole kneeling trailing figure coming around in a beautiful right curve, crouching, the legs shot forward and back, the body leaning out against the swing, the sticks accenting the curve like points of light, all in a wild cloud of snow. (cited in Christensen *Notes* 8)

But Christensen is at pains to show that right-branching syntax is widespread and functional in nonfiction and even academic writing. Joe Williams also affirms the value of this kind of syntax: "Avoid opening sentences with long introductory clauses or phrases" (*Style* 86). Here's an example of right branching of syntax from the academic linguist, Wally Chafe:

> In spite of problematic cases, intonation units emerge from the stream of speech with a high degree of satisfying consistency, not just in English, but in all languages I have been able to observe and in fact in all styles of speaking, whether conversation, storytelling, oration, the performance of rituals, or even (or especially) reading aloud. (*Discourse* 62)

5. Unplanned Spoken Language Tends toward *Parataxis* rather than *Hypotaxis*

I've had to learn and relearn these technical Greek terms, but they name a distinction that is interesting and important:

Parataxis: *God said: Let there be light, and there was light*

Hypotaxis: *Because God said Let there be light, therefore there was light.*

Here's a more down-to-earth example:

Parataxis: *The driver stepped on the gas. The car lurched forward.*

Hypotaxis: *The driver stepped on the gas and therefore the car lurched forward.* (Or *After he hit the gas, the car lurched forward.*)

In parataxis, the elements simply sit "side by side" ("para" = "next to"). But in hypotaxis the elements are hierarchical so that one gets to be on top and the other must lie "under" ("hypo"= "under"). So hypotaxis insists on *articulating the relationship* between the two elements and usually insists that one element is dominant and the other embedded. The paratactic form is simpler and leaves the relationship unexpressed or implied—setting the elements democratically side by side rather than with one on top.

As linguists note, side by side paratactic structure is more common in everyday speech than hierarchical hypotactic structure. We say one thing; and then we say another (as in right-branching syntax). As we converse, we don't take planning time to work out hierarchical or subordinate relationships between elements before opening our mouths. But when we write, we can take more planning time. As children get older, parataxis turns up more frequently in their writing.

Perhaps it's not surprising then that hypotaxis and embedding came to be generally accepted as representing "syntactic maturity." And so in the 1970s there grew up a huge movement among teachers and theorists of writing—almost an industry—championing *sentence combining* exercises. These exercises give students two or three sentences in a "flat" paratactic relationship to each other and then ask them to turn them into a single hierarchically embedded hypotactic sentence. (Strictly speaking, sentence combining *can* produce long *paratactic* sentences, but the exercises were almost always set up to demand hypotaxis and embedding.)

Enthusiasts for sentence combining made a number of nontrivial arguments. The exercises force students to *articulate* the logical relationship between the various elements of a sentence. *Don't just let the elements sit there and "lazily"* imply *how they are related. You must figure out how they are actually related and make it clear to the reader.* Fair enough. Hypotaxis demands more explicit thinking.

But there was a second argument that was potently silent—and not so fair. They simply had to use that key phrase, "syntactic maturity." (*Raise your hand if you are against maturity.*) In our present culture of literacy, there seems to be a solid consensus that essayist and academic writing should have lots of hypotaxis. I think this helps explain why there is more hypotaxis in children's writing as they get older.

If someone like me complains that hypotactic embedding makes sentences harder to read, fans might argue back like this: "*Sure, hypotaxis is harder not just for writers but also for readers, but writers need to spell out syntactic complexity if they want to convey complex meaning. Writers and readers will just have to suck it up.*" But hypotaxis doesn't always add precision; sometimes it just adds mud. Here is something from the very pamphlet of the National Council of Teachers of English that argues for sentence combining. Students are given two clauses and asked to combine them into a single sentence. Here is the model answer: *James Watt's discovery that steam is a powerful source of energy led to Britain's establishing an industrial society* (O'Hare 86). I'd argue that readers are better served by syntax that's more like what comes out of people's mouths in everyday speech—something more naturally paratactic and unnominalized, perhaps something like this: *James Watt discovered that steam is a powerful source of energy and this discovery led Britain to establish an industrial society.* No precision is lost.

Besides, is it always better to spell out all relationships? Some are obvious and it can be pompous to spell them out. (Hypotactic: *Because the driver stepped on the gas, the car lurched forward.* Surely it's better paratactic: *The driver stepped on the gas; the car lurched forward.* Hypotactic: *She works in social services and plans to get a master's degree in social work so she can help others.* Paratactic: *she plans to get a master's degree in social work. She wants to help others.*) Parataxis creates energy; hypotaxis reduces it. It's especially clogging when sentence combining encourages writers to turn an action ("Watt discovers that steam is a source of energy") into an abstract static noun ("Watt's discovery that steam is a powerful source of energy")—and make the whole lumpen nominalization into the subject of the poor little verb, "led."

And is it really more "mature" to use parataxis and embedding? Yes it represents *one* kind of maturity or sophistication, but not the only kind. Consider this question: What serious professional writing in our culture is *most* wise and mature? I'd claim that the answer is *good literature*. Good stories, poems, and creative nonfiction get a good deal of their power by leaving things implied. When something is implied, the reader is pulled in and *participates* more deeply in the meaning—*experiences* the meaning—rather than just understanding it. (See Tannen's "Relative Focus.") And many good writers of expository and academic writing do *not* succumb to the syntactic bias among writing theorists in favor of hypotaxis, embedding, and left-branching syntax. Writers reach readers better when they *also* know how to call on the rhetorical virtues of parataxis and right-branching syntax that's so common in everyday speaking.

I fear that hypotaxis serves the machine grading of student writing. The software can't read; all it can do is count observable features. (Should I have written, "*Since it cannot read, counting is all it can do*"?) You can bet that one of the things they count are words and phrases that signal hypotaxis: *for example, therefore, because, as a result, moreover, nevertheless.*

> Here is part of Erich Auerbach's wise meditation on hypotaxis and parataxis in his classic study, *Mimesis*:
>
> > [W]e are reminded of certain Biblical passages, which in the mirror of the Vulgate become: *Dixitque Deus: fiat lux, et facta est lux* [Genesis 1: 3 And God said: Let there be light, and there was light]; . . . [other examples] *aperuit Dominus os asinae, et locuta est* (Num. 22: 28) [The Lord opened the mouth of the ass, and she spoke]. In all of these instances there is, instead of the causal or at least temporal hypotaxis which we should expect in classical Latin (whether with *cum* or *postquam*, whether with an ablative absolute or a participial construction) a parataxis with *et*; and this procedure, far from weakening the interdependence of the two events, brings it out most emphatically; just as in English it is more dramatically effective to say: He opened his eyes and was struck . . . than: When he opened his eyes, or: Upon opening his eyes, he was struck. . . . (61–62)

6. Unplanned Spoken Language Is Good for Pith, Gists, and Nutshells

In the chapter before this one, I told how most writing teachers learn to ask students "What are you really trying to say here?" when the essay is a tangle. Students usually blurt out the point in clear language. But that chapter was about the process of speaking. Now I want to focus on the product: what are the linguistic features that create condensed clarity about the main point?

Admittedly, plenty of casual spontaneous speech is diffuse—rambling and digressive. We often speak three words or phrases instead of taking the time to decide which is the right one. We don't have the time to decide what we really mean because the listener is right there waiting for us to finish the sentence. Besides, listeners are "enablers" for imprecision. They can tell us when we're not clear, ask us what we were trying to get at, and play the midwife to what we really mean—or what we should have meant but didn't.

Still, there seems to be something about everyday spoken language that can lead us to pithy directness. Spit it out. Hit the nail on the head. Think of "sayings." Sayings are *said*. They have a nutshell quality. Sayings take lots of experience and meaning and coil them up into a tight energized spring. Sayings came from someone's mouth—and they live in mouths. Nice guys finish last. Winning isn't the main thing, it's the only thing. Cut to the quick. I recently heard this one from Iraq: If you are hunting for rabbit, take a rabbit. If you're hunting for gazelle, take a rabbit.

The rhythmic and intonational habits we learn in speaking give people the rhetorical structures they can use to package well-digested insights. Speech provides the ideal *potential* for sayings; we have pith coiled up in our tongues. We can see it in some tweets. Here are two examples I recently saw from people reflecting on the internet: "Sadly, I think less and google more"; "I think about more things for shorter amounts of time."

Ben Franklin exploited this dimension of spoken language to create some of his sayings. In *Poor Richard's Almanac*, he did what I'm arguing for in this book: he used writing, but exploited the natural rhythmic resources of speech to make better sayings. Jill Lepore has the evidence: Franklin took "A Man in Passion rides a horse that runs away with him," and turned it into "A Man in a Passion rides a mad Horse." Here's a borrowing that was already pretty good—"Many things are wanting to them that desire many things"—but he made it better still: "If you desire many things, many things will seem but a few" (Lepore "The Creed" 80.)

So in fact we can find a quality of oral pithiness in everyday spoken language even when much talk is windy and round about. Consider this example from the *Anchorage Daily News*. Jason Lange was driving his snowplow late at night in a blinding snowstorm. In his headlights, a moose and its calf suddenly appeared. He jammed on his brakes but couldn't keep from skidding—and neither could they. The reporter quotes Jason: "Their feet were moving 100 miles an hour but they weren't going anywhere" (Section B, p. 1, Sunday, December 28, 2004).

Imagine the context for this single sentence. Some reporter hears about the overnight moose-kill and interviews Jason—perhaps even the very next morning when he's sleepy. The reporter turns on the tape recorder and asks questions. If the reporter was any good, he invited Jason to ramble on—letting him interrupt himself, move back and forth in time, move around between events and feelings and opinions—and even vent. The tape recorder probably captured some other eloquent bits, but the reporter shrewdly pounced on this one for his first paragraph. It's a perfect example of how, even in the midst of unfocused rambling, our tongues can be an organ for power, precision, and compression.

Imagine if Jason Lange were set the job of writing an essay about his evening's plowing. He might have been. He might be in college—driving his plow for a night job. From my experience as a teacher of students like Jason, I can say that he would be much less likely to have come up with a formulation so pithy if he were writing an essay. I see plenty of good writing—but not many formulations as forceful and condensed as what came out of Jason's mouth. It's a nutshelling that is characteristic of speech at its best. It took free-flowing conversation to produce this "saying."

Perhaps you'll say that I'm falling into the stereotype of assuming that the unskilled uneducated working-class Alaska snowplow driver can only be eloquent when he speaks. Not at all. There's every chance that Jason is actually a Ph.D. academic, who fled the Lower Forty-eight because he couldn't find a good academic job or got tired of the academic ratrace. Alaska is full of such folks and they often have jobs like driving snowplows all night (sometimes enjoying life far more than they did before!). Consider even the most educated academics—prominent leaders in their fields who have written influential books and articles in their disciplines. I read lots of their writing too, and they are seldom any better at hitting the nail on the head in their writing than the college freshmen I teach. Actually the freshmen pull it off more frequently because lots of them still use their tongues for writing.

It's not that economists or physicists are hobbled by the complexity of their thinking. If you hear them in a bar talking about their ideas with friendly listeners, they *can* hit the nail on the head. They can express complicated ideas in clear condensed pithy words. Some of these formulations between sips of beer are slang, but many of them would be perfectly appropriate on the pages of their most learned books or articles. These academics would probably do pretty well with a reporter who puts a tape recorder on the table. But for all their learning and skill with words, these learned, authoritative writers can't usually manage to nutshell while they write. They seem to lack pith because they feel they have to "write writing." It would have been the same story if Jason Lange were a software engineer, a Wall Street trader, or a business executive—as he might well be in Alaska. It would have taken speaking.

There's one significant exception to all these stories I'm telling about various Jason Langes. He might well be driving that plow because he's a fiction writer or poet. Alaska is also full of these folks with jobs like driving snowplows at night. (The reporter himself probably has a drawer full of stories and a novel he's finishing.) Poets and fiction writers *do* learn to hit the nail on the head with their hands, not just their mouths. But—to telegraph the point of the book—it's the power of their mouths that they've learned to harness with their fingers.

But my argument here is that nonfiction writers—people writing memos, committee reports, *and* academic papers—can do the same thing. Here's an academic historian who knows how to get coiled up spoken energy into careful prose (it's Richard Hofstadter on Teddy Roosevelt):

> The straddle was built like functional furniture into his thinking. He was honestly against the abuse of big business, but he was also sincerely against indiscriminate trust-busting; he was in favor of reform, but disliked the militant reformers. He wanted clean government and honest business, but he shamed as "muckrakers" those who exposed corrupt government and dishonest business. . . . Such equivocations are the life of practical politics, but . . . Roosevelt had a way of giving them a fine aggressive surge. (From *The American Political Tradition*; quoted in Benfey 24)

Of course, Hofstadter needed careful revising and editing to harvest the fruits of what he learned from his mouth and ear. See Chapter 10 on care and 11 and 12 on revising with mouth and ear.)

Why do some people seem to come up more often with pithy sayings? Mere practice can't explain it since so many prolific speakers and writers are windy and verbose. The answer is a mystery, but I can't help thinking about Wordsworth's infamously sentimental generalization in the Preface to *Lyrical Ballads*: that poetry needs the "real" language of "uneducated country folk." It's easy to argue against such a wild generalization, but I wonder if solitude and silence may not help invite pungent speech. New Hampshire farmers and Maine fishermen are famous for their laconic zingers. I suspect that something useful happens to our thinking and language when we have to spend lots of time alone in our own heads—talking only to ourselves. I was once invited to co-lead a weekend workshop on silence and voice at a Quaker retreat center at Pendle Hill near Philadelphia. "You bring *voice* and we'll provide *silence*," my Quaker host told me. Throughout the weekend, we experimented in all kinds of ways with both writing and silence, and after a while it seemed clear that eloquence was enhanced by periods of silence. Consider "Caedmon's Hymn"—a lovely Anglo-Saxon prayer to God. He was a poor simple herder of animals but God bade him speak. He gives God credit for his simple profound words, but he also said it came from "chewing his cud," presumably in silence, like the cows he took care of. (See my "Silence: A Collage.")

---

7. Spoken Language Is More Coherent than Written Language

What? Can this be true? Spoken language seems so messy. Yes, but it also has a certain *cohesion*. It takes the form of what linguists call the "*given-new contract*" that governs most spontaneous speech. That is, as speakers say one phrase or clause and then move to a new one, they characteristically start the new one with something already given in the previous one. ("The general formulation for the structure of an information unit is '(Given +) New'." [Halliday and Greaves 56].) Here's a particularly obvious example in words that rolled off my fingers as I was speaking onto the page:

But that's not really the main thing. The main thing is that . . .

After looking at a large sample of speech, Chafe makes this observation about given-new structure:

What we do *not* find are intonation units in which both the subject and predicate express new information. . . . If this is a limitation on what the speaker can do, it may also be a limitation for the listener as well. It may well be that neither the speaker nor the listeners is able to handle more than one new idea at a time." (Chafe *Discourse* 108–109)

Thus, as speakers we learn to adapt to listeners stuck in real time with no leisure to go back and re-hear what we say. Our habits of speech have been shaped throughout our lives by listeners saying "What? Slow down" when we've gone too fast for them. Haviland and Clark note that "the speaker tries, to the best of his ability, to make the structure of his utterance congruent with his knowledge of the listener's mental world" (Clark and Haviland, quoted in Chafe *Discourse* 169). So speakers typically use a kind of linking structure: they grease the skids for something new by starting with a reference to what's old or "*given*" in the previous phrase (or easily accessible or recoverable or already prominent in the conversation).

As Chafe writes,

> It would make sense that one would employ as a starting point a referent that is already active in the discourse. And indeed one of the most striking properties of subjects [or starting points] in conversational language is the fact that such a high proportion of them do express given information. (*Discourse* 85)

Of course, speakers aren't always as blatant with their given-new as when I wrote, "But that's not the main thing. The main thing is . . ." Here's an extended example of a young woman speaking about a party she was at. I wouldn't have noticed the given-new structure in this passage before I began to study spoken language. I'll explain it below. (In transcribing continuous speech, Chafe gives each intonational unit its own line. More about intonation units in the next chapter):

1. I started talking to another guy,
2. when Bill walked off.
3. And all of a sudden I'm realizing,
4. this guy is stringing complicated sentences together,
5. and he's dropping literary terms,
6. and names,
7. and I'm kind of going,
8. where are you from?
9. He's an army brat.
10. He speaks fluent German.
11. He's lived in about thirty places.
12. And I said,
13. you must have an easy time making new friends,
14. it's easy for you,
15. and he said oh yeah.
16. But also what it had done,
17. it caused him to be introverted,
18. so he read a lot,
19. when he was a kid.
20. So he's really self taught. (Example from Chafe; email May 10,)

Most of these intonation units start off referring to this unnamed "another guy." (That's not true in line one, but the starting point there is "I"—a given in the conversation. But after line one "this guy" functions as a "given"—easily accessible to consciousness. When Chafe looked at a large sample of spoken sentences, "ninety-eight percent of these given subjects were, in fact, pronouns"—which by definition refer back to something already mentioned (*Discourse* 85).

In this passage, we can see another striking feature of unplanned speaking that correlates with the given-new structure. The new element always gets the stress—saying to the listener, in effect, "Listen up. This is new." Thus even as reader, you can probably hear that virtually all these intonation units start from nonstress and build to stress—to what's new. (As we read the silent text, we're tempted to see line 2 as an exception and put the stress on "Bill." But Chafe notes that in the recording of the actual speech, "Bill" was in fact *unstressed*. The stress fell on "walked off" which was the news here—and of course "Bill" was "old" from what the speaker had been saying before our extract began.)

When speakers decide to violate the given-new pattern (which of course they sometimes do for rhetorical or other reason), they alert listeners by starting off with an unexpected stress (*Listen up. I'm starting with something new*). Halliday also gives prominence to this given-new structure in speech and is particularly interested in the role of intonation.

By stressing this fine-grained element of coherence that is characteristic of human speech, it might look as though I'm pretending that we're always clear when we talk—as of course we notoriously are not. But the passage we've just looked at gives us a good illustration of how we confuse listeners when we speak spontaneously. The young woman speaker plays fast and loose with "it" in lines 14, 16, and 17. In line 14, "it" refers back to "easy time making friends," but in 16 and 17 "it" refers *further* back to "lived in thirty places." Both meanings for "it" had been activated in the conversation and thus are easily accessible—*to her*—but she forgot to notify the listener that she was switching between "it"s. In fact—with stress as a signal—her live listener *might* not have been confused. Still, there's no gainsaying how often we confuse our listeners by playing fast and loose with pronouns like "it" and "he."

This "given-new" structure in spoken language fits with what Paul Grice called the "cooperative principle" in discourse. He's referring to a wide variety of conversational structures that increase the chances of successful communication.

❖   ❖   ❖

I've been talking about the given-new habit in speech. What about writing? Speakers use the habit unconsciously in speaking, but our conscious decisions often differ from our unconscious habits. So it's not surprising that writers often fail to create given-new links when they choose and plan their words—especially in revising when they consciously add and cut and rearrange words to try to get the thinking right. But when we fail to link our clauses and sentences in this way—we destroy the coherence or flow that is natural in spontaneous speaking and thereby make readers work harder to process our language.

Joe Williams explicitly preaches the need for given-new in writing. He links it to the concept of cohesion:

We feel one sentence is cohesive with the next when we see at the beginning of a second sentence information that appeared toward the end of the previous one. That's what creates our experience of "flow." (*Style* 80)

To illustrate this advice, he gives a problem passage of three sentences. The second and third ones are harder to process because they start off with what's *new*:

> Some astonishing questions about the nature of the universe have been raised by scientists studying black holes in space. The collapse of a dead star into a point perhaps no larger than a marble creates a black hole. The fabric of space is changed in puzzling ways when so much matter is compressed into so little volume. (80)

Here's his improved version where the second and third sentences flow better because they start with meanings that are already given and thus active in the reader's mind:

> Some astonishing questions about the nature of the universe have been raised by scientists studying black holes in space. A black hole is created by the collapse of a dead star into a point perhaps no larger than a marble. So much matter compressed into so little volume changes the fabric of space in puzzling ways.

Note the passive construction in the middle sentence ("A black hole is created"). Williams observes that writers often make their writing *less* coherent and harder to understand when they are too preoccupied with the ubiquitous advice to change all passive sentences to active form. By making every sentence active, they often violate the "given-new contract" and make the language harder for readers. In fact, passive sentences are often just what we need for creating helpful given-new links between sentences by "lightening the load" at the start of the new sentence.

Here are two sentences I found in a rough freewritten draft:

> We lose touch with mouth and ear. This leads to writing without flow.

Notice how my "this" is a nakedly helpful example of a given-new link—and very characteristic of spoken conversation (after all, I "spoke" it onto the page). Sticklers might accuse me of the crime of using a pronoun without a precise antecedent. My "this" doesn't point to a specific word but generally to the whole thought. But it points clearly to what is given and makes it a "light subject" or "starting place" for the new element I am introducing ("writing without flow") Because I was freewriting, I didn't have to consciously plan this pattern of linking coherence or flow; I just had to recognize it and value it. (Of course this process involves rejecting or changing spoken usages that don't work—and genuinely vague pronoun use is common in speech.)

We can learn and consciously follow the *rule* from people like Joe Williams: start new sentences with an element from previous sentences. But we can get the *feel* of this reader-friendly, given-new pattern that comes for free in our speaking. We will find it in our speaking onto the page and also if we read aloud to revise as described In Chapters 11 and 12.

8. Spoken Language Is More Coherent than Written Language in a Different and Surprisingly Obvious Way

If we look at the words people *actually write*—before they clean up their drafts into a revision—we see language that is often far more incoherent than their spoken discourse. That is, the process of writing often leads to *more* false starts, interruptions, cross-outs, and changes of direction than speech. In the case of unskilled writers, sometimes even the *final* drafts are less coherent than their speech. (Admittedly, a few writers won't write down a sentence till they've cleaned it up in their heads; see the case of McEwan in Chapter 10.) Halliday points out that writing is

> characterized by hesitations, revision, change of direction, and other sim-
> ilar features; these tend to arise when attention is being paid to the process
> of text production. Since highly monitored discourse is typically written,
> these features are actually more characteristic of writing than of speech;
> but because most written text becomes public only in its final edited form,
> the hesitations and discards are lost and the reader is shielded from seeing
> the process at work. ("Spoken and Written" 70–71)

Halliday's larger point is that incoherence comes not from speaking as a mode but rather from the mental process of self-monitoring. This variable of *mentality* cuts across the difference between speaking or writing:

> Speech, we are told, is marked by hesitations, false starts, anacolutha,
> slips and trips of the tongue, and a formidable paraphernalia of so-called
> performance errors. . . . There is no disputing the fact that these things
> occur, although they are much less prevalent than we are asked to believe.
> They are characteristic of the rather self-conscious, closely self-monitored
> speech that goes, for example, with academic seminars, where I suspect
> much of the observation and recording has taken place. If you are con-
> sciously planning your speech as it goes along and listening to check the
> outcome, then you naturally tend to lose your way: to hesitate, back up,
> cross out, and stumble over the words. But these things are not a partic-
> ular feature of natural spontaneous discourse, which tends to be fluent,
> highly organized and grammatically well formed. If you are interacting
> spontaneously and without self-consciousness, then the clause complexes
> tend to flow smoothly without you falling down or changing direction in
> the middle. ("Spoken and Written" 68)

When I think about this point—how planned and careful language breaks down more often than unplanned unselfconscious language—I understand something that has always intrigued me about the writing of students: I can virtually always understand their freewriting, however messy and jumpy it might seem, whereas I often can't understand their carefully revised texts. Halliday is eloquent on this feature of unplanned language:

> This [point] . . . runs counter to our received attitudes toward speech. . . .
> [S]peech allows for such a considerable degree of intricacy; when speakers
> exploit this potential, they seem very rarely to flounder or get lost in it. In

the great majority of instances, expectations are met, dependencies resolved, and there are no loose ends. The intricacy of the spoken language is matched by the orderliness of spoken discourse. (67)

How can we harness the coherence of our oral "blundering" to help our careful writing? All too often, I've found myself deeply engaged in revising something important—revising it more and more—and gradually getting more and more tangled in a swamp. Suddenly I remembered that I had earlier *spoken* this train of thought in a conversation—or even more fully to a class or a conference audience. As I was tangled up in my revising swamp, I realized that my spoken version was actually *clearer* than the struggled-over words in front of me on the page. The spoken version may have been messy and lacking much of the precision, development, and careful qualification that writing can give, yet my life would have been easier if I'd started "talking" my thinking through my fingers—or even used a transcript of my talking—and *then* revised so as to bring in the benefits of the slower writing gear: more details, richer development, and more effective organization.

9. Spoken Language Has the Advantage of Representing the World as *Process*

As he so frequently does, Halliday gives us an evenhanded comparison:

> Spoken language represents phenomena as if they were processes [while] written language represents phenomena as if they were products. ("Spoken and Written" 74)

(Remember: he's not pretending to talk about *all* spoken or written language; "spoken" for him means unselfconscious, unmonitored language; "written" means monitored and self-conscious. More about his usage in the Introduction to Part Two.)

On the one hand, he underlines the virtue of written language for how it represents the world (especially with all the nominalizations):

> So the written language has always tended to make the world look like itself: stable, solid, dense, with recognizable chunks that may get built into substantial and complex structures. This was highly functional at the birth of experimental science, where the world needed to be held still so that it could be observed, measured, and reasoned about. (*Complementarities* 167)

But on the other hand, he underlines the virtue of spoken language for its opposite gift—and actually says that this spoken quality is *more* valuable for representing the world:

> I am inclined to think the written language of the future will go back (or rather forward) to being more processlike; not only because the traditional objectlike nature of written discourse is itself changing . . . but also because our understanding of the physical world has been moving in that direction, ever since Einstein substituted space-time for space and time. ("Spoken and Written" 79)

If those two claims sound overgeneralized and merely abstract and theoretical, look again at the written and spoken versions of the sentence about stars that I explored earlier (in the section about nominalizations). Notice how the written version creates a crystalline *stasis,* while the spoken version transforms it into *action* or *motion.*

> [written] *The conversion of hydrogen to helium in the interiors of stars* is *the source of energy for their immense output of light and heat.*

> [spoken] *When stars <u>convert</u> hydrogen into helium in their cores, they <u>get</u> the energy they need for <u>putting out</u> so much light and heat.* (or) *Stars <u>convert</u> hydrogen into helium at their centers. That's how they <u>get</u> so much energy to <u>put out</u> light and heat.*

In the written version, two entities are connected by an equal sign spelled "is." In the spoken version, we have a *story* about action and energy. When Halliday compares a different example of written and spoken renderings of the same thought, he concludes, "the written variant tells the story in nouns: *visit, sense, risk, attempt, action* whereas the spoken version tells it in verbs: *visited, ended up feeling, might get hurt, tried to do.*"

When Halliday praises the process-oriented tendency in spoken language, his interest is theoretical and epistemological. He argues that reality, as modern physics shows it to us, is more about *events* than *objects.* I agree, but my interest is less theoretical. My concern is with effective writing. Language usually gets its meaning into the minds of listeners or readers when it embodies movement or change through time. Putting this crudely: stories tend to help us experience a meaning better—even a conceptual meaning—than purely conceptual language.

Halliday's contrast between stasis and movement fits with Christensen's contrast between left-branching and right-branching syntax. Left-branching syntax gives us the static periodic sentence—"conceived, pondered over, reshaped, packaged" (Francis Christensen 6) that "represents phenomena as if they were products" (Halliday "Spoken and Written" 74). Right-branching syntax gives us the cumulative sentence—"dynamic rather than static, representing the mind thinking" (Francis Christensen 6) that tends to "represent phenomena as if they were processes" (Halliday 74).

When we write we are told to figure out ahead of time what we want to say (*Start by making an outline*) and let the writing represent the fruits of *completed* thinking. When we talk, on the other hand, we are often still working out our thinking: our words represent thinking in process. The advice to writers is understandable since our spoken attempts to figure out what we mean often create a linguistic mess. Yet language is more lively and energetic when it represents thinking going on. This kind of language helps readers *experience* our meanings. It turns out that we can get the best of both worlds: we can speak onto the page at the early stages, and then in revising save the best of spoken thinking-in-action—but shape it and organize it so it's coherent. (I focus on this issue—theoretically and pragmatically—in Chapter 15.)

Halliday writes further:

> I have usually had recourse to metaphors of *structure* versus *movement*, saying, for example, that the spoken language is choreographic. The complexity of spoken language is in its flow, the dynamic mobility whereby each figure provides context for the next one, not only defining its point of departure but also setting the conventions by reference to which it is to be interpreted.
>
> With the sentence of written language, there is solidarity among its parts such that each equally prehends and is prehended by all the others. It is a *structure*, and is not essentially violated by being represented synoptically, as a structural unit [all at once—outside of time]. With the clause complex of spoken language, there is no such solidarity, no mutual prehension among all its parts. Its mode of being is as process, not as product. . . . We have not yet learnt to write choreographic grammars; so we look at spoken language through the lens of a grammar designed for writing. ("Spoken and Written" 66–67 my emphases)

Halliday traces the more static, nominalized grammatical style to seventeenth-century scientific writing, a kind of writing that worked more at "the construction of an 'objectivized' world through the grammar of the written language" ("Linguistic Perspectives" 16). See also Adolf and Olson on this historical development in style.

The Complementarity of Speech and Writing

After all this defense of virtues in typically spoken language, I'll end by stressing again the virtues in *both* speaking and writing. Halliday is eloquent in spinning out the many "complementarities" of the two—indeed that's the central word in the title of his new book.

> The complementarity of speaking and writing is not a case of reciprocity. They do two different things; not the same thing in two different ways. (*Complementarities* 168)
>
> Spoken language is liquid . . . and transitory; written language is solid and permanent. There are many other such pairs we could use as analogy: mercurial versus crystalline, river versus glacier, dance versus sculpture. What any such pair of terms *must* suggest is that both states of being are equally rich and equally complex. . . .
>
> So writing is at one and the same time both more constraining and more enabling than speaking, and the fullest semiotic potential of the human brain, as we have inherited it, requires both. (168)

This last point is the theme of my book: to get the best writing, we require the benefits of *both* speaking and writing.

Implications for Teachers and Writers

So we can't get good writing by just speaking easily onto the page or using transcripts of speech. What we need are the *resources* of speech that I've been describing here: involvement features that connect words better to the audience; flexible lively syntax; direct concrete language rather than clogged nominalizations; right-branching syntax; parataxis; greater coherence; and a rendering of the world as process more than as product.

In my teaching I have used lots of freewriting or speaking onto the page and I think I see it gradually infecting students' careful writing for the better. By some kind of simple osmosis, students seem to begin to get into their careful writing more of the lively energy, directness, clarity, and voice that exists naturally in their speech and freewriting. It sneaks into their ear too and can thus provide a basis for their revising (if they trust their ear). Many other teachers have seen the same thing. (See Hilgers for striking careful empirical research demonstrating that students who were given practice in freewriting wrote essays judged better than students who were given other practice exercises.)

How can we get the benefits of these resources into our careful writing? My main answer comes in Part Three about reading aloud to revise. That's where we learn to harvest the resources of speech for careful writing.

The techniques in Part Three rely most on the mouth and ear. But I'll mention here a few more cognitive analytic exercises that can also help reap the resources of speaking onto the page:

- Read over your fast careless textual speaking onto the page (even if it's produced by voice-transcribing software) and look for linguistic virtues. There's no need for technical terms (*Let's see: Where is there parataxis and right-branching syntax? Where are the nominalizations?*). No, just look for passages that feel strong, lively, and clear. When new users look at their freewriting, sometimes they can't see anything but a mess: perhaps wandering, digressive and too wordy. But if we keep our ear out for linguistic virtues in freewriting, we'll find them.
- Compare pieces of our fast careless writing with pieces of careful writing we've already finished or with pieces of published writing. What are the different strengths and weaknesses we notice? It's fruitful to discuss with others what might be different perceptions of strong and weak passages.
- Simply look for strong passages and create a collage as I describe in Chapter 10.

❈   ❈   ❈

There's one more remarkably powerful virtue in spoken language and I'll treat it in the next chapter: intonation.

LITERACY STORY

How We Got Spaces between Our Words

The early Canaanites and Semites who invented the alphabet did not yet use vowels. Saenger argues that this is one big reason why they put spaces between their written words. A text consisting of continuous words written only with consonants—without vowels—would be too hard to decipher. Try that last sentence this way:

atxtcnsstngfcntnswrdswrttnnlwthcnsnntswthtvwlswldbthrdtdcphr.

But when the Greeks introduced vowels into the Semitic alphabet, it became much easier to read writing with no spaces between the words. Try that earlier sentence with the vowels added:

Atextconsistingofcontinuouswordswrittenonlywithconsonantswithout-vowelswouldbetoohardtodecipher.

Still, writing with no spaces strikes us as weird and difficult. We need to remember that "reading" was a different business in Greece and Rome from how we think of it:

> Unlike modern reading of a text, ancient reading remained an oral activity even when it was performed privately. Totally silent reading, without movement of the tongue and lips, was only very rarely practiced in Greco-Latin antiquity. A skilled reader prepared his text orally in a soft voice in advance so that he could pronounce it aloud to an audience without stumbling. The wealthy relied on educated slaves to read to them. . . .
>
> Oral reading also reflected the ancient Greek and Roman aesthetics that placed great value on the musical qualities of elegantly written metered prose and verse that would have been lost in the silent scanning of the text. Reading was thus a quasi performance and not simply the visual extraction of meaning from graphic signs. (Saenger "History" 11–12)

There's a famous story that Augustine tells in his *Confessions* (CE 400) of being amazed when he happened upon Ambrose, Bishop of Milan, reading his manuscripts—silently: "His eyes travelled across the pages and his heart searched out the meaning, but his voice and tongue stayed still" (Book Six, Chapter 3). Nevertheless scribes *sometimes* put spaces between words for non-elite people who couldn't afford slave readers and had to do their own reading. So some early copies of the New Testament and some funerary inscriptions did have spacing (Saenger 12).

But things were different in Ireland. As early as the seventh century, Irish monks began putting spaces between the words they copied—and also added some syntactic punctuation that demarcated units of meaning. Presumably they did this because, unlike everyone else in Europe, Latin was not their mother tongue, so they had a much harder time copying and reading it. For Europeans, a Latin text was a phonetic transcription of the language in their bones—the language they spoke—and hence it looked relatively familiar spelled out on paper. A word-separated text also freed the Irish copiers and readers from having to orally pronounce a text as they worked with it. They used this word-separated technique in developing a new genre of prayer book intended for personal silent prayer. Another reason for the unusual Irish spacing is that they sometimes copied Syriac bibles from the Middle East, and these *had* spacing.

This Irish practice spread to England as the Irish came to train Anglo-Saxon scribes. But the English Channel was harder than the Irish Sea for word spacing to cross:

This word-separated text format remained a unique phenomenon of the British Isles until the tenth century. Outside of Brittany and isolated Celtic and Anglo-Saxon monastic colonies, this format was unknown on the European Continent. (12)

It took even longer for fully separated text to circulate around Europe. (Needless to say, I'm drawing here on Paul Saenger's "History of Reading." He went onto write *Space between Words: The Origins of Silent Reading.*)

5 Intonation

A Virtue for Writing at the Root of Everyday Speech

INTONATION IS A virtue in speech that may provide a bigger payoff for writing than any of the nine virtues I described in the last chapter. Intonation is the rich music we all use to sing almost every word we speak. I like to illustrate intonation for students with a mini-workshop. I ask everyone in class to say the single word, "Hello," but in each case to try to send a slightly different message. After each "performance" we see what listeners heard. Besides the various obvious seductive forms of "hello," there is the Sherlock Holmes's "hellll-o" that says "Here's an interesting fact." And the "hellooooo" that says, "Wake up, dummy." Other words work well for this mini-workshop: "no," "maybe," "yes." It's amazing how many messages human speakers can send with the *sound* of just one word—a word that is *silent* on the written page.

Virtually everyone is a master of intonation, yet consider how complex this musical instrument is that we can all play unconsciously. There is pitch (low, high), volume (soft, loud), speed (slow, fast), accent (stress, no stress), intensity (relaxed, tense), timbre (breathy, shrill, nasal, and many more), pausing (long, short). Note that these are not binary items, for in each case there is a full continuum between extremes (e.g., between low and high, slow and fast, loud and soft). There are glides and jumps. Also, there are patterned sequences. For example, tune is a *pattern* of pitches; rhythm is a *pattern* of speed and accent. Combinations of all of these elements create a rich music for conveying subtle (and not so subtle) meanings.

Very small children who are learning to talk seem preoccupied with intonation. They continually practice and often exaggerate the vocal music that goes with speech. I remember a very small child saying, "*Actually*, I don't think I *want* to go to bed right now"—not angry or even recalcitrant, just firm. His whole sentence—especially his "actually" and "want"—created a richly musical performance that was far more dramatic and expressive than anything I'd ever heard come out of his parents' mouths. There is reason to suspect that intonation is a favored doorway for children into the mastery of syntax. ("It is well known that young children are more sensitive to tone and context of an utterance than to its precise verbal form" [Olson *World on Paper* 92]).

It's rare for people to speak without intonation; and even *no-intonation* or monotone is a kind of intonation that usually sends its own message. I notice that faculty meetings are often dominated by monotone where people often take all the music out of their speech. It's a sign of being on guard. (*Don't let anyone get a glimpse of how you really feel. This is a dangerous place.*) Bakhtin was fascinated with intonation and speaks of how we lose it if we don't have "choral support" from our listeners. The "stiffness" of stiff adults often brings restricted intonation. Wooden politicians like Al Gore and John Kerry spend a good deal of time with coaches who try to teach them to be even half as intonationally expressive as they were at age five. When we can't understand people who speak a different language or dialect, we often understand their intonation just fine. In his extended and remarkably clear treatment of intonation, Bolinger notes that even speakers of tonal languages like Chinese use plenty of additional intonation.

Two Methods that Linguists Use for Representing Intonation

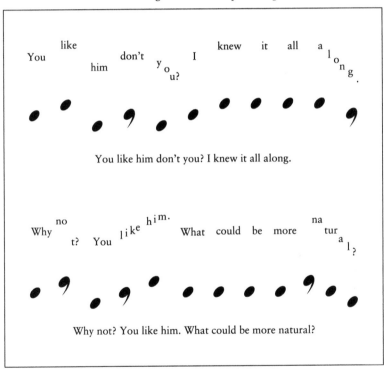

You like him don't you? I knew it all along.

Why not? You like him. What could be more natural?

The "seasick typewriter" examples come from Bolinger *Uses* 117. The other method is sometimes called the "tadpole" technique.

Intonation and Meaning

People most commonly associate intonation with what is expressive, interpersonal, or emotional—revealing, for example, whether the speaker feels happy or lonely—or whether the person is characteristically peppy or depressed. It's notable how often our intonation betrays our real feeling or character even when we try to sound otherwise.

About terminology. Linguists sometimes use the word "intonation" in a strict and narrow sense—limiting it to mean pitch or melody alone. In that sense it's a subcategory of the larger concept of "prosody": the complete range of all audible features that speakers can use with spoken words, such as varying the speed, lengthening syllables, accent, and silent pausing. I've opted to use the term "intonation" rather than prosody because it's a more familiar and less technical term. Besides, in literary theory, "prosody" has a confusingly different meaning altogether, describing features of poetic versification like meter and rhythm. Besides, I see people like Bolinger and Chafe sometimes letting "intonation" cover a wide range of audible effects. Bakhtin too prefers the term and starts off an important essay ("Discourse in Life") by exploring the rich complex messages conveyed in a single empty word, "well." (For this book, I have no need for a technical investigation of the difference between intonation and prosody, narrowly defined.)

About monotone or the avoidance of intonation. I've always been struck with T. S. Eliot's flat readings of his poetry. Alan Bennett speaks of

> sitting on winter afternoons in the nave of Ely or Lincoln [cathedrals] and hearing from the (so-called) loudspeaker a dry, reedy, unfleshed voice taking evensong. And one was grateful that the voice was without feeling—no more emotion than from an announcer giving the times of the departure of trains: the words themselves so powerful that they do not need feeling injected into them, any more than poetry does. Or, as T. S. Eliot said, who had that style of delivery himself, "Speak the word, speak the word only." (544)

Eliot's "liturgical" style of reading seeks to remove any sense of a particular *person*—or even a particular interpretation—between his actual words and the listener. He was a champion of "impersonality" in poetry.

Catherine Madsen writes a fascinating study of language written for liturgy. The goal, she says, is language that bears listening again and again over decades or more—language that will yield constantly changing meanings that are deep and lasting. She writes of the use of a "liturgical monotone" that "allow[s] several readings without comment—without 'privileging' any one over the others. . . . In liturgy, intimate secrets can be simultaneously spoken and concealed" (157).

But in this book, my interest is in how intonation relates not so much to feeling as to grammatical, syntactical, semantic, and connotational meaning. As just one example, consider how this sentence has different meanings—depending on mere emphasis:

> The prime minister *wasn't* selected [as opposed to expectations that he would be]
> The *prime minister* wasn't selected [as opposed to someone else who was elected]
> The prime minister wasn't *selected* [as opposed to some other process of choosing him]

That is, intonational stress causes an (often unstated) meaning to light up in the mind of the listener. Meaning shifts as intonation shifts. The sound of irony or sarcasm causes a particularly strong shift: it turns a positive meaning into a negative one. We embed quiet subtle meanings into sound at every instant of natural speech.

The different stresses in the sentence about the prime minister are crude compared to all the possible subtleties of meaning that intonation can create. So when we hear natural appropriate intonation, we get the gift of *hearing meaning* as opposed to having to *construct* meaning: the music of intonation enacts a rhythm and melody of meaning. As listeners, we often feel as though the speaker and the language are doing the work of getting the meanings into our heads.

As *readers*, however—stuck with a silent *text*—we often feel that *we* have to do the work of extracting the meaning. That's why people tend to understand naturally spoken language more easily than they understand silent writing. Consider a sentence in this book that you've had to read twice. If I or someone else had given even a decent reading of it out loud, the meaning would have jumped right into your head on the first hearing. Shakespeare is often difficult on the page but clear when spoken well.

Poor sad writing. The cat has its tongue. How can silent text on the page carry any of this rich audible intonation that's so helpful for communicating meaning? Of course we *could* send a recording with every text we write; readers could get all these audible aids to comprehension—and pleasure. That's why so many people like books on tape. But my goal in this book is to get the best of *both* speaking and writing. If we insist that readers listen to a recording, we lose two central virtues of writing that are lacking in books on tape—speed and flexibility: readers of silent text can go fast, skip passages, and jump around to read sections in any order. But I'll argue below that we *can* get some of the benefits of intonation even onto the silent page.

Intonation and Voice

Intonation doesn't just give us the sound of *meaning*; it also gives us the sound of *people*. When we listen to talk, we tend to *hear* a kind of person: eager? sarcastic? hesitant? guarded? We tend to *hear* personal traits like honesty, untrustworthiness, arrogance, open mindedness. Many people have been struck with how Eudora Welty began her memoir:

> Ever since I was first read to, then started reading to myself, there has never been a line read that I didn't *hear*. As my eyes followed the sentence, a voice was saying it silently to me. It isn't my mother's voice, or the voice of any person I can identify, certainly not my own. It is human, but inward, and it is inwardly that I listen to it. It is to me the voice of the story or the poem itself. The cadence, whatever it is that asks you to believe, the feeling that resides in the printed word, reaches me through the reader-voice.

Some sophisticated scholars want us to stop hearing that way—stop reading that way:

> No, *we* don't hear *a voice or an attitude or a personality—we* infer *it. And we should stop doing that because we are so often wrong. Don't pay attention to anything but the* meaning.

True. Strictly speaking, we *don't* hear attitude or personality in words. But if we take that line of reasoning, we have to realize that we don't even hear *meaning* in words—we have to infer it too—read it in. We hear the sound *dear*, but the sound itself doesn't tell us if it means "dear" or "deer." We read it in. When a German hears the same sound, he hears "you" ("dir"). Meanings are not in words, they are in people.

So it's hopeless to tell people to stop "hearing" attitude and character on the page. The only sensible goal is to help people hear better—which means helping them be more aware of the attitude or personality or tone of voice that those words tempt them to read in—and to question themselves about what's genuinely implied by the words and what they are temperamentally prone to hear. When purists pay attention to meaning alone, they tend not to notice how strongly influenced they are by the voice they are "not hearing." Teachers, for example, often find more mistakes and weaknesses in student essays where the voice unconsciously irritates them or turns them off. Their only hope of fairness comes from learning to notice how they have been reacting (perhaps unawarely) to the voice.

Voice is a complex and controversial topic. (I've recently tried to sum up conflicting issues and opinions in my "Voice in Writing.") But the bottom line for writers is pretty obvious. Readers tend to enjoy texts better and keep reading longer when they hear a voice or a person in a text—as long as it's not the wrong voice for the job. An effective voice can pull readers through difficult or unwelcome ideas. The voice is a matter of all those "silent sounds" that intonation can put into silent writing.

But even though I'm an enthusiast for voice, I must end with an important warning for other enthusiasts who are tempted to think it's the main thing. Intonational phrasing and sound and voice are big pluses for writing, but they aren't enough in themselves to make writing *good*. Some of the emptiest, wrongest, and most dangerous writing is full of intonational phrasing, sound, and voice.

By the way, in a review of linguistic research about intonation and gender, Sally McConnell-Ginet found evidence that women used somewhat more intonation in their speaking than men. The differences were not extreme, but women used a wider range of ups and downs. She related that to her hypothesis that women show themselves more aware of status. She made some other interesting observations or claims about how people perceive intonation. "[T]he group heard as effeminate used a significantly wider range of speaking pitches and changed pitch more frequently." One- and two-way glides on single syllables tended to be perceived as nonmasculine. Interestingly, "[a]dult males whose speech was heard as effeminate by judges had, on the average, slightly lower-pitched voices than a matched group of males whom judges heard as nonremarkably masculine in their speech" (549). On this intonational gender difference, see also Wolfram, Adger, Christian 49.

Intonation Units

If we are interested in writing, the most fruitful way to look at intonation is to look at the little packages it comes in. For it turns out that when humans speak, whether casually or carefully or even reading aloud, they tend to chunk their speech into little musical spurts of sound that are commonly called intonation units. (Crystal calls them "tone units"; Halliday calls them "tone units or information units.")

Here is a passage of spontaneous speech. (I printed it in Chapter 1 from an interview in a retirement community.) As with much transcription by linguists, each intonation unit is given its own line.

> NEAL
> the last time we talked you said you were a world traveler.
> you've been all over the [place] [overlapping speech in brackets]
>
> ALBERTINE
> [oh yes] yes yes
> that was after I married.
> and we decided-
> I wanted to know the great question that was on my mind-
> I'll never forget-
> that's folk curiosity.
> I wanted to know
> what makes people tick.
> and so ah
> my husband loved to travel.
> so ah . .
> the same I
> so we went out to find-
> what makes people tick. {chuckles}
> and of all our travels
> we all came back home after many many years.
> that there was just one answer
> everybody ticks alike. {chuckling}
> There's no difference.

Chafe writes that intonation units

> occur as spurts of vocalization that typically contain one or more intonation peaks, that end in any one of a variety of terminal pitch contours, and that usually but not always are separated from each other by pauses."
> ("Punctuation" 397)

Chafe is particularly interested in how widespread this feature of language seems to be:

> In spite of problematic cases, intonation units emerge from the stream of speech with a high degree of satisfying consistency, not just in English, but in all languages I have been able to observe and in fact in all styles of speaking, whether conversation, storytelling, oration, the performance of

rituals, or even (or especially) reading aloud. That fact suggests that they play an important functional role in the production and comprehension of language. (*Discourse* 62)

Here's another illustrative passage from Chafe. It records an academic speaker at a conference. First she stands off to the side because she's shorter than the podium—and she speaks in a casual extemporaneous way. Then as she starts reading her paper, she moves back behind the podium. Yet the intonational pausing persists across these two forms of speech. (He uses initial periods to represent tenths of a second of pause.)

> . . . I'm standing over here to talk to you,
> because,
> (laugh) I'm too short to be seen,
> (laugh) you know over the podium.
> . . . (laugh)
> . . . You-
> most people have,
> . . . uh,
> . . . an image of me,
> . . . mainly cowlick and eyebrows,
> . . . and,
> . . . so this,
> . . . this is a good compromise.
> [then moving behind the podium, she starts to read]
> . . . .Now most students,
> . . of human development,
> . . seek to discover.
> . . what is universal,
> . . . in the developmental process.
> . . . no matter what aspect of human development,
> . . they happen to be investigating.
> . . . They assume that the course of development,
> . . . to one extent or another,
> . . . is largely shaped.
> . . . by biological dis- predispositions.

In this passage, "the intonation units in both the spoken and read-aloud portions were almost identical in length, in each case averaging 1.9 seconds, a figure that is typical of spoken English in general, regardless of how it is produced" (Chafe, "Reading Aloud" 9). Even when speech is coherent and flowing, we still see intonation units of more or less the same duration.

Chafe argues that this intonational habit reflects cognitive limitations for both speakers and listeners. Intonational pausing reflects "in a gross way a strong constraint on the capacity of active consciousness" (*Discourse* 65). Thus speakers focus their full attention or active consciousness on one piece of meaning as they articulate it, but then it takes cognitive effort to shift their focus of attention to another bit of meaning and create another unit—usually but not always with a tiny pause or gap between them. Sometimes the whole intonational "phrase" is no more than "uhhh" or "well," but speakers create this kind of "place-holder" intonation unit when they are giving their limited attention to the problem of figuring out what to say next.

> Intonation units represent the amount of information to which a person can devote his central attention at any one time. ("Cognitive Constraints" 180)

Chafe has studied intonation units extensively. See Chapter Five in his *Discourse, Consciousness, and Time* for a clear and extended treatment. Chafe notes that there can sometimes be some ambiguity in identifying the beginning and end of a unit; some are fragments. But he argues that they are usually clear to an attentive listener of recorded speech who considers the variety of factors that usually characterize a unit: usually a brief pause at the end; almost always a kind of closure "tune" ("terminal pitch contour"); usually an accent or pitch prominence—occasionally more than one; often they start with a bit of speed up and then gradually slow down; they often move from a higher pitch toward a lowering; often they end with a change in voice *quality* like a tiny creak. About 60 percent of the units that Chafe has looked at among large samples represent a clause. He hypothesizes that we tend to start out with the intention of building a clause into an intonation unit—but very often we get derailed. He notes that intonation units can be substantive ("but isn't she healthy?"), or regulatory ("well"), or fragmentary ("I mean she").

Still the linguistics of intonation units or "tone units" is complex (as Chafe implies when he says that identification can be ambiguous). Halliday and Greaves have studied intonation in even finer technical detail than Chafe and they disagree with him about pausing: "[T]here are typically no pauses between tone units; the melodic contour of spoken discourse is continuous, and a pause is much more likely to occur in the middle of a tone unit—for example before a rare or unexpected word—than at the point where the tone unit ends" (58). I can't decide among these professional linguists. I rely on Chafe because I find him easier to understand.

To illustrate how speakers don't always manage to shift their focus of attention so smoothly from one bit of meaning to the next, I'll reprint the fragment of dinner table conversation that I printed in from Chafe in Chapter 1. He notes pauses in fractions of a second—and also strong and weak stresses:

   . . . (0.3) Some élephants and these

   . . . (0.1) they

   . . . (0.7) there

these gáls were in a Vólkswagen,

   . . . (0.4) and uh,

   . . . (0.3) they uh kept hónkin' the hórn,

   . . . (0.2) hóotin' the hóoter,

   . . . (0.6) and uh,

   . . . (0.4) and the élephant was in frónt of em,

so he jùst procèeded to sit dòwn on the VW̌.

We encounter this limitation every day when we ask people for their phone number. It's extremely hard to speak or hear or remember a phone number without breaking it into intonation units. Even if it's just seven digits, we seem to need two pieces of intonational grammar. European phone numbers are often laid out all in a row with no breaks, and that makes them hard even to take in.

But it's not just speakers who have limited attention. Listeners also have limits on how much information *they* can focus full attention on during any one instant. So even if speakers do manage to get their minds around a big chunk of meaning and language that they *could* rattle off nonstop for much longer than two seconds (or can read the words off a page), they mostly don't rattle on nonstop. Experience has taught them, for the most part unconsciously, that listeners tune out or don't understand if they speak too long without any pauses or changes of pitch or accents. A stream of language with none of that intonational architecture is hard to understand and deadening in its effect. Consider our sample astronomy sentence from the previous chapter:

> The conversion of hydrogen to helium in the interiors of stars is the source of energy for their immense output of light and heat.

For a written text, it's far from awful, but people don't *say* sentences like this in everyday conversation—and it doesn't carry much implicit intonational chunking to help silent readers. If an academic wanted to read it out loud in a conference paper, he *could* make it clear if he "read with careful expression"—which would probably mean making brief pauses where I've inserted slashes:

> The conversion of hydrogen to helium / in the interiors of stars / is the source of energy for their immense output of light and heat.

But this reading is a bit clunky; it's creating some intonational music that's not actually built into the silent written sentence. (Academics in many areas of the humanities and social sciences often jettison the intonational wisdom they have in their bones and read papers nonstop out loud at academic conferences. Scientists, interestingly, often use a more "human" language modality at their conferences and *talk* from slides and notes—rather than read papers. They are often amazed to hear about the unhuman linguistic practices at conferences in other fields.)

Whether or not Chafe is right in his ambitious hypothesis that intonational chunking has been favored by evolution, he has the psychological and philosophical wisdom to stand back and notice that it's actually a miracle that one speaker can get a piece of meaning almost instantaneously from his mind into someone else's mind where it didn't exist. Intonational chunking increases the likelihood of this miracle.

The title of Chafe's book on this topic shows his interest in time: *Discourse, Consciousness, and Time: The Flow and Displacement of Conscious Experience in Speaking and Writing*. He points out the obvious fact that speech happens *in time*—"online," as the jargon has it. Time won't pause while we speak and listen, so *we* must pause and chunk our language into intonational music because of the limits on how much information we and our listeners can process at any instant.

Consciousness is another key word in his title. By focusing on cognitive constraints in speakers' minds, Chafe is of course building part of his theory on what is not observable—what's inside speakers' heads. He understands the dangers of this kind of hypothesizing, but still he gently chides most linguists and social scientists for a timid form of empiricism that limits them to observable language. He argues that we cannot have an adequate theory of speech without making hypotheses about the consciousness of speakers. (See his eloquent methodological introduction.)

He hypothesizes three limitations on people as they speak to each other: (a) It takes mental effort to get a new idea into consciousness (calling this *activation cost*). (b) Thus it's hard to start off an intonation unit except with what's already in mind (calling this the *light subject constraint*). (c) And there's only so much information we can focus on at one moment (calling this the *one-new idea* constraint). He says that these three constraints "involve the expenditure of a minimum amount of mental effort in the activation of subject referents" (*Consciousness* 289).

Intonation Units and Writing

But things are different, notes Chafe, when we move from speech to writing. Writers and readers work "off line" and therefore don't need this chunking. Writers can take as much time as they want to pack meanings into their clauses and sentences, and readers can take as much time as they need to unpack and swallow and digest the contents of those rich unchunked stretches of language. Chafe's view here is common—almost universal—and it has two obvious arguments to support it. First, writers and readers *can* take as much time as they want. Second, most writing—or at least most essayist expository writing—*does* have longer more complex sentences and clauses than we find in speech.

Linguists, teachers, and copy editors tend to smile benignly on this difference between speech and expository writing. But I don't smile. They affirm a kind of wall between speaking and writing that I want to knock down. I say that writers should *exploit* this gift for intonational chunking that we've learned all our lives from the pressures of time and listener presence. For reading is *not* immune to time. The text may be laid out in space, but readers are wholly constrained by time. Since they can take in only a few words at once, the reading process is a temporal process: really, it's more like listening to speech than what people unconsciously think of as "reading"—more like listening to music than looking at a picture (more about this in Chapter 15 and my "Music of Form"). Do readers really have all the time in the world? They're usually in a hurry. Often enough they stop reading if they have to reread sentences to figure out the meaning. They appreciate language they can understand first time around—which means language sculpted into intonational units. Most writers want readers to keep reading.

Besides it's no good saying that writers should emulate an *average* of *all* expository writing. Our goal ought to be *good* expository writing. I think I see *good* writers making their writing clearer by using more of the intonational instincts they learn from speaking. Why shouldn't writing heed the "strong constraints" imposed by human consciousness? Of course the intonation units in writing can be longer than the two-second needs of speech, but good writing needs units short enough that readers don't have to take extra time to extract the meaning.

This sounds like an argument for simple plain writing. It is. Simpler would be lovely, even for academic writing. Note the short intonation units in the preceding three sentences. For most of my writing, I allow myself longer ones— but I hope I'm right in thinking that intonational phrasing makes the writing easier to understand.

But calling on the intonational wisdom in our bones does not mean we have to write simple prose. *Highly* complex prose, when it's effective, will harness intonational architecture and the constraints of consciousness. The pauses in complex prose can even grow out of self-interruptions—a feature characteristic of speech. Look again at the remarkably complex sentence from a late Henry James novel with all its intonational pausing (I quoted it in the last chapter to illustrate left-branching and right-branching syntax). I've underlined separate intonational units and put slashes at points of greatest implied pause:

> But she saved herself in time, / conscious above all that she was in the presence of still deeper things than she had yet dared to fear, / that there was "more in it" than any admission she had made represented—/ and she had held herself familiar with admissions: / so that, not to seem to understand where she couldn't accept, / and not to seem to accept where she couldn't approve, / and could still less / with precipitation, advise, / she invoked the mere appearance of casting no weight whatever into the scales of her young friend's consistency. (*Golden Bowl* 184)

He builds astounding intricacy out of a deeply *spoken* habit of intonational pausing and chunking. In much seventeenth- and eighteenth-century prose too (for example, in Hume or Gibbon), we see a similar complexity of syntax that nevertheless builds elegantly on the intonational chunking characteristic of speech. And by the same token, we see it in good contemporary writers who favor rich flexible syntax. Note Geertz:

> The recent tsunami in southern Asia, in which perhaps a quarter-million people of all ages and conditions were swept indifferently away by a blind cataclysm, has, at least for the moment—perhaps only for the moment—concentrated our minds. (5)

In short, the goal for writers is to do what speakers do: chunk language into intonational units.

A written intonational unit is a phrase that's comfortably sayable in one nonstop piece of rhythm: a phrase with a bit of musical shape or intonational rhythm to it, and a phrase that probably ends with at least a tiny natural pause. It might be as short as *still less* (James), or as long as *perhaps a quarter-million people of all ages and conditions* (Geertz). But of course readers have full choice about how to read or hear a sentence. So we might decide that there are *two* intonation units in that Geertz phrase: *perhaps a quarter-million people [/] of all ages and conditions*—or this one: *swept indifferently away [/] by a blind cataclysm.* For strictly considered, intonation is a purely *audible* matter and doesn't exist in silent writing—or it exists only in oral performance of writing (outwardly or in the inner ear).

So even though intonation in writing is a matter of hypothesis or estimation, nevertheless there is a huge practical payoff for writers: syntax can strongly *suggest* how it wants to be performed; written words can be shaped so that they *invite* helpful intonational shaping and pausing in readers' ears, even without punctuation marks. Writing that lacks this kind of intonational shaping is harder on readers—clunky, less comfortable to say, harder to process.

Intonation Units and Syntactic Glue

Look again at this bit from Albertine's talk about why she likes to travel. It shows why people so often badmouth speech. The syntax is strained and broken:

> that was after I married.
> and we decided-
> I wanted to know
> the great question that was on my mind-
> I'll never forget-
> that's folk curiosity.
> I wanted to know

People do speak that way, often enough. (But don't forget the research by Labov and Halliday [60, 77] showing that spoken language is not as much of a syntactic mess as it's often accused of being. This messy patch is only a small part of Albertine's monologue.) I certainly speak lots of this messy syntax. Often after we've just started to say one thing, we break off and start something new because we have a new thought or a qualification or a little story. The connections between phrases are often weak or faulty.

However, what's important to notice is that most of these bad connections come *between* intonation units—where there's often a pause—when the speaker is shifting attention from one bit of meaning to another. Weak glue. Grammar crime.

But look *inside* the intonation units. Strong glue, strong connections: the words inside the intonation unit follow each other with smooth natural syntax. So look again at that "broken illiterate speech" from Albertine in the retirement community. Notice this time how *unbroken* the links are within each intonation unit:

> that was after I married.
> and we decided-
> I wanted to know
> the great question that was on my mind-
> I'll never forget-
> that's folk curiosity.
> I wanted to know

Lines of poetry are often highly indebted to intonational chunking. John Ashbery has won just about every poetry prize on earth for poems that often give the effect of seemingly random strings of very spoken intonation units. Here is the opening stanza of a poem called "The Virgin King":

> They know so much more, and so much less
> "innocent details" and other. It was time to
> put up or shut up. Claymation is so over,
> the king thought. The watercolor virus
> sidetracked tens.

Why is the syntactic glue so strong between words inside intonational phrases? The answer is a little startling at first: because of nonplanning. The words came in a "spurt," to use Chafe's word. We give birth to the whole phrase as a unit and utter the words more or less without choosing them. Of course we might have consciously chosen the new piece of meaning and even a key word or two, but once we launch ourselves into an intonation unit, the words tend to unroll on their own. Often enough, we don't even have any awareness of the words we are in the act of not choosing. When we utter one word, the next word is pulled along or just pops out—no effort or forethought. The unplanned words in an intonational phrase usually blend syntactic and semantic meaning at a finer level than we see in planned or monitored or "constructed" language. The sequence feels natural and unplanned because it *was* natural and unplanned. The syntactic glue is so strong because we made it with so little work.

Some words are even more tightly glued because they come in ready-made clumps like "paying attention" or "as we speak." In recent years, linguists have become more and more interested in these "lexical bundles" or "familiar collocations" as basic building blocks in a language. But these clumps explain only a small part of the glue in intonation units.

In other words, intonation units help readers not just because of the pausing that I celebrated in the previous section—the pausing that helps listeners and readers catch their syntactic and semantic breath. In addition, intonational chunking generates powerful glue between words within the units. So if we want to talk about the syntactic coherence in unplanned spoken language, we can't just complain about weak "ungrammatical" glue *between* the phrases; we have to celebrate the strong glue *within* the phrases.

What's so good about the well-glued words within an intonation unit? I'll put my answer crudely: if words *came out* of one mind easily all together, then they'll *go into* another mind easily too. Or at least they will if the speaker and listener share the same language or dialect or speech community—that is, if the listener has a mind that's organized by the same syntactic structures as the speaker's mind. For example, unplanned intonational language by computer geeks won't sound so natural and easy to computer-phobes—even when they are brother and sister.

Because Halliday is a highly technical linguist, he doesn't settle for a crude answer. He shows how the many patterns of intonation are really reflections of *grammar* or *syntax*. He works this out in great detail by mapping different patterns of stress and pitch contour onto different syntactic structures.

> Intonation is not phonetic icing on the real lexicogrammatical cake. There are such icings, for example the quality of voice which expresses anger or sorrow or whatever. But intonation doesn't work that way. It is a system of [lexicogrammatical] choices which you can and must choose from whenever you speak. (Email to me, 1/10, from William Greaves, co-author with Halliday of *Intonation in the Grammar of English*.)

(The Halliday model of intonation is fascinating but highly complex—a bit more technically detailed than I can comfortably master. See the co-authored book length analysis. Also Halliday/Matthiessen, pp. 87–94. David Crystal argues, by the way, that Halliday goes a bit too far in linking intonation so very deeply to grammar.)

In short, the grammatical links *between intonation units* may be highly problematic, but the grammatical links *within intonation units* are strong and basic to the syntax of the language. It's this strong glue that helps written language attain the ideal that some writers since Aristotle have set: to sound natural and not carefully planned.

SponTax

So if we want *written* words to be clearest and easiest for readers to understand, then here's another virtue of intonation chunking: writing is clearer and stronger when we have that unplanned connection between word A and word B that we find inside intonation units—those natural, almost unsplittable links. Consider Henry James's phrase *"still deeper things than she had yet dared to fear"*; or Geertz's *"perhaps only for a moment."* They might have well labored over the wording, but if so, they were laboring to replicate the linguistic virtue of a natural intonational phrase. And that virtue is clarity and ease of comprehension.

The syntactic quality I'm interested in here is like something we see in graceful human walking, or good running by a dog, or good lying down by a cat. Each submovement follows the one before *efficiently:* unplanned and without rehearsal or control. So by the same token, the sequence of unplanned words in an intonation unit is "syntactically efficient" for both the human *production* of language and human *reception*.

This quality that's so helpful in writing, then, is *spontaneous syntax*. It's this sinewy bond between individual words in unplanned speech that helps both writers and readers. Let's bottle it!

SponTax.

Spontaneous Syntactic Glue. Extract of Speech. Available in liquid or tablet form. Consult your doctor to see what SponTax can do for you. Possible side effects include clichés, logorrhea, and bored listeners. If writing persists for more than thirty-six hours, consult your physician.

With a few well-placed bribes, perhaps we could get the Language and Drug Administration to approve it. The demographic is brilliant: it works for all ages and populations. We could get rich!

But damn! We have a problem. It's free. All humans from the age of three or four already have an infinite supply of SponTax coursing through their veins. People never run out. In truth, the bureaucrats have been pushing the other way. Long ago, some group bribed the Language and Drug Administration into *discouraging* the use of SponTax—the taint of speech—in all "serious writing." A good deal of money has been made getting people to fear the strong clear effective syntax they get for free. Everyone has been subjected to a campaign that says, "Writing means conscious vigilance. Never use an unplanned unchosen word. Never let words just come."

I can illustrate the deep cultural prejudice against spontaneous syntax from firsthand experience. Here are two phrases that I used in my writing that were changed by copy editors in such a way as to destroy SponTax. I wrote *always comes with* and it was changed to *is always accompanied by*. I wrote *who has a strong sense of* and it was changed to *who retains a deep conviction that*. There was no *mistake* for the copy editor to root out (I'm always grateful when they do). He or she was rooting out SponTax—or what I like to call (in a phrase that's best said with a wrinkled nose) "the *taint* of speech." Academic copy editors sometimes say they are fighting "too much informality" or "low register." And SponTax is often strong in casual or slangy speech. But my offending phrases were not low or slangy—except for those people who call *all* natural speech low by definition. In fact, plenty of SponTax is available in non-casual, nonslangy language. (Let me quickly note that the Oxford copy editor for this book, Patterson Lamb, didn't go in for this kind of thing. She was sensitive and deft.)

Hand-crafted SponTax

Some readers will charge me with romantic sentimentality for my praise of spontaneity—and I cannot deny the charge. Yet I can turn around and insist on my equal love for conscious sophisticated craft. There's no conflict between my two loves. The fact is that good writers down through the ages have been using careful conscious craft to *synthesize* SponTax in their home laboratories. In Chapter 3 I quoted even Aristotle on the goal of working hard and consciously to create language that sounds genuinely spontaneous and natural.

Good writers sometimes use SponTax in an interestingly oblique way. That is, they try for language that is obviously *not* spontaneous or unplanned while at the same time creating the *feel* of unplanned syntax. Look at this poem by Robert Hass:

Mouth Slightly Open
The body a yellow brilliance and a head
Some orange color from a Chinese painting
Dipped in sunset by the summer gods
Who are also producing that twitchy shiver

In the cottonwoods, less wind than river,
Where the bird you thought you saw
Was, whether you believe what you thought
You saw or not, and then was not, had
Absconded, leaving behind the emptiness
That hums a little in you now, and is not bad
Or sad, and only just resembles awe or fear.
The bird is elsewhere now, and you are here.

The poem is largely made of well-shaped intonation units within which the words are well glued. But look at some of those phrases: *dipped in sunset* and *twitchy shiver* and *less wind than river* and *the emptiness that hums a little in you now*. They are intonation units that give the *feeling* of "naturalness" and even spontaneity—that kind of rhythm and audible architecture—and yet they also give us the pleasure of the unexpected that's created by conscious elegant craft. They use the same glue that makes clichés work—but they are as far away as you can get from clichés. Hass's language is not speech, but he crafts his written elegance out of the *resources* or *features* of everyday speech. Spontaneous syntax follows well-used grooves, but writers can consciously choose unexpected words to lay down in well-used syntactic grooves.

Clichés are built out of SponTax, but that's not their problem; their problem is in being overused as total word-packages. The actual syntax in clichés is precious for writing. (In many or even most other cultures, people welcome clichés or sayings in serious writing. See Fox.)

As a poet, Hass exploits even the naughty *weak* glue that speakers so often use between intonation units—the weak glue that creates the "bad grammar" that grows like weeds in careless speech:

Where the bird you thought you saw
Was, whether you believe what you thought
You saw or not, and then was not, had
Absconded

Understandably, we aren't allowed to write that kind of grammar for most purposes and I've tried to avoid it in this book. Hass purposely confuses us into a breakdown or misunderstanding in our first reading—and in this way he makes us go back and *say* and *hear* the words because speaking/hearing is the only way to understand the syntax. (We wouldn't have been much confused if we heard it in a good performance—with full intonational stress, rhythm, and melody.) I love how he puts the rhythm and illegal syntax of careless speech in a highly wrought poem. He exploits the *intricacy* of casual spoken grammar—a grammar that highlights the music of intonation. And his larger strategy is to insist that we *hear* his poem, not just take it in conceptually. In this way, he builds pleasure in the counterpoint between the spoken rhythm and his line breaks.

The Goal for Writers of Prose?

It's the same as I stated earlier: create intonation units. But now I can be more specific. *Inside* your phrases, use strong glue—like that found in unplanned spoken language. But *between* your phrases, use better, stronger glue than we find in lots of unplanned speaking. This last point, crudely translated, means "use good grammar," but I hope my analysis in terms of intonation units can show scared or inexperienced writers that they can get correct grammar and still not be stuck with simplistic "Dick-and-Jane" grammar.

In short, SponTax comes to us free when we speak, but it disappears when we are struggling to work out a difficult train of thought in writing. If I'm trying to be clear about an idea that is buried or tangled in a draft—for example, if I'm trying to figure out why X seems true and Y seems true but X and Y contradict each other—I find I often have to choose individual words, slowly and painfully, one word, then the next; then sometimes discover I need to stick another word between those two. I have to change words, change the order of words, and try to muscle words into saying some idea or distinction that I'm struggling to understand. This process kills SponTax every time. It's what must have happened to the writer of this sentence:

> My own research shows that in a model simultaneously accounting for both House and presidential on-year voting in terms of voters' issue preferences, partisanship, economic evaluations, assessments of the presidential candidates' personal qualities, and demographic characteristics, the electoral value of being an incumbent rather than an open-seat candidate fell to 16 percent, on average, from 1980–88 to 1992–2000.

So I'm not arguing against conscious choosing and deciding. In the end, as we revise and edit, we are doing nothing *but* making conscious decisions. (See Chapter 10 on care.) My argument is against the powerful forces that tell writers *never* to use unplanned syntax. Indeed, the reason skilled writers are good at careful revising is *because* they learned the feel of *unplanned* syntax in their mouths and ears.

So we need a later stage of revising to harness a different kind of conscious planning to make language sound as though it came naturally and easily to the mouth as an uttering human—even if that language is making some thought or distinction that we struggled hard to untangle. In Part Three of this book, I'll explore that precious later stage of writing.

Final warning (to be printed on the labels of SponTax bottles). The strong syntactic glue found inside spoken intonation units will give clarity and energy to writing, but it will not create good writing. Clear energetic writing may be expressing nonsense.

Summary Illustration of the Virtues of Speech

I'll try to illustrate the virtues of speech that I've described in this and the preceding chapter by recasting three sentences from Chafe's book. He's a good academic writer whom I admire not just for his insights and research but for his writing. He's not one of those who are painful and frustrating to read. But I'll try to make some of his sentences even clearer and stronger by calling on the virtues of speech.

CHAFE: [E]ach intonation unit verbalizes the information active in the speaker's mind at its onset. Let us hypothesize that an intonation unit verbalizes the speaker's focus of consciousness at that moment.

SPEECH GEAR REVISION: When speakers create intonation units, they are finding words for the meanings that are active in their minds at that moment.

CHAFE: At the completion of an intonation unit the speaker must intend that a reasonable facsimile of his or her focus of consciousness will have become active in one or more other minds.

SPEECH GEAR REVISION: At the end of an intonation unit, the speaker hopes to have gotten his or her focus of consciousness into the active consciousness of a listener.

CHAFE: It is through this dynamic process of successive activations, first for the speaker and then, through the utterance of an intonation unit, for the listener, that language is able to provide an imperfect bridge between one mind and another.

SPEECH GEAR REVISION: When speakers shape their words into intonation units, each unit represents a speaker's focus of attention, and each does what it can to help the listener to create the same focus of attention. This dynamic way of structuring speech increases the chances that one mind will understand another.

It's surely obvious that I didn't get these revisions by just blithely speaking onto the page—just as I didn't rewrite that astronomy sentence in the previous chapter except by conscious effort and deliberation. In both cases, I had to try phrasing after phrasing in my mind's ear (or out loud). It took conscious work. Often it wasn't quick. But my goal in this work was to reproduce the syntactic *quality* that I've learned to value by paying attention to what comes free in casual conversation. If we speak our words onto the page using our nonplanning speaking gear, we will get language with lots of intonation units, but this unplanned language won't itself work for careful writing. In Chapters 11 and 12 I'll explore more concretely and practically how to harvest intonation—and the other virtues described in the previous chapter—for careful effective writing.

I think I might be able to teach a meta-lesson with my revisions of Chafe. It strikes me (only at a late stage of revising this book) that Chafe's third sentence is better than my alleged improvement. His is effectively elegant and it's syntax carries his meaning well; my revision is a bit clunky and deaf. I speak in Chapter 12 of the dangers when stylists are too governed by a theory and not enough by their ear.

✻   ✻   ✻

Intonation will turn up as central in Chapters 11–14—about reading aloud.

LITERACY STORY

How Charlemagne and Alcuin Robbed Latin of Its Name

By 800 Charlemagne had conquered virtually all of Europe. The Pope gave him the title "Holy Roman Emperor" and his territory came to be called the Carolingian Empire. He seemed to like to reform and regularize things; he reformed the education system in his empire, particularly in the Church. As a conqueror and ruler, he didn't like too much mess. When he noticed the linguistic mess in his empire he wanted to fix it.

Latin hadn't shown much dialectal variation while the Roman Empire lasted (up till the fifth century), but then with no strong administrative center in Rome, Latin began to diverge somewhat into multiple "Latins"—depending on whether it was spoken in the regions we call Italy, Spain, Germany, or the eastern reaches. That's what troubled Charlemagne—all these different Latins that people spoke all around his "European Union." He wanted something tidier and more linguistically unified. (He didn't know when he was well off: what would he think of the European Union now with some twenty official languages?) So he sought out the best authority on Latin that anyone could find for him. This turned out to be a monk named Alcuin—way off in England, a far corner of the empire.

For whereas everyone in Europe grew up learning Latin as their native spoken language, most people in England spoke Old English or Celtic or some other non-Latin. The Latin known by Alcuin and the few highly literate English folk in England was the classical Roman version preserved in Roman manuscripts. No doubt that's why their version of Latin was admired. It had all the features of "good" language: it was old and it came from books—and no one spoke it (except sometimes for some purposes inside monasteries). It stayed still instead of changing all the time.

So Alcuin brought his old "real Latin" over from England and Charlemagne authorized that this should now count as Latin throughout the empire:

> This decision, to standardize Church and educational Latin on such an archaic model gradually extended out from the Carolingian realms until it became the basis of the so-called Twelfth-Century Renaissance all over Europe, which was what led to this antiquarian variety of Latin (rather than the contemporary Romance [the evolved Latin]) becoming the "international" language of education. . . . This archaizing Latin—whose oral mode involved the Germanic spelling pronunciation which had long been the norm in the Anglo-Saxon [English] church—was in Romance eras an innovation. (Wright 4)
>
> By the twelfth century Latin was used very extensively in writing all over Europe, also in several countries that had never belonged to the Roman Empire, such as present-day Germany, Poland, and Denmark. It was the dominant written language everywhere; in many countries no other language was written. It was no one's native language by this time, but Latin was much used as a spoken language, particularly within the Church. Spoken and written Latin was taught in school. (Janson 101–102)

What a success Charlemagne wrought with Alcuin's help: a huge standardization of a language that was coming apart. It came to be a written language of amazing longevity. Yet if we consider Charlemagne's original goal, the whole enterprise was a complete failure. They discovered—as so many governments and bureaucrats have found—that it's impossible to curb people's tongues. Almost no one in Charlemagne's EU *talked* the new/old/better Latin. Some priests gave sermons in it, but parishioners found them difficult or impossible to understand.

The only effect on everyone's spoken language that Charlemagne and Alcuin managed to achieve was to steal its name—the name that everyone had called it for at least ten centuries prior to 800: "Latin." The new/archaic *written* language took this name while the spoken language was left nameless. This shift in labels must have been confusing and gradual as people struggled not to call their Latin "Latin" any more. But after a while they stopped and the new labeling stuck, and eventually the various former-Latins—vernacular languages—took on different names: *Spanish, Portuguese, French, Italian, Romanian, Catalan, Galician,* and so on. For the interim orphan language, scholars came later to use the term "romance."

Wright points out that it's a misconception to call Latin a "dead language":

> [T]he essential truth is that all these languages (which are indeed now thought of as being different languages from each other [e.g., Spanish, Portuguese, French and so on]) are direct continuations of spoken Latin, in the same way as modern Greek is a direct continuation of spoken Ancient Greek . . ., and just as Modern English is a direct continuation of Old English. [See the Literacy Story about Greek following Chapter 15.]
>
> Greek and English are not dead [though they have changed]; and they have not changed their name. . . . The difference is that English and Greek have not fragmented and Latin *has*, for political reasons. . . . If there had not been this change of name and the label *latinus* had not come after the 9th century A.D. to be reserved for the archaizing register (a non-native language used by literate English people), it is possible that the Romance languages might not have fragmented conceptually and their variety could have remained language-internal—as Chinese has remained in the minds of most Chinese-speakers, since they all use the same written system. . . . (Wright 4–5)
>
> "Classical" Latin was written by very few people during a relatively brief period . . ., whereas "Vulgar Latin" refers to the speech of millions of people over hundreds of years. (8)
>
> [A] living evolving language whose speakers cover over a quarter of the world's land surface can hardly be called dead. (6)

This is the story of the political imposition of an archaic book version of language upon a huge kingdom of native speakers of that language. With this act of imposition, everyone's native spoken version of the same language came to be judged problematic. For me, the important point is that their native language gets ruled wrong for writing. "By prescription of school statutes Latin had become Learned Latin, a language completely controlled by writing" (Ong *Orality* 113).

6 Can We Really Have the Best of Both Worlds?

I'VE SPENT THE last five chapters trying to describe the best things about writing and speaking. Can we have a kind of writing that keeps all the best things I described in Chapter 2 (it's good for revising, reworking, and communicating complexity, and it carries prestige, safety, privacy, and more)—but at the same time a kind of writing that is as easy as speaking and that has all the other advantages of speech that I described in Chapters 3, 4, and 5 (liveliness, natural connection with audience, intonation that magically carries meaning, and all the other virtues)? Can I embrace my new love, speech, and bring her home to live with me and my longtime committed love, writing?

No.

I need to acknowledge from the outset that my goal for this book is unattainable—it's utopian, an impossible dream. By acknowledging this, I'm trying to make it clear that I'm utopian, but not *just* a utopian; a dreamer, but also a realist.

Idealism: Going for the Utopian Dream

I'm working from a premise that's too often neglected: just because a goal is unattainable, that doesn't mean we can't take it *as* a goal and make progress toward it. If we decide it's desirable, we can figure out which steps move us closer—even though we'll never actually get there.

This is a premise that guides many natural scientists. They know it's impossible to get absolute proof and objective certainty, but they don't throw up their hands and say, "Well then, it's all a matter of opinion or feeling, no theory is any better than any other." They take objectivity and proof as *goals* and gather evidence about competing theories to see which seem closer—even though that evidence will always be arguable, never certain.

In much of my teaching, I'm trying for a utopian space where students can be safe in two different ways: safe to say and write whatever they need, but also safe in never being disrespected. These two safeties are unattainable because they conflict with each other. I may want *free* speech, but I have to curb it in order to outlaw *disrespectful* speech. But unattainability is no reason not to fight toward utopian conditions.

Surely, lots of teaching is utopian: an attempt to set up "unrealistic" class-rooms where students can develop fragile capacities that wouldn't survive in unprotected "real" conditions. Freewriting (see the next chapter) is writing, but it creates "unrealistic" protection. Water is like freewriting. It's a utopian space for physically disabled or rehabilitating people: the buoyancy of water allows them to move their limbs in conditions that are unrealistically free from the full force of gravity.

Most of us have utopian impulses. We don't have to give them up. I'm insist-ing I can be both utopian and realistic in this book. My overall argument is that we can go a long way toward the unattainable goal of bringing the best of speaking to the best of writing. Lincoln made a comparable argument speaking in Philadelphia on the way to taking up the presidency. He said that the signers of the Declaration "did not intend to declare all men equal *in all respects* [nor even] mean to assert the obvious untruth" that men were equal in rights and opportunities. Rather

> they meant to set up a standard maxim for free society, which should be . . . constantly looked to, constantly labored for, and even though never per-fectly attained, constantly approximated, and thereby constantly spreading and deepening its influence, and augmenting the happiness and value of life to all people of all colors everywhere.

Utopia is a rich concept. Thomas More gave this name to his (partly satirical) picture of an ideal society—coining a word that means both "no place" and "good place." (The Greek word behind his "U" means "good" but also "not.") David Bartholomae ac-cuses me of seeking "an institutional space free from institutional pressures, a cultural process free from the influence of culture, an historical moment outside of history, an academic setting free from academic writing" (64). Probably. And I've probably not acknowledged enough that it's unattainable. But see Fredric Jameson's *Marxism and Form* for a defense from the left of utopian thinking. Art may often reflect dominant values, but it also gives glimpses of how things could be. See Herbert Marcuse on the impossibility of revolution without play. See also Russell Jacoby's *Picture Imperfect: Uto-pian Thought for an Anti-Utopian Age*.

Realism: Facing Facts

In my pursuit of the unattainable, I'm also facing facts. In this section I'll bounce back and forth like a ping-pong ball between what I see as an idealist versus what I see as a realist.

As idealist, I see that writing *can* be virtually as easy as speaking. The wide-spread use of freewriting has taught countless people what I struggled to learn: to write fast without worrying—as though engaged in easy speaking through the fingers. Of course writing takes a bit more physical effort than speaking unless we use voice-activated software on our computer. But it's not true that you have to learn the conventions of correct writing to write. Even tiny chil-dren can do lots of writing. All around the country there are lots of them in kindergartens and first grades. In Chapter 3, I used the example of the kindergartener who wrote that lovely story about the creation of the earth—starting out, "1 DAY VVAL IF THAR WAS A DAY. THAR WASSAND AND DAST AND ROK SSTONS AND SUM ATHR TYGS AND IT WAS A TUNDR CLAPS! AND APLANIT BEGAN TO RIS AN THA COD IT EARTH." ("One day, well if there was a day. There was sand and dust and rocks and stones and some other things. And it was a thunderclaps! And a planet began to rise. And they called it Earth.")

As realist, I may acknowledge that every child masters the central linguistic complexities of his or her native language by age four, but I can't forget that a law somehow got passed in our culture and many others: no one can use his or her native language for serious or prestige writing. Even my native language—so-called standard White upper middle class New Jersey spoken English—is wrong for edited written English. "Correct writing" is no one's mother tongue. So for most serious writing tasks that matter (which means most writing for school and for the workplace and much writing for the wider world), none of us can avoid having to translate our thinking into "correct" language.

So "easy writing" or "mere writing" or vernacular writing won't get us two crucial benefits of writing that I described in Chapter 2, namely, prestige and authority. We don't get much prestige if our committee memo or school essay looks like a thank you letter from a five-year-old to her grandmother. I do lots of easy mere writing—not just for journal writing but even in drafts for articles and this book. But readers won't read my easy writing—or if they do they'll think it's terrible. Most of my easy writing is neither good nor "correct." And I don't like to read rambling disorganized writing myself—or even well-shaped writing with spelling or grammar that's random and confusing.

But as idealist, I insist that vernacular writing *is writing*. This is not just sophistical wordtrickery. The real wordtrickery happened when the concept of "correct" was secretly smuggled into the word "writing." Is it not writing that the kindergartener produced? Is it not writing when Captain John Smith writes this nonsentence about his meeting with the Powhatan Indians during his early exploration of Virginia?

> Arriving at Weramocomoco, their Emperour proudly lying uppon a Bedstead a foote high, upon tenne or twelves Mattes, richly hung with Manie Chaynes of great Pearles about his necke, and covered with a great Covering of Rahaughcums. [racoons] (quoted in Crystal *Stories* 301)

That kindergartener and John Smith engaged in *writing*. They found visible words for their mental or audible words, and they got those words on paper or some other surface so they were readable (though the first grader's writing is only readable by someone who cares about him). Shakespeare (or the printers who put out his plays) produced *writing*—even if not consistent spelling and grammar. When people realize that "writing" doesn't have to mean "correct writing," they will realize that they can write *any* thoughts or feelings they can say. They don't have to worry about whether it's good or meets some standard for "correct writing."

When we realize that *writing* doesn't mean *correct writing,* we can notice that vernacular writing actually has many of the *other* important advantages of writing I described in Chapter 2. It's good for diaries, and some letters, emails, and blogs—even for many online sites like e-pinions. It's self-reinforcing and thus helps people learn to enjoy writing. It's excellent for privacy; teachers can use lots of it to get students to do low-stakes writing that helps them learn and think about the concepts they are studying. And it's particularly good for helping people see and resist pervasive cultural and institutional forces that try to control them.

As realist, I welcome those advantages, but I insist on noticing how all that writing is *careless.* No one but the writer would read it.

As idealist, I deny that point. That is, vernacular writing doesn't *have* to be fast or careless. We can write slowly and revise and get careful thinking and effective organization. We can even seek feedback from ally readers and revise and still use only our vernacular spoken language. This kind of careful vernacular writing will no longer have the advantages of speed and easiness (though it can build on a fast easy first draft), but in return it will gain a huge advantage: it will be inviting for friendly readers to read—though they will have to be tolerant of whatever "incorrectnesses" or "mistakes" the writer happens to make. (Some users of slow vernacular writing will not make many.)

So *careless* vernacular writing is writing, and *careful* vernacular writing will be more widely acknowledged as writing. When people can say "I'm a writer for I can get my thoughts down quickly and easily and I can take more time and work them out carefully"—when they can tell themselves this, they will be hugely empowered. They can even insist that they have *entered the world of literacy* (refusing that surreptitious link between "literacy" and "correctness").

Besides, if people have gotten this far with their vernacular speech, they will be braver about adding another bit of work and get it standardized or "correct." There are many ways to get help in this process. Many teachers don't like to talk about them, but they are widely used. If writers have already worked hard to get their meaning clear and strong, it's a pretty quick job for someone else to edit the spelling and grammar. (The spell checker on computers can help, but it fails on many homophones. Style-and-grammar checkers tend to be confusing, misleading, and not trustworthy.)

- Typists will usually handle grammar and spelling as part of the job. After all, people in authority sometimes have secretaries who do this. And when you get good enough so people want to publish what you write, publishers will lay on copy editors. Plenty of published writers cannot get rid of all their "mistakes"—including me. (But if you submit a manuscript full of "mistakes," most publishers will turn it down.)
- You can often find a friend or loved one who will copy edit as a favor or a trade.
- Many people will actually enjoy reading what you write if you *leave* it in your home version of English (for example, African American Language or some form of Latino English). It will be appreciated not just by fellow members of your speech community but by many

mainstream readers. (See Appendix II for examples of published writing in nonmainstream versions of English.)

As Realist, however, I have to point out that careful revising and correct language are not always enough. Writing is always in a context of genre and audience. For many genres, there are substantive conventions that must be learned—conventions that can be subtler and more complex than the spelling and grammar conventions. Are you writing a memo, a committee report, a grant application, or an essay? The conventions are different for each. How should it be organized or structured? What counts as an effective argument or even a "fact"? What kind of tone or level of formality is needed. Each of these kinds of writing implies a genre and a community of readers with definite expectations. (For a rich interesting exploration of different genres for writing, see John Trimbur's *The Call to Write*.)

Take even a single genre—the academic essay: the standards and conventions are different for different disciplines and realms (psychology? nursing? English? physics?). Another seemingly narrow genre: an essay for wide circulation magazines. The conventions differ (*Harper's? Cosmopolitan? Slate? Outdoor Life?*). As realist I have to acknowledge that there's no way around *learning* or *figuring out* what these various communities of readers require before they are even willing to consider a piece of writing. You can't ask a typist or close friend to do this kind of work for you. We need additional learning that the mother tongue cannot give us. (See Creme and Lea for a list of sixty kinds or genres of academic writing.)

As idealist, yes, but let's not forget about easier genres that many people want to use: memoir, story, creative nonfiction, poetry—and even the op-ed. Scholars of literacy like to analyze subtle conventions in such genres, but in fact these conventions are routinely violated in published instances. These genres are essentially *freeform* or anarchic.

As realist, however, I must acknowledge that most inexperienced writers don't *realize* that they have almost complete freedom in these genres. It takes some learning and experience to get the confidence to realize the absence of real limits or constraints. And then there are all those other genres that *do* require lots of knowledge that don't come with the mother tongue.

As idealist, I won't let myself be boxed into a corner where I'm supposedly against *work*. Using vernacular speech for writing does not conflict with work. Once people have the experience of getting all their words and thoughts on paper with no struggle, they are more likely to want to work hard at slow careful revising of some of what they are saying. Then when they learn they can revise some of these words and thoughts and make them inviting to readers, they are more likely to want to work at learning about the conventions needed for some particular genre. If people feel they can't start out till they understand a genre, they are likely never to start out.

As realist, I point to the single standard of correctness in our culture. This requires that all serious writing should use a language that differs from everyone's vernacular. As realist, I don't like it and consider it to be an oppression that bears on everyone—most unfairly of course on those without the privileges of class and race. I'm sad that I feel I have to devote so much of my book to helping writers and potential writers buckle under to this unfair standard. (My capitulation is not just sad to me; it seems oppressive or even racist to some people who see it as a kind of Uncle Tom stance. It seems to them that if I am helping people *serve* an unfair status quo, I am helping *maintain* that unfair status quo. How can I change a standard by giving in to it?)

As idealist, however, I am stubborn and insist that facts change. That is, I'm *not* fully giving in to the standard. With this book, I am working to *change* facts—to change the conventions of literacy in our culture so that the only standard for writing will be goodness, not correctness. This change won't happen overnight, but it's coming much sooner than most people think (as I try to show in my final section, Part Four). I think of Dante's long-range rhetorical strategy: when he wrote his celebration of vernacular speech, he used Latin; he pragmatically accepted the reigning standards so as to reach his audience. But when he wrote the *Divine Comedy* in his local vernacular, he insisted on a stubborn utopian idealistic fight for cultural change—and it came.

Realistic idealism. My idealism and realism get more and more tangled up together. An ineffectual idealist might settle for good arguments: *Here are seven good reasons why the single standard is unfair and harmful.* But as realist I know that good arguments seldom dent the values of a culture. The ineffectual idealist might raise a flag and issue eloquent rallying cries: *To hell with our culture's values! Let's all be like Dante and write so well that we force change.* But as realist, I know it's useless to say, "Write as well as Dante"—especially to people who feel writing is out of their reach.

My functioning stance in this book is a kind of realistic idealism. That is, the work I'm trying to do here is to *create conditions* that will actually lead to change. I can show people how to use their gift of easy speaking for both the early and the late stages of writing. Vernacular speech will help them get words on the page (Part Two) and then later get their language strong and clear (Part Three). It will help them get writing good before the *final* step of making it "correct" and getting it to fit the conventions of the readers.

These processes I'm suggesting will make writing easier and better not only for people who already write but others who don't. When such people discover that writing is indeed available and learn to do the extra work needed to get their writing to pass muster with mainstream readers, they will realize that what's good about their writing has nothing to do with conformity to narrow standards of "correct" literacy—often not even to genre conventions. They will be braver about stopping when they've managed to create *good* writing in their own vernacular spoken language or mother tongue. They'll see that there are audiences for such writing. And some of the writing will be so good that it wins mainstream readers. The goal of my book is to create a world where more people have more good things to say and get them in print in more versions of English.

That may sound ambitious enough but I won't stop there. I have my eye on a higher peak. As a lifelong academic, I insist that it's finally become a realistic goal to make *academic* writing more welcoming to the sound of the ordinary human voice. If more academics have a better time writing and learn to bring more of their vernacular voices to their texts, it will help melt certain ritualized conventions that don't really benefit the academy.

A final note of blunt realism. Even after we've gotten rid of a single standard for serious correct writing—even after everyone can write serious pieces in his or her own home language and have their version of English recognized by all readers as proper, serious, and appropriate—everyone will *still* have a big problem. We'll all be left with the hardest writing job of all, writing well: creating good thinking or a good story, effective organization and evidence, and learning about specialized genre conventions. When *correct* is gone, we'll still have to struggle with *good*.

Summing up the best of both worlds. I started with this question: Can we bring to writing all the advantages of speaking—and still keep all the advantages of writing? I answer *No,* but insist that if we aim *toward* that goal, we can make things a lot better for people who write or want to write. For the immediate future there is no way to remove the embargo against everyone's native vernacular language for serious writing, so for most of the book, I'll be showing ways to *use* that vernacular speech even to create "correct writing." And there will never be a way to make good writing easy, but working at it will be more inviting when we get to use our own language.

✻   ✻   ✻

An Objection. I've been sensing someone like John McWhorter waiting to interrupt with a scornful response:

> *Stop casting yourself as a dramatic hero struggling bravely toward an unattainable goal. Your goal is dubious and it's already won. Literacy has already welcomed speech. Speech has already degraded writing.*

In a book called *Doing Our Own Thing: The Degradation of Language and Music and Why We Should, Like, Care,* McWhorter has written a criticism of "our national shift from a written to an oral culture" (xxii). He is passionate to defend what he calls "high language" (xx) or even "written-style language" (xxiv). He feels that we've lost our pride or love of "artful language" (xxi). McWhorter gives interesting and entertaining evidence of how we've seen a "written-to-spoken shift" in the writing of our culture (xxiii). He's right; I agree. There are many elements of "talkiness" and casual informality not just online but in our serious books, newspapers, and magazines—even in some academic writing—talkiness that would have seemed out of place fifty or a hundred years ago. I'm not willing to join the chorus of people who cry, "Standards are falling," but surely the "single standard" for correct writing and "good writing" have both been getting shaky. It's this change that I'll explore in my final section.

So I don't much fight his description of what's been happening—nor do I fight his goal. He's not one of those fastidious purists who *hate* the colloquial or informal or low style. As a linguist, he *defends* spoken language against fussy-minded detractors; he goes so far as to say that speech is *never* ungrammatical (unless the speaker is brain damaged or a tiny child or not a native speaker). In fact he writes his own book in a remarkably talky style; his very title is pure slang (*Doing Our*

Own Thing: The Degradation of Language and Music and Why We Should, Like, Care). His battle is against what he sees as a near *monopoly* of the low style for writing. He's probably right about this, and in his sense that few people love or work at eloquence in writing or oratory any more. I think he's right in an interesting additional lament: that Americans don't *love* English the way so many speakers of other tongues are passionately in love with their language. What's surprising, though, is that he admits to the same thing: "I sense myself as suffused with the same lack of linguistic self-love I have chronicled around me" (235). (I hope this book betrays how deeply in love I am with the English language.)

He wants more writing and speaking in the high artful style—writing in its "Sunday best." And so do I. While I welcome the informal style, I also love high, elegant, artful writing in its Sunday best—as long as it's actually good and not just pretentious. Where we differ is about the role of the tongue in writing. He sees speech as a force that pulls writing down. I see it as a force that can improve writing. I'm arguing that if we harness the tongue for writing, we won't just bring more casual speech to the page (though we will); we will also bring more high artful language. In Part Three I think I can show that the lack of art and eloquence in writing that he complains of is due to a *neglect* of the tongue, not an over-reliance on it.

❉   ❉   ❉

Four Hybrids that Suggest Paths toward the Best of Both Worlds
It's helpful to notice four common forms of writing that already enlist speech for writing.

1. *Email.* This often represents physical writing driven by mental speaking (more about this point in the Introduction to Part Two). Some people don't think of email *as* writing because it's too much like speech. But email is a powerful example of how it's possible to bring the *ease* of speaking to the activity of writing. Many people think that emails, chat room writing, blogs, and other forms of fast online writing are degrading our culture. I don't see anything wrong with this kind of writing when the audience and context are appropriate. The writing can be careless or unclear, and sometimes lead to misunderstanding, but we don't usually look to these kinds of writing for precision.

2. *Quotation.* Writers in all sorts of genres have a simple, useful way to bring speech to writing: simply *quote* it. The interview or profile is a genre that tends to be lively because it includes so much quoted speech. In my first-year writing classes, I've made a habit of assigning an interview essay:

> Find someone on campus or at home who likes to write and cares about it and does quite a lot of it. Interview them about what they write, how they write, and how they feel about writing. Make sure to include lots of quotations from what they say.

I think I see students' prose getting a bit richer and more flexible just because they are picking out the most interesting and lively passages of speech, writing them out—and writing their own prose cheek by jowl with this imported speech. (More about this assignment in Elbow and Belanoff *Being a Writer*.) Many newspaper stories give a central role to quotations.

Quoted speech turns out to be the doorway through which stigmatized languages make their way into "proper published literacy." First we have writers like Zora Neale Hurston who *quote* characters using stigmatized vernacular speech. Then we have writers who *narrate* whole books through the voice of a character who uses a vernacular dialect (such as Twain's *Huckleberry Finn* and Sapphire's *Push*—both told by an adolescent speaker of stigmatized English, or James Kelman's *How Late It Was, How Late*, told by a down-and-out Glaswegian). Finally we get books like Gloria Anzaldúa's *Borderlands / La Frontera*, where the author herself writes in her own vernacular nonmainstream voice. Robert Burns's poetry was once denigrated for its dialect, but over the years, it's become canonical. Henry Louis Gates notes an interesting progression from Zora Neale Hurston's *Their Eyes Were Watching God* to Alice Walker's *The Color Purple*. He says that Hurston's narrator *speaks* "herself to a personal freedom and to a remarkable level of articulation in the dialect voice," but Alice Walker's narrator "*writes* her way" to this freedom (169).

3. *The Recorded Interview and Oral History.* Consider again the long passage that I quoted in Chapter 2 where Michael Eric Dyson reflects on the important benefits of writing and literacy—not just for culture in general but specifically for Black culture. Were his printed words speech or writing? He *spoke* the words in an interview, but those audible words were recorded and then transcribed into *writing*. This writing formed a chapter in a book made up mostly of interviews. We end up with a hybrid form—and another example of where I'm headed in this book. Dyson speaks directly to this hybridity in the Preface of his book:

> I am especially fond of the interview because . . . [it] blends the virtues of the written and spoken word. In this form, one may freestyle on ideas. . . . [It] showcases rhetorical improvisation in its purest incarnation. (xix–xx)

In order to produce this mixed form, he exploited the obvious and powerful benefits of *writing:* he could look at the transcript and reflect and ponder and even get feedback for written revision.

Yet of course he reaped the benefits of *speech*. His speech situation was almost ideal in its fruitful ambiguity or doubleness between high-stakes and low-stakes language use. It was high stakes because he was speaking for a microphone and tape recorder for the purpose of publication while being interviewed by an editor of a scholarly journal. But the stakes were low because he could take the kind of improvisational risks we use in casual conversation: he knew he could go over the transcript and make whatever changes he wanted—not just rewriting but also omitting and adding. He probably deleted half or even more of his recorded speech. Good interviewers usually work hard to help their subjects be comfortable, and the whole interview reads as though the editor was supportive and encouraging. It's clear that Dyson enjoys the lively spontaneity and immediacy that speech invites (calling it "rhetorical improvisation"). Note one of his long sentences:

It makes a huge difference to think about our ideas in relation to written words that anger us, that inspire us, that cajole us to agree or argue with what's being communicated, whether it's the writings of Ellison, or the writings of Foucault, or the writings of Baldwin, or the writings of Hurston. (26)

He creates a rhythmic energy and syntax typical of fast-moving lively speech; note how he riffs on writers' names in a speechy audible way. (The syntax is notably "right branching.)

Dyson did his own work to create writing out of his comfortable speaking. But it's fairly common for someone else to do the work. Studs Terkel is the master of this form with his many books of oral history. He carves compelling informal written prose out of people's rambling talk. He doesn't have to rewrite, just cut and rearrange; the good stuff is there to find.

Of course part of Terkel's gift is to *elicit* good talk by taking people so seriously and listening so well. But Terkel's gift is one that we can learn to internalize for ourselves: to take our own words and thinking seriously and to *listen* to ourselves with a welcoming, caring attitude. When people start to write, it's common that they become hypercritical of themselves, but this is not necessary. Writers sometimes learn to seek out friends with some of Terkel's skills when they are preparing to write something. (The *Paris Review* has published a useful series of volumes of interviews with well-known writers as they reflect on their practice.) Dyson knew how to harness the powers of speech for the sake of writing.

But there's a drawback of speech that Dyson couldn't evade even in these lovely conditions. He could delete and revise all he wanted for his wider audience, but nothing prevented him from inadvertently blurting something that his interviewer—alive and present at the scene—considered stupid or offensive. He could say, "Strike that from the record"—but he can't strike it from the editor's memory. He could have had more safety if he'd asked the editor for written questions and then taped himself talking in private. People do this. But as with all hybrids, there are trade-offs. He would have lost the energy and immediacy that comes from face-to-face dialogue.

4. *Using Oral Presentations to Improve Written Essays.* At a recent conference of writing teachers, I heard three teachers from different colleges (Brittany Boykin, Shay Brawn, and Rebecca de Wind Mattingly) describe yet another way to improve writing with speech. In assigning an essay, they went through this progression: first students write a draft; then they revise the draft into *notes* for an oral presentation, which they give to the class; and finally they revise it into a written essay.

The students' oral presentations were not just conversation or dialogue, they were spoken monologues—quite informal yet often scary to give. But the process harnessed some powerful virtues of speaking that improved the students' final written papers. Here's why:

- As students planned their talks, gave their talks, and listened to fellow students doing the same, they gained a far more palpable sense of audience than they tend to have when they write. They didn't need that usually futile advice from a rhetoric teacher: *"Pay attention to your audience!"* They couldn't *help* paying attention to the audience literally in their faces. They could see and feel when their listeners seemed interested and when they began to tune out. They could feel how their sentences had to work on a first hearing—which is exactly the standard we should have for written sentences. One student said, "Once I lose the attention of my audience, I can't get it back." When the students returned to the form of written essay, they often hung on to this recent memory of trying to say these ideas to live people.

- The spoken version had to be much shorter than the papers; students had only five to eight minutes. They had to cut out lots that they had in their drafts. This forced them to find—or, more often, figure out—their central points and argument. They had to simplify and clarify to a core skeleton of thinking. In doing this, they had to figure out how to *subordinate*, for you can't have too many "main ideas" for a short talk. And when they were listening to the oral reports by classmates, they could notice listeners tuning out when a talk was all generalizations and no examples—or all stories and examples and no conceptual skeleton. So when they finally revised to their own final longer *written* versions, they could hold on to the clarity that an oral presentation forced them to carve out. Many of them made some of the cuts permanent so as to give more development to fewer main points.

- You can *hide* when you are writing, but not when speaking to live listeners. Having to give a spoken talk made them take more ownership of their thinking. Some of them remarked how it was easier to bullshit in writing—to spin out ho-hum uninvested thinking.

This way of teaching made it obvious that speaking versus writing is not an either/or matter. The spoken presentations helped the writing, but they were valuable in themselves. The students were grateful for the practice in a rhetorical form that they will often have to use in later life.

When I heard these three teachers, I was impressed at their creativity. They had invented a good teaching technique that I'd never had the sense to use. Yet now—during a final revision of this chapter—I suddenly see what they did through a new lens. I take nothing away from their ingenuity to note that they are merely bringing to the classroom a way that most academics and professionals have used speech to help their writing. That is, when academics and professionals have an idea they want to write up, very commonly they manage to try out a version of it as a short conference presentation. The benefits are just what I've described. (But academics and professionals sometimes blunt the benefits by taking two more years to write the essay—and by this time they've sometimes lost the benefits of the live talking to a live audience.)

Another hybrid: audio books. These also bring the advantages of speech to writing, but in this case it's readers who benefit from the speech, not writers. Audio books may be spoken, but they are not recordings of live speech such as in senate hearings, public speeches, or TV and radio programs. Yet the spoken versions bring some of the energy and intonation of speech to a text and thereby often make the meaning clearer and easier to understand. It's not surprising that many people like to *hear* writing out loud.

✻　　✻　　✻

To summarize this chapter: I've just described four suggestive hybrids that point the way to this book's utopian goal: harnessing what's best about speaking and bringing it to writing. It's an unattainable goal, but the utopian impulse makes me seek it, and this helps me clarify two goals that *can* be attained: the short-term goal of making it easier and more satisfying to write while still meeting existing standards for correct acceptable writing; and the long-term goal of changing our culture's standards for acceptable writing.

LITERACY STORY

Two Stories of How Early Standard English Was Born

The most widely circulated story goes like this: we all inherited London's form of English as "standard English" because London became the economic and political center of England in the late fourteenth century. But it turns out that this is not quite right. The language that emerged as standard—even for speaking—was an artificial hybrid mixture that *corresponded to no one's speech*, much less a Londoner's speech. It was an idealization. It borrowed spoken features from different regional dialects and also written features that didn't exist in speech anywhere. Here's a linguistic historian Jonathan Hope:

> [T]he linguistic data does not support the notion that Standard English evolved from a single dialect—as most historians of the language accept. Standard English features can be traced to an inconveniently wide range of dialects. (50)

Hope goes on to quote the words of two respected linguists (Pyles and Algeo) as they tell the conventional "single-ancestor" story.

> It is not surprising that a type of speech—that of London—essentially East Midlandish in its characteristics, though showing Northern and to a lesser extent Southern influences, should in time have become a standard for all of England. (Hope 50, quoting Pyles and Algeo)

But Hope was quoting those scholars in order to skewer them with this satirical response:

It is tempting to ask what dialects are *not* present in this Londonish-East Midlandish-Northernish-Southernish "single" ancestor. (50)

Hope shows that the form of Standard English that got itself established in this period had the effect of making *everyone's speech wrong*:

> The "selection" process of standardization is not the selection of a single dialect, but the selection of single linguistic features from a range of dialects—features which are then recombined into a new dialect which lacks a common ancestor. . . . *Selection* becomes *selections*, and this accords much more closely with the observed nature of Standard English (the mixing of northern and southern forms, for example). (51)

Hope goes so far as to argue that the forms that became Standard English were "selected" (seldom consciously) *because* they were not common, comfortable, or natural. "A number of the variants [that end up in] Standard English can be characterized as the *least* likely to have been selected (if 'naturalness' or frequency is a criterion) from a pool of variation" (52).

He gives these examples of features that got chosen even though they were almost certainly different from how most people talked.

• Double negatives were somehow ruled wrong or nonstandard—"despite their frequency in speech and dialects" (53). In other words, most Londoners—like most people in England—took double negatives for granted. Indeed I gather that virtually all spoken languages use double negatives, *n'est pas?* I've never known a child who didn't naturally use double negatives.

• *What* as a relativiser gets dropped—in effect telling folks at the time that it was okay to say, *I gave him what he asked me for*, but they must *not* say, *I gave him the money what he asked me for*. This locution got "de-selected" even though it is used "by most (perhaps all) non-standard dialects" (52). Like double negatives, the locution continues to thrive in "bad" dialects—but that's because it's so linguistically natural.

• All verb endings get dropped except for an obligatory "s" for third person singular (*I run, you run, he runs*). Hope says that it was unusual—"typologically unlikely"—to mark off just the third person singular form as different from all the rest.

• A *five-person* pronoun system gets selected. Thus we have

singular	*I*	*she/he/it*
singular/plural	*you*	[EMPTY]
plural	*we*	*they*

It was very odd, Hope argues, to leave that empty hole, especially when it was always filled in the preceding dialects (Middle English and Early Modern English) and also in most present-day dialects. He gives these examples: *thou/you, you/ youse, you/you-all* (52).

• "Why, in choosing the form of spelling for the past tense ending, does Standard English select *-ed* from the range of possible choices: *-ed -d -'d -t -'t?* Especially given that *-ed* corresponds to the phonetically *least* common form" (54–55).

Another historical linguist, Jim Milroy, makes the same crucial point in a more general or universal form:

> [S]tandard "varieties" appear as idealizations that exist at a high level of abstraction. . . . [T]hey do not conform exactly to the usage of any particular speaker. Indeed the most palpable manifestation of the standard is not in the speech community at all, but in the writing system. (11)

Even now, the rules for "correct speech" tend to be found in books meant largely to guide writing.

It's hard to avoid the naive question: Who *decided* to have a Standard English that made everyone's speech wrong? There was no *Academie Anglaise* in London in the late thirteenth and fourteenth century to make rules (though Norman French was not totally dead yet). We'll never know, but these historical linguists imply a process that's actually not so hard to imagine: the "better sort of people"—when faced with a choice between forms—tend to opt for locutions that differ from the speech of the masses—even if it means they have to adjust their own speech habits a bit:

> When two equivalent structures have a salient existence in the speech community, such as *you were* and *you was* or *I saw* and *I seen*, one is accepted and the other rejected—on grounds that are linguistically arbitrary, but socially non-arbitrary. Thus standard languages are high-level idealisations, in which uniformity or invariance is valued above all things. One consequence of this is that no one actually speaks a standard language. (Milroy 13)

Milroy notes that the new emerging standard

> was overtly used in gatekeeping functions in order to exclude the majority of the population from upward social and professional mobility—so much so that Abercrombie (1963), in an excellent and prescient essay first published in 1951, could speak of an "accent bar" as parallel to the "colour bar." (20)

For this literacy story I am drawing material from a fascinating book, *The Development of Standard English 1300–1800: Theories, Descriptions, Conflicts*, edited by Laura Wright.

PART TWO

SPEAKING ONTO THE PAGE

A Role for the Tongue in the Early Stages of Writing

Introduction: Speaking and Writing as Mental Activities

The argument of this book is simple: that we can enlist the language activity most people find easiest, *speaking,* for the language activity most people find hardest, *writing.* In Part One, I explored the potentialities of both ways of using language. I used just one chapter to explore the virtues of writing because there isn't so much news there. I spent three chapters exploring the virtues of speech because they are far too little recognized.

Now I will explore ways to bring these virtues to writing. Here in Part Two, I focus on the early stages of writing where it is possible to do what I call "unplanned speaking onto the page," or using our "speaking gear" for writing—as in freewriting. Then in Part Three, I will focus on the late revising stages of writing where we can harness the resources of the tongue by reading aloud.

More Defining

In the Introduction to Part One, I looked at the differences between speaking and writing along three dimensions:

- *Speaking and writing as different physical activities:* moving our mouths versus moving our fingers;
- *Speaking and writing as different sensory modalities or media:* language consisting of audible sounds existing in time versus visible marks existing in space;

- *Speaking and writing as different linguistic products:* the kinds of words that come from mouths versus from fingers. Here the difference is not so clear. If we consider the *full* range of language that humans produce, there is an almost complete overlap between what is spoken and what is written. But if we focus only on two common kinds of speaking and writing—casual conversation and careful expository prose—then there are rich and interesting differences between speech and writing.

Some readers will suggest that I also need to contrast speaking and writing as *social* or *contextual* processes, pointing out that speech is usually a social dialogue with present-time listeners and writing is usually a solitary activity addressed to absent readers or no one in particular. It's true that these conditions are common in our culture (and many others) and have deeply influenced most people's experience and conception of speech and writing. But these conditions give a somewhat restricted picture of the possible conditions for human speaking and writing. Furthermore, my main argument here is that we can radically change the social uses of speech and writing. I began this line of thinking in a 1985 essay called "The Shifting Relationships between Speech and Writing."

Now I need to explore a fourth dimension in which speaking and writing can be contrasted: *speaking and writing as* <u>*mental*</u> *activities, not physical activities.* This distinction is central for my argument. And it happens to clear up a puzzle I mentioned earlier: when we *dictate* are we speaking or writing? Let's look more carefully.

Consider some famous writers. Isocrates helped shape the earliest sense of written prose in the West, and like so many ancient "writers," he seldom physically *wrote.* He mostly dictated spoken words to a slave. (Dictation was a common practice through much of antiquity, but scholars think that Isocrates occasionally did put stylus to papyrus himself. See W. V. Harris.) Milton was blind when he wrote *Paradise Lost,* and dictated it to his daughter. People in modern offices have traditionally dictated letters for secretaries to type. And now we can buy voice-activated software and just talk and the computer turns our audible speech into visible writing.

When people dictate letters, essays, poems, or other texts they are making noises with their mouths, but often they *experience* themselves *mentally* as writing. As they speak their words, they are mentally creating *written sentences* or *written lines of a poem.* They think about where the sentences begin and end; sometimes they speak the punctuation aloud (one of the options with voice-activated software). Should we say to Milton, "Face it, John, you didn't *write Paradise Lost,* you spoke it"? Can we imagine that Milton let his daughter decide where to end his lines and how to punctuate? These observations fit my own experience too. I've sometimes *written* by dictating into a tape recorder or into my computer for a secretary, or used voice-activated software as I've just described—*feeling* my words as written sentences and sometimes *seeing* them in my head, even saying my punctuation aloud. I've been *mentally writing.*

But this isn't the whole story. Sometimes as I engaged in this mental process of careful writing, I got frustrated and tangled up trying to speak "sentences"—indeed, correct sentences—trying to speak written words. Sometimes I just gave up and said to myself, "The heck with this. I'm just going to *talk*." So I just "let go" and stopped trying to "write." I stopped thinking of my words as parts of a sentence. This gave me a completely different mental experience of using language. When I had been trying to dictate writing, I often had to pause and decide on the right word. But when I let myself dictate by just talking and I got going in the process, I no longer had to pause and often didn't even choose my words. They just *came*—out of my mental sense of having something I wanted to say. In fact I often stopped having any awareness of the words coming out of my mouth *as words;* I just felt myself uttering *thoughts* or *meanings*. This different process produced an observably different product, different language. The words looked much more like casual speech.

So if we want an adequate understanding of how people use their mouths and hands for language (and if we want to understand borderline cases like dictation), we need to distinguish the *inner mental* process from the *outer physical* process. This distinction has been made by a prominent linguist, M. A. K. Halliday. When he discusses the obvious differences between casual speech and careful writing, what interests him are the inner, mental differences that usually accompany them. He uses the words "natural," "un-self-monitored," "flowing," and "spontaneous" to describe the mental process we tend to use when we speak in casual safe conversation in real time without pausing or worrying. And he uses the terms "self-monitoring" and "controlled" and "self-conscious" to describe the more careful, deliberate, "choosing" mental process we tend to use for careful writing. In writing, we can pause as long as we want—ponder and change our minds—before deciding on a word or phrase or even a whole structure ("Spoken and Written" 66, 79).

By paying special attention to the mental dimension of how we produce language, Halliday shows that the mental and physical dimensions don't have to match each other. That is, as we speak with our mouths, we don't *always* natter along without pausing or choosing; we *sometimes* plan or rehearse or monitor our words (as in a job interview or dangerous argument). And as we write with our fingers, we don't *always* choose words with care; we *sometimes* put out language in an unplanned or unselfmonitored or spontaneous way (as in some emailing, diary writing, and freewriting).

If it seems odd or unrealistic to talk about a *mental* language use that differs from a *physical* language use, I would insist that we see it every day in something

---

Halliday goes so far in his terminology that (somewhat confusingly) he lets the mental dimension trump the physical dimension. That is, he uses the term "spoken language" for *any* language we produce with our mental process of spontaneous language production—even if we are using our fingers to write; and he uses the term "written language" for *any* language we produce with our mental process of self-conscious, monitored language production—even if we are using our mouths to talk:

> Speech and writing as forms of discourse are typically associated with the two modal points on the continuum from most spontaneous to most self-monitored language: spontaneous discourse is usually spoken, [while] self-monitored discourse is usually written. We can therefore conveniently label these two modal points "spoken" and "written" language. ("Spoken and Written" 69, my emphasis)

But having identified spoken and written language with *mentality*, he carefully acknowledges that the physical dimension can differ from the mental one:

> The more natural, un-self-monitored the discourse, the more intricate the grammatical patterns that can be woven. Usually, this kind of discourse will be spoken, because writing is in essence a more conscious process than speaking. But there are self-conscious modes of speech, whose output resembles what we think of as written language, and there are relatively spontaneous kinds of writing; spoken and written discourse are the *outward* forms that are typically associated with the critical variable, which is that of [*inward*] consciousness. . . . The complexity of spoken language is in its flow, the dynamic mobility whereby each figure provides context for the next one. ("Spoken and Written" 66, my emphasis)

Oesterreicher, too, spends a good deal of time on this crucial distinction between the mental and the physical: the "conceptual [mental] aspect of language must be strictly distinguished from the medium aspect of language" (191). He cites various other linguists who "all insist that the *conceptional* profiles of any discourse are, as a matter of principle, independent of the *medium of discourse*" (191 my emphasis):

> Similar distinctions are made by M.A.K. Halliday, Wallace Chafe, Elinor Ochs, Deborah Tannen, and other scholars. They use—more or less systematically—the terms spoken versus written to mark the medium-opposition, and terms like oral versus literate, informal versus formal, or unplanned versus planned to denote aspects of the linguistic [and mental] conception. In addition, Basil Bernstein's distinction between restricted and elaborated code reflects differences in linguistic conception too. (Oesterreicher 191–192)

French linguists actually have separate *terms* for the mental and physical dimensions of language. In fact they set out *two* dichotomies: *langue parlee* versus *langue écrite* and *code phonique* versus *code graphique*.

quite ordinary: "talking" inside our heads. Most people comfortably recognize that they speak *mentally* inside their heads while *physically* saying nothing.

In future references to these two mental processes of generating language, I will often allow myself some metaphors—imprecise of course, but helpful.

Some might object that inner speaking is not "normal" speaking because it's monologue rather than dialogue. But spoken monologue is a common human activity too—as in telling stories to friends, giving directions, explaining complex procedures, teaching classes, lecturing, or allowing ourselves to be interviewed. For such monologues, there's usually a present audience—either face to face or on the phone. But there's an interesting form of spoken monologue with *no* live audience that's becoming more and more common in our culture: the phone message. Phone messages provide a good illustration of how language use changes with time and culture. At first we had no history or genre of phone messages, and most of us were flustered when we had to leave one. "What am I doing?—writing a note or saying something to someone?" (I often find myself ending a phone message with, "Bye bye, this is Peter"—as though I were signing my name at the bottom of a letter.) But now people are becoming adept and treating phone messages as a genre and even an art form.

And plenty of our inner speaking is strongly dialogic because it's directly addressed to an audience—which we supply—real or imagined. I love the French phrase, *l'esprit de l'escalier*, that refers to the common experience of leaving a party or a meeting and walking down the stairs (l'escalier) and suddenly finding in our minds exactly the brilliant or witty (l'esprit) remark we *should* have made but didn't. As we speak inside our heads, we see how brilliant we would have been—leaving our crestfallen listener flustered and speechless. Similarly, when we know we'll have to say something difficult or awkward in a face-to-face encounter, we sometimes rehearse words in our heads—often imagining a full dialogue that includes the other person's words. No sounds, yet we hear sounds in our heads. During this inner speaking, people sometimes even form silent words with their mouths (I'm often startled to find my lips doing this).

Of course, plenty of our inner speech is purely to ourselves. We try to figure out what to do next or we find we need to describe for ourselves something that happened. Troublesome events sometimes lead us to tell them to ourselves over and over. This kind of talk can merge with or transform itself into inner thinking. Vygotsky charts the developmental route in children from outer speech to inner speech to thinking. He and others have good examples of children talking to themselves as they try to solve problems.

Some language-happy theorists claim that *all* thinking is in words. Most people don't see it this way and the common experience of artists and musicians (and the behavior of animals!) seems a sufficient rebuttal to such an unlikely idea. We can trust the commonsense view: sometimes we think with internal speech and sometimes without language at all. (See Pinker, *Stuff of Thought,* for strong arguments against the peculiarly narrow view that all thinking is in language.)

I like to say that we have a choice between two mental *gears:* a "mental speaking gear" and a "mental writing gear"—and we can use either gear whether we are physically speaking or writing. For example, in a job interview, we might start out comfortably chit-chatting in our speaking gear. But then the interviewer says, "Now tell me why you consider yourself qualified for this job." Suddenly we have to downshift into our writing gear so we can use care in planning, choosing, and monitoring our words.

Conversely, when we are writing with our fingers—pausing and choosing words with care—we can decide to upshift into our speaking gear and let words roll out unplanned or unmonitored, sometimes almost of their own accord. We allow ourselves to write just as spontaneously and uncarefully as we often do in safe conversation. This fluent process is what I'll focus on in the next chapter where I treat freewriting. Freewriting is an exercise designed, among other things, to bump ourselves into the mental speaking gear as we write. It's not that freewriting yields exactly the language of talking. But it harnesses the essential *resource* of talking that I'm interested in here: unplanned words.

There's another metaphorical contrast that I find very helpful: *uttering* language (i.e., using the speaking gear) versus *constructing* language (using the writing gear). The word "utter" helps imply the mouth-based nonplanning spontaneous process we so often use in comfortable speaking. The words "construct" and "compose" imply the more careful hand-based mental process most people use when they consciously choose words and phrases. I often use this metaphor when I'm responding to student writing. I point to sentences that are particularly tangled and clogged and say something like this:

> I found this sentence difficult and unpleasant to read. Notice how *"constructed"* it is. You would never *utter* a sentence like this. I sensed that as you were writing it, you paused or interrupted yourself quite often to ponder which words or phrases to use—or how the grammar ought to go. You *chose* words, but you didn't then get them to follow the kind of comfortable clear sequence that is natural to your mouth. You haven't broken any grammar rules, but your words don't hang together. Try *uttering* your thought, and your sentences will be much clearer and more inviting for readers.

My distinction between constructing versus uttering doesn't map *precisely* onto Halliday's distinction between self-conscious monitored language versus unplanned spontaneous language. For one *can* utter or speak onto the page in a slow, deliberate, planning way, with conscious awareness of every word. For example, the writing of a tricky personal letter is sometimes a slow affair: most people do a lot of pausing, pondering, choosing, crossing out, changing their minds when they write a Dear John letter or a proposal of marriage—and sometimes just an invitation to dinner. And yet these letters tend to be written in uttered syntax or represent speaking onto the page.

The Continuum between the Speaking Gear and the Writing Gear

My metaphors, speaking gear versus writing gear or uttering versus constructing, imply a binary, either/or choice. In the physical realm we're pretty much stuck with a binary choice between using the mouth or the fingers; in a bike or car with gears, we're in one gear or another. But in the mental realm, we have a full spectrum or continuum between our inner writing gear and our inner speaking gear—uttering and constructing—between full spontaneity and full planning. Whether we are speaking or writing, we spend lots of time at intermediate points—partly planning and partly blurting. Our choice among mental "gears" is not digital but analogue. As Halliday put it (in the previous box), "[mental] speaking" and "[mental] writing" are "modal points on a continuum." We sometimes sort-of monitor or "watch our language" but still go fast without much pausing or planning—or vice versa.

Still, activity along a busy gamut does not deny the reality of the terminal points at each end. For instance, in my dictating experience, I felt an abrupt change of mental gears from constructing to uttering when I stopped trying mentally to "write." Suddenly I could stop thinking about words and let my mind focus on meanings, and the words took care of themselves. I stopped being conscious of what a sentence was—where it started and ended and how to punctuate it. As a result, I could find more words without struggle. It's probably more accurate to say that I didn't so much decide to *engage* my speech gear as *disengage* my writing gear. It was my writing gear that was distracting me and inhibiting language—even inhibiting thinking. The same thing happens in writing when I'm struggling to figure out how to say what I intend and choose my words—and I get slower and more stuck in molasses. Suddenly I remember I can just freewrite, and so I let go and let words tumble out; I seem to be able to "utter" my way through my perplexities. The process may not yield precise thinking, but it gives me words that will *lead* me to precision. And amazingly enough, occasionally precision is just what I get from the nonplanning.

Summing Up the Definitions

In the Introduction to Part One, I pointed out that when linguists look at a huge corpus of human discourse, they can't find a clear dividing line between words that were spoken and those that were written. Humans are flexible. They can blurt unplanned language, whether speaking or writing—or "watch their tongues" in either modality.

Now in this Introduction to Part Two, I've shown where this flexibility comes from: it comes from the *mental* realm. We can engage in "*mental speaking*" and produce unplanned language—whether we use our mouths or our fingers; and we can engage in "*mental writing*"—and produce carefully monitored language—whether we use our mouths or our fingers. We have linguistic choices in our heads that need not be governed by the physical mode of producing language.

The theme of the book is *choice*. There's almost nothing we can't do with our fingers and our mouths and our minds. I'm fighting against too much material determinism. And I'm fighting too much cultural determinism—in particular about writing: let's not be restricted by how our culture (or any culture) uses writing.

7 What Is Speaking onto the Page and How Does Freewriting Teach It?

"SPEAKING ONTO THE page." This odd metaphor first came to me as part of the germ for this book. I was freewriting my way out of a tangle of perplexity and I startled myself with a new thought: "I'm not just *writing*, I'm *speaking* . . . onto the page." I realized that I was using the linguistic gear I normally use for talking. It's a miraculous ability we take for granted in casual conversation: the gift of finding words without trying, without looking for them, without planning. This realization opened up a new way to see freewriting—*hear* freewriting—and at the same time it also opened up a new way to think about the very nature of speaking and writing.

When we speak onto the page, we use our fingers to put words onto the page or screen, but the words come to mind fluently, nonstop, without planning or conscious choosing. Halliday explicitly notes that we can write with the mental "unselfmonitored" process he calls "speaking" ("Spoken and Written" 66).

Just as unplanned speaking sometimes leads to disrupted language and sometimes to fluent coherent language, so too with speaking onto the page. (Actually, I think I notice that freewriting leads to extended passages of fluent connected language more often than we produce in actual speaking. For freewriting is a monologue with the safety that no one else is listening.) Plenty of people talk easily onto the page when they write in diaries, email, chat rooms, and for some letters. But many find it hard to exploit the ease of unplanned speaking when they are trying to write something serious that demands a lot of thought. If you ask them about their serious topic, they can usually *speak* lots of thoughts and words, but they don't feel they can do the same thing on paper. They feel they have to get their thoughts right and put them into proper words. *"If I throw down careless imprecise words on a topic where I need care, it'll make my mind flabby and I'll never be able to carve the precision I need."* These are understandable feelings; but for scores of years disciplined writers have used freewriting and still maintained their discipline in revising.

Throughout the world of writing, even very serious writing, we'll find plenty of unplanned words that were spoken onto the page. But we can't actually *identify* those unplanned words. For when we look at writing by other people—published or not—we never really know how any passage of words was actually produced. Much of it was written with care, and most of it got serious care as it was revised and edited. Yet some or even much of it might well have been spoken fluently onto the page without much care or planning. We just can't tell because of the pesky fact that unplanned freewriting can yield such excellent writing.

In the next chapter I'll look at many of these places in the world of writing where we are likely to find unplanned language. But in this chapter I'll focus only on freewriting because I want to focus more directly on words we *know* were produced without planning. Freewriting teaches how to use the unplanned speaking gear as a disciplined practice for part of the writing process, even when the topic is thorny. Freewriting is an invitation to not worry, an invitation to forget standards or rules. (When I introduce it, I sometimes even say, "invite garbage"—to show that I mean it.) Yet because of that very freedom, it often leads to good writing. And even when it is broken and syntactically messy, it will invite the linguistic virtues that I described in Chapters 4 and 5.

First I'll look at freewriting as pure exercise: it helps people learn this peculiar ability to exploit for *writing* the unplanned fluency that is natural in safe comfortable speech. Then I'll look at freewriting as something that many experienced writers use for getting important writing done—freewriting for serious results.

Freewriting as an Exercise

Freewriting is a simple artificial writing exercise—classically ten minutes by the clock. The goal has always been to make the process of writing easier and more comfortable while also bringing out livelier and more natural language. In a moment I'll provide a couple of samples to show what unplanned language can look like under exercise conditions, but first let me say more about the exercise process. The terms are simple:

• Write without stopping. If you feel *nothing* in mind—or if you don't want to write what comes to mind—just describe your shoes or write something over and over ("nothing nothing nothing" or "I hate this I hate this"—or even "shit shit shit"). "Don't stop" doesn't mean "Rush." It's fine to breathe deeply, untense your muscles, pause briefly now and then to let a feeling deepen. The goal is not some kind of pure mental nakedness or perfect psychiatric free association; the goal is the easy nonplanning of language and—gradually—easy movement of thinking.

• It's private. You *can* decide tomorrow or next week to share what you write today, but write now with the expectation of *not* sharing.

• Don't worry about any standards for writing. Freely accept carelessness, meaninglessness, or even garbage.

There are two useful variations on normal freewriting:

• *Focused freewriting.* Try to stay on one topic. You'll probably wander off, but just pull yourself back when you notice. This process is helpful when you face a particular writing project. It helps you get going and produce lots of words and thoughts on the topic. Also, many teachers improve class discussions by giving students five minutes of private focused freewriting on a topic or a question before inviting discussion. Students invariably have much more to say after they've blurted their first thoughts privately on paper.

• *Public freewriting*. Write with the expectation of sharing. This makes freewriting less safe, so you might let yourself make brief stops and cross-outs and engage in a bit more conscious planning. Public freewriting works best if there is already some trust in the group—or considerable courage. And when it comes to sharing, you can always "pass." ("Marriage Encounter" groups make good use of something close to public freewriting: couples more-or-less freewrite and then share the results. This practice calls on the central principle of Outward Bound: growth often results from deliberately imposed risk. But using risk in this way involves some danger and it takes good direction or supervision.)

Because freewriting makes us put out language without stopping, it pushes most of us into our mental speaking gear where we can't plan or rehearse words before uttering them. In short, it forcibly interrupts that deep habitual connection between the physical act of writing and our mental habit of planning and choosing words. Even though some people are mentally quick and agile and can do *some* planning while they talk or write fast, most people who freewrite for more than a little while are popped into a way of generating language that they experience as quite different from even quick agile planning and monitoring.

A Quick Glance at the Pedigree of Freewriting

Ken Macrorie was the first to bring what he called "free writing" to the attention of the field of composition (*Writing to Be Read*, 1968). He wanted to help students stop writing stale, stilted, dead language—what he called "Engfish." He prescribed a ten-minute exercise of nonstop writing where you just put down the words that come to you, not trying for good or correct writing. He wasn't thinking about speaking onto the page or about using the speaking gear for writing. And neither was I for the three decades I spent celebrating freewriting and exploring its possibilities.

Macrorie became one of the first prominent figures in the brand-new field of composition in the 1960s and an early editor of our main journal, *College Composition and Communication*. But he has always been at pains to insist that he didn't invent freewriting. He gives credit to two women writing in the 1930s who can be thought of as the unrecognized founders of the so-called "writing process": Dorothea Brande and Brenda Ueland. But he points in particular to a 1936 essay by William Carlos Williams, "How to Write," that has this key passage:

> One takes a piece of paper, anything, the flat of a shingle, slate, cardboard and with anything handy to the purpose begins to put down the words after the desired expression in mind. This is the anarchical phase of writing. . . . Write, write anything: it is all in all probability worthless anyhow, it is never hard to destroy written characters. But it is absolutely

essential to the writing of anything worthwhile that the mind be fluid and release itself to the task.

Forget all rules, forget all restrictions, as to taste, as to what ought to be said, write for the pleasure of it—whether slowly or fast—every form of resistance to a complete release should be abandoned. . . .

[Critical, conscious attention to words] is dealt with in the colleges and in all forms of teaching but nowhere does it seem to be realized that without its spring from the deeper strata of the personality, all the teaching and learning in the world can make nothing of the result. . . . I am not speaking of two persons, a poet and critic, I am speaking of the same person, the writer. He has written with his deepest mind, now the object is there and he is attacking it with his most recent mind, the fore-brain, the seat of memory and ratiocination, the so-called intelligence. (Quoted in Belanoff, Elbow, and Fontaine 171–172, but see Williams "How to Write.")

And Macrorie points to a remarkable essay by S. I. Hayakawa. This man became a conservative U.S. senator from California, but he started out interested in language and general semantics and wrote a book I remember as interesting when I was starting out: *Language in Thought and Action.* In a 1962 essay in *College Composition and Communication,* Hayakawa wrote these striking words:

How, then, shall writing be taught? I am just about coming to the conclusion that it should not be taught at all. I believe that instruction in grammar, spelling, sentence structure, paragraphing and such should be abandoned in Freshman English. The students should be told that the lid is off, that they can write and spell and punctuate any damn way they please—but that they must write daily and copiously.

A favorite exercise of mine (the idea comes from Paul Eluard and the surrealist poets) is to give students a specified period—say fifteen or twenty minutes—and tell them to write rapidly and continuously for that length of time, without pausing, without taking thought, without revising, without taking pen from paper. If the student runs out of things to say, he is to write the last words he wrote over and over again over and over again over and over again until he can find other things to say. (Quoted in Macrorie "Freewriting Relationship" 177, but see Hayakawa "Learning to Think"—the passage is on 8.)

None of these forebears called it freewriting or saw it as a way to enlist speech for writing. But Hayakawa noted: "In a matter of weeks, student writings, at first so labored and self-conscious, become fluid, expressive, and resonant with the rhythms of the spoken American language" (Macrorie *Writing to Be Read* 8). And when Macrorie praises a piece of freewriting, he writes, "here is a real girl speaking"—"an individual person seems to be speaking" (10).

As Hayakawa indicates, they all more or less stole the activity of "automatic writing" from surrealists and dada-ists. Yeats famously got his wife to write automatically while in a trance. (See Boice and Meyers.)

Some readers might want to read Appendix I, "How Freewriting Went from Dangerous to No Big Deal in the Composition and Rhetoric Community."

What Does Freewriting Look Like When Produced as an Exercise?

Here are two pieces of freewriting by first-year college students in a classroom setting. By looking at what's produced by less experienced writers, I can show even better how freewriting brings the virtues of speech to the page. First, a plain example of ordinary no-assigned-topic freewriting. The teacher who elicited the following piece began every class with a ten-minute freewrite—in effect, "Write whatever comes to mind or whatever you need to write about today. Don't stop." As Richard Haswell and Pat Belanoff both note, students who are new to freewriting often stay fairly close to the conventions of ordinary writing until they gradually learn to exploit the potential freedom:

> Mark called me this morning at 8:00. I couldn't believe it. When Charlene came and knocked on the door and said it was for me. I knew it had to be him. He called me last night at 11, but I wasn't in. I was at the reading Room ironically writing about him. I got back at 11:25. We talked about school and stuff, but something is wrong. Ever since Terry and I talked about Mark and I, I've been having crazy feelings about do I really love him or not? I do, I say, but is it really real. Damn, I guess this is normal, but I don't want to even think this way. Maybe since I'm not close to him these thoughts run around my mind. I don't know, it's so hard, Sometimes I even think that I'm with him just because he's good to me. Is that being selfish or is it the way I'm supposed to feel? (Fontaine 8)

You may ask how we can publish private writing. The teacher, Sheryl Fontaine, was a researcher and didn't reveal her research interest to her class till after she'd had the same group for two semesters. At the very end, having established lots of trust, she asked her students if they would give her examples of their private freewrites. Most of them gave her many examples. For Fontaine's essay and other interesting explorations of the topic, see the volume on freewriting edited by Belanoff, Elbow, and Fontaine.

For another example, here's a piece of focused freewriting. Students were given a standard essay prompt and told to use freewriting for generating ideas.

> OK Why do I really think that the governt should limit the amount of violence on TV? I think it is obvious. Just turn on your TV and you see the most awful, violent, sick really stuff. Crazed lunatic captures young child in mall and threatens to do awful things, or stalker threatens to rape woman. Police everywhere, guns going off this is crazy. I just don't think this is everyday stuff. Sure somewhere things like this go on, but I've never seen a high speed chase or even a gun going off other than for hunting.

It seems like TV glorifies violence or maybe rubs there face in it like it was a cow pie smelly and foul. ok keep writing keep writing. I don't know who watches this stuff. Yes I do. My dad does and I've been caught too. They have lots of action and suspense that they draw you into them. It's like there's some magnetic force. Don't these shows manipulate us, show us things that are so violent so strange so fearful that we have to look. But how does that affect us to look? For us as adults I think it needlessly puts us through a bad experience. The big losers are kids. Here's my strongest point. They are so impressionable that they don't know the difference between right and wrong. I've seen kids after watching the ninja turtles come out kicking and fighting like that's ok. Violence in the cause of right. Yuck. the the the the Also young kids can't tell the difference between fantasy and reality. Like that kid that set fire to his home after seeing it done on bvis and but head. Boy I bet his parents were upset. We obviously have an epidemic of teen violence now already. Where is it coming from? I think TV has got to be a contributing factor. (The Write Place)

But Where Are the Virtues in This Writing?

When I and others have praised the benefits of freewriting, we have tended to fall back on words like "lively," "energetic," and "possessing a voice"—contrasting it with so much of the stiff and sometimes muddy English that is so common among students, professionals, and others. But now, on the basis of the linguistic analysis I did in Chapters 3, 4, and 5, I can show more clearly where the "life" of freewriting comes from and how it effortlessly captures onto the page some of the precious virtues of unplanned spoken language. In what follows I do some extended analysis of these freewrites in terms of some of the virtues I mentioned in Chapters 4 and 5: intonation units, coherence, parataxis, flexibility of syntax, avoiding left-branching syntax and too much nominalization, language that connects with the audience, gisting or talking turkey, and reality as process. I find it fascinating and it provides a useful further window on those virtues of speech. But I will put it in a long box because some readers will take my word for it and prefer to move on.

• *Intonation units.* Because the language of freewriting is unplanned—as in speaking—it falls naturally into strong clear intonational phrases. (*"ha. no small order, there. But I do believe it." "crazy feelings about do I really love him or not? I do, I say, but is it really real. Damn, I guess this is normal, but I don't want to even think this way." "Police everywhere, guns going off this is crazy. I just don't think this is everyday stuff."*) This is why you can so often "hear" the intonation in freewriting. This kind of intonation tends to carry the sound tangled up in the words and make comprehension almost effortless.

• *Coherence.* Less messiness. These freewrites illustrate Halliday's startling claim that speech is more coherent than most writing. Like speech, these freewrites have many fewer crossouts and false starts than we see in the texts of writers who have time to pause, change their minds, and revise. And yet for the same reason, freewriters instinctively tend to make it easy to follow transitions from one sentence to the next. Even when one sentence is jammed up against another that says the opposite ("I don't know who watches this stuff. Yes I do."), this "failure of logical planning" functions as a remarkably "coherent" transition. Both syntax and logic are transparent.

• *Parataxis.* This is a potent source of *energy* in language: "connecting" clauses and thoughts with each other without connection—without articulating how they relate. "I don't know who watches this stuff. Yes I do." Consider the comparative limpness of a "properly written" version: "I don't know who watches this stuff; however, I have to admit that my father does and I sometimes do too." The fact is that the opposite form—syntactic embedding or hypotaxis or hierarchy—often *saps* energy. Another example: "The big losers are kids. Here's my strongest point. They are so impressionable . . ." And the young woman writing about Mark doesn't have time to give hierarchical logic to her conflicting feelings and falls into repeated paratactic contradiction: "

> I've been having crazy feelings about do I really love him or not? I do, I say, but is it really real. Damn, I guess this is normal, but I don't want to even think this way. . . . I don't know, it's so hard, Sometimes I even think that I'm with him just because he's good to me. Is that being selfish or is it the way I'm supposed to feel?

• In a sentence I omitted from that passage, she does use hypotaxis, but it's the kind of simple, clear variety that's common in speech and doesn't sap energy: "Maybe since I'm not close to him these thoughts run around my mind."

• *Flexibility of syntax.* The second writer more than the first one exploits some of the flexibility of typical speech—break-offs and sudden swerves. But even though the first writer's prose looks simple at first, in fact it is far from the Dick-and-Jane simple repetitive syntax that students so often fall into when they write timidly and fear mistakes. It's full of comfortable spoken flexibility.

• *Avoiding the clogging effects of left-branching syntax and too much nominalization.* These benefits come naturally from the lack of time for planning. Right-branching syntax and verbs rather than nouns: these help explain why freewriting tends to be easy to understand. (Admittedly, academic or professional writers who are used to thinking in highly nominalized abstract or even jargon-ridden language will produce freewriting with some of those features, yet the clogging factor is usually much lower.)

• *Language that connects with audience.* You might think that private freewriting wouldn't be very audience oriented, and yet look at that second writer's habitual "you." It could be called just a habitual verbal tic, but it's a habit of orienting one's language to an audience.

• *Gisting or talking turkey.* Freewriting can be digressive and when it's imposed on reluctant students, I sometimes call it "compulsory writing." Some of them just walk the dog in language. I don't complain about that because it's still doing its work of helping students feel comfortable as they write. Nevertheless, most freewriting, as here, *does* tend to get around to some blunt summings up. "Do I really love him?" the first writer asks—and then gives blunt answers. The fact that her answers conflict with each other gives them added point and accuracy. "Good writing" is supposed to be consistent and to "have a thesis," and this, paradoxically, can lead to some fudging and lack of thrust. The second writer—even on the fly—gives a quick summary punch: "Here's my strongest point."

• *Reality as process.* I'll slightly bend Halliday's interesting philosophical claim that spoken language gets truer to reality by representing things as process. I want to point out one of the features of freewriting that I find most precious and helpful for good writing: freewriting tends to enact *thinking in process.* For "good writing" they tell us to begin by "making up your mind," "figuring out your point," "getting a clear thesis." Okay; yet this can be one of the main sources of syntactic and intellectual deadness in so much writing. Freewriting doesn't give us the time to make up our minds, but it gives us the privacy to acknowledge our ambivalence. (As Chaucer says, "The tongue explores the aching tooth.") So even though the conventional argument against freewriting is that it enforces thoughtlessness, Sheridan Blau argues (below) that it actually *invites* thinking that is active and productive. You don't have time to run away from all the thoughts, feelings, and experiences that contradict the way you like to see things. (The speaking gear yields thinking in process; the writing gear yields considered thinking.)

Here's an intriguing minimal claim for freewriting: I've almost never seen a freewrite I couldn't understand—even if it's full of "ungrammatical" language and unexpected swerves and jumps. But I've seen *lots* of carefully composed and revised writing that was too incoherent to understand. This points to a deep fact about writing and language: the incoherence that comes from nonplanning is minor compared to the incoherence that comes from careful planning—unless it's quite skilled. (See essays by Belanoff and Haswell on coherence in freewriting. As writers get more skilled, they seem to exploit better the potentials for productive chaos in freewriting.) I'm fascinated with freewriting and believe that it's too little explored, but again I'll help some readers move along quickly by using an extended box for some further observations about it and for an example of my own freewriting.

• Exercises have an interesting paradoxical relationship to goals. They are "pragmatic" and "useful" and yet they often feel as though they have no goal. For the goal is in the doing. When we practice musical scales or run wind sprints, the goal is not to make music or get to the other end of the field. The goal is to improve our ability to make music and to develop running speed and lung capacity. And sometimes the goal of an exercise is oblique. Simone Weil wrote that struggling over mathematics homework *with care* is a good way to get closer to God. A Buddhist sage famously asked an acolyte to focus full attention on cutting up carrots—as a road toward enlightenment. Those interested in Alexander Technique would say that freewriting is an exercise in *not trying—avoiding "end-gaining"*—learning to move or behave *not* toward an end or goal. The goal is going-through-the-motions.

Thus, thinkers and mystics down through the ages have noted the power of *nonchoosing* or *nonplanning* for deeper insight. Teachers of drawing have long used a visual equivalent of freewriting: the sixty-second sketch where you must keep moving the pencil or charcoal and not lift it from the paper. Here's another example, applied to the writing of poetry. At a conference, Gabriel Rico read us a good poem twice: the first time was just for listening; the second time, she asked us simply to write down the words that struck us as pleasing or powerful. Then she gave us only three minutes to write a poem of our own—on any topic that somehow emerged from having to use all the words we'd written down. The products were often surprisingly successful—even from people who never dared write poetry. Gabriel savored the paradox: she said that the problem with writing poetry is often that we have too much time. (See Works Cited for some of Rico's interesting and important work.)

• By the way, when teachers ask students to freewrite, it's crucial that they join in too. Otherwise students assume that freewriting is just a "baby" exercise that professionals don't need—or a way for stuck teachers to keep students busy. In fact, freewriting usually bears the most fruit for experienced writers. When I'm somewhat nervous while leading a class or a workshop or giving a talk and I ask others to freewrite, of course I make myself freewrite, but the result is often incoherent. I can't harness my mind—or rather, that little harbor of safety gives me permission to *not* harness it. Here's a tiny stretch of something I wrote under these conditions:

What's up what's up what's up what's up what am I doing hello hello hello how am I doing I don't know I don't know I don't know nothing nothing nothing

• When I want people to think about the effect of audience awareness in writing, I ask for a private freewrite and then a public one. The contrast helps most people realize how often their normal writing is permeated by awareness of an audience—and often some anxiety. The contrasting experiences help them realize that they aren't taking enough advantage of the inherent privacy of any early draft piece of writing.

• There are a few people whose freewriting doesn't seem very related to speaking. They write without stopping or planning, but they seem to use a more *conceptual* gear—maybe even a visual gear—than a speaking gear. They just list words or phrases and don't use syntax to connect those words and phrases. They make a kind of generative list. And often there's little sense of voice or any sound in the language they produce. Some people learn this kind of freewriting from a different exercise that's also valuable, and deeply visual: *wordwebbing* or *conceptual mapping*. Write the word or phrase you want to explore in the middle of a sheet of paper; then—quickly, without thinking too much—put down as many other words and phrases as come to mind. If they seem close to the main idea, write them nearer the center; if they seem more distant, write them farther away on the sheet.

• Freewriting has gotten very mainstream. A TV episode of *NCIS* turned on it. A writer was blocked and so did lots and lots of freewriting. A criminal stole the typewriter tapes and committed murders that followed this secret script and thus implicated the writer. It's a little startling that the character uses a typewriter rather than a computer, and that his writing can be read from it. It strikes me that the person who wrote this episode was working hard to get freewriting into a TV show. (See "Cover Story.")

Freewriting for Serious Results

Freewriting is not just an exercise. Speaking onto the page is the way many skilled writers come up with a strong first draft. They do this for a number of reasons:

- It's a fast easy way to get a first draft. Often it's good, occasionally very good.

- It's a good way to avoid the reluctance and procrastination that so often stop us when we want to *start* writing something. Instead of standing shivering on the edge of the cold water—just jump in and move your arms and legs fast.

- It frees us from constant nagging by the internal editor—nagging that tries to make us stop and correct or change the words we've just written—sometimes stopping us from putting down any words. We may not learn to *turn off* that voice for a while, but freewriting lets us refuse imperiously to obey it.

- Freewriting gives us access to the unconscious. When we use a conscious process for writing—deliberately figuring out what we mean and how to say it and choosing our words as we write—we almost invariably close the door to the unconscious. But if we learn to let words tumble onto the page, the process often leads to words and thoughts we didn't expect to write: thoughts or memories or feelings that surprise us. When I lead people who are new to freewriting exercises, I always ask how many wrote things they didn't expect to write or that surprised them. It's usually at least half—and the number goes up as people get more experienced.

- Freewriting frees us from being too impeded or hypnotized by the thought, "I am sitting down to write an important essay [or memo, chapter, book, or poem]." Even if it's our explicit goal to produce one of those entities, freewriting lets us redefine our job right now: simply trying to produce a "stretch of writing," "a few bushels of words." If you'll use freewriting this way, you'll find it's not so hard to move from these "ingredients" to the more defined and structured piece you want to end up with. Of course it might then become hard to shape what you've written into a particular genre for a particular purpose or audience—but it would have been at least as hard if you had set off to produce it directly. And the freewriting will help the final result be better.

As one example of how an experienced writer uses freewriting for serious results, here's what Janet Bean wrote to develop a train of thinking for a project. Her audience is partly herself, but as you'll see, it's also public freewriting directed at me. It started off a collaboration between us and grew into an article we published together (see Bean and Elbow).

> . . . why am I so drawn to this idea of free speech/free writing? I think because I have the feeling that free speech actually WORKS as a widely held concept, but people really don't believe in free writing. We may do a little, undisciplined freewriting in our classrooms, but in the end, it's really all about standardizing language. That's what's school's about.
>
> We must recognize that it's not enough to stand up in front of a classroom and say "freewrite," expecting that this will somehow create an environment that is "free." I think we have to talk about the politics of standardization, about dialect and value, about the relativity of correctness. (you might disagree with me here. I think it's possible, perhaps, to do this through showing—not so explicitly. By having students read diverse,

hybrid texts. By valuing students language in the classroom. I would still argue that you'd be doing political work by action. With Af-Am students, though, what has worked for me is the explicit—along with the action.)

freewriting is transgressive, by its very nature.

we need to free writing (like those posters, FREE MANDELA, FREE THE WHALES)—free writing from the racist and classist practices of educational institutions. ha. no small order, there. But I do believe it. We have to stop believing in a pure standard English. Monocultural language practices. I see my main purpose as a teacher in this learning community for Af.Am. students is to show them that they can draw on Black rhetorical and intellectual traditions. That to be a writer and thinker is to embrace their identity as African Americans.

Freewriting is in many ways the antithesis of "schooled" writing. Yet it helps make good academic writing possible, I think, in the way it makes connections. I'm leaning toward seeing freewriting as a hybrid—that's my goal. I'm guessing that you might disagree with me here—that you like the idea of getting as much speech as possible on the page?

The writer is an academic exploring issues she's long pondered, but you can see how freewriting helped her push them—and in addition how her language has many speech virtues that I explored with the student freewrites.

Here's what she said about how she wrote it when I asked her afterward:

> I wrote it straight through, right on the computer, with pauses to think, but no recursivity in terms of, say, going back to the first paragraph and adding or deleting. I was definitely writing it to you, but in a particular way. I think what I do when I'm writing freely like this is invoke the kind of intimate communication style of conversation. So the idea of audience is important, as is the context of friendship. I'm thinking of your response, as when I say, you might disagree with me here. It does have an auditory feel for me, but not so much "speaking on the page" but "speaking to you on the page." But even as I say that, I can see that some of the way I'm using sentence fragments is more like I'm writing to myself. (Email correspondence)

So far, I've neglected the role of freewriting in producing *form* or *structure*. I've tended to imply that it gives us only *content*—leaving only formlessness or even mess. That happens often enough of course, but sometimes freewriting is a rich source of form, structure, and *craft*. For example, there are quite a few times when I feel I've figured out a good structure or an outline for what I'm trying to write (which is never at the beginning of a project—see Chapter 10, "The Need for Care"); but then I notice how freewriting leads me into a more sophisticated larger structure of thinking or narration or imagining than what I had been able to figure out consciously.

I've only recently noticed a tiny gift of craft that the unconscious has been giving me for a long time. When I sit and try to figure out how to say or write even a very small idea, I often consciously try one phrasing after another—and none of them are satisfactory. But as soon as I write fast out of the *feeling* of what I'm trying to say, I often find better language—sometimes even a metaphor or deft turn of language—that says more accurately what I'm trying to say. Somehow a deft shape of wording hadn't been available to me through thinking.

To illustrate how the unconscious can give us sophisticated writerly structure and craft—not just ingredients or content—consider the following piece.

The Sun Room

Sitting on the floor next to my grandfather in the sun room. Why did he always bring me there first? He would always want to know, "Well, what can I cook you for breakfast?" Mom's off to work. Dad's out of town again.

Christine stays with me. She's the one who always takes my pain. Oh no, after breakfast I hope we go for a walk first, not back to the sun room. By now the blinds were down, and all I could see is the rocking chair blanket on the floor. Not again. I can see only the dark sun shine through the blinds. This time I can't enter this room. I'll let Christine go for me. She always helps me out.

Grandpa says, "Come sit here with me—hold me, lay on top of me." always ending up in a gooey mess. I have to tell Christine to go take a shower before my mom comes home. O, shit, here she is now. Go faster Christine is in the bathroom. Mom's looking for us. God, hurry up, clean up. Mom pulls open the shower curtain to see Christine and says, "Corinna, I told you to be ready when I got home. You have an appointment . . ."

Christine is never around when anyone else is. Christine is my other self.

Corinna Spenard

This is the piece as Spenard published it in the journal *Flying Horse*. But it's virtually word for word what she freewrote in a workshop led by Pat Schneider for low-income women living in the projects. (At the time of writing, Spennard was a single mother with three children and hadn't gone past tenth grade. Subsequently she got her GED degree and is prospering in college. Writing workshops opened the door to writing and played an important larger role.)

Here's the actual text as she wrote it that evening:

[Written at the top of the page] Choose a room in the house you grew up in [this was the prompt]

    [circled] Sunroom
    glass windows
    dark sun
    rocking chair
    [In the upper right side of the page, there's the outline of a five-pointed star with a question mark inside and "I wish. I wish" written above it]

Schneider runs writing workshops or classes that last for eight or ten weekly sessions. She speaks of how freewriting helps her and others to keep on writing, to push away all thoughts of criticism, and to stay attentive to the unconscious. She says the process helps get us sometimes to the place where "the words are white hot."

Schneider has developed a set of conditions that are particularly fruitful for using freewriting to produce good first drafts. In multiple sessions, people write together in each other's presence; she provides leadership to create a supportive climate where people are peers even though some participants are clearly more skilled than others, a spirit of trust in what comes through freewriting, an invitation at the end for everyone to share if they want. The goal of sharing is simply to listen and appreciate, or sometimes to mention a phrase you remember as strong or a section that touched you. (For more about how to set up a group to help everyone write, see her book, *Writing Alone and with Others*. Schneider founded the organization *Amherst Writers and Artists*.)

I'm struck and pleased at how many writers' groups spring up around the country and the world. But it makes me sad that so many people seem to assume that the only point of a writers' group is to critique each other's writing. Writing groups work better—even if only for the sake of critiquing—if some time is devoted to *everyone* doing some writing together and being invited to share at least a scrap of what they have written. This helps people keep in touch with the vulnerability of writing and stay in a very peer relationship. The activity of writing itself, especially freewriting, is a *leveling* activity that tends to put skilled and unskilled writers on the same psychological footing.

As an example of how an experienced published poet uses freewriting for creating a marriage of craft and ideas, here is a poem by Pat Schneider. She published it without a single change from the original nonstop freewrite in one of those sessions. (It's about her relationship to the religious traditions she grew up with, and she reprinted it in her *Writing as a Spiritual Practice,* in press.)

HUSH

Hush. Slow down. Say the names
of those for whom your candle burns.
Say them into the attentive ear
of memory, or of God.
Oddly, now, either one will do.
You are no longer required to believe.
Receive the gift of listening.
Belief is as hard as a hickory nut
that, cracked, holds many mansions.
The faces that you love are chalices.
Hush. Slow down. Tip the chalice,
sip the wine and say it:
all that I remember now are mine.

Two Cousins of Freewriting: Inkshedding and Invisible Writing

Inkshedding: An Application of Freewriting that Foregrounds Speech

It took me many years to see the connection between freewriting and speech, but two brilliant Canadian teachers of writing saw it immediately. Jim Reither and Russ Hunt started with a wild experiment whose explicit purpose was to hi-jack for writing some of the advantages of speech. They taught an entire writing course—from first day to last—during which everyone was forbidden to speak a word. All transactions had to be in writing. "Please open your books to page fifty-seven." Such words were never spoken or heard; they had to be written on the board or put on a handout (and this was before photocopy machines). "Which book?" "I missed last class because I was sick." Students couldn't say these words—only write them on little notes (as though they were deaf). Reither and Hunt were consciously trying to heighten the social and dialogic dimension of writing. They were rubbing students' noses in a conception of writing that was new to most of them: writing isn't just a one-way piece of language that goes from the student and stops with a teacher who grades it— and where the whole purpose of writing is in order to be judged. Long before computers were used for writing, this had an effect we now see in email and online courses: it de-fanged the act of writing and made into a no-big-deal medium of communication between humans.

They called this writing *inkshedding,* borrowing the term from seventeenth-century slang (but generously noting their debt to freewriting). Inkshedding is public focused freewriting for academic purposes. Hunt writes:

> Briefly, it entails informal or impromptu writing that is immediately read and used and responded to by others, and then discarded. A typical ink-shedding situation might occur as a response to a conference paper—the

audience might immediately write for a few minutes, then read a half-dozen other participants' [inksheds], and then move to oral discussion based on the reading. The writing might then be thrown away. (249)

They were consciously and explicitly developing a hybrid between speech and writing—developing the ability to speak onto the page, though I don't see them using that phrase. Reither and Hunt figured out how *speech* evades many of the problems of writing—problems that come from its permanence and cultural weight—especially in the classroom. In speaking, we generate language and thoughts for an audience, but we throw away the words after they have done their work. We let the sound waves dissipate without bothering to save them. Speech as "self-consuming discourse." Hunt and Reither were trying to bottle the advantages of "no-big-deal" language for writing.

But of course they were preserving some of the advantages of writing. They saw some pragmatic efficiencies in writing that speech lacks. Suppose you are leading a classroom or a meeting and your goal is the obvious one that we often avow: we want everyone to learn as much as possible from the thinking of others. Speech isn't very good for this job. In a meeting or discussion only one person can speak at a time—even if there are no floor hogs. With inkshedding, everyone writes simultaneously and quickly, and then the texts are passed around the room and everyone reads simultaneously. The process is surprisingly fast and efficient and it yields the maximum interchange of thoughts in the minimum time. It's not designed to preclude discussion; it can be an ideal prelude to it.

> Inkshedding addresses two difficulties that some people have with freewriting. First, some people feel that the stakes are too low in freewriting: it feels too much like a *mere* exercise—a waste of time. Feeling this way, they have trouble focusing any effort or concentration; mental doors fail to open for them. Second, interestingly enough, a few people feel that freewriting raises the stakes too *high*. They find private writing *more* threatening than shared writing, for they experience *themselves* as the most damning reader of all. They find it easier to write for a reader, even a critical reader, than to be left alone with their own words.

Nowadays we can get the same effect with networked computers or chat rooms, but this technology is not so common in the rooms where we have our meetings or conference sessions. (And Reither and Hunt developed inkshedding way before any of that technology.) Since 1984, the annual conferences of Canadian writing teachers (the Association for Study of Language and Learning) have been titled *Inkshed*. I attended *Inkshed 18* in the spring of 2001 and saw inksheds from individual sessions typed up and put on the bulletin boards by the next morning so they could be read by people who had gone to a different session. For an extended definition and history of inkshedding, see http://www.stthomasu.ca/~hunt/dialogic/inkshed.html.

Invisible Writing: A Version of Freewriting that Foregrounds the Role of Attention

Many things that seem natural and inevitable are artificial. Writing itself, for one. But now writing feels natural and inevitable—and with it, the fact that we can *see* what we write. In 1975, James Britton and some colleagues did some experiments to confirm their natural assumption that the ability to see what you write "is an indispensable feature of the composing process for all writers and for all but the most cognitively simple writing tasks" (quoted in Blau "Thinking and the Liberation of Attention" 284). They used 1970s technology for this experiment: they wrote with spent ball point pens and put carbon paper between two sheets of blank paper. Thus they couldn't see what they wrote, but the words were recorded by the carbon paper. Britton described the experience as completely disruptive: "We just could not hold the thread of an argument or the shape of a poem in our minds, because scanning back was impossible" (quoted in Blau 284).

Britton et al. were English and perhaps it took someone in California, Sheridan Blau, to foster a completely different experience with invisible writing. He repeated Britton's experiment many times:

> At first to my embarrassment and then to my amazement my students, using empty ballpoint pens and carbon paper, wrote competently and with increasing enthusiasm even as they progressed along an [elaborated] sequence of increasingly difficult writing assignments. ("Thinking and the Liberation of Attention" 284)

Why did these peculiar conditions help them?

> Several of them reported that the constraints of the invisible writing procedure actually enhanced their fluency and spurred their creativity. The invisibility of the text seemed to force them to give more concentrated and sustained attention to their emerging thoughts than they usually gave when writing. (284–285)

Computers now make invisible writing easy: just turn down your screen.

Invisible writing reveals the interesting fact that writing is not just writing; it's usually *both-writing-and-reading*. Invisible writing blocks the reading, and this forces us to engage in *nothing-but-writing* (as a disease, this is *alexia sine agraphia*, according to Oliver Sacks). This turns out to boost concentration and intensity of mind. I sometimes use invisible writing when I find myself flagging on a pragmatic less-than-epic writing task such as writing duty letters: I am tired or I don't want to write them. When I turn off the screen, I *can't* stop, and this makes me quickly get my thoughts down—no matter how unlovely their form. It gets me to complete a rough rough draft very quickly, and I find it's not so hard to clean it up. Invisible writing is a particularly crucial exercise for people whose writing is hobbled because they are too finicky. They spend too much time sitting there, trying to decide, crossing out, and reading back over what they've already written. Not-writing is a powerful trap for unskilled and unconfident writers:

> The fact that unskilled writers in their composing tend to reread (on the average) after every four or five words (Schneider), compared to thirty

or forty words for skilled writers (Pianko), suggests that poor writers compose without much of a sense of where they are going, without the kind of tacit or felt sense of an idea that seems to impel the writing of more skilled writers. Unskilled writers seem to compose instead by constantly consulting what they have just said as the basis for what they will say next. (294)

It's easy to see how invisible writing helps brute productivity. We can't dither or we'll lose track of what we are saying. But Blau goes on to make a more striking claim: that invisible writing helps *thinking*. Sounds wrong; and of course it doesn't help precise and careful thinking, which requires slow pondering. What it helps is *productive* thinking—the ability to come up with lots of ideas and to explore them in creative and fruitful ways. He explains this by noting the role of *attention* in thinking and how attention is a limited resource. (Note how Chafe made the same point: we pause in speaking because we can't give full attention to more than one bit of meaning at a time.) Blau argues that if we stop attending to the *written words* (and especially if we stop worrying about issues of correctness), we can give more attention and concentration to our *thinking*—to the incipient *meanings* we are trying to put into words.

> We must not become so numbed by our own educational propaganda about how writing is an instrument for the improvement of thinking (although it is) to forget the irony of the fact that the act of writing is itself one of the principal obstacles to focused, sustained, and insightful thinking for many writers, novice and experienced alike. What invisible writing and freewriting offer us are techniques for overcoming impediments to thinking that are posed most devastatingly for beginning writers but that also challenge most of the rest of us, when faced with the task of producing extended written discourse for a public audience. ("Thinking and the Liberation of Attention" 289)

I never expected to hear something similar from two prolific dedicated empirical researchers, Marlene Scardamalia and Carl Bereiter, because they have been such tireless champions of writing.

> It is indeed worth contemplating the possibility that for most people writing is an impediment rather than an aid to thought. While we have no direct evidence of this, it has been suggested to us continually through comparing what students produce in writing and what they are able to come forth with in interviews and discussions. These oral interchanges reveal substantial pools of knowledge not drawn on in composition.
>
> The contribution of writing to thought is quite possibly a contribution enjoyed only by the highly literate few (not even all who could be called skilled writers). (309)

(On the crucial but subtle experience of attending to meaning apart from the words, see my "Felt Sense.")

I've spent most of my career trying to figure out things that help writing, but I've never come up with anything as useful as Ken Macrorie's simple crude exercise of freewriting. To anyone who has read this far, I make the following announcement in a firm tone:

> Do *not* read (or write) any further till you have really tried out freewriting. Too many people, teachers especially, have come to think, "Oh yes, freewriting. I'll tell my weak scared students about it. I'll introduce it and do it once on the first or second day of the semester and that's all. But it's not for me."
>
> You need to test it out in a disciplined and consistent way—at least half a dozen times—both as a pure exercise and as a way to get words, ideas, and even drafts for a serious project.

I hope that my advice to *try it* will carry more weight when I make it clear that I'm not trying to get you to *marry it*. That is, nothing in this book argues against writing with constant conscious vigilance to every word. In Chapter 10, I argue that conscious care is one essential ingredient for good writing. And if you can produce good writing with *nothing but* unrelenting vigilance, do it. The only thing I'm against is the idea that constant vigilance is the *right* way or the *only* way to write. Especially if you are a teacher who has been tempted to tell students, "Never let down your guard."

And you'll have noticed that I bend over backward not to claim that freewriting always leads to *good* writing. And I especially don't want readers to hear me saying, "If it's spontaneous, it must be good." Still, almost everyone who uses freewriting finds passages they are grateful to have and that they can use with little change. (See Darwin's testimony in the next chapter.) And lengthy freewrites sometimes lead to usable *structures* or organizations that we can't find in our best "careful outlining" mentality.

❖   ❖   ❖

Now that I've given a better sense of what it means to use unplanned language for writing and what the results often look like, I'll use the next chapter to explore other places in the written language all around us where unplanned language can often be found.

I'll list here the places where I write about freewriting. Citations for these titles can be found in the Works Cited. *Writing Without Teachers*, 1973. *Writing With Power*, 1981. "About Resistance to Freewriting and Feedback Groups," 1982. "Toward a Phenomenology of Freewriting," 1989. *Nothing Begins with N: New Investigations of Freewriting* (with Pat Belanoff and Sheryl Fontaine), 1990. "Freewriting and the Problem of the Wheat and the Tares," 1992. "Freewriting" for the *Encyclopedia of English Studies and Language Arts*, 1994. *Writing about Media: Teaching Writing, Teaching Media*, 2008. (With Janet Bean) "Freewriting and Free Speech: A Pragmatic Perspective," 2010.

LITERACY STORY

The Linguistic Brightness of the So-called Dark Ages

I draw on two remarkable books by Maria Rosa Menocal (cited at the end). In both of them she shows that something bright, surprising, and civilized was going on in the period most of us have been taught to call the "Dark Ages." She describes a culture—really a *multi*-culture—that flourished in a huge area of southern Europe and North Africa. It spread up from North Africa through Spain and right around across the north side of the Mediterranean to Italy. It was a huge fluid territory because it was not yet carved up by nation states like Spain and France. The center was Al-Andalus or Andalusia—Islamic Spain. The whole area she calls *Romania*. (Remember the Literacy Story after Chapter 5 about Charlemagne and Alcuin? About how the name "Latin" was stolen from the Latin that was a living spoken vernacular and given to the archaic nonspoken book Latin imported from England? Well "Romance" is what the people's language came to be called. *Romania* is where the "Romance" language prospered—before it divided more fully into Spanish, French, Portuguese, and Italian.)

Menocal's books are learned hymns to a time and place of remarkable multiculturalism and toleration. Muslims, Jews, and Christians lived together throughout the huge region in relationships of remarkable toleration and mutual respect. There was a surprising flowering of Arabic, Hebrew, and Latin culture: all strong and respected—cheek by jowl. And not only did the three great religions live together with little religious conflict; homosexuals and also dark-skinned Muslims from North Africa mixed freely with the other Muslims, Jews, and Christians. As the three main cultures flourished, people moved freely throughout a region of no borders, no nations.

This North African/Southern European culture flourished for something like five hundred years, ending with the non-symbolic date of 1492. In other words, Menocal is focusing on the period that comes just before what we've been taught to call the Renaissance—the "rebirth." It was from the Renaissance that we got the story that the previous era was so "dark." Menocal argues that things were bright in this unrecognized pre-Renaissance period and region—and that the "dawn" of the Renaissance carried a great deal of darkness.

Menocal is particularly interested in language and literature. What she finds are mixings that had mostly been neglected by previous scholars and historians. Most striking was how the three international languages—Arabic, Hebrew, and Latin—permeated this huge region. Arabic was the lingua franca for the whole region, but people of any learning tended to know all three. When Columbus sailed from Spain to "India," he took with him a learned Jew fluent in Arabic—specifically in order to talk to the "Indians" he planned to encounter. He assumed that they, like any civilized people, would speak Arabic:

> [T]he first official diplomatic conversation in the New World took place between Luis de Torres, a Jew of recent conversion, speaking in the lovely Romance-accented Arabic that was the language of both high culture

and stunning nostalgia—and a Taíno chief in the hinterlands of Cuba. (*Shards* 11)

But what particularly interests Menocal is the array of flourishing *indigenous* languages around Romania, for example, Provençal, Catalan, Languedoc—along with the rich bodies of oral and written literature in all of them. (Dante admired and expressed his indebtedness to literatures in Languedoc and Provençal and writers like Arnaut Daniel.) The national languages of Spain and France had not yet suppressed those vernacular languages and massacred many of the speakers.

She celebrates how writers and singers in this culture often created linguistic hybrids—"mongrel poetry" in "mixed" and "bastard" forms that "incorporate the other." The poems engage in the kind of code meshing and switching that have occurred in language contact situations throughout history all over the world. (We seem to inherit in the Western Hemisphere a tradition of code shifting and code mixing among Hispanic and Latino/a speakers.) She celebrates the "aesthetics of difference" and links all this writing with love songs and oral language.

One of the reasons we don't have many of the texts she's unearthing is that they were seen as popular *song* perhaps more than as poetry. That is, they weren't intended as timeless texts to save. She quotes a historian of Arabic poetry who calls this kind of work, "poetry born as song."

> [I]t developed as something heard and not read, sung and not written. The voice in this poetry was the breath of life—"body music." . . . It conveyed speech and also that which written speech in particular is incapable of conveying. This is an indication of the richness and complexity of the relationship between the voice and speech, and between the poet and his voice. It is the relationship between the individuality of the poet and the physical actuality of the voice, both of which are hard to define. When we hear speech in the form of a song, we do not hear individual words but the uttering of them. (*Shards* 260)

To illustrate this linguistic and aesthetic melting pot, she cites a poem/song in one of the main languages of the time and region, Provençal (a language later lost in the bloodshed of establishing "France" as a nation, but now being revived in its homelands). The poem's refrain had always been seen as nonsense syllables—a kind of medieval "hey nonny nonny." Only recently did a European medieval scholar think to knock on the door of a scholar of medieval Hebrew. They discovered the refrain was actually in Hebrew. Menocal and other scholars are working to recover more of this oral poetry.

Darkening

So how and when did we lose this rich tolerant culture? We don't usually ask the question because so many "educated people" didn't know it existed.

Menocal focuses on 1492, the deadline that Queen Isabella and her government and the Church set for all Jews to leave Spain. Columbus couldn't sail from Spain's best port nor get the best ships and sailors because most were being used by thousands of fleeing Jews. At the same time, Spain was also expelling the very Arabs who had earlier been the dominant political and cultural group.

The mood had turned toward *orthodoxy;* religious pluralism needed to be cleansed. The institution of the Spanish Inquisition had been set up more than a dozen years before 1492 to test the "purity" of the faith of Jews who had converted. But the Inquisition didn't take on its horrific intensity till after the expulsion decrees of 1492.

This was also the date of the first grammar of a vernacular language on its way to being the language of the new nation states. Castilian was the language and Nebrija the grammarian, and in the next Literacy Story I'll focus on how he sold his thinking to Queen Isabella. Nebrija's goal was to curb the "*bad*" and *mixed* versions of this language—and all the other flourishing vernacular languages. People would need to go to school to learn to get their language right. Columbus wrote his famous log in the vernacular, but it was corrected into proper grammar by a grammarian soon after he returned, and his original was not deemed fit to save. The "correct" version is all we have. The taste for orthodoxy spread. This was the period when nation states were being born, "national" languages were being imposed on large groups, and other vernaculars were being wiped out. So these national languages needed to be "right" and consistent—not too mixed or variable.

When people value orthodoxy and purity, they often get preoccupied with *language*—no doubt because it is so inherently impure, plural, and constantly changing. In this period, there came to be a privileging of "good language" and grammar and mono-lingualism—and an ultimately victorious desire to write the linguistic riches of Al-Andalus and Romania out of history. There wasn't room any more for the "messy, cacophonous, and painfully disruptive" oral grammar, language, and poetry.

So Menocal resists the orthodox historical story of the Renaissance, calling it a "smoothing over" of history. Muslims and Jews are written out of "our Western" history, and that's why no one ever noticed that the "nonsense" refrain was actually Hebrew. "[W]hat survives is the palimpsest, the accentless narration, . . . [a story of] moving purposefully—struggling inexorably—toward pristine Castilian, or pure Italian, or perfect French" (13–14). She speaks of the enduring power of what she calls the "Renaissance paradigm" or "a powerful ideology that has called itself 'Renaissance'" (*Shards* 13).

It's important to notice that the new Renaissance values she describes are exactly the ones that have been enshrined in most cultures and institutions of schooling everywhere: correctness and purity. Distancing of self and lack of presence in texts was another Renaissance value—whereas presence in language was characteristic of the speech and writing in Romania and Al-Andalus.

Menocal keeps coming back to Petrarch as central and symbolic of the beginning of the Renaissance—1492 also being a year when he was at his height as an influential scholar and poet. He admires the newfound classical texts from Greece and Rome and ancient literary language (unearthing some ancient texts himself). He is repelled by the chaos of cultures and languages all around him—the mongrelism of all the oral poetry and vernacular.

> In his role as arbiter of high cultural standards, Petrarch . . . and the tradition that follows him all the way into our classrooms is horrified by all

the same things that horrify others today: the reveling in pluralities; the refusals to cultivate the great tradition; the writing of literature in the crass dialects instead of the great literary language; the embrace of the popular and ungrammatical into the exclusive clubs only the learned could once join; an ethnic and religious variety that would be unequaled in Europe thereafter. (*Shards* 37)

But it turns out that Petrarch "alone in his room in the dead of night is very much the lover of vulgarity and scatteredness" (37).

> Long were the nights he stayed up until dawn, writing superb love sonnets in the vernacular, and then he got up in the morning and lamented the fragmentation of the self that the invention of the sonnet and poetry in the vernaculars had wrought on his culture, his age. . . . [For this lament] the language of his narrative and his idealized past [was] taut and orderly. (49)

So even though most of Petrarch's work was in Latin, he is best known and admired for his poetry in the *Canzoniere*—written in the vernacular language he thought inferior to Latin and unfit for poetry. These love poems played a dominant role in the invention of the sonnet as a form.

Menocal shows how the spirit of the incipient Renaissance is ominously analogous to our own. Europeans began to want to "fix grammar" and think of the previous age as a "dark" time of bad language and bad grammar. There were forces in the air "calling for clear distinctions, loyalties to self and hatred of others, and, most of all, belief in the public and legal discourses of single languages and single states" (89).

Menocal has two books about this area and period: *Shards of Love: Exile and the Origins of the Lyric* and *The Ornament of the World: How Muslims, Jews and Christians Created a Culture of Tolerance in Medieval Spain*. The first is a rather scholarly book that focuses on lyric poetry and song, but with this focus she builds a rich picture of the remarkable history in the large region she calls *Romania*. The second book aims at a larger general audience and focuses more particularly on *Al-Andalus*. But it also gives a rich sense of the larger multiculture by giving stories of illustrative key persons. There's some danger that in my enthusiasm for her work, I've been too broad brushed. I hope I can encourage readers to go to her books themselves.

8 Where Else Do We See Unplanned Speaking onto the Page?

WITH MY FOCUS on freewriting in the last chapter—especially freewriting as an exercise—I might have given the impression that careless speaking onto the page is an unusual and recent activity. It's not. If we consider all the writing we see or have seen, we can safely assume that a good deal of it was unplanned speaking onto the page. Noticing this will give us a richer sense of the role of speech in writing.

The trouble is that we cannot so easily "notice" whether writing was crafted with care or spoken onto the page in an unplanned process. Think about playwrights and novelists who struggle and revise and tinker to make their dialogue *look* as though it were spontaneously blurted. James Wood argues that if dialogue really looks like speech, it surely was not. He says that Richard Price's

> dialogue shines precisely because it isn't how we speak. . . . Actual speech tends to be dribblingly repetitive, and relatively nonfigurative, nonpictorial. Price, by contrast, awards his characters great figurative powers, endows them with an ability to take everyone's cliches and customize them into something gleaming and fresh. . . . Price reminds us that great comedy is made by the confusion of written and spoken language. (James Wood 79, 81)

(His disparaging generalizations about spoken language are a little exaggerated—fueled by our cultural blindness to the linguistic coherence of speech.)

On the other hand, some passages of writing are eloquently complex but *not* labored: the writer was warmed up and hitting on all eight cylinders and "spoke" that excellent prose without planning or monitoring or crafting. Excellent writers testify to this happy experience, and unskilled writers sometimes find themselves surpassing their most careful work with unplanned freewriting. Charles Darwin makes this comment in his *Autobiography:*

> There seems to be a sort of fatality in my mind leading me to put at first my statement or proposition in a wrong or awkward form. Formerly I used to think about my sentences before writing them down; but for several years I have found that it saves time to scribble in a vile hand whole pages as quickly as I possibly can, contracting half the words; and then

correct deliberately. Sentences thus scribbled down are often better ones than I could have written deliberately. (159)

He marvels that he can get good prose by blurting—by exploiting his mental ability to *not-plan* or *not-control* language. But of course we can be sure that he doesn't hold back from revising when the blurting isn't so clear or graceful. The general principle here is this: it's virtually impossible to tell from looking at words on the page how they were generated; you can't tell the process from the product. (Again, I don't want to imply a simplistic contrast—as though words are wholly blurted or wholly planned. Obviously there is a continuum here. Much writing is produced by a mental process halfway between those extremes, sort of free and sort of planned—or planned here and blurted there.)

In what follows, I'll describe many kinds of writing all around us where we can be fairly confident that people *often* spoke the words onto the page without much careful planning.

Email. An obvious site. In addition, lots of people take part in chat rooms and other e-locations where they sometimes feel they are talking more than writing.

Letters. It's safe to say that *many* letters are spoken in an easy unplanned way through the fingers. When Biber surveyed all spoken and written language (see the Introduction to Part One), letters were one of the most prominent examples of "cross-over" language: *writing* that is more "speech like" than much speech.

Diaries and journals. These are classic sites for easy speaking onto the page. They invite the word "spontaneous" in all its eruptive force. Even though many people write diaries slowly and carefully (sometimes dreaming of their publication or even carefully planning it), I'd bet that most people reading this book have at least sometimes done a bit of nonstop "speaking" onto diary pages—if only for venting.

I see no reason to doubt Virginia Woolf when she insists that she often generated words spontaneously in her diaries. (We might suspect some writers of fibbing about the spontaneity in their diaries, but Woolf wrote so many volumes of diary on top of so much writing—in an interrupted life—that she didn't have time to pretty the picture.)

> I got out this diary, & read as one always does read one's own writing, with a kind of guilty intensity. I confess that the rough & random style of it, often so ungrammatical, crying for a word altered, afflicted me somewhat. I am trying to tell whichever self it is that reads this hereafter that I can write very much better; & and take no time over this; & and forbid her to let the eye of man behold it. . . . But what is more to the point is my belief that the habit of writing thus for my own eye only is good practice. It loosens the ligaments. Never mind the misses & the stumbles. Going at such a pace as I do I must make the most direct & instant shots at my object, & thus have to lay hands on words, choose them, & shoot them with no more pause than is needed to put my pen in the ink. I believe that during the past year I can trace some increase of ease in my professional writing which I attribute to my casual half hours after tea. (Bell; Entry for "Sunday (Easter) 20 April")

Diarists sometimes talk to others or to themselves in their diaries. Anne Frank began her entries, "Dear Kitty." (For a collection of diary and journal writing down through the centuries, see Mallon, *A Book of One's Own.*)

I don't keep a regular journal, but I make periodic journal entries when I'm struggling or perplexed about writing or teaching or life. And occasionally I'll make entries when I feel I've figured something out. Usually they are freewritten—speaking onto the page. Here's a fairly typical entry where I explore my frustration about teaching. I'm using writing not so much to reach a conclusion as simply to explore my perplexity—to try to do justice to the discontinuities in experience.

Now [i.e., finally] I feel comfortable and confident writing. I trust it. I always feel <u>un</u>comfortable, <u>un</u>confident in my teaching. Yet nevertheless—though I don't know how to explain this—I still feel teaching is my profession. I feel deeply cathected to it. I can't just walk away from it. If I were to stop teaching and do nothing but write— and were fully successful and respected as a writer—rich and famous even—I would still feel like a failure because I couldn't figure out how to teach.

Maybe that's the germ of <u>Writing Without Teachers</u>: that I'm simply allergic to teaching. I guess that's true; at least in certain senses. Certainly I have an allergy to making people do things. I just get stuck and anxious when I'm trying to do that. I <u>am</u> comfortable helping people do things they've decided for themselves that they want to do. Yet I have lots of ways I want to push or get people to do things. Lots of wonderful ideas for assignments and even more ideas for what to <u>make</u> people do during an hour or five hours of workshop time.

The germs for my 1973 *Writing Without Teachers* were journal reflections on my struggles with writing.

Blogs. Some blogs are obviously written with great care, but some look as though they were probably spoken spontaneously onto the page. Here's a passage from a blog:

> so I saw superman returns last night, btw . . . seriously. it was as if this film had taken the exact blueprint of my movements, and speed and mapped them out of my dreams. the gentleness and impossible speed, the suspension of gravity. the strength I took from the sun's rays, how they entered my chest. the towering cloud formations, and gathering storms, lightning in the stratosphere and over horizons. everything . . . (Boxer 18)

The language is not like conversational dialogue, but I doubt the language was planned. It usefully exploits the resources of speech. In the last half, the writer seemed to have happened upon a feeling or a meaning-impulse and let unplanned language roll out. Notice all the right-branching syntax. In commenting on it, Sarah Boxer names many of the features of spontaneous conversation:

> The very tone of most blogs—reactive, punch, conversational, knowing, and free associative—is predicated on linkiness. . . . Bloggers assume that if you're reading them, you're one of their friends, or at least in on the

gossip, the joke, or the names they drop. They often begin their posts mid-thought or mid-rant—in medias craze. They don't care if they leave you in the dust. (17)

But just in case we thought that these linguistic features arrive only from the hip regions of the internet, she goes on to show how Plato's *Republic* begins the same way!

Written exams. "*Discuss the causes of the French Revolution. You have one hour.*" It's worth noticing how often exam writing makes students use their tongues for speaking quickly onto the page. When we have only twenty minutes or an hour to write an essay, we *may* do some initial planning, consciously drafting an opening sentence or two, and perhaps some quick final editing (as our teachers urged us to do). But with the pressure of time, soon it's blurting, uttering, "talking onto the page." The final product is often very like informal speech.

I'm intrigued with timed written exams as a genre. Because exam conditions can often give rise to careless language and shallow thinking, many teachers forget to notice that their students' exam writing is almost always *clearer* than their essay writing. Mina Shaughnessy famously explored the placement exams of poorly prepared open-admissions students at City College in New York City and remarks in passing that "it was not unusual to find students at this level doing better on their test essays than on outside assignments" (*Errors* 5).

As a student at Oxford, I spent month after month unable to produce essays for my tutor even though I had a whole week with nothing much else to do. But when I got to the final exams I didn't have time to agonize, I wrote.

Speaking-to-write workshops. Robert Wolf teaches workshops around the country where he encourages participants to do what people in all cultures so often do: *tell* uninterrupted spoken stories of something that seems important to them. But in his workshops, this is only the first step. Afterward he gets participants to sit down and *write* their stories with no struggle.

> [T]hey are urged to write them as closely as possible to the way they told them. This takes all the mystery out of writing. It emphasizes story line, and tells people that they don't need special training to write intelligibly. . . .
>
> To get a reluctant person to attend a workshop I tell them that anyone who can tell a story can write one. Once they realize that writing consists of imitating oral tellings, the problem of getting them to write is usually solved. Very few of those who attend a workshop have not followed through with a written piece. (Wolf, *American Mosaic* 3; see also his *Jump Start: How to Write from Everyday Life*)

Unplanned speaking onto the page that we never see. I alluded earlier to hidden *care*: language that looks unplanned but was actually labored over—which is especially likely when playwrights and novelists struggle to create "spontaneous" dialogue. But now let's look at the opposite kind of hiding—and it's surely much more common: hidden *carelessness*. Much of the excellent well-crafted language we encounter didn't get excellent or well crafted till the revising stage. It started out as careless unplanned freewriting or speaking onto the page—a product of exploratory writing and early drafts. We never see the mess. And let's not forget that some of that crafted writing was actually blurted.

Here's an extended passage from a story Jerry Kelly wrote in a Wolf workshop. Kelly works in real estate and doesn't think of himself as a writer:

[FROM] A CHANGING NEIGHBORHOOD

Where do all these people driving down U.S. 18 come from? Where are they headed? Have they passed through our little town before, or will they come again? Think back to the last trip you took through towns large and small, towns that you had never seen before. What were the impressions that stayed with you, and why? Think about it. Rewind that video tape in your mind and pay closer attention this time. Why can one village stand out so much clearer in your mind than all those other nameless, faceless ones? And which do you suppose our dear Clermont is to most of those passing through in that constant, never-ending parade called U.S. 18. (Wolf *American Mosaic* 166)

It's possible that the participants in Wolf's workshops sometimes wrote slowly and consciously in an attempt to remember the words as they had earlier spoken them, but surely most of them learned to simply trust the nonplanning tongue that had served them well earlier.

Native speakers of writing. Do you remember pig-Latin? When I first heard it from the big kids, I was baffled. But soon I learned to speak it fluently in real time without having to monitor or watch my language. This is a perfect model for how people can learn automaticity in any nonnative or nonvernacular language. "Correct Edited Written English" is no one's mother tongue, but it can be learned and fully internalized. Pig-Latin is easier because we don't have to use different words or grammar—we just have to reverse some sounds. Given all the languages that humans can learn, it's not surprising that some people learn even to *speak* absolutely correct edited written English in real time without pausing or giving any attention to the rules and conventions of written grammar. Usually these are people who write a great deal or do a lot of public speaking. Or they grew up in a family or attended a school where it was required—like wearing a tie.

William Buckley was probably ten years old before he learned to "speak writing," and he learned it well—and this surely helped him become a prolific writer. He once boasted that he "knock[ed] out his column in 20 minutes flat—three times a week for 260 newspapers." When Morton Kondracke needled him about this in *Newsweek*, Buckley wrote a response and spoke of his training at Yale in the class called "Daily Themes" in 1948, "whose single assignment, in addition to attending two lectures per week, was to write a 500- to 600-word piece of descriptive prose every day."

Every few years, I bring out a collection of previous published work, and this of course requires me to reread everything I have done in order to make that season's selection. It transpires that it is impossible to distinguish a column written very quickly from a column written very slowly. Perhaps that is because none is written very slowly. A column that requires two hours to write is one which was interrupted by phone calls or the need to check a fact. I write fast—but not, I'd maintain, remarkably fast. . . .

Anthony Trollope rose at 5 every morning, drank his tea, performed his toilette and looked at the work done the preceding day. He would then begin to write at 6. He set himself the task of writing 250 words every 15 minutes for three and one-half hours. Indeed it is somewhere recorded that if he had not, at the end of 15 minutes, written the required 250 words he would simply "speed up" the next quarter-hour, because he was most emphatic in his insistence on his personally imposed daily quote: 3,500 words. (Buckley "With All Deliberate Speed")

So Buckley and Trollope and many other experienced writers do a good deal of *speaking onto the page*, but it's also hidden. When people are native speakers/writers of correct writing, their prose is liable to be literally *fluent*: it "flows" because they weren't having to pick and choose their words on the basis of rules of grammar. (This explains why so many teachers are tempted to try for the will-o'-the-wisp goal of getting their students to learn the rules so well as to become second nature. Few of those teachers have actually attained this goal themselves.)

> I generalized that we can never tell the writing process by looking at the written product, and I pointed to how humans can learn to speak any language onto the page. But when we see writing with certain large and complex syntactic constructions, we are probably safe in saying that they were constructed, not uttered. As an example, I keep remembering the architecturally chiseled prose of the Chicago/Aristotelian critic R. S. Crane:
>
> > [A] poet does not write poetry but individual poems. And these are inevitably, as finished wholes, instances of one or another poetic kind, differentiated not by any necessities of the linguistic instrument of poetry but primarily by the nature of the poet's conception, as finally embodied in his poem, of a particular form to be achieved through the representation, in speech used dramatically or otherwise, of some distinctive state of feeling, of moral choice, or action, complete in itself and productive of a certain emotion or complex of emotions in the reader. (96)
>
> Matthew Bailey argues that he can distinguish truly oral medieval epics from translations that are only pretending to be oral. He compares versions of the same passages and shows where later writers use subordinating conjunctions and hypotaxis that are absent in the oral version that uses more parataxis (265).

Speaking *excellent* prose onto the page. Trollope and Buckley often achieved more than correctness; they often produced *quality:* writing that is remarkably polished, elegant, and well structured. And yet they often "spoke" it with fluent nonconscious nonplanning. Their words *look* as though they must have been carefully crafted. We see this gift most strikingly in musicians who improvise brilliantly: they create rich, new, intricate, elegantly structured music—on the fly.

Looking at her voluminous diaries (at least five volumes), it's clear that Virginia Woolf developed the ability to relinquish care and planning and still produce prose of remarkable clarity and force—sometimes economy. I cannot help but feel that even when she was writing her great novels, she sometimes got warmed and "rolling" and found herself producing excellent writing without monitoring or planning every word. Of course she was a careful reviser, so when we look at her "careful" published works, some of what we see is carelessness *doubly* hidden: what was careless for her was good—and then she hid some of *that* by making it better still when she revised.

How do people produce good writing fluently and without planning? Is it the quickness of their thinking and decision making—the kind of thing people ascribe to a champion tennis player or quarterback? Humans *can* learn to think very fast, but research on some of those excellent sports figures seems to reveal something else. Some of these remarkable athletes speak not so much of speed (except when they say "I was going so fast, but it *felt* very slow"), but rather of a kind of ease or even calmness. They don't speak of rush or strain but of an intense, all-absorbing concentration that destroys all sense of time.

Mihaly Csikszentmihalyi and a crew of colleagues have done extensive and valuable research that gives scholarly substance to the vague and popular word "flow." They have investigated (and prolifically reported on) all realms of activity—from sports to music to highly intellectual mental tasks—and found that people can somehow manage to get so absorbed in a task in a special way that they can fluently (flowingly) do better than they normally manage—and lose all sense of time, conscious planning, and decision making.

These researchers go on to describe empirically the conditions that seem conducive to this state of transformative concentration and absorption in a task. For one thing, the task must be hard but not too hard. If it's too hard, it stops people; if it's too easy, it doesn't engage enough effort and even struggle. But if the task elicits a certain deep investment, it can produce "a narrowing of the focus of awareness, so that irrelevant perceptions and thoughts are filtered out by loss of self-consciousness" (Csikszentmihalyi *Between Boredom and Anxiety* 72; note the title). When critics speak of a kind of "white heat" in some passages of Virginia Woolf's great novels (and other great work), I can't resist thinking they might have been written in a kind of "flow" condition of heightened intensity.

In the realm of writing, the ancients had a simple word for the process of surpassing one's own normal abilities: "inspiration"—a higher power was "breathing into" the writer (*spire* as *breathe*). But if we don't believe in the Gods, we have to read people like Csikszentmihalyi (and learn to pronounce his name). Two scholars in my field give a good description of what this remarkable process looks like for writers. They point out how people sometimes have the experience of seeming to become one with the text or the writing—the words coming, as it were, on their own. This ideal of flow—fluency—is not aided but undermined when a writer attempts to intervene consciously in the unconscious aspects of the process. (Colomb and Griffin 293)

It's important to note that these two scholars are not "far out" new age types. In fact they reveal their conservative orthodoxy by slipping into what I would call a traditional mis-understanding. They argue that this experience of flow or spontaneity is available only to those who have steeped themselves in *conscious training*:

> As the research unequivocally shows, moments of flow in writing and elsewhere are rare, transient, and the product of past experience and present preparation. In other words, it's the conscious work people have done and now do that makes possible moments of difficult, unconscious achievement—something every thoughtful sports coach, dance or music teacher, and writer knows. (293)

This claim holds up for many skilled activities. You can't play a single decent note on a violin or an oboe without good training. Good tennis players, pitchers, soccer players need lots of training before they can get to a condition of skilled flow. But I doubt whether research has "unequivocally shown" what the two scholars claim when it comes to *producing language*. When they make their conservative claim, they blind themselves to the common experience of many people who lack training but who can nevertheless get to a place of intense involvement in speaking or writing where they "seem to become one with the text"—in which the words "come as it were, on their own." The same goes for singing. It's obvious that people without special training sometimes speak or write or sing in a state of deep concentration, relinquishing conscious planning and control, yet produce excellent work in the way that Csikszentmihalyi describes. (Of course Colomb and Griffin could wriggle out of my objection by pointing to all the talking and singing that most humans do—as a *kind* of "training." But that admission would undermine their obvious teacherly prejudice that only good boys and girls who do all their homework have any hope of writing well.)

"Flow" is a slippery and problematic term especially because it's used so loosely. Many teachers hate it when students praise writing as "having flow." Csikszentmihalyi and his colleagues are referring to "flow" as a mental *process*, not so much to words or product. By the way, the kind of flow state they describe can happen not just in putting out words, but even (as in my experience) in revising or editing.

Dictation: mental speaking or mental writing? Toward the end of his life, Mark Twain would lie in bed each morning with a cigar and dictate his autobiography to a secretary:

You will never know how much enjoyment you have lost until you get to dictating your autobiography; then you will realize, with a pang, that you might have been doing it all your life if you had only had the knack to think of it. And you will be astonished (& charmed) to see how like talk it is, and how real it sounds, how well & compactly & sequentially it constructs itself, & what dewy & breezy & woodsy freshness it has, & what a darling & and worshipful absence of the signs of starch, and flatiron, & labor & fuss & the other artificialities! Mrs. Clemens is an exacting critic, but I have not talked a sentence yet that she has wanted altered. There are little slips here & there, little inexactnesses, & and many desertions of a thought before the end of it has been reached, but these are not blemishes, they are merits, and their removal would take away the naturalness of the flow & banish the very thing—the nameless something—which differentiates real narrative from artificial narrative & makes the one so vastly better than the other—the subtle something which makes good talk so much better than the best imitations of it that can be done with a pen. (Clemens 370–371)

There's no proof that he actually dictated these words (they're from a letter), but everything in the language points to dictation. And who can resist the picture: Twain propped up in bed dictating to a dutiful woman sitting nearby— her dress showing "signs of starch and flatiron" in honor of the great man—the aura of speech mingling with the smell of his cigar. (In our tradition, it seems always to be the woman who takes dictation from the man, but Henry James dictated to a man.)

So when a businessman says, "Take a letter, Lillian," he might proceed to speak careful correct writing; but there's every chance he's implicitly saying something more like this: "Take down my careless informal speech and make writing out of it—literate and correct." It has been common for women to know proper grammar better than men—and for the wife to have responsibility for writing the letters. It is a commonplace that the job of secretary involves knowing more than the boss about how to make writing correct. Twenty and thirty years ago, students in my writing classes sometimes said to me, "I don't have to learn how to write. I'm going to have a secretary and she'll take care of that for me." Nowadays I don't hear this excuse. Many people who used to get secretaries have personal computers now and are expected to turn out final drafts of their own letters.

Let me linger a moment on this image of an overpaid boss who can't write decent prose and relies on an underpaid secretary who can. It's not a pretty picture. He might well be quietly saying to her, "It's not worth wasting *my* high powered executive mind on trivialities of clear prose, grammar, spelling, and punctuation. That's for someone of your low status." (Note, by the way, how often in various cultures, the job of knowing correct language was given to a low-status underling; in the classical world, writing was often enough the job of a slave.)

Yet I can remove the ugliness in this image by internalizing it as a kind of allegory. It strikes me now that as I try to write, I pretend that I'm an overpaid insouciant boss. I just open my mouth and rattle out language with no worries at all about what's right, because "she" will later fix everything for me. This fiction helps me not worry. But of course then I have to turn around and consent to be that "she." At a certain point—tomorrow, next week, next month—I have to try to enter into the mentality of a person who is skeptical, hard-assed, down to earth, critical, probing, and well organized—whose job is to make this writing effective, appropriate, and correct and keep the boss from looking stupid or uneducated. So at this point my image breaks down because as I revise, I can't be a "mere" secretary afraid to challenge the boss's very thinking. I have to be able to say, "The old man can't think straight; he was dead wrong about all kinds of things and sloppy in his logic. I'll have to think it through and cut out some of the stupid things he wanted to say." In short, as reviser we have to be willing to overturn what the dictator said.

Other Dictators—Henry James. I was amazed to learn that James *dictated* the rich prose that he produced in the second half of his career. When he worked on *What Maisie Knew* around 1896, his wrist became too stiff and he hired a stenographer to take down his words. After a month of dictating, he invited the stenographer to take dictation directly onto the newfangled typewriter—instead of taking shorthand to transcribe later. From then on, James dictated to the typist most of what he published.

As you'll see I'm struck with how much of the "good writing" we see has been dictated. But I'm not trying to pretend that dictation always involves unplanned language ("mental speaking"). Some dictating is slow and careful ("mental writing"). But I suspect that even painstaking dictators get certain features into their labored language that benefit from their passage through the mouth.

For example, it's tempting to assume that Twain dictated unplanned language with his mental speaking gear and James dictated carefully with his mental writing gear. Twain's letter is so "speakerly" and James' prose so "writerly." We can imagine Twain letting his words tumble happily along, unstoppable—and James speaking carefully, and continually interrupting himself with a good deal of mental rehearsing and backtracking. But when I look again at James's late prose through the lens of my current interest in speech, I cannot help seeing—hearing—the effects of a *speaking gear*. This perception is supported by a recent biographer of James:

> His practice in the last two decades of his life, of dictating almost everything he wrote, to the stimulating click of the typewriter, means that there is an unparalleled continuity of effect between his published writing, his private writing in letters and journals, and the accounts we have of his conversation. . . . [Arthur Benson reflects on] "the whole process of his thought, the qualifications, the resumptions, the interlineations . . . laid bare. . . . It was like being present at the actual construction of a little palace of thought, of improvised yet perfect design." (Hollinghurst 29)

Note how his late interruptive prose cries out for a good reader's voice to bring the syntactic drama to life. We need to *hear* the complex music of the intonation. His early prose was simpler when he wrote longhand.

Leon Edel, the magisterial biographer of James, notes that

Henry James writing, and Henry James dictating, were different persons. His sentences were to become, in time, elaborate—one might indeed say baroque—filled with qualifications and parentheses; he seemed often in a letter to begin a sentence

> without knowing what its end would be, and he allowed it to meander river-like into surprising turns and loops. . . . Certain indirections and qualifications had always existed. But the spoken voice was to be heard henceforth in James' prose, not only in the rhythm and ultimate perfection of his verbal music, but in his use of colloquialisms and in a more extravagant play of fancy, a greater indulgence in elaborate and figured metaphor, and in great proliferating similes. (176–177; quoted in Honeycutt 309)

Richard Feynman. This eminent physicist was very much a writer—yet in a sense he almost couldn't write. Freeman Dyson tells a surprising story of how Feynman wrote the essay that earned him a Nobel Prize. He was visiting friends who had heard him present the groundbreaking train of thinking that he continued to *not* write up. They finally locked him in a room and wouldn't let him out till he had at least a good draft. Dyson then explains that most of his published books were produced by a *kind* of dictation:

> His many books were not written by him but transcribed and edited by others from recordings of his talks. The technical books were records of his classroom lectures, and the popular books were records of his stories. He preferred to publish his scientific discoveries in lectures rather than in papers. (Dyson "Wise Man" 4)

Note the title of his classic two-volume introduction to the field of physics: *The Feynman Lectures on Physics.* Perhaps in the beginning, Feynman didn't think of his classroom talk and lecturing *as writing,* but after he had published a number of books this way, he surely knew he was using his mouth for writing. And we can be sure he didn't say to himself, "I better speak slowly and *carefully* because this is *writing* that I'm creating with my mouth." Slow care is what *prevented* him from writing. What saved him as a writer, in fact, was his ability to get rolling and open his mouth and speak words that often became fluent—even though they were about technical scientific matters.

Bertrand Russell. It turns out that he dictated *Our Knowledge of the External World.* He tells the story of how it came about:

> I had undertaken to give the Lowell Lectures at Boston, and had chosen as my subject "Our Knowledge of the External World." Throughout 1913 I thought about this topic. In term time in my rooms at Cambridge, in vacations in a quiet inn on the upper reaches of the Thames, I concentrated with such intensity that I sometimes forgot to breathe and emerged panting as from a trance. But all to no avail. To every theory that I could think of I could perceive fatal objections. At last, in despair, I went off to Rome for Christmas, hoping that a holiday would revive my flagging energy. I got back to Cambridge on the last day of 1913, and although my difficulties were still completely unresolved I arranged, because the remaining time was short, to dictate as best as I could to a stenographer. Next morning, as she came in at the door, I suddenly saw exactly what I had to say, and proceeded to dictate the whole book without a moment's hesitation.

I do not want to convey an exaggerated impression. The book was very imperfect, and I now think that it contains serious errors. But it was the best that I could have done at that time, and a more leisurely method (within the time at my disposal) would almost certainly have produced something worse. Whatever may be true of other people, this is the right method for me. Flaubert and Pater [who advised slow scrupulous care in writing], I have found, are best forgotten so far as I am concerned.

Of Ford Madox Ford, Edmund White writes this:

> Like James he often dictated all or part of his novels. . . . Ford fervently believed—and persuaded Pound—that a writer should write "nothing, *nothing*, that you couldn't in some circumstance, in the stess of some emotion, *actually say.*" Indeed Ford's prose, more than that of any other writer of his period, sounds spoken. . . . [H]e tried to evolve for himself "a vernacular of an extreme quietness that would suggest someone of some refinement talking in a low voice near the ear of some else he liked a good deal." This could just as easily be a Jamesian precept and in our own day Colm Tóibín (especially in *The Master* and *Brooklyn*) seems to be subscribing to this hypnotic practice. (29)

Of Dostoevsky, David Remnick says this:

> [Dostoevsky] wrote "Crime and Punishment" and "The Gambler" simultaneously. He knew that if he didn't finish "The Gambler" on time he would lose the rights to all his future books for the next nine years. That's when he hired his future wife as a stenographer and dictated it ["Crime and Punishment"] to her. (Remnick 103)

Tolstoy evidently dictated his novel *Resurrection*.

Isaiah Berlin was famous for his voluminous and brilliant letters, but a jealous fellow historian, A. L. Rowse, called him "dictaphone don" because he dictated them.

An eminent scholar on Emerson points out, "His essays all began as lectures. His writing was first speaking" (Richardson, quoted in Banville 34).

Chandler writes about the widespread use of dictation in the business world (starting, interestingly with Adam Smith). He says relatively few literary writers use the process, but mentions a nontrivial list of notable exceptions: Milton, Goethe, Walter Scott, Edgar Wallace, Paul Gallico, James Thurber, Eugene Ionesco, and popular English romance writer Barbara Cartland. (Chandler 1992c, cited in Honeycutt)

I struggled for my Ph.D. in English literature and worked much of my career in a field devoted to the study of writing, so it's striking to me that I had no idea till now of how much serious writing was produced by dictation. Perhaps it's just my undiligent study, but I suspect that *most of us* have been living in a culture of literacy where the collective memory has forgotten how much important writing started out *spoken*.

Dictation with voice-activated software. When IBM first brought out their "dictaphone," they advertised with a slogan like "Speaking Is a Better Way to Write." (Unfortunately this is from memory and I can't find a definitive source.) Now we have voice-activated software so we can turn our talk straight into text—bypassing the need for a dictaphone and typist. (The makers of *Dragon Naturally Speaking*, probably the best such program, advertise with a slogan that's terrible because no one ever put it to what Flaubert called "the test of the mouth"! "[J]ust say the word and Dragon Naturally Speaking will transform your productivity.")

Voice-activated software works much better than it used to. Originally, you had to speak your words carefully and somewhat separately. But I recently tried a version, and it gets better and better at deciphering your accent and speaking habits as you "train it." The program thus lets you talk comfortably and fast, and after it gets to know your voice, the results are amazingly close to correct. A few words come out wrong because the program misheard your speech (if you said "four door Chevrolet," it might give you "Ford or Chevrolet"). But every wrong word is spelled impeccably and it virtually never misses longer more technical words. Of course it won't give you "correct written English" unless you speak "correct written English." The technology has made plenty of executives wish they still had a secretary.

Ordinary dictation to a human transcriber (whether directly or onto a tape) has long been used by people who have to do quick "write ups" of their observations or findings: doctors, dentists, social workers, and inspectors of various kinds. These documents are often very important as records—sometimes even with legal standing. But they don't need formal language or even necessarily complete sentences—as long as the wording is not ambiguous or imprecise. In many of these workplace contexts, it's fine to speak onto the page quickly and not worry at all about careful organization or the conventions of correct writing. People can speak into a tiny digital recorder that will feed the files to a computer with voice-activated software for transcription into text.

As voice-activated software for writing gradually becomes more reliable and available, it's being used more. Some people who use this technology for more substantial or high-stakes writing (such as serious memos, reports, essays, and even books) try to speak correct writing into the microphone. But the technology naturally invites the kind of rough two- or three-stage writing process that I've used for so long and that I celebrate in this book: speaking or uttering onto the page without trying to get things "right"—often not even worrying about planning or organizing. Then after there's lots of rough but valuable material, revising for thinking, organization, and style, and finally for surface features. (On dictation in the workplace, see Honeycutt and Tebeaux.)

The successful novelist, Richard Powers, wrote a column in the *New York Times Book Review* in 2007 that starts off, "Except for brief moments of duress, I haven't touched a keyboard for years." Powers goes on:

> No fingers were tortured in producing these words—or the last half a million words of my published fiction. By rough count, I've sent 10,000 e-mail messages without typing. . . . I write these words from bed, under the covers with my knees up, my head propped and my three-pound PC—just a shade heavier than a hardcover—resting in my lap, almost forgettable. . . . You'd be hard-pressed to invent a greater barrier to cognitive flow [than having to type everything]. . . . I can live above the level of the phrase, thinking in full paragraphs and capturing the rhythmic arcs before they fade.

He acknowledges that "I needed weeks to get over the oddness of auditioning myself in an empty room, to trust to the flow of speech, to learn to hear myself think all over again."

Amy Butler Greenfield was a writer who came down with lupus and decided to use voice-activated software to carry on her writing career. She used it to produce her excellent and well-received nonfiction book, *A Perfect Red: Empire, Espionage, and the Quest for the Color of Desire*. She used the software for a literal "speaking onto the screen/page"—thereby creating a text with fairly informal language and sentences and ideas that needed reorganizing. For the process of revising and editing, she used her fingers rather than her voice. She had to be strategic at this stage and try to conserve her physical resources. She could only type for an hour or so on many days. But as she put it to me, "Dictation serves as a broad brush. Typing is better for fine changes" (phone interview, October 15, 2006).

Sometimes, in fact, she spoke what functioned as a "*pre*-draft." She dictated her thinking till she found herself in a position to start a new, more focused draft—sometimes by dictation, sometimes by hand or keyboard. She also used dictation for meta-comments to herself: something along the lines of "I'm thinking this, but then I'm wondering about that—and I'm not sure how much sense X makes." She told me that she speaks each day into what she calls a log, letting herself jumble issues from her work and her life.

She used this technology-assisted process not only for *Red* but also for a novel. Even though she cannot use dictation to produce final drafts of texts for readers, she finds she *can* use the software to write the final drafts of speeches for listeners—texts that she herself will speak to the audience (phone interview, October 15, 2006).

When Greenfield sometimes dictates a pre-draft and then abandons it, she is bringing to writing another one of the advantages of speaking. In writing, our goal is usually a product, a text, but in speaking our goal is very often not the words but what we learn from speaking the words.

❋   ❋   ❋

Given my enthusiasms and how my work is sometimes described simplistically, I'd better be explicit again in acknowledging what I hope is already clear: I am not arguing that speaking onto the page (or using mental speaking) is enough for good writing. Darwin kept some of his "carelessly written sentences"—but only after looking at them and deciding consciously that they are good as they are. If we want good writing, we will virtually always need conscious care for revising and editing (mental writing). Chapter 10 focuses on the need for care.

LITERACY STORY

Another Successful Rhetorician in the Court of Queen Isabella

This story helps flesh out the sad ending of the "bright" pre-Renaissance, multicultural realm of Romania that I described in the previous Literacy Story. In that story I mentioned the grammarian Nebrija. He was the first man to write the grammar of a current vernacular spoken language—and as it turns out, of a European national language. This language was Castilian, the mother tongue of his queen, Isabella. In 1492, he told her that her reputation would soon wither unless her language, Castilian, were imposed on all the peoples of her realm—for a variety of different languages and dialects were being spoken throughout the queen's large realm. In fact, Spain was in the process of expelling all Moors and Jews in 1492 and enlarging its territory. "Language has always been the consort of empire, and forever shall remain its mate," he wrote to the queen (Illich 33).

Nabrija also argued to the queen that this Castilian language that was to be imposed on all her subjects must be *regularized*:

> This our language has been left loose and unruly and, therefore, in just a few centuries this language has changed beyond recognition. . . . By means of my grammar, they shall learn artificial Castilian, not difficult to do, since it is built up on the base of a language they know; and, then, Latin will come easily. (34, 37)

Because he was a grammarian of Greek and Latin, Nebrija felt confident that he could tell when grammar was "bad" in any language—among other reasons because he mistakenly thought Greek and Latin were settled unified unchanging languages. (Nebrija's *Gramatica Castellana* was printed in Salamanca on August 18, just fifteen days after Columbus sailed. It is available online. See Nebrija.)

He knew that Isabella was a woman of taste and learning. Illich tells us that

> [h]e is aware that she reads Cicero, Seneca, and Livy in the original for her own pleasure; and that she possesses a sensibility that unites the physical and spiritual into what she herself called "good taste." Indeed, historians claim that she was the first to use the expression. (Illich 34)

So when she initially rejects Nebrija's proposal, she does so from a position of high literacy.

> The queen praised the humanist for having provided the Castilian tongue with what had been reserved to the languages of Scripture, Hebrew, Greek, and Latin. But . . . she was unable to see any practical use for such

an undertaking. . . . In her royal view of linguistics, every subject of her many kingdoms was so made by nature that during his lifetime he would reach perfect dominion over his own tongue *on his own*. (Illich and Sanders 69)

We might assume that Nebrija was partly motivated by concern for the needs of a new technology, printing. Gutenberg had set up his first press fifty years earlier. Perhaps Nebrija thought (as we might) that printing can't flourish without the standardization of language. As Nicholas Ostler points out, the development of printing at this very time should have reinforced the hegemony of Latin as the only legitimate language for writing. But, surprisingly, it turned out that printing seriously *undermined* Latin. Printing turned out to be the medium for lots of romance novels in various vernaculars for new audiences of middle-class readers. In fact it was the *success* of printing that disturbed Nebrija. He was

> upset because people who speak in dozens of distinct vernacular tongues have become the victims of a reading epidemic. They waste their leisure, throwing away their time on books that circulate outside of any possible bureaucratic control. "Your Majesty," [people of our kingdom] waste their time on novels and fancy stories full of lies." (Illich 35)

In short, Nebrija saw printing as a danger. Up till recently, when books had to be copied by hand, they were relatively rare and precious and could therefore easily be suppressed. But with books printed in many copies in many vernaculars, they could not be stamped out.

> It is estimated that before 1500 [only sixty years after Gutenberg], more than seventeen hundred presses in almost three hundred European towns had produced one or more books. Almost forty thousand editions were published during the fifteenth century, comprising somewhere between fifteen and twenty million copies. About one-third of these were published in the various vernacular languages of Europe. This portion of printed books is the source of Nebrija's concern. . . . Vernacular allied to printing would challenge the nation state. (36)

His situation was just like ours as we face the internet. We cannot control what goes onto the internet.

But like Columbus, another good rhetorician, Nebrija won over the queen. As a result schools began for the first time to teach children "correct" Castilian, using Nebrija's grammar. So thanks to the insight of a grammarian who thought all language should be like Greek and Latin, and the power of a strong queen, we now take for granted something that both Illich and Sanders insist is new under the sun: that children and adults cannot be trusted to speak their native language properly unless they get help from professionals—that is, grammarians and schoolteachers.

> Outside of those societies that we now call Modern European, no attempt was [ever] made to impose on entire populations an everyday language that would be subject to the control of paid teachers or announcers. Everyday language, until recently, was nowhere the product of design; it was nowhere paid for and delivered like a commodity. And while

every historian who deals with the origins of nation-states pays attention to the imposition of a national tongue, economists generally overlook the fact that this taught mother tongue is the earliest of specifically modern commodities, the model of all "basic needs" to come." (47)

Henceforth, people will have to rely on the language they receive from above, rather than to develop a tongue in common with one another. The switch from the vernacular to an officially taught mother tongue is perhaps the most significant—and therefore, least researched—event in the coming of a commodity-intensive society. . . . Formerly there had been no salvation outside the Church; now, there would be no reading, no writing—if possible, no speaking—outside the educational sphere. . . . Both the citizen of the modern state and his state-provided language come into being for the first time—both are without precedent anywhere in history. (Illich 36)

As a result of the exceptional events Nabrija set in motion, few people in our culture feel they can operate safely in their mother tongue. Even "cultured speakers" worry about whether they make "mistakes" in what you'd think was their own language. (More about this issue in Chapter 17.)

9 Considering Objections to Speaking onto the Page

NOT SURPRISINGLY, MANY teachers and authorities on writing disagree with the idea of using our speaking gear for writing—putting down words in the unplanned, uncareful, almost spontaneous way we use in casual speech. Those early calls by William Carlos Williams and Hayakawa for fast easy writing (quoted in Chapter 7) haven't been much heard or heeded. Janet Emig is an influential teacher and scholar of writing who declares that

> there are hazards, conceptually and pedagogically, in creating too complete an analogy between talking and writing, in blurring the very real differences between the two. (124)

In this chapter, I'll describe some objections and then work out my responses.

First Objection: Speaking onto the Page Yields Language that's Wrong for Writing

This is obviously true. The vernacular speech that comes most easily to the mouths of even the most mainstream or privileged White speakers is not right for correct writing. (For more on what people mean by "standard" see the Introduction to Part Three.) In our culture we have a situation of *diglossia*—two languages—as do many other cultures: one for speaking, one for writing. This diglossia is very mild for mainstream speakers; many people pretend it's not there. But class and ethnicity give many people a version of spoken English that's much further from correct writing.

In light of this situation it's not surprising to see the traditional approach in teaching writing: *keep speech and writing separate*. I call this the "two-gear approach": use one mental gear for speaking and another mental gear for writing. This approach is widely taken for granted. Teachers traditionally warn students not to confuse speech and writing.

No one can deny that this traditional two-gear approach to writing has worked for many people. Surely much of the good writing we find in the world was produced by the two-gear method. And this traditional approach has an obvious appeal. When we develop a separate gear for writing, we are nudged toward what has always been a tempting ideal: to become a *"native writer of writing."*

What a bother to start off with speech on the page and then have to revise it into writing. Why not learn the language of literate writing early, learn it well, and then use it without having to think about it. Just cruise along in your writing gear. You'll still have to revise early drafts, but you'll be revising only the content, not the language, for those drafts will already be in the language and style or register or mode of writing, not speech. You won't have to ponder which kind of grammar, syntax, and vocabulary are allowable in speech and which are required for writing. This will make life easier. You will have learned automaticity in writing.

No wonder the two-gear approach has become traditional and lurks in our mother's milk. It simply seems obvious that we ought to start out writing in the language of writing.

My Response

I'm not trying to eliminate the two-gear approach for those who find it effective. But I'm disturbed when teachers or others think it's the *only* right way to write. I want another option easily available to all: starting by freewriting or speaking freely onto the page and waiting till the late editing stage to get Edited Written English. Here are some of the advantages I see:

• When people learn to write by speaking onto the page without worrying about correctness, it helps them do what they so often postpone or even dread: *start off* writing projects. Few people can learn to write really well unless they write a great deal and with some pleasure, and few can manage that unless they feel writing to be as comfortable as an old shoe—something they can slip into naturally and without pinching. The traditional method of starting off with proper language may have worked for some, but it's impeded many others—making them feel writing as an alien, uncomfortable, or even impossible enterprise.

• When I speak to teachers about writing, I like to startle them with a provocative challenge: "I'll bet that very few of you have ever written with full attention on what you are trying to say." It's an obvious yet somehow neglected fact that while most people are writing, they are unable to keep their attention from always leaking away from the *meaning* or *thought* they are trying to articulate as they keep trying to notice whether they are writing *well* or *correctly*. It's not just inexperienced insecure writers who always hear that loud interruptive internal voice: "*Wrong word*" or "*Unclear*" or "*Grammar!*" or "*Look it up.*"

• Walter Ong points to the obvious fact that the mother tongue is more deeply connected to the unconscious than any dialect or language we learn later. This is a rich source of not only of memories, thoughts, and images; writing also gains energy, life, and voice when it is fed by the grammar and vocabulary that permeate the unconscious.

• When students and others follow traditional advice and try for correctness at every moment, their language is often stiff, awkward, and unclear. Their attempts sometimes even lead them to the kind of peculiar mistakes people make when they try to use a language they don't know well. Because of this, many people try to play it safe and stick to relatively simple sentences. When teachers look at student texts with this kind simplified or plodding language, they sometimes blame speech—when really it was *fear* of speech that impoverished the syntax. When people let themselves genuinely speak onto the page, their language is more flexible and complex and sometimes eloquent.

• The traditional approach seldom yields what people hope for: the dream of becoming a native writer of correct writing and not having to think about grammar or punctuation or right language as we write. As with any new language, we don't get to be native users unless we use it every day and a great deal. For every William Buckley, there are thousands who write a lot but still often have to stop and ponder a matter of correctness. In fact, the more you sensitize your instincts to help you automatically choose what's correct, the more often you notice tricky problem situations where it's not clear what is correct. (*It depends on who/whom they mean.*) English teachers and copy editors tend to interrupt themselves more than others. For pieces that have to end up in standardized English, there's no way to avoid thinking about the rules. But at least we can postpone that thinking till the end—after we've managed to work out exactly what we are trying to say. The traditional method is supposed to "reduce language interference" by having students ignore their speech as they write, but speaking onto the page in a home language entirely *eliminates* language interference while we write.

• In fact there *is* no single version of "correct, edited, written English" to learn and make unconscious. EWE is not a single monolithic dialect with a single set of rules to learn. Teachers and publishers are notoriously variable in what they insist on as "correct." As with the spoken "standard," it's often not so much a matter of what to include but which "violations" to *exclude*. Some teachers and publishers outlaw all informality, such as using the first person or narrative or statements of feeling—even contractions. Yet other teachers and publishers call it stuffy to *avoid* these features of writing. The dividing line between speech and writing is constantly shifting. More and more serious writers shift back and forth between formal and colloquial language for conscious rhetorical effect—sometimes cheek by jowl. (Here is David Brooks in a serious *New York Times* op-ed column about economic policy: "The doctrine has vanished because this recession is deeper than others and we've run out of other stuff to do.")

• So instead of trying to lock ourselves into a single bland one-size-fits-all "correct writing gear" that we use unconsciously, we're better off delaying till the end many of these decisions about correctness and degrees of formality. Only after we have worked out our thinking, reflected consciously about audience, occasion, and genre, and looked back over a good draft of what we are writing—only then are we finally in a good position to make flexible conscious choices about where to place our text on the spectrum from "high formal" edited "correct written" English to "idiomatic" vernacular-inflected language—and how much hybridization to use.

• The final process of editing and correcting provides an ideal occasion for noticing and comparing the subtle differences in grammar, lexicon, and other conventions between speech and proper writing. This practice in comparative linguistics is a natural way to develop a more sophisticated meta-awareness of language variation and the relationship between speech and writing.

Besides, the grammar of "proper" English is much easier to learn and remember when you compare it and relate it to the grammar we get when we aren't even noticing the words we use. With just a little help from teachers or some readings, students can begin to develop conscious knowledge of the grammar and syntax of *both* systems and see that the rules for correct edited writing are simple and primitive compared to the rich complex rules of spoken English that they've already mastered.

A Deeper Objection: Speech and Writing Are Not Just Different Languages or Dialects. They Are but Different Ways of Thinking or Using the Mind

This objection can be spelled out further:

> If vernacular speakers draft in their home language, they can't "just edit" into EWE. The difference between vernacular speech and what is required for most serious school or workplace essays is not a small matter of syntax and lexicon. As Frantz Fanon famously observed, "every dialect, every language, is a way of thinking." To end up with essayist prose or an academic essay, writers who freewrite or speak onto the page will have to change the very modes of thinking, arguing, reasoning, and organizing that are built into the fabric of their vernacular drafts.

Here is further support for this objection. Vygotsky writes:

> Our investigation has shown that the development of writing does not repeat the developmental history of speaking. Written speech is a separate linguistic function, differing from oral speech in both structure and mode of functioning . . . even its minimal development requires a high level of abstraction. (1962, 98)

Janet Emig writes (in the essay that I quoted at the start of this chapter):

> [T]o say writing is talk recorded [is] an inaccuracy. . . . Rather, a number of contemporary trans-disciplinary sources suggest that talking and writing may emanate from different organic sources and represent quite different, possibly distinct, language functions. (124)

In the Introduction to Part One, I listed these features of careful writing that distinguish it from everyday speech. It is more structurally complex and elaborate; more explicit in having more complete idea units; more decontextualized or autonomous and less dependent on a shared situation or background knowledge; less personally involved, more detached and abstract; more deliberately organized and planned; and characterized by a higher concentration of new information (Biber *Variation* 47). When Olson argued in 1977 that teachers should teach the distinct language of writing, his essay was very influential.

My Response

The premise here is valid: writing in vernacular speech *does* yield thinking and rhetoric that's wrong for essays, reports, memos, and most serious expository writing. (The premise of the first objection was valid too.) But this true premise does not compel the traditional conclusion: that we should try to keep speech and writing apart. It's perfectly feasible to end up with final drafts that represent good essayist rhetoric or academic thinking if we write early drafts woven from vernacular language, thinking, and rhetoric.

I'll point to the history of *freewriting*. Freewriting leads not just to "wrong language" but to wrong thinking and rhetoric: too personal, careless, experience-based, rambling, and repetitive—and unattentive to the needs of genre, audience, and rhetorical situation. Yet for many years, many people have found freewriting a helpful way to start off on the journey to an essay that conforms to a very different kind of thinking and rhetoric. They have learned that it's worth putting up with the early wrongness because of all the benefits. In the early days of freewriting people said that users would be ruined if they got in the *habit* of writing carelessly and ignoring audience and genre—if they began to confuse the easy looseness of freewriting and the kind of thinking that essayist writing demands. But as we've seen, when people learn to exploit the benefits of freewriting, they learn to treat it—loose habits and all—not as the whole job of writing but as a productive stage that leads to revising and editing.

Indeed, one of the nontrivial benefits of freewriting is how it almost forces people to do substantive revising—not the mere tinkering and surface correcting that so many students settle for. When students draft with the language of vernacular speech, they are forced to give explicit and conscious attention to issues of reasoning, genre, audience, and register that are needed for whatever essayist or academic paper they are working on. I love the way I can startle all my students with how I phrase my assignment to revise:

> Your job here is to take your first draft or mid process draft and use feedback from me and your classmates and make the very best essay you can. Work on the substance of your thinking and organization. What kind of reasoning and analysis or arguing does this essay call for? By the way, forget about all issues of grammar, spelling, or correctness for now. I'll ask you to focus on them later.

For I always require what I call a "final final draft"—where the only task is grammar and copy editing.

So I think we've already won this battle. No one fights against freewriting any more—not even the scholars and theorists who call "freedom" a meaningless and harmful word. (See Appendix I, "How Freewriting Went from Dangerous to No Big Deal in the Composition and Rhetoric Community.") Authorities in the field have declared, in effect, that it's legal to write wrong—even at the level of rhetoric and thinking; and countless teachers and students have found it positively *helpful* to write wrong on the way to right writing. One of the most celebrated and photocopied essays about writing is "Shitty First Drafts" by a writer of the first order, Anne Lamott. (It's a chapter in her useful book about writing, *Bird by Bird*.) Consider also the wide success of Natalie Goldberg's *Writing Down the Bones* where she tells writers, "*Don't cross out. . . . Don't worry about spelling, punctuation, grammar. . . . Lose control. . . . Don't think. Don't get logical*" (8). Bruce Ballenger is another advocate of this approach who offers many useful ideas especially for student writers.

Of course there's one argument against speaking onto the page or freewriting or shitty first drafts that's unbeatable:

> *I get along fine using the traditional method of keeping speech and writing apart and starting off writing everything right.*

If someone can say that the traditional two-gear method leads them to genuinely good writing in a process they find satisfying, more power to them. Writing is mysterious and people should stick to any method that works. *But if they have success this way, it doesn't mean they should try to make everyone else* write this way. The fact is, many teachers who tell students to write with constant vigilance cannot themselves write well—and often don't write at all.

Perhaps Quintillian was the first to argue against freewriting—indeed against the idea of rough first drafts:

> A different fault is that of those who wish first of all, to run through their subject with as rapid a pen as possible, and, yielding to the ardor and impetuosity of their imagination, write off their thoughts, extemporaneously, producing what they call a rough copy, which they then go over again, and arrange what they have hastily poured forth; but though the words and rhythm of the sentences are mended, there still remains the same want of solid connection that there was originally in the parts hurriedly thrown together. (from his *Institutes of Oratory*, Bizzell and Herzberg, 405)

James Gee might be called a recent critic of freewriting, at least by implication. That is, he emphasizes that the mode of thinking and rhetoric and seeing the world that goes along with a language or dialect—he calls the whole package a "Discourse"—is something that lives in our bones. He implies that we can't change writing in the wrong Discourse into the right Discourse by a mere process of conscious revising. Presumably, if we want to create writing in that target Discourse, our only hope is to try to learn to *live in it* and *use* it as much as possible.

Another Objection: Speaking onto the Page Will Hasten Impurity and Change in Written Language

It's a truism in linguistics that spoken language changes more quickly than written language. And if people use more of their mouths and ears for writing, this will surely lead to change in the written language. Indeed in my final chapter I invite us to foster rather than fight the process by which our culture is evolving toward a multidialectal literacy that some fear as "anarchy."

My Response: About the Hunger for Purity and Permanence

Here, I agree with the objection itself—that enlisting more of speech will often change written language—but it's the premise I question. Is it so bad for language to change—even written language? The hunger for permanence and purity in language is perennial and deep and has been memorably expressed. Samuel Johnson wrote that the "one great end of this undertaking [his famous dictionary] is to fix the English language." Jonathan Swift agreed, and hoped there would be some way of "ascertaining and fixing our language for ever."

> But Johnson admits that as his work proceeded he came to see that language could not be "fixed" and its continual change could not be halted. The lexicographer finds that the dictionary cannot "embalm his language." The sharing of language by all classes means that language, like manners, must inevitably be depraved, for example by its use in commerce; and its depravity must spread to all its users. The maker of dictionaries cannot cure obsolescence or prevent novelty; all he or she can hope for is to palliate what cannot be cured. Having understood that, says Johnson, "let us make some struggles for our language." (Kermode 29)

As I reflect on people throughout the ages who have complained about change and corruption in language, I think of teachers trading stories of student bad writing: *You think that's bad? Listen to what one of my students wrote!* No one really believes they can stop language from changing; so it must be that we get some relief from complaining. McWhorter likes to complain about the damage caused by spoken language, yet even he cannot resist the fun and energy that speech offers for his writing and for his title: *Doing Our Own Thing: The Degradation of Language and Music and Why We Should, Like, Care.*

Few people go so far now as to say, "I want *purity* in language." But plenty of people feel comfortable saying things like this: "I'm a purist when it comes to [say] split infinitives or prepositions at the end of a sentence." Indeed the ideal of purity goes deep in our culture—and many others. It's helpful here to call on Lakoff and Johnson's notion of "metaphors we live by": unconscious metaphors that permeate not just our language but our thinking. For instance, why should we assume that *unmixed* is better than *mixed*? But *mixed* connotes adulterated or bastardized or sullied. (Steel is stronger than iron because it's a mixture. Sexual reproduction was a big advance over a-sexual reproduction because it mixes the genes of two parents.) For another ingrained metaphor, it's worth noticing how often teachers and others use metaphors of *dirty* for grammar they consider bad ("sloppy, slovenly, slipshod") and *clean* for "correct" grammar. I find myself falling into this metaphor when I hear myself saying that I want to "clean up this draft." (I say I like "clean prose," but that's not really about grammar.)

Richard Boyd has written striking essays on the ideal of "purity" among teachers and language authorities. The title of one of his essays quotes some of this language: "'Grammatical Monstrosities' and 'Contemptible Miscreants': Sacrificial Violence in the Late Nineteenth-Century Usage Handbook."

There was a tradition that ran strong among many nineteenth-century English and German philologists who sought to preserve an alleged "Northern" or "Saxon" purity in the English language. They cherished the "strong sinews" and energy they felt natural to the Anglo-Saxon strain, and they fought to save this from the "effeminate" softening or weakening influences of French and Latinate language. I yield to no one in my love of the blunt energy of the Anglo-Saxon element in English, but I love equally the other more sinuous and intricate flavors that the English language has also taken on in its deep hybridity. (See Richard Lanham's *Style* for a much needed appreciation of rich, more latinate complexities in prose that is not "clean.")

If present-day purists complain about all the neologisms that computers brought in, I reply that they have actually *invigorated* the Anglo-Saxon flavor of English. Some readers will remember when the limitations of the byte forced everyone to use file names no longer than eight letters. This led to short words and energetic wordjamming as in *WordStar*. Even when the technology finally permitted longer file names, there persisted a strong cultural yen for a "tech-y" flavor of short, punchy, hybrid words. People still seem to feel that it's cool to use names like MicroSoft, WordPerfect, TurboTax, YouTube, Facebook, PowerPoint, FedEx, OxFam, Twitter, and so on. Note how words like these often produce trochee wordjams that are perfect echoes of Anglo-Saxon poetry, which is full of words like "whaleroad" for "sea."

Change and Hybridity Are Not the Problem

If we worried less about change and hybridity, we could bring more energy and wisdom to the problem of producing *good* writing, not just correct writing. I can't define "good writing"; I doubt it can be done. But if change is "debasement," then Shakespeare debased English.

It's not just that change is inevitable; in fact there's no such thing as purity in language; what people want to *protect from change* is invariably a product of change. Language changes and then the changed bits intermingle and change more. Carelessness is probably the main engine for change. Thousands of different languages started out as the single Indo-European language. Was that pure? Or was Adam and Eve's language the only pure one? Language evolves and becomes hybrid depending on who the speakers hang out with, what valley they live in, what year it is—and who they get conquered by. The English language is probably more bastardized than most: it's famous for its early mixtures of Anglo-Saxon and Norman French—not to mention Celtic and Viking and even Arabic. In subsequent eras, it's taken on more "alien" borrowing from the rest of the world. This results in a huge vocabulary. English has about 200,000 words in common use, German 184,000, French 100,000.

Because the Vikings visited at various times, we got three words out of just one of theirs: *channel, kennel,* and *canal.* Because the French won in 1066 we have both *pig* and *pork, cow,* and *beef.* But all languages are shaped by these processes of change and hybridity. "No language has ever been found which displays lexical purity: there is always a mixture, arising from the contact of its speakers with other communities at different periods in its history" (Crystal *Stories* 57).

Turning from vocabulary to grammar, it turns out that so-called standard English grammar, right from its origins in London in the late medieval period was an artificial hybrid mixture that corresponded to no one's spoken language. (See Hope in the Literacy Story after Chapter 6. More about this in Chapter 17.) Even the grammar that purists feel as "clean" or "pure" or "correct" is really hybrid and contingent. Consider all the randomisms that resulted from various attempts to "improve" English in the eighteenth century. Language authorities talked about trying to purify, but often they were actually trying to make English more *hybrid* with Latin. *Stop spelling dout that way; it's closer to Latin dubitas if we stick in a "b" to make doubt. Stop spelling amiral that way; it's closer to Latin admirabilis if we add "d" to make admiral.* (No matter that *amiral* was an already accepted Arab word, *amir-al,* meaning the chief or the leader. Other examples in Chapter 17.)

> For an interesting example of hidden grammatical impurity, consider the "s" we put on verbs in the third-person present singular form (*I fall, you fall, he falls*). This third person "s" is commonly explained as the last surviving remnant of the Anglo-Saxon verb system—which put endings on *every* verb form (as in Latin and German). Black speakers are commonly blamed for omitting the "s"—or sometimes praised for simply carrying English grammar where it's been headed all along. (*He fall* sounds unmistakably "Black" to many ears.)
>
> It turns out that this nice "historical" story serves to cover up the fact that third-person singular "s" (so crucial for good grammar) is actually a *heathen error.* The "correct" ending is the "th" form we see in Shakespeare ("she falleth"). "S" was an *Old Norse* form that corrupted our good sturdy Anglo-Saxon "th." When this began to happen, medieval English purists must have gone around muttering, "Why must kids these days speak gutter Norse and degrade our pure English language?" (Or did they call it "terrorist Norse" since the Vikings had wreaked such havoc in the land?) In a comparable lament, medieval purists must have also muttered about low-class types who said "*ask.*" For it turns out that the original verb was Anglo-Saxon *acsian*—which of course we still have in Black English *axe* (*I'll axe him is he coming*). (For both corruptions, see Crystal *Stories* 77.)

Some people think of writing as more pure than speaking. Writing is (allegedly) stable and unchanging—it has rules—while speech is prey to this week's fashion. This mentality led early philologists and linguists to look to *written* texts as the true picture of a language. But writing could be called even more hybrid and random than speaking. Writing is a new and peculiar thing to do with the language that humans had been speaking for thousands of years earlier. Most languages have never been written. The very process of inventing visual languages gave rise to impurities. For it turns out that *no* written language we know of is pure in its basic system for the visual representation of spoken words. We like to brag that we have a purely "phonographic" writing system where our alphabetic letters represent sounds; the Chinese like to brag they have a purely "logographic" writing system where their characters are blessedly *unrelated* to spoken sounds—and thus can be used across different spoken languages. But in fact neither of these claims is true. "[A]ll writing systems use a mixture of phonetic and semantic signs. What differs [from one written language to another] . . . is the *proportion*" (Robinson 14). (For more on this, see the Literacy Story following Chapter 1.)

Look at academic literacy. Each academic discipline has different conventions for writing—conventions that go from the micro-level (footnoting and citations) to the macro-level (what counts as evidence, ways of making an argument, ways of organizing a whole train of thought). No doubt some of the differences stem from differences in the scholarly enterprises, but many of them are contingent and arbitrary.

We see this hybridity even within branches of the same field. Literary biographers get to call Hemingway *Ernest,* but most other literary critics must call him *Hemingway.* When students write "Ernest" in their literature papers they are often felt to be hopelessly naive and inept at any kind of literary work. (How many teachers get around to telling students, "Don't say 'Ernest' unless you are writing biography.") Another example: it is fine to focus attention on your subjective, idiosyncratic feelings when writing psychoanalytic or reader response literary criticism, but it's mostly inappropriate to do so in other modes of literary criticism (even though the critic's feelings often determine the analysis).

In truth, this whole book is a celebration of hybridity and impurity. What could be more hybrid than the process of mentally speaking for the sake of physical writing:

- "Real speaking" is usually out loud with the mouth, but here we speak silently and use our fingers to produce a text.
- "Real speaking" is usually public and dialogic, aimed at listeners in real time, but speaking onto the page is private and may never go to anyone.
- "Real speaking" is not usually for making a text, but that's the goal of speaking onto the page.
- "Real writing" is usually careful and monitored, but speaking onto the page is often blurted and uncareful.

Here is a brief meditation on hybridity from a cultural anthropologist, Renato Rosaldo:

> On the one hand, hybridity can imply a space betwixt and between two zones of purity in a manner that follows biological usage that distinguishes two [discrete] species and the hybrid pseudo species that results from their combination. . . . On the other hand, hybridity can be understood as the ongoing condition of all human cultures, which contain no zones of purity because they undergo continuous processes of transculturation (two-way borrowing and lending between cultures). Instead of hybridity versus purity, it is hybridity all the way down. (Foreword)

Deeper Still: A Final Objection to Speaking onto the Page

I don't think resistance to speech for writing would persist if the only objections were the ones I've addressed. I can't help seeing the resistance as part of something else in our culture of literacy (and in the culture of literacy in many societies): speech is for everyone, but literacy is an exclusionary club. Literacy represents a deep prejudice against what is "low" and "vulgar." (*Vulgar* originally meant "of the people.") Speech—the unfettered human voice—is owned by everyone and is often felt as "common" by "literate" "cultured" people. Everybody masters his or her native language and is fluent in speech at an early age; very few people—even skilled and talented writers—become actually comfortable at correct writing. We get lots of talk about the goal of universal literacy in the United States, but I'd say that literacy still *functions* as a way to keep people out—a way to reinforce privilege, power, and class. (I develop this argument more fully in Part Four.)

LITERACY STORY

Everyone Complains about Language, but No One Does Anything about It—Except Now and Then

Around the fifth century BCE, Koreans began using Chinese characters for writing Korean speech. They didn't have writing at the time and the Chinese had a venerable and well-developed system. Many centuries later, in CE 1446 King Sejong was troubled by how difficult literacy was in this situation.

He gathered the best authorities on language and got them to create a new script that was better for representing Korean speech with no confusions or ambiguities—something easy to learn and easy to read. In promulgating the system, he stressed how different Korean was from Chinese—and how Chinese writing made most Koreans illiterate. Only privileged aristocrats could read and write fluently.

He and his scholars came up with a new system for writing. When it was originally promulgated in 1446, it was called *eonmun*, "vulgar script." In 1912 the name was changed to *Han'gul*, "great script." The creators were

> inspired by the block format of Chinese characters and by the alphabetic principle of Mongol or Tibetan Buddhist writing. However, King Sejong invented the forms of han'gul letters and several unique features of his alphabet, including the grouping of letters by syllables into square blocks, the use of related letter shapes to represent related vowel or consonant sounds, and the shapes of consonant letters that depict the position in which the lips or tongue are held to pronounce that consonant. (Diamond 230)

That is, Han'gul uses *"letters"* that represent individual sounds (phonemes—as our letters do). But they are clumped together into square blocks that each represent *syllables*—larger clumps of sound that actually have meaning. This blocking system makes it easy to see the boundaries between syllables. (Note how English alphabetic writing often obscures the boundaries between syllables. But English isn't as bad as German since that language so often runs together so *many* syllables into one word. Speed limit comes out *Hoechsgeschwindigkeitsbegrenzung*.) As Diamond indicates, some of the individual "letters" inside the blocks even show where or how the mouth produces this particular sound.

In the official 1446 promulgation of the language, it is written, "A wise man can acquaint himself with [it] before the morning is over; a stupid man can learn [it] in the space of ten days." Jason Epstein tells us that King Sejong himself celebrated the new language thus: "A wise man may acquaint himself with it before the morning is over, even the sound of the winds, the cry of the crane, the barking of the dog, all may be written" ("Reply"). DeFrancis calls Han'gul the best, "most scientific" form of writing, saying that it combines the best features of an alphabet and a syllabary (17, 290). The Koreans remain understandably proud of this remarkable form of writing and now mark the very date of its fifteenth-century promulgation as a national holiday (October 9).

The subsequent history bears thumbnailing. At first, Han'gul was opposed by conservative Confucian scholars for obvious reasons. But it took root and soon came to be used widely, especially by women and writers of popular fiction. Perhaps for that very reason, a sixteenth-century king banned its use. But in the late sixteenth century, it was revived and used for many Han'gul novels. In the 1800s it was officially adopted for official government documents. During the occupation of Korea by Japan during World War II, however, it was banned again.

Later in the twentieth century there was a Western-looking movement to give up the block structures and use the Korean letters strung out from left to right—as in English and most Western writing. But Koreans refused to abandon the block syllables, though they adopted the Western convention of writing these blocks from left to write instead of using vertical columns as in Chinese.

Despite the firm establishment of Han'gul, Chinese characters can still be found in South Korean newspapers, and children still learn nearly two thousand Chinese characters in high school. But North Korea abolished Chinese characters in public writing in 1949.

So Korea presents us with a remarkable example of a person with great political power utterly changing a writing system in order to make writing and reading widely available to people without privilege. And in the face of subsequent resistance, the country hung on to this form of writing—a form that invites speech for writing. It's a lovely example showing that it's not really so hard to make a progressive change in writing.

(I've done no firsthand reading about this topic and so in this short account I am relying more heavily than usual on the Wikipedia entry for "Han'gul" [as of November 11, 2010]). The entry is long and extremely detailed, but the writer is a great fan of Han'gul and very enthusiastic—so possibly we should be skeptical of some points. Yet the account seems to rely substantially on a scholarly source, "The Korean Writing System: An Alphabet? A Syllabary? A Logography?" by Insup Taylor.)

10 The Need for Care

Easy Speaking onto the Page Is Never Enough

YOU COULD CALL this book one sided. There's only one chapter on care while I devote all the rest, in effect, to non-care: to what the tongue can do without planning. But I've made it one sided because the need for care is old news and doesn't need my help.

Yet I also imagine a very different critique. Someone might make fun of my main argument in this way:

> You're pretending to be radical, but your whole argument is just a disguised rehash of a venerable old tradition. Aristotle and Hazlitt speak for it—a tradition that says good writing <u>should</u> look like unstudied speech. But these folks had the wisdom and honesty to insist that it takes care and hard work to produce what looks like it came without trying. They don't naively pretend we can get this kind of good writing by trusting what comes for free.

The Venerable Tradition of Care

I don't disagree with that venerable goal in itself. In fact I'll spell it out a bit more. But then I'll argue against some thinking associated with this tradition.

So here is Aristotle:

> We can now see that a writer must disguise his art and give the impression of speaking naturally and not artificially. Naturalness is persuasive, artificiality is the contrary; for our hearers are prejudiced and think we have some design against them, as if we were mixing their wines for them. (*Rhetoric* Book III, 1404b)

Richard Graff summarizes this tradition in the Classical period:

> Throughout antiquity, spontaneity or apparent spontaneity, was held out as an ideal for oratory, an ideal embodied in the famous doctrine that "art should conceal art." For the orator, this demand for naturalness could be fulfilled in at least two ways, either by perfecting his skill in true oral improvisation or by mastering the ability to compose a written text and manage his oral delivery of it so as to make the whole performance seem spontaneous.

In the first sentence of perhaps his most famous essay, Hazlitt in the eighteenth century asks us "to write as any one would speak in common conversation":

> It is not easy to write a familiar style. Many people mistake a familiar for a vulgar style, and suppose that to write without affectation is to write at random. On the contrary, there is nothing that requires more precision, and, if I may so say, purity of expression, than the style I am speaking of. It utterly rejects not only all unmeaning pomp, but all low, cant phrases, and loose, unconnected, slipshod allusions. It is not to take the first word that offers, but the best word in common use; it is not to throw words together in any combinations we please, but to follow and avail ourselves of the true idiom of the language. To write a genuine familiar or truly English style, is to write as any one would speak in common conversation who had a thorough command and choice of words, or who could discourse with ease, force, and perspicuity, setting aside all pedantic and oratorical flourishes. ("Essay VIII. On Familiar Style")

I agree that it often takes great care to produce language that *looks* spontaneous. Novelists and dramatists testify as much. Alan Bennett writes plays that brilliantly render spontaneous careless speech, and his "Talking Heads" are masterful and touching monologues. I'd gotten to know Bennett a bit when I studied at Oxford and have had the occasional tea with him since then; so a few years ago I proudly sent him an article of mine about freewriting or speech in writing. He thanked me on a postcard saying something like this: "I read with grateful pleasure your interesting words about quicker easier writing. Meanwhile, I'm afraid I spend all day trying to write just a sentence or two."

When I listen to the radio or watch TV, I sometimes like to think about all the *writing* in what I hear. Writers produced that text for Diane Sawyer to say—text that is supposed to sound completely unplanned and "naturally" spoken. Not easy; it can't be tossed off. We notice when the writer says something "off" or stumbles with a sentence that's too complicated for natural speech. (At Stanford University, Andrea Lunsford teaches a course on writing for radio.) Consider writers for *Glamour* or teen magazines. They are often highly educated and exert self-conscious sophisticated skill to produce unselfconscious-sounding gushy "teenspeak." When you call up the bus company and ask for help with schedules, you sometimes get the pre-recorded voice of a perky young woman who starts out, "Okay, let's see. I'll do my best to help you." Someone had to write those words. A good critic, Louis Menand, writes:

> [C]hattiness, slanginess, in-your-face-ness, and any other features of writing that are conventionally characterized as "like speech" are usually the results of laborious experimentation, revision, calibration, walks around the block, unnecessary phone calls, and recalibration." ("Bad Comma" 104)

So I'm not fighting the argument for care. The need for care is the theme of this chapter and a premise for the whole book. And I understand why teachers and stylists advise care so relentlessly. Think of all the careless writing in our email boxes, online, in rushed daily newspapers—not to mention careless writing in scholarly articles and student papers.

The Doctrine of Eternal Vigilance

Eternal vigilance may be the price of liberty, but not, I'd argue, the price of good writing. Eternal vigilance may help some people write well; more power to them. But I'm fighting against the doctrine of eternal vigilance as a monopoly: the feeling made to live in so many people's heads that it's the *only* way to write well: *never* let down your guard. As a monopoly it does considerable harm.

Yes, someone like Ian McEwan can make eternal vigilance work. He says that he writes

> without a pen in my hand, framing a sentence in my mind, often losing the beginning as I reached the end, and only when the thing was secure and complete would I set it down. I would stare at it suspiciously. Did it really say what I meant? Did it contain an error or an ambiguity that I could not see? Was it making a fool of me? (quoted in Zalewski 55)

He wrote *Atonement* this way, and many other good and successful novels.

But it strikes me that eternal vigilance will only work if you have what McEwan has: enormous skill, a highly developed conscious taste, limitless stamina—*and* what might be even *more* crucial: the gift of full faith in yourself to believe that you actually *can* find the right thoughts and words. Otherwise, you join the ranks of so many people of talent who give up before they manage to write what they could write. Some teachers and writers will respond, "Of course. No one should pick up a pen unless they have great skill, stamina, and faith in themselves." But that dictum excludes me and it excludes many others who could otherwise write well.

Most of us need *relief* from vigilance if we want to write productively— some time for *no care* in putting down words. Otherwise we choke off the rich supply that is actually available to us all. Most of us write better when we allow ourselves to write down words and ideas before knowing whether they are acceptable or good. I like to tell students that eternal vigilance makes sense in driving; every other car might have a drunk driver who will kill you. But while you write each sentence, it's not so helpful to assume that it could get you in trouble. No one can harm you for a draft you never show them. Wait till revising for that kind of vigilance.

My point in this chapter is that we don't have to choose between vigilance and unplanned vernacular language. Carelessness alone leads to sloppy bad writing. Vigilance alone—staying always on guard even while we are trying to find words and ideas—can lead to unsuccessful writing and it also drags many people down to where they hate or even stop writing.

Here is some writing that was surely produced with unrelenting care. The writer manages to say with complete precision exactly what she wants to say in flawless grammar. Indeed, she is a leading authority on grammar in writing. She's saying that writing is more "developed" if we use a "writtenlike, dense clausal structure." But do we want to read prose like this when she could have said it so much more clearly by using some of the "undeveloped" capacities of speech?

This view of syntactic complexity, capturing the insight that more developed writing packs more information into each clause, and that this density of information is achieved by taking information that might be presented by a less mature writer in a whole clause and constructing it as a modifying element or subordinate clause, became very influential, stimulating other researchers to investigate syntactic complexity. Haswell's (2000) recent large-scale study, a reanalysis of 80 variables from studies of undergraduate writing using factor analysis to develop clusters of features that demonstrate maturity and development, also found increased length and density associated with postnominal modification, prepositional strings, and other structural features. The characterization of written language development as a movement from a more oral-like clause-chaining style to a more writtenlike, dense clausal structure has been useful for researchers in analyzing the written language of developing writers. (Schleppergrell 554)

Yet cold vigilance is exactly what we all need during the revising and editing stages. And we need plenty of it, because revising and editing almost always take *longer* than generating. I spend many more of my writing hours revising than unplanned speaking onto the page. But I need speaking onto the page not only in order to get things written in the first place, but also because it is a mysterious doorway to all the linguistic and rhetorical virtues that I'm trying to show in this book.

My overall goal is to find what's best about speaking and bring it to what's best about writing. One of the *best* things about writing is how it invites care. It gives us time for detached scrutiny and slow, careful, conscious, decision making. When we speak with natural spontaneity or use our speaking gear to write, we mostly *give up* the linguistic virtues of care. But just because we give up care during early stages of the writing process, that doesn't mean we have to give it up entirely. It's not either/or when it comes to care and carelessness. If we want to create good writing, we need *both* mental processes. In fact if we use both, we get a powerful dialectical benefit. That is, it's easier to relinquish careful planning and be creatively and fruitfully generative if we know we are going to come back tomorrow or next month and apply single-minded, scrutinizing care. And it's easier to be rigorously and indeed *negatively* careful when nonplanning has given us a rich fund of words and diverse ideas to choose from—even wild and wrong ideas.

Why Care Is Indispensable

So it's a very traditional view that I affirm: if we want something good, we can't get along without cold scrutinizing vigilance and careful decision making. That is, even though easy freewriting, emailing, and blogging *can* yield short stretches of smart, powerful, charming, and rhetorically effective pieces of writing— even though Darwin *could* sometimes get better sentences with blurting than with care—nevertheless we can't get *sustained* pieces of good writing without the use of deliberate conscious care. Care is particularly needed if you accept my invitation in Part Two to *relinquish* care during the early stages of writing.

In truth, care is *more* essential than carelessness. That is, quite a number of people have written brilliantly using *only* vigilant care, while very few have written well without it. Perhaps it looked in Chapter 8 as though Buckley and Trollope and Woolf learned to write well without care: they became so practiced and skilled as native writers of careful skilled writing that they could produce it as fluently as most of us can speak. Perhaps these writers were so practiced that they could make decisions at lightning speed, or perhaps they knew how to get into an almost tranced "flow" condition where "decisions get made" without any need for conscious attention. Nevertheless, if they wanted to be sure their writing was good, they could not avoid *reviewing with care* what they had written so quickly and well. And even if that review didn't result in any change, it involved a cold careful *decision not to change,* based on a shrewd expert examination. In Chapter 6, I pointed to the good writing that Michael Dyson and many others have produced from spoken interviews where much of the language was surely uncareful speech. But Dyson had to use careful deliberation to choose and organize the good bits—and cut or edit the rest.

Note that careful reviewing is not so much a process of *producing* language as of *examining* it—from the outside as it were—with a detached monitoring, critical mentality. The problem with the doctrine of eternal vigilance for many of us is that it asks us, in effect, to generate language from the outside.

Two Procedures for Using Care to Bring Coherence Out of Chaos

When people first try freewriting or speaking onto the page, they sometimes terrify themselves with the results. They feel overwhelmed by too many informal, inexact words. All these ideas, memories, and images are in the order they came to mind—some of them wrong and some inappropriate for the piece in hand. Ideas, arguments, memories, or plot events are sometimes tangled together and seem inseparable or unorganizable.

For this situation I will suggest two ways to harness care for creating coherence. The first procedure—using collage form—is the quickest and easiest; it leads to a coherent and pleasing piece of writing but not a fully explicit and logically organized essay. It yields a "collage essay"—often an effective way to present thinking or even an argument. But collages are also ideal for stories, memoirs, poems, travel pieces, and interviews. (Dyson's interview essays that I referred to in Chapter 6 border on being collages. See also the collage obituary from *The New Yorker* that I've put at the end of this chapter.) The second procedure is what I call the skeleton process: it's a more consciously conceptual process and a powerful way to create a careful and more traditionally organized essay.

❖   ❖   ❖

Using the *Collage* to Get from Chaos to Coherence

A "collage" in the original sense—as used by painters and other artists—is a picture produced not by painting or drawing but by gluing actual objects on the canvas: bits of colored paper or cardboard or metal or even things like theater tickets. (*Kolla* is Greek for "glue.") For a *written* collage, writers bring together separate, disconnected bits of writing rather than one continuous, connected piece. Often there are spaces or asterisks or decorative dingbats between the separate bits. (Dingbats are the decorative text-separators that you see just above this section.) That may not sound like good writing, but finished collages are often remarkably satisfying and rhetorically effective. At a symposium on fiction, Donald Barthelme said, "The principle of collage is one of the central principles of art in this century and it seems also to me to be one of the central principles of literature" (Menand "Saved" 74).

You'll find many written collages in the world—even though lots of them are not labeled as such. Many articles in newspapers or magazines are really collages. They contain many quick changes of focus but those nontransitions are not marked except with a change of paragraph—yet readers take these jumps in stride. Feature stories in newspapers and magazines lend themselves particularly to collage form. We've all read something like "A Portrait of Lower Manhattan" where the article skips from street scenes to clothing shops to atmosphere to history—from wide-shot overviews to close-up portraits—all with no clunky transition sentences. TV documentaries are almost always collages: they continually jump us from one clip to the next with no transition, and we take this in stride. The collage form is alive and works well. Interviews and interview-based essays are often not so far from the associative, somewhat random collage structure.

A collage can serve as a quick and simple way to produce a finished piece. That is, after you have done a lot of freely and carelessly generated writing, you can just pick out the passages you like best, do minimal revising or editing, and put them together in whatever order strikes you as intuitively interesting or fruitful. Mark Twain thought he was making a joke, but really he was describing the collage: "Writing is easy. All you have to do is cross out the wrong words."

Creating a written collage is fairly quick and painless. It has the added benefit of showing you that there was good stuff buried in all that unplanned, unorganized speaking onto the page that might be discouraging you. It helps you clear away all the distracting clutter and see the virtues.

In truth, the collage form lets us *avoid* the hardest jobs in writing:

- Revising weak passages. For a collage, just throw them away. (You can "cheat" and improve a couple of passages that are weak but seem indispensable.)
- Figuring out the main point and stating it clearly. A collage can work very well even if you haven't figured out your main point or what you are actually saying!
- Figuring out the best logical order for the bits. Instead, let yourself decide intuitively on an order that seems fruitful or intriguing.
- Making good transitions between the sections. The collage dispenses with transitions. (Actually there *are* transitions—invisible but effective: gaps that function by surprise, opposition, juxtaposition, or sly allusion.)

Here are the concrete steps that will yield a collage:

1. Look through all the rough writing (speaking onto the page) that you have written for this piece and choose the bits you like best. Some will be as short as a sentence or two, some as long as a page. If you are working on paper, cut them out with scissors. On a computer, put these passages into a new file and put asterisks or dingbats between them. (Be sure to keep the original file unchanged; you may want to raid it again.)

2. Lay them out in front of you so you can see them all. If you've been working onscreen, print them out and cut them into pieces that you can physically rearrange. Then read through them—slowly, respectfully, even meditatively.

3. Then arrange them in what feels like a pleasing or compelling or interesting order.

4. At this point, you may see you need a couple more bits: missing thoughts or images or stories you want to add. Fine. Perhaps you see your core idea better now and can say it with clarity; or you are moved to write a reflection on it. Or you remember a badly written bit you threw away and see that it's needed. Or maybe you see a good way to write something for an opening or closing bit. But remember that good collages can get along without "introductions" or "conclusions": you simply need a bit that works as a way to "jump into" your piece and another to "close the door" at the end.

5. Next, revise it all—but invite a kind of minimal and purely "negative" approach. See how much you can do by just *leaving out* words, phrases, sentences, or passages that don't work. Omission usually adds energy; addition usually saps it. Of course you'll do some rephrasing, perhaps for clarity or energy, but see how far you can get without heavy rewriting (unless there's some particular section you really want to rework). Reading your words out loud is best for this process.

6. Instead of trying to make nice connections or transitions between your pieces, just leave spaces for asterisks or dingbats.

7. If you want a finished piece, copy edit your collage carefully and type and format it to make it look its best.

By the way, there's a continuum that stretches between collage and essay, so one option is to start with a bare, scanty, and merely suggestive collage—and then revise it *in the direction of* an explicit essay.

Collage is an ideal form for collaborative writing—particularly for people who are scared of writing with others. The collage invites an interesting mix of individual and cooperative tasks. Individually, each person is wholly in charge of her passages; no one has to bend her ideas or style to fit the others; there's no need for any of those frustrating arguments over single words or phrases. (These arguments are often what make people give up collaborative writing. However, solo authors can get feedback on their bits from the others—if they want it.) But everyone collaborates in deciding which pieces to use and what order to put them in. A collaborative collage is often stronger and more interesting if it shows sharp contrasts or even conflicts between different people's visions, points of view, ideas—and even voices and writing styles. It becomes a dialogue or conversation, not a monologue. (See my "Collaborative Collage.")

Using the Skeleton Process for Building a Coherent, Well-Organized Essay from Disorganized Exploratory Writing

With my metaphor of "skeleton," I'm suggesting a process where you start by looking for stray bones lying around on the ground and then gradually build them into a strong coherent "skeleton" that's actually alive. The process leads gradually from chaos to order and uses an especially productive kind of outlining.

1. *Find promising passages.* Read slowly through all the rough writing that pertains to the topic. Read it in whatever random order you find it. Look for any passages that somehow feel pertinent or important. They may be long or short—occasionally just a sentence. Many will be important because they contain a thought or idea or point (big or small); but some will be important because they contain *stories* or *examples* rather than ideas or reasons.

2. *Create bones.* For each important passage, create a tiny summary *germ sentence.* Make it as brief and pithy as possible. If a passage contains more than one idea or point (perhaps it's a longer passage), summarize them all. You can write germ sentences when you choose each passage or wait till you've chosen them all.

In writing these summary sentences, you may need to spell out a point or idea that's not clear or perhaps only implied in your rough writing. If the important passage tells not a thought but rather an illustrative story or example, summarize it too. But try to *say* what it is "about." For example, don't just say "The ad for Coca-cola"; say "The Coke ad implies that Coke will improve your health."

The main thing is this: if a passage of rough fast writing *feels* important in some way for the topic you are writing about, force it to yield a germ sentence. You are creating bones.

Insist that you summarize them in *sentences—with verbs*—not just in single words or phrases. Don't just write "blue-collar salaries"; write "some blue-collar workers earned more than some white-collar workers." The goal of this activity is to create ingredients that will later help you see the *logic* of your thinking. You won't be able to see the *logic* if you just write "the Coke ad" or "blue-collar salaries." Germ sentences might well be questions: "How come some blue collars earned more than some white collars?" It's particularly valuable to make a germ sentence out of an implied perplexity—something you don't understand. Single words or short phrases are mute and merely *point* to an *implied* concept or idea. A little sentence *says something* and has conceptual or semantic energy that helps get you from one idea to the next. Verbs strongarm you into thinking.

Most of all, germ sentences will help you later when you are trying to figure out a sequence or organization. And short is good. That's why I find that informal language is good—even better. To make these ideas as *pointed* as possible, I try to turn them into *blurted speech.* I find that the mental energy I need to crunch my points into *short* kernel sentences with verbs makes my ideas stronger and clearer. Even if a particular "point" is nothing but an example or illustration, the sentence still helps; for example, "he spoke monotone—but his words had power." If you come across the same idea or example again (which often happens with freewriting or easy speaking onto the page), there's no need to write another sentence—except that sometimes a better, more pointed germ sentence springs to mind.

This process will yield a long list of short sentences. They'll be in random order. Fine. You aren't worrying about sequence or organization yet. You aren't even trying to figure out your main point yet—nor decide which other ideas to keep or drop. (If you write these on index cards, it's easy to arrange them in different orders—but I usually get along just writing them on regular paper—which makes it easier to see them all at once.)

3. *Figure out a main idea.* Now look through this long list of kernel sentences or bones—in the order you find them. First just mark or underline the ones that feel important or central. This will help you if you still don't know your main idea—and in fact if you think you know your main idea, you may change your mind if you start by just marking the passages that feel important.

Look through these marked ones and figure out your main idea. Maybe it's obvious at this point. But maybe you still can't figure it out. This happens to me a lot. Maybe all that exploratory writing and thinking has led you through ideas you've thought of before, but now you can see that these ideas are taking you on a journey toward an idea that you've never had before. But you *still* don't quite have it. Maybe there's a kind of *felt but absent* main idea that's been gently tugging at you, tickling you, driving you in your exploratory writing. It's an idea that's trying to hold all this interesting material together, but it isn't here yet. That's a good sign; you are on your way to a piece of new thinking.

But now you have to figure it out. Perhaps *now* you can write out this implied main idea in a crude short germ sentence. But that may be difficult even now. You can sort of feel it—sense the shape of the hole where it belongs—but you can't yet *say* it. In that case then, freewrite some more out of this *feeling* so you can work your way to it. Or talk it through with someone. When you finally have it, you can move on to step four.

Notice, by the way, that if you had made an outline *before* doing the exploratory writing, you never would have come up with this interesting new idea you're now trying to figure out. We're often advised to start off a writing project by making an outline, but that's almost never worked for me. I can never make a useful outline till *after* I've done a lot of exploratory writing. And even then, outlines don't become useful for me till I learn to build them out of germ sentences instead of single words or phrases.

4. *Build the skeleton*—a sequence. Now that you have a sentence for your main point (and of course your main point *can* change later as you write—which can also be a good sign), you can begin to work out a good sequence for your bones, that is, for your ideas, reasons, examples, or stories.

Start by just looking at your main idea and the germ sentences that seem most important. Because you forced yourself to write your points in the form of *sentences*, it will be much easier to figure out how to string those sentences together so they make good sense or tell a good story. More ideas may well come to you during this process—ideas for more germ sentences.

You could call this an outline, but I find it helpful to think of it as a *story outline.* It's made of sentences that tell a kind of *story of thinking*—a story that feels coherent and sensible. It's an outline of *thoughts,* not just single words or single phrases that point to mere *topics* or *areas.* The idea of "story outline" helps me realize that there's no "correct" sequence for my ideas. I'm not trying to write a perfect piece of geometry. I'm trying to build a good sequence of sentences where each point *follows* the previous one naturally, and where the whole sequence is going somewhere and has a felt shape—like a good story.

Most good essays are actually more like stories of thinking than pieces of lockstep logic. There are lots of ways to tell a story well. Good stories can start in the beginning of the events, the middle, or the end. So too with good stories of thinking and good essays. They can start at the beginning, but they can also work well if you start in the middle or with some random interesting story—or even start with the conclusion and then tell the story of how you got there.

As you arrange your sentences to tell a good story of thinking, you may find that there are some gaps—some ideas or points that are missing if you want them all to follow each other in a coherent way. If so, you'll have to write these missing sentences now. It's very common to need more examples and illustrations, though you may not see that need till you actually start to write a coherent draft.

5. *Create a coherent draft.* When I used to make conventional outlines of words or phrases instead of sentences, I always had a hard time writing a draft from them. Somehow the "points" wouldn't "go" into prose. I've found that a story outline of actual sentences works much better. Some germ sentences can even serve as little titles or subheads for a section.

Using the skeleton process for revising or feedback. I've been describing the skeleton process as an early procedure for creating a draft. But it can also be useful late in the process for *revising* a draft essay that you've already worked on or even finished—but which somehow doesn't work. Perhaps you gave the draft to readers and they are dissatisfied, but they gave you all kinds of suggestions that conflict with each other or that you mostly don't trust. If you use the skeleton process this way, it becomes a way to revise a draft or even an already finished piece.

❊ ❊ ❊

The collage form and the skeleton process are disciplined ways to use *care*—not the tongue but conscious cognitive critical scrutiny. They involve standing back and figuring out what we are *trying* to say or *ought* to say, figuring out what order things should go in, and changing or cutting what doesn't work or doesn't belong. They help us come at language with critical detachment from the outside—extricating ourselves from being caught up inside the language and thinking we are generating.

Applying Care and Planning to the *Process* of Writing

I see this chapter as the conceptual hinge of the whole book: no one can get sustained good writing without vigilant, cold, sharp-eyed care. Still, my larger message is that few can write well unless they also know how to *relinquish* care, especially during the early stages of a writing project. Most of us need to welcome unplanned, unvetted, probably-wrong words and ideas onto the page if we want to find rich enough fodder for the vigilance and care we need later. But we can't give up care.

The practical problem then is this: how can we plan and not plan?—be careful and careless? How can we harness the best of both? It's hard enough to learn to pat the top of your head and rub your belly at the same time—and these activities don't fully exclude each other. But when processes exclude each other, like care and carelessness, *time* comes to the rescue: we can be careless and careful at different moments or stages of a writing process.

It turns out that many people who rail against carelessness are not actually very careful about the *process* they use for writing. Some even scorn attention to "process" (just as professors of a disciplinary subject sometimes scorn attention to "pedagogy"). They just carry on writing the way they've always done ("carefully" they'd say) without really thinking it through from a position of critical consciousness. In this final section of the chapter, I want to argue for more conscious care about the very *process* we use for getting things written. Process is a realm where thoughtful deliberation is particularly appropriate.

Conscious conceptual thinking has shown me a writing process in which carelessness and care can interact in a fruitful way. It's a process that is implicit throughout the book.

1. *Generating.* This stage is for exploring on paper and early drafting, speaking onto the page or freewriting in whatever language comes most easily and comfortably to the mind and mouth. The goal is to get down as much material as possible in one way or another.

2. *Substantive revising.* This is often a slow, difficult process of digging in and thinking hard. It's likely to involve plenty of slow pondering. I often find a story outline helpful at this point (rather than at the beginning). In substantive revising, we deal with issues of organization and even genre. For many genres, we need to think about the expectations of those who feel they "own" the genre. As an essay, for example, is this more argument or analysis? As a piece about scientific or sociological process, is it a lab report or an analytical or even argumentative essay about research procedures? As a memoir or personal essay, is it trying to fit a particular tradition or just take its own path—and is it trying for facts and verisimilitude or a purely subjective point of view?

   As narrative, how explicitly present do you want to be as teller? In this book, I mostly neglect substantive revising since I don't see a special role there for the tongue. A big exception, however, is my plea for story outlines. They are built out of spoken sentences rather than static words or phrases. And the notion of *story* outline acknowledges that readers are operating in time, whereas conventional outlines imply the space dimension. (See Chapter 15 for more on this.)

3. *Late revising.* This is for clarity and style. I'll focus on this stage next in Part Three (in Chapters 11 through 14).

4. *Final editing of surface features.* Such features are usually matters of convention. So if the piece needs to end up in "correct" Edited

Written English, this is the time to make the changes that are needed. How formal or informal should it be in register or tone? Even if a piece doesn't have to be in Edited Written English, this final editing step is still needed for typing mistakes and other oversights like inconsistent spelling. (But keep your eye out for the point that emerges in the next section—the Introduction to Part Three: "correct writing" doesn't require knowing *everything* in the rule books; it only requires knowing the relatively small number of no-no's that set off the "error alarm" in the heads of mainstream readers.)

This is the process I've learned to use for writing essays for publication and for this book. Of course when I want to do certain other kinds of writing—diary or journal writing, emailing, and exploratory writing—I can settle for the first step alone. And when I want to write informal pieces that don't matter so much—some letters, quick memos, slightly more important emails, and the like—I can skimp on steps 3 and 4.

In listing four linear steps, I don't mean to sound too simplistic or rigid. If writing is going well, there may be no need to follow this sequence. That is, in the middle of loose freewriting or easy talking onto the page, you might find that you don't get too distracted from your thinking if you stop and do some revising or editing: fix some spelling; completely rewrite some sentences or paragraphs to make them clearer or logical; ponder at length to revise a thought that is elusive or seems wrong. If that works for you, fine.

But if you are not satisfied with your experience of writing—if you are having what feels like too much trouble or anxiety or even pain—what you need may be some genuine rigidity. As you generate words and thoughts, you may need to forcibly *stop* yourself from fixing spelling, improving phrases, or trying to get your thinking clear. For me, unless my writing is going perfectly, I often need to hold a kind of gun to my head and rigidly prevent myself from trying to rewrite a sentence that is positively ugly or stupid sounding when I'm trying to generate ideas or even draft. Otherwise I lose all momentum or even grind to a halt. The thing that slows most writers down—discourages, frustrates, and sometimes swamps them altogether—is the process of continually becoming distracted or derailed by a problem that they could forget for now. Just keep going.

What's most damaging (except for the Ian McEwans of the world) is trying to perfect each sentence before moving on to the next. Face it; you can't know till later how this sentence ought to look. Indeed, you may well have to cut it later, so why struggle now to improve it. Worse yet, you may find later that you really *should* cut it—but you can't bring yourself to do that because you sacrificed so much effort on it and have come to love it as your baby.

It often happens as we write that we come up with an idea (or memory or turn of the story)—but then suddenly suspect that it's not quite right, and this leads us to write a different version or idea. We can't quite figure out which is right. Unless you are feeling very good about your process at the moment, I'd suggest *not* stopping to try to ponder it out. Better, usually, to leave both versions there. Just keep writing out what you are writing. This may even lead to a third version. At this generating stage of things, you are not in a good position even to *know* whether the first, second, or third idea is better. Wait till the revising stage to fix all matters of careful thinking and organization. And wait till the late revising stage for all matters of style and phrasing and tone; *and* wait till the editing stage for all issues of grammar and spelling. I consciously try to stay pretty well within these linear stages and advise others to do the same. I sometimes turn off the automatic spell check and use it only at the end.

Note however: this linear rigidity is only needed in *one direction*. That is, my main problems come from jumping *forward* into revising and editing as I generate. Jumping *backward*—from some kind of revising back into generating—is useful at any point. That is, during any later stages of writing—even when I thought I had finished—I've found it useful to allow myself to notice problems in thinking, organizing, or style. At these moments, I have to be willing to plunge back into the chaos of new generating or organizing—either by talking onto the page or by slow deliberate revisionary thinking. It sometimes takes a page of exploratory writing to help me simply clarify the logic in a single paragraph that's "off." Here then is why all writers tend to breathe a sigh of relief to discover there's no more time left. Without deadlines it's hard to finish anything.

A mainstream journal once turned down an article I submitted because they complained that I seemed to advocate a writing process that was "simplistically linear" and too one-step-at-a-time. Hadn't I heard of all the research about experienced and professional writers using a more "recursive" writing process?

I admit that this overall writing process might seem too much like "cookbook" writing. The skeleton process in particular is a refinement of what I described in *Writing Without Teachers* as a way to get something written when my mind had shut down—because of the panic of a deadline or my sense that I could never figure out my thoughts. I called it "desperation writing" (60ff). Some folks never need this kind of deliberate care over process; occasionally I don't. But scholars and psychologists have often noted how *many* different mental processes need to go on for writing to occur—not to mention halfway decent writing. So maybe it's a useful fiction to proceed as though the task of writing makes it hard to fire on all eight cylinders at once.

Besides, when scholars scorn any talk about "linear steps" in the writing process and wave the banner of recursiveness among "skilled practitioners," they are invoking a misleading empiricism. Are "skilled practitioners" always our best models for the writing process? Many of them experience unnecessary pain and delay—and plenty of them write pretty sad, clunky articles or essays (I remember research involving writers for *Seventeen* magazine). And should we all try to write like Ian McEwan? If I were researching "the practices of skilled writers," I'd explore a practice that's probably more central to success in good writing: the courage to *throw away* what one has labored over with sweat and blood.

The former first violinist of the Juilliard String Quartet, Robert Mann, played brilliantly, but it would be crazy for any student to imitate the ungainly inefficient physical technique he somehow managed to wield. Sondra Perl did foundational research showing how recursiveness tends to be a huge *problem* with novice writers: they tended to stop after almost every sentence or two to read back over what they had written and worry that it might be wrong.

LITERACY STORY

An Example of a Collage from The New Yorker (July 5, 1982)

ROBERT BINGHAM (1925–82)

HE was a tall man of swift humor whose generally instant responses reached far into memory and wide for analogy. Not much missed the attention of his remarkably luminous and steady eyes. He carried with him an education from the Boston Latin School, Phillips Exeter Academy, Harvard College—and a full year under the sky with no shelter as an infantryman in France in the Second World War. Arriving there, he left his rifle on the boat.

One of his lifelong friends, a popular novelist, once asked him why he had given up work as a reporter in order to become an editor.

"I decided that I would rather be a first-rate editor than a second-rate writer," he answered.

The novelist, drawing himself up indignantly, said, "And what is the matter with being a second-rate writer?"

Nothing, of course. But it is given to few people to be a Robert Bingham.

To our considerable good fortune, for nearly twenty years he was a part of *The New Yorker*, primarily as an editor of factual writing. In that time, he addressed millions of words with individual attention, giving each a whisk on the shoulders before sending it into print. He worked closely with many writers and, by their testimony, he may have been the most resonant sounding board any sounder ever had. Adroit as he was in reacting to sentences before him, most of his practice was a subtle form of catalysis done before he saw a manuscript.

Talking on the telephone with a writer in the slough of despond, he would say, "Come, now, it can't be that bad. Nothing could be *that* bad. Why don't you try it on me?"

"But you don't have time to listen to it."

"We'll make time. I'll call you back after I finish this proof."

"Will you?"

"Certainly."

•

"In the winter and spring of 1970, I read sixty thousand words to him over the telephone."

•

"If you were in his presence, he could edit with the corners of his mouth. Just by angling them down a bit, he could erase something upon which you might otherwise try to insist. If you saw that look, you would be in a hurry to delete the cause of his disdain. In some years, he had a mustache. When he had a mustache, he was a little less effective with that method of editing, but effective nonetheless."

•

"I turned in a story that contained a fetid pun. He said we should take that out. He said it was a terrible line. I said, 'A person has a right to make a pun once in a while, and even to be a little coarse.' He said, 'The line is not on the level of the rest of the piece and therefore seems out of place.' I said, 'That may be, but I want it in there.' He said, 'Very well. It's your piece.' Next day, he said, 'I think I ought to tell you I haven't changed my mind about that. It's an unfortunate line.' I said, 'Listen, Bobby. We discussed that. It's funny. I want to use it. If I'm embarrassing anybody, I'm embarrassing myself.' He said, 'O.K. I just work here.' The day after that, I came in and said to him, 'That joke. Let's take that out. I think that ought to come

out.' 'Very well,' he said, with no hint of triumph in his eye."

•

"As an editor, he wanted to keep his tabula rasa. He was mindful of his presence between writer and reader, and he wished to remain invisible while representing each. He deliberately made no move to join the journeys of research. His writers travelled to interesting places. He might have gone, too. But he never did, because he would not have been able to see the written story from a reader's point of view."

•

"Frequently, he wrote me the same note. The note said, 'Mr. ——, my patience is not inexhaustible.' But his patience *was* inexhaustible. When a piece was going to press, he stayed long into the evening while I fumbled with prose under correction. He had pointed out some unarguable flaw. The fabric of the writing needed invisible mending, and I was trying to do it with him in a way satisfactory to him and to the over-all story. He waited because he respected the fact that the writing had taken as much as five months, or even five years, and now he was giving this or that part of it just another five minutes."

•

"Edmund Wilson once said that a writer can sometimes be made effective 'only by the intervention of one who is guileless enough and human enough to treat him, not as a monster, nor yet as a mere magical property which is wanted for accomplishing some end, but simply as another man, whose sufferings elicit his sympathy and whose courage and pride he admires.' When writers are said to be gifted, possibly such intervention has been the foremost of the gifts."

PART THREE

READING ALOUD TO REVISE

*A Role for the Tongue during Late Stages
of Writing*

Introduction: What Is Standard English?

In Part Two ("Speaking onto the Page") I focused on the early stages of exploring and drafting; here in Part Three I focus on the late stage of revising. The theme for Part Two was *treating speaking as writing:* using the speaking gear to get words onto the page. Here the theme is *treating writing as speaking:* taking our good written draft and speaking it to make sure it speaks well. In effect I'm suggesting a circular sequence: at the early stages, language comes from the mouth to the page; at the late stage it goes from the page back into the mouth.

In Part Two, I worked hard to justify an idea that might have sounded wrong: that we can speak unplanned nonliterate language onto the page even when our goal is to produce "correct" writing that is different from speech. Here in Part Three, I have an easier sell: late revising by reading aloud is a venerable practice that has been advocated by good writers and teachers down through the ages. But new interesting issues will arise as I explore this simple, mother-and-apple-pie way of using the tongue for revising.

I want to underline the word *late* here. This reading aloud process for revising doesn't make much sense until *after* we've revised our way into figuring out what we're really trying to say and how to organize it. I pretty much ignore in this book the crucial process of deliberate substantive revising—except for what I wrote in Chapter 10 on care. For *late* stage revising that I turn to now, some people even use the words "stylistic editing" rather than revising. That is, revising by reading aloud is most obviously about getting clear and forceful language. But I insist that the process also leads to clarification of thinking.

A welcome to careful writers. Some of you will find that you simply *cannot* bring yourselves to write by freewriting or using unplanned speaking onto the page as I suggest in Part Two. You cannot stand to produce disorganized and sometimes chaotic writing or let it stay there on the page. I want to assure you that you will probably enjoy the technique I suggest here in Part Three. It is very different from what has gone on before and does not ask you to tolerate even a little chaos. So even if you draft very slowly and carefully, it's almost certain that your late drafts will benefit from the careful reading aloud process I describe in the next two chapters.

One Last Definitional Task: What Is "Standard English"?

Actually there are two "standards" that need exploring because they are both slippery, arguable, or even dubious: "standard written English" and "standard spoken English."

It might be nice to think of the word "standard" as merely neutral—like the platinum rod locked away in a Paris safe that is the "true standard" for what we call a meter. It's merely arbitrary, right? There's nothing *superior* or *inherently correct* about how long that rod is. But it's hard to stop feelings of inherent correctness from creeping into whatever seems merely conventional. In fact, the allegedly neutral "true meter" locked up in Paris is said to be *exactly* one/ten-millionth of the distance from the equator to the north pole along a meridian running through (naturally) Paris. Any other length for measurement would of course be irrational or vulgar. In the United States and England, we don't go in for French hyper-rationality and we use a more arbitrary measure of distance, namely, "feet." But even here there are wisps of "correctness": twelve inches is said to be the length of Charlemagne's foot. That's probably a myth, but wouldn't it be handy to have Charlemagne's foot locked away in a safe! Still, we ran into Charlemagne before for the well-documented act of language standardization that had enormous consequences across Europe (see Literacy Story, Chapter 5).

Most linguists agree that *all* versions of English are equally rich and complex—as long as they've gone through the threshing floor of children's language-creating brains—that is, as long as they are not incomplete pidgins. So I'm tempted to go along with a custom among many sophisticated scholars to completely avoid the word "standard." It's a word that does harm in our culture by silently implying that other varieties of English are inferior or bad or lacking—substandard or "vulgar." So I will often use the term "*standardized* English."

Yet I won't run away from the word "standard" either because it's not the word that does harm; it's the cultural assumption. In fact I find the word indispensable to use now and then because it brings out into the open the erroneous and harmful assumption of superiority. In order to make some of the arguments that are central to this book, I have to look at how our culture uses and thinks about speech and writing. I need some open-eyed, anthropological, critical distance for describing the enormous power that the terms "standard written English" and "standard spoken English" exert. The terms are socially constructed, but that doesn't make them less real or powerful. Implications of royal superiority are more naked in England where they talk about the "Queen's English." But even here, the term "standard English" has enormous ritual power to make many people *want* it and work hard to *get* it, and look down on those who don't have it. (I found it helpful to learn the surprising history of how we got our Standard English in the late Middle Ages—Literacy Story, Chapter 6.)

Standard or standardized <u>written</u> English (SWE). It's alive and well in our culture, but what does it mean? Many varieties of English get into print in various contexts, but "standard" doesn't refer to all of them—not even to everything published in mainstream books and magazines. It refers only to one slice of mainstream writing—but an incredibly important and powerful slice: the slice that people happen to *call* "correct edited written English." When people champion Standard Written English, they sometimes call it "proper" or "correct" or "literate" writing. Some linguists label it the "grapholect" (E. D. Hirsch). To describe it more fully, I'll call on the linguists, Walt Wolfram, Carolyn Adger, and Donna Christian:

> [It] tends to be based on the written language of established writers and is typically codified in English grammar texts. It is perpetuated to a large extent in formal institutions such as schools, by those responsible for English language education. (10)

These three linguists don't actually call it *written* English; they call it *Formal Standard English* or *Prescriptive Standard English*. But they acknowledge that it's essentially written by saying "There are virtually no speakers who consistently speak formal standard English as prescribed in the grammar books" (10). So it's a language that is found only on paper—and only in the texts of certain "established writers," and its rules are in grammar books. So again: standardized written English (or prescriptive standard English) is *no one's* mother tongue.

Standard or standardized <u>spoken</u> English. In the British Isles there might seem to be a clearer sense than here of what standard spoken English is—but that impression might come from the fact that there are so many regional dialects in England that are so different and spoken by so many people. In any event, the British have somehow worked out a language culture that defines the vast majority of speakers' language as nonstandard. "BBC English" is spoken by probably less than a quarter of speakers in the British Isles; "RP English" ("Received Pronunciation"—the highest prestige form that people associate with Eton, Harrow, and the Queen), is now spoken by only 3 percent of the population (Crystal *Encyclopedia English* 365). But these days in England, there is far less stigma than there used to be about nonstandard spoken Englishes—particularly as speakers of various nonstandard versions become prominent in politics and business and often occupy positions of leadership. But I don't sense much tendency yet to grant the term "standard" to all these versions of English that people nevertheless accept as normal and nonshameful. Yet no doubt because of the great power that "good English" used to hold to make people feel ashamed, there's now a good deal of satire and ridicule of it. I know of children who were brought up to speak the best English who adopt at a fairly young age a noticeably divergent or "wrong" accent—which they keep as adults.

You may have noticed that I've managed to write that long paragraph without a word of definition. But defining standard spoken English is notoriously hard. The entry on "standard English" in *The Oxford Companion to the English Language* starts out saying it is "a widely used term that resists easy definition but is used as if most educated people nonetheless know precisely what it refers to." In the United States, defining standard spoken English is even harder. U.S. versions of English are less wildly different than in England, and perhaps there's more of an unspoken assumption that if important people in society speak in a certain way, it must be more or less standard. In fact, standard spoken English in the United States can only be defined negatively:

> If native speakers from Michigan, New England, and Arkansas avoid the use of socially stigmatized grammatical structures such as "double negatives" (e.g., *They didn't do nothing*), different verb agreement patterns (e.g., *They's okay*), and different irregular verb forms (e.g., *She done it*), there is a good chance they will be considered standard English speakers. . . . In this way, informal standard English is defined negatively. In other words if a person's speech is free of structures that can be identified as nonstandard, then it is considered standard. (Wolfram, Adger, and Christian 12)

They point out how this is different from the situation in England:

> The basic contrast in North America exists between negatively valued dialects and those without negative value, not between those with prestige value and those without. . . . North Americans in commenting on different dialects of American English, are much more likely to make comments about nonstandardness ("That person doesn't talk correct English") than they are to comment on standardness (e.g., "That person really speaks correct English"). (12)

It's as though mainstream speakers walk around saying, "I don't know much about standard spoken English, but I know it when I don't hear it." Yet their ears are not very sensitive. There are *relatively* few matters of grammar or accent that set off the "bad English alarm bell."

Here's a story from Geneva Smitherman illustrating the way educated Americans assume that "standard English" means correct grammar—while in fact they mostly don't notice deviations from it (though they tend to listen harder when speakers have a different ethnicity). Smitherman was seeking funding to study employer attitudes toward Black speech, but she was turned down by the head of a research team. He maintained that everybody knew that you had to speak the King's English to get ahead in

America. With my research proposal thus dismissed, I started to leave. As I did so, the research division head turned to his assistant and said, "Listen, can you stay a few minutes? You and me have some work to do." Now, me bein me, I had to correct my man's "bad grammar," I said, "Hey, watch yo' dialect—it's you and I have some work to do." He turned fifty shades o' red, and I split. Naturally, that siggin of mine had shonufff blowed the possibility of me gitten any grant money! (*Talkin* 199)

The man who turned her down assumed that since he had gotten ahead in America, his English must have been standard and correct. This story is quoted by Vershawn Young (68), who goes on to tell a different story. A woman candidate for teaching first-year writing was turned down. She didn't use a piece of invisible bad grammar, she used a piece of *alarm-bell grammar*: "he don't" (70). The committee ears were sharper because she was Black, but that particular usage could have cooked the goose of a White candidate too—implying low class.

Thus *standard* English turns out to cover a wide *range* or *plurality* of different Englishes. In the last fifty years, *writing* too has been moving in this direction of being something that can only be defined negatively: you get a good deal of choice about which forms are acceptable—*as long as* you avoid the no-no's. This development helps support the approach to writing that I have been suggesting in this book (and previously too). If we want to end up with a piece of writing that is called "correct," we can speak onto the page in our most comfortable language or mother tongue and then make the relatively few adjustments that are needed. That is, to achieve correctness, we don't have to *write in it*—we don't have to "upload" an entire language or dialect into our minds. Indeed our final "correct" writing will tend to be clearer and more lively if we use the mentality of our vernacular speech and then get rid of the usages that set off the "bad English alarm" in mainstream readers. (I'm suspecting that the situation in other "colonial" nations, like Canada, Australia, South Africa, might be like that in the United States: that people are willing to use the word "standard" for a broader range of versions of English than in England. Crystal gives a short clear treatment of "standard English" in his *Encyclopedia of the English Language*, 110ff. His *Stories of English* is particularly good for a richer treatment of "standardness." For more about "standard English" and its interesting history, see the early part of Chapter 17.)

11 Revising by Reading Aloud:

What the Mouth and Ear Know

SAMUEL BUTLER IS one in a long line of writers through the ages who have celebrated reading aloud:

> I feel weak places at once when I read aloud where I thought, as long as I read to myself only, that the passage was all right. . . . If Moliere ever did read to [his house maid], it was because the mere act of reading aloud put his work before him in a new light and, by constraining his attention to every line, made him judge it more rigorously. (138)

Joe Williams and Richard Lanham are recent theorists of style who insist on the benefit of reading aloud.

For others who discuss the importance of reading aloud for revision, see Mina Shaughnessy (*Errors and Expectations: A Guide for the Teacher of Basic Writing*), Joseph Williams ("The Phenomenology of Error"), Flower and Hayes et al. ("Detection, Diagnosis, and the Strategies of Revision"), and Muriel Harris ("Teaching One-to-One: The Writing Conference"). Eric Havelock stresses the importance of reading aloud in his "Orality, Literacy, and Star Wars" (141). See Sally Gibson for her "Reading Aloud: A Useful Tool for Learning?"

Here are some composition textbooks that recommend reading aloud as a technique that improves revision: Kenneth Bruffee's 2007 *A Short Course in Writing: Composition, Collaborative Learning and Constructive Reading*, 4th ed.; Linda Flower's 1998 *Problem-Solving Strategies for Writing in College and Community*; Diana Hacker's 2007 *A Writer's Reference*, 6th ed. Richard Lanham's 2006 *The Longman Guide to Revising Prose*; Donald Murray's 2004 *The Craft of Revision*, 5th ed.; Judith Nadell, John Langan, and Eliza A. Comodromos's 2006 *The Longman Writer: Rhetoric, Reader, Handbook*, 6th ed.; Joy M. Reid's 2000, *The Process of Composition*, 3rd ed.; Lynn Quitman Troyka w / Douglas Hesse's 2005 *Simon and Schuster's Handbook for Writers*, 7th ed.; Joseph Williams's 2005 *Style: Ten Lessons in Clarity and Grace*, 8th ed. Thanks to Debbie Rowe for these citations.

Consider the long tradition at Oxford and Cambridge where virtually all undergraduate writing is read aloud to a tutor who (in my day at least) never saw the writing. Most of those colleges now save money by having group tutorials, but I gather that even so, students still read their essays aloud. Because of the power and prestige that Oxford and Cambridge had down through the centuries (graduates were given, in effect, *two* votes in national elections until 1935), a large portion of prominent politicians, scholars, and leaders of society up till recent times had undergone three years of this weekly ritual: writing essays that they had to read aloud and that were evaluated entirely on the basis of hearing. I think this may explain something I've noticed till recently about English scholarly and political writing: it seems more accessible, spoken, and free of jargon than the same genres in German and U.S. academic writing. Even the most scholarly of English academic books have, at least until recently, tended to avoid what we often think of as "normal" academic tangledness.

Down through the ages, one of the most venerable exercises for learning to write has been to imitate the style of a respected writer—and this exercise often begins with reading aloud passages from the model author. Reading aloud is how you get a style into your bones so you can reproduce it without planning.

Reading aloud works best for revising when we read to live listeners. Their presence sucks us into somehow hearing as though through *their* ears. Still, solitary reading aloud is remarkably powerful for late revising. It's even powerful to "read aloud inside our heads"—not making sounds but moving our lips. I confess I sometimes settle for this; but it's an imperfect shortcut, and I always get better results if I can force myself to say the words out loud.

In this chapter and the next, I'll describe some concrete practical workshop activities for teaching the practice. For reading aloud is not so effective unless it's somewhat disciplined—not haphazard. But the chapters are animated by a larger slightly theoretical question: how does reading aloud improve prose? A satisfactory answer turns out to be complex and interesting, but I'll begin with the simple claim that I use with first-year students:

> Readers will find your writing clearer and more inviting when your language is *comfortable to say aloud*. When it is, readers don't have to work as hard to understand your words. They seem to *hear* the meaning come up off the page.

I find that when students have the repeated experience of reading their writing aloud, they are more likely to write sentences that are inviting and comfortable to recite—which in turn makes the sentences better for readers who get them in silence. Putting this differently, the *sound* of written words is a crucial benefit for silent readers, yet too few students *hear* the words they write. When they have to read their writing aloud frequently and thus hear it, they tend to *listen* more as they write—and readers *hear* more meaning as they read.

In my teaching, therefore, I build in as many occasions as I can for reading aloud—using all stages of the writing process. Most of these occasions involve no feedback. Thus the reading aloud takes very little class time:

- When I get the whole class to do public freewriting or inkshedding (not private writing), I almost always have us all read our words aloud in pairs or small groups.
- When students are working on essays, I have them read very early drafts to each other in pairs and small groups—not for any feedback

but simply so people can hear their draft thinking aloud. If the essays are on the same topic, they can discuss the topic after they've heard two or three drafts.

- For feedback, I have them read their middle drafts in pairs or groups. For feedback, people need to read their draft twice. (See *Writing With Power* for ways to handle this.)
- Even when I ask students to give paper copies of their drafts to each other for feedback to be written at home, I always ask them to prepare the ground by reading their drafts aloud to their responders in class before taking the paper copies home.
- When students have finished final drafts, I often ask them to read the whole thing in pairs—again, not for feedback but simply to celebrate being done. (Even at this final stage, students often hear problems in what they wrote, but after all the revising they've done I love saying, "We can't revise forever. Let's just call it done for now.")
- Sometimes I ask everyone to give a celebratory reading of a paragraph or two of their final draft to the whole class.

Furthermore, it's become a staple in my teaching of first-year writing to have frequent ten- or fifteen-minute conferences with students during which they read aloud whatever version of the current essay they have in hand. (I meet with half the class each week.) When they stumble over a tangle—or even just mumble—I say, "Read it slowly, read it lovingly, pay attention to how it feels." Then I can say, "Try another way to say this. See if you can say it so it feels good in your mouth and sounds right in your ear." One of the great benefits of writing centers is that tutors normally ask students to read their writing aloud.

Of course many people have had painful experiences reading aloud in school. It functioned as a test of reading and they were criticized for every mistake. So now they need support for all this reading aloud. But when I'm present (as when they read to me alone or to the whole class or when I visit a small group), I struggle for a way to be supportive while I push hard. I'll sometimes stop them: "Please, please, stop rushing, stop mumbling. Don't be so *mean* to us. We want to *hear* your words. Don't trash your own writing." With the whole class I sometimes use some odd but effective micro-exercises that I learned from John Schultz, in what he calls "Story Workshops." For example, make your voice go way up and way down on every other syllable or every other word; or read alternate syllables very loud and very soft. These are exercises in artificiality, in letting yourself sound foolish, in getting over embarrassment. The goal is to try to stop running away from the sound of your own voice—even revel in it. The moral is radical: you can't write well unless you are willing to make a fool of yourself—especially if you want your writing to do more than merely soothe readers into staying comfortable with how they already see things. These odd exercises improve student reading very quickly.

In the end, the easiest way to ask people to read aloud well is to insist on this formulation: read your words so that a listener without the text will understand them perfectly. This formulation gets away from distracting issues like "acting skill" or "sincerity" or "good expression." It's all about the blunt reality of *felt meaning*. To read aloud well, the central phenomenological event is to get yourself to *feel* the meaning. This turns out to make your voice do what's needed for the listeners to *hear* the meaning without the help of their eyes.

The Process Itself

My overall claim here is clearest when I say it the way I like: *if people read aloud carefully each sentence they've written and keep revising or fiddling with it till it feels right in the mouth and sounds right in the ear, the resulting sentence will be clear and strong.* If pressed by a skeptic, I resort to a more careful translation: the resulting sentence will be *much* clearer and stronger than if the writers relied only on their *understanding* of what sentences are supposed to look like—that is, clearer and stronger than if they relied only on their knowledge of rules or principles.

Of course "clear and strong" is not the same as "correct." "Aint *nobody* don't use double negatives." This is a strong clear sentence—and true. Plenty of students hear no problem with "she know." There's still a need for final copy editing for surface features like spelling and grammar and perhaps register—and this requires calling on knowledge that the mouth and ear don't have. But the goal of revising by mouth and ear is not "correct grammar" but clarity and strength. The process is about meaning, not propriety. (More on this qualification at the end of the next chapter.)

I find I need to use mini-workshops to help students learn the discipline of relying on their tongues and ears. Many people have been warned to *distrust* these organs for writing; many have a hard time *overriding* their sense of rules and principles. Yet they often don't really understand the rules and principles they try to use—and in truth, the rules need to be taken with a grain of salt. But when I investigate the process used by those students who seem most "naturally skilled" as writers, I usually discover that they have always instinctively tested everything they wrote against mouth and ear.

We work on sample sentences and longer passages that need revising. I like to start out with examples from published writing to show students that they can vastly improve the work of professionals. Here's one sample:

> The newness of bilingual education means that the aim of research is more likely to be an account of what occurs when bilingual education is introduced than a demonstration of outcomes.

I start by getting students to read it aloud in pairs—without changes—for practice in reading aloud and to try to get a physical feel for meaning. Most of them hear pretty quickly that the sentence kind of bogs down and loses focus, and the meaning gets a little fogged over. Of course a good performance can make a bad sentence better—and I like to reward good readings; we all need practice in putting our bodies into written language. But even when we hear a really good reading that tries to give life to the sentence, I find most students can still feel a kind of mashed potatoes quality after "the aim of research." So then I ask students to continue in pairs and craft new versions—trying to use *only* the mouth and ear as tools. Here's a nice revision that came from this process:

> Bilingual education is new. As a result, research on it is more likely to show what happens when it's introduced. Research on long-term effects will be harder to get.

This kind of revising takes practice. I use a number of these mini-workshops over the weeks. I sometimes put students to work on examples from my own writing. I want them to understand that sad prose is something we all naturally produce. Here's something I wrote when I was speaking onto the page and trying to get down as much of my thinking as I could, so I let the language run on and on:

> When I set up my classes so that students have to read some of their words aloud—read their drafts, read their revisions, read short exploratory pieces—read something at least once a week in pairs or small groups or even in ten- or fifteen-minute conferences with me—I think I see them more often writing words in which readers hear meaning—words that do a better job of silently giving meaning to readers.

Once people read it aloud they can feel the repetition and loss of energy because I kept piling on caboose phrases that make the sentence go on and on. (It's a good example of how right-branching syntax naturally runs wild in speech. Right-branching is a good *kind* of syntax for writing, but we don't want everything it gives us.) Using mouth and ear, someone revised it to this:

> I set up my first-year writing classes so that students have to read some of their writing aloud every week. They read a draft, a revision, an exploratory exercise; they read in pairs, in small groups, or they read to me in mini-conferences of ten or fifteen minutes.

I also make sure to use a sample of something I've revised. I want them to realize that tangled language comes as often from *careful revising* as from careless speaking onto the page. Revising often leads us to *construct* sentences that have lost all connection to the mouth: we piece sentences together word by word—as we try to wrestle them into meaning what we are trying to mean.

Most people need a bit of training to notice weaknesses when the writing is not awful: how to notice what's merely limp and lifeless and how to get the best of what their mouth and ears can provide. If people give wholehearted attention to working on a few sentences that they didn't write themselves, their mouths and ears get better at noticing where meaning gets muffled. And if people can work on sentences in small groups, they learn from the ears of others.

I sometimes give them longer examples. Here's a piece of published writing by someone who seems to have lost the use of his organs for speech and hearing. (This is longer and worse than I normally use for in-class exercises with students. You'll see in the next chapter why I include it here.)

> My own research shows that in a model simultaneously accounting for both House and presidential on-year voting in terms of voters' issue

preferences, partisanship, economic evaluations, assessments of the presidential candidates' personal qualities, and demographic characteristics, the electoral value of being an incumbent rather than an open-seat candidate fell to 16 percent, on average, from 1980–88 to 1992–2000. An analogous model of midterm voting, necessarily absent the presidential voting equation and the presidential candidate variables, reveals comparable decline in the power of incumbency from 1978–86 to 1990–98. (This was written by a professor for more general readers—i.e., in a college alumni magazine.)

It's hard work to improve this. Here's my attempt:

In national elections, incumbents generally fare better than candidates competing for an open seat. But this advantage can decline. My research shows how it declined by 16 percent over about twenty years (from 1980–88 to 1992–2000). I saw a similar decline when I looked at twenty years of midterm elections (when the presidency is not on the ballot) from 1978–86 to 1990–98. For this research, I looked at years when only representatives were running for election (midterm elections) and years when both the president and representatives were on the ballot (on-year elections). I also looked at the following factors: partisanship, economic evaluations, demographic features, the issues voters preferred, and assessments of the presidential candidates' personal qualities.

After lots of this kind of practice, I can point students to any tangled sentences and passages in their drafts and say "I'm having to struggle to read this. It feels clogged. Remember our workshops? Make it right for your mouth and ear. Make it speakable."

Of course "strong and clear" are not the same for everyone. Style is subjective and mouths and ears differ—especially across groups. In fact, it's interesting to hear students argue about which versions of a sentence are better. When they argue on the basis of rules, guidelines, or grammar, the outcome is very unpredictable and even scary: the sentence that most of them call right is often very sad. But when they argue on the basis of mouth and ear, I find the result encouraging—even when they vote against the version I prefer. It's usually strong and clear even if it's not the music I like—and most heartening of all—the conversation is very *writerly*. It helps them grow as stylists.

Even sympathetic readers of this chapter will think of other possible problems with this over-simple technique, but I'm waiting till the end of the next chapter to explore objections and my own qualifications.

It's worth noting that some people "revise by reading aloud" while in the act of generating words for the first time. That is, many writers who insist on a slow and deliberate process for putting words onto the page test every word against the needs of mouth and ear. Of such writers we are likely to say, "She writes sentences slowly and carefully, but she always builds highly speakable, natural sounding, comfortable, clear sentences." They don't use rapid unplanned speech for generating language; they use slow planned speaking.

Revising Longer Passages and Whole Essays with the Mouth and Ear

The mouth and ear tell us not only about individual sentences but also about problems in longer passages. For example we might work on two individual sentences and make each one strong and clear, but now when we read one after the other, we hear something wrong at the joint. Perhaps there's a slight contradiction in meaning or emphasis, or they need a transition, or they need to be in a different sequence. Or perhaps each one has a lovely rhythm, but the two rhythms work against each other—as when two sentences cry out to be parallel but we didn't notice the possibility because we worked so hard on each one individually.

Many writing teachers hate the term "flow." It's so vague, and when students are asked why they like a certain passage they often settle for saying, "It flows better." But the term is useful because it points to very subtle issues of connection that we can hear but which are hard to analyze. For example, I noted earlier that unplanned speech tends naturally to follow a "given/new" sequence. Speakers tend to start a second sentence with information given by the first one—which gives a better foundation for the new information that comes second (see Chapter 4, 93ff). When we get better at revising by reading aloud, the ear learns to notice deviations from this useful structure, something that comes free in speaking. Here is a sequence that violates given/new:

> *If writing were merely the creating of diagrams, it wouldn't matter. You can start from anywhere in a diagram.*

When students have done some of this training, their ears might hear the slight gap, and their tongues might find an improvement like this:

> *If writing were merely the creating of diagrams, it wouldn't matter. In a diagram, you can start from anywhere.*

But with reading aloud, we don't have to do this kind of conscious analysis.

I hear a reader complaining:

Peter, you're assuming a very trained ear that catches subtle problems that most unskilled writers will miss. You love music and your ear is very tuned to subtleties.

Yes, I love music and I've worked on my ear, and I've chosen an example here where the problem might seem small and the solution minor. If this process doesn't help unskilled writers with small problems like this—but helps them only with more glaringly awkward or unclear writing—that's okay. But at the end of the next chapter I treat more fully my reasons for granting more trust to the ears of unskilled writers, as long as they get good ear-and-mouth practice by working consistently with it.

Reading aloud also helps us hear problems in the larger structures of overall organization. As we revise and try to get our reasoning right, we do lots of stopping and starting. As we follow the twists and turns of the micro-organization, we lose sight of the macro–organization; we can't see the forest for the trees. Even though reasoning and logic seem much more matters of analysis than hearing—more mind than body—nevertheless we can often *hear* a lapse in logic. That is, we can hear when the train leaves the tracks, whether they are organizational tracks or logical tracks.

Reading aloud can even help us hear a general loss of energy or focus or presence—the air gradually seeping out of the tire. The mouth and ear can lead us to say, "Okay, everything's fairly clear here, but you're taking too long. Spit it out, get to the point quicker. You're tiring me."

❊   ❊   ❊

In the last section of this chapter, I'll give more examples of problems that reading aloud can help with. And I'll also compare what we learn from the mouth and ear with advice from respected authorities on style. But first, consider this interesting question.

How Does Reading Aloud Relate to Ordinary Speaking?

No one would confuse reading aloud and ordinary speaking. So when we read aloud to revise our writing, we seldom come up with everyday speech. The process makes our written sentences *sayable,* but they are seldom sentences we *say.* Everyday speech is usually informal and sometimes rambling or disjointed, but the practice of revising by reading aloud steers our writing toward what's well formed (even if the well-formed phrasing uses slang or an informal register). Thus if we take a transcript of our everyday speech and read it aloud, it will seldom feel right to the mouth—yet all the language came from the mouth. Here's a piece of actual speech from a smart linguist speaking off the cuff (in a seminar about the function of repetition in spoken language):

> Yeah. I think that the function is open and, to talk about general function, I think the function in general is to direct, so that—a pointing function— to direct a hearer back to something and say, "Pay attention to this again. This is still salient; this is still—has potential meaning or some kind of potential that can be exploited by us and let's make use of it in some way." (Johnstone 67)

This is worthy of the Nixon tapes. The tongue produced it, but it's not acceptable to the tongue. Even if we looked at an example of more fluent speech, it too would most likely be unacceptable to the mouth and ear in the revising process. (The linguist's speech is an example of what Halliday and Labov referred in Chapter 3 when they noted that the most disjointed speech tends to come from academics. And in a *sense* it's not really "spontaneous" since he keeps changing his syntactic mind in mid-phrase. Yet most of us in more spontaneous speech do occasionally make this kind of syntactic change in mid-phrase.)

There's an interesting perplexity here about speakers' knowledge of their native language. On the one hand, the deeply internalized and virtually kinesthetic or bodily knowledge that we carry in our tongues produces somewhat "messy" syntax when we are caught up in everyday speech; but on the other hand, this same tongue *rejects* what it produced when we ask it to choose what pleases it. An exploration of this paradox would surely enrich and complicate our conception of both spoken language and a native language.

Anyway, when we use the mouth and ear for revising, we discover that they seem to like *form*—even formality. The process often gives us language a bit more elevated than everyday speech—sometimes even slightly artificial. We might say that revising by reading aloud gives us not *spoken* language but language that's *inviting to speak*.

I mustn't seem to imply that all speech is informal. At least *some* speech, even in our culture, is more formal than some writing. (See the Introduction to Part One for statistical evidence from linguists on this point.) Humans seem to like the sound and the feel of elegant language in their mouths and ears. Wallace Chafe works with various Native American languages and writes about the tradition of ceremonial and ritual speech in different cultures (see Chafe "Differences between Colloquial and Ritual"). Consider this example of formal Indian oratory—from a speech made by the Delawares to the Mohicans in 1804, and printed in an old missionary magazine:

> When I look upon you I see your head is hanging down, and your tears running down and your heart upset; therefore remembering the custom of our forefathers, I stretch my hand, and wipe your eyes, that you may see your grandfather [the Delawares] clearly, and unstop your ears, that you may hear, and set your tongue and heart right that you may understand right, and make your bed good, that you may rest yourself. I sweep clean the path before your face. (Six strings of wampum were then delivered to the Mohicans. See *Panoplist*. Thanks to Lion Miles for this example.)

Even if the nineteenth-century translator heightened the language, there can be little doubt that the speaker was reaching for well-shaped language—and that listeners expected it.

In short, writing has no monopoly on formality. We can find it in some speech. And reading aloud is a doorway that can take us there.

How Does Revising by Reading Aloud Relate to the Contrast between Body and Mind?

A not-too-hidden subtheme of this book is that the *body* or *kinesthetic sense* has lots of linguistic knowledge that good writing needs—and that it's a mistake to insist that all writing decisions come from conscious deliberation. I love how freewriting allows us to find words and ideas without planning—some of them very good. And I love how this revising process lets us improve our sentences under the guidance of mouth and ear—not just using conscious knowledge of grammar or style to figure out what good sentences are supposed to look like. The diagnostic process we use involves the body (reading aloud), and the criterion we use for judging revisions is also kinesthetic or body-based.

Perhaps everyone is tired of the ubiquitous research about the intelligence of the body. I remember reading about research showing that soldiers hit their targets more often when they just raised their rifle and shot "by feel" than when they took time for careful aiming. Here's a recent example:

> [A]dults are asked to predict where a ball that rolls around and around a circular ramp will finally come out. Adults, she said, are "terrible at it if they're asked to draw the path the ball took, or make a verbal prediction of the path it will take. But if they are asked to reach in and find the ball, their hand automatically goes to the right place. With their motor system, they can anticipate correctly, but that knowledge isn't accessible to them verbally." (Talbot 97)

Thus spoken language, though it's language, is rooted in the body. It has access to things that conscious thinking cannot find. This is most obvious with how our mouths follow rules of grammar that our minds cannot tell us about. I remember reading about teachers working with Cockney kids in London who discovered that they could find "correct grammar" when asked to "pretend to talk posh." See also the example in Chapter 3 about how children internalize very early the difference between stative and nonstative verbs—learning to say "I am going out" but not "I am loving you."

I know that when I imply a distinction between the body and the mind, here and elsewhere, I seem to be using something between exaggeration and metaphor. I know: The mind is more than conscious thinking. When we behave or choose without conscious thinking, it doesn't mean we are not also using the mind. We get a helpful corrective from a Chomskyan linguist on this point: "The body is just an extension of the mind" (Roeper 20—see also Mark Johnson, *The Body in the Mind*).

But let me fight back a bit and defend my "crude, naïve" usage: it's equally an exaggeration or metaphor to say that the body is just an extension of the mind. The difference between body and mind is something that most people experience in a crude everyday commonsense way. It's rooted in ordinary language and deep categories.

This ongoing argument is not about facts, it's about *lenses* or what I call "lens claims." (Kenneth Burke spoke of "terministic screens.") We can use different lenses for talking about something—in this case a lens that sees the obvious difference between body and mind or else a lens that denies the difference. We need different lenses because each lens tends to highlight what other lenses obscure.

So I will persist in using a lens that permits me to say that "the mouth and ear decide when language is weak or strong." I think we need this lens in a culture where schools and "language correctness authorities" give a kind of monopoly to conscious thinking and fail to credit what the body can do with language. (For more on lens claims see my "In Defense of Private Writing.")

So it might look as though I'm saying that we have no need for conscious careful deliberation in this revising process—we can rely entirely on the mouth and ear or the body. But it's not that simple. There is a central role for conscious deliberation in this kind of revising. I found I had written this sentence:

> People fear that the invitation to the process of using invented spelling will destroy any hope that kids will learn to spell right.

My mouth and ear alerted me to the problem and many others would notice it too, especially if they'd done some of the practice or training that I've described.

The phrase has a kind of soggy wordiness and lack of energy. (If we used theory to analyze the problem, we could speak of too much nominalization and the lack of well-formed intonation units.)

But even though the mouth and ear can find the problem all by themselves, the mouth and ear often cannot *fix* the problem without help from conscious thinking. I often feel trapped or hypnotized when I've written words that *finally* say exactly what I am trying to say—and it was a struggle to find them. They may not please my tongue, but how can I find a better substitute without losing the meaning I struggled to find?

Sometimes it's enough to grab and shake myself, as it were, and demand a solution: *Damn it, just say this thought to a friend during a walk in the woods or over a beer.* This can work. But plenty of times it doesn't. My search for a solution is often more like solving an intellectual puzzle: *What are some ways I could rearrange these words and find others and still say what I want to say?* I have to start fiddling with the words in a brute random way. *What if I started with the final phrase? What different words could I use?* It's often a process of trial and error. This doesn't count as sophisticated intellection, but it's very much a conscious deliberate thinking process—very far from just letting the body take over.

In this case, the fiddling around didn't work and I had to think consciously about different ways of saying it. This led me to this improvement:

> People fear that if we invite kids to use invented spelling, they'll never learn to spell right.

So my argument in this section is that the mouth and ear are central, but they cannot do the whole job without conscious deliberation.

Some Specific Problems that Reading Aloud Can Cure

In this section I consider a few typical problems; in the final section, I compare the advice we get from leading authorities on style to the advice we tend to get from the mouth and ear. Thus readers who only want to follow my argument and train of thinking and skip specific examples could now jump to the next chapter—where I explore why and how this process of outloud revising actually works.

Here then are some common stylistic problems that are usually improved by careful reading aloud:

• Bureaucratic prose. Here is a "learning outcome" that a university adopted as a goal for all students: *Students enter, participate in, and exit a community in ways that do not reinforce systemic injustice.* When I asked an undergraduate class there to work on this with their tongues and mouths, Dana Arvig came up with this lovely improvement: *Students participate in a community without reinforcing systemic injustice.*

• Roundabout or long-winded language. Here's a good sentence for training. *The overall plan of this study was to test whether sentence-combining practice that was in no way dependent on the students' formal knowledge of transformational grammar would increase the normal rate of growth of syntactic maturity in the students' freewriting in an experiment at the seventh grade level over a period of eight months.* (This scholar is arguing for sentence-combining exercises. Seems to me like an argument for sentence-decombining. See my "Challenge for Sentence Combining.") The tongue will naturally look for ways to break it down and "spit out" the meaning.

• Repetition or "clang." In writing (and especially in revising when we work at the micro-level and lose perspective), we can easily fall into using the same word or phrase too often. Handbooks commonly advise writers to "vary the wording, avoid repetition." This explains why writers so often turn to a thesaurus. The ear is good at hearing the annoying clang of repetition. Here's a short passage I found I had written: *Reading aloud makes us hear words. It intensifies our own experience of our own words.* Immediately my mouth and ear heard the problem of "words" "words."

Yet the ear can also recognize when repetition is no problem or even effective. Repetition can feel natural and give punch. I heard "own" "own" in the second sentence but I heard it as a source of strength.

It turns out that Tolstoy used many features of spoken language in his writing. In particular he sensed the power of repetition in spoken language. The most widespread translations were done in the nineteenth century and the repetitions were removed. But there's a recent translation (by Pevear and Volokhonsky) that gives us a better sense of how Tolstoy wanted to sound. Orlando Figes praises this version and points to the way previous translators had run away from this strong feature "in the interests of 'good writing'" (6).

> In the scene before Prince Andre's coffin . . . where Tolstoy uses the past tense of the verb "to weep" (*plakat'*) no less than seven times, Pevear and Volokhonsky are the only translators not to flinch from using "wept" throughout: Garnett says "cried" four times and "wept" three; Louise Aylmer Maude says both words three times each, omitting one verb altogether; Edmonds has "wept" four times and "cried" thrice; while Anthony Briggs says "wept" five times, omits one verb, and then breaks the repetition with "gave way to tears." (Figes 6)

Forceful writing doesn't fear repetition and a truly good writer judges not by abstract guidelines but by what effect she wants and what works for mouth and ear. Observe how the following sentence fastidiously avoids repetition by changing "known as" first to "called" and then to "denoted."

> Short sections were <u>known as</u> *comma*, longer ones <u>called</u> *colon*, and the longest sections <u>denoted</u> as *periodos*.

This is called "elegant variation" but what's wrong with "known as . . . known as . . . known as"? The meaning would be easier to process and the language more energetic. Of course, mouths and ears differ in different cultures. I've been told that Japanese readers enjoy hearing more repetition than most of us do in our mainstream culture.

> The larger principle emerges: don't go by rule or fashion—see what works best for mouth and ear.

- Interruptions that impede the natural flow of syntax and slow understanding. Problem interruptions are most frequent when there is some kind of data to report:

> NAEP reported that students who read the most fluently (rated 4 on a 4-point scale) scored much higher on standardized tests of reading proficiency than students who read less fluently (rated 1 on a 4-point scale).

When we enlist the tongue and ear—or at least a tongue and ear that have undergone the kind of training I discuss above—we get something more like this:

> NAEP reported that students who read the most fluently scored much higher on standardized tests of reading proficiency—compared to less-fluent readers. On a 4-point scale, fluent readers scored 4 while less-fluent ones scored only 1.

Here's a kind of interruption that is tempting because it seems driven by logic and the writer probably thought she was saving a few words:

> We want our students to have a critical understanding of, and the ability to produce, the kinds of writing that will be required of them.

But the mouth and ear take the kink out of the syntax and provide something more energetic and easier to process. And it's no longer:

> We want our students to have a critical understanding of the kinds of writing that will be required of them, and the ability to produce it.

Our mouths need to finish chewing a syntactic bite before taking on another bite—even if it is small. Perhaps the following example is too trivial or fussy, but it illustrates the principle more nakedly. I wrote,

> There's that important word *give* again.

My tongue and ear felt a tiny unwanted interruption that sapped energy. It seemed stronger if I delayed the interruption:

> There's that important word again, *give*.

It's not that interruption is necessarily bad; it's a question of when an interruption gets in the way and when it does no harm—or even adds grace or elegance or interesting rhythm. The tongue and ear know the difference. Of course, tastes will differ; we get to make our own decisions about how we want readers to perform our language. But it needs to be a decision based on performance, not on theory. Many present-day writers and copy editors want fewer interruptions than David Hume used in the eighteenth century:

> It is sufficient for our present purpose, if it be allowed, what sure, without the greatest absurdity, cannot be disputed, that there is some benevolence, however small, infused into our bosom; some spark of friendship for human kind; some particle of the dove, kneaded into our frame, along with the elements of the wolf and the serpent. Let these generous sentiments be supposed ever so weak; let them be insufficient to move even a hand or finger of our body; they must still direct the determinations of our mind, and where everything else is equal, produce a cool preference of what is useful and serviceable to mankind, above what is pernicious and dangerous. (Quoted in Denby 96)

Yet what pleasure we get (at least I do) from these elegant syntactic interruptions and from how they fit the music of intonational phrasing. Hume probably revised by reading it aloud, since that was such a celebrated practice in his era. Even when Henry James interrupts his syntax too much for me to enjoy, I still appreciate his intonational architecture—in contrast to the randomness we see in so much other writing, especially scholarly writing.

> The frequent interruptions for data or information play a big role in clogging up academic, technical, and legal writing. The inserted bits often consist of technical information that work better if postponed till a natural pause at the ends of phrases or major syntactical units: that way, most readers can pretty much ignore the detailed information, and those readers who need it can use it just as well or better when it's postponed till a natural pause.
>
>> But a close reading of these scholars, especially Goody (1968) and Goody and Watt (1963), leaves some room for questioning the picture we just saw of consistent and universal processes or products—individual or societal—of literacy. Goody pointed out that in any traditional society, factors such as secrecy, religious ideology, limited social mobility, lack of access to writing materials and alphabetic scripts could lead to restricted literacy.
>
> The last sentence is especially annoying because the interruptions delay the arrival of the verb we were needing. We can bring in the verb where it belongs and save the interruptions till the tongue finds a natural pause:
>
>> But if we read these scholars closely (especially Goody [1968] and Goody and Watt [1963]), we'll have some questions about the picture we just saw. We'll question whether the processes or products of literacy were universal to whole societies or just to individuals. Goody pointed out many factors that might serve to restrict literacy in traditional societies—factors like secrecy, religious ideology, limited social mobility, lack of access to writing materials and alphabetic scripts.

Comparing What We Learn from the Mouth and Ear with Advice from Respected Authorities on Style

The most respected guidebook on style is probably Joseph Williams's *Style: Ten Lessons in Clarity and Grace*. It's gone through many editions and is chock-full of excellent advice and interesting examples. But I'd argue that the mouth and ear will give us *most* of what he offers, and we can get it without the grammatical knowledge needed for following his advice. Here is Williams's advice for avoiding nominalizations:

> When the nominalization is the subject of an empty verb, change the nominalization to a verb and find a new subject. (16)

He gives a good example, but I don't find I can easily understand his principle and use it. Not many who need the advice will do any better at using his grammaticalized algorithm as they write or revise. Yet the mouth and ear—if sensitized with some practice—can usually get rid of a nominalization when it is a serious problem, that is, when it muffles up a piece of meaning inside an abstract noun and blunts the energy. (For examples, see my treatment of nominalizations in Chapter 4.)

We also get good advice from Richard Lanham's various excellent books on style. *Revising Prose* is the most practical. But revising by mouth and ear is much simpler and more pleasing than following his conceptual advice—which he summarizes repeatedly as follows:

1. Circle the prepositions.
2. Circle the "is" forms.
3. Ask, "Who is kicking who?"
4. Put this "kicking" action in a simple (not compound) active verb.
5. Start fast—no mindless introductions.
6. Write out the sentence on a blank sheet of paper and look at its shape.
7. Read the sentence aloud with emphasis and feeling.

The advice we get from Williams and Lanham is largely excellent and they certainly know far more about grammar and style than I do. But I prefer the test of mouth and ear not only because it's so much easier to use, but because in many cases it's actually more trustworthy. Williams and Lanham rely on theoretical principles of grammar, but principles cut indiscriminately. Here are some cases where I'd say the principles break down or needn't be trusted:

• When Williams follows his own advice about nominalizations, he says we should change *Our discussion concerned a tax cut* into *We discussed a tax cut.* But surely *Our discussion concerned a tax cut* is perfectly strong and clear and it would be just fine in most contexts. Plenty of nominalizations work well.

• Williams rules against the following sentence:

Scientists the world over, because they deliberately write in a style that is aloof, impersonal, and objective, have difficulty communicating with lay people ignorant of scientific method. (Style 92)

He says to replace it with this one:

Because scientists the world over deliberately write in a style that is aloof, impersonal, and objective, they have difficulty communicating with lay people ignorant of scientific method. (92)

What he suggests is clean prose, but my mouth and ear prefer his "wrong" version. It has a better music of meaning.

• Williams lays down the general grammatical principle that we should not separate an adjective from the phrase that ought to follow it. Following this principle, he says we shouldn't slip intervening words into the following holes: "as accurate . . . as any" and "more serious . . . than what." Thus he advises the following improvements.

—Change *"The accountant has given as accurate **a projection** as any that could be provided"* into *"The accountant has given **a projection** as accurate as any that could have been provided."*

—Similarly, he asks us to change *"We are facing a more serious **decision** than what you described earlier"* into *"We are facing a **decision** more serious than what you described earlier. (Style 94)*.

His improvements are acceptable austere prose, but why go to the trouble to remember and consciously apply his principle and rewrite those sentences when the resulting improvements—at least to my mouth and ear—are really no better.

What I sense in his "improvements" is the operation of a larger but hidden general principle—I wonder if he would acknowledge it: for good style, you must remove "the taint of speech." I can't find any errors or other problems in some of his "wrong" versions—except that they are more natural to the tongue. He seems bothered if writing smacks of speech.

At this point one of my readers objected. *You're just quibbling. Why argue? These are all matters of taste or style—or as Williams frames it, "grace."* But I do argue. If it's all a matter of taste and not error, why are things so often framed as *rules*? Does the passage that follows look like an invitation to develop or improve taste?

1. **Diagnose.** To predict how a reader will judge your writing, do this:
   a. Ignoring short (four- or five-word) introductory phrases, underline the first seven or eight words in each sentence. [Note how Williams should have delayed the parenthesis.]
   b. Look for two things:
   • Those underlined words include abstract nouns.
   • You have to read at least six or seven words before you get to a verb.
2. **Analyze.** If you find such sentences, do this:
   a. Decide who your cast of characters is, particularly flesh-and-blood characters.
   b. Find the actions that those characters perform.
3. **Revise.**
   a. If the actions are nominalizations, change them into verbs.
   b. Make the characters the subjects of verbs.
   c. Rewrite the sentence with conjunctions like because, if, when, although, why, how, whether, or that. (Williams *Style* 41)

How can such advice help but reinforce the common feeling that writing is all about following complex rules? It seems fair to invoke Bourdieu's argument that *difficulty* is an important feature in a wide range of cultural activities from cooking to art appreciation that serves to distinguish what is "higher" from what is "lower" (see his *Distinction: A Social Critique of the Judgement of Taste*).

If we want to help people develop taste and grace, surely it's better to ask them to practice using their mouths and ears so they become gradually more sensitive and skilled—more graceful. This would be a way of helping them develop and improve their *own* style and taste—instead of following mechanical principles, algorithms, or systems in order to mimic someone else's voice or notion of style.

Williams and Lanham acknowledge occasionally that we should consult the ear, but most of their decisions are based on analysis of grammatical principles.

Williams highlights *grace* in the title of his book, but I sense that he prefers what is merely *clean,* even when it's sometimes unmusical or wooden. More often I prefer Lanham's advice. His own voice and style are more lively and human. Because of his lifelong work on the prose, poetry, and rhetoric of the English Renaissance, he makes more use of the mouth and ear. He is more flexible and catholic in his thinking about language, and more sensitive to the limitations of blanket principles of style. One of his early and most interesting books has a title that says a lot about his approach: *Style: An Anti-Textbook.*

✣   ✣   ✣

In the next chapter I'll ask the interesting questions of *how* and *why* reading aloud improves written language.

LITERACY STORY

Syllabaries and Sequoyah's Invention in Arkansas in 1820

Am I the only one to be surprised to learn that writing was (evidently) invented only three times? We see so many kinds of writing in the world and they seem so different. But Russell Bernard argues that much of this diversity comes from a process he calls "stimulus diffusion." The Indus Valley is thought by some scholars to have been the site of a fourth case of inventing writing, but Bernard says it's a matter of people coming up with something that seems new—and is indeed new—but they were inventing on the basis of a borrowed model.

> [L]anguage contact brings the *idea* of writing and literacy, but the development of a script is then entirely local. Rather than adapting a Semitic script, the ancient Harappans of the Indus civilization may have gotten the *idea* of writing from trade with Semitic-speaking peoples and then developed their own [very different] script. (26)

Close to home, we find a remarkable case in point. In Arkansas around 1820, a Native American Cherokee named Sequoyah got the idea of writing from what he saw around him (though he couldn't read or write) and then forged his own system. He devised an original syllabary for writing the Cherokee language. He had no way of knowing that the Minoans of Crete had already invented a syllabary 3,500 years earlier. (See the Literacy Story following Chapter 1 for a description of the syllabic system in contrast with the alphabetic and logographic writing systems.)

Here is an excerpt from Jared Diamond's *Guns, Germs, and Steel:*

> Sequoyah observed that white people made marks on paper, and that they derived great advantage by using those marks to record and repeat lengthy speeches. However the detailed operations of those marks remained a mystery to him, since (like most Cherokees before 1820) Sequoyah was illiterate and could neither speak nor read English. Because

he was a blacksmith, Sequoyah began by devising an accounting system to help him keep track of his customers' debts. [Thus he recapitulates the original process we saw in the Middle East: financial record keeping as the seed for the invention of writing.]

He . . . began by drawing pictures, but gave them up as too complicated and too artistically demanding. He next started to invent separate signs for each word, and again became dissatisfied when he had coined thousands of signs and still needed more.

Finally, Sequoyah realized that words were made up of modest numbers of different sound bites that recurred in many different words—what we would call syllables. He initially devised 200 syllabic signs and gradually reduced them to 85, most of them for combinations of one consonant and one vowel.

As one source of the signs themselves, Sequoyah practiced copying the letters from an English spelling book given to him by a school teacher. About two dozen of his Cherokee syllabic signs were taken directly from those letters, though of course with complete changed meanings [sounds], since Sequoyah did not know the English meanings [sounds]. . . .

Sequoyah's syllabary is widely admired by professional linguists for its good fit to Cherokee sounds, and for the ease with which it can be learned. [Cree speakers were able to develop a rich literacy in only a matter of months!] Within a short time, the Cherokee achieved almost 100 percent literacy, bought a printing press, had Sequoyah's signs cast as type, and began printing books and newspapers. (228–230)

In his book on writing systems, Florian Coulmas looks at various syllabaries. The Japanese have two different syllabaries, *hiragana* and *katakana*. (They also have a third writing system that uses Chinese characters, *kanji*—which means "characters.") Syllabaries are well suited to spoken Japanese because it has so few syllables: 113. In comparison, Chinese speech has 400 without tones—1,277 if you count the different tones for the same syllable (DeFrancis 42).

Coulmas says that most syllabaries could be called defective or incomplete if the goal is an exactly accurate rendering of all syllables used. But he notes that such a limitation or defect is irrelevant to the practical balance between economy and ease of interpretation. The reason why court stenographers and TV captioners can turn rapid speech into text is that their machines permit them to put down *syllables* with just one stroke. (Also a few whole words. For more on Sequoyah, see Lepore, *A Is for American*.)

12 How Does Revising by Reading Aloud Actually Work?

I'LL TRY TO explain here what goes on when we read aloud and revise under the guidance of mouth and ear. The chapter is not a practical aid to helping people engage in the activity; rather, I'm trying to look under the hood and see what makes the car go. Essentially, I'm finding a lot of complex reasons for why such a simple process works. I think the analysis is fascinating—and crucial for understanding how speech can help writing. But I won't let my enthusiasm obscure some serious objections readers might have—and qualifications I need to make. I'll turn to these at the end of the chapter.

Why Is It So Helpful to Read Our Own Writing Aloud?

> *I feel weak places at once when I read aloud where I thought, as long as I read to myself only, that the passage was all right.*

Samuel Butler's words point to the most obvious benefit. It intensifies our own experience of our own words through multiple channels of perception. We don't just see them with our eyes and understand them with our minds; we feel them with our mouths and hear them in our ears—and indeed experience them proprioceptively in our bodies. Flaubert made a soundproof room for testing his prose by reading it aloud and spoke of putting his writing "a l'epreuve du gueuloir" (putting it to the test of his *gullet* or *trap*—slang words for mouth).

I'll point to four other advantages of reading aloud:

• All too often people write ineffectually because they don't fully "own" or "inhabit" their words. This is a common problem with students since so often they write only because someone (like me) is making them write. When they feel "It wasn't *my* idea to write this damn paper," it's all too easy for them to feel, "It's not really *my* paper—I'm just writing what I'm supposed to say." The result is often dead.

In many workplace settings too, people have to write what they're supposed to write. When people in this situation try to read aloud what they have written and try to give it any care, they can usually *feel* the blah, blah, blah—the lack of investment. Of course, reading aloud won't help if they *really* don't give a damn about the writing. But if they actually want their writing to be any good (even merely for the sake of a grade or a good job evaluation), they'll realize that they need to find words they *can* read with conviction. There's some mysterious act of self-investment that goes along with good writing—and reading aloud can help us notice when it's not there.

• When reading aloud helps us experience our own words, it helps us experience how *others* will experience them. Why do we so commonly glance in a mirror as we pass by? It's not just vanity—in fact it's often not vanity at all. More often than not, we want a glimpse of how others see us. Reading aloud gives us that glimpse. When I speak aloud the words I've written, it's almost as though I've magically brought another person into the room. When we read and experience our words with those multiple channels of perception, we vastly increase our awareness of audience.

• When we read writing aloud it increases our chance of noticing any mismatches or friction between the outer *physical* experience of *hearing the sound* of our words and the inner *mental* or *cognitive* experience of *feeling the meaning*. After practicing the activity of reading aloud to revise, we begin to learn to notice when the fit is not so good between words and meaning—a sense of our feet swimming a bit in shoes that are too large—a sense of sounds sort of flapping around a bit and slightly muffling the meaning. For example, I think many people would be able to hear this kind of flapping or static when they read these words aloud, even though it's not a horrible phrase:

> *My own research shows that in a model simultaneously accounting for both House and presidential on-year voting . . .*

Our kinesthetic experience tells us that this passage will make readers work harder than they should. As we consciously try out different wordings on our tongues and ears, we are looking for a better marriage between physical sound and mental meaning—as in this modestly improved version:

> *In my research, I used a model that accounts for both House and presidential on-year voting.*

When there's a better fit between sound and meaning, we come closer to the *embodiment of meaning*; we give readers a better chance of *experiencing* our meaning. (About the mysterious business of "feeling meaning," see Gendlin and Perl on "felt sense," and my "Felt Sense and the Wrong Word.")

Another small example. I frequently find some static between sound and meaning in uses of "former . . . latter" as a way to structure a sentence:

> This argument comes perilously close to equating local food systems with sustainable food systems, when the former is merely one ingredient of the latter.

This isn't tangled, in fact it's neat or even elegant; but the meaning seems to me to lag behind. I always have to waste mental energy to go back and check to see which is former and which is latter. Notice that "former . . . latter" virtually never turns up in spoken language. I think that shows how the locution is derived from the logical, spatial, and visual dimension—and that it's not a locution that embeds its meaning very well in sound and time. (See Chapter 15.)

- Reading aloud helps even with the visual surface of writing: spelling, grammar, carelessly omitted or repeated words, and conventions of grammar and usage. Some of these matters, like spelling, are purely visual, and yet the mouth and ear help us catch what our eyes miss. (Joseph Williams advises reading aloud as an easy way to fix errors in his "Phenomenology of Error.")

Debbie Rowe is doing interesting research on how students can revise better by getting computers to read their writing aloud—and computers are getting better and better at the task. It's clear that this process is helpful: the computer reads it more clearly and coherently than many people will do without practice and courage; and the computer makes you *hear* tiny mistakes that you often don't see when you read aloud and make tiny unconscious corrections. But even Rowe is forced by her research to acknowledge an important loss when we bypass the crucial process of getting the language and meaning into our *bodies*.

By the way, the ability to read aloud has been shown to correlate with success in various school subjects, even math (see Wood). Here are Crawford, Tindal, and Stieber:

NAEP reported that students who read the most fluently (rated 4 on a 4-point scale) scored much higher on standardized tests of reading proficiency than students who read less fluently (rated 1 on a 4-point scale).

. . . earlier research has demonstrated that [out loud] reading achievement is a strong predictor of math achievement . . ., and . . . initial research on accommodations indicates that reading math multiple-choice tests aloud may help students with reading problems. (307)

The Role of Intonation Units

The goal of reading aloud is to find places that feel wrong or tangled or dead. But finding problems is just the first step. Then we have to fix them. I turn now from the process of reading aloud to the process of revising, but please remember that every time we try out a possible improvement, we *test* it by reading it aloud.

To understand the power of revising under the direction of mouth and ear, we need to look at the role of intonation units. I'll explore three ways in which reading aloud uses intonation to improve writing:

1. In Chapter 5, I showed how speech produces intonation units with good grammatical glue between the words *inside* them, but often bad grammatical glue *between* the intonation units themselves. Remember Albertine's words (quoted in both Chapter 1 and 5)?

> *and we decided-*
> *I wanted to know*
> *the great question that was on my mind-*
> *I'll never forget-*
> *that's folk curiosity.*

If we read aloud, we *hear* those bad grammatical joints between units. And when we then try to revise—no longer forced to keep on speaking to a listener—we can try out one version after another. The mouth and ear are not satisfied till we find language with good grammatical glue between intonation units.

2. Those intonation units in Albertine's speech are *fairly* complete and coherent as phrases. But in Chapter 1 I also gave an example of dinner table conversation with more broken and incoherent intonation units:

Speaker 2 again:

> . . . *(0.3) Some élephants and these*
> . . . *(0.1) they*
> . . . *(0.7) there*
> *these gáls were in a Vólkswagen,*
> . . . *(0.4) and uh,*

The untutored tongue produced this language and Chafe notes that it is grouped into intonation units, but these are the kinds of fragmentary units that speakers produce when they are searching for words—when they are butting up against the limits of what the mind can figure out during any given instant of time. Needless to say, when we read this aloud to revise and have time to try out alternatives, we avoid such incoherence.

Those two samples are taken from speech. They are somewhat extreme in their problems if considered for writing. The units and the joints between them are more unsatisfactory than we usually produce as we write. Nevertheless, if we freewrite fast or freely, speaking onto the page, we sometimes produce problems of this *kind,* and reading aloud comes to the rescue.

3. But when we *write* words consciously on the page—especially while revising in a painstaking way—we often create comparable problems from an intonational point of view. We may succeed in ending up with grammar that is 100 percent legal and correct, but in our efforts to find precision for our meaning—often choosing one word at a time, changing our mind and using another, or using a phrase instead of a word, adjusting it all again, and making further adjustments to get rid of a grammatical mistake—we often end up with tangled language that doesn't fit into clear, coherent intonational phrases.

Revising by reading aloud comes to the rescue here too. When we take the time to insist that every sentence feel right in the mouth and sound right in the ear, the process cajoles our written language into comfortable intonation units. This means that the phrasing fits comfortably into the natural grammatical patterns of the language. ("The tone unit [intonation unit] in phonology realizes the information unit in the grammar" [Halliday and Greaves 58].) And when the language is well fitted to the grammar, the *meaning* is well fitted to the words. This makes them easier to process and usually more pleasing to the ear. Halliday and Greaves spell out in enormous detail the deep intricacies of the intimate marriage between intonation units and the grammar of English in their remarkable book and CD, *Intonation in the Grammar of English.*)

To illustrate, here's a problem sentence:

> Soon after that article was printed, the financial edifice Mr. Weill took credit for helping to build collapsed, inflicting immense collateral damage in the process.

Most of the intonation units here are natural and comfortable and embody meaning well, but not this central part:

> the financial edifice Mr. Weill took credit for helping to build collapsed.

This is the kind of grammar we create when our mind's eye is on the meaning and our ear is not listening to the rhythm of intonation. It's natural enough; we need to keep our eye on the meaning. But when I revise by mouth and ear (not in some magical kinesthetic process but just by fiddling and trying out one rewording after another), I get this:

> Soon after that article was printed, we saw the collapse of the financial edifice that Mr. Weill took credit for helping to build, a collapse that inflicted immense collateral damage.

I found better intonation units that carry meaning better, but I wasn't thinking in these terms; I was just trying to please my tongue and ear.

Here then is my essential line of argument:

- Written words can be arranged or shaped so that they *invite* well-shaped intonational phrases in the mouths of anyone who speaks them or in the ears of any reader who reads them (outer ear or inner ear).
- Intonation units are deeply linked to the grammar of the language; this means that good intonational shaping means good grammatical shaping—which makes the words easier to process and usually more pleasing.
- There is some evidence that even fast silent readers get some fragmentary subliminal auditory response when they read. (See Chafe *Discourse* 288 and "Punctuation"; also Fodor.) But even if some readers *hear* nothing at all, they benefit from good grammatical patterning.

Let me reflect for a moment on this contrast between *real* intonation units and what I'm *hypothesizing* as comfortable intonational phrasing that fits the mouth and the natural grammatical patterns of the language. In truth, we can't *see* intonation units in silent writing. Intonation units are entities of *sound* in spoken language. So if I want to talk about written language that falls into good intonational patterns—and that's central to my argument—I'm hypothesizing. Readers are free to read written words with any intonation they want. In short, good intonational phrasing is subject to debate, but the best *evidence* in trying to decide how good it is will come from the mouth and the ear—not from abstract principles.

Here's another concrete example to illustrate what I mean by better and worse intonation units: two passages by the same author (Stephen Booth) in the same book:

(1) Any reader committed to reading and paying attention to the book that follows can profitably skip this introduction. Everything I want the introduction to do is done in the essays it introduces. I am writing an introduction only because experience has taught me that people who read academic criticism—usually authors of academic criticism—do not so much read critical studies as "check them out." (*Precious Nonsense* 1)

(2) The difficulty in dealing with the relation of *shall not perish from the earth* and the Bible is that the specificity of the evidence can overwhelm its presenter and lead him to posit an audience as finely tuned to biblical echoes as his research has recently and temporarily made him. (32)

Surely the second passage is less successful as writing—more work to comprehend, less grammatically and semantically satisfying. The traditional diagnosis of the problem would focus on grammar. The passage is all one single sentence that's too long; its subject is a big lumpy clause; its object is a bigger lumpier clause launched by a flimsy "that"; and the main verb—poor little "*is*"—struggles to hold these two verbal masses into a single piece of felt meaning. Traditional analysis leads to traditional advice for writers: "Don't let your sentences be too long; don't use large compound clauses for subjects and objects; and use active verbs instead of the verb *to be*." But writing *can* be strong even when it violates every one of those grammar-oriented rules.

My argument is that we get a more helpful diagnosis of the problem if we look at intonation units in both passages. I'd argue that the words in Booth's first passage invite most readers (if they are native speakers of English) to hear or read them in fairly comfortable intonation units. I've underlined them:

<u>Any reader committed to reading</u> and <u>paying attention to the book that follows</u> can <u>profitably skip this introduction.</u> <u>Everything I want the introduction to do</u> is done <u>in the essays it introduces.</u> <u>I am writing an introduction</u> only because <u>experience has taught me</u> that <u>people who read academic criticism</u>—usually <u>authors of academic criticism</u>—<u>do not so much read critical studies</u> as "<u>check them out.</u>"

It seems to me that this phrasing—the comfortable grouping of words and tiny pauses—explains why the passage is fairly comfortable to process or understand by the reader. Compare the second passage:

The difficulty in dealing with the relation of *shall not perish from the earth* and the Bible is that the specificity of the evidence can overwhelm its presenter and lead him to posit an audience as finely tuned to biblical echoes as his research has recently and temporarily made him.

I'd suggest that the language here does not group itself or invite the same kinds of comfortable intonational phrasing. It's not clear whether the first unit is very short ("The difficulty")—or longer ("The difficulty in dealing with")—or perhaps too too long, running all the way to "perish from the earth." That uncertainty arises because the words don't really hang together very well. The grammatical patterning is weak or ambiguous. Thus we don't have strong grammatical glue holding words together and we don't get natural comfortable pauses. (Or we could say that we hear a lot of static between the sound of the words and the felt meaning they are trying to communicate.)

If Booth had read this sentence aloud with care, surely his mouth and ear and body would have felt the problem. And if he had used these kinesthetic senses to look for what was more satisfying, he would have come up with stronger and clearer intonational phrasing. Here is my attempt to revise with mouth and ear. It would take a more major recasting of the whole context to make something genuinely pleasing:

> Difficulties arise when someone tries to show the relations between *shall not perish from the earth* and the Bible. The specificity of the linguistic evidence can overwhelm him. And the process might tempt him to assume an audience as finely tuned to biblical echoes as he is—or at least as finely tuned as his research has recently and temporarily made him.

Booth's problematic passage is a good example of what we often get from revising. It's so clearly *constructed* rather than uttered. That's why the words don't fall into coherent tone units. He found words for all the things he wanted to say, he made them say exactly what he wanted to say, and he *built* them into the grammar for a perfectly legal sentence. But not a good sentence for readers.

Revising is probably the biggest source of the weak or unsatisfactory intonation units in a late draft. When we revise—trying to correct what's wrong or imprecise in our earlier drafts—we push words around, we cut words, and we add new ones. The process is usually slow and deliberate—*cognitive* and *conceptual*—and often not tuned to the mouth and ear. Revising is all about the mentality of *care* that I celebrated in Chapter 10, but careful writing often leads to phrasing without clear intonation units—or ones that are too long, ungainly, and tenuously glued together. (We also get problematic intonational phrasing from unplanned speaking onto the page.)

So when we take written passages that don't satisfy the tongue and ear and fiddle with them till they feel right, readers will tend to hear coherence within the intonation units *and* between them. Even well-shaped intonation units can have weak glue *between* them so they don't follow nicely; we feel a bump or gap between the phrases—not just in rhythm but in meaning. But we can rework the problem sequence of phrases till the connections between them also satisfy the mouth and ear.

Bakhtin underlines the central force of intonation. He opens an essay with a picture of two speakers sitting in a room in Russia when one notices snowflakes starting to fall outside the window—in May! "Well, . . ." says one of the speakers. Bakhtin meditates on the rich complex shared meanings that are communicated by that allegedly meaningless syllable.

> [Spoken] words are impregnated with assumed and unarticulated qualities. . . . Intonation lies on the border between life and the verbal aspect of the utterance; . . . [intonation] pumps energy from a life situation into the verbal discourse, . . . [intonation]

endows everything linguistically stable with living historical momentum and unique-
ness. ("Discourse in Life" 106)

Also:

Intonation establishes a firm link between verbal discourse and the extraverbal
context—genuine, living intonation moves verbal discourse beyond the border of the
verbal, so to speak. (6)

(Bakhtin is particularly interested in how intonation carries wider cultural meanings; I
settle here for how it carries simple literal meaning.)

Bakhtin doesn't just explore how intonation carries meaning. He stresses something
else important about vocal intonation: the need for what he calls "choral support."
That is, the intonational wind usually goes out of our voice if we feel that others will
criticize us or think we're stupid or make us feel unsafe in some other way. That's why
so many committee meetings and faculty meetings are dominated by gravely monotone speech—and why students often mumble their speech in class. These settings are
so often experienced as unsafe. However, Bakhtin fails to note an important exception:
when people are in the grip of passionate feelings they sometimes speak with powerfully musical intonation even if they are at risk or in great danger—that is, when there
is *no* "choral support." (In Chapter 3, I gave an example of this in the words Fannie Lou
Hamer spoke at the Democratic National Convention.)

Intonation Units and Sound

Sound is a huge advantage for language. Spoken words have many more semiotic channels than written words for carrying meaning (see the opening of
Chapter 5 for a partial list of the sonic resources of speech). It's sound that
provides those channels. That's why linguists sometimes call writing an "impoverished system." If we want to write well, we have to do more with less. A
harpsichord can't shade volume and tone the way a piano can, yet harpsi-
chordists use subtle cues of rhythm and timing to communicate the kind of
thing that pianos communicate with volume and tone. For another musical
analogy, Mozart had fewer harmonic resources at his disposal than Brahms,
but he did at least as well at creating harmonic richness.

When a text is hard to understand and we read it silently, we usually feel as
though we have to do all the work of getting the meaning off the page and
into our heads. But if someone gives a decent reading of the same text, we
usually feel as though those *sounds* are doing some of the work of getting
those meanings into our heads. Ease of comprehension is one of the attrac-
tions of books on tape—and one of the reasons people go to lectures when
they could save time by staying home and just reading what the lecturer wrote.

Let me try to illustrate my point by "reading aloud" some hard prose for
you. With artificial signs, I can help you *hear* that tangled passage about election results that I quoted in the last chapter. I'll represent intonation units by
giving each one its own line; I'll represent the length of pauses by the number
of "#"s at the end of each line; I'll represent loudness or stress with bold type;
and I'll represent a lowered voice with italics and smaller font (creating a *"parenthetical" aside*).

My own **research** #
shows #
that in a model #
simultaneously accounting for both **House** and **presidential** on-year voting #
  in terms of voters' issue preferences, #
  partisanship, #
  economic evaluations, #
  assessments of the presidential candidates' personal qualities, #
  and demographic characteristics, ###
the electoral value of being an incumbent #
rather than an open-seat candidate #
fell to 16 percent
  on average, #
  from 1980–88 to 1992–2000. ####
An **analogous model of midterm voting,** ##
  necessarily absent the presidential voting equation #
  and the presidential candidate variables, ##
reveals a comparable decline in the **power of incumbency**
from 1978–86 to 1990–98.

These are just visual tricks to evoke sound in your ears. Of course writing hasn't neglected visual tricks. For hundreds of years we've used commas, periods, colons, and semi-colons to help us hear pauses—each with a slightly different sound. Underlining, italics, and bold type help us hear emphasis and a louder voice. Parentheses help us hear a lowered voice for insertions or interruptions (by the way, I'll explore punctuation in more detail in the next two chapters). Poets use line breaks to create a subtle counterpoint between vision and hearing.

There are other commonly used visual cues—not necessarily for sound, but nevertheless to enrich meaning. Kids in school famously use double and triple underlines, circles, shiny stars, wiggly lines, and bigger or smaller letters. The web has brought us emoticons <:) >. (A recent grad student, Joe Berenguel, created a new one that he calls "mustache man" to mark sarcasm; <:)) >. Fernando Poyatos seriously proposes six new symbols of punctuation—for example to mark "quick tempo, stress, whisper, laughing, crying" [107]—but he doesn't seem to get many takers. With computers, people sometimes vary their fonts and use other kinds of formatting with semiotic effect, for example, using Comic Sans for informal language and Times New Roman to emphasize proper formality. Font is like handwriting—which sometimes gives a cue about the writer's mood or even character.

But "proper literacy" tells us not to exploit too many "childish" visual features to convey the sounds of spoken language. I use lots of italics when I write (speaking onto the page). I remove quite a few as I revise; and copy editors always remove more. Indeed, starting sometime in the twentieth century, the conventions for comma use began to change and, in effect, copy editors began removing commas—pruning the fairly rich use of commas up through the nineteenth century.

This "light comma" style is often praised as "modern, streamlined, clean" (rather than "fussy and old-fashioned"), but Chafe shows how it actually increases the *work* that readers must do in order to extract meaning from a text. For when writers follow the older rhetorical tradition and use more commas, they help signal a bit of the prosody of speech and thereby

> increase the transparency of their [written] language. By signaling the boundaries of normal processing units [intonational phrases] they relieve readers of the necessity of *creating those boundaries for themselves*, and thus allow the ideas behind the language to show through without interposing the language as something else to pay attention to. [In contrast, a writer who follows the modern style and uses fewer commas] forces his readers to create their own processing units. ("Punctuation and the Prosody of Written Language" 420; italics added)

In short, our culture of literacy seems to have a feeling that writing should be in some sense "clean" or "pure" and it tends to frown on efforts to help the ear *hear* written language. "Clean" and "pure" thus tend to imply, "steer clear of what's audible and temporal; try to make text as wholly visual and spatial as possible." (By the way, it took thousands of years before scribes started lightening the work load and helping us hear a text by putting spaces between words. See the Literacy Story after Chapter 4 for more on this).

Chafe relates our comma diet to a change in the culture of reading. The comma-rich style was related to the widespread habit of reading aloud, as described, for example, by Walter Ong (1982):

> The famous *McGuffey's Readers*, published in the United States in some 120 million copies between 1836 and 1920, were designed as remedial readers to improve not the reading for comprehension that we idealize today, but oral declamatory reading. . . . They provided endless oral pronunciation and breathing drills. (115–116)

My larger point in this section is that sound carries meaning and that we *can* get some sound into our silent writing. Few would deny that *some* stretches of silent words seem to lead most readers to hear them in their inner ear—without any extra effort. Why? One reason is familiarity. If the silent words are familiar enough, readers can scarcely help hearing them:

> *Get your paper. Hear all about it.*
> *Nice guys finish last.*
> *We value your business. Please stay on the line and the next service agent will be with you momentarily.*

Because of past hearing, some silent words trigger sound. Even if the words are hard to say, they can arouse aural memories: *Forgive us our trespasses as we forgive those who trespass against us.*

But if we want the advantage of sound for our writing, we need to get readers to hear what *we* write—to hear unfamiliar sequences of words in their inner ears. We know it's possible because almost all of us have noticed the phenomenon. When we read certain passages of words we've never read before, we are likely to say, "I hear a voice on the page." Robert Frost made a kind of voice manifesto:

> All that can save [sentences] is the speaking tone of voice somehow entangled in the words and fastened to the page for the ear of the imagination (Preface).

He once said that he wanted his poetry to capture the effect of hearing a conversation in the next room—where you don't hear the meaning but you get the music. Readers, writers, and critics can't seem to avoid the vexed concept of writers "finding a voice."

Musicians speak of certain passages of notes being easier to play because the notes "lie under the fingers." When players sight-read unfamiliar passages with notes of this sort, they find their fingers falling easily and naturally into the patterns or sequences that are called for. In the same way, unfamiliar words and phrases can "lie under our intonational fingers." If writing that is new to us is shaped into coherent intonation units that are comfortable and familiar to our mouths and ears (and thus central to the grammar of the language), we will tend to hear them. Thus the elegance we saw in Hass's poem ("Mouth Slightly Open" 118): he created comfortable and familiar intonational and syntactic patterns, while nevertheless choosing unusual and idiosyncratic sequences of words: *dipped in sunset, twitchy shiver, less wind than river,* and *the emptiness that hums a little in you now.*

The unfamiliar words fit the intonational and grammatical patterns that are in our language and almost in the bones of readers who are native speakers of English. So when we revise by mouth and ear and create comfortable intonation units, we help readers *hear* our writing. If you look back a couple of pages to the two passages by Booth, I'd suspect that the first one is not just easier to understand but that you are more likely to hear the words.

Of course different people will have different intonational habits. Grace Paley's subtle New York Yiddish intonation units will not ring in the ears of readers who've heard only Southern speech. The British phrase "in hospital" seems odd to American ears—and not just the words but the intonation that goes with them. Black English speakers tend to follow somewhat different intonational patterns. But despite differences, there is a huge overlap in intonational habits among English speakers from countries as distinct as the United States, Canada, England, Australia, and South Africa. So I'd argue that most of those underlined phrases in the first passage from Booth fit the intonational habits of lots of English speakers of the last century or so.

John Trimbur charitably observes that in my explorations of what the mouth and ear can do, I am gesturing toward a theory of style: something grounded not in metronomic meter or grammatical or rhetorical rules but in intonation units, the body, and ultimately the breath. He suggests exploring links with William Carlos Williams and his interest in the "variable foot"—something he felt he learned from American speech. One thinks also of Charles Olson's theories of "projective verse" also grounded in the breath.

Intonation Units and Music

Where there's sound, there's liable to be music. The sounds might be nonmusic if they are random (like a garbage can rolling down the street) or merely regular (like the ticking of a clock). But if they are organized or patterned in some rich, intricate, and explainable way, I'd call them music—or at least one kind of music. (Someone once complained to John Cage that the traffic noises outside his New York apartment were annoying, but he replied, "They're playing my music.") The patterns of intonational sound that speakers of English naturally use *are* rich, intricate, and logically ordered—in ways that are extensively laid out by Halliday and Greaves in their *Intonation in the Grammar of English*. They show how native speakers of English develop an acutely sophisticated sense of pitch, rhythm, and patterning. (Surely this must be true with other languages.) On the CD that comes with their book, some of the subtle differences of intonation (linked always to grammar) are so subtle that they are hard to hear. And yet it's undeniably clear that native speakers *make* these subtle differentiations as part of everyday unplanned talking—and that listeners *register* these same subtle "hard to hear" differentiations. (The reason they are sometimes hard to hear on the CD is that they are often presented out of the normal context of more extended speech. In live speech, we all speak them and hear them.)

In short, there's a subtle and intricate music that's integral to everyone's everyday language. I posit therefore that everyone who speaks a native language comfortably has a strong musical sense. I assume that this is one reason why music is so central to humans and why music has such power over us.

But can we get music into *writing*. I'd argue that we actually do manage that when we write language that invites readers to clump it into well-formed and well-connected intonation units. Till now I've stressed only how well-formed intonation units are a help to comprehension because they are linked to grammar and thus carry meaning. But now I add that they have a further benefit of giving esthetic pleasure. There are various reasons why it's a pleasure to read the language of some writers, but surely music is one of them.

The music of intonation has always been enjoyed though only recently been explained, but there's a more obvious kind of music in spoken and written language that has been the focus of intense conscious interest by serious speakers and writers for at least two thousand years. I'm referring of course to the "figures" or "flowers" or "tropes" (meaning "turns") of rhetoric. With their forbidding Greek names (e.g., anaphora, apagoresis, chiasmus), these can seem obscure and marginal (and some are). But speakers and writers have been fascinated because their music has power. Kennedy: *Ask not what your country can do for you . . .*; Churchill: *We shall fight on the beaches, we shall fight on the landing grounds, we shall fight in the fields and in the streets . . .*; Roosevelt: *We have nothing to fear but fear itself.* For a grand and useful assembly of classic and interesting examples of rhetorical tropes, see *Farnsworth's Classical English Rhetoric*.

In fact, music in spoken and written language can be so powerful that it is a danger. Music can overpower us; it can seem like magic. Plato disapproved of rhetoric and referred to its music as a drug. He wanted speakers to avoid rhetoric and use only dialectic because it relies on logic, not music. Plato noted correctly that rhetoric provides the music whereby a bad argument can defeat a good one—whereby a skilled lawyer can persuade a judge or jury that the innocent person is guilty, or vice versa. He was all too aware of how the music of rhetoric tricked the Athenians into a disastrous war. It was a combination of rhetoric and fear that tricked us also into a disastrous war or two. In the eighteenth century, the influential Royal Society promoted "plain prose," saying, in effect, that we can't do science if we are too in love with the music of language.

For all my celebration of reading aloud, I recognize that the very music of language can sabotage it. Occasionally I find I get too preoccupied with the sound and can't keep my mind on the meaning. Perhaps I'm reading a child's book out loud too many times; or I'm too nervous because I'm reading to a scary audience. For a related problem, notice how some inveterate public speakers become suckers for the sound of their own voice singing the music of the words. It seems that religious preachers are more than usually prey to this seduction. We can *hear* them paying too much vain attention to the music of their own words and voices, and it curdles the meaning and prevents us from paying full attention.

I think I see the same seduction happen sometimes in the performance of music itself. I think I hear certain performers—especially when they have astounding technique—getting so preoccupied with the beauty of the sound they make that this hyper-awareness gets between us and the music they are playing. I experience the pianist Glenn Gould as a paradoxical case. In some performances he seems to me a musical genius at getting musical meaning *into* every note he plays—sometimes just striking a single key with more than usual meaning. But then sometimes I feel him so preoccupied with his technique and his interpretation that he gets between me and Bach.

So how do these ruminations about music in language apply to the main theme of these two chapters: reading our writing aloud and revising it under the guidance of mouth and ear? When we manage to shape our language into well-formed intonation units, we are creating music. But music alone is not enough. We need a music well married to meaning—a marriage of sound and meaning or the audible embodiment of meaning. So when we read aloud to revise, it's crucial to keep attention on meaning, not just on sound. We need to treat mouth and ear as carriers of *meaning*—not just as sources of music. In a trivial example, we get a brisk music from this sentence (from Pinker, *The Language Instinct*): "Time flies like an arrow; fruit flies like a banana." But the music short-circuits the meaning.

Intonation Units through the Ages

An obvious objection wells up:

> *You are grounding your understanding of good prose on what we learn from the mouth and ear. This is foolhardy. The sound of good English prose has radically changed through the ages.*

Yes, the sound has changed. Here is an idiosyncratic view of major changes in the history of English prose style—seen as it were from the distance of the moon:

> There are two great tectonic shifts in English writing. One occurs in the early eighteenth century, when Addison and Steele begin *The Spectator* and the stop-and-start Elizabethan-Stuart prose becomes the smooth, Latinate, elegantly wrought ironic style that dominated English writing for two centuries. Gibbon made it sly and ornate; Johnson gave it sinew and muscle; Dickens mocked it at elaborate comic length. But the style—formal address, long windups, balance sought for and achieved—was still a sort of default, the voice in which leader pages more or less wrote themselves.
>
> The second big shift occurred just after the First World War, when, under American and Irish pressure, and thanks to the French (Flaubert doing his work through early Joyce and Hemingway), a new form of aerodynamic prose came into being. The new style could be as limpid as Waugh or as blunt as Orwell or as funny as White and Benchley, but it dethroned the old orotundity as surely as Addison had killed off the old asymmetry. . . . The new style prized understatement, to be filled in by the reader. What had seemed charming and obviously theatrical twenty years before now could sound like puff and noise. ("The Back of the World" 58)

(This is Adam Gopnik in *The New Yorker*. In the early pages of each issue, we see the magazine reveling in idiosyncratic freeze-dried micro-summaries of movies and plays. Gopnik uses that style—as though looking through a telescope from the wrong end.)

Whether or not his thumbnail generalizations are fair, the history of writing in English could be called the history of changes in what people want writing to *sound* like. Nevertheless, it's my hypothesis that if we examine widely admired passages of prose in those very different styles from various ages, we will find one common element: coherent, speakable intonation units. I'll use a box to present a tiny sampler of representative passages on the next page.

So in my analysis of how intonation units bear on good writing, I'm not favoring one style or music at all. But I'm hypothesizing that good written music of all sorts is fueled by well-formed intonation units; that strong prose in any style tends to rely on coherent sayable intonational phrases, coherently linked. Is this huge claim too broad to be valid? Perhaps, but it will nevertheless prove helpful if you want to write strong prose that fits at least *one* very widely acceptable style.

- From John Lyly—a passage spoken by Euphues himself:

> Ah Euphues, into what misfortune art thou brought! In what sudden misery art thou wrapped! It is like to fare with thee as with the eagle, which dieth neither for age nor with sickness but with famine, for although thy stomach hunger, thy heart will not suffer thee to eat. And why shouldst thou torment thyself for one in whom is neither faith not fervency? Oh the counterfeit love of women! Oh inconstant sex! I have lost Philautus. I have lost Lucilla. I have lost that which I shall hardly find again: a faithful friend. Ah, foolish Euphues! Why didst thou leave Athens, the nurse of wisdom, to inhabit Naples, the nourisher of wantonness? Had it not been better for thee to have eaten salt with the philosophers in Greece than sugar with the courtiers in Italy?

Surely we see here a symphony of intonation units—even if the tone and the modes of connection are quite different from those in other styles of good writing.

- From the middle period where Gopnik speaks of "elegantly wrought" prose, we already saw a good example of Hume's somewhat noble prose (231). Here is a fussier journalistic sample from an 1825 review of Edmund Kean playing Richard II:

> The irresolute changeable monarch was exhibited with great force and truth, while the reflecting and moralizing parts, which, from the lips of an inferior performer, would have been scarcely endurable, were, by Mr. Kean's varied and pointed delivery, made the most interesting part of the performance. (See Reviewer "Richard II")

Even though the larger music here—the style and tone—is not to the taste of many readers now, the central ingredient is coherent, well-shaped intonation units. Some are long, some very short, but they work well with the mouth and the ear. Because of that—I'm arguing—they work well with the mind.

- Now we are heirs of a process that could be said to have started with the Royal Society's celebration of plain prose in the eighteenth century. Members of this emerging culture of scientists were suspicious of writing with music. "Strunk and White"—the famous "little book"—surely more often assigned and bought than any other in the last hundred years—celebrates and embodies this taste for restrained prose. Here is a piece of classic E. B. White plain prose:

> In the summer of 1957, I wrote a piece for *The New Yorker* about a textbook I had used when I was a student at Cornell. The book dealt with usage and style; the author was William Strunk, Jr., who had been my friend and teacher. . . . Professor Strunk was a positive man. His book contained rules of grammar phrased as direct orders. In the main I have not attempted to soften his commands, or modify his pronouncements, or delete the special objects of his scorn. I have tried, instead, to preserve the flavor of his discontent, while slightly enlarging the scope of the discussion. (Strunk and White v).

This is a blunter yet quieter prose, but it still relies on coherent sayable intonational phrasing that helps the meaning come through, and it still gives a kind of intonational music. (White loves the trick of insisting for a while on plain nonelegance, so that when minor elegance finally comes, it's very felt.)

Reading Aloud for the Study of Literature

I want to note the application of this kind of reading aloud to the literature classroom. Our longest and usually deepest experience of how words carry meaning involves felt bodily experience, not just intellectual understanding. I harness this principle when I want to teach rich literary texts—for example, sonnets by Shakespeare or Donne or lyrics by Emily Dickinson. I used to give the traditional homework task:

> Please read and study the words of the poem very carefully till you really understand them. Then we can discuss those words in class.

I've learned that most students understand the poem far better when I set a different task for homework:

> Practice reading the poem aloud over and over till you can make it *work* for a listener who can't see the text. When we gather in class, everyone will have to perform it—in a small group or for all of us. Your goal is to *say* those words in such a way that you *give* the meaning to a listener who can't look at the words.

Students get closer to the poem this way; class goes better than before. Besides, this approach helps students do something they often can't do in regular "literary" discussions: restate the literal meaning. After we hear some of the readings we discuss preferences for one rendering or another. This discussion takes us not just to clarification of meaning, denotative and connotative, but also to most of the literary and theoretical issues that are central to literary analysis: tone, irony, the narrator's voice, reliable narrator, and so on. We can even discuss deep cultural assumptions (e.g., sexism, individualism) by exploring why the text asks to be read in certain ways—and why other ways of reading it go "against the grain" of the text and perhaps of the culture that supports it.

What every literature teacher wants is for students to *experience* the meaning—and also experience the sensory effects of the words in their connotations and music. This out loud approach is simple and it gets me further than I've been able to get with more traditional approaches. (*Traditional?* What could be more traditional than asking students to read literary texts out loud?)

I love the way that frequent reading aloud helps make people better readers. Not only do they notice more; they are more likely to get *pleasure* from reading. Among the various reason why lots of people don't read so much, one is often overlooked. Too few people hear the drama of voices and the music of intonation lurking on the silent page.

Six Objections to My Argument—and Some Qualifications that I Need to Make

There are various objections that readers might make, and some of them are valid. I acknowledge that revising by reading aloud will sometimes fail.

(1) *The process may not work well for ESL students—or for people whose native language is not English.* No doubt. People who come to English after

adolescence—and there are many of them in our classrooms now—will probably be slow to develop the intonational habits of native English speakers, and so they cannot put so much trust in their mouths and ears. But I look forward to research and have a hunch the process may be of some use even for students of this sort. I have the following email from a tutor in a university writing center who said that the process improved all his students:

> One student in particular, who has only been speaking English for 4 years, was able to almost eliminate all of his sentences that sounded awkward. He told me that when he revised, he would read his essay aloud and would reword anything that sounded a bit off. In doing this, his writing improved significantly by the end of the quarter. (David Fontaine-Boyd, email 5/20/09)

(2) *Look at horrible grammar that comes out of everyone's mouth these days!* But the goal of revising by mouth and ear is not "correct grammar"; it's clarity and strength. Appalachian and Black dialect will sound strong and fine to many. So too, *The prime minister would of declared war if he'd of had more support.* Look at this example of Jamaican English from the narrator of Andrea Levy's excellent novel, *Small Island*:

> Yet there was Mrs Blight kneeling before Gilbert and I, her pretty blue eyes dissolving . . . while glaring on we too Jamaicans, waiting anxious to see if we would lift our thumb or drop it" (523).

Reading aloud may also yield the "wrong register" or level of formality for any given situation. Slang and vulgarity can be strong and clear. Many sentence fragments and split infinitives will sound just fine to most people. Whatever is strong and clear will pass this test.

After all, there's a necessary step that comes after revising by mouth and ear: editing for the surface features like grammar. There's no escape from having to know how to avoid those relatively few grammatical uses that set off the "error" buzzer if you want to reach most teachers and most employers these days and many other standard readers (even if you want to experiment with the approach called "code meshing," see Chapter 16, 320–22). But the job of making language correct for conservative readers is much easier for most people *after* they have revised with mouth and ear. It's a process that cures many "grammar mistakes"—especially the many that come from carelessness or struggles with meaning or struggles with trying to write "correct" language.

(3) *My students just can't read aloud. They stumble or mumble so the process doesn't help their writing.* Yes. But the very fact that so many people are scared to read their words aloud—much less with conviction—leads to one of the main *benefits* of revising by reading aloud. That is, if people want the benefit badly enough (or we can push them successfully enough) so that they learn to *give* their words with their mouths, they get braver about giving their words with their *minds* or *wills*. They stop *mentally* mumbling. In a literal sense, this process makes people *put their body where their words are.*

What made it possible for me to write my first book on writing in 1973 was being tired of not being heard. A good teacher I know, Jenifer Auger, has a simple but effective technique for the writing classroom. When her students have blah voiceless writing, she makes them speak the following words to her before reading their text: "*Listen* to me, I have something to tell you." (personal letter 1/06/11). She sometimes asks students to write essays in the form of a letter to someone they care about. In the next chapter, I'll describe some out loud punctuation exercises that help students be braver about putting their bodies into written words.

In this connection, it clears the mind to think about writers who needed *real* courage to write:

> The threat of martyrdom hangs over all the early Protestant writings, and concentrates them; writers who could die for their theology, or even for translating the Bible, "meant what they said." (Madsen 71. For their translations, William Tyndale was executed and Thomas Cranmer burned.)

(4) *Reading aloud can disguise weak or unclear writing.* It can. A bad sentence read well can work well for listeners. Here's a striking example from a published essay: *Divine predetermination of what shall be imposed constraints on both thought and behavior.* No doubt the writer *heard* a nice sentence; he provided a good pause after *what shall be.* He overlooked the booby trap for readers who read *what shall be imposed* as a unit. Here's a more striking example: *The fat people eat accumulates.* Because I love intonation so much, I'm actually fond of this sentence—and how it creates its pungent meaning with only the tiniest intonational rise on "eat" and the tiniest pause after it. But of course it's a disaster in writing.

Pronouns that are a big problem in writing often disappear in the spoken version. Look at this example from the Old Testament.

> *All who see me laugh me to scorn; They curl their lips and wag their heads, saying, He trusted in the Lord; let him deliver him; let him rescue him, if he delights in him.* (Psalm 22)

I love how this passage highlights the way intonation carries meaning. All those ambiguous "him"s are clear if we receive them as the writer assumed we would, that is, out loud. Or if spoken on stage, the passage would be no problem at all. The actor would say "*let him deliver him; let him rescue him,*" and listeners would *hear* that these "*him*"s refer to the Lord. (The passage also shows how ancient writers took it for granted that we'd hear their texts out loud.)

So reading aloud won't fix everything. My very efforts to get students to put themselves enthusiastically *into* a bodily reading of their own words can sometimes blind them to a problem for silent readers. But I'm unrepentant. Invested reading aloud improves ten bad sentences for every one it protects. Besides, when we read aloud to revise, we're not confused about the goal. We're not trying to compensate for bad writing; we're trying to improve it. We're not trying to perform an unchangeable text so it works well (as when we read a difficult Shakespeare passage aloud), we're trying to *change* the text to make it easier to process. We're using our mouths and ears to try to feel obstruction or friction between the meaning and the words—to feel where the verbal clothing is not a good fit with the body of felt intention beneath the words.

(5) *Revising by reading aloud plays into a weakness for language that's elegant, slick, overblown, or shallow.* It can. It can tempt writers to neglect careful close thinking and be seduced by a clever, facile, or even elegant sound. Much second-rate professional writing falls into this trap. "Airline magazine prose," I call it, and it can sound pretty good. So advertisers, political speech writers, and spinmeisters don't need my arguments. They always already revise by reading aloud. What "sounds good" can lull us into staying vague about meaning.

Like most teachers, I've seen a certain number of students with a knack for "catchy prose" who think this knack is enough for good writing. Their writing has sometimes been unreservedly praised by teachers who feel beaten down by years of awkward clunky prose. But let's think carefully about this alleged problem. There is nothing wrong with the "mere" ability to make prose that sounds good; in truth, it's precious. The problem comes from thinking that this is *enough.* As teachers and readers, we can demand hard clear thinking *in addition* to syntax that sounds good. Writers of advertising copy are paid better than we are for producing catchy syntax. We might condemn how they *use* their skill, but not the skill itself.

In fact, I want to fight back a bit on this issue. Yes, people can sometimes be seduced by word music. But I answer by reiterating the main point of this chapter: a good invested reading out loud will more often *expose* empty or shoddy thinking than hide it. Sound and intonation *are* meaning—embodied. And reading aloud can also help us hear problems in larger meanings as we read aloud longer passages or whole essays—hear the *logic* and the *organization* of a text.

(6) *Some people have tin ears and can't tell a clear strong sentence from an awkward, ungainly one.* It's true that some people have better ears than others. But that's no argument for failing to use this powerful tool. Here are some reasons for putting more trust in the ears around us.

• People's ears can get better with a little training in a practice that is probably new to them. Even the haughty Fowler, in his entry on "rhythm," insists that people can learn:

> [T]he prose writer's best guide to rhythm is not his own experiments in, or other people's rules for, particular cadences & stress-schemes, but an instinct for the difference between what sounds right & what sounds wrong. It is an instinct cultivable by those on whom nature has not bestowed it, but on one condition only—that they will make a practice of reading aloud. That test soon divides matter, even for a far from sensitive ear, into what reads well & what reads tamely, haltingly, jerkily, lopsidedly, top-heavily, or otherwise badly. (from his entry on rhythm)

• People have been *listening* to language all their lives. They've noticed when they had trouble understanding the meaning, and this develops audible *clarity* as a criterion they can intuitively call on. And they've noticed when spoken words made them tune out, and this develops audible *strength* as a criterion they can call on. So when they notice that a sentence isn't strong and clear, they don't need the ability to *magically generate* elegant sentences; they just need to work out alternative versions—even randomly by trial and error—and test them against their criteria of clarity and strength.

• But more categorically, I refuse to accept what are usually facile accusations that so many of "them" ("others") have tin ears. Let's examine what usually counts for evidence in these charges.

—But they speak so badly! Yes. But the words that come out of our mouths in spontaneous speech are no measure of what the mouth *likes* when it is invited to make slow deliberate judgments. Remember the ludicrous jumble of broken speech that came out of that Ph.D. linguist's mouth (256). Fragmented speech is what flies out of many mouths in spontaneous speech.

—But they write such abominable prose! Yes, many people do—some of them very educated. But most bad writing comes because people have been advised to turn off their mouths and ear. Instead, they try to follow rules they don't really understand; or they fearfully try to play it safe with wooden, repetitive Dick-and-Jane sentences.

—But they like such awful music! Most music that people like to call "awful" is actually strong and clear. Strong and clear doesn't mean elegant or sophisticated. I can't get myself to like grand opera nor those pieces by Debussy and Ravel that seem shimmery and pulseless. But people with excellent taste love both. A different taste in music is not the same as a tin ear.

I'd insist that none of these factors (bad speech, bad writing, music you hate) will stand up as evidence that people can't use their mouths and ears effectively in the kind of deliberate focused way that I'm suggesting.

When it comes to producing tin-eared language, the culprit is likely to be schooling. When people earn membership in a professional group they are sometimes tempted to use a language that functions to exclude nonmembers. I'm thinking particularly of some academics who seem to *prefer* the sound and feel of what's unclear and weak. Consider this sentence from an essay in *The Publications of the Modern Language Association* (a sentence that turns out to be saying something that's actually useful!):

The discourse of common sense becomes available for appropriation and for the transformative rearticulation of the egalitarian imaginary by historically marginalized subjects (e.g., women and members of racial, religious sexual, and class minorities) not comprehended practically in its original enabling fiction. (Slaughter 154)

I guess it's possible to prefer this "music": for the way it sounds *special* and echoes the "music" of fashionable theorists. In graduate school, you can learn to love this sound. The eminent sociologist, Howard Becker, wrote a terrific book on writing in the social sciences. He describes a graduate seminar where they worked on a sentence from someone's paper and finally got it strong and clear. At this point a grad student blurts, "Gee, Howie, when you say it this way, it looks like something anybody could write." Becker's comment: "You bet" (7).

If you are a teacher and don't want to try out this kind of revising because you fear that your students have tin ears, remember, it's not an either/or choice. You don't have to abandon other methods in order to try out reading aloud in addition. If you try more than one method, I wager you'll end up with more trust in their ears and mouths.

I don't deny that some people have better ears than others. My viola teacher hears a subtle difference between how I play two phrases, but I can't hear it. And then with her help I can. Catherine Madsen (in a remarkably interesting book about better and worse liturgical language) hears a difference that I couldn't hear—and then I could:

> The opening collect of the Anglican communion service was treated in this way. The old form—
>
> > "Almighty God, unto whom all hearts are open, all desires known, and from whom no secrets are hid—"
>
> built both grammatically and emotionally toward a state of humility and receptiveness:
>
> > "Cleanse the thoughts of our hearts by the inspiration of thy Holy Spirit, that we may perfectly love thee, and worthily magnify thy holy Name."
>
> In the revision it is only slightly altered:
>
> > "Almighty God, to you all hearts are open, all desires known, and from you no secrets are hid: Cleanse the thoughts of our hearts by the inspiration of your Holy Spirit, that we may perfectly love you, and worthily magnify your holy Name."
>
> The changes are few and simple—you can miss them if you read quickly with the eye—but to the voice and the ear they are fatally inane. The tension of the old version's subordinate clauses, which peel the heart like the layers of an onion, is flattened into a plain set of descriptors; God cleanses the thoughts of our hearts more or less automatically, because it's his job, not in response to our plea. (14)

My hypothesis in these past two chapters is that we can learn to help our silent texts read themselves out loud to silent readers.

LITERACY STORY

When They Stopped Teaching Grammar

Ever since the flowering of Greek literacy in the fifth century BCE, everyone with learning and authority has assumed that if you want to learn a language or know about it, you must use your *eyes* and study the *written* form of that language. This means that language learners have traditionally been taught a conscious understanding of grammar. Our "grammar schools" were intended to teach language in this way. It wasn't till late in the nineteenth century that people broke free of this pervasive and powerful assumption.

A Swiss man, François Gouin, was engaged in trying to learn a language he didn't know when he noticed that his three-year-old nephew was learning a new language more quickly and easily. In 1880 he wrote *The Art of Learning and Studying Foreign Languages,* proposing what came to be called the "Series Method." It called on the ear more than the eye. The teacher engaged in sequences of simple doings and sayings: *I put my hand on the doorknob. I turn the doorknob. I open the door. I walk in.* Learners repeat the words as they repeat the actions.

His work was rather widely ignored (though people in the twentieth century eventually got interested in it). But at the end of the nineteenth century—a generation after Gouin—Charles Berlitz developed what he called the "direct method." As most people know, this was all about speaking and listening, not learning grammar or studying how to write and spell. Berlitz's method was popular for a while, but it too faded. The traditional eye-and-grammar approach to learning a language has huge momentum that was hard to resist. But early in World War II, the U.S. Army took up Berlitz's approach and it became called the "audiolingual method" or the "army method." Largely as a result of this wide usage and institutional backing, this non-grammar approach to learning language finally became popular and took permanent root.

So it was a long slow fight to loosen the stranglehold of the literate assumption that we must use the eye and conscious thinking to learn a language—to loosen the literate blindness to how children learn native and new languages with their ears and mouths. This approach is now widely used in many school and college classrooms, independent language schools, and audio programs like Pimsleur and Rosetta Stone.

13 Punctuation

Living with Two Traditions

TO MOST PEOPLE, punctuation seems to be all about rules that are a little mysterious and hard to understand. Yet many people settle for a kind of "voice/pause" technique: *Say the words and listen to the pause. If the pause is short, use a comma; if it's long, use a period.*

Virtually all authorities condemn this approach. Martha Kolln, a widely respected authority on grammar who is far from old-fashioned, gives us this warning: "It's often tempting to insert a comma wherever a pause occurs in a long sentence, but that technique will lead to errors: Every pause is not a comma pause" (159). Clark and Ivanic spell it out further:

> A very common way of explaining punctuation is that it marks "pauses." However, the punctuation of written English does not coincide exactly with the tone units of the language. . . . [They cite various studies to this effect, e.g., Bolinger and Sears, and insist that if we want accurate punctuation, we need] knowledge of such things as which conjunctions signal the beginning of a subordinate clause, which sorts of verbs count as a finite verb and which do not, the difference between relative and other types of pronoun, and the way in which some clauses can be embedded within others. [We] do not want to muddle learners with over-technical detail. But the truth is that, in order to operate the punctuation conventions perfectly, everyone *must* acquire at least an intuitive knowledge of these syntactic considerations. (1997, 209–210)

These are humane and politically progressive scholars who seek to *extend* literacy—not conservative protectors of literacy against the unwashed. But when I read that passage about subordinate clauses and finite verbs, I start to feel a little unwashed myself—helpless even with my Ph.D. in English. Imagine the reactions of weak students who have often experienced failure. If we need to know the subtleties of grammar in order to punctuate rationally, we shouldn't be surprised to find insecure writers taking wild guesses. Mina Shaughnessy looked at lots of punctuation from weak students hoping to enter the City University of New York during the period of open admissions. She reflects on what she noticed:

> [T]here often appears to be a psychological resistance to the period—perhaps because it imposes an end on a unit the writer has usually had

difficulty beginning or doesn't want to finish. It says that the writer must mobilize himself for another beginning, almost always a formidable task for an inexperienced writer. Commas, however, are not final, yet they hold things together. (*Errors* 18)

> [A] student may give the marks of punctuation different structural power than the conventional system allows—using commas, perhaps . . . to separate the sentences of a thought cluster and periods to mark the end of a thought cluster or paragraph. . . . Still another student, taken with the accessibility of some marks and the austerity of others, generously scattered commas about his sentences "because," he explained, "they are so cheap."
> Put a comma before "and" said a teacher once, and the student learned to write "Hortense, and I."
> Put a comma where you breathe, said another, with of course no guide-lines. . . . So the short winded produce a deluge of commas and the long-distance runners none. . . .
> What such errors reveal is that students who have learned not to trust their intuitions tend to follow instructions literally, even where intuition or common sense might be more illuminating guides. ("Basic Writing" quoted on 303–304 of Maher)

We must realize that her samples were written under exam conditions where students had time constraints and were often anxious. Their punctuation was probably more impulsive than usual.

Some very small children who are just beginning to experiment with writing put just one period at the end of each page. Sounds crazy, but they were imitating the only model they knew. They saw only children's books with a picture and one sentence on each page. Of course: there was just one period at the bottom of each page.

When people take the time and energy to really investigate the mysteries of punctuation, they sometimes get surprisingly hooked. I never thought this would happen to me, and I look forward to getting over it (as does my wife). But punctuation is fascinating because it's where a certain kind of rubber hits a certain kind of road. It appeals to something deep in our relationship with language because it's the only visual cue that takes us from silent, timeless *visual symbols* on the page to audible, in-time, mouth-moving *performance* in our bodies. It's where the mind meets the body, where the eyes meet the mouth, where space meets time.

In the chapter following this one, I'll suggest a specific, concrete technique for punctuating by reading aloud and listening carefully. It's fairly simple and orderly—almost rational, though it takes work and discipline. But to prepare the ground, I'll look at some history to show why our present situation is so vexed—and why it makes sense to use reading aloud for punctuation. In order to understand our current difficulties in punctuation and how to avoid many of them, we need to see how we are presently caught between two conflicting traditions. (Readers who want only the proposals—no background—can skip now to the next chapter.)

A Prologue to Two Traditions in Punctuation: Two Traditions in Grammar

When I explain our punctuational conflict to students or teachers, I find it helpful to start with a short prologue about a different linguistic conflict that also tangles us up. That is, we are also caught between two conflicting traditions about grammar: an older word-*ending* tradition and a newer word-*order* tradition.

- *The older word-<u>ending</u> tradition.* This leaves us with two different forms of the same word, for example, *who* and *whom* or *I* and *me*. The tradition derives from Old English—which was a language with lots of different endings or forms for the same word, depending on its grammatical function at the moment (as we see in Latin or German). Thus we are supposed to say *who* when it's the subject of a verb (*"Who is coming to the party?"*), and we're supposed to say *whom* when it is the object of a verb or a preposition (*"Whom did you invite to the party?"*).

- *The newer word-<u>order</u> tradition.* Over centuries of talking, the older word endings dropped away (*People <u>will</u> talk sloppily, don't you know*), and English came to rely on word *order* to signal the grammatical function. For example, *The dog bites the man* now means that the dog did the biting. In Anglo-Saxon or German or Latin, that same sentence could mean either that the dog is biting the man or that the man is biting the dog—depending on the word endings.

Over time, endings melted away—almost. The word-order tradition now dominates the functioning spirit of English—almost. For there are a few pesky conflicts.

If we say *Who is coming to the party?* we're fine because it conforms to both traditions: "who" is the subject of the verb and it also comes before the verb. And we're also fine if we say *You invited whom?* because *whom* is the object and it comes after the verb. But in some situations the traditions clash. Because English is now dominated by the word-order tradition, we often say *Who did you invite to the party?* But this is called wrong. We're supposed to say <u>whom</u> *did you invite* because the old word-ending tradition "owns" *who* and *whom*, and in this sentence, *whom* is obligatory because it is the object of *invite*.

So even though the word order tends to guide our tongues and is considered the living spirit or "genius" of present-day English, the word-ending tradition still claims sovereignty over those situations where there are two forms for the same word. The good news is that English has very few of these words that have two forms or endings. The bad news is that they turn up every other minute: *I/me, he/him, she/her, who/whom.* (We've only "recently" lost *thou/thee.*) This conflict between two grammatical traditions creates a double bind: damned if we *who,* damned if we *whom.* That is, if we say *Whom did you invite?* we sound a bit stuffy; we'll sometimes be laughed at not only by "the man in the street" but even by sophisticates who care about the living spirit of present-day English. But if we follow that living spirit of English and say *Who did you invite?* we are in fact violating a law that's still on the books, and we run a risk of being arrested as ignorant or sloppy. Woe is me. (Woe is I?—which is the title of a helpful amusing book on language [see O'Connor].)

And that's not the worst of it. The word-ending tradition is not just harder for most of us than the word-order tradition; it has a tricky additional complication. It doesn't settle for always using subjective forms for the subjects of a sentence (e.g., *I kissed Mary*) and objective forms for the objects of a sentence (e.g., *Mary kissed me*). It turns out that *sometimes* we're supposed to use *subjective* forms for the *objects* of certain sentences—or at least what feel like the objects (e.g., *It's I*; or *If it were she in charge, everything would run better*). To decide which rule to follow, you have to distinguish "active doing verbs" like *kiss* or *bite* and "being or linking verbs" like *be* or *is* or *seems*. Doing verbs are "normal" and take objective forms. But being verbs are different and take subjective forms after the verb.

Needless to say, this complication is annoying. The vast majority of verbs are active and normal, but verbs of being like *is* come up every other minute and require a form that our tongue resists. People have been corrected so often for saying *"It's me"* instead of *"It's I,"* that it's as though they have begun to engage in a kind of sitdown strike:

> If you are going to slap my wrist for saying "it's me" and ask my tongue to use the word "I" when it's just not natural, then I'm going to start saying *nothing but* "I"—"I, I, I"— even when you don't want me to. I'm going to say sentences like "The committee elected Mary and I"—"They threw a part for Oscar and I." I don't care if it sets your teeth on edge.

Caught between Two Traditions of Punctuation

The story of two grammar traditions sets the stage nicely for the story of how we are caught between two *punctuation* traditions: an older tradition of *rhetorical* or *elocutionary* punctuation and a newer tradition of *grammatical* or *syntactic* punctuation.

- *The older rhetorical or elocutionary tradition.* In this tradition, punctuation was designed to help people read aloud or to *hear* how the sentence is supposed to sound. It is punctuation of the voice and of the tongue. It grew up as a response to the earliest uses of writing where there was no punctuation at all. Indeed the very earliest writing often didn't even have spaces between words and itlookedjustlikethiscanyouimagineitbutthatshowtheywrote. But since most writing was read out loud (even in solitude), people needed help in deciding where to pause.

- *The newer grammatical or syntactic tradition.* In this tradition, punctuation is designed to reflect the grammar or syntax that underlies a sentence. Scholes and Willis explain that

> [t]he [older] elocutionary function of critical marks (commas, colons, periods, etc.) appears to have been predominant until the middle of the 16th century, when Aldo Manuzio the Younger enunciated the claim that the main object of punctuation was the *clarification of syntax*. The rules for

the use of such marks in contemporary English were first codified in 1740 in Samuel Johnson's *English Grammar* and have remained relatively unchanged since then. (13, my emphasis)

In short, the grammatical tradition of punctuation is the "means by which a grammar of English is represented in orthography" (Scholes and Willis 19).

In *A Manual of Composition and Rhetoric*, 1892, John Seely Hart wrote this:

It is sometimes stated in works on Rhetoric and Grammar, that the points are for the purpose of elocution, and directions are given to pupils to pause a certain time at each of the stops. It is true that a pause required for elocutionary purposes does sometimes coincide with a grammatical point, and so the one aids the other. Yet it should not be forgotten that the first and main ends of the points is to mark grammatical divisions. Good elocution often requires a pause where there is no break whatever in the grammatical continuity, and where the insertion of a point would make nonsense. (quoted by Nordquist)

The big practical difference between these traditions in punctuation comes in how much *choice* they give us as writers. The older rhetorical tradition invites lots of choice because it doesn't bind writers to the grammar of a sentence. It recognizes that a writer might want two different performances and sets of pauses for the same sentence or for sentences with the same grammatical structure —because of a difference in context and rhetorical goal. For example, the rhetorical tradition offers options here:

The party will re-draw the congressional district if the incumbent is re-elected.

The party will re-draw the congressional district, if the incumbent is re-elected.

The party will re-draw the congressional district. If the incumbent is re-elected.

The same sentence can do different rhetorical jobs, depending on the context or writer. In one situation a writer might use no comma to tell a simple obvious story—"of course." But in another situation the writer might want a story that emphasizes doubt about the re-election. It's a question of how a writer wants the reader to hear not just the language but even the meaning.

In contrast, the newer grammatical tradition rules the last sentence *wrong*. This tradition offers much less choice—sometimes no choice at all—because the grammar of a sentence is built in and unchanging, no matter the context or writer.

Most authorities on English say that the newer grammatical tradition is in charge of our punctuational world now, but it's not so simple. That tradition does indeed write the rules, but those rules turn out to give considerable space for the rhetorical tradition. So in fact the rhetorical tradition is still alive and vigorous, but in a somewhat underground way: its existence is not well recognized. In truth, we live now with *both* traditions existing uneasily—as with the word-ending and word-order traditions. Often they agree, but sometimes they clash.

Harmony between the Two Traditions

What most of us need to know is that there's more harmony than we are led to believe. For example, when it comes to periods, there's a remarkable congruence between the allegedly strict demands of the newer grammatical tradition and the flexibility offered by the older rhetorical tradition. Consider our options for punctuating this potential sentence:

> *First it was 9/11 then it was the war in Iraq and then it was the stock market slide.*

If we think in terms of the rhetorical needs of different writers and different contexts, we might want any of four different punctuations:

> *First it was 9/11, then it was the war in Iraq, and then it was the market slide.*
>
> *First it was 9/11. Then it was the war in Iraq. And then it was the stock market slide.*
>
> *First it was 9/11, then it was the war in Iraq. And then it was the stock market slide.*
>
> *First it was 9/11. Then it was the war in Iraq, and then it was the stock market slide.*

Permission granted! It turns out that these are all fine by the "rigid" grammar rule book. How nice. It looks as though the grammar tradition is really quite generous and gives lots of flexibility to the voice.

But it's not really generosity. It's more accurate to say that the grammar tradition is actually trapped in a kind of corner and *has* to cut a good deal of slack for the rhetorical voice when it comes to sentences. For it turns out that the grammar tradition lacks any coherent or consistent grammatical definition of what a sentence actually is. The sentence is not really a clear or stable part of the grammar of the English language! "[T]he construct *sentence* evolved with writing systems as an orthographic convention, and is not a unit of the grammar itself." This is a summary of Halliday and Matthiessen (1985) by one of the most authoritative scholars of English grammar, Mary Schleppegrell (in Bazerman's authoritative handbook of research on writing). Dawkins cites what he calls the most exhaustive study we have of the punctuation of sentences:

> Levinson's evidence proves [that] the written sentence is not a grammatical entity (8, 121–126), nor can its punctuation be grammatically characterized (141, 154); as an entity, it is *created by* punctuation, "an operation on a text" (120), specifically a capital letter and a sentence-final mark. . . .
>
> In fact, the concept of a written sentence did not exist at the time of Shakespeare. . . . The concept we are all familiar with (subject and predicate, complete thought) developed out of the growing desire in the 17th and 18th centuries for a standard of correct English . . . ("Modern Sentence" 2, emphasis added)

"*Correct English*" is the key term here. It depends on an abstract notion of grammar—a theory of how English is *supposed* to be structured. But it didn't fit how English actually worked—nor does it now. Eighteenth-century grammarians sought to ennoble English on the model of a "true" and "superior" grammar—that is, Latin grammar. In the authoritative *Cambridge Encyclopedia of Language*, David Crystal points to holes in all subsequent attempts to define the sentence—grammatically or logically:

> Despite all the difficulties, we continue to employ the notion of "sentence," and modern syntacticians try to make sense of it. But [finding] a satisfactory definition of "sentence" . . . [is] an enterprise that is unlikely to succeed, with over 200 such definitions on record to date. (94)

It's the *clause*, not the sentence that linguists study because the clause is the basic unit that structures English grammar. And lo and behold, the clause, being a much more reliable unit of grammar than the sentence, tends to be marked by the *voice* as part of the intonation of natural speech.

So we are left with a confusing situation. The rules tell us to put periods at the end of every sentence and use grammar to decide where a sentence ends, but grammar cannot give a coherent picture of a sentence. For this reason, the rules often stand aside and allow us to use *intonation* or the *voice* to decide where periods and commas should go. That's why we get all that lovely choice in punctuating the 9/11 sentence.

Here's an illustration of the incoherence in how the "written sentence" is officially defined. The second, third, and fourth sentences here (from an editorial in the English *Guardian* newspaper) are obviously *not* sentences according to the official rules—but they clearly *are* sentences according to the *actual*, functioning grammar of English—a grammar that is reflected better by the rhetorically based intonation and clause grammar than the makeshift "grammar of the sentence":

> [I]t is difficult to maintain that there is no need to change the organizations that govern security in Europe. First, because there are still disputed borders in Europe and they have to be dealt with. Second, because . . . . And third, because . . . .

We're not supposed to make sentences out of "mere clauses" like "Because the argument wasn't logical." But the grammar police tend to stand aside and allow sentences like these.

I wish I could say that the shaky status of the sentence gives *completely* free rein to the voice for the punctuation of sentences. It doesn't. The voice can lead us into violations of the rules that will result in a ticket for a "moving violation." But these rules for punctuation cannot claim to be fully based on grammar. When it comes to the sentence, they are based on an artificial construct (somewhat based on Latin) that doesn't really fit English grammar.

Where the Two Traditions Conflict

In our culture and in our schools, the grammatical tradition is dominant and it can bite. There are plenty of places where if we serve our rhetorical needs, we break the grammatical law, but if we conform to the grammatical law, we undermine our rhetorical needs.

Consider this example:

Pollsters were surprised by her victory, they had forecast low results.

The comma is ruled an error by most people who know and feel the force of the grammatical tradition (like many teachers). But many good writers find themselves in certain rhetorical situations where they decide this punctuation is what they need. Perhaps there's a kind of momentum in the train of thinking in the preceding sentences that makes this "comma splice" seem just right. The writer wants to keep the two clauses linked and create a larger single unit of meaning (thus asking readers to hear only a comma pause). When the context is different, the same writer might insist on a period—to set off the two clauses as very separate units of meaning (thus asking readers to hear a closure pause).

For another example of a clash between the two punctuational traditions, there are many sentences where speakers naturally pause and sometimes writers want a pause, but where a comma is illegal. In particular, speakers very often put a comma pause between a bulky subject phrase and the verb that follows it. For example, most speakers pause distinctly after "had passed" in this sentence:

The man who was finally appointed long after the deadline had passed[,] was dishonest.

In fact, most readers would welcome that comma. Without it, they might well stumble in their silent reading. But the comma is ruled an error. Even when the subject is shorter, people are often tempted to put in a comma:

The man who was finally appointed[,] was dishonest.

In effect, virtually all legal commas match a speech pause, but not all speech pauses are allowed to have a comma. Yet despite these conflicts, the grammatical tradition *sometimes* stands graciously aside and says, in effect, "Silly me! Of course your voice gets to decide—your rhetorical principle takes precedence over my grammatical prohibition of commas between the subject and verb." For example, the rule books acknowledge that the prohibition causes a train wreck for readers in a sentence like this:

Those who can do; those who can't teach.

The rule books say "Go ahead and listen to your voice":

Those who can, do; those who can't, teach.

(Note, however, that with the current fashion for micro-sized handbooks for students to stick in their back pockets, these important exceptions are apt to be left out.)

So we live in a world where the rhetorical and grammatical traditions of punctuation sometimes clash. Writers who rely on their voice are sometimes fine, but sometimes they are fined for disobeying the rules of the grammar tradition—a tradition that currently has sovereignty.

Parkes, in his definitive history of punctuation, remarks that modern Finnish punctuation is *wholly* grammatical. For example, *every* clause is marked by commas (*She said to him, that she would run for congress.* See Parkes 92). I guess if we want consistency, we should move to Finland. For the Finns also radically reformed their spelling in the twentieth century. Modern written Finnish is evidently closer than any other language to the goal of accurately representing spoken Finnish. But which *version* of spoken Finnish is honored in this way? Besides, the Finns, in their hunger for consistency, have wandered into a conflict. Spelling reform brings speech and writing closer, but a wholly grammatical system of punctuation drives a wedge between speech and writing.

This History Leaves Us with Some Potent Illusions

Most grammar books, teachers, and "cultured" people would describe English punctuation as follows:

> We have consistent rules of punctuation that skilled writers follow and unskilled writers break. The rules are consistent because they reflect the grammatical tradition, not the rhetorical tradition.

But this dominant picture is illusory. And the illusion does harm.

First of all, we *don't* have consistent conventions of punctuation that real writers follow. The pervasive illusion of consistency comes from a convention among publishers of books, newspapers, magazines, and professional journals. They have turned over responsibility for punctuation to professional copy editors who see it as their job to enforce the *same* rules and conventions. (Admittedly, there are a few subtle variations among publishing houses, but those differences are more about citation systems than about meat and potatoes of punctuation.) As a result, we almost never *see* how good writers actually punctuate their writing.

This startling thought is Dawkins's important insight. (His seminal essays, "Teaching Punctuation as a Rhetorical Tool" and "Punctuation: Some Informing History" have been central to my understanding of punctuation.) But sometimes, as he points out, we actually *do* see how skilled writers punctuate. That's because of another convention among publishers. When copy editors deal with *literary* prose—fiction, personal writing, creative nonfiction, and of course poetry—they permit all kinds of inconsistent and "wrong punctuation."

This looks like special homage to creative writing, but I wonder if it doesn't really imply that creative writing doesn't count as "serious writing." And some editors can't resist "correcting" even creative writers. Robert Frost used this punctuation in his famous poem, "Stopping by Woods":

His house is in the village though

But for the first edition, his editor insisted on the grammatical rule (or one interpretation of the grammatical rule) and "corrected" it like this:

His house is in the village, though

Frost's rhetorical intention was finally honored in a later edition. See Pritchard for the story.

That is, our present culture of literacy has adopted an assumption that "creative" writers are allowed to "take liberties" and punctuate as they wish.

So when we see "creative" punctuation in literary prose, we are usually seeing punctuation that skilled, competent writers *chose* in order to create the rhetorical effects and intonational subtleties of meaning that *they* want. Dawkins has gathered an eye-opening collection of examples of punctuation that literary writers have used that violate the grammar-based standards. Here's a particularly striking passage from James Agee that Chafe quotes to show how rhetorically effective it can be to violate the standards:

> He has been dead all night while I was asleep and now it is morning and I am awake but he is still dead and he will stay right on being dead all afternoon and all night and all tomorrow while I am asleep again and wake up again and go to sleep again and he can't come back home again ever any more but I will see him once more before he is taken away ("Punctuation" 418).

He also quotes a passage from Hemingway who is insisting on no commas at all for rhetorical effect:

> Earlier in the evening he had taken the ax and gone outside of the cave and walked through the new snow to the edge of the clearing and cut down a small spruce tree. (*For Whom the Bell Tolls* 258; Chafe "Punctuation and the Prosody of Written Language" 400)

> I've noticed that many small-budget scholarly journals in Europe don't use copy editors. In these journals, then, we are seeing author-chosen punctuation in non-creative writing. But often these academic writers are simply trying to follow ill-understood rules rather than actually trying to decide on the rhetorical effect they want to have on readers. (Also, there are some differences in rules or conventions from country to country—as we just saw in the case of Finland.) In the United States, small scholarly journals are getting poorer so we are seeing less copy editing in them. Some publishers go so far as to get scholars to send in camera-ready copy in order to save even the cost of formatting.

Lynn Truss presents herself as a champion of correct grammar-based punctuation. With her blockbuster, *Eats Shoots and Leaves,* she made a fortune professing outrage over mistakes. But let's look more closely. She constantly breaks the very rules that she says she is fighting to preserve. Here is only part of Louis Menand's long mischievous list of examples:

> The preface, by Truss, includes a misplaced apostrophe . . . and two misused semicolons: . . . About half the semicolons in the rest of the book are either unnecessary or ungrammatical, and the comma is deployed as the mood strikes. Sometimes phrases such as "of course" are set off by commas; sometimes they are not. Doubtful, distracting,

and unwarranted commas turn up in front of restrictive phrases . . ., before correlative conjunctions . . ., and in prepositional phrases. . . . Where you most expect punctuation, it may not show up at all. ("Bad Comma" 102)

Menand counts these as violations of *grammar*-based *rules*. But he recognizes that most of them are probably examples of what most good writers do when they resist the rules: doing what the voice demands. As Menand puts it, "Truss is right (despite what she preaches) when she implies, by her own practice, that the [grammar-based] rules don't really have that much to do with it [good writing] (102)." So we can count Truss as a covert champion of *rhetorically* based punctuation.

She is not alone in falling into what I'm tempted to call the "Truss syndrome": on the one hand decry how "mistakes" are invading us from everywhere and threatening literacy—and blame them on ignorance or carelessness (or low class). But on the other hand, freely violate the rules if you have enough authority to do so; no one will notice. Your violations will make your writing better, while lots of people make their writing worse by trying to follow the rules.

Where people like Truss and grammarians and conservative readers tend to see nothing but ignorant carelessness in deviations from the rules, Chafe, like Dawkins, insists on seeing good rhetorical reasons for overriding the grammatical rules of punctuation.

The question should not be put in terms of "sloppiness versus care, but in terms of the extent to which writers are guided by their inner voices—by auditory imagery—versus the extent to which they are guided by imposed rules." ("Punctuation" 402)

Chafe bluntly contests this pervasive assumption that grammatical rules govern punctuation and insists, surprisingly, that modern English punctuation as we see it in print (not as it's usually explained to us) serves primarily to convey writers' prosodic intentions for how they want readers to hear their words. He knows this sounds crazy and that it's the complete opposite of what authorities say. Thus he starts by quoting from the *Comprehensive Grammar of the English Language* by Quirk, Greenbaum, Leech, and Svartvik: "Punctuation practice is governed primarily by grammatical considerations." These grammarians go on to speak of violations of these punctuational conventions as "inconsistencies . . . that would not be permitted in most printed material" (in Chafe "Punctuation" 402, quoting from 1611[!]).

But then Chafe argues that these very grammarians provide the data to contradict their claim that "punctuation practice is governed primarily by grammatical considerations." The four scholars look at a large representative sample of published English and find that 45 percent of the marks are periods. Chafe then notes that periods almost invariably represent a falling pitch in the intonation of speech (i.e., that they fit the prosodic tradition). The grammarians also find that 47 percent of the marks are commas. But the grammarians themselves concede that "a great deal of flexibility [is] possible in the use of the comma. . . . The comma in fact provides considerable opportunity for personal taste" (Chafe 4, quoting 1611).

Chafe then does the math and insists that 92 percent of published punctuation represents either a definite falling pitch (where the grammatical tradition obeys the rhetorical need for a period), or a spot where "personal taste" takes over—and personal taste tends to reflect rhetorical or prosodic needs.

As a prime piece of evidence, Chafe calls attention to the grammarians' own sentence just quoted: *"The comma in fact provides considerable opportunity for personal taste."* They purposely broke their own rule and omitted the conventionally mandatory commas around "in fact" (copy editors had surely penciled them in) because they wanted to minimize pauses in their readers' ears. Chafe goes on to provide evidence for how grammar sometimes does and sometimes does not govern punctuation—and how reputable writers sometimes use the Truss syndrome and insist on letting their voice override the rule.

Here's a striking example I found to match Agee and Hemingway's avoidance of punctuation. Jonathan Bate, a literary biographer and academic of impressive reputation and accomplishment, wrote this passage in a recent biography of Shakespeare:

> The office of William Cecil, Lord Burghley. First minister of state, eyes and ears of Her Majesty. A table piled high with state papers; a steady stream of officials coming in with reports, requesting signatures on letters for dispatch out into the regions. (From *Soul of the Age: A Biography of the Mind of William Shakespeare*; quoted by Greenblatt)

Dawkins gives other examples from writers? like E. B. White.

Nicholson Baker provides another interesting example from an authoritative historian of punctuation, Malcolm Parkes—someone Nicholson calls an "eagle-eyed paleographer who has worked so hard to 'raise a reader's consciousness of what punctuation is and does'!" Parkes wrote:

> *Pausing therefore was part of the process of reading not copying.* (Baker 78)

Parkes must have held a gun to the head of the copy editor to insist on dropping the comma before the final two words—wanting to make readers hear the sentence with as little pausing as possible. Baker recounts other stories of his own and other writers' negotiations with copy editors over punctuation. And he agrees with Chafe's claim that

> most writing most of the time does use punctuation in a way that respects the prosody of written language. . . . In the end . . . the most satisfying guidance comes from listening to the inner voice itself. Nurturing that listening can only improve the quality of written language. ("Punctuation" 425)

Why *should* all writers punctuate in the same way? Or even be consistent from work to work? Writers create and vary their written *style* for the sake of giving readers particular kinds of rhetorical experience. Also their voice, register, and persona. Is not punctuation part of style?

Nicholson Baker is fond of a punctuational practice widely used in the past but now taken away from us: a comma *along with* a dash. (Baker calls this a "dashtard.") He is happy when Eric Partridge cautiously accepts them.

> There was a glimmer of hope in Eric Partridges's *You Have a Point There* (1953)—he advised that, yes, compound points should be used with "caution and moderation," but he had the courage to admit that "occasionally [they] are, in fact, unavoidable" (87). [Note Baker's use of the dash.]

I love Partridge's use of the word "*unavoidable.*" It's mostly used by authorities to tell us that we cannot avoid some piece of correct punctuation. What a treat it is to see Partridge, a scholar of language in a book about punctuation, insisting that sometimes *breaking* the law is unavoidable.

❖   ❖   ❖

So here's the point of my history: we live in a culture of literacy where grammar books, authorities, and teachers all think that *grammar* is the predominant guide to punctuation; they universally declare that it's ignorant and naïve to use our voices to punctuate. But if we look more carefully at history and at published writing, we learn that, in fact, the grammatical rules fit surprisingly often with the needs of the voice—and indeed that the rules sometimes stand aside for the needs of the voice—the needs of meaning. And we see that good writers often insist on consciously breaking rules that conflict with the needs of the voice.

Of course irreconcilable conflicts *do* sometimes stand between grammar and the voice, but these conflicts seem to have hypnotized teachers and grammar books and the public into believing that you can't punctuate or even write well without special knowledge of grammar and the rules.

In the next chapter, I'll describe a disciplined method for punctuating by using the mouth and ear without having to know grammar or consult rule books. I'll show where this method works and where it sometimes fails. I'll argue that this method, if used in a disciplined way, will yield "good enough" or "adequate" punctuation: that is, the results will be *mostly* "correct." Where they are "wrong," those errors will be mostly inoffensive or even helpful to readers—not the kind of glaring mistake that gets the writer seen as stupid or grossly illiterate. Those more damaging mistakes are the ones people make when they try to follow complex rules they haven't mastered.

LITERACY STORY

The Rule about That and Which

The tricky rule about *that* and *which* turns out not to have been one of the ten commandments given to Moses. It first appeared in 1906 in Henry and Francis Fowler's *The King's English.* Twenty years later, after Francis had died, Henry produced his magisterial work, *A Dictionary of Modern English Usage*. The original edition still sells in many copies and continues to provide help and pleasure. (Fowler's text has also been revised: lightly by Ernest Gowers in 1965; substantially by Robert Burchfield in 2004.)

In the 1926 *Dictionary* Henry explains what had motivated him and his brother twenty years earlier when they set in motion more turmoil than they had ever imagined:

> The relations between *that, who, & which,* have come to us from our forefathers as an odd jumble, & plainly show that the language has not been neatly constructed by a master builder who could create each part to do the exact work required of it, neither overlapped nor overlapping. (Entry for "**that** rel. pron")

He goes on for seven more densely packed pages to explain and illustrate the "principle" that he and his brother had promulgated—a principle he says writers might follow if they want to unjumble the linguistic mess left us by our forefathers. But over the intervening twenty years, the principle had, unsurprising, come to be seen as a "rule." (I explain it in the next chapter, 14, but I will argue there that even if we want to obey the rule, we don't need to understand it.)

Like many rules that are slippery and complex, this one took deep root—especially on this side of the Atlantic. It bedevils many people, and rule books and grammar books always give space to it. But there is a huge irony in this story. Early in his seven-page treatment in 1926, Fowler quietly takes it back and says that it cannot be understood as a meaningful rule. That is, he inserts this wistful note:

> Some there are who follow this principle now; but it would be idle to pretend that it is the practice either of most or of the best writers. (635)

He's alluding to the fact that the "principle" has been on the books for twenty years since 1906 in *The King's English*—but it's been ineffectual.

What's interesting here is the role of the Atlantic Ocean with regard to his quiet recantation. It was heard in England but never heard on these shores. American grammar and usage books almost universally enforce the rule (though recently there have been a few small dispensations). But authorities in Britain soon declared that British subjects were *excused* from having to follow it. In the British manual, *New Hart's Rules: The Handbook of Style for Writers and Editors*, British readers are given free choice between *that* and *which* (68). (*Hart's Rules*, 2005, is adapted from *The Oxford Handbook of Style for Writers and Editors*, 2002.) In other words the highest authorities smile on the same old chaos handed down from the forefathers.

But immediately after those handbooks say that there's no need to worry about any difference between *that* and *which*, they add (somewhat disdainfully?): "In US English *which* is used only for non-restrictive clauses" (*Hart's* 68).

Still, invidious distinctions are irresistible. Amazingly, the style guide for the left-leaning *Guardian* newspaper in England still clings to the distinction. It gives a beguilingly simple explanation: "That defines, which informs." (See *Guardian* in Works Cited for the web address of an impressive and interesting resource.) But try *using* this explanation; I think you'll find that it comes apart in your hands when you try it on lots of actual sentences. In the massive *Cambridge Grammar of the English Language*, Huddleston and Pullum insist that it's a "fallacious" and "unhistorical" principle to require "that" for restrictive clauses.

Joe Williams carefully explains the rule for *that/which*, but then notes just as carefully how it is not followed. He concludes:

> A rule can have no force when someone as eminent as Barzun asserts it on one page and unselfconsciously violates it on the next, and that "erroneous" *which* is never caught, not by his editors, not by his proofreaders, not even by Barzun himself. (*Style* 18)

But then Williams makes a confession that illustrates the cultural power of an *alleged* rule—the kind of rule that helps people look down on others:

> Having said that, I confess I follow Fowler's advice, not because I think that a restrictive *which* is an error, but because *that* is softer and because the Grammar Police subject those who write about language to withering (and often uninformed) scrutiny. (19)

Katherine White illustrates a different confusion over *that* and *which*. (She was an editor at *The New Yorker* and wife of E. B. White.) She got mixed up about the direction of trade across the Atlantic. She thought the *British* had to follow Fowler's principle, but that *we* could be looser in the United States—perhaps because of our Revolution. When Richard Wilbur had a poem accepted as a young man at *The New Yorker*,

> Katherine White said to him, "You don't seem to have any understanding of the difference between *which* and *that*," she began. "I don't at all," Wilbur admitted. *"Which* sounds like a brisk word and *that* is a soft-sounding word." White replied, "Fowler wouldn't find that acceptable," then added, "But Fowler was British, wasn't he, and we're an American magazine, so we'll let it go." (Lambert 38)

❊   ❊   ❊

Joe Williams goes on to give a helpful list of other bugbears that intimidate so many writers and cause so many ignorant readers and teachers to find nonexistent faults. Here are some items he calls *"folklore."* "A rule is folklore," he says, "when vast numbers of otherwise careful readers and writers ignore it":

- "Don't begin sentences with *and* or *but.*"
- "Use *fewer* with nouns you count, *less* with nouns you can't."
- "Use *since* and *while* only to refer to time, not to mean *because* or *although.*"

(*Style* 17–20)

In contrast to "folklore" he has a list of what he calls *"options."* Of these he says: "On the most formal occasions, when you are under the closest public scrutiny, you might choose to observe these rules. Ordinarily, though, they are ignored by most careful writers, which is to say they are not rules at all" (22).

- "Do not split infinitives."
- "Use *whom* as the OBJECT of a preposition. . . . Purists would condemn William Zinsser for this use of *who*: . . . . **'Who** am I writing for?' [instead of] 'For **whom** am I writing?'"

- "Do not end a sentence with a preposition." [He points out that the editor of the second edition of Fowler, Sir Ernest Gowers, doesn't consistently observe this principle.]

  - "Use the singular with *none* and *any*." (20–22)

I treasure this big/little story about *that/which*. From a practical perspective, it demonstrates the grammatical sophistication of the *tongue*—which I will show at the start of the next chapter. From a linguistic perspective, it demonstrates that many "rules" and "principles" of written language are contingent—made up and randomly imposed. And from a cultural perspective it demonstrates the point made by Thorstein Veblen and Pierre Bourdieu: what is hard to learn and takes training to accomplish and causes much confusion turns out to be ideal for showing who has prestige and who can be looked down on.

It also illustrates the difference between two meanings of the word *grammar*. For linguists, grammar consists of rules that native speakers can't help but follow: in effect, they are in our bodies because our mouths follow them but our conscious minds don't understand them. But for schoolmarms and the rest of us, grammar consists of rules that we *don't* naturally follow. We have to think conceptually to understand them and often fail nevertheless to follow them.

14 Good Enough Punctuation by Careful Reading Aloud and Listening

My Claim

Authorities on punctuation seem to agree that we should stop trying to follow the voice and buckle down and learn the grammar-based rules. (See Clark and Ivanic at the opening of the last chapter.) My claim here is that most punctuation mistakes come not from paying too much attention to the voice but rather too *little*—too little of a kind of disciplined attention that I'll describe here. As I argued in the two chapters on reading aloud to revise (11 and 12), carefully spoken language gives us a better window onto meaning and intention than we get from grammar. For this reason, I'll try to show that careful reading aloud— since it is a way of serving rhetorical and intonational needs—yields punctuation that is at least *good enough*. Good enough even for the grammar-based rules. It's much better than what people get when they are careless or just act on feelings, and also better than what people get when they try to follow rules they don't fully understand or remember. In fact it's better than some punctuation we see in print.

Here is a more precise statement of my argument:

- If you *don't* know, understand, or remember the grammar rules for punctuation, this method will lead to *some* errors, but almost none of the glaring errors that tempt teachers and other readers to think you are stupid or illiterate.
- If you *do* know the rules, this technique will improve your punctuation by guiding you when the rules are ambiguous (as they often are), or when the rules actually need to be broken (as they sometimes do).

If you want to eliminate *all* errors, you will have to understand the rules of punctuation and the principles of grammar they rest on. My clinching argument is most pragmatic of all. Most people will *not* know the rules and they *will* punctuate by voice, no matter how often they are warned against it. But they'll use the voice naively and badly. So our best hope is to learn how to use the voice in a careful disciplined way.

I learned exactly this pragmatic line of thinking from a presentation by Janet Bean, who argued that students *will* use grammar checkers on their computers no matter how much we warn them of the dangers. Our only choice is between closing our eyes to the fact they are doing it (and badly), or showing them how to do it *well* (which is not so hard).

I am also implicitly drawing on W. D. Winnicott's concept of "good enough." He was a brilliant and useful British psychoanalyst, and in one part of his extensive work, he fought against the pressure that mothers often feel to be *perfect* in meeting the needs of their babies and toddlers. He showed instead how infants actually do better with mothers who are "good enough" and gradually stop meeting every need.

I can't offer empirical proof that my claim is true. What I'm trying to offer are good reasons. Thus, really, the chapter is a call for research.

Illustrating the Claim with the Rule about *That* and *Which*

I can highlight the guts of my claim by pointing to the pesky problem of *that* versus *which*. Of course *that/which* errors are far from life-threatening. But the problem shows a lot about how punctuation works. Consider the two possibilities here:

The concert that is taking place on Saturday night is sold out.
The concert, which is taking place on Saturday night, is sold out.

Which is wrong?

It turns out that neither is wrong. Both are correct—or rather each is correct depending on the context—that is, depending the writer's *intended meaning*. In most contexts, one will be wrong. If you want to choose the right one for a given context, you have to understand the rule that most people find difficult. (Note that I could also have written, *You have to understand the rule, which most people find difficult*).

But in fact we don't have to understand the rule. Reading aloud with care gives us a rule that is simpler and more reliable: *If your voice pauses, use which and commas; if it doesn't, use that and no commas.* The important point is that the distinction between a restrictive and nonrestrictive clause (the basis of the grammar rule) really depends on the speaker's or writer's *intended meaning*— on how the language user *felt* "Saturday night" in her sentence about the sold out concert. Did she feel "Saturday night" as an essential part of the message or an added bit that could be left out? If you want to see how complex the rule is, I welcome you to this box.

The essential rule *can* be stated in a simple tidy package: *That goes with restrictive clauses; which goes with nonrestrictive clauses*. But I've always found it difficult to open that package. Here is the explanation given by Diana Hacker in one of the most commonly assigned student handbooks:

Word groups describing nouns or pronouns (adjective clauses, adjective phrases, and appositives) are restrictive or nonrestrictive. A *restrictive* element defines or limits the meaning of the word it modifies and is therefore essential to the meaning of the sentence. Because it contains essential information, a restrictive element is not set off with commas. [Then she gives an example.] If you remove a restrictive element from a sentence, the meaning changes significantly, becoming more general than you intended. . . .

A *nonrestrictive* element describes a noun or pronoun whose meaning has already been clearly defined or limited. Because it contains nonessential or parenthetical information, a nonrestrictive element is set off with commas. [She gives another example.] If you remove a nonrestrictive element from a sentence, the meaning does not change dramatically. Some meaning is lost, to be sure, but the defining characteristics of the person or thinking described remain the same as before. (Hacker 148).

I guess there's a clear distinction in this passage (if we can understand it—not all students are happy they had to buy this expensive book), but the author has the grace to acknowledge that theory sometimes breaks down in practice. Thus she adds:

Often it is difficult to tell whether a word group is restrictive or nonrestrictive without seeing it in context and considering your meaning. Should you write "The dessert, made with fresh raspberries, was delicious" or "The dessert made with fresh raspberries was delicious"? That depends. If the phrase *made with fresh raspberries* tells readers which of several desserts you're referring to, you would omit the commas. If the phrase merely adds information about the one dessert served with the meal, you would use the commas. (149)

I'm tempted to throw up my hands. I don't always understand which clauses are subordinate, which verbs are finite, and which pronouns are relative. (See Literacy Story, Chapter 13, for the peculiar history of how the *that/which* distinction was originally imposed in England—and then rescinded there but left on the books in the United States.)

Diana Hacker's explanation actually ends up a little looser about this rule than many other U.S. handbooks. In effect, she abandons *half* of the rule. She writes, "Use *that* only with restrictive clauses. Many writers prefer to use *which* only with nonrestrictive clauses, but usage varies." (If she'd had a little more courage, she might have suggested a simpler blunter rule that I sometimes offer students: *Always use "that," never use "which." "That" will almost never get you in trouble*.)

My favorite usage guide is one that doesn't try to teach me; it just gives me quick answers—answers that are usually easier to find than in regular handbooks that want to improve me. Not surprisingly, it's the *Reference Manual for Stenographers and Typists* by Gavin and Sabin. And when they do feel they have to explain a rule, they are clearer than most handbooks. It's characteristic of them simply to avoid the slippery terms, *restrictive* and *nonrestrictive*, and talk more simply about *essential* and *nonessential* clauses (9–10).

Rodney Huddleston and Geoffrey Pullum spent ten years writing the eighteen-hundred-page *Cambridge Grammar of the English Language* (2003). Their main and almost only argument for studying grammar is that it is necessary *if you want to understand writing books and advice manuals*! Yet this example beautifully illustrates a central fact about punctuation. Many or even most punctuation rules in grammar books are *imperfect* attempts to do justice to what matters: the writer's inner intended meaning.

And intended meaning manifests itself most clearly and reliably when people speak their meanings carefully aloud. When we punctuate our own writing, *we* know our intended meaning better than anyone else. (We seldom have to punctuate anyone else's writing—except on punctuation tests! And even then, reading aloud is the best way to estimate the writer's intention.)

Let me summarize the point of this introductory dalliance with *that* and *which*. The grammatical rule is tricky, rubbery, and not easy to understand. But the reading aloud rule is simple and helpful. It's a striking case of what we can get if we harness the mystery of *intonation* for punctuation.

Training the Voice and the Ear

But the reading aloud technique I'm suggesting requires some training. If we use our voices casually and settle for unconsidered decisions based on spoken pauses, we will almost surely use too many commas since we pause so often in speaking. And sometimes we'll use too few periods because sometimes we don't feel a closure pause where the grammar rule demands a period—that is, in situations where informal speaking has led us to gather into a single larger intonational alliance what grammar calls a "run-on sentence" or a "comma splice."

Most people need to train both their voices and their ears. Voice training requires thoughtful reading aloud, not casual speaking as in everyday speech. Many students have had unpleasant classroom experiences when asked by teachers to read aloud, and many adults are shy about giving vocal prominence to the words they've written. I have to keep repeating: *Say the words lovingly. Don't settle for a timid or halting or uncomfortable performance. Try to be <u>convincing</u>.* (I avoid saying, "Read it with expression" because that phrase so often means "Read it with a fake pretense.") The training also requires testing out *different* ways to perform the same sentence. We need to read the alternative versions with loving care and then listen carefully to subtle differences.

Let's start with a simple example from Dawkins ("Teaching Punctuation"):

First it was rain then it was snow.

I ask students to come up with as many different performances of these words as possible. It's as though this sentence is a little song, and we're looking for the maximum number of ways to sing it. Or it's a micro-Shakespeare play that we might stage with different interpretations. What we are seeking, in the end, is one or more versions that seem right or at least acceptable. But I urge them to try out marginal or weird versions too, so we can find where the limits are. (Besides it's fun to see how far you can stretch a performance. What can we learn about the play if Hamlet is portrayed as a girl?)

So for a marginal possibility, we hear a loving performance with absolutely no pause anywhere. Also we need to hear a loving rendition of *First. It was rain. Then. It was snow.* Some students stick up for marginal renderings like these, and one can invent rhetorical situations that make them tempting. But most vote that those two marginal readings aren't quite right for the mouth and ear on that sentence.

But there are multiple readings that most people accept, and they are all correct (more below about punctuational choice). It's good news when there are multiple acceptable readings. It means more choices for punctuating. But remember, it's not a question of pure *sound*. It's the marriage of sound and *meaning* that we seek with reading aloud—and that punctuation is meant to convey. We are looking for the out loud performance that best *matches* the meaning—that *is* or *enacts* the meaning.

So as we try out variations in pausing, stress, and intonation, we get to listen for slightly different shades of meaning or emphasis. We often have a choice among them, and we're looking for the *sound of the particular meaning* we really prefer or intend. So as we randomly or playfully try out variations, we sometimes uncover a *new* shade of meaning we'd never thought of. We might even conclude that this new shade is the one we'd been looking for all along; we had *intended* it but not quite said it. (It's this internal state of affairs that leads people so often to say, "You know what I mean?" or "You *know* what I mean!" This intended-but-unsaid meaning is a "felt sense." See my "Felt Sense"—where I explore the intricacy and precision of felt bodily meanings that are sometimes unarticulated in words.)

This exercise in playfully trying out different and even nutty versions helps students not settle for timid, mumbling, monotone readings. We can't make good decisions about what's "acceptable" unless we hear good faith or even loving readings that try to be convincing. (In truth, it can be helpful to work on these punctuation exercises *before* working on the more general process of reading aloud for revising described in Chapters 11 and 12. These punctuation exercises get students into the spirit of brave and invested reading.)

※　　　※　　　※

Ear training is just as important as voice training. People need to *listen closely* to performances till they learn to hear the subtle but genuine difference between the sound of closure and delay or pause—that is, between "period intonation" and "comma intonation." (These are terms that Chafe and Danielewicz use in their linguistic research on speech and punctuation ["'Normal' Speaking" 215].) Comma intonation and period intonation represent the kinds of pause that we usually represent in writing with a comma and a period.

Many students think that *short* equals "comma" and *long* equals "period." This misconception explains most of the mistakes people make when they punctuate by voice in a casual and undisciplined way. Duration is a red herring. With training—and for some it takes repeated sessions—people gradually learn to ignore how long the pause lasts and listen instead for the often subtle difference between the *sound* of closure or letting go (the sound of period intonation), and the *sound* of non-closure or not-quite-letting-go or still-hanging-on (the sound of comma intonation).

The difference can be quite subtle. In teaching, I often find myself doing little bits of exaggerated micro-singing or intonational moaning to illustrate the difference between letting-go and not-quite-letting-go—all the while varying the duration of the pause. For students need to hear how *not-letting-go* can stretch out for a long period of time, and *letting-go* can slip past you almost before you hear it. (And of course there are subtle marginal cases of "not quite letting go, but not quite hanging on." This is why God invented the semi-colon.)

When I say that some students are slow in learning to discriminate between the sound of the comma and of the period, this may reinforce a general lament among "cultured" folk: *Young people these days have tin ears.* Or even: *Your method asks for musical sophistication, and some people will never have it.* But that's wrong. The knowledge I'm trying to get them to use is not new to them; they already have it. They've been using exactly these delicate vocal cues to communicate fine distinctions of meaning in their speaking throughout most of their lives. And they've been *registering* distinctions of meaning on the basis of these subtle cues—even when the comma pauses are long and the period pauses are short. It can be useful to capture their natural uses of subtle intonation on tape and point out short lettings-go and long holdings-on.

But this knowledge, like so many of the complex rules of grammar that every child learns from an early age, tends to be tacit. It emerges in performance but isn't found by conscious introspection. Students have been using it but not consciously attending to it—and certainly not applying it consciously to written punctuation in a classroom. I'm tempted to think that there's an inherent musical subtlety—especially rhythmic—in all humans who learn a native language. Note, however, that I'm not claiming that their casually *spoken* periods and commas always match correct *written* punctuation, merely that their casually spoken language depends on these subtle differentiations between closure and nonclosure. Casual speaking leads people to put closures and nonclosures where grammar says they shouldn't.

When we train with different renderings of the same sentence and can't quite find one that pleases the mouth and ear, we have come up against a useful principle for writers: when we are perplexed about punctuation, we probably have a bad sentence. It needs to be rewritten in such a way that the punctuation is obvious. Ernest Gowers has a chapter on punctuation in his classic 1948 short pamphlet for His Majesty's Stationery Office, *Plain Words: A Guide to the Use of English.* He sets a wonderfully austere goal: try to write each sentence so clearly that it doesn't need *any* punctuation but the final period. And Cicero: who would have thought that the father of the periodic sentence was of the same mind? But Baker notes that

> Cicero himself disdained punctuation, insisting that the well-cadenced sentence would audibly manifest its own terminus, without the need of any mere "stroke interposed by a copyist." (77)

Everyday Speech versus Reading Aloud
The leverage in this technique comes from the difference between two ways of uttering words: casual everyday speaking and careful reading aloud. In everyday speaking, we frequently pause. Some of these pauses have a natural logic even though they violate the rules for punctuation (such as pausing between a long subject and its following verb). Others result because we speak in "real time" and often pause while trying to find thoughts and words and create

syntax on the fly. ("Speakers are unable to verbalize within a single intonation unit more than one concept that has been recalled from long-term memory" [Chafe and Danielewicz "'Normal' Speaking" 218]). Speakers pause when they run out of cognitive steam or feel the tickle of a related thought or momentary doubt or qualification. As Chafe remarks, we often start off a sentence with nothing but a gamble that we can finish it (*Pear Stories* 30). For all these reasons, people are often tempted to use too many commas when they let their casual speaking voices guide their punctuation.

Careful reading aloud is a far different use of spoken language—as we learn from the training I describe here and in the previous three chapters. When we read aloud lovingly for the sake of working on our writing, we can take time to try out *alternative* readings—and we can plan or rehearse the words in mind before speaking them. We don't have time for this in natural conversation—and not even when we read aloud for listeners. So when we read carefully aloud for the sake of revising our own writing, we are not so tempted to make a comma pause every time we might pause in casual speaking. Our goal in these exercises is not to mimic speech but to create the best musical performance of a set of words—the performance that best *sings* the meaning. In this process—with time for planning and rehearsing and multiple versions—we naturally create longer intonation units and these units usually reflect natural structures of syntax and the semantic shapes of our intended meaning. In effect, we're trying for the "ideal performance" of a string of words.

So when Chafe and Danielewicz discover punctuation errors in student writing and blame it on the use of voice, their culprit is *casual everyday speech*.

> We have seen that the way inexperienced writers use punctuation often reproduces patterns found in spoken language. . . . [C]arrying over spoken prosodic habits into the punctuation of writing often leads to nonstandard, and sometimes infelicitous results. ("'Normal' Speaking" 224)

When unskilled writers use too many commas and periods (and occasionally too few), it's because they aren't stopping to read their sentences lovingly aloud; they're not trying out multiple performances and listening for closure versus nonclosure pauses; and they're not going on to use *conscious considered listening* for deciding where pauses are *really* needed. If you are using this disciplined process, you are very far from casual everyday speaking.

Scholes and Willis also investigate student punctuation mistakes and they too blame the use of voice. They show that students don't understand the "syntactic" function of punctuation. They conclude that "despite 250 years of instruction and practice, a large number of otherwise educated writers remain relatively ignorant of the orthographic [or grammar-based] function of punctuation" (18).

But let's look at the peculiar test they used. They used reading tests and asked students to interpret sentences whose meaning depended on punctuation. In their test, students were given a sentence and asked to choose between interpretations A and B:

The player was on drugs the whole season and that it was known by the coach was unforgivable.

> A. The coach's knowledge was unforgivable.
> B. The player's drug use was unforgivable.

Then students were given another version of the same sentence and asked again to choose between A and B:

> The player was on drugs the whole season and that, it was known by the coach, was unforgivable.
> A. The coach's knowledge was unforgivable.
> B. The player's drug use was unforgivable.

These sentences are surely rather artificial—unlike what almost anyone would ever want to write. And students naturally tended to make decisions based on intuitions from normal speaking. They weren't even shown the two sentences *together*—which would have made it easier to compare them, even in the absence of training. *If* they'd used the disciplined technique I'm describing here—that is, if they read the two sentences lovingly aloud with careful listening and gone back and forth between them—then they would have had a fighting chance at *feeling* the meaning and how it shifts between sentences. And if (for some sad reason) they had been trying to *write* sentences like these, they would have *generated* them naturally with the pauses built in. They would have had no need to understand the rules of what Scholes and Willis call "orthographic punctuation"; their mouths and ears would have felt the meaning and where to put the pauses and the punctuation. In short, careful reading aloud is very different from casual speech. (These are exactly the kinds of sentences Gowers was talking about: the difficulty in punctuation sends a message: "Rewrite this sentence.")

Punctuation as an Inviting Meadow for the Voice

What emerges from good training samples is what we saw from the history I recounted at the head of the previous chapter: punctuation often gives us an inviting meadow with various correct and acceptable choices. That is, even though people tend to feel punctuation to be the realm of rules—above all, the realm of *error*—nevertheless we have more choice than we are usually led to believe. As Chafe argues, there is far less conflict than most people realize between the rules of grammar and the older tradition that follows the rhetorical needs of the voice. (During the Vietnam War, I applied in good faith for status as a conscientious objector. My draft board refused me, even after an interview and appeal. It might be that they sensed that I would turn into the violent creature I've become: someone who wants to *shoot* teachers who call a piece of punctuation or grammar *wrong* when, in fact, the rule books do not call it wrong.)

John Dawkins highlights the *rhetorical* dimension of punctuation. The rhetorical lens shows that when we speak and write, we don't so much follow rules as make choices—choices about the meaning we want to convey, how to say it, and how to get the rhetorical effect we want. He lays out a "hierarchy of functional punctuation marks" that run from the greatest separation to the greatest connection: period, question mark, exclamation mark, semicolon, colon, dash, comma, and zero or no punctuation. He shows that *every* mark of punctuation is valid between the clauses of *First it was rain then it was snow* (including question marks). Only with zero punctuation do we get a conflict between the rules and the voice, since most teachers call it an error in any context. But Dawkins illustrates good nonfiction writers using zero punctuation in this kind of sentence for particular rhetorical effects. In certain situations a writer might want even this variation: *First it was rain then it was—snow!* This is legal also with ellipses instead of the dash. (Comma or period would be illegal here, but the tongue is not much tempted to use them.)

I also like to train with samples that have choices you don't even notice till you explore options. For example:

> *During the recession the stock price began fluctuating more and more wildly.*

Creative sharp-eared students come up with what seems odd but is actually a common enough intonational pattern in speech and even in good writing:

> *. . . the stock price began fluctuating more—and more wildly.*

We get to discuss how this version doesn't just change the rhythm; it reflects a subtle and interesting change in meaning. You could call my exercise artificial because the writer always knows how his own sentence should sound. But in fact that's not true. We all write sentences sometimes that can be improved with a performance we hadn't considered. This always leads us to the inevitable chestnut: *A woman without her man is nothing.* Sometimes I have to linger with this sample and press for possibilities no one has found. I'm always curious to see the gender of the student who finally comes up with the famous version: *A woman. Without her, man is nothing.* Anyway, all of this work is about the hearing and the bodily enactment of meaning.

Objection. *But you're deluding students. You're leading them down the primrose path to an artificial meadow of choice. You've stacked the deck with training sentences where all options are legal.*

Yes. Even though we have more punctuational choice than most people realize, nevertheless there are buried land mines in this inviting meadow. The artificially safe training sentences are for tuning the mouth and ear, but we need to go on to practice sentences where there is a conflict between the desires of the tongue and the grammatical rules.

Punctuating Defensively

So how should we deal with the land mines that even careful reading aloud won't save us from? Here are five possible responses. I move from what's easiest to what's hardest.

1. *Don't worry.* Just use careful reading aloud and listening. It won't lead to *many* mistakes. And those few mistakes are not so damaging. They aren't the kind that lead some teachers and other readers to consider you illiterate or stupid—which *does* happen with the mistakes people make when they are careless or guided by feelings or by rules they don't really understand. Few readers actually know the rules well enough to catch most mistakes.

2. *Follow a few simple guidelines.* Sticklers will scorn them as *oversimple,* but they help a lot:

- *About commas: When in doubt, leave it out.* Careful reading aloud will help us avoid most of the extra commas that come from the pauses in casual speech, but some will creep in. This "leave-it-out" guideline is especially appropriate now since copy editors in the last fifty years have come to favor as few commas as possible.

- *Stick to periods, commas, and question marks.* These minimize the chances for infraction, yet they are all we need for excellent writing—even for subtle shades of meaning and emphasis. Of course it's lovely to have elegant punctuation that calls itself to the reader's attention; and students can get brownie points from some teachers for a well deployed semi-colon. But the most realistic goal for punctuation is the same one for spelling: *not* to be noticed.

- *Never use <u>which</u>.* Most that/which tickets are issued for illegal *which*s. It turns out that the more workaday *that* is fine for most of what we normally write. In the few cases where *that* is legally wrong, very few readers will know or care enough to ticket it. (Intriguingly, many academics let themselves be seduced into the opposite policy of overusing *which.* Michael Bulley did extensive research on *that* and *which* in published writing and found that "in some parts of the academic world, there is nowadays a preference for the polite-sounding *which* over the more workaday *that*" [47]. These academics probably feel that they sound more learned and impressive with *which.*)

- *And then there are dashes.* When you are perplexed about what your mouth and ear are telling you, try Emily Dickinson's one-size-fit's all punctuation—the dash. A dash is *never* wrong from a strictly legal point of view if used in any spot where you pause in careful reading aloud. Sticklers will often accept a dash for a speaking pause where they would ticket an illegal comma or period. When people hate dashes, they can't usually call them *wrong,* merely lazy bad taste. Dashes are particularly good for representing the parenthetical interjections that are so common in speech—like this—that good writers often use. (You will have noticed that I am guilty of what many people of taste will consider dash promiscuity. But then Emily is my neighbor.)

3. *Learn just a few real rules.* Once you can read aloud with investment and listen with sensitivity—which means that you have developed a working competence with the powerful principles at the heart of most punctuation—you'll find it's not so hard to learn one or two rules from the *grammatical* tradition.

- *Never put a comma between the subject and its verb.* This rule requires a bit of grammar awareness, and some exceptions are allowed, but many students can benefit from hearing it—once they are no longer flummoxed by punctuation.

- *Semi-colons are useful and easy* for a sequence of items that need to be separated when there are also pauses inside some of those items. A common example is with dates: *January 11, 2002; September 4, 2003; November 1, 2005; and April 20, 2006.* They are also useful for a series of phrases, e.g., *They called off the picnic for three reasons: because it was raining; because the food was stale; and because they didn't even want to go.*

By learning a few rules like these, students can treat punctuation as the realm of thoughtful rhetorical *choice*—but still avoid most of the few mistakes that reading aloud alone might lead to.

4. *Look hard at the long final section of this chapter* which is simply a collection of examples where reading aloud succeeds and fails. If you examine it thoughtfully you can get a *feel* for possible problems and how to avoid them. Feeling is actually what most people use when they've learned to follow all the intricate rules.

5. *Learn all rules and how to follow them.* I can't recommend this route unless you love verbal and grammatical complexity. For learning the rules also means learning the rules for exceptions to the rules. Grammar itself is deeply interesting, but the rules for punctuation yield little intellectual reward.

The Danger of a Defensive Mentality

It's hard to avoid thinking defensively about punctuation since it's so often taught as a set of rules. And we're never told when we got it right, only when we got it wrong. But if writers write too defensively and worry too much about land mines and rules, it often makes writing unpleasant for them and saps their writing of energy. Careful reading aloud is a way to avoid most errors without this negative effect—and indeed it improves style.

A much better goal here is the one that Dawkins celebrates: to learn to treat punctuation as a *positive rhetorical act,* not just a defensive attempt to avoid error. We write better when we can think of ourselves as theater-directors or movie-*auteurs* and make choices about how we want readers to *perform* our sentences and *experience* our meaning. This approach to punctuation keeps the emphasis on the important writerly question: *What do I really mean—especially now that I've listened more carefully? And how do I want readers to experience my meaning?* Besides, when readers hear and feel our meanings, they don't have to work so hard to understand words on the page.

It's worth noting that this approach to punctuation follows the Deweyan tradition of progressive education: don't treat learners as blank slates and make teaching a process of giving students new rules to learn and understand. Instead, build on what students already know and can do. In the case of punctuation, learners can use the intonation that comes to their tongues for free. This carries tacit mastery of the amazingly complex syntactic rules of their native language.

But of course we are not *consciously aware* of most of the rules that our tongues follow. Dewey insists that we learn from experience—but not from experience in itself—only by reflecting on experience. The disciplined process of reading aloud and listening carefully and comparing alternative performances of the same sentence: these activities help us reflect consciously on how intonation and pausing relate to nuances of meaning and emphasis. We don't need new information for learning to punctuate well—we don't need to learn the rules—but we need to learn to reflect consciously on what we can already do. The process takes discipline, time, and attentive reflection.

> Of course I am not the first to argue for this approach. Francis Christensen notes that Wallace Anderson called the "pitch-pause method" the most effective way for dealing with restrictive and nonrestrictive modifiers, and Christensen says he prefers it too. But he notes that it is "an oral method and is therefore limited generally to situations where the teacher can ask the student to read the sentence aloud." (97)

Good Enough Punctuation: A Concluding Collection of Examples Where Reading Aloud Succeeds and Fails

I'll prolong this chapter with a long catalogue of examples. Readers who are interested in my argument but don't care about disputed or fuzzy issues in punctuation might just as well go on to Chapter 15.

Sentence Fragments

According to conventional grammatical rules for correct revised Edited English, sentence fragments are illegal. Careful reading aloud will reject most of them—but not all. It will sometimes allow fragments like these:

> *The test results were announced yesterday. After students had waited three weeks.*
>
> *He wants voters to see what he actually is. That is, a strong independent member of the senate.*

The good news is that these errors are not so damaging. We see them in lots of published writing—because they work rhetorically. What's more, the mouth and ear almost always *reject* "illiterate fragments" like these:

> *If the incumbent is re-elected. The party will redraw the congressional district.*
>
> *Before we can make a decision. We must wait three weeks.*

Students who don't consult mouth and ear and are careless or confused by punctuation sometimes write damaging fragments like these. But careful reading aloud will accept only viable or "acceptable" fragments like the two I started with—or ones like this:

> *First it was rain, then it was snow. Which finally put a halt to our plans.*
>
> *The party will re-draw the congressional district. If the incumbent is re-elected.*
>
> *They called off the picnic for three reasons. Because it was raining. Because the food was stale. And because they didn't even want to go.*

According to the strict rules of the grammatical tradition, such sentences are wrong—and a fair number of teachers will hand out a ticket. But fragments like these are commonly used by good writers in their published writing. (Earlier, I noted exactly this punctuation used by the English *Guardian* newspaper.)

Henry James goes so far as to begin the last paragraph of his *Portrait of a Lady* with a fragment that many mouths and ears would reject: *On which he looked up at her.* This was for the 1881 version, and when he revised the novel for the late massive New York edition of all his novels, he let the extreme fragment hang out there longer: *On which he looked up at her—but only to guess, from her face, with a revulsion, that she simply meant he was young.*

Run-on Sentences or Comma Splices

If people read aloud carefully and really listen to alternative readings, they will avoid most run-ons. But again, not all. The good news is that a careful reading always gives us a pause of some sort where writing demands a period, so at least there is no danger of the kind of unbridled run-on that naive students can make when they use no punctuation at all, for example,

> *He had waited hours for everyone to assemble for a long committee meeting he got annoyed and drove off.*

But the bad news is that even a careful considered decision based on the mouth and ear can invite a comma where most teachers and many readers will insist on a period:

> *Pollsters were surprised by her victory, they had forecast low results.*

Dawkins shows plenty of good writers insisting on overriding the rule with this kind of "comma splice" in order to increase connectedness between clauses. But many teachers and readers who know the rules are unforgiving about run-ons. For some reason, run-ons seem to scream *"bad punctuation"*! Teachers find it hard to accept that students might have good rhetorical reasons for violating the rule. Teachers' eyes are pre-tuned to look for errors in students writing. Joseph Williams tricked teachers into *not* noticing errors by surreptitiously embedding them in an essay he published ("Phenomenology of Error"). (In Chapter 17 you'll see a delicious passage from Fowler with a striking comma splice. It might have been avoided with careful reading aloud—though I mustn't assume too much about 1920s spoken English in England.) So even though reading aloud will prevent most run-on sentences, it has a slight weakness for comma-based run-ons. This might be the biggest danger for the reading aloud technique. I haven't figured out a good preventive slogan (like the one for preventing too many commas: "If in doubt, leave it out"). I alert students to the danger, but I don't want to put too much emphasis on "For goodness sake, be careful!" because I don't want to make them defensive punctuators who will start distrusting their most valuable tools: the tongue and the ear.

> There's an interesting larger theoretical issue here. If someone uses reading aloud in a careful considered way and writes an illegal comma run-on sentence instead of "correctly" making two sentences, it doesn't mean that her tongue is stupid; it means that her tongue has insisted that these two clauses are actually *functioning*—grammatically—as a single sentence. The real problem is not with the tongue; the problem is, as we've seen, that the grammar of correct writing has a shaky idiosyncratic basis—especially when it comes to the concept of "sentence." I'd argue that, in truth, the careful tongue gives a better window into the *actual* grammar of English than can be found in the rules for correct sentences.

Too Many Commas—Especially between Subject and Verb

This might be the most frequent "error" that reading aloud will lead to. Ordinary speaking is littered with pauses between subjects and verbs, sometimes even when the subject is very short, for example,

> *He* [pause] *is the culprit.*

But if you use careful reading aloud rather than just listening to casual speech, you'll avoid many of those illegal commas. Still, you'll probably end up with some. For example, even with a careful loving reading, you might want *He, is the culprit* if the context is very dramatic. But a more likely danger is something like this:

> *The man who was appointed way after the deadline had passed, was dishonest.*

Many readers will accept this comma and perhaps even be grateful, but those who know and care will call this punctuation definitely wrong. The rule is unforgiving. We're left with a perplexity. How to proceed? One option is to learn the rules. But I don't think that's really an option for most people—especially with my goal of inviting more people to write. For most of us, then, I make two suggestions. First, punctuate with careful reading aloud. We will end up with a few "extra" commas between subject and verb and occasionally between verb and object. In most cases, readers will benefit from them without noticing them. The only readers who will object are those who know the rule and also care more about it than about ease of reading. For example, here's an illegal comma that few will complain about:

> *An effective administrator thinks first, and never lets herself be hurried.*

(The clause after the comma is not an independent one.) Here's an example from this book where, even after much careful revising, I left a comma between a long subject and the verb that follows.

> *By age four or earlier, every human child who isn't brain damaged or left in the woods to be raised by wolves, has mastered the essential complex structures of a native language-or two or even three.*

The copy editor removed the offending comma. I'd call it "good enough punctuation" but I accepted her help. One less crime on my record.

Second, always keep in mind this general rule of thumb for commas: *When in doubt, leave it out.*

I want to illustrate how complex and discouraging the rules are, but I'll resort to a box because I suspect most readers will take my word for it.

Here is Martha Kolln:

[N]ever separate

- the subject from the verb
- the direct object from the objective complement
- the indirect object from the direct object
- the verb from the subjective complement

. . . Even though the [extended subjects] . . . may be long—they may even require a pause for breath—the slots are never separated by commas. (Kolln 15)

(Note that she calls this zone a "slot" even while insisting that nothing belongs in it.)

She calls her book *Rhetorical Grammar: Grammatical Choices, Rhetorical Effects*, but when it comes to punctuation, she's clearly guided more by rules than by the rhetorical tradition. Here's a bit more:

[W]ith one exception, never separate the verb from the direct object. [The exception is with quotations, as with "He said, "I love you."] (15)

Use a comma with the coordinating conjunction between the clauses of a compound sentence. Use no comma with *and* between the parts of a two-part compound structure within the sentence." (186)

As we saw earlier, many rule books tell us to skip the no-subject-verb-comma rule if it causes too much confusion—as in *Those who can do; those who can't teach*. So the writer is left in the tricky position of trying to decide *when* a sentence creates *"enough confusion"* to justify overriding the "never" rule. In effect, the rule giver asks us to call on our mouth and ear—though it also asks us call on our knowledge of psychology, since we must decide how much our readers will care about the rules and whether they will consider us smart or stupid to break them.

I'd argue the rules tempt too many writers into too *few* commas. Here, for example, is a sentence from *The New Yorker* that serves readers badly for lack of a comma after the long subject ending in "civilization":

Throughout the eighteen-thirties, the give-and-take between Carlyle's deeply pessimistic sense of the primal violence that lay beneath the surface of civilization and Mill's insistence that the cure for the primal illness was more civilization was one of the creative engines of English thought. (Gopnik "Right Again" 87)

It says a lot that a writer as good as Gopnik (or the sophisticated copy editor at *The New Yorker*) insisted wrongheadedly on the rule. The real problem, of course, is not the punctuation but the sentence. If the writer had revised by reading aloud, he would have insisted on a much better sentence.

Chafe would like to relax the rule against commas between subject and verb when those commas are helpful to readers, but he's also realistic about what is feasible at the moment:

It is very tempting in these cases to recommend that the prohibition be relaxed so that contemporary authors would be free to follow the practice of their nineteenth-century predecessors. The rule, however, is by now so entrenched that it would be difficult to repeal. For writing teachers, the best practice may be to teach it as an arbitrary rule, while at the same time allowing students to recognize the discrepancy for what it is. ("Punctuation" 421)

He advises teachers to show "a tolerance or even respect for writers who are sensitive enough to follow what their inner voices 'say'" (423).

But and However and Similar Words

There are some pesky ambiguities about how to punctuate these little words, whether they occur at the start, the middle, or even the end of a sentence.

After an introductory phrase, rule books are more tolerant than they used to be about letting us skip commas. (Hacker says, "If a conjunctive adverb or transitional expression blends smoothly with the rest of the sentence, calling for little or no pause in reading, it does not need to be set off with a comma" (151). She lists examples like *also, at least, certainly,* and many others. But she doesn't answer the question, "How smoothly does it have to blend?" She alleges she's giving a rule, but really, she's calling on the mouth and ear to decide. Yet she doesn't put *however* on her list. So we're left with the conventional rule that won't let a "however" go naked. Because I'm a published author, I can refuse a copy editor's comma after "however." (*Most people believed him. However he never told the truth.*) You'll notice me consistently skipping these kinds of commas where I don't want a pause.

But new authors may feel fragile and beaten down by difficulties they endured getting their first article accepted. They may not dare or even be allowed to refuse this "help." And teachers will call students wrong for this usage. Students are seldom in a position to point out to their teachers that authorities disagree. It's not so hard to remember to put a comma after *however,* but if the punishment for error is not too great, why not stick with the rhetorical tradition that asks *How do I want my readers to hear my meaning?* Even readers who know the rule don't usually consider it a capital crime.

When words like *however* don't start the sentence, we see similar perplexities. For example, is it okay to leave out a comma after "Freud" in this sentence?

> *Freud however, wrote brilliantly in German and talked in everyday language about the es, ich, and uber-ich rather than using the more technical sounding Latin of id, ego, and superego.*

Careful reading aloud makes me omit the comma and thus commit what is technically an error, but again it's not lethal and it helps the reader hear the meaning as intended.

As for such words at the end, remember Frost's line, *His house is in the village though.* His rhetorical meaning was travestied when an editor inserted a comma. And in the following sentence, there's no good reason for a comma after "declined" if the writer doesn't want readers to hear an intonational break:

> *The president suggested an amendment. The senators declined however.*
> *Bottom line: the tongue can sometimes lead to errors.*

And *or* But *with Interjected Phrases*

Consider this elegant (verbless) (non)sentence about vodka from *The Joy of Cooking:*

> *Another spirit, this, as blithe and potent as whisky and gin and, next to gin, perhaps the most versatile of "mixers"* (Rombauer and Becker 39).

The commas around "this" are a lovely example of harmony between the rule and the needs of the voice. The punctuation captures beautifully how the sentence is meant to be heard. But when I get to the comma between *and* and *gin (potent as whisky and, next to gin),* I am thrown off balance by the fastidious rule. It violates the rhetorical needs of voice and ear. We need to hear *and next to gin* as a single intonational phrase—a single unit of intonational meaning.

Speaking of being fastidious, consider Wordsworth's Lucy poem:

> *But she is in her grave, and, oh,*
> *The difference to me!*

He had a poet's good ear and praised the speech of ordinary people. Could he really have wanted readers to hear *three* pauses near the end of the first line? Perhaps. But the rest of us must surely have permission to avoid this kind of comma.

Another example. If writers carefully follow the rules of punctuation, they will end up with a sentence like this:

> *Her interpretation was best, but, surprisingly, it was disqualified.*

(It would be punctuated the same with *and* instead of *but*.) But if writers carefully read aloud to punctuate, they are likely to use only two commas, not three:

> *Her interpretation was best, but surprisingly, it was disqualified.*

Some might even skip that last comma to get readers to hear the final clause as one unit of intonational-based meaning.

I am conducting my own little war against these commas that obey the strict law and thereby ruin the intonational shape. But some teachers will take out the red pen and declare error. Still, not many readers worry about this particular rule. So, here again, we're in the realm of "good enough." Careful reading aloud can lead to errors, but they are errors that fit the writer's rhetorical preferences (because of the shape of meaning) and make things easier for readers. So these errors don't usually get writers in much trouble except with that small number of readers who both know the rule and also care a lot about it. Unfortunately, many of them are teachers.

Commas in a Series

The reading out loud method confirms what is probably the most accepted answer to the perennial debate about whether to put a comma before the last item in a series ("*The President, the Senate[,] and the House of Representatives*"). I'd argue that the voice is wise when it usually pauses before even the last item. This is a big help when the last two words in a series *function* as one item: our mouths and ears know enough *not* to pause near the end of this sentence: *For supper we'll have ham, eggs, spinach, and bread and butter.* Occasionally, we *want* readers to understand bread and butter as separate items. If so, the mouth and ear will effortlessly guide us to a comma and give readers the understanding we are trying to convey. Here is the larger theme again: rules are too rigid; the voice is the best window onto intended meaning or rhetorical need.

But what about this example:

> *The podium was draped in red, white, and blue.*

The final comma looks stupid. But remember I'm not defending a rigid rule (always put a comma before the last in a series), I'm defending what the voice wants—which is probably no comma.

> Note, however: when we speak the phrase normally, we don't pause at all after *white*—not even after *red*. But if we give a careful loving reading (rather than just speak casually), we might well pause after white. There might be a rhetorical situation where we want readers to hear a pause.
>
> Kolln recognizes the central role of voice in the matter of commas in a series:
>
> > These commas represent the pauses and slight changes of pitch that occur in the production of the series. You can hear the commas in your voice when you compare the series of three with a two-part compound structure. . . . [W]hen people *omit* a comma between the last two items in a series, they are implying a closer connection than actually exists between the last two elements of the series, and [the absence] ignores the pitch change, however slight, represented by the comma. (168–169)

Still, there's an extremely subtle rule that the careful voice will sometimes violate. It turns out that while most adjectives in a series are supposed to get commas, some are not. Consider these two sentences. Both are punctuated according to the rule even though the second one has no comma between the adjectives.

> *Some postcards feature appealing, dramatic scenes.*
> *Other postcards feature famous historical scenes.* (Troyka 127)

A gold star goes to anyone who can explain why. I don't get a gold star, but I found this in a book. The answer is that the first one involves "coordinate adjectives" and the second one "cumulative adjectives." I can't get it straight myself and I think the tongue and ear will do at least as well even as people who have more or less understood the rule. (Authorities admit that it's often hard to decide whether an adjective is "coordinate" or "cumulative.") Reading aloud will sometimes be wrong, but the issue is so picayune that mistakes are seldom recognized and even less often prosecuted.

> The handbook by Keene and Adams charmingly explains the order in which we should put no-comma cumulative adjectives: (1) articles, pronouns, quantity words, and possessives; (2) evaluative words; (3) words about size; (4) words about length and shape; (5) words about age; (6) words about color; (7) words about nationality; (8) words about religion; (9) words about material makeup; (10) nouns used as adjectives; (11) and finally the noun being modified. (336)
>
> This is exactly the kind of analysis that linguists use to explain the subtle rules that native speakers pick up when young and follow without trying. That is, most people *instinctively* speak the following adjectives in this order: *The beautiful blond French actress.* And the voice knows when we should use a different sequence. That is, if we're talking about actresses from two different countries, we'll instinctively say, *The French beautiful blond actress.*

Parenthetical Elements

Francis Christensen notes the wisdom of the voice for various kinds of punctuation. About parenthetical elements he writes: "In reading a sentence, one 'drops his voice' in order to bridge over the parenthetical element, and when he has bridged over it and picks up the thread of the sentence, he resumes his normal tone of voice" (104). Also: "Quotations and quoted titles are usually managed accurately in speech but often are not in writing" (101). For example, in speaking our voices know instinctively that a comma is not needed in the first sentence but is needed in the second.

> *He was called the dictator of the New World*
> *He was called, "The Dictator of the New World."*

Writing does well to learn the wisdom of the voice in this distinction.

Restrictive and Nonrestrictive Clauses

This is the *that/which* question that I visited at the start of the chapter. (Or should it be this way: This is the *that/which* question, *which* I visited at the start of the chapter?) But there are other cases to consider. Restrictive and non-restrictive clauses constitute a realm full of pitfalls. (It would help to follow Gavin and Sabin and change the terminology to "essential" and "nonessential" clauses.) Christensen gives a couple of examples of error from published writing. He is exercised because they genuinely distort the meaning:

> *Robert Frost was the winner of four Pulitzer Prizes more than any other poet.* (99–100)
> *Pilots, whose minds are dull, do not live long.* (taken from Gowers)

What's striking is that these mistakes got past good writers and copy editors—yet they would *not* have gotten past most people who read them out loud lovingly and listened carefully to the meaning carried by the voice. The mouth and ear would have revealed that the intended meaning was *not* that Frost got four more Pulitzer prizes than any other poet or that all pilots have dull minds. Were the writer and copy editor both careless? Were they trying to follow rules they didn't understand? We don't know, but I think we can confidently say that their attention was too exclusively visual, textual, and conceptual, and they made themselves dear to everything auditory and physical.

Christensen brings up another situation, however, where careful reading will sometimes fall down on the job. He is interested in the distinction revealed by these two phrases that he quotes from published writing:

> *Wordsworth's brother John*
> *his sister, Dorothy*

Both are right. The first phrase correctly *omits* the comma in order to imply that he had more than one brother; the second *needs* the comma in order to imply that he had only one sister (98).

This made me sit up and listen carefully to a passage where I'd written the phrase *my wife Cami*. I'd made no pause and used no comma—which turns out to imply I had multiple wives. Certainly in casual conversation we tend to omit the comma (*I'd like you to meet my wife Cami*). If I'd read it carefully aloud, I *might* have avoided error and made a pause. Probably not. Here is a case where many people—even when speaking and listening with loving care—will get the punctuation wrong. But again, of those who detect the crime, few will prosecute.

Someone might use this example to try to undermine my whole argument. They might say,

> See, you can't trust the mouth and ear. The body doesn't understand syntax. It couldn't hear an implied difference in meaning. For writing we have to use our conscious minds.

But even here, I will doggedly defend the syntactic wisdom of the voice. My mistake didn't come from a failure of my mouth and ear; it came from a failure of my *mind*. That is, when I fail to pause before *Cami*—where logic and the rule demand a comma—it's not that my mouth doesn't register how many wives I have; my *mind* is failing to register it. My mind fell into a thoughtless unawareness of how many wives I had. If my mind had actually been consciously aware of how many wives I have, my mouth and ear might well have gotten the pause right and put in the correct comma.

Indeed, I'd challenge sticklers like Christensen not to be too quick or too rigid in blowing the whistle with this rule. For I might in fact be talking about my wife Cami *as opposed to* my *former* wife Linda. Similarly, someone might write about "our president Barack Obama" with no comma and be pounced on—when in fact the writer was expressing his awareness of Obama compared to other presidents we've had.

If any teacher cares enough about this noncrucial Veblenesque rule to have training sessions on it, I suspect she'll find interesting results. Start by working on a single sentence like this—*He awarded the contract to his brother John*—and don't raise the finicky issue of whether there is more than one brother. No one will notice it. But as always, press for alternative valid readings. When we compare careful readings with a pause and without one, most people will surely agree that both versions are okay. But then try pushing them to decide whether one reading is better or preferable. There's a good chance that someone will notice a slightly different *meaning-feeling* between the two versions. If people discuss the difference, there's a good chance that someone will notice that the no-pause reading opens a door to the idea that there is another brother. This multi-brother meaning is unmistakable if someone tries putting a stress on *John*. Anyway, if we read with full care and investment and if we are halfway lucky, our voices will help us follow *even* this slippery rule.

LITERACY STORY

Languages Dying and Being Reborn

Christopher Moseley is editor-in-chief of the *Atlas of the World's Languages in Danger* and he writes:

> [E]ach language is a uniquely structured world of thought, with its own associations, metaphors, ways of thinking, vocabulary, sound system and grammar—all working together in a marvelous architectural structure which is so fragile that it could easily be lost for ever. (Davies)

Linguist Kenneth Rehg goes on:

> It is likely that linguists of the future will remember this century as a time when a major extinction event took place, as an era when thousands of languages were abandoned by their speakers in favor of languages of

wider communication. . . . Will we be admired for having conscientiously responded to this crisis, or will we be ridiculed for having thoughtlessly ignored our evident duty? (Matsushima)

It turns out that 94 percent of the world uses only 6 percent of its 6,900 ancestral languages. "Chinese, English, Spanish, Russian, Hindi, and Arabic are first or second languages for 55 percent of the world's population" (Bernard 26). Many of the remaining hosts of languages are on the verge of disappearing as globalization and modernization push minority and under-documented languages aside for the more dominant ones. The National Science Foundation estimates that by the end of the century, half of the languages will disappear; other estimates are even more bleak.

To take just one example, 1974 saw the death of the last native speaker of Manx (a Gaelic language spoken on the British Isle of Man). But that man recorded much of his language before he died. There are two kinds of good news I struggle to keep in mind even as so many languages die. I try to avoid the trap of despair.

1. Sometimes it's not so bad when a language dies or is radically cut back. In his *The Last Lingua Franca*, Nicholas Ostler tells the striking case of Persian. It used to be the legal language in Indian courtrooms, but the British simply dropped it and decreed the use of local languages. They decided there could be no real justice if people can't understand how they are being treated by the law. Persian was also decreed away by the Soviet Union after the revolution in these regions: Kazakhstan, Turkmenistan, Uzbekistan, Tajikistan, and Kyrgyzstan. The revolutionary government drew the borders of these soviets in terms of the language spoken in each. Literacy went up from less than 10 percent to almost 100 percent by 1959.

In 1928 in Turkey, Ataturk got rid of the Perso-Arabic script and decreed the Roman alphabet. The Ottoman Perso-Arabic script is an abjad; it lacks vowels. Turkish speech cannot be well represented in writing without more clarity about vowel sounds than are provided by written Arabic or Persian.

2. Some languages are being reborn. Davies notes that

> A country with adequate state support and a willingness on the part of the people can encourage its languages to flourish independently. Papua New Guinea is a fine example of this: although the nation with the greatest linguistic diversity on the planet, it has relatively few endangered languages. Even Livonian, with its single native speaker, is being taught on Latvia's Kurzeme peninsula and is now being used by poets to write verses and by parents to chat with their children. (7)

Here are other notable languages that have been reborn: Hebrew, Celtic, Catalan, Breton, Hawaiian, and Ecuador's Andoa. I'll look more closely at Hebrew, Hawaiian, and Celtic.

Hebrew

Hebrew is one of the oldest of languages; it was spoken during the period of the Hebrew Bible or Old Testament. In the Literacy Story about the invention of the alphabet, we saw the invention of the Semitic alphabet used for *writing* Hebrew (a process starting roughly in 1700 BCE). But around 250 BCE, spoken Hebrew began to die out as Aramaic became the spoken language of the Jews. Even though Hebrew was scarcely spoken afterward except in religious ceremonies, it continued as the written language of the Jewish religion. And it continued to flourish in these ways:

> Historically, Jews have . . . adapted Hebrew (maintained in religious study) to *write* the national languages they spoke. These include Yiddish (derived primarily from German), Judeo-Arabic (spoken by Jews across the Arabic-speaking world), Judeo-Spanish (based on Spanish before 1492 when the Jews were expelled from Spain), and JudeoTat (spoken by perhaps twenty thousand Jews in Russia and Azerbaijan) (Harris 1994). In these cases, the social isolation of an ethnic group, in constant economic contact with dominant groups, produced corpora of written words that encouraged and supported literacy—and that were wholly inaccessible (written in Hebrew character) to members of the dominant cultures. (Bernard 23)

Starting in the late nineteenth century, a single man, Eliezer ben Yehudah, revived Hebrew as a spoken language—and now a national language. He devoted his life to the revival. In the process he adapted it for modern use through the introduction of thousands of modern terms. Gradually the language was used by more and more of the Jewish settlers in Palestine and in 1948 became the official language of the State of Israel.

When the novelist S. Yizhar was a child in the 1920s, only 20 percent of Jews in Palestine had mastered Hebrew. By the time of his first novel, 1938, 70 percent said they primarily spoke Hebrew. Something like three million people speak Hebrew either as their mother tongue or adopted tongue. Israel has set up an extensive system of courses for new immigrants to learn the language.

Here are some words from Hebrew that have become part of English: hallelujah, sabbath, cherub, seraph, Satan, shibboleth, and behemoth.

Celtic

When the Romans took over the British Isles, the Celts were pushed west to Ireland and Wales, north to Scotland, and south to Cornwall. Some of these Cornish speakers got in boats and settled in Normandy France. Some also went to the Isle of man (Manx)—and more recently to Cape Breton Island (North America) and Patagonia (South America). In effect, Celtic speakers were pushed to the fringes of western Europe.

The rich tradition of Celtic oral literature is one of the oldest in Europe and can be traced back to the sixth century CE. But during the nineteenth century, the various spoken forms of the Celtic language seemed on their way to extinction. In the British Isles, this was due largely to British rule and the migrations in and out caused by the industrial revolution. Yet large numbers of speakers remained in the western regions of Ireland, Wales, Scotland, Cornwall, and French Brittany. And despite the death of the last speaker of Manx, there has been an ongoing and increasingly successful effort in all these regions to stage a Gaelic revival: festivals; courses for adolescents and adults; monolingual nursery schools and even some regular schools; radio and TV programs and newspapers in Gaelic.

I'll look at Wales for an example. Up until 1900 almost half the population still spoke Welsh; in some western regions up to 80 percent of the people *still* speak it. The Eisteddfod Welsh festival has never stopped, and it maintains the ancient tradition of competing to see who is most skilled—"inspired" really—at composing poetry on the spot. In 1967, the Welsh Language Act was passed, making Welsh an official national language. (This happened with Gaelic in Ireland much earlier, 1922, with the founding of the nation.) In 1988 the Welsh Language Board was established to help ensure the rebirth of Welsh. Similar things are happening in the four regions of Britain and even to some degree in Normandy. The western areas of all these regions are where the most native speakers of Celtic languages are found.

And written Celtic? In the very earliest times, there was some writing in the Ogham alphabet, and a few inscriptions remain. But when St. Patrick brought Christianity to Ireland in the fifth century, Irish writers began to write Irish literature in the Latin alphabet—and this was in a period when literacy in Europe was crumbling. Irish Gaelic was the first vernacular language in Europe to develop a written form. By medieval times, Celts had developed the Uncial alphabet for manuscripts—using letters that are a variant of the Latin alphabet. This alphabet was used for printed Irish until quite recently and is still seen on road signs and public notices throughout Ireland and Scotland: it's the kind of "poetic looking" Irish you see on banners and other celebratory sites. But in the twentieth century, Ireland and Scotland developed a "standard" spelling that uses conventional Roman letters.

We have little of the sixth-century Irish literature left because of Viking raids. But starting in the tenth century, the body of written Celtic literature increased greatly and continues.

Hawaiian

Hawaiian is a language brought from Polynesia to the Islands as early as 300 CE by remarkable explorers sailing on rafts and using the stars to guide them.

Written Hawaiian starts with American Christian missionaries in the 1820s who worked out a spelling system for the language. Hawaiian is a liquid-sounding language, and the missionaries ended up using all five of our vowels but only seven consonants (plus the *okina,* an apostrophe that signals a glottal stop—note its use in the word *Hawai'i*). The missionaries wanted their "heathen converts" to be able to read the Bible. Hawaiian royalty converted to Christianity, and with it to literacy in Hawaiian. Most Hawaiians came along.

Hawaiians could now read and write their language. The Bible was translated into Hawaiian in 1839, and Hawai'i became one of the most literate kingdoms in the world. There were Hawaiian dictionaries, literary magazines, and musical lyrics; people wrote diaries, and the affairs of state were largely conducted in Hawaiian (though the monarchs and the missionaries who held executive positions in the government often used English in addition). Mark Twain, in his memoir about his visit to Hawai'i, writes about hearing the legislature function bi-lingually.

But in 1893, the U.S. government and business interests arrested the Queen and overthrew the Kingdom of Hawai'i and annexed the territory. In 1898 the Hawaiian language was banned from public schools and the government. The language was not allowed to be taught even in the Kamehameha schools reserved for children of Hawaiian descent. Yet many people continued to speak it and fourteen newspapers continued to print exclusively in Hawaiian.

But the suppression even of *spoken* Hawaiian was eventually successful. Both spoken and written Hawaiian were near death by the mid 1960s; a true native speaker of the language was hard to find. But shortly after this time, Hawaiian activists began a revival of the language. Before long they established immersion schools for young children. They started out with only the kindergartens and each year they moved the language up one grade. During my year of teaching at the University of Hawai'i, I saw TV coverage of the first graduating high school seniors giving speeches in Hawaiian. It's not uncommon now to hear children and parents chatting in the language. The archives of written Hawaiian are being opened up. Previously untranslated material is coming to light. All this is part of the renaissance of Hawaiian culture. (For much of this I am indebted to email from Suzie Jacobs who has taught and studied Hawaiian literacy.)

15 How Speech Can Improve the Organization of Writing

Form as Energy

Writing as a Way to Elude the Temporal Nature of Speech

Speech exists in time and time is a prison. Throughout our entire lives we are always—at every instant—stuck in that single instant of time: the present. We can't "see ahead" to the future, and our memories of the past are notoriously unreliable. In contrast, space gives us lots of freedom and perspective: we can see ahead and behind, left and right, up and down—often to great distances. In the realm of time, there's only one thing that we can reliably know outside our present instant: we were born and we will die.

Because our audible words are stuck in the prison of time, they disappear the moment they leave our mouths. It's hard to examine them, revise them, analyze them, or save them. But the glory of writing is its spatial nature. It eludes the problems of time in the following ways:

- We can step away from the words we've written and put them out of mind for a while, but they'll still be there. We can look at them again, think about them, and revise them.
- Writing helps us carry words *across* space and time to places our voices can't reach. Now of course we have the technology to record speech and transmit it, but recorded speech is nowhere near as convenient as writing if we want to revise and manipulate our words.
- We can close our eyes but not our ears. Consider our experience on buses, trains, and planes when someone keeps talking loudly to a neighbor or on a cell phone.
- Writing escapes the slowness of speech. Readers can take in words enormously faster than listeners can.
- Readers can jump all around in a text—or pause and re-read— instead of having to listen to each word stuck in its sequence. (Books on tape can be lovely, but only if we have lots of time and don't want flexibility.)
- When we speak there's almost always a listener who will hear us, and we often end up regretting what we said. With writing we don't have to give our words to *anyone* till we decide we want to—and till we

have made them the way we want them. Yet we can give early drafts to ally readers and get feedback to help us revise a *later* draft for difficult or hostile readers.

- In speech, it's hard to keep track of logic: inconsistencies and contradictions slip past in the seductive flow of persuasive speech. Writing helps us *see* the timeless dimension of logic—especially when we make use of visual outlines or charts or use the special language of symbolic logic.
- Our spoken words die with us, but (as Shakespeare noted over and over) writing gives us hope of living for ever through visible words.

In all these ways then, spatial and visual writing eludes time.

But Writing *Doesn't* Elude Time

Even though we can look at a page of writing all at once, and even though essays, poems, and books are spatially laid out so all the words sit-there-all-at-once, nevertheless a reader's *experience* of writing is not all-at-once. Readers can take in only a relatively few words at a time. Reading is inevitably *temporal*. When we read a text, we are like ants on a painting: we can crawl all around the canvas but we can never see more than one small part of the painting.

Clever readers use various methods to try to escape the temporal nature of reading:

- "Non-reading." I've met scientists and engineers who brag, *I never read. I look through the abstract, glance over tables and graphs, check out the bibliography, and browse the discussion. That's all I need.* In effect, such "readers" are trying to *see* the article all at once. They're trying for a bird's-eye view of the painting. They do save time, but the best they can manage is to be grasshoppers rather than ants. They can strategically jump around and skim and skip. Many academics and professionals often "read" by just glancing through texts to look for what might be useful.
- Speed reading. A few people can read at mind-boggling rates without boggling their minds. They run their eyes quickly down a page and understand lots (or all?) in very few seconds. This shows that human minds—or at least a few of them—are capable of exploiting the spatial nature of print to an amazing degree. They can accelerate reading *toward* the "speed of sight." And all of us can take training to accelerate our reading—though I soon lost the small gains that I got from Evelyn Wood in graduate school. (She taught me to use my finger for pulling my eyes faster down the page, but now that I've fallen back to my old ways, it feels as though my finger is slowing me down.)
- Notes and outlines. When we make notes or outlines for writing or taking notes as we read, we're often trying to transform a long temporal experience into a visible representation that we can take in quickly at some later time—sometimes even at a glance.

Yet the fact remains that readers are stuck in time. There is no way they can take in a text all at once. It takes time even to glance through a table of contents or read an abstract or understand a graph.

We tend to think of sight as a quicker, richer, and more sophisticated medium than hearing—especially because it came so much later in our evolutionary development. Sight is linked to the outer and more recent layer of the brain, the cerebellum; hearing is tied to the older, inner, and more primitive parts of the brain. But when it comes to speed, new sight is the tortoise and old hearing the rabbit. Jeff Goldberg reports on striking research:

> "In order to be able to process sounds at the highest frequency range of human hearing, hair cells must be able to turn current on and off 20,000 times per second. They are capable of even more astonishing speeds in bats and whales, which can distinguish sounds at frequencies as high as 200,000 cycles per second," says Hudspeth.
>
> Photoreceptors in the eye are much slower, he points out. "The visual system is so slow that when you look at a movie at 24 frames per second, it seems continuous, without any flicker. Contrast 24 frames per second with 20,000 cycles per second. The auditory system is a thousand times faster."

Roy Harris fights the idea of writing as temporal and insists that it is *wholly* and *essentially* spatial. He insists on defining writing not so much as the representation of speech, but as the representation of semiotic *information*. As prime models or illustrations of writing, he points to things like graphs, tables, and electrical or knitting diagrams: elegant and efficient ways to convey information that cannot be spoken. The first forms of writing were financial records and didn't represent speech or syntax. It's accidental to the *nature* of writing, he insists, that it came to be used so often to represent speech. (I mentioned in Chapter 2 his intriguing observation that mathematics was hobbled until it stopped using spoken words for numbers and started using Arabic numerals that can be manipulated in space and not be tied to any spoken language.) Harris's argument depends on a rather narrow model of writing, and even diagrams or mathematical formulas take time to process.

In contrast, Stanley Fish insists that for texts, "everything depends on the temporal dimension" (159). "[R]eadings proceed in time" (3). The notion that a text "can be taken in at a single glance [is] positivist, holistic, and spatial" (158). He uncovers many problems of interpretation that stem from the mistaken notion that interpretation is "what a reader understands at the end of a unit of sense (a line, a sentence, a paragraph, a poem)" (158). An interpretation is a process of understanding that constantly unfolds.

In this chapter, then, I'm making two arguments.

1. Because writing seems so visual and spatial, most people misunderstand the nature of *organization* in writing. Unconsciously, they see it as a spatial matter—as though it were the *arrangement of objects in space*. In fact, we don't get a good understanding of the organization of writing unless we realize that it involves the *ordering of events in time*. To understand better how organization works in time, we need to consider media more obviously rooted in time: spoken language (speeches and plays), music, and movies.

2. If we bring more speech to writing in the two ways I'm suggesting in this book, we are more likely to *experience* the temporal dimension of writing. This will encourage us naturally to organize our texts more effectively for readers

trapped in time. That is, when we speak onto the page and read aloud to revise, we are more likely to experience how writing is not a matter of creating timeless logic but of creating sequences of words that *make things happen* in the realm of time.

Organization in Writing

The concept itself—*organization*—is hostage to space. When we talk about organization, we tend to use words like *structure* and *shape* and *form*—words that are essentially visual. Ask someone to figure out the organization of a play or movie or symphony. She is likely to take out pencil and paper and make a *visual spatial* diagram. Spatial diagrams work for spatial objects like paintings and photos, but they carry the unspoken implication that organization itself is a matter of the arrangement of elements in space. They privilege spatial symmetry.

But speeches, plays, movies, and pieces of music function in the realm of time. If we want to represent how they are organized, we have to find a way to talk about *events in time* and how they are sequenced. I find music particularly helpful for exploring temporal organization. Music makes a good analogy to writing because of course it *can* be written down on paper in space—just like ordinary language. But when we ask why a piece of music seems well organized, we know that organization is not actually in the written version; it's something in the arrangement of audible *sounds* in the realm of time. It is the sounds that seem "well held together" for listeners—not the notes on the page. The sound sequences *cohere*; we experience them as temporally bound.

So if we want to think better about the organization of temporal media—music, speeches, movies, plays, *and writing!*—we should avoid words like *shape* and *structure* and *form* with their visual bias. It helps to use a word like *coherence*: it's a word for organization that is not in hock to space. The concept, *organization*, is confused because it conflates two ideas that are quite different: how objects are organized in space and how events are bound together in time.

So how *are* events held together in time so that we experience them as coherent? I'll use this chapter to give some specific answers and try to show in each case how speaking onto the page and reading aloud will tend to promote coherence in writing.

But first let's have a quick simple lesson about coherence. Imagine the melody of "Happy Birthday" written out or diagrammed on paper. (Our copyright laws restrict its use.) We see four nicely related visual shapes. Roughly speaking, the first three phrases each go up and then go down—each one rising higher than the one before.

> *Happy birthday to you* (it rises and then falls)
> *Happy birthday to you* (starting on the same note, it rises and fall similarly, but gets one note higher)
> *Happy birthday dear Abigail* (again from the same note, it rises much higher—and then falls lower)

But the fourth melody is upside down:

Happy birthday to you. (Starting higher than the others, it mostly falls)

Admittedly, this well-shaped visual architecture plays a role in our experience of "Happy Birthday" as coherent. But if we actually *listen* to the melody (and you should pause to hum it to yourself), we experience something more powerful, and it operates in the realm of time. At the end of each of the first three phrases, the melody leaves us hanging—unsatisfied and wanting more. After each phrase, it's as though we are pulled forward by the future. But at the end of the fourth melody, we get the opposite temporal experience: rest, satisfaction, closure, home: no pull forward in time.

The coherence of this little song depends on how both the melody and harmony create a pattern of yearning and relief, dissonance and consonance, itch and scratch. This pattern or sequence holds the four phrases together and keeps them from floating off separately—it keeps us experiencing them as a single coherent entity. Kenneth Burke put this into a famous theoretical formulation: "[F]orm is the creation of an appetite in the mind of the auditor, and the adequate satisfying of that appetite. . . . This is the psychology of form as distinguished from the psychology of information" (*Counter-Statement* 31–33). Very little music that we admire as coherent is so simple and visually neat as the melody of "Happy Birthday." Most interesting and pleasing music is actually rather *messy* if we look at a visual diagram of all the notes. Composers don't try to avoid or remove mess; they create a coherent pattern of energy or dynamism that harnesses what might seem a messy plethora of notes. It's a *dynamism* that holds a complex sequence of sounds together so we experience a *temporal architecture* as a single whole.

So too with good speeches. Some *may* look neat and symmetrical if seen from a sufficient height ("first A, then B" or "Three main points"), but this simplicity usually belies a texture of messiness that is common in good speeches: a succession of looking forward and backward, of zooming in and panning out. Good speakers find a way to *bind time* and pull us through their often messy words and give us an experience of coherence.

My argument is this. If we want to improve the organization of *writing*, we need to pay better attention to the binding of time through dynamism: imbued energy. My theme is *organization as energy*. How then can we bind time with written words? Good writers—consciously or not—tend to remember that readers have an experience that is more temporal than spatial. So where do writers find the energy that binds written words together so as to pull readers along from one part to the next and make them experience the text as a coherent whole? Since reading is a series of events in time, my claim is that the answer is the same one that applies to music. Successful writers lead us on a journey to satisfaction by way of expectations, frustrations, half satisfactions, and temporary satisfactions: a well-planned sequence of yearnings and reliefs, itches and scratches. Again Burke: "Form, having to do with the creation and gratification of needs, is 'correct' in so far as it gratifies the needs it creates" (*Counter-Statement* 138).

Admittedly, we can use visual features to give *some* degree of organization to a text. We can vary the length of paragraphs; vary the fonts; use bullets, subheads, and charts. Visual designers give us striking or complex page layouts to liven up a text. Technical and business writers stress how important it is to break up the page with visual interest. But in truth, if most designers had their way, they'd *banish* full pages of text—which they tend to call "boring." That just reveals how deeply they are tempted to treat the organization of written words as wholly spatial. When we are faced with ten or a hundred full pages to read rather than skim, there's relatively little help we can get from visual design. (Mary Hocks gives interesting insights about visual rhetoric in *digital* or *online* texts, but for this chapter, I'm concerned with conventional linear texts—whether we read them on paper or on a screen.)

Traditional Advice for Organization: Outlines and Signposts

The traditional advice for organizing essays is to use outlines and signposts. Both techniques are useful but their usefulness is limited because they have a spatial bias and writing is stuck in time.

Both words, "signpost" and "outline," are visual metaphors that imply a spatial perspective on organization. We use *signs on posts* to guide us as we walk or drive through space; we draw *lines around the outside* of complex paintings or photos to free ourselves from the welter of details or when we want to get perspective—in effect a "bird's-eye view." It's not that outlines are no help to us as writers. They help *us* clarify our thinking—help us figure out our main point and try to work out a coherent sequence for all the subsidiary points we are trying to make. But the help they give to readers is indirect and sometimes ineffectual.

For when we use an outline for writing an essay, the spatial bias often leads to a problem. The outline gets us to put everything related to A in the A section, and everything related to B in the B section, and the same for C. *We*—being the outliners—have a good "bird's-eye view," but we forget that our readers cannot escape their ant's-eye view. While they are reading the A section, they can't see into B or C; while in B they can't see into A or C—and so on. Of course we can remember *some* of A while we are in B, but our memory fades. The reader-ant has no perspective. That is, when we are frustrated as readers, it's often because we need some hints about what's coming, or we need to be reminded of what the writer already told us but we forgot. Outlines often make us avoid the "messiness" of repeating ourselves or recursively doubling backward and forward, but some tangled messy redundancy is often what readers need. (Speech has *too much* redundancy for writing, but that has tempted many writers to use too little.)

Good speeches often have useful elements of "mess": traces of the theme are scattered throughout or we hear some oft-repeated phrase or motif. We see the same thing in music. In the common structure called "sonata form," for example, we get A material and then B material—and then A and B varied and explored together in the development section—and finally A and B again in the recapitulation. Very repetitious. Conventional outlining promotes the common visual seeing-it-all-at-once assumption about organization; it neglects the mysterious question of where the *dynamism* or *energy* comes from that binds long stretches of language into felt forms through time. Things may be beautifully *structured* into A, B, C, and D, but what makes us want to keep reading through the long A section—to keep going on to B and C? When people successfully explain their thinking in conversation, they often *don't* use the segregational structure of outlines and instead jump back and forth between large generalizations and very concrete low-level points or examples.

Signposting is another staple of traditional advice for organization: *"In this essay I will demonstrate the following claim: . . . "* or *"In the next section, I will . . . "* or *"In this essay I've tried to show . . . "*. Obviously signposts (despite their spatial etymology) *do* help with time: they help readers trapped ant-like in the prison of time. That is, if we get a good signpost at the beginning of a section or even a whole essay, we are much less likely to get bogged down and lost, even if the argument is not so clearly made and the parts are not well arranged. The signpost helps us *experience* some coherence even in what is not so clearly presented. So too for signposts at the end: *Oh now I see what she was getting at.*" Signposts are particularly helpful for skimmers who want to elude as much time as possible. Long essays often start with short abstracts.

But where to put your signs? At beginnings, pointing forward—or at endings, looking back. This is a dilemma for writers, given that essays can only be read in the realm of time. Signposts are best at preventing confusion if they come first (*"In this essay I will . . ."*). But initial signposting can make an essay seem flat-footed, naive, and stiff. Indeed, introductory signposts tend to put the scratch before the itch and thus may well prevent any time-binding itch from cropping up. Textbooks are likely to be beautifully organized in these non-energy-producing ways—especially with signposts—but they often put readers to sleep. All scratch, no itch. Even if a piece of writing is perfectly mapped and signposted and utterly clear (no mean trick!), what will pull readers to keep reading? What will make the ant *want* to keep walking around on that painting? (Admittedly, *some* initial summaries provide an itch to draw readers on: *"In this essay I will demonstrate that two and two add up to five."*) But if we put signposts at the end of sections, we aren't doing much to prevent confusion for readers as they make their way through.

Signposting can certainly help us climb up a tree and peer over the temporal linear underbrush of words by giving us "instantaneous" previews and summaries. Nevertheless, what I'm particularly interested in are the more *dynamic* or *energy-based* techniques of organization that don't so much try to elude or evade time as actually *harness* or *bind* time.

Binding Time with Story: Story Outlines

When we look across the universe of writing, it's easy to see the most common and powerful way that writers bind words and pull readers through a text. Story. Narrative is a universal pattern of language that creates sequences of expectation and satisfaction—itch and scratch. *"Once upon a time there was a little girl whose parents died and left her unprotected. . . ."* *"He found his eye drawn to the corner of the room to the kind of woman he almost never noticed."* Even when we already know the story of *Oedipus* or *Hamlet,* the narrative thread can exert its dynamism and pull us along. Fairy tales and archetypal folk stories are particularly good at harnessing the energy even of familiar narratives.

But what if we are writing an essay or report or some other piece of nonfiction where there is no narrative? How do we bind time when we are trying to explain, persuade, or analyze? But in truth, we don't have to give up the benefits of story for such writing—nor the benefits of outlining and signposting. For there's a kind of outlining that is different from conventional outlining, one that's become essential to me in my writing: *story outlining* or *sentence outlining*. I described this technique as part of the "skeleton process" in Chapter 10—how to create a story outline for building coherence out of chaos. Here I'll focus on how a story outline creates the dynamism of expectation and relief that harnesses time.

The key to the story outline is the *sentence* with its *verb*. The sentence can make assertions or claims—pose problems or work through a solution. The sentence is a little piece of energy or music; it has the rhythm and melody that can pull us along—just as in music. Or rather it has energy, rhythm, and melody if the writer has been successful.

There are certain simple paradigm sentences that carry the cognitive seeds of a whole essay—sentences like *Most people think . . ., but really. . . .*; or *It used to be . . ., but now. . . .*; or *Even though the theory seems to explain most of the data, it turns out that . . .* (Ponsot and Deen had this powerful insight.) With this kind of syntax, the writer plants an expectation or itch. Notice how these sentences are stories of thinking.

In contrast, a conventional outline consists of mere words or phrases, so it can only *point* or *name* an area. Thus the spatial visual trap that so often leads to a static structure. Words and phrases without verbs lack the energy that drives a train of thinking and pulls the reader along. They don't articulate conceptual or semantic energy that gets you from this point to the next one.

And logic? Conventional word-and-phrase outlines aspire to all-at-once logic. Sentence outlines aspire instead to a "story of thinking": a train of thinking where one point *follows* the next in an order that is convincing or reasonable and doesn't contradict logic. Many good analytic or expository essays—even academic essays—are really stories of thinking where the individual steps may often be logical—or at least not in violation of logic—but the longer trains of thinking seldom follow a sequence of true inductive or deductive logic. Productive and interesting essays are more often informed by a narrative flavor than by a static scheme like, "Here are three reasons for X." (We do no favor to logic or clear thinking if we use the word *logical* for good essays that are merely well argued or convincing or not self-contradictory.)

There is an important link to speech here. Sentence outlines can be thought of as "talking outlines" because they ask for the kind of syntax you'd use if you wanted to *say* your thoughts to someone—which is of course an excellent idea. When we talk, we don't use single words or phrases; we say sentences that can pull a listener through our progression of thoughts. In contrast, conventional outlines with single words and phrases are usually "unspeakable." The process of creating and testing a good story outline is the same as for reading aloud to revise: keep fiddling till it sounds right. The test of a sentence outline is to read it aloud; it should work in sound through time. By reading aloud, we can hear whether we have a coherent convincing train of thought that draws a reader through the ideas or argument. We can feel and hear if the cars on the train are connected, are in the right order, and are going somewhere.

Let me illustrate how a story or sentence outline differs from a traditional one. For the previous section of this chapter, I had to struggle to work out my thinking and I made good use of sentence-outlining. I had already done lots of writing—indeed, I was borrowing a good deal from an essay I had published—but for this book I needed to reorganize it. A story outline helped me out. I moved back and forth from outline to text. Sometimes the prose showed me a flaw in the outline; sometimes the outline showed me a flaw in the text. Here is how a **conventional outline** for the section might look:

Traditional Advice: Outlines and Signposts
Nonfiction
Traditional advice
Benefits of outlines
Shortcomings
Benefits of signposts
Shortcomings

Here is the **story outline** that I gradually worked out. Notice how it is more speakable and dynamic.

Traditional Advice: Outlines and Signposts
How can we bind time or create coherence for essays?
Traditional advice says to use outlines
They help writer with thinking
But they create *spatial* neatness that often doesn't work for readers trapped in time
Signposting is also traditional advice
It's another visual metaphor, but it *does* help readers stuck in time—help them feel coherence even if the writing is confusing
But where to put signposts? First is best for preventing confusion; but if so, they often don't give itch, they destroy itch
If last, they don't prevent confusion well
They try to elude time; I want dynamic energy-based organization that harnesses time

---

I use story outlines not just for small sections where I'm trying to untangle little knots of thinking. I often force myself to make a story outline for whole essays. For this book, I've made a story outline for most chapters as a whole—again, going back and forth dialectically between outline and text. By way of example, here is the first half of my story outline for this chapter (at one stage, anyway):

Can Writing Get Around the Temporal Problems of Speech?
— Here are temporal problems of speech—and how writing eludes them; it even helps with time as existential prison

---

Yet Writing Doesn't Really Elude Time
— We can only read a few words at a time &c &c
— Readers try to escape time by speeding up (skimming &c), but still reading is temporal
— Footnote exception; Harris: writing not as language but information

Organization in Writing
— The concept of organization is hostage to time: pleasing arrangement of objects in space vs. coherence of events in time
— For understanding organization in writing, look to temporal forms: speeches, music, plays, movies
— What makes events cohere?
— Quick general answer: Happy Birthday
— Really it's in the alternation of expectation/satisfaction, scratch/itch. Burke
— It's all about dynamic vs. static; form as energy

Traditional Advice: Outlines and Signposts
— Outlines often help the writer (with thinking) more than the reader
— But outlines imply a visualist birds-eye view—and lead to segregational neatness of arrangement (A, B, C) that often doesn't work for readers because of the temporal nature of reading
— Signposts *do* help in the order of time—they can give experience of coherence even with incoherent text
— But they have nothing to do with organization as coherence in time. They don't tell us how to arrange the sections of an essay. They can go anywhere; they can help no matter how sections are placed
— Signposting dilemma: put them first to prevent confusion? but if so, they are flat-footed and prevent itch

Binding Time with Story
— It's the most traditional and powerful way to hold words together in time. But what about nonfiction?
— Don't have to give up story or outlining: a different kind of outline works better in time: story or sentence outline
— Conventional outlines are spatial—words or phrases just point. Story outlines use sentences and verbs; they have energy, they pull "story of thinking"
— "Train of thought" (movement) is better for coherence than "photo of thought" (timeless—static)
— I can't outline usefully till I have done lots of writing where I'm not bound by an outline

Binding Time with Perplexity

There's one more point about outlining and *time*. The advice we most often hear is this: "*Don't start your serious writing till your thinking is clear; to clarify your thinking, use an outline.*" I find it useless to begin this way. And I see lots of weak writing from students who outlined *before* they wrote: they have only one and a half good ideas, but they tried to build them into an outline with three main points, A, B, and C. Before they are ready for an outline, they need to do more exploratory writing (or talking) in order to get enough good ideas. *Then* the story outline works well.

Binding Time with Perplexity

If we don't have an actual story to drive our essay, the most obvious way to create a "story of thinking" is to start with an itch: not a claim or a policy but a question or problem or perplexity. Writers sometimes do this in a somewhat artificial way: *I'm not perplexed by my topic any more, but here's a question I can start with to "hook" the reader.* This can work, but there's a danger of it sounding like a gimmick: readers can sense that there's no real perplexity generating energy.

What I want to celebrate is the process of inviting *genuine* perplexity into the writing process—dynamic itch—especially during early stages. Too few writers do this because of the pervasive assumption that writing is for what you've already figured out, not for uncertainty. *Perplexity and confusion are fine for casual talk, but writing is only for what's clear.* Thus, when most people are engaged in the act of writing, they stop writing whenever they feel perplexed. They start again after they've gotten over their uncertainty. *Writing is a record: why record confusion?*

In his book, *Induction and Intuition in Scientific Thought,* the Nobel biologist Peter Medawar points out that the conventions of scientific writing tend to suppress the element of inquiry and perplexity. When scientists publish, they are led to use the conceptual format they used for testing and proving. The goal is to make the claim seem impregnable—Q.E.D. This form tends to leach away most of the energy-driven uncertainty that drove the actual thinking and experimenting. The dynamism is lost that could elicit energy in readers. In journalism, the term *hook* has become a cliché, and many journalistic hooks are corny and involve no perplexity. The best hook for an essay is a piece of genuine uncertainty.

Speaking onto the page during early drafting helps us naturally articulate the perplexity that is driving us to write in the first place. Of course it may happen that we *don't* feel perplexed when we start writing; perhaps it is a strong feeling or settled conviction that drives us to write: X is a good idea or Y is a wrong policy. But even in this situation, if we talk comfortably onto the page without trying to plan things out, we are very likely to wander into saying something—some point or detail or story—that actually undermines our initial conviction. Exploratory unplanned writing on different days is particularly good for generating perplexity. We find ourselves saying on Tuesday what contradicts what we wrote on Monday. This forces us to probe more deeply and not settle for the simplistic thinking that people so often create when they make a standard outline and suppress troublesome details, stories, or thoughts. The five-paragraph essay tends to function as an anti-perplexity machine. Speaking onto the page helps keep us in touch with the fact that "inquiry" actually means inquiring.

When a writer articulates perplexity, we see someone, in effect, of two minds (or more than two). Speaking onto the page helps us do justice to both our minds or multiple opinions—one at a time or in debate. Thus it harnesses not just narrative but drama. It's sad how many essays are shallow because the writer had only one mind—succumbing to the pressure to make it up before starting. Students often say, "I had this other idea, but I couldn't figure out where to put it" or "it seemed to undermine my point." And even when perplexity leads us eventually to a single and exact conclusion that could be stated all-at-once in a bird's-eye claim, we have a better chance of making readers *experience* that claim and be pulled through our text if we find some way to do justice to the conflict that gave rise to it.

This has been my situation with this book. I've been writing and drafting and revising it for so long (and boring family and friends) that I've more or less worked my way into enormous conviction. Yet I have allowed myself to retain traces of the myriad perplexities and mind-changes throughout. And of course I remain deeply perplexed about whether I can make headway with others (change the culture!) by making such an ambitious argument for which I could never have enough learning or authority.

But perplexity itself is not enough. A literal record of our speaking onto the page will often be a confusing zigzag record of different and sometimes contradictory thoughts and feelings—even an incoherent mess. We need to build out of our perplexity a focused story and economical line of thinking.

> More and more teachers are learning to help students do short pieces of "writing to learn"—where the goal is to explore and process new ideas they are encountering in a course—not to create coherent or settled texts for readers. This valuable practice helps students learn to write into and through perplexity.
>
> When we allow ourselves to speak ourselves into perplexity, we increase the chances that we will get to the remarkable focused and energized mental condition that Mihaly Csikszentmihalyi calls the "flow state."

Binding Time with Voice

The topic of voice in writing has become theoretically vexed in my field, but for my purposes here I can stick to what is simple and inarguable. Any text can be spoken aloud, but only some texts somehow lead readers to "hear a voice" even in silent reading. When readers hear a voice in a text—whether or not they like that voice—it creates a sense of coherence in time. The sense of voice in a text increases the experience of rhythm, movement, and immediacy in the words. It tends to draw readers into and through the words, increasing the sense of energy. And audible language is more easily understood (as I explored in the chapters on intonation and reading aloud). The spoken sound of words carries meaning. It doesn't take away from this point that readers will often differ as to whether they hear a voice or the nature of the voice they hear. (See Roland Barthes on the drawing power of what he calls "the grain of the voice.")

In addition, some texts lead readers to sense a person or speaker in the words. Even if an essay is not well unified, structurally or conceptually—even if it shifts in point of view—it can be successful with readers if it gives them the sense of a single person exploring these ideas that are in dialogue or even in conflict with each other. Even if readers don't like the voice they hear, it can still give coherence to the text. The Socratic dialogues could be said to wander in a disunified way, but they are held together by the voice and persona.

Of course, a strong and believable dramatic voice may not stop readers from complaining about incoherent thinking. Voice doesn't cancel thinking: *ethos* doesn't cancel *logos*. But as Aristotle observed, *ethos* is the most powerful of the three sources of persuasion and can have a stronger effect than *logos*. Sometimes a convincing voice handled well can make a reader actually *welcome* movement to a new point of view, rather than complain that the ending doesn't fit the beginning. Ever since Bakhtin's work became prominent, theorists have used *dialogic* as a term of praise. The very term implies the sound of voices.

A reliable way to bring voice to a text is through the two techniques that I'm celebrating in this book. Speaking onto the page brings out the movement, energy, and *sound* of voice. Still, the process can lead to voices that are impulsive, unconsidered, and sometimes at cross purposes. But the second technique—revising by reading aloud—helps us listen thoughtfully to the voices we produce by speaking onto the page (and the emptiness or muddiness of voice we produced by painstaking revising), and this can help us craft our final draft into a coherent voice that works. We notice limp or tangled passages that are unspeakable. We hear changes of voice and get to decide whether we want this sudden bit of irony or uncertainty or anger.

Binding Time with Words that Enact Rather than Record

There's a subtle but powerful difference between language that *records* past thinking and language that *enacts* present thinking—as it's going on. Of course any good writing must be a record of past thinking. (This follows from my argument in Chapter 10 on the necessity of thoughtful care in writing.) Present thinking is often messy—perhaps wandering, and redundant (as in some freewriting, journal writing, and email). But those of us who have looked without prejudice at freewriting and other kinds of unplanned speaking onto the page have noticed something interesting and valuable: a distinctive energy and voice that gives readers a heightened sense of *contact* with the consciousness of the writer. It's the enactment of ongoing thinking that produces these effects. It often includes perplexity. Such writing tends to give a sense of *movement* through time.

Is it possible to have the advantages of both—a well-ordered record of carefully considered past thinking that nevertheless enacts the life, presence, and energy of present thinking in process? Yes. It happens in many various and subtle ways, but for one example, consider this sentence:

> *Sentences are little pieces of energy or music—they have rhythm and melody—even in writing. Or rather they have energy, rhythm, and melody if the writer has been successful.*

It came from freewriting or speaking onto the page—putting down my thinking in process. When I revised, I noticed what might seem a problem: an initial statement followed by a statement that calls the first inaccurate. *Why waste time saying it wrong and then right when you could say it right the first time?* But my mouth and ear told me to keep both sentences.

In doing so, I wasn't consciously using the theory I am laying out here. But what my mouth and ear preferred, it now strikes me, is the fact that this and other kinds of thinking in action, if handled successfully, can pull a reader along without annoyance because of a sense of *shared* mental action. It turns out that this is quite a common pattern in writing and is often effective:

> *By the end of the 1880s Henry [James] had become increasingly anxious about the progress of his career as a novelist—or rather, about his lack of progress.* (Lodge 94)
>
> *Rum is distilled from sugar cane—or rather, molasses.* (Rombauer and Becker 39).

Why didn't the writers edit out the lies or first thoughts ("progress" and "sugar cane")? If they had, they would have ended up with simpler clearer sentences. But they instinctively sought to retain the energy of thinking-going-on—and to convey some of that energy into the reader's mind.

We can also describe this pattern in terms of voice: the writing enacts a dialogue in which we hear a change of voice as the later bit responds to the earlier bit, or makes a meta-comment. (See Palacas on voice and intonation in parentheticals; and Crismore on voice in metadiscourse.)

It might seem as though thinking-in-action would undermine clarity. *Don't confuse me with a voyage through ideas you've already discarded. Just tell me your conclusions.* But those examples show that such "voyages" can be rhetorically effective. Indeed, thinking-in-action can actually *aid* comprehension. Notice the pattern in my example above: *I assert X. Well, actually, not quite X, but a complication of X.* One of the best ways to help readers understand a complex idea is to start with an oversimplification. A simple claim is easily stated and easily grasped; complications and qualifications can be added later. This strategy can function not just in sentences but in paragraphs or even whole essays:

> *Roughly speaking, my claim is X:* . . . [stated in a sentence—or a paragraph]. *But it's not that simple* [and then comes a new paragraph or even a new section].

Teachers and academics like to pounce on sentences that are simple enough to be easily attacked. Simple sentences are likely to be false, almost by definition. The truth is usually complex. Teachers often feel it's their job to find attackable sentences. But when writers worry too much about preventing attack, they forget something basic about rhetoric: it's not really so bad if readers resist or disagree at first, for in resisting they involve themselves and contribute energy to the process of understanding a train of thought.

Good orators often consciously startle an audience with something that seems wrong or even *is* wrong. Public speakers pay more conscious attention than many writers do to an essential rhetorical problem: keeping the audience awake and involved. Speakers look out at their audience and see them slump or yawn; they know that it's usually boring and ineffectual to build a speech out of nothing but sentences that listeners already agree with or can't dispute. (Two exceptions: speakers at a pep rally for an audience who all share a passionate view—*polluters are terrible* or *health care reform is terrible*. They are looking for nothing but cheers. Second, it's often bad for students when teachers resist even temporarily.)

The pressure to avoid attackable sentences tempts many academics and students to create sentences with all the needed qualifications and complications already built in. This is one reason that academic prose is often difficult or laborious to follow. The spatial and visual bias reinforces the mistaken goal of trying for all-at-once-ness. But when we build in all the qualifications so our sentences are fully true or valid, we usually end up with sentences that are too complicated—and also too boring because of their lack of energy or pull.

> The danger of attack is particularly strong in the field of philosophy. Here is one philosopher's ambivalent praise for a colleague's ability to write steel-plated prose:
>
> > The argument is heavily armored, both in its range of reference and in the structure of its sentences, which almost always coil around some anticipated objection and skewer it; [Bernard] Williams is always one step ahead of his reader. Every sentence seems constructed in such a way as never to need withdrawing: it is fully shielded, immune from refutation. Williams is so well protected that it is sometimes hard to make out the shape of his position. The sentences seldom descend to elegance, and lucidity seems less highly prized than impregnability, though there are certainly flashes of humor and no lack of verbal resource. (McGinn 70)

When we speak onto the page, we seldom create the problem of all-at-once sentences with every qualification already built in. Speaking doesn't give us time for this kind of pre-planning. And when we revise by reading aloud at the late stage of revising, we can hear when a sentence is tangled or dead because we tried to pack too much into it as we were revising. We can hear whether our sentences have the energy to pull readers through time.

The mouth and ear prefer careful and revised language that nevertheless enacts large scale thinking-in-process—language that dramatizes a change from one position to another:

> *X seems clearly true for the following good reasons* [and spell those out]. *But if we look again more closely, we can see that really Y is a better conclusion for these reasons.* . . .

Some writers harness time for a structure that's even more complex:

> *A. But no, B. Yet consider the force of C. Nevertheless D.*

When writers use this kind of dialogic form that moves through time, they are often able to convey to readers a stronger felt presence of a mind in action. (Of course, this kind of form *can* be wooden: the writer starts by pretending to have views that she didn't really take seriously—mouthing positions that are merely "straw men.")

In Chapter 4, I described the advantages of the "right-branching" syntax we often get from unplanned speaking: starting off by saying the kernel phrase or clause that gave rise to the impulse to speak—and then adding more phrases, clauses, and thoughts as they come to mind. Here now is one more reason this kind of syntax can be effective in writing if it is well shaped through out-loud revising: it conveys to readers the energy and dynamism of a mind in action. As Francis Christensen notes, "[The right-branching sentence] does not represent the idea as conceived, pondered over, reshaped, packaged, and delivered cold. It is dynamic rather than static, representing the mind thinking" (6).

Concluding Reflection: Singing in Our Cage

Nothing I say in this chapter is meant to undermine the larger fact I opened the chapter with: writing *does* give writers and readers some relief from the intractable medium of time. The goal of this book is not just to enlist speech but also to *keep* what's best about writing. Written language is far less tangled in the glue of time than spoken language. When we learn to organize our texts with traditional techniques of structure, signposting, and mapping, we give readers some respite from the temporal prison of reading. Writing lets us preserve words through time instead of always losing them at the moment of utterance. Yet if we can *harness time* rather than trying to elude it—if we can give readers an experience of coherence and satisfaction *in* that intractable medium of time—we will give them an experience of deeper coherence and satisfaction. We will have brought organization and coherence to the realm of greater existential helplessness.

Good writers have always used dynamic modes of form as a source of energy to bind time and give a sense of coherence to large and complex texts. They have learned to let words have the dynamism that Walter Ong highlights in speech:

> Deeply typographic folk forget to think of words as . . . events, and hence as necessarily powered: for them, words tend rather to be assimilated to things, "out there" on a flat surface. Such "things" are not . . . actions but are in a radical sense dead. . . . The fact that oral peoples commonly and in all likelihood universally consider words to have magical potency is clearly tied in, at least unconsciously, with their sense of the word as necessarily spoken, sounded, and hence power-driven. (Orality 32–33)

(See Burke: "The titular word for our own method is 'Dramatism,' [which] . . . treats language and thought primarily as modes of action" [*Grammar* xxii].)

We're told that angels can communicate with each other instantaneously. They zap rich complex meanings all at once from one consciousness to another. How nice. Computers are almost as good as angels: their 1's and 0's may be arranged in linear sequences, but they move *fast!* We poor humans are stuck in the communicative slow lane—in both speaking and writing.

But think again about this cage of time and linearity in language—this inherent prissiness that says "You mustn't put more than one byte in your mouth at once": in truth, it is the glory of syntax and language. And of music! Imagine saying, "Let's get away from linearity in music." Without linearity, no rhythm.

Rhythm declares to each beat, "You must wait for your proper turn: not too soon, not too late." Without linearity, there is no experience of energy or dynamism in language—spoken or written. Consider Lear's version of bliss with Cordelia: "We'll sing like birds in a cage."

LITERACY STORY
Three Countries with Competing Official Written Languages

Greece

From the earliest preclassical days, there were at least three Greek dialects, Aeolian, Doric, and Attic. Speakers in all three could understand each other, but each language was written in its own way. In fact, a tradition developed that certain kinds of writing belonged in certain dialects. So the Attic playwrights, Aeschylus, Sophocles, and Euripides, wrote their plays mainly in Attic, but they used Doric for the songs and choral recitations (Janson 80. For Greece and Norway, I'm following his account. Page numbers are from him).

In preclassical and classical times, Greece consisted of different city states rather than a single state, yet the people in all of them had a sense of themselves as *Hellenes* (Greek)—and others as barbarian. "So a uniform language and a single state are not necessary conditions for people to feel that they belong together" (79).

We are accustomed to the idea of *written* classical Greek having spread far and wide through history. Think of all the remarkable classical texts left us in literature, history, and other fields. But a worldwide spread of *spoken* Greek? This, however, is just what Alexander the Great managed—at least throughout his known world. He was from Macedonia and spoke that language, but, famously, he was tutored by Aristotle. Throughout the astoundingly large territory he conquered, he used Attic Greek as the official language. All military and administrative people had to learn to speak Greek (81). "Thus [written *and* spoken Greek] was in use without interruption from Alexander the Great to the mid fifteenth century, that is for more than 1,700 years" (83).

When Greece became a state in the nineteenth century, written Greek emerged again as an official language. But spoken Greek had changed over the centuries, and the Greeks somehow decided they couldn't use the old written form. (There are plenty of examples of states keeping speech and writing far apart, but Greece didn't take that path.) Somehow,

> [i]n the course of the nineteenth century, there appeared . . . two competing written languages. One is called *dimotiki* ("the popular language") and is reasonably close to modern spoken Greek. The other one is called *kathareuousa* ("the purified language"), and it includes many more words and forms from classical Greek. (84)

Greeks fought over the two written languages, at times bitterly. When the generals took over the government in 1967, the "purified" form was declared the official obligatory language for all state business and in the schools. But when the military junta fell in 1976, *dimotiki* was declared official.

So the Greeks have two written languages, but only one is given state sponsorship at a given time. We see here a pattern that occurs over and over: languages serve as the focus of political struggle. Not surprisingly, conservative factions tend to struggle to preserve more traditional written languages—often with more links to past literature. More radical or left-leaning groups often struggle to promote forms closer to the people's speech—and this often goes along with a tolerance or even desire for change.

Norway

The Scandinavian languages all sprang from a common early ancestor, but dialectal differences grew up early. In the thirteenth and fourteenth centuries, the kingdoms of Denmark, Norway, and Sweden developed three distinct written languages. But the Norwegian version died out as Norway came to be dominated by both Sweden and Denmark. Starting in the sixteenth century Danish became Norway's written language.

In the twentieth century, after independence, influential Norwegians began consciously introducing spoken Norwegian words into their written language till "the Danish written language gradually became more similar to spoken urban Norwegian" (221). But

> [t]here was also a competing, more revolutionary movement. Its goal was to created an entirely new Norwegian written language, based upon Norwegian rural dialects and to some extent on the medieval Norwegian written language. . . . [Eventually] two written languages emerged in Norway within a half a century after the disappearance of the Danish influence. . . . What was called Danish-Norwegian in the nineteenth century is now officially called *bokmål* ("book language"). The language dubbed *landsmål* ["country language"] by Aasen is nowadays called *nynorsk* ("new Norwegian") (222).

So Norway resembles Greece in having two different written languages, one closer to speech. But in Norway, both of them are officially tolerated and widely used.

Vietnam

The Vietnamese Buddhists used Chinese characters for more than a thousand years when Vietnam was colonized by China (111 BCE to 939 CE). They used it to write material in classical Chinese, but they pronounced the words with Vietnamese sounds. But in the fourteenth century *Chu Nom* was developed—a character-based writing system for writing the Vietnamese language.

In the seventeenth century, however, a French Jesuit, Alexandre de Rhodes, went to Vietnam and developed a written script using Roman letters rather than characters: *Quoc Ngu.* When the French ruled Vietnam (1861–1945), they naturally used the Western letter-based *Quoc Ngu.* But the anti-colonialists fighting the French used traditional *Chu Nom* writing for their resistance literature. Nevertheless, Ho Chi Minh and some other resistance fighters favored the letter-based *Quoc Ngu* for the sake of mass literacy. "In 1945, immediately after the declaration of independence against the French, Ho Chi Minh launched a campaign of mass literacy explicitly to enlist people in the struggle against the colonials." (The quotation is from Bernard, 26—and in my account I am relying on him.)

16 Summary Chapter

The Benefits of Speaking onto the Page and Reading Aloud

I'M AN ENTHUSIAST. I think that everyone can write better and with less frustration and anxiety if they harness the enormous powers of their vernacular speech: speaking onto the page for the early stages of writing and reading aloud to revise during the late stages of writing. In this chapter, however, I'll focus on the benefits for three particular groups: newcomers to literacy; fairly competent writers who speak the mainstream variety of English; and speakers of nonsanctioned, nonstandardized, or stigmatized versions of English.

1. Newcomers to Literacy

About very small children, people often say, "They haven't learned to write yet." But in fact, small children *can* write if only they are given a little key to unlock the door. All they need is a rough idea of the alphabet and some of the sounds that go with the letters—and the encouragement not to worry about spelling. With that, they can *write their speech*—speak onto the page. (I focus here on small children, but what I write applies also to adults who have not yet learned to read or write.) Here is an example of a child's writing as he produced it. And here are his words in grown-up spelling:

> One day, well if there was a day, there was sand and dust and rocks and stones and some other things. And it was a thunderclaps! And a planet began to rise. And they called it Earth. And do you know what? It rained and rained and rained for thirty days in the big holes. And see we began to grow. And the first animal was a little dinosaur. When the Earth turns around the sun, the sun turns around the Earth. The sun isn't really a big ball. It is really a giant star. It is really far and so it looks like a circle. Don't listen to the newspaperman, all that about the sun. Don't be afraid because the sun will last for ever. That's all there is. (Calkins 49)

(For another example, see Katie Ray's "When Kids Make Books" 17.)

For children, it turns out that drawing a picture is often the generative germ for the words. Listen to what Chris said:

> Five-year-old Chris opened his book to a blank page and took hold of his pencil. Cheerfully, I asked, "What are you going to write?" The boy stared

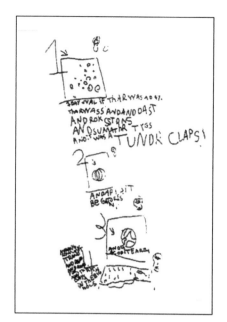

at me as if astounded by the stupidity of my question. "How should I know," he said. "I haven't drawed it yet." [Calkins *The Art of Teaching Writing* 47 and 50])

First-grade teachers or parent helpers often type these texts into standard grown-up spelling and then bind the pages together with hard covers and make little books of them. As children write more books over the months, teachers usually make a prominent classroom library. Thus in many classrooms around

the country, kindergarteners and first graders are not just writing stories but "publishing" their own books. They learn to read by reading their own books and those of their classmates. There is a much-told story of a reporter visiting one of these classrooms where the first graders eagerly show him their books. "Have you really written a book?" the reporter bends down to ask with a bit of condescending surprise. The child looks up and says, "Haven't you?" It has become common in many kindergartens and first grades across the country (and adult literacy centers) to encourage this kind of writing.

Some call this "illiterate writing." But isn't that an oxymoron? I question how our culture has defined "literacy" (a job I will take on in Part Four). For now, we simply have to acknowledge that even though children like this are not as good at forming letters and spelling words as most older people are, nevertheless they write easily and confidently and (dare I say it?) often more forcefully than many of their elders.

This approach to writing and reading is well documented now. Researchers have shown that the stories written by children in these classrooms are at a higher level of cognitive development and linguistic sophistication than the stories they can read. For more about this approach and other examples, see Calkins; Ray; Ray and Cleaveland; Harste, Woodward, and Burke. There's an interesting parallel here to the successful Suzuki approach to teaching violin and other instruments: trying to learn by ear before trying to learn to read notes on a page.

When children write in this fashion, shall we say they are "speaking onto the page"? In one sense, they clearly are; speech is the only fully workable language they have at this point. But on the other hand, they can't yet physically write quickly and fluently, and may even be taking time to plan and monitor each word rather than just letting words come without care or planning as in casual talking. We can't know the process behind words we find on the page. Perhaps the distinction is moot in the light of the findings of two researchers:

[W]e have found that with 8- to 11-year-olds, that is, children who are still mastering the basics of writing, few differences are apparent between their oral and their written narratives. . . . [D]uring the early grades the processes involved in both oral and written production are generally common to both modalities. (Hildyard and Hidi 303)

In any event, it's obvious that little children benefit from the invitation to use their only language for writing.

In California this invitation to speak onto the page has been largely discouraged because of the widespread criticism that it is a "whole language" method. "Whole language" activities are feared because of the emphasis on reading by sight rather than reading by sounding out. Yet when children are invited to write before they read, the process is all about the ear and phonics: it's nothing *but* the sounding out of letters and words.

This practice is not available to little Chinese children and others who don't use an alphabet or syllabary for writing. You can't use spoken language for writing if there is no link between the sounds of your spoken words and your writing system.

Writing as the Doorway to Literacy

When "illiterate" children learn to write by speaking onto the page, a principle of profound simplicity emerges: writing comes naturally before reading! Very young children can write before they can read, they can write more than they can read, and they can write more easily than they can read. For they can write any word or sentence they can say. All they need is an invitation to use whatever letters come easily—using invented spelling or kid spelling or "approximations." In contrast, their usable vocabulary for reading is very limited. They can read only the few words they have already learned—or that they can sound out. Even younger children who don't know the alphabet can write if they have seen other people write: they just scribble, scribble, scribble—but with meaning. Often they can "read" their scribbles back to you.

This new literacy practice—the explicit invitation to write before reading—strikes me as the most far-reaching change in education, indeed in literacy itself, that has happened in centuries. But why did it take people so long to discover this root, brute, always-true fact that writing is easier than reading and thus naturally precedes reading (at least in cultures that use an alphabet or syllabary)? Donald Graves and Lucy Calkins and several others deserve enormous credit for figuring it out (see Calkins; Graves; Harste, Woodward, and Burke). But why wasn't it obvious for centuries? Surely lots of children in literate households down through history have scribbled meaningfully before they could read or spell. Plenty of grown-ups must have noticed children sometimes using letters to make meaningful words and sentences. But the grown-ups somehow couldn't see it as writing. There's something about our culture of literacy (all cultures of literacy?) that made these simple facts difficult to see and reflect upon. But once these researchers (and thinkers!) help us use a new lens for looking at this ubiquitous and doubtless ancient children's activity, we can see that writing is a much wider doorway into literacy than reading (see my "Write First" and "War between Reading and Writing").

Small children who read what they and their classmates have written often get more involved in reading and more quickly competent at it than those who read only published textbooks brought in from outside and written by people they have never met (especially basal reading textbooks). In this process, learning is faster and kids have a healthier stance toward reading—a stance that says,

> Hey, these things called books are written by regular people—they are what *we* write. Let's read books to see what other people like us have to say.

In these classrooms, children don't get saddled with the attitude that is so common in schools: that books are merely occasions for being tested—impersonal products coming from a corporate, faceless "they"—like arithmetic workbooks. In short, speaking their native language onto the page can help children quickly feel that full literacy is natural and comfortable.

But wait. If we invite kids to spell wrong, they'll never learn to spell right. This is an understandable fear, but not a valid one. This approach to literacy does not ignore correct spelling or pretend it doesn't matter. When little children read typed up versions of their own and each other's books, they see what they knew anyway: that this carefully typed up "grown-up spelling" is different from their own "kid spelling." The write-before-read approach doesn't invite teachers to say "Spelling doesn't matter." (A few rebellious souls have said this, but they started way before the start of the movement I'm talking about.) Rather, the approach invites teachers to say, "Spelling doesn't matter *while* you are doing these first drafts; but it matters a lot for final copies. They should look good." Most children care a lot that any final copy should "look right." (In fact, there are a few children who feel that way so strongly that they can't bring themselves to write any word till they find out the correct spelling.)

Some people want to blame this new practice for all the bad spelling we see, but spelling in English has always been a problem. Correct spelling really depends very much on the eye. Perhaps spelling ability has declined as reading has declined among people of all ages. Yet most "bad spellers" do better than Shakespeare or Lewis and Clark (see Chapter 1, 28) or John Smith (see Chapter 6, 126).

See Gunther Kress for interesting and lucid scholarship on spelling. The regularization of English spelling didn't really happen, he shows, till the late sixteenth and early seventeenth centuries. It was the work of "inkhorn grammarians" during the centralization of the British State under the Tudors. He also demonstrates how most misspellings by children reflect closer and more accurate listening to spoken words than most of us literates manage. We tend to tune out the real sounds of spoken words because we think of written words as more real. Kress also shows how public worry over bad spelling goes up and down with history. During periods when people feel a sense of national decline, there is more worry about errors and calls for tightening standards. In periods of confidence and exuberance, there is less worry over spelling. (See Frank Summers's *Wholly, Holey, Holy: An Adult American Spelling Book* for a compilation of the *many* cases where dictionaries disagree about spelling.)

Montessori schools usually encourage children to write before they read—not worrying about spelling for a while. They do lots of preparatory sensory work such as explorations of sandpaper versions of the letters of the alphabet. When Waldorf schools invite children to read, they take pains to get students fluent in performing songs and stories, body movement, and playing music. I admire this insistence that children integrate language with the body—which is, in a way, the seat of language. (In human development, children learn gesture and intonation in their bodies before they learn grammar.) But I'm sad to be told that even in these progressive Waldorf schools, some teachers haven't escaped our cultural habit of assuming that the doorway to literacy involves learning visible language by reading, not audible language through writing. Writing is a powerful way to heighten the goal of integrating literacy with the body and the whole person—not just the head.

Voluminous reading is the best route to good spelling, and reading is one of the main beneficiaries of this write-to-read approach. Reading benefits enormously from the reading aloud in these early grade classrooms when the class frequently gathers around the "author's chair" to hear the author read her story or short book—sometimes following along the text (correctly spelled) with their eyes. This helps them see reading as a friendly human social process. One reason so many people are bored with reading is that when they pass their eyes silently and quickly over texts, they don't *hear* any of the music and drama of the human voice. In school contexts especially, children too often feel that reading is mere fodder for tests and that the point is merely to *extract information* as quickly as possible. There are too few practices that help them feel reading as pleasure. Writing before reading helps children feel much sooner that they are members of what Frank Smith brilliantly called "the literacy club." The only sure way to help people learn to spell better is to promote practices that make them read more. Spelling tests and reading tests won't do the job.

When we encourage children to notice that they can write more than they can read and thus can write *before* they read—can use writing as a doorway to literacy—this is not just practical pedagogy or a "good technique." The approach overturns an ingrained hierarchy between reading and writing. The traditional phrase "reading and writing" makes reading the horse and writing the cart: reading always comes first. If we question this relationship, we'll notice some deep cultural assumptions embedded in schooling and literacy:

- Reading means that someone else chose the words; writing means that the learner chooses the words. Reading asks, "What do *they* have to say?" where writing asks, "What do *you* have to say?"
- Reading implies "Sit still and pay attention," whereas writing implies "Get in there and do something." People often fall asleep while reading, never while writing.

- Reading means consumption; writing means production. When reading always comes first, we set up a "banking" model of education that says there's nothing in learners' heads till we put it there.
- Reading encourages passivity by locating agency and authority away from the student and keeping it in the teacher, institution, and culture. When reading always comes first, this locks schools into sending students a pervasive message: "Don't speak until spoken to, and don't write your own ideas until you prove you can reproduce correctly the ideas of others." When we invite students to talk onto the page and thereby let writing naturally precede reading, we help students break out of their characteristically passive stance in school and learning.
- Reading implies that the eye is the central organ for language; writing by young children brings out the centrality of the tongue and ear for language.
- When reading always comes first, it lulls people into thinking that "literacy" is all about mastering the code and conventions of Edited Written English. *Literacy* actually means *letters*, and the generative core is the ability to get your thoughts into letters or visible language. The power-giving core of literacy involves agency and activity rather than passivity.

If we try to undo this powerfully ingrained hierarchy of reading over writing, there are likely to be strong objections from the powerful companies that make textbooks in general and basal readers in particular—and the test-making companies that are uncomfortably linked to the textbook companies. We might see objections also from many literary critics and English departments where the priority of reading is part of the wallpaper.

Extensive reading is a wonderful help for writing (and spelling)—possibly the best help of all—but it's not actually *necessary*. People who don't read can call on a rich complex verbal ability in their speaking and listening, and this ability can be the basis of good writing. Probably not very "literary" writing, but there's a lot of good writing these days that's not very "literary"—and there's going to be more. In short—with adults as with small children—reading isn't the only or sometimes even the best doorway to literacy; writing works as well, and sometimes better.

I grant the usefulness of a formulation that has been fashionable among some theorists, namely, that "reading is really writing" (actively creating meaning), and "writing is really reading" (passively finding what culture and history have inscribed in our heads). This formulation carries some useful truth—this lens shows us some things that the commonsense lens obscures—but in the end, writing promotes more psychological and physical engagement than reading. And anything that helps preserve the cultural dominance of reading over writing helps preserve our unhelpful assumption that the only doorway to literacy is to listen to authoritative voices and be tested about whether we understand them accurately.

There are many *adults* who are not yet literate. The approach I'm describing is even more promising for them. They are likely to have even more things to write than small children—more experiences they have undergone, more opinions that have built up. They can naturally start their journey to literacy by writing out their experiences and thoughts. Then with some help, their words can be put into conventional spelling and they can learn to read by reading their own and each other's writings. The world of reading will open more invitingly once they gain that felt link between physically spoken and heard words and silent words on the page.

2. Fairly Competent Writers Who Speak the Mainstream Variety of English

Everyone likes to complain about all the bad writing in the world. (See, for example, E. L. Godkin writing in 1897 about "the illiteracy of American boys." This was the title of a piece he wrote in an eminent educational journal. He was editor of *The Nation* and one of the authors of a Harvard report that also noted the poor preparation of entering students.) But let's turn our attention away from bad writing—and also from all the truly excellent writing in the world. Instead, let's think about all the *more or less competent* writers in the world. There are lots of them, despite all the literate handwringing. *Some* managers at H&R Block and Blackwater write good reports; *some* people in Habitat for Humanity and other nonprofit agencies write good exploratory studies and grant proposals. The same for CitiBank, the State Department, town governments—even in schools and colleges. Many engineers write effective reports and proposals. And think about all the students at all levels who actually write fairly well.

It's salutary to put our minds on all the fairly competent writers in the world. Researchers in my field have long reveled in documenting how *much* writing is done in virtually all the professions. I know from visits to many campuses that when writing program directors try to encourage writing across the curriculum, they often get more cooperation from schools of engineering and business than some English departments. I like to startle my first-year writing students by telling them: "If you hate writing, you're better off becoming an English teacher than an engineer. Research shows that the average engineer spends between a quarter and a third of the week writing."

Now a simple question: how many of these fairly competent writers feel genuinely at home as they write? I invite you to consider what I have found overwhelmingly true in a long career during which I can't seem to resist talking about writing to everyone I meet: a large proportion of skilled competent writers (most?) don't really feel quite comfortable or in their element as they write. They don't feel writing as something that belongs to them or fits them. Yes, some do; and a few *love* to write and do it whenever they get a chance—a handful of them writing so much that they become "native speakers of written English." And some competent writers feel *sort of* at home as they write—just as some carpenters or accountants or plumbers who don't love their work nevertheless learn to feel more or less at home as they go about their jobs.

But I think I see that *most* fairly competent writers put off writing as long as they can and undertake the job with some reluctance, often some anxiety. I'm talking about people who *know* they are competent even when sometimes *feeling* incompetent: they know they've managed many times to produce competent or successful writing and they know they can do it again. But they don't feel writing is really "theirs." It's as though someone else—or some other group—"owns" writing; they are only sort of visiting or "making use of it." That first grader writing "illiterately" about dinosaurs and volcanoes was much more at home in writing than many *competent* grown-ups. I'm suggesting then that it's not just unskilled, unpracticed writers who will benefit from the practice of drafting by speaking onto the page and revising by reading aloud; even competent writers need the benefits of this approach.

Deborah Brandt interviewed a large sample of people in her classic study of *Literacy in American Lives* and found that

> [m]any people took pride in calling themselves an "avid reader" or "quite a reader" or "always reading." Yet there was a reticence among the people I spoke with—including a well-established, published poet—to regard themselves as writers, despite avid energy in their pursuit of writing. (159–160)
>
> [A]cross the generations, school-based writing was widely associated with pain, belittlement, and perplexity. (164. See also Aldrich on anxiety and discomfort among adult writers in the workplace.)

What is it about writing that keeps people from being at home even if they are skilled and have written over and over? It's my argument that they feel that writing means having to use a language or a linguistic gear that is not theirs. I see over and over that many writers, even when they know they are *competent*, don't feel comfortable having to "write writing"—write "correct written English"—a different language from the one they feel most at home in. And for most people, the process of writing has gotten all tangled up with being judged—judged for wrong language and imprecise thinking. Part of the problem is that so many people have deeply embedded memories of teachers finding and correcting errors and other problems in everything they write. In fact, it looks at first as though writing, *as a medium*—inherently and inevitably—invites judgment: writing leaves a permanent record. What we produced carelessly, or even with great care, often sits there for a long time where anyone can see faults.

But this assumption rests in faulty thinking. If more people realized that they could talk onto the page or freewrite in a gear and a language that they feel *is* their own—and that nothing they write this way will be put out to readers for critical judgment—their relationship to writing would vastly improve. I've seen this happen again and again. Of course people still need to be painstaking when they revise and edit so as to get ready for judgment, but they can learn to feel much more at home writing because so much of the process involves using their comfortable language and *not* being judged.

I notice this situation for myself as a writer. I have a mother tongue much closer to Edited Written English than many others have. But the words and constructions that come naturally to my tongue are often wrong for writing.

I'm an experienced, competent writer, but I find I cannot give my full attention to figuring out my thinking till I ignore questions of what's right for written language or this audience or this genre, and let myself speak or freewrite onto the page. I've learned to write with language that is not just safe but that *welcomes* whatever comes to my mouth—no matter who might frown on it.

3. Speakers of Nonsanctioned, Nonstandardized, or Stigmatized Languages

There are many versions of spoken English, but none of them match Edited Written English. Some are closer and others further away. Children who grew up in "better" families in the southern counties of England speak a version of English that's closer to EWE than mine.

Consider this Glaswegian version of spoken Scottish English that James Kelman writes in his novel, *How Late It Was, How Late:*

> Mind you but getting blootered, it would be one way of making it home. Weans and drunks man know what I'm saying, the auld god fellow, the central authority, that's who he looks after. Sometimes that was what the bevy was like but a magic carpet. Othertimes it wasnay. (45 Vintage 1998)
> ("Weans" = wee ones; "man" = must; "bevy" = drink)

Or these excerpts from "Aunt Roachy Seh" by the remarkable Jamaican poet, Louise Bennett:

> Meck me get it straight, Mas Charlie,
> For me no quite understan —
> Yuh gwine kill all English dialec
> Or jus Jamaica one?
>
> . . .
>
> Ef yuh cyann sing 'Linstead Market' [cyann = can't]
> And 'Water come a me yeye'
> You wi haffi tap sing 'Auld lang syne' [tap = stop]
> and "Comin through the rye'.
>
> Dah language weh yuh proud a,
> Weh yuh honor and respec —
> Po Mas Charlie, yuh no know seh [you don't know to see]
> Dat it spring from dialec!
>
> . . .
>
> Yuh wi haffi get the Oxford Book
> A English Verse, an tear
> Out Chaucer, Burns, Lady Rizelle
> An plenty a Shakespeare!
> *Aunt Roachy Seh*, 1993.

Certain forms of spoken English are more stigmatized than others. Scots dialects are far less stigmatized than they used to be in England (Kelman's novel was nominated for the prestigious Booker Prize). For a long time, Robert

Burns's poetry was considered almost trash by "literate" folk in England and many even in Scotland. U.S. rural Southern speech and urban working-class speech are often stigmatized. Many who grew up in the South or the Ozarks manage to "lose" the rich powerful form of speech that is actually still in their bones. "Literate" people love to make fun of Bronx, Brooklyn, and Queens speech—not just the grammar and vocabulary but especially the accent.

But *Black English* or African American Language (AAL) has tended to be particularly stigmatized—sometimes more so than "Black" skin. It's not so uncommon for mainstream White people to find themselves assuming that someone is unintelligent if he "speaks Black." This stigmatization has been so pervasive as to be internalized by quite a few African Americans. Jesse Jackson famously called Ebonics "trash talk" and Bill Cosby prominently said (and later repeated) these words (using "it" to refer to young speakers of this language):

> It's standing on da corner. It can't speak English. It doesn't want to speak English. I can't even talk the way these people talk. "Why you ain't, where you is go . . ." I don't know who these people are. (Dyson xii)

Many names have been given to this language: Black English, African American Vernacular English (a term often used by linguists), and African American English (a term used in two respected books about the language [Lisa Green; Theresa Redd and Karen Webb]. I am using the term African American Language (AAL)—the title of an active and ambitious center established by the linguistics department at the University of Massachusetts at Amherst. I also seek to honor the huge contribution of Geneva Smitherman and some others who are refusing a lens that suggests too fully that the language is just a poor stepchild of English. The most controversial term is Ebonics. When Robert Williams coined it, he used it to apply to a spectrum of languages including those of the Caribbean. He says that Ebonics refers to the

> linguistic and paralinguistic features which on a concentric continuum represent the communicative competence of the West African, Caribbean, and United States slave descendants of African origin. It includes the various idioms, patois, argots, ideolects, and social dialects of black people, especially those who have been forced to adapt to colonial circumstances. (Quoted in Smitherman "Black English/Ebonics" 29)

See Lisa Green's introduction to her *African American English* for a good treatment of the naming issues. And for explorations of Black culture and hip hop language, see Alim and Alim, Baugh, and Smitherman.

We see the same kind of stigmatization of various Hispanic-inflected versions of English (Latino or Mexican American or Puerto Rican), of various Caribbean creoles or "patois" dialects of English, and of Hawaiian Creole English (often called "Pidgin"). Spanish speakers from Spain who make "Spanish mistakes" in English will not feel what many North American Hispanic speakers can scarcely avoid feeling: that their "mistakes" make them sound stupid in many mainstream ears. It has been found that teachers sometimes penalize students more for "Black mistakes" or "Latino mistakes" than for garden variety "White mistakes" or "ESL mistakes." "Asian mistakes" are often experienced by teachers as poetic and insightful. Stigmatization of "lower class" language betrays itself in many ways, but here's a curious practice. When writers present the speech of lower class speakers, they often use words like "wuz," "enuff," "offen." The words are pronounced just this way by mainstream people, but seldom represented this way. *Respelling* as condescension (see Behrens).

Writing in Black English or AAE or Other Stigmatized Vernaculars

Since the growth of the process movement in the teaching of writing in the 1960s and 1970s (more about this in Appendix I about the field of composition), lots and lots of teachers have come to invite students to use everyday speech for writing. It's not that they say, "write in speech." They say something more like this: "Try freewriting for exploratory and early draft writing. Don't struggle for correct language or stop to figure out grammar problems." When students follow this advice, they naturally use their everyday spoken language.

Yet this approach has *not* been so widely adopted for speakers of Black English and other heavily stigmatized languages. These languages are so highly "marked" by race that many teachers (some of them speakers of Black English) find it wrong or scary to invite students to write in them—even for exploratory early drafts. Thus the approach for student speakers of stigmatized languages has tended to be the traditional two-gear method: *keep speech and writing apart.* Work toward comfort and fluency in using language that's right for writing. When speakers of stigmatized languages *are* invited to freewrite, it's often not so much an invitation to use Black English but rather something more like this: "*Use freewriting to help you get more comfortable and less anxious trying to use the <u>right</u> language for writing. Freewriting will help you go faster and not worry about mistakes in your efforts to write in White English.*"

This traditional "two-gear" approach—start off using "correct" English—can obviously work. It's probably produced much of the good writing in mainstream English by Black writers and speakers of other stigmatized languages. And it's an approach favored by some progressive and sophisticated linguists and scholars. Here is Marcia Farr, who has been a notable fighter against the stigmatization of nonstandardized versions of English:

> I worry a bit about trying to get them to write in their "mother dialect." . . . [U]sing it in the classroom (unless in creative writing) confuses form with function. I think it's more important to get them to fully realize the adequacy of all dialects. "Leave their oral language alone," as it were, but teach writing in SE. (Email response in 2000 to my 1999 "Inviting the Mother Tongue")

Advantages of Speaking onto the Page for Speakers of Stigmatized Englishes

Even though we know that the two-gear method can work for some students, I'd argue that it has worked *against* most speakers of stigmatized languages. I'll use this section to describe some of the advantages. Since so many mainstream students have been invited to start off writing projects more comfortably in their everyday vernacular speech—which of course means using "wrong language" for writing—it's surely time to invite speakers of *any* spoken version of English to do the same. (I'm drawing here on my recent essay, "Why Deny to Speakers of African American Language a Choice Most of Us Offer Other Students?")

First I'll summarize briefly some of the advantages that I spelled more fully in Chapter 9 as I responded to objections against speaking onto the page:

- When people are invited to write in the language that comes most easily to mouth and mind, they can write more easily and find more words and ideas.
- When students try to write in a language that's not comfortable to them, they often produce stiff, awkward, unclear writing, and even make peculiar errors.
- The traditional approach seldom yields what people hope for: the dream of becoming a native writer of correct writing and never having to think about the rules as we write.
- In fact there *is* no single version of "correct, edited, written English" to learn and make automatic. Writers need the opportunity to make conscious rhetorical choices about levels of correctness and formality (and in this case "Whiteness") for any particular piece of writing, given the audience and occasion.

Some students who speak a language that is strongly stigmatized may understandably *decline* any invitation to use it for writing in school. Some may not want to use it for academic tasks because it feels like an intimate, precious home language—especially when the school tasks feel impersonal, abstract, or "square." Some may feel they have too few allies in the class and so fear that classmates will look down on them for using their vernacular language. Some may not want to use it because they are trying to become fluent in EWE and are willing to give up comfort and fluency for the sake of working toward this goal. Many speakers of a stigmatized language might decide not to use it at all in writing because they are comfortable fluent code switchers into a version of mainstream sanctioned spoken English. And finally, a few may *themselves* disapprove of their own language and feel that it's wrong, bad, defective, or broken. Some have family members pushing them to learn "good English." The mother they learned it from—the very mother whose tongue it is—may call it "bad broken English." I don't feel this a good reason for not using it, but I feel I have to tread very carefully when the student herself feels it strongly.

I see six other advantages of speaking stigmatized English onto the page:

1. When speakers of stigmatized languages start off trying to write in "proper English," their efforts to follow unfamiliar rules often lead them into odd or fractured words or impossible constructions: language that would never come

out of anyone's mouth. (An example of hypercorrection is *loveded* written by a speaker who must feel, "Uh oh, I'm always criticized for leaving off endings. See Baugh, *Black Street Speech*.) Teachers often read this kind of accidental nonlanguage as a "cognitive deficit," that is, stupidity. If the students had simply written the vernacular grammar that came easily to mouth, their words would at least have been clear and strong. And very often the vernacular form would have been *right* for correct written English (in this case *loved*). Teachers and students (and linguists?) are so preoccupied with the *differences* between Black and White English that they forget to notice that the vernacular grammar is usually *right* for White English—and often even for Edited Written English. Crystal points out that

> [o]nly about 1 percent of the grammatical rules of English (such as the proscription of *ain't*, or of double negatives . . .) are actually relevant to [for?] the distinction between standard and nonstandard, and debate can rage about the correctness or otherwise of some of the proscriptions (such as the concern over "split infinitives" . . .). Similarly, only a small number of dialect or slang words, by comparison with the lexicon as a whole, have a status as nonstandard. . . . The standardness of English is actually characterized with reference to a very small part—chiefly in spelling and grammar—of the language's structural resources. (*Stories* 224–225. The little bracketed "debate" between *to* and *for* is Crystal himself trying to illustrate arbitrary language debates.)

2. Speakers of highly stigmatized languages can discover to their benefit that writing is a safer mode for language than speech. When they *speak* with mainstream listeners, they risk stigmatization unless they have the unusual skill of removing even subtle traces of accent and intonation. But they can *write* safely and comfortably in their comfortable vernacular without fear of prejudice—and wait till the end to make changes into Edited Written English. Making those changes is easier than most people think. Remember what I quoted from the linguists Wolfram, Adger, and Christian (216 in the Introduction to Part Three):

> If native speakers from Michigan, New England, and Arkansas avoid the use of socially stigmatized grammatical structures such as "double negatives" (e.g., *They didn't do nothing*), different verb agreement patterns (e.g., *They's okay*), and different irregular verb forms (e.g., *She done it*), there is a good chance they will be considered standard English speakers. . . . In this way, informal standard English is defined negatively. In other words if a person's speech is free of structures that can be identified as nonstandard, then it is considered standard. (12)

Preventing mainstream readers from saying "That's *wrong*" is often a matter of learning to fix a limited number of socially (often racially) stigmatized features.

Code switching versus *code meshing*. There's an interesting and complicated discussion going about these two practices. Code switching (in this context) means speaking or writing entirely in the mainstream language when a mainstream audience expects or needs it—and thus avoiding *all* Black language or grammar. Code meshing, in contrast, means *keeping* some Black language and grammar: "blending, merging, meshing dialects" (Young 72). Vershawn Young and Suresh Canagarajah make strong arguments for code meshing. Their two main points are compelling. First, they insist that if we try to make speakers of AAE avoid all Black language for a piece of writing, even a final draft for other professors, it reinforces racism and "double consciousness" (Du Bois)—sending the message, in effect, "You must learn to operate in two consciousnesses and implicitly accept one of them as superior." Second, they point out that in many cases, writers can actually enhance their writing by using some noticeably Black language. Young gives these examples from Geneva Smitherman's published professional writing:

> It's been a long time coming, as the old song goes, but the change done come
>   In writing that is rich and powerful—and funky and bold when it bees necessary—
> they dissect black writing and black speech. (Young 58)

As I read Canagarajah and Young, I see the following premise in their arguments: if speakers of AAE can show enough skill and control to make a text conform *mostly* to the conventions of Edited Written English, why should they hide their Black language and the fact that they are Black? Why pretend to be White? Their code meshing is comparable to the technique we saw in Krugman, Safire, and Dowd—who are, in effect, code meshing vernacular *White* speech with standard correct writing. Canagarajah and Young also make the crucial point that the traffic between discourses moves productively in both directions. "Standard" discourses have always been changed and enlivened by writers using "nonstandard" discourses.

But I see Young quietly acknowledging that code meshing won't be successful unless the writer has control over language. He makes an appeal to teachers "to teach how the semantics and rhetoric of AAE are compatible/combinable with features of standard English" (71). And he and Canagarajah recognize that this kind of racially marked code meshing can only work in our present culture if the writer has some authority. If the code meshing turns up in work from a mainstream book or magazine publisher, that gives considerable authority. Even before Smitherman was well known to most people in the composition community, she used this kind of code meshing in some of her articles in the academic journal *College English*. Since student writing is so commonly read through a teacher-lens that looks for problems, student code meshing probably won't be so successful unless the student has convinced the teacher that she is skilled and sophisticated and in control of her written language. That is, Young makes it clear that the culture has to change before the technique will work pragmatically for most students. He says that people who use Black English shouldn't be punished for it but "the fact that AAE is still subject to racism is the issue to correct" (65). "[W]e should abandon [the regressive practice of] codes switching [but] for this to happen requires a movement" (67).

Canagarajah and Young somewhat neglect two issues I'm interested in: first, the importance of making lots of room where students can write *wholly unplanned* vernacular language—with *no* need for linguistic sophistication or control; second, the possibilities for what might be called "*invisible*" or "under the radar" code meshing. That is, what I've learned from Wolfram, Adger, and Christian (earlier) is that people can use quite a lot of their comfortable spoken vernacular if they avoid certain usages that trigger the error alarm. Such usages by AAE speakers will often *not* be heard by mainstream readers as "Black"—merely a little informal (as with Krugman).

I suspect that the value of this kind of "invisible" code meshing is confirmed by some remarkable research by Smitherman and her team. They looked at thousands of papers on the nationwide NAEP exams and showed that "Black expressive discourse style" correlated with *higher scores*—as long it wasn't accompanied by the Black syntax or grammar—and this was twenty years ago ("The Blacker the Berry"). If you look at her list of stylistic features in that article, you'll see that many are not very specific to AAE. It was the "Black grammar" that was racially marked and served to lower scores. So Young and Canagarajah are right to pursue the value and importance of what might be called "in your face" code meshing, but writers at this very cultural moment will have a much easier time writing for conventional readers, especially teachers and employers,if they learn how to "fix" the few features of their vernacular that set off error alarms.

For a recent, valuable, and extensive collection of essays about the virtues of code meshing, see Young and Martinez. (In that collection, however, Elaine Richardson, a prominent African American scholar, chooses not to use the term code meshing and prefers "code switching" and "code mixing" [241].)

3. When speakers of, say, Black English start off speaking their vernacular language onto the page, their final process of editing and correcting into EWE provides an ideal occasion for repeatedly noticing and consciously comparing the differences between Black English and EWE—differences in grammar, lexicon, and other conventions.

- The grammar of correct Edited Written English is much easier to learn and remember when you compare it and relate it to the grammar of what comes out of our mouths when we aren't even noticing the words we use.
- Students can easily be helped to see that their home language—so often denigrated—is a rich, rule-governed, complete language—indeed a language with subtleties of tense and aspect that are lacking in standard spoken or written English. (These linguistic sophistications lacking in standard English are explained in most studies of AAE, e.g., Baugh, Green, Palacas, Redd.)
- This practice in comparative linguistics is a natural way to develop a more sophisticated meta-awareness of language variation and the nature of speech and writing. (This kind of work in contrastive rhetoric and grammar is recommended by the following researchers in the volume by Nero: John Rickford for AAE speakers; Pratt Johnson for Jamaican Creole speakers; Anam Govardhan for Indian English speakers. See also Carol Severino.)

4. When people use their stigmatized vernaculars for writing it will help them take pride in their own language and help overcome the alienation or ambivalence that many of them might have about a language that the culture denigrates. Even for the essays that they must copy edit into "White" "correct written English," the use of a home language for exploring and drafting can

help foster pride. And when they look at their good drafts that they've not yet copy edited into EWE, they'll scarcely be able to help noticing that it's good—and good *in* their home language. They'll see that good serious writing does not *have* to end up "correct" White English.

In my teaching of first-year writing, I put a lot of emphasis on the task of carefully revising and copy editing students' three or four major essays. But I invite everyone to revise and copy edit at least one of those essays into their vernacular spoken language, not Edited Written English. (Remember, mainstream White speakers have a home vernacular, and it's helpful for them to learn to be conscious of how it differs from correct writing.) I want all students, but especially speakers of stigmatized languages, to understand that revising and editing have no inherent link with "correct edited written English." I want them to learn to revise and edit for good thinking, clarity, liveliness, wit, and consistency—and to realize that EWE has no monopoly on those virtues. Indeed they sometimes notice that EWE can get in the way of clarity, liveliness, and wit. When they accept this invitation, they end up with a carefully revised and copy edited paper in their home or vernacular comfortable language.

There's been a good deal of important published writing in AAL and other stigmatized versions of English in recent years (see Appendix II for examples). But somehow teachers have tended to assume that all this published writing in stigmatized versions of English is irrelevant to the writing lives of students in our classrooms who speak those languages. In my writing classes, I publish three or four class magazines each semester. These are ideal sites for various versions and registers of English—and they often lead to useful discussions about language difference and ideology. But there are more and more opportunities for *wider* publication even of student writing in other versions of English. School newspapers, school literary magazines, and even some local Sunday papers are good sites for publishing good, well-revised and edited feature pieces in nonmainstream versions of English. And of course the internet offers limitless opportunities, for example, websites, blogs, and instant distribution to friends and family. If students are required to do all their drafting in so-called standard English—if they are not given the choice of writing in their home vernacular—they are stuck with only this one writing gear.

Victor Villanueva, one time chair of CCCC, writes:

I am fifty now, maybe a third of my life left, I wonder if I'll die without ever being fluent in the language that first met my ears. English is the only language that I know, really. Yet [NewYorkan] Spanish is the language of my ear, of my soul. I'm saddened by my loss. It wasn't necessary. One gives up nothing being adept at two languages or more. One gains. So many have had to give up so much to be part of the US. (quoted in Kells 35)

5. For all these reasons then, speakers of stigmatized languages seem to do better in school settings if they are invited to use their vernacular spoken language. Arthur Palacas is a linguist and composition scholar at the University of Akron who has long taught a first-year writing course where students read and write Black English. They also study the syntax and lex-

icon of that language in comparison to standardized English. When this course came under fire, he researched and discovered that over a period of about ten years, the Black students in his course had a much higher retention rate at the university than Black students who had taken a different first-year writing course—and possibly a greater retention rate than the average for university-wide White students ("Saying Yes").

Consider also the remarkable research by Patricia Irvine and Nan Elsasser. They taught basic and honors writing classes at the College of the Virgin Islands (CVI) where almost all their students were native speakers of the local Caribbean Creole vernacular English. The college insisted on standard English for virtually all student work and didn't permit credit for the first-year writing course unless students passed a conventional grammar test on standardized written English. But Irving and Elsasser had their students reading and writing and studying their stigmatized vernacular English and exploring comparisons with the prestige version of English. Not only did their students in both remedial and honors classes write better essays than students in their "control" classes but these students had a higher passing rate in the grammar test of *standard* English! Irvine and Elsasser write:

> Although many educators acknowledge the problems inherent in the so-ciolinguistic status quo, they hesitate to challenge it because of the deep-seated belief that any time devoted to Creole literacy takes away time that could be spent in English instruction, and so interferes with students' understanding of English. However, our experience with freshmen remedial and honors students at CVI does not corroborate this assumption. In fact, confronting and challenging sociolinguistic norms through the study and use of Creole effected a change in stance and attitude toward learning in general and writing in particular. Both remedial and honors students wrote more, and wrote more carefully and convincingly, in the Creole-centered courses [and did far better on exit exams in standard English,] than did our students in the English-centered classes. (310; see also Irvine and Elsasser)

6. One of my larger goals is for nonsanctioned versions of any major language to survive and flourish *as languages*. Few languages manage this unless they are used for writing.

But What about Careful or Academic Thinking?

In Chapter 9 I addressed the important objection that vernacular speech and expository writing are not just different languages or dialects but they are different ways of using the mind. Writers who speak onto the page with their vernacular speech cannot create an essayist text or an academic essay unless they change the very modes of thinking, arguing, reasoning, and organizing that they've woven into the fabric of their vernacular-based drafts. I need to address this objection a bit further here because so many people feel it more acutely for students whose native language is stigmatized. In classic research, Arnetha Ball found that high school speakers of AAE used modes of thinking that are not adequate for academic essays.

But this objection applies also to mainstream White students who are invited to freewrite when they draft. Whatever version of vernacular English students speak, they will need a strong revision process. When speakers of stigmatized dialects are asked to revise, their job will be exactly the same as it is for mainstream students. Take that statement of feelings and rewrite it as conceptual point or claim with clear supporting reasons and examples; reframe that story so it functions more clearly as supporting evidence for a more conceptually stated point. This is a completely different job from fixing grammar and spelling.

This kind of revising is hard work for mainstream students and vernacular speakers alike. But for most essay writing, it's the most important work—whether the writing is for school or business or the wider world. And when vernacular speakers do this work, they demonstrate the interesting distinction that Geneva Smitherman makes between two dimensions of AAE: Black English Vernacular *discourse style* and Black English Vernacular *grammar*. Using this distinction, she explicitly recommends the approach I am talking about and writes this:

> I am often asked "how far" does the teacher go with this kind of writing pedagogy. My answer: as far as you can. Once you have pushed your students to rewrite, revise; rewrite, revise; rewrite, revise; and once they have produced the most powerful essay possible, then and only then should you have them turn their attention to B[lack] E[nglish] V[ernacular] grammar and matters of punctuation, spelling, and mechanics. ("Black English/Ebonics" 29)

The important point here is that the use of a dialect or language does not lock someone into one mode of thinking or organizing or rhetoric. There may be significant links between language, thinking, culture, and identity. But links are not chains. The central premise here is that people can use any variety of English for any cognitive or rhetorical task. Does mainstream English—or EWE—"own" certain kinds of thinking and certain discourses? Must people give up their cultural identity to take on certain rhetorical or intellectual or cognitive tasks? Surely we can validly invite speakers of stigmatized spoken versions of English (or any language) to take on academic tasks and write an academic essay in

---

Lisa Delpit is sometimes cited as a blanket critic of all uses of Black English in school, but her famous objections are more nuanced. In fact she writes specifically in favor of the kind of writing approach that I'm advocating:

> Unlike unplanned oral language or public reading, writing lends itself to editing. While conversational talk is spontaneous and must be responsive to an immediate context, writing is a mediated process which may be written and rewritten any number of times before being introduced to public scrutiny. Consequently, writing is more amenable to rule application—one may first write freely to get one's thoughts down, and then edit to hone the message and apply specific spelling, syntactical, or punctuation rules. (25)

Thomas Farrell shone an astringently bright light on this idea by denying it. He claimed that low essay scores by African American students were explained by the "impoverished" version of the verb *to be* in their language—arguing in effect, that people cannot analyze or think abstractly in AAE. Smitherman was at pains to contradict this notion in almost all of her writing.

Note a related case. The discourses of abstract analysis and logic are deeply linked to White, male, Western culture, yet plenty of women have insisted that they don't have to give up their identity as women to use these discourses. See Nussbaum for a vigorous statement of this position.

their home dialects—as Latinos, African Americans, or Caribbeans. The general principle here is that people can keep their writerly identity—indeed their ethnic identity if they wish—and still work in various genres and produce language in which conservative readers will find no "mistakes." Writing with "an accent" doesn't have to be "wrong writing."

Revising by Reading Aloud: Advantages for Speakers of Stigmatized Englishes

Many speakers of a stigmatized language have been corrected for wrong writing so often that they have lost their bodily compass for written language. They have come to turn off their mouths and ears when they write. They have lost any clear sense of what written language can *feel like* in the body. Their only relationship to written language is like their relationship to a purely cognitive task—or even to a puzzle that's designed to trick them. They have to make theoretical and abstract decisions, answering questions like these: *Is this natural sounding word going to be another one that teachers call wrong? What was that wording they said was correct?* Arthur Palacas once told of going through an essay with one of his African American students, and at one point he said, "Oh I see now. If it sounds right to me, it's wrong. If it sounds wrong to me, it's right!"

Revising by speaking aloud can restore that compass. It invites speakers of stigmatized languages to give their mouths and ears the *central* role in writing that they should have. Yes, of course the mouth and ear will sometimes yield nonstandardized grammar ("wrong grammar"), but students will learn that these organs are actually the best source of what's needed most for good writing: strength and clarity of language. They can *own* this strong clear language—claim it for their bodies—and learn to put off till later the minor editing needed to make this good language pass muster as EWE.

LITERACY STORY

Chairman Mao Tries to Make Literacy More Available to the Chinese

Despite the fact that most Chinese characters have visual cues as to sound (see the Literacy Story following Chapter 1, about different writing systems), Chinese visual characters don't map onto Chinese spoken words. Whether you want to read characters or write them, you cannot sound them out from spoken language. Chinese children learn spoken Chinese "for free"—as all children learn their mother tongue—but for writing and reading, they have to learn all the visual characters through a completely different and mostly conscious process of memorization.

But Mao Zedong wanted to change this and make literacy much more available to the masses of Chinese. He wanted to replace the traditional characters with the Roman or Latin letters used for English and so many other languages. He may not have talked about "speaking onto the page," but his goal was to create a way of writing Chinese where the symbols would represent the sounds of spoken Chinese. Speaking to Edgar Snow in 1936 he said:

> We believe Latinization is a good instrument with which to overcome illiteracy. Chinese characters are so difficult to learn that even the best system of rudimentary characters, or simplified teaching, does not equip the people with a really efficient and rich [written] vocabulary. Sooner or later, we believe, we will have to abandon characters altogether if we are to create a new social culture in which the masses fully participate. (Quoted in Robinson 196)

That was from a private interview, but Mao said the same thing in a semi-public speech. But his remarks were suppressed and kept secret till 1981. Here's a passage:

> Because such [Roman] letters are few in number, only twenty-odd, and are written in one direction, they are simple and clear. Our Chinese characters certainly cannot compare with them in this respect. If they can't compare, well then they can't compare, and one mustn't think that Chinese characters are so good. (DeFrancis 252)

He goes on to ridicule the idea that written Chinese is the best system in the world; he argues that past dynasties have taken good things from the West and that it makes good sense to do so for writing.

But it didn't work out. Mao abandoned the plan in 1950. DeFrancis calls it "the Great Leap Backwards" (257). There seems to be no record of his motives, but it's assumed that pressure was put on him by the Red Guard, accusing him of kowtowing to the West. It's known that the Red Guard denounced the use of Roman letters for Chinese (DeFrancis 270). Eventually Mao settled for some simplifications in the traditional Chinese characters so that it took fewer strokes to write many of them. Robinson deplores the result:

> Today, the Chinese probably have the worst of both worlds: chaos in the [simplified] character script and an uncertain status for the romanized script. (196)

Because of the new set of simplified characters, Chinese growing up in the last fifty years have not been able to read the classical literature written in the older classical characters. (See also the article on this topic in *The New Yorker*, February 16 and 23, 2004).

In 1958—after Mao changed his mind and after the introduction of simplified characters—the People's Republic of China made a momentous decision. It finally did mandate the use of the Roman alphabet for Chinese writing—it's called *pinyin* ("spell-sound")—but *only* with striking limitations and for certain limited purposes. First, the government decreed that pinyin spelling of Chinese characters must match the speech of the version of Chinese spoken only in the north, including Beijing: *Mandarin*—or in Chinese *potunghua*. This made pinyin a foreign language for the majority of Chinese speakers—that is, for speakers of the half dozen or more other mutually unintelligible languages all called "Chinese." Pinyin was also to be used in first grade to help children start to learn characters, and especially to help children of all dialects all around China to learn how to *pronounce* the Mandarin characters. So pinyin was to serve as a standard or universal language for all of China, but it didn't at all standardize spoken Chinese.

When the Mandarin dialect of Chinese was *first* officially imposed as the only acceptable pronunciation for pinyin spelling, it was actually based on the speech of one man in Beijing:

> In the 1920s Y. R. Chao, a phonetician and all around linguist of note, as a member of a group of scholars concerned with language standardization, made some phonograph recordings of his own speech as a help in fixing the norm. As he himself was only semifacetiously fond of saying, he was for a while the only speaker of the Chinese national language. (DeFrancis 53)

Theoretically, the use of Roman letters for writing *would have* permitted *all* Chinese speakers to write in their own separate and very different spoken dialects or languages. After all, any form of spoken Chinese can be spelled out in the Roman pinyin letters. Some prominent authorities argued strongly for this course of action. But with the requirement that pinyin reflect only Mandarin, the government made a huge move toward standardization in writing. (Notice how this government policy shares certain features with what Charlemagne decreed in 800. He made Latin a universal language, but it didn't standardize spoken Latin at all.)

Pinyin has made it possible to write Chinese on computers. But typing Chinese requires an extra step. You start by typing your word in pinyin—that is, typing the sounds of the spoken word in Beijing's Mandarin dialect (virtually always one syllable). But you have not finished. Virtually all Chinese spoken words come in four or more spoken "tones" or intonational tunes. A single word spelled in pinyin can have four or more completely different meanings, depending on the tune it's given. So after you type in your "almost word," a screen pops up showing you the four or more traditional nonalphabetic *characters* that your pinyin word *might* mean. You then click on the character that fits the word/tune you have in mind (or literally have in mouth).

In the subsequent years after 1958, after pinyin had been introduced and used in all schools, and after people in China had become used to writing it on the computer, we might think that the nation would have gone on to take the step that Chairman Mao pulled back from taking: abolish the old characters and use a fully Romanized system of writing. The advantages for mass literacy would have been enormous. But Chinese characters are infinitely beautiful, interesting, and rich in connotation—and it's a writing system that has been in continuous use longer than any other. (The Western alphabet *started* earlier, but the Chinese were the first to develop a functional writing system.) Most literate Chinese feel deep pride in

I am relying heavily throughout this account on DeFrancis in his book about the Chinese language. In particular, he tells many of the interesting details of the ideological and literary struggles between radical and conservative scholarly and political voices in China about whether to give up characters.

Here are a few more observations about Chinese that many readers might appreciate:

• Chinese is a paratactic language in that it leaves out lots of connectives like *if*, *then*, *however*. This has led some people to call Chinese primitive because it also lacks many tenses and conjunctions. It sounds like a pidgin. "You go New York tomorrow." Or "You go New York yesterday." Needless to say, it's a fully complex developed language.

• In *written* Chinese, every character has its own meaning and its own sound. There is no danger of homophones, that is, of the same sign having different meanings or sounds. As a result, written Chinese can be very terse. It's quite the opposite with *spoken* Chinese where there are lots of homophones. Almost all spoken words are monosyllables, and there's a limit to how many different monosyllables one can devise. Even after you assign four different "tones" to each word, there are still lots of homophones.

• Language is very often a source of potent political and cultural conflict. DeFrancis points to Chinese as an example of huge language differences that don't *necessarily* create political divisions. The Chinese used and continue to use very different and mutually unintelligible languages ("dialects") that are no closer than French and English, but without large political disputes or tensions about the language. No doubt this situation stems from the power of ruling emperors down through the ages and continuing today in a powerful government. DeFrancis argues that language disputes usually stem from political difference (as between France and Spain), or religious difference (as between French Catholics and English Protestants in Canada), or between economic difference (between French-speaking Walloons and Dutch-speaking Flemish in Belgium; see 56–57).

their writing system. In contrast, most of us literate Westerners—even if we happen to feel pride in our language or in the alphabet as a *system*—don't see anything beautiful or emotionally touching in the actual letters we handle so casually. In fact, many English speakers feel some irritation or even shame associated with the letters of our alphabet because English spelling is such a muddle.

From *Goatperson and Other Tales.* by Michael Leunig.

PART FOUR

VERNACULAR LITERACY

Introduction: Dante's Vulgar Eloquence

When Dante produced his masterpiece, *The Divine Comedy* in 1308, late in his life, he finally used the spoken vernacular language that he'd previously celebrated in *De Vulgari Eloquentia*. It was the local dialect of his native Florence; he had called it the language of children and nursemaids. He had argued that it was *nobler* than Latin—which was then the only language deemed proper for serious writing. So when he finally used this low, spoken vernacular language for the highest religious and philosophical epic—a poem many now call the greatest work of all time—many people of learning and influence derided his decision. He

> was criticized for having written such a work in the vulgar tongue, the speech of the street. . . . Giovanni del Virgilio accused Dante of throwing his pearls before swine. . . . A later and more famous classicist, Francesco Petrarca would also claim to pity . . . [Dante] whose writings are lacerated and corrupted by the horrendous pronunciation of "idiots" (the unlettered) in taverns and squares. (Cornish 176)

I want to call attention to what Dante demonstrated: that a local spoken language that was scorned for writing could be used for writing of the highest seriousness and quality; and that such a language could eventually become a language that *everyone* considers right for writing. For of course this "vulgar" vernacular of Dante's poem *became* modern Italian: the sanctioned official literate language used throughout modern Italy. Present-day Italians can read *The Divine Comedy* more easily than we can read Chaucer—another fourteenth-century writer.

But this process of acceptance took many hundred years. And by the time Dante's dialect finally became legitimate, it started declaring that most other spoken vernaculars in Italy are *illegitimate* for writing! Children all over Italy who speak different local dialects of Italian are forced to use official Italian for their spoken and written schoolwork. Indeed, the literate cultures of *all* the upstart European national languages—like French, Spanish, and Portuguese (along with English)—forgetting their "illiterate" roots—now have the gall to turn around and try to exclude present-day vernacular spoken languages and call them illiterate and unfit for writing.

In Chapter 17, I will explore some of the problems with *our* existing culture of proper literacy and how it is hostile to speech. In the final chapter, 18, I will argue that we are moving with surprising speed toward a new culture of *vernacular literacy* that will welcome speech—in fact multiple spoken languages—for writing. In this new culture, all the different versions of spoken English will be considered appropriate for serious writing.

17 How Our Culture of Proper Literacy Tries to Exclude Speech

What Is Literacy?

I am writing a book about slithery words, *speech* and *writing*. And now *literacy*. What does that word mean?

Literacy originally referred to the mere ability to put words into writing. Spelling and grammar didn't much matter. (In certain medieval times and places, people were called literate if they could sign their names.) This was the literacy we saw in the passages from Lewis and Clark and John Smith (see 28 and 126). I call this skill "mere" literacy or *vernacular literacy* or *vulgar literacy*. It's a kind of literacy I want to celebrate. When I hear people call someone's writing "illiterate," I want to answer, "No, that's impossible. If it's writing, it's literacy."

But of course people talk about "illiterate writing" all the time in our culture. It signals a new higher bar for literacy. The term now means the ability to produce not just written language but *correct standard* written language. (See the Introduction to Part Three for definitions of "standard.") "Literate writing" also carries restrictions of vocabulary and register. That is, literate writing should avoid *words* that are too undignified or vulgar. This is the version of literacy that permeates our culture: I call it *proper literacy*.

And still the bar keeps going up. In recent decades, an important academic movement has emerged that treats literacy as something richer and more complex—and more interesting. This movement is often called New Literacy Studies, and it has been spearheaded by scholars in England (see New London Group). There are now whole academic departments and programs with the title *Literacy Studies*. The central point in all this recent work boils down to something like this: every "discourse community" has its *own* literacy—its own complex set of conventions for speech and writing that must be met before you are admitted to membership. Discourse communities are often professions—for example, physicists or physicians or pilots—but also less formal groups like bikers and hackers and bird-watchers. If you want your essay for a bird-watching journal or newsletter to be respected—or even accepted—you will have to know how to follow the written conventions of that group.

This line of thinking leads inevitably to the concept of *multiple literacies* or *multiliteracies*. For example, you'll be "illiterate" among rap poets if you are too "literate" in the traditional sense. Notice how the word "literacy" continues to go through a common linguistic process. In its basic meaning, the word applies to writing or texts, since it so obviously derives from "letters." But the word began to be applied metaphorically, as when people refer to speech as "illiterate" or to "visual literacy" or "mathematical literacy." There are no letters in speech, yet in our culture, people often judge spoken words by whether they *hear* the proper letters or grammar in them. None of these phrases feel metaphorical any more.

Even one of the prime London Group scholars, Brian Street, argues that it's not helpful to use the word "literacy" on pictures and other nonverbal phenomena. I have another reason that I'm troubled by expanding the uses of this word. I hate to see people using a word that is essentially about *writing* or *letters* to talk about other skills or competences. "She's so illiterate about make-up." Do we really want to reinforce the ominous implication—already in the air—that all intelligence and skill means correctness with letters and writing?

By the way, we see here how metaphors "disappear." To feel something as metaphor, we have to feel that it's the wrong word. See Walker Percy's useful essay, "Metaphor as Mistake."

The new literacy scholars have their own literacy of course (as they would be first to acknowledge), and they tend to see a theme of social justice as central to their work. They are saying, in effect:

> Stop deluding the public into believing that nonliterate people will be accepted as literate members of our culture if we teach them to read and write correct English. That's never enough. Not only are there other subtle forms of literacy they need if they want to be accepted in most literate discourse communities. In addition, there are seemingly extraneous requirements—usually involving class and race—that will often bar people even if they can write well. Stop pretending that "literacy campaigns" led by presidents' wives can catapult everyone into middle class "good behavior." Writing is not a neutral technology. Writing always exists in situations of differential power—and power often trumps writing.

These literacy scholars have done important and useful substantive work about how writing functions differentially in many different realms. (For an overview, see a useful collection: Cushman et al., *Literacy: A Critical Sourcebook.*) So yes, there is a logic to talking about multiple literacies—many of them subtle and hidden; literacy is very complex.

But in this last section of the book, Part Four, I want to wrest our attention back to the two simpler meanings: *vernacular* literacy (or "mere" literacy—producing writing at all), and *proper literacy* (producing "correct" writing). I'm preoccupied with mere vernacular literacy because it's so undervalued; and

I'm preoccupied with proper literacy because it's so overvalued. My desire to narrow my focus this way is not far from the reason that New Literacy scholars broadened their focus. They and I are both worried about how "proper literacy"—correct spelling and grammar—has tended to dominate our culture and cloud people's minds.

Proper literacy is linked with deep power—even with magic. *Grammar* and *glamour* are actually the same word. (In the Middle Ages, you could escape hanging for a serious crime if you could recite the Lord's Prayer in Latin.) The New Literacy scholars and I are both saying, "Let's explore how literacy *really functions* in our culture."

They're looking at the odd, interesting, and sometimes random linguistic features and skills that are actually required for acceptance in various literate communities. For example, different professions and academic disciplines have different ideas for what counts as "a good argument" or "good organization" or "good evidence" in writing. But I'm looking at how literacy really functions in our culture too: how proper literacy—surface correctness in language—is so deeply rooted in most people's minds, even in the minds of people who scorn it or feel they'll never get it.

If we look at how readers actually read, we'll see that the surface of language is often *more* important than substance. The surface is what people see first; or rather they see it first *if* they see something wrong or different about it (i.e., if it's "marked"). Otherwise they don't see it. It's the same with speech: we notice an accent or dialect first—but only if it's "other"; ditto for skin color or hair or clothing. People often have more psychic energy tied up in surface than in substance. They can be less tolerant of *language* they disapprove of (grammar, spelling, dialect, accent) than of *ideas* they disapprove of. (*I can deal with her being a transvestite communist, but her <u>language!</u> Ugh.*) Surface is often linked to identity, as with skin color: "who I am," "who they are," "who is 'one of us' or 'in our family.'"

A Long-Running "Literacy Campaign": Against Speech Itself

Here's the story that most knowledgeable people tell about speech and proper literacy. Certain groups have attained power and privilege, and this is why their spoken language is adopted as the standard for correct writing. Power and privilege often derive from race and class, so attitudes about language often carry prejudices of race and class. For example, most White people accept that they mustn't think that people are stupid if they have a darker skin, yet many White people comfortably think that someone is stupid who speaks Black English or some other vernacular stigmatized by race or class.

There's no denying this important story, and I've published essays and given talks about the need for teachers to invite speakers of stigmatized languages to write in their vernacular spoken language. But I want to focus on a different story here. I'm arguing that proper literacy is not just at war with the speech of nonprivileged or stigmatized groups: it's at war with spoken language itself—*even* with the spoken language of privileged or mainstream speakers. I can't resist repeating the mantra: *proper writing is no one's mother tongue.* It took me a long time to realize what had been staring me in the face all along: that my privileged "standard" spoken English was not right for writing.

It's worth noting a revealing parallel here between these two stories and the two stories I told earlier about the development of fourteenth-century Standard English:

- People assume that fourteenth-century Standard English was at war with the speech of everyone who didn't live in London; but the historical linguists showed that it was at war with everyone's speech, even those in London. (See the Literacy Story, Chapter 6.)
- People assume that present-day literacy is at war with the speech of stigmatized people; but my claim is that it's at war with everyone's speech.

In the rest of this section I'll try to support my perhaps startling argument that proper written literacy is at war with speech itself—even the speech of privileged speakers. I'll look at three kinds of writing: school writing, academic writing, and "generally literate" writing.

School writing. People often use the term "academic writing" for what students are supposed to write, but faculty members have traditionally refused to accept from students many of the linguistic and rhetorical features that they readily accept from their academic peers in articles and books. Some teachers insist on essays that announce their thesis in the first paragraph—or even insist on five-paragraph essays—when they don't ask that of colleagues or themselves in published academic writing. The tacit assumption here is what I call "the Picasso principle": you aren't allowed to draw funny looking bulls till you learn to draw proper looking bulls. Wolfram, Adger, and Christian lay out some of the anti-speech restrictions in school writing. When they describe features of the "written language style that a student must eventually learn," they lay down some specific do's and don't's. Avoid phrases like "a lot of trouble," and write instead "a good deal of difficulty." Avoid the first person as in "I find soccer to be very popular," and write instead "Soccer seems to be very popular" or "It seems that soccer is very popular"(129–130). And of course it's still common for quite a few teachers to outlaw "I" even though the APA handbook that governs writing in the natural and social sciences specifically recommends "I" when it's appropriate, such as in referring to one's own experimental procedures.

Note that their warning is not against *stigmatized* dialects of spoken English; it's against mainstream spoken English of privileged speakers. This helps explain the widely noted fact that most comments by teachers on student writing are corrections of language.

Janis and Richard Haswell looked at eight hundred pages of evaluative teacher comments and found that two-thirds of them were noting violations of "correctness": violations of a "conventionally correct or stylistically approved text" ([4]; see also Janis Haswell; also Connors and Lunsford who looked at written comments on three hundred papers. Most comments focused on correcting and editing—not just for errors but for "deviation from algorithms and often rigid 'rhetorical' rules" [217].) I'm not saying that all these mistakes would have been normal in speech; many would have been odd or wrong for speaking too. But when students try to operate in a language they aren't comfortable with and don't know in their bones, they create all kinds of grammatical tangles and oddities.

I spoke recently with a writing teacher in a familiar dilemma. She wanted to give a good grade to a student because he wrote so well, but she felt she couldn't do so because he made so many mistakes.

Consider again what happens when we call a student into our office and ask, "But what are you trying to *say* here?" and the student blurts her main point in clear speech. Somehow this kind of language and speaking was unavailable to her for writing. She felt she had to use *written language* for her thinking, and this led her to create opaque tangles of language and thinking.

How about "you"? Second person constructions are an interesting marker of the difference between speech and the dialect for school writing. All teachers stress the importance of remembering audience, but most of them turn around and enforce the convention that excludes "you" in school and college essays. Students are understandably tempted to feel they are addressing their written words to the teacher (usually the *only* actual flesh and blood reader, and the important one because she is the grader), but they learn they are not supposed to write, "In your lecture last week, you argued. . . ." Even if they have learned a more sophisticated stance (the teacher is not really the audience and you should be addressing a fictional audience of "educated" or "general" readers) there is still a natural temptation to use "you" even for those readers—as in, "Because of the widespread veneration of Lincoln in our country, you probably assume. . . ." So students are in a bind: they must learn the tricky and unnatural skill of writing *to* an audience while not *syntactically addressing* anyone at all.

There are further perversities in the audience situation for student writers. School writing is mostly *not* private and safe since it has to be handed to a teacher—often graded. Yet much school writing goes *only* to the teacher—whose only job is to judge—so this seldom feels to students like communicating with an actual human. When James Britton and colleagues examined masses of school writing, they noticed that the students tend to write as though to no audience.

Academic writing. What about the language that academics use when they (we) write for academic journals and books? We give ourselves more freedom than is usually given to students. For example we don't so widely exclude second person direct address. "You" is common in textbooks, not infrequent even in our academic articles, and ubiquitous in our written comments to students. Yet we are generally supposed to avoid the language of speech. I've already illustrated this convention with examples of changes made by copy editors of academic journals to some of my manuscripts on their way into print (Chapter 5). Two other examples:

- *when I dropped out of graduate school* was changed to *when I interrupted my graduate education*
- *who has a strong sense of* was changed to *who retains a deep conviction that*

In the first one, the copy editor didn't outlaw "I" but tried to enforce the convention of *distance* in academic writing. The second correction represents the convention that academic writing should use language that would not come comfortably out of anyone's mouth—not even the mouth of a privileged person speaking his native language.

In short, the prose that teachers require of students for important essays and the prose that academics use for publication consist of dialects or registers that are inimical to the language of speech. Most teachers feel it's their duty to teach students to master this kind of prose—even if it's a bit restrictive.

> *Come on, Peter! Times have changed. Teachers and academic journals aren't so stuffy any more.*

Escalating My Claim: "Generally Literate Writing"

Yes, plenty of teachers aren't so linguistically conservative any more, and much academic writing has become adventuresome—some of it notably experimental. Indeed, my larger argument is that more and more speech is seeping into writing that counts as "correct"—and seeping fast—even in the academy. Our culture of literacy is changing perhaps faster than any other literate culture has ever changed—and I'll try to describe that change in the next chapter. The goal of this book is to hasten it and help people realize that spoken language is available to them as they write.

But it would be a mistake to underestimate the grip of proper literacy. Because readers in the field of composition and rhetoric hear so much progressive talk about language from each other (for most conference presentations and journal articles take a progressive stance), they may forget the narrow restrictive language standards that so many faculty members wield in English and other departments in schools and colleges and universities.

In fact, instead of retreating at this point, I'll escalate my claim. It's *not only* students and academics who feel they must avoid speech-inflected language for serious writing. I'll argue that our culture of literacy leads *most people* to feel they must avoid spoken language when they want to write almost anything they'd call serious or literate. They tend to feel this restriction even if they speak the mainstream privileged brand of spoken English, and even if they have successfully finished schooling.

> *But this is absurd. Look at the informal and colloquial language currently published all over the place—even in high prestige sites like the* New York Times *and* The New Yorker. *We see lots of written language infused with spoken registers in publications of high prestige and wide circulation. John McWhorter takes an entire book to describe and mourn the colloquialization of published writing. He writes, "we live in an America with a distinctly*

different relationship to the English language than an America still within living memory" (167).

Yes, yes, I accept the point. I myself have been busily collecting samples that would seem to refute my own claim that serious writing outside the academy is at war with speech. *The New Yorker* is famous for its editorial attentiveness to style, correctness, and taste, yet listen to this sentence I copied from there: "Which only shows how far things have sunk." An in-your-face sentence fragment. More striking, it begins a new paragraph. It's *trying* to sound like blurted speech. For another example, we sometimes see attempts in mainstream serious writing to mimic a speech breakdown: "This school of criticism seems to disapprove of, well . . . everything." And here's another invasion from spoken grammar: *Let's continue to try to shape the world, but let's not be so stupid about it, is the general idea* ("Breaking Away" 84). The writer is Louis Menand, a sophisticated literary critic and historian and staff writer at *The New Yorker*. His sentence exploits an interesting efficiency that's common in the syntax of unplanned syntax. We start off with an opening sentence (or two!) and then in mid-course we realize that we want to use everything we've said so far as the *grammatical subject* for a different sentence that says (what we suddenly realize in mid-course) we really want to say.

Here is William Safire as early as 1999 in his "On Language" column in the prestige pages of the *New York Times* (and Safire's rulings on language policy are often quite conservative). He's having fun with language by being deliberately chatty:

> Although I am quite able to set this word out of my mind as I write this column, let me *prattle* awhile [and then he jumps into a parenthesis of impersonal scholarly etymology] (from the Low German *pratten*, "to pout," and then "to prate, babble, talk idly").

He likes to swerve suddenly into and out of personal speech, especially in chatty asides, and he clearly celebrates the clash of registers. The next paragraph starts off,

> In the age of multiculturalism and interdisciplinarianism (there's a new one), most of the nonscientific uses of the term have been pejorative.

He starts another section of the same column by writing a one-sentence paragraph in Yiddish flavored syntax:

> You pay for good linguistic lawyering, you get it.

And he ends the section with yet a shorter paragraph:

> I spell it *tchotchki*. Do I need a lawyer?

Listen to Paul Krugman defining what economists mean by the term "money": *"Currency—pieces of green paper with pictures of dead presidents on them—is money, and so are bank deposits on which you can write checks"* (28). I love Krugman's sentence. I think it's good *because* he exploits some of the interesting resources of casual speech. He's enjoying the way spoken syntax interrupts itself, and how it revels in blunt, concrete low-register language. My larger project is to help *more* people do what these writers do—to use the syntactic flexibility we see in Menand, the fun-with-chattiness we see in Safire, and the pungently concrete almost-slang definition we see in Krugman. I want all writers to feel they have permission to call on the resources of their spoken language.

> Notice too how all three examples exploit a more general rhetorical principle that is characteristic of speech and sometimes confused with mere informality: the refusal of *distance* from the audience. Burke made much of the distinction here between solidarity with the audience versus social distance—what he terms "identification" and "division." Menand, Safire, and Krugman are all refusing the language that comes from an "expert speaking from on high." (I'm indebted to John Trimbur for this insight.)

But I'm writing this book *because* I think we still have a very long way to go before most people feel they can write this way. When financial planners, doctors, lawyers, engineers, social workers, or members of city councils are writing memos, reports, and grant proposals—even letters to clients—I don't think many of them feel they ought to write sentences like Krugman's—or the jaunty sentences by Maureen Dowd or Thomas Friedman—or indeed the brazenly chatty sentences that William Safire sometimes uses to argue for linguistic *conservatism*! Few citizens writing a report feel they should use a phrase like "green paper with pictures of dead presidents on them" when they want to define a central theoretic concept in a report or essay or grant proposal.

So, odd as it sounds, I'm arguing that these sentences written in prestige magazines and newspapers by prominent writers like Krugman, Menand, Dowd, Friedman, and Safire are *not*—or not yet—an accurate picture of what counts as proper writing. Not, at least, in the minds of most people who don't already define themselves as writers. After all, why should they feel they can enjoy using speech-inflected language like Krugman's or Menand's when they have been so consistently warned against it? *Let's continue to try to shape the world, but let's not be so stupid about it, is the general idea.* Many everyday people might love a sentence like this (though they're likely to call it a mistake if they see it in a report or memo rather than in *The New Yorker*), but when it comes to their own writing, they are more likely to feel, "Well 'real writers' can take these liberties, but not me."

It's not that municipal committee reports or H&R Block memos ought necessarily to use language that's quite so playful or in your face. But workaday texts like those could comfortably benefit from everyday spoken language—such as I used in some of my definitional work:

> This is where things get muddy. People commonly assume that the language that comes from people's fingers is not like the language that comes from their mouths. But linguists have shown that strictly considered, there is no real difference between them. That is, any kind of language is sometimes spoken and sometimes written. Linguists show the vast overlap by collecting huge "corpora" of millions of strings of spoken and

written language. When they jumble together all the strings, they find they can't usually identify which ones were spoken and which were written. That is, when we look at spoken and written language that was produced in a full range of human contexts and purposes, the dividing line between spoken and written pretty much disappears. (Introduction to Part One)

By giving examples like those from Krugman, Menand, and Safire, I'm trying to illustrate how even very informal speechy language has begun to be accepted in prestige literate sites.

For school is the doorway to careful or important writing, and school is where the no-speech standards are taught and enforced. Most writing teachers don't feel they've "taught writing"—nor do most biologists feel they've "insisted on good writing" in their biology course (as we hope they will do)—*unless* they insist on correct edited proper English. Most people don't feel they have "learned to write" unless they have learned to use this somewhat formal restricted dialect needed for school and college essays. If they happen to make a bad grammatical mistake on their job or write something seriously tangled or unclear, they are likely to hear someone say, "What did they teach you in school, anyway?"

And think about large-scale high-stakes testing. In their sixteen years of schooling on the way to becoming "an educated person," students are blitzed with more and more statewide and nationwide tests—and more in English than in any other subject. Even when these tests use human graders rather than machines, and even when testing officials maintain that correctness isn't the main thing, all that testing makes teachers and students preoccupied with correctness. Here is a *criterion of good writing* that's given to people who grade a statewide test of student writing:

> the writer's ability to form competent, appropriately mature sentences and the use of word level features that cause written language to be acceptable and effective for standard discourse. This includes the system of symbols and cuing devices a writer uses to help readers make meaning.

This is a lovely example of *one kind* of skilled writing: it deftly manages never to use the word "correct" or "rule"—and yet keep those words front and center in graders' minds. Sixteen years of this kind of testing (and the tests have a huge impact on what the teachers teach) make it all the harder for most folks to use the resources of speech as Krugman or Safire or Dowd do. Teachers often tell me, "I can't do freewriting any more. There's too much pressure from these high-stakes timed essay tests."

In Chapter 11, I looked a bit at the advice in Joseph Williams's *Style: Ten Lessons in Clarity and Grace*—the influential style guide that's gone through more than a dozen editions and is widely used in businesses and colleges. He gives this sentence as a problem to fix: *There is no need for our further study of this problem.* I agree that it's a problem, but look at his solution: *We need not study this problem further* (42). It's a good clean sentence (though timid and lacking any rhythmic shape), but the thing to notice is how hard it runs away from spoken language. It seems as though he couldn't even imagine the obvious solution: *We don't have to study this problem any more.* It's perfectly correct—no violations; it's plain and direct and the register is not "low." It's just the kind of sentence that anyone should feel free to write in their committee report or memo or academic essay.

But Williams doesn't seem to be able to imagine it as a solution—presumably because it has the taint of speech. Who would ever *utter* what he suggests: *We need not study this problem further* unless they were consciously or unconsciously trying to avoid the taint of speech. My claim is that this kind of advice leads people to feel they can't use their own natural inborn language for writing.

Another objection:

> *Give it up. The internet has changed all this. Look at all the bloggers who write talky language every day.*

And again I reply Yes. Things are changing and this makes me happy—at least when the talky writing happens to be clear and strong. And I will consider the amazing force of the internet in the next chapter. Many of those bloggers *have* already come to feel at home when they write *because* they no longer feel they have to avoid the resources of speech. But I fear that most of them feel this freedom to "speak" freely with their fingers only because they are on the net—and not writing the kinds of essays, articles, reports, memos, or proposals most people "normally" have to produce on paper. Even though lots of the blogging is very serious, say, about politics or the economy or health, I'm betting that most bloggers don't feel they can linguistically blogify when writing "serious texts" ("literate texts") off the net—even if they are privileged people who grew up with mainstream spoken English and were successful in school and college.

Indeed, it's the skilled and well-educated people who often worry most. Consider these words from someone we'd expect to be most confident about language, a longtime skilled, published English teacher who is an "English language coordinator" in her district:

> For years I've played word cop on myself. I stop what I'm saying to think "Objective or subjective case? Do I need *I* or *me* here? Hmmm. There's a *lay* coming up. What word can I substitute for it? *Recline?*
>
> And I've studied this stuff. After all I've been an English teacher for almost 20 years. . . . The problem is that every time I pause, I stop the momentum of my thinking. I'm no longer pursuing content, no longer engaged in trying to persuade or entertain or clarify. Instead I'm pulling Warriner's or Mrs. Delaney out of my head and trying to figure out how to say something." (Linda Christensen, "Whose Standard?" 142)

The fact that correct literate writing calls on language that has to obey rules that differ in slippery ways from the rules people follow in their spoken language often distracts even well-schooled mainstream speakers. They are so often nervous about using the right grammar and language that they stop and check the spelling or worry, for instance, about whether *whom* is really needed here. And it's not just grammar and spelling—it's the assumption that writing requires "*better*" language.

Dawkins reflects on how small and tricky some of the rules are (e.g., at the end of a quotation, put punctuation inside the quotation marks—except if it's a semicolon or colon and then put punctuation outside the marks). He writes this:

When reflecting on these questions one begins to smell a classism that was analyzed a hundred years ago by Thorstein Veblen in *The Theory of the Leisure Class*. The less useful something is—an object, a behavior, a skill—the better it serves to mark one a member of the upper classes, and the harder it is to learn—especially in a school setting—for anyone raised in the marginalized cultures of urban or rural America. ("Punctuation" 60)

Another objection:

> *Peter, of course most people aren't comfortable writing, but that's not for fear of impropriety. It's because serious writing simply asks for more* precision. *Writing asks us to struggle for more careful thinking, more effective organization, and clearer sentences than we need when we speak comfortably.*

True enough. But if that were the only difficulty with writing, people would have the following feeling: *Writing is hard and takes a lot of work—sometimes it's even a painful struggle. But still I feel at home with the task because the language I'm struggling with is my language.*

I'm happy to say that I finally feel that way—and what a relief. For I've learned to use my spoken language for all early and middle drafts, and even during much revising. And I use a good deal of it in this book since I haven't tried to get it accepted in a scholarly journal. Some of you feel it when you write. But I'll bet that a huge proportion of you do not. We've always known that speakers of low-status versions of English—especially stigmatized versions—couldn't write with the rich intricate spoken language they are at home with—the language that comes to their mouths naturally and easily. But I'm insisting that this is true for many mainstream speakers too. We're not getting lots of good writing that many people of all sorts could produce if writing invited more of the resources of speech.

Propriety Anxiety

Why does "propriety" have such a strong hold on so many people? Who knows? Perhaps it has something to do with the deep human hunger to be *accepted*—accepted as members of society in good standing and not be looked down on or rejected. It's rare for us not to feel a desire to be accepted by people we care about or admire—junior high school writ large. The demand for correct language is one of the deepest and most pervasive ways that a culture tries to instill "propriety."

"Why Are You Shamed by Your Mistakes in English?" This is the headline for "probably the longest-running advert in newspaper history [for it has] managed to survive for nearly 50 years." It advertises a correspondence course in various English newspapers (the *Guardian*). Needless to say, propriety is deeply tangled with class. I quoted Ian McEwan in Chapter 10 on the enormous slow care with which he works out every sentence in his head before he writes it down, and then when he finally does, "stares suspiciously" at it and asks, will it be "making a fool of me?" (Zalewski 55). He went on to relate this care to class anxiety. He told of how his mother, "[a]shamed of her working-class accent, . . . spoke with absurd slowness in front of posh women, treating the

English language as 'something that might go off in her face, like a letter bomb.'" (52)

Lynn Bloom has explored the middle-class ethos that pervades the profession of writing teachers and how this gives them the job of instilling propriety. Among the eleven middle-class values that she sees saturating the field, she points to these: *respectability, decorum or propriety, moderation or temperance, cleanliness,* and *delayed gratification.* Despite any protestations to the contrary, we English teachers tend to be the tongue guards of our culture.

I'm intrigued to notice how, even in the Wild West we call the internet, people can't seem to stop instilling middle-class propriety. I'm thinking of the internet convention that says YOU MUSTN'T WRITE IN ALL CAPS. If you do, you are guilty of "SHOUTING." I've heard net-sophisticates make snide comments about shouters, and they didn't think of themselves as guardians of middle-class culture. But what else are they but schoolmarms in the new Wild West trying to keep the lid on the unshaven cowboys when they come into town? The metaphor of "shouting" says it all. Most rules of proper literacy are rules against making a loud noise: keep it down, don't make a racket. What's wrong with noise in writing?

When I am in buses, trains, and subways in the United States, I think I *hear* this middle-class, "literate" pressure not to "raise your voice." I think I notice that middle-class speakers who have mastered proper literacy use a more limited range of intonational highs and lows, louds and softs, while those working-class or lower-class or ethnic speakers who use a primarily oral version of English are more likely to speak with more vociferous intonation. (*Vociferous,* literally, means full of voice.) I take it as a deeply human trait to use the natural resources of intonational music to let our emotions show in our speaking. Unrestrained children use lots of intonation. *LOTS!* But I think I see speakers who consider themselves cultured assuming they should show fewer ups and downs and intensities and emphases even in their speaking. (This seems to be an Anglo-Saxon cultural assumption, for it doesn't seem to function in Italy and France and other European countries where the culture of literacy is no bar against *high* intonational expressiveness in speech.)

So there's an insidious double bind that comes from the culture of propriety in writing: *really good writing*—even when it's proper or correct—needs those eruptions of energy, vociferousness, and even spontaneity. It's what makes writing alive and forceful. Yet those eruptions have to conform to the standards of correctness and propriety (even if we're now seeing more leeway in prestige sites like *The New Yorker*). That's why truly good writing is so hard: you have to get back into your writing what you had to work hard to take out of it in order to pass through the initial doorway into literacy. Sadly, many people who have passed through that door—who have learned to be perfectly competent at writing correctly and who may write a great deal—haven't learned this trick of getting back into their literate writing some of the intonational energy and enthusiasm they used as children.

Not Just Writing but Speaking Too

One of the biggest sources of language anxiety was born in Queen Isabella's Spanish court at the time of Columbus. See the Literacy Story in Chapter 8 about how the grammarian Nebrija persuaded the queen to set in motion a cultural practice that she found weird at first but which we now take for granted: the idea that people are not qualified to speak their native language unless they go school and find out from professionals how to do it right.

Propriety anxiety wouldn't strike so deep if it struck only writing. Sadly, many people feel they must guard against impropriety or error in their *speech* too: the rich, intricate, spoken language that they know in their bones. They sometimes feel danger, even when they converse informally with family or friends. Just the other day a literate friend said something like this in a very casual setting: "I was really happy and elated! Oh, I guess I'm being redundant." He had internalized that red ink comment in the margin: *Redundant!*

Every English teacher who strikes up a conversation with a stranger knows about this: *Oh, you teach English. I better watch my tongue.* But if you really do watch your tongue and stumble into an uncertainty about a usage and look up the rule in a handbook, the answer is usually a rule for writing. Somehow the propriety conventions in our culture say that good speech should be like good writing. (And of course this dates back to the fourteenth century, as I showed in the Literacy Story following Chapter 6 about the birth of "Standard English.") And yet few of those who speak what seems like "standard spoken English"—whose speech sounds fine to most others—actually follow the rules in the rule book. As a result, our tongues are often faced with double binds—situations where you can't win. For example, when we are talking informally—or even in a more formal situation—should we say

> The audience to whom Darwin felt he was speaking?
>
> or
>
> The audience Darwin felt he was speaking to?

The first version sounds pretty stilted and artificial—almost like nonspeaking—and a fair number of handbooks will tell us to go ahead and end your sentence with a preposition. (Churchill—a serious writer who made heavy use of reading aloud—helped fight prissiness with his famous riposte: *This is the kind of nonsense up with which I will not put.*) But out in the real world of literate civilians, you can be corrected or condescended to for doing that. Spoken English is always under pressure from propriety and written English.

I feel the double bind when I answer the phone. Someone asks, "Is Peter Elbow there," and I've tended to answer what I learned was right: "This is he." But in recent years, I've come to feel an uncomfortable prickle in that locution: it feels too much like self-conscious correctness—as though I'm not talking my native language. Yet I'm finding it hard to decide what I would prefer. "I'm me" sounds weird; "Speaking" or "Here" sound like something from the movies. So now I tend to say something like, "That's me." And yet—such are the complexities in the concept of "native language" and the effects of living in the belly of the culture of propriety—sometimes I forget and blurt out what grew into a sort of naturalness, "This is he." What have we come to when I have to engage in complex thinking and still can't quite figure out how to speak my native language?

Here's another double bind. In the second sentence of this book I write that ". . . our present culture of 'proper literacy' tells everyone that they are not supposed to do their serious writing in the mother tongue they know best and possess in their bones." This (of course?) is grammatically wrong: I used a plural "their" to refer to singular "everyone." But to avoid the "mistake" we would need to use the sexist "his," the ungainly "all persons," or the clumsy "his or her." This "lack of concord" between pronouns is everywhere in speech and is beginning to be accepted even by some rule books. I think the best guide to grammar and usage problems is Garner's *Dictionary of Modern American Usage,*" where he writes "Disturbing though these developments may be to purists, they're irreversible. And nothing that a grammarian says will change anything" (529, entry for "Pronouns, D").

Yet—and this is the kicker!—folks of *high prestige* will look down on you for being "*too correct.*" If you *really* care about propriety and are sensitive to language, you know that *correctness* can get you in trouble with the folks of *highest* taste. Consider this delicious short passage from Fowler's much longer entry on split infinitives (in his monumental *Modern English Usage*):

1. Those who neither know nor care [whether they split infinitives] are the vast majority, & are a happy folk, to be envied by most of the minority classes; "to really understand" comes readier to their lips & pens than "really to understand", they see no reason why they should not say it (small blame to them, seeing that reasons are not their critics' strong point), & they do say it, to the discomfort of some among us, but not to their own. [Note the British punctuation after "understand."]

2. To the second class, those who do not know but do care, who would as soon be caught putting their knives in their mouths as splitting an infinitive but have hazy notions of what constitutes that deplorable breach of etiquette, this article is chiefly addressed. These people betray by their practice that their aversion to the split infinitive springs not from instinctive good taste, but from tame acceptance of the misinterpreted opinions of others; for they will subject their sentences to the queerest distortions, all to escape imaginary split infinitives. (558)

The key, says Fowler, is "instinctive good taste." But where do we get that? "Good breeding" no doubt—which means, of course, being born into the right family and class. Or does it? Often the best "breeding" for propriety is carried out by those who lack prestige but want it for their children. And in truth, many people of the very best taste didn't get "good breeding" even from upwardly mobile parents. They "bred themselves up from their bootstraps"— working hard and conscientiously to develop their taste—in this case, their ear. Fowler is playing the classic game of class: scorning "middle-class" efforts to appear proper—yet writing a book addressed precisely to middle-class people who are striving for propriety.

I can't resist thinking that the largest language-oriented organization in the world, the Modern Language Association, lives off propriety anxiety. Most of their books make little or no profit, but their *Style Manual* and *Handbook* sell massively. And they are frequently revised (*Uh oh. I better not settle for four-year-old correctness!*).

It's interesting to compare England and the United States when it comes to linguistic propriety. On the one hand, England is much more deeply riven than we are by dialectal differences of class. And English stigmatization can be more cutting. But on the other hand, the United States still shows its colonial roots: we in the colonies often work harder to prove fidelity to the motherland and its standards. U.S. bookstores are awash in handbooks for correct language, but John Boe (editor of an interesting journal called *Writing on the Edge*) went into Blackwells, perhaps the greatest English bookstore, and asked for a grammar book. The clerk asked, "Do you mean ESL?" "No, I want English grammar for the English." The clerk was baffled and finally said he thought maybe he could find one. So even though it often looks as though linguistic propriety counts for more in England than in the United States, the English are sometimes more casual. (See the Literacy Story of Fowler and *that/which*, Chapter 13.)

Resistance and the Allure of Wrongness

Some of the most telling evidence for propriety anxiety is negative—and it's everywhere. I'm talking about a pervasive *resistance* to propriety in written language. Consider *Toys R Us, Kwik Kleeners, E-Z Car Wash, 7-Eleven,* and *Sheer Kuts*. People cannot seem to resist flaunting wrongness—even in neon. "Literate" or cultured people like to think that mistakes always stem from ignorance and lack of care. *Eats, Shoots and Leaves* sold hundreds of thousands of copies by dramatizing outrage at wrong punctuation. But I think that these gilt and flashing store signs betray a common but seldom acknowledged deep *pleasure* in wrong language. (It's this kind of micro-resistance to pervasive authority that Michel de Certeau writes about in *The Practice of Everyday Life*. Kermit Campbell speaks of hip-hop as "the mental activity of oppressed creativity." See also Olivo on hip-hop. See too unwords.com, a huge cache of words that don't exist but are trying to exist. Their slogan: "Change English, one word at a time.")

As for me, I've had to admit to myself that *bad* and *wrong* have somehow come to be positive words for me. So when I talk positively about "writing garbage" in this book, I find I've bothered some people who've read drafts. My friend Pat Schneider wrote me this note (she's author of one of the best books on writing, *Writing Alone and with Others*):

> I work all the time to help undo the feelings in so many writers—especially my students from the projects—that they "write garbage." It troubles me to hear you say anything good about writing garbage.

So why do I like *wrong, bad, garbage*? For I also love elegant *rightness*. As a fairly naive child, I played during the summer months with children of college professors and was intimidated by the culture at their fingertips—hearing, for example, of how they used to stage Shakespeare with puppets in their homes.

As an English major at an elite private college, I strove to develop good taste. I developed a sensitive radar for what is culturally "right" and "better." And I have to confess that I love passages like the one I just quoted from Fowler. His arrogance carries poison, but there's something wonderful about a *total* self-confidence that helps him skewer people who care *too much* about propriety.

But the truth is, I've also grown to love "wrongness"—even for its own sake. I certainly had a firsthand taste of linguistic snobbery and chauvinism when I studied at Oxford in the uptight pre-Beatles era when my tutor remarked that I spoke "like a colonial" and said (when I read aloud a passage from Marvel), "Maybe that's why you don't understand poetry, Elbow, you don't know what it *sounds* like." (A cynical reader could call this book my wounded reaction to having failed in my initial attempts to become uncomplicatedly *"in"* as a cultured intellectual.)

But why encourage "garbage"? It's because I sense that pressure from propriety in our culture has done so much harm. I find that when I say to people, "Don't worry about correctness or any kind of judgment when you freewrite or do a draft," it isn't quite enough. For most of us have actually *breathed in* or *swallowed* all these judgments about impropriety and badness; they are woven into the very fabric of our minds. They constantly filter our words and thoughts at a level of nonawareness. The only way to get through the filters is to actually *invite garbage* or *badness*. When I teach, I tell people that speaking onto the page will produce some writing that they hate (because of the internalized judging). Yet almost always, some of the very language they hate will be good. They'll probably have trouble seeing the goodness, but if they are willing to share some of this kind of writing with others (who also share their own very rough writing), readers will sometimes pounce on some "garbage passage" and see that it's good. Making this point most broadly: I don't think many people manage to write really good stuff unless they also write garbage.

In addition, good writing often involves simple *power* in words. As children, our strongest voice is often annoying or threatening to the grown-ups. Face it, children can be deafening. It was hard not to spend a good deal of my parenting time saying "Shhh!" Most people have a lot of verbal power tied up with what's discouraged, forbidden, or bad. Sometimes we can't get the power without the garbage. In the end, my goal is not wrongness but *really good* writing—something better than writing with no faults. If writing is really good it will probably *have* faults. Almost certainly it will have grown from drafts with lots of faults. Think of all the school writing that gets a good grade for simply avoiding faults. How often is "A writing" actually worth reading?

If we invite garbage, maybe we can actually destroy the concept of *bad writing*. Consider: when we read someone's writing and say, "That's terrific," we may be terribly wrong, but we seldom do harm. In fact we often do good. Almost every time I find adults who are enthusiastic writers, they usually give credit to someone who gave enthusiastic praise when they were younger. Yet that praiser probably had "extremely bad taste" in the eyes of many sophisticates—sophisticates who like to wring their hands at "all this misguided talk about *self-esteem*."

But are there any benefits that come from calling a piece of writing *bad*? It often does harm. We are very likely to be wrong or have poor taste, yet the writer will often take our words seriously. Besides, what *is* bad writing? It's as impossible to define as good writing. Most of us find it hard to forget criticism; easy to forget praise. So I see nothing illogical about a writing world where it's fine to say "That's terrific" when we are moved to do so, but where we refrain from ever saying "That's bad"—even if we are somehow convinced that it is bad.

Concluding

After exploring all these interesting literacy issues, I want to highlight the main theme: we live in a culture of proper literacy where serious writing does not accept spoken language. Even spoken language does not accept spoken language. That is, the rules for *acceptable* or *good* speech tend to come from *writing* and they don't fit anyone's actual talk—not even the talk of privileged mainstream folk. This has been true ever since fourteenth-century London (and no doubt earlier). The pressure for propriety in language makes it harder for people to bring their best linguistic strengths to writing and even to speaking.

Things are changing fast, however, and that's the argument I'll make in the next chapter.

|||||||||||||||||||||||||||||||||||||||||||||||||||||||||||||||||||||||||||||||||||||||||||||||||||||||||||||||||||||||||||||||||||||||||||||||||||||||||

LITERACY STORY

Illegal Alphabets

Here are two puzzles to think about as you hear this story

1.

Avivac	ahorita regreso
camvak	volver
tumach	demasiado
mach	mucho
limisi	dejamever
aidono	yo no se
guariyyusei	que dice uste
brouken	roto
aijef	tengo
gimi	deme
noder	no ay
lrero	poquito
jit	el

pedes	foozi
figido	lepara
pulli	honir
pulcins	honchli
callus	hano
galina	hanin
pridias	uuanti
mufflas	handschoh
implenuus est	fol ist
manneiras	parta
maartel	hammar
puticla	flasca
fidelli	chalpir
fomeras	uuaganso
radi meo parba	skir minan part (Kalmar 62)

On a very hot night in July 1980 in Cobden, Illinois, there was a notable meeting in Su Casa Grocery Store between some Mexican immigrant workers and some Anglos. This begins the series of events told by Tomás Mario Kalmar in his book, *Illegal Alphabets and Adult Biliteracy: Latino Migrants Crossing the Linguistic Border.* (All page citations are to his book.) Even though members of both groups had already played a bit of basketball together, both the Mexicans and the Anglos were very shy with each other. There was a lot of pregnant silence as they stood around together. Some energy and ease finally came into the room when some of the Mexican men began to sing. Kalmar notes, "These corridos are invariably learned *líricamente*—'lyrically,' that is to say by heart, by 'word of mouth,' orally, not from written texts" (5). Kalmar and a couple of friends had brought a guitar and banjo, and so then they began to sing some American songs. People joined in on both sides and learned a bit of each other's songs.

These meetings continued, and on a later evening, Raúl and Alfredo wanted to write down the words of "You Picked a Fine Time to Leave Me." They had learned it *líricamente* but wanted the text *toda la letra.* Then one young man, Panchito, who had his eye on a pretty young Anglo girl, wanted another text *toda la letra.*

> [H]e came over to where we were singing. In the softest possible voice, he asked, "¿Como se dice en inglés ¿donde vives??" . . . *Where do you live?* [Panchito] mimicked [the answer] until he got it off by heart, *líricamente.* He borrowed a ball-point pen and a scrap of paper from Alfredo. He wrote JUELLULIB. (9)

Remembering this tiny phrase might seem easier than remembering the lyrics of an entire song, but when you want to try even this little bit of a new language on a stranger girl from a wholly different culture, it's easy to forget. This was the opening move in what Kalmar speaks of as a "language game" taken up by a bunch of the migrant people: they wanted to be able "to write English como de veras se oye, the way it really sounds" (23). For Panchito, the written letters *"juel-lulib"* were the truest visual way to represent the sounds, *"Where d'you live?"*

Using the same process, a group of the migrants gradually drew up lists of English words—"the way they really sound," using letters of the alphabet but following Spanish conventions for how to represent sounds. Indeed, as different individuals wrote their version of the English word, there were many discussions about which sequences of letters gave the most accurate representation of the sound. For instance, they discussed the merits of different ways of writing "the law" (as in the sentence they were discussing, "The law doesn't protect us"!): *dolor, dolod, doloc, doló,* and *toloon.* Eventually they made small dictionaries.

The first puzzle that I put at the head of this Literacy Story is an example of one small dictionary they made.

What about the second puzzle? It's an ancient historical document. Kalmar often uses it when he does workshops with teachers. It turns out to be the early medieval "Kassell Glossary" (from about the time of Charlemagne—see the Literacy Story following Chapter 5). "It was written in Europe in the ninth century, [but] nothing at all is known about who wrote this text, when, where, why or how (60)." But it clearly translates words from Late Vulgar Latin or early "Romance" to a "barbarian" [Germanic] language, "Old Bavarian." Kalmar imagines the scene to be the same as occurred thirteen centuries later in Cobden, Illinois. For he says that the handling of consonants shows that it was written by the "barbarians," not the Romance-speakers:

> The Kassell glossary is therefore, like the Cobden glossaries, coded in a "home-made" hybrid alphabet, and if we can decode it today, it is thanks to a "folk" tradition of using the Roman alphabet as a sort of generic International Phonetic Alphabet from the ninth century to the present. (64)

I apologize for telling only the tiniest bit of Kalmar's brief intriguing book. I recommend it. It's rich in human interest narrative and linguistic and educational theorizing. For me, it leads to two different reactions.

On the one hand, I see it as a powerful story of what I call "mere literacy": people insisting on what has always been true: that it's not hard for anyone to find written form for spoken words. In effect, the migrants are insisting that

> [w]e can do "mere literacy" even for a language we don't know. We don't care about how the authorities say we're *supposed* to spell words. Those official spellings get in our way. We can take charge of our literacy.

On the other hand, the story leaves me deeply sad. I lament what it says about literate societies. The story shows how the magical power of *written words* creeps into every pore and cell of everyone who lives in a literate culture. Ever since humans could talk, children have learned their native language with amazing speed, just by *listening* and *speaking.* And ever since human speech divided into different languages, humans in multilingual settings—even adults past the ideal age for language learning—have learned second and third languages by *listening* and *speaking.*

The goal of these immigrant workers in Cobden was to learn some English *como de veras se oye*—the way it really sounds (23). But they felt they had to have *written words* to look at. They knew that English spelling was an impediment, but they were convinced that *spelling* is what they needed. (*Spell* means magic.) Did they realize that these transliterations into Spanish orthography actually *interfered* with the goal of learning to say English words the way Anglos say them? If they put half as much effort into ear work as they put into eye work, they would surely have done better at learning English the way it really sounds.

Or would they reply to me, "*We can't just learn by ear; we also have to know how to read—at least to read signs.*" (I don't remember Kalmar saying they had this goal.) But of course the approach they took made it *harder* to read signs or write notes to Anglos. And for notes to each other, Spanish was better.

But they had a third goal too—though not so much mentioned in the book—a goal that justified their approach: to *remember* language. Even to remember how to say "Where do you live" when you are fifteen and face to face with a pretty girl whose skin is a different color and whose culture looks down on yours. But as Plato pointed out, our weak memories are a byproduct of literacy.

So though this lens for the story makes me sad, it doesn't make me feel any blame. I am *not* trying to say

> *Why didn't they <u>realize</u> they were doing it all wrong? They were as misguided as all the scholars and teachers who think the only way to learn a language is to study the grammar!*

No, once you are in a culture of literacy, there's virtually no way to remove these feelings and assumptions from your pores and cells—no way to prevent that short-circuit between ear and eye. Indeed, David Olson reports what perhaps we shouldn't be surprised at (and he cites reputable research for it): that in literate cultures, children's first understanding of words as words is tied to their written form—not their spoken form (*World on Paper* 77).

I suppose I should celebrate the fact that literacy is so deeply and pervasively powerful; after all, my main goal is writing. But I am sad nevertheless, because my argument in this book is that writing itself *suffers* in literate societies because literacy itself (as we now have it) so deafens people to their primary form of language: speech.

I recently read an account of a very young middle-class man who was trying to help an older poor man who was having lots of trouble in various aspects of his life. The older man finally admitted, with great shame, that he couldn't read. As they talked about this, he blurted in a moment of exasperation, "I have no *words!*" I feel *his* words like a kick in the stomach. For in truth, like all persons, he was running over with words. Indeed, it became clear in reading the story that he was far more linguistically eloquent than the kid helping him. But he didn't *feel* he had any words because he had no grasp or power over what to him was the *reality* of words. Spoken words don't count.

18 A New Culture of Vernacular Literacy on the Horizon

IN THE LAST chapter I described problems and anxieties that stem from our current culture of proper literacy, a culture that makes writing less available than it should be. The culture rejects spoken language for writing; indeed, it's somewhat scornful of speech itself—as "vulgar" compared to dignified writing. This culture imposes a more or less single standard of correctness for writing. This is a dialect ("grapholect") that differs from the easy natural spoken languages used by virtually everyone—even those in privileged classes.

But of course our "current" culture is not wholly current: things are changing. "Correct written language" has been under strain for a while, and this is not just because people make mistakes and copy editors don't catch them all. In fact our very "standards" for correctness have been changing and getting more flexible. Quite a few teachers and copy editors accept grammatical constructions they wouldn't have accepted a generation ago. *The New Yorker* and the *New York Times* sanction the kinds of talky informal prose that I pointed to in the last chapter.

What's going on? *Things are falling apart.* That's what it looks like to people who are committed to strict standards. That's what change always looks like when your frame of reference is the previous order of things. But I want to suggest a frame of reference oriented more in the future. This helps me see that our culture of literacy has been moving for some time now toward a very different culture of literacy—a culture that will accept and even welcome spoken language for writing. And not just mainstream spoken English: *all* versions of spoken English will be considered acceptable for serious public writing before too very long. This means we'll no longer have a *single* language for what's valid for serious writing.

Such a development is hard to believe. After all, authoritative and even progressive linguists like to opine that a single standard is inevitable. Wolfram, Adger, and Christian speak of the "inevitability of dialect diversity and language standardization":

> Whether we like it or not, some type of language standardization seems inevitable. This conclusion comes not just from examining the situation in the United States or in English-speaking areas, but from surveying language situations throughout the world. (115–116)

These are recent, progressive linguists. Another one, Janson, says that without a standard, schooling is impossible. "Where there are schools with elementary instruction in reading and writing, there must also be orthographies and other established language norms" (228). How can teachers correct someone's language if there is no such thing as correct? If a teacher had students who spoke eight different dialects of English, she would have to accept final drafts in all of them—many she didn't know very well. This is a Wilder West than McWhorter fears. The death of good writing, the degeneration of the English language! Surely human nature itself resists linguistic chaos and seeks some order and standardization—especially when it comes to writing.

Or does it? I'd ask you to *consider* the vision I'm presenting here, even if only as a hypothesis. For in fact those linguists I just quoted should not have said that standardization is inevitable; they should have said it's *common*. To argue for my vision, I need to turn to history. We've had a Babel of Englishes in the past and it didn't kill writing or language or civilization. It won't this time either. A single standard for written language that differs from spoken dialects is not built into the universe or the nature of language; it's something that has *sometimes* emerged. In cycles. Usually it's been imposed. I'll look at historical examples of the tension between divergence and standardization, considering first spoken language and then written language.

Spoken Language: Divergence and Standardization

Attempts to Standardize

For one important example of the push/pull between divergence and standardization—and between vernacular language and writing, I'll summarize the Literacy Story I told about Charlemagne, Alcuin, and Latin (Chapter 5). Latin didn't diverge much till the end of the Roman empire in the fifth century, but then as it lived on as the spoken language throughout Europe, it began to diverge somewhat into multiple "Latins." But when Charlemagne conquered his huge kingdom in 800, he brought in Alcuin from England. Alcuin brought in "good Latin" because it came from books; it didn't have all the "problems" that come from a language being a spoken as a native tongue. Charlemagne mandated it for his whole empire.

From one point of view, Charlemagne's and Alcuin's attempt to standardize Latin was a big success. They stabilized it as an amazingly potent international *written* language that lived on as the only language for serious writing for virtually ten more centuries! Newton wrote in Latin. But from another point of view, Charlemagne and Alcuin utterly failed to stop the divergence of language. People did *not* change their spoken Latin to make it more like what Alcuin could speak because he learned it from books. The multiple Latins Charlemagne hoped to standardize kept on diverging more and more—as the living spoken languages of most people throughout Europe.

It's not so easy to curb how people talk. The odd mixture of success and failure set in motion by Charlemagne and Alcuin marked the beginning in European history of a gulf between spoken vernaculars and serious writing.

But where Charlemagne's attempt to standardize the spoken vernacular in 800 was a failure, it's easy to find some successes. All around the globe, the growth or fanning of national feeling and the imposition of nation states has standardized languages over and over. Part of the success lay in actually killing off thriving local languages (and sometimes the speakers). During the "formation" of France, a number of strong languages were wiped out—many of them with rich literatures (such as that of Provencal, Catalan, Occitan). Of course the current dominance of English around the globe may be killing more languages than local nationalisms have managed in the past—but it's probably a close contest.

Nebrija, enlisting the help of Queen Isabella in Spain, had more success in standardizing the current unruly version of Castilian—and in suppressing what he thought of as the even more unruly diversity of other dialects throughout Spain (see the Literacy Story, Chapter 8).

Webster wanted an "American English," but he celebrated it as more single and pure than what people spoke in England—closer to Chaucer and the uncorrupted English that existed before 1066 (see Lepore). He wasn't offering license, he was offering a new standard. He was very scornful of "mistakes" in the spelling of American English.

> In a stroke of linguistic nationalism, Webster makes American English historically antecedent to British English. As Webster says in his *Dissertations on the English Language,* published in 1789, there is a "surprising similarity between the idioms of the New England people and those of Chaucer, Shakespeare, &c. who wrote in the true English stile" (108). (Trimbur "Linguistic Memory" 582)

The "English Only" campaign in the United States seems to derive from a potent mixture of nationalism and insecurity—fear of the "alien." It's touching when speakers of English argue for purity in language since English is probably the most impure bastardized language there's ever been. It's slept with every language it ever encountered, even casually. The strength of English comes from how many babies it's had with how many partners.

Supporters of "English Only" tend to forget that the United States has already managed to stamp out other languages:

> The history of the German language in the United States is an important part of understanding the development of a politics of linguistic unity in that country. At the time of the American Revolutionary War, after all, not all that many people in the colonies were English-speakers. (Some scholars say that English-speakers numbered fewer than 40 percent; others point out that the German-speakers in one state numbered more than 50 percent.) Many German-Americans believed that German would eventually become an official American language; a few people argued that all Americans should learn to speak German; several endorsed the view of Benjamin Rush (a "founding father") that there should be a German-language national college; hundreds hoped to found a New Germany following the model of New France or New England. In any event, by 1900, there were millions of German-speakers in the United States. German-Americans had

published tens of thousands of German-language books and pamphlets. The German-American ethnic group was well educated, wealthy, and influential. (Shell 258–259)

This is from an important collection called *Multilingual America* (Sollors). It took the anti-German frenzy during the First World War to erase the prominence of German in our country. That's when the many towns and cities named "Ber<u>lin</u>" got rechristened "<u>Ber</u>lin."

See also *The Multilingual Anthology of American Literature: A Reader of Original Texts with English Translations* (Shell and Sollors); also *Herencia: The Anthology of Hispanic Literature of the United States* (Kanellos). And for the neglected story of how the profession of composition in the United States is complicit in the English-only process, see Trimbur's "Linguistic Memory."

Patterns in Divergence and Standardization in Spoken Language

In the face of these mixed results about success and failure in the standardizing of spoken language, can we generalize? We can. If we stand back and look at the history of human spoken language—using both a microscope and a telescope—we see a continual tug of war between divergence and standardization. Consider the root process by which languages continue: babies and toddlers learn the language around them. But babies and toddlers always get things wrong: they use the wrong pronunciation, the wrong syntax, the wrong word, and the wrong meaning for a word. But their mistakes are continually corrected toward what's right—namely, the standard—for that family or group. Divergence is overcome.

But as standard-lovers continually recognize with a sigh, the job of rooting out divergence—that is to say, *error*—is never done. In Chapter 9 I described Dr. Johnson's mood of resignation:

> The lexicographer finds that the dictionary cannot "embalm his language." The sharing of language by all classes means that language, like manners, must inevitably be depraved, for example by its use in commerce; and its depravity must spread to all its users. . . . Having understood that, says Johnson, "let us make some struggles for our language." (Kermode 29)

Pesky children don't just get things wrong; sometimes they say things wrong on purpose. The tug of war between infants and their families enacts a general process that continues after babies grow up. Individuals are a force for divergence while groups are a force for conservation or conservatism and tend to keep individuals in check. And of course the same dialectical tension exists between small groups and large groups.

One might conclude that standardization always wins out. After all, languages hold together and persist. But no. Sometimes the individual or the small group wins. Individuals or small groups who talk "wrong" are *usually* pushed back in line—corrected, ignored, or not understood. But if their "wrongness" is sufficiently effective or attractive in that context—or if the individual or small group has special power or prestige—the wrongness can catch on. The large group gives in and changes its standard to match the small group or even individual. (This dialectic tug of war was a premise at the heart of my 1973 *Writing Without Teachers;* see 151ff.)

Someone had to have been the first person to use *cool* to mean "good" or use "villain" to mean bad (it used to be a neutral word for a man). Idiosyncratic usages can infect and take root. No doubt cool-as-good started out as a *metaphor*, for every new metaphor is a word used with a "wrong" sense. Similarly, some Roman must have been the first person to say he was bothered by a *"scruple"* nagging his mind or conscience. But he knew that "scruple" just meant "pebble." He wasn't talking about pebbles, he was saying that something was nagging at his mind the way a pebble nags when it's caught in your sandal or shoe.

Those are trivial examples, but languages would never change if it weren't for the triumphs of deviance or error. If human speakers always pruned away new shoots, we would all still be speaking the language that Adam and Eve spoke in Eden or in the Rift Valley of Africa. (It's fun to think of Indo-European as just a debased regional offshoot of an earlier "true language.") Only deviance and wrongness explain the existence of different languages. Every different dialect or language in the world represents a failure at standardization.

It's time and space that fertilize the roots of wrongness:

- *Time.* After fifty or a hundred years, people even in the same village usually talk a somewhat different language. The dynamics are many and interesting, but more often than not, young people are the force for change and elders a force for conservation. Interestingly, the smaller the village or region, the more the language changes. (Janson 234)
- *Space* too brings divergence. When people from this village move over to the next valley—or country or continent—their language often diverges from the language they left behind.

Time and space, between them, give rise to different dialects—and then to different languages. In some cases, time trumps space: the home language may change faster than the "colonial" version. When I studied at Oxford in the 1950s, I used to say "I guess," and people made fun of my "colonial English." I felt a gleeful satisfaction when I found it in Chaucer.

What we see in this process is just another application of the second law of thermodynamics: what is ordered tends to become disordered. Physicists point out that we can't create or even maintain order without adding energy. It takes work to keep the socks in order in the top drawer. So in the realm of language, divergence *happens* unless someone exerts force to impose or maintain standardization.

Sometimes the force is wielded by individuals with power—like Charlemagne, or like Ataturk who imposed the Roman alphabet on Turkey, or like the Korean king who imposed a brand new writing system (see the literacy story following Chapter 9). People in charge tend to feel more secure when things are standardized. With authority, they can impose it. Sometimes the force comes from a group—though the group may be spearheaded by individuals. The force that spreads English around the world is more subtle—economic and social and cultural. When one tribe or country overruns another, it often wipes out the conquered language—even in those cases when it doesn't wipe out the people. (Crystal tells the interesting story of why the French conquest of England didn't wipe out English. See his *Stories*.)

In our mainstream monolingual U.S. culture, most people assume that we *need* convergence and single standards. *"Without a standard, we couldn't understand each other. Everything would grind to a halt!"* But when it comes to the different versions of English used in the United States, misunderstandings seldom derive from difference itself. When people misunderstand each other's English, it's more often a case of *psychological* interference. That is, people who speak the dominant version sometimes listen to other versions through a stance of disapproval of what they think of as *alien* and bad English. And people who *speak* stigmatized versions would sometimes just as soon not be understood by mainstreamers. When stigmatization is not in force, humans usually take dialectal variation in their stride and understand each other without struggle. Most real misunderstanding stems not from speakers who grew up with different dialects of English but from speakers who started out speaking entirely different languages. Speakers of English as a second language sometimes have a very strong accent and a weak command of the grammar. (Literate people like to say, "If you don't spell right, readers won't understand you," but there's plenty of recent research showing that it's actually quite easy to understand wildly misspelled writing.)

Even in cultures where fully different languages are spoken (rather than merely different dialects), people tend to learn a good deal of each other's languages if there's not too much stigmatization going on. As Mary Louise Pratt argues, bi-lingualism and multi-lingualism are the rule rather than the exception in human communities. George Steiner points out that almost every culture has a "Babel myth": a story of the gods *punishing* humans by giving them divergent languages. But he argues that language difference is actually one of the greatest human blessings.

Written Language: Divergence and Standardization

In the case of writing, we can see the same tension between diversity and standardization. But because writing somehow seems so "official"—often supported by the government or the schools—the forces for standardization are often stronger.

In England before 1000 CE,

> there were no attempts at creating a common standard for the written language. On the contrary, each writer employed his own dialect, so there are texts in Kentish, in West Saxon, in Northumbrian, and so on. . . . Even though the writers of Britain probably all knew the strictly standardized written Latin language, they did not try to create anything similar.
>
> This is quite similar to the situation in Greece before the Macedonian conquest, and to some extent also to that of Italy before Dante. Where there is no political unity, the idea of a common standard for a written language is not very close at hand. (Janson 145)

But by about 1000, King Alfred had amassed power beyond his immediate realm and made West Saxon the standard for writing for much of England. Once he'd managed this, scribes from all over England wrote in the West Saxon version of English, and indeed his scribes recopied various existing written texts into this "proper" language. This gave a sense of uniformity; it was an early way of "enforcing standards." This recopying fooled later scholars into thinking that there was more linguistic homogeneity in England than had actually existed (see Crystal *Stories* 55).

But then with the French conquest in 1066, England lost this standard form of written English. Norman French became the language of everyone in court or government circles. The many people who dealt with people in either realm had to learn it. But most English folk didn't live in court or government circles and went on talking the vernacular English of the time. And some of them *wrote*, despite all the official and literary writing in French that went on:

> From around 1200 and onwards, people wrote in English again. However, the texts were quite different from those produced before the Conquest. There was no standard language any more: the fairly uniform spelling and grammar based on West Saxon speech that dominated in the tenth and eleventh centuries had disappeared altogether. Instead, each author seemed to write and spell more or less according to his own spoken dialect. For a period of about 200 years, there were again many written dialects, just as in the earliest period of written English. (Janson 155)

This diversity stares us in the face if we want to read Middle English literature. We see very different forms of English if we read Chaucer (from near London), Henryson (from Scotland), the poet of *Gawain and the Green Knight* (from the north), and the poet of *Piers Plowman* (probably from the South Midlands). Linguists can see from Middle English texts—hear, actually—what region of England or Scotland the writers called home. But many nineteenth-century scholarly editors changed many Middle English texts to conform to an alleged "standard"—which again helped people forget how much diversity there had been in written English for such a long time (Roger Wright 3).

But it's not till the eighteenth century that we get the most powerful, pervasive, and conscious imposition of standardization in written English. This was the age when dictionaries were born. And with them, for the first time in English history, came a powerful ideology of *prescriptivism*. As the historical linguist, Hope, writes, prescriptivism is

> not in itself a linguistic process. . . . [It's] "*language-external*": a cultural, ideological phenomenon which plays itself out *in* language. . . . Prescriptivism . . . has been highly successful as a social ideology while failing to account for linguistic data. (51, 54, my emphasis)

But isn't this a perennial human tendency?

No. It's true that humans (prey to insecurity) have always been tempted to ridicule or even scorn people who speak differently. The Greeks called non-Greeks "barbarians" because their talk sounded like *bar-bar-bar-bar*. In our culture, many people can't seem to get tired of laughing at Brooklyn or Bronx speech. Nevertheless, prescriptivism is different because it insists on a *moral* dimension in the disapproval of "wrong" language. Till the eighteenth century in England, there had never been such a widespread deeply rooted moralism about "bad language."

This is the period when we see a huge flowering of metaphors of uncleanness, corruptness, and immorality for wrong language. Well before Samuel Johnson wrote his dictionary, Ben Johnson wrote: "Wheresoever manners and fashions are corrupted, language is. It imitates the public riot" (quoted in Kermode 28). (See Richard Boyd's research on nineteenth century-handbooks where scholars talked about "grammatical monstrosities" and "contemptible miscreants.")

Till the eighteenth century, there was no consistency in spelling and very little consistency in written grammar (even Alfred's monolithic Anglo-Saxon wasn't fully standard). But with the eighteenth century, those who cared about language wanted to make English not just regular but noble and good—and that meant that it should be like book Latin. (I mentioned some of these attempts in Chapter 9: don't split infinitives because they are not split in Latin; add "b" to *dout* and "d" to *amiral* to make them sound like Latin.) Yet the English language and English literature flourished before the eighteenth century—without benefit of standardization. (It may well have flourished less in the eighteenth century!)

Eighteenth-century Scottish rhetoricians laid down guidelines for the proper use of English, and these took firm hold throughout England and the United States. (Eighteenth-century Scotland saw a flowering of rhetorical studies that focused on *English* writing. Prominent figures were Hugh Blair, George Campbell, and Alexander Bain. Till then, rhetoric—part of the medieval *trivium*—had focused mostly on ancient Greek and Latin and medieval sermons.) Thomas Miller points out that the native language spoken by these influential rhetoricians, *Scots* or *Scottish*, was ridiculed and scorned by literate English people as forcefully as some people have ridiculed and scorned Black English.

Miller suggests that the linguistic and cultural defensiveness or insecurity of these learned Scots scholars might have given them the drive to establish an aggressively *proper* standard for rhetoric and language (Miller, chapters 3 and 4). I cannot resist sensing a parallel between this influential language work coming from Scotland and Alcuin's importation of "good Latin" from England to central Europe (thanks to Charlemagne): the most fiercely imposed standards often come from the margins. In Alcuin's time (800), England was the wild margin of the European universe; in the eighteenth century, Scotland was the wild margin of the cultivated English universe.

Interestingly, however, the eighteenth-century prescriptivist drive did not seem to regularize accent in prestige *speech*. Until late in the nineteenth century, there was no single standard for elite spoken English in England. Even prominent figures like prime ministers Gladstone and Peele spoke publicly in their strong regional accents—including, no doubt, some "nonstandard" bits of grammar; so too Thomas Arnold, headmaster of Rugby school, and Thomas Hardy in their different accents. But with the Education Act of 1870, elite schools were open to the general public (or at least those who could pay), and this somehow led to the promulgation of an elite "proper" *spoken* English. Any-

The greatest example of standardization in writing comes from China. Because of the size and power of the various early empires, a standard form of Chinese characters has been used from the Shang dynasty around 1200 BCE (more fully standardized in the Han dynasty around 200 CE) through to the present—and this throughout the largest country in the world, and also for many centuries in Japan, Korea, and much of southeast Asia! Chinese is not the oldest form of writing, but it's been used the longest, most continuously, and by most people. This is a case of standardized writing used by people who spoke a huge diversity of spoken languages (though of course literacy was *relatively* rare among these millions and millions of people).

The standardization of writing in China involved not just the form of the visual characters but even the *language* or *dialect* used:

> Until the early 20th century, all dialects of Chinese were written in a [single] literary dialect that dated to the late Old Chinese period, about 1100 BCE to 100 CE. This meant that literate Chinese wrote in a way they themselves did not speak. This form persisted, in part, because of the Chinese civil service's power in creating and maintaining the written standard for some 2,000 years. (Schmandt-Besserat and Erard 16)

In the 1950s, the People's Republic made a remarkable move that might have *ended* this massive standardization when it decreed that pinyin or Roman letters could be used for writing. This would have permitted speakers of the eight or more very different versions of spoken Chinese to *write* their dialect or language. A number of leading figures argued for this policy and it's presumably what Mao intended—till he changed his mind and turned against his own suggestion for changing Chinese writing entirely into pinyin. Instead the government decreed another massive standardization. All use of pinyin throughout China must conform to the dialect or language of Beijing and the north. Everyone who wants to use pinyin for Chinese (and now this means everyone who wants to use a computer for writing) must spell out their words in that one dialect (Potunqua). (For more on Chinese, see the Literacy Story in Chapter 16. DeFrancis tells this story well and in detail.)

So What?

What can we conclude from these stories? It's clear that as humans use language, there is a recurring and repeating tug of war between divergence and convergence—the kind of thing we see in families, groups, communities, regions, and nations. (Bakhtin was struck with how language moves from diversity to conformity but conformity leads back to diversity: "Every utterance participates in the 'unitary language' (in its centripetal forces and tendencies) and at the same time partakes of social and historical heteroglossia (the centrifugal, stratifying forces)" [272].) Divergence is the norm in both spoken and written language (thanks to human carelessness and to the second law of thermodynamics). But standardization is somewhat more frequently achieved with writing than speaking. But it's not always achieved.

So the linguists I quoted earlier were wrong when they said that standardization is inevitable in spoken language, but they might feel more justified if they applied their judgment to writing—where standardization seems to have better odds. The very stories I just told all describe the eventual imposition of a single standard for writing: the power of the early emperors in China led to a single system of written characters throughout that vast land; Charlemagne's importation of Alcuin in 800 led to a single standard for writing in Latin throughout Europe; King Alfred's dominance in England in 1000 created a single standard for writing in England; the powerful eighteenth-century prescriptivists managed to impose a far more narrow single standard for English writing.

So should I give up my vision of a coming divergence in written English that welcomes different spoken versions of the language? I decline. (Surprise!) Instead, I insist that to some degree, the stories also *support* my vision.

- They show that standardization is *not* inevitable. Standardization is not built into the way humans use language. There were long periods of divergence—periods that sometimes followed an imposed standardization. Linguistic divergence and multiplicity—the lack of a single standard for writing—is also normal. So I'd say we are now in a period when it's getting increasingly normal to have a growing diversity of forms of English writing.

- They show that it takes strong force (usually political, sometimes military) to squash the inevitable human linguistic tendency toward divergence. In our present culture, I don't see any political or military force waiting in the wings that might forcibly impose uniformity or help maintain our current and crumbling single standard for correct writing. Teachers and copy editors have tried their best for quite a while and they haven't managed to stem the tide of diversity in written English.

- The stories show that richly expressive language and the best literature we have ever known can all flourish during times of diversity in written forms of English. Think of Middle English literature and especially Chaucer; think of Shakespeare who also wrote in a time of diversity in grammar and spelling.

World Englishes
So what can we look forward to? I will soon turn to the main argument of this chapter: that in the United States we are moving toward a new *divergent* culture of vernacular literacy with no single standard for writing.

But first I must try to do justice to a process of mass *convergence*. English—spoken and written—has taken over more and more of the world, helping hasten the death of quite a few languages and undermining many more. As we might expect, this doesn't happen without the imposition of force. In this case the force can seem subtle (*Isn't it charming? People just seem to _want_ English!*), but of course it's all being driven by obvious economic and political force. More and more countries and individuals are feeling they must take on English to survive. It's a frightening and tragic prospect. One can read of parents in certain Asian countries having doctors cut a small ligament in the tongues of their babies in the belief that this will help them learn to say English words better. One of the big battles in quite a few nondeveloped countries is between authorities who favor immersing children in English in the earliest grades and other authorities who argue (rightly, I believe), that children will learn better—even learn English better—if they do lots of their schooling in their home language.

> Wagner's (1993) research in Morocco shows the ease with which multiple literacy can be achieved. . . . This finding is particularly striking since French and Arabic differ radically in lexicon, syntax, and script. This provides support for the interdependence thesis (Cummins 1979): that learning to read in any language produces skills that are transferable to any other language, thus making it easier for children to become biliterate or multiliterate. . . . [I]n an era of economic globalization and cultural heterogeneity, multiple literacy (rather than language homogenization) appears to be spreading rapidly. (Bernard 27)

And even though spoken English is playing a huge role in the drift toward massive homogenization in human language, this is not, in fact, a case of *standardizing English*. The results of this worldwide Englification are notably unstandardized: not English but *Englishes*. (Recall how Latin evolved into Latins in the early centuries of the Common Era and finally gave rise to all our "romance" languages.) The vast majority of speakers of English in the world are African and Asian and don't have English as their first language. The linguist, Liesel Hibbert, argues that Black South African English is emerging as its own new standard, different from British English (35). (She also calls attention to the weaker cultural and political status of African American Language in our country.) There is a growing movement around the world to prefer teachers of English who are *not* from the Anglo-American "homelands" and *don't* have English as their first language. Local teachers not from the metropole are sought because their speech is closer to what is used in that region. The authority on world English, David Gradol, writes that "[l]arge numbers of people will learn English as a foreign language in the 21st century and they will need teachers, dictionaries and grammar books. But will they continue to look towards the native speaker for authoritative norms of usage?" ("The Decline of the Native Speaker" 68). His answer is No.

So it doesn't seem as though a highly standardized *spoken* English will blanket the globe in the future (especially with the wild freedom on the internet). And it's instructive also to look at the past:

The original Lingua Franca was a variable Romance mode loosely based on mid-medieval Catalan, used among the maritime peoples of the Western Mediterranean. The name [lingua franca] arose because the Catalans were often called "Franks," perhaps pejoratively at first but eventually without such connotations. The virtue of the *lingua franca* in its original context lay precisely in its versatility and flexibility. The very last thing to be useful there would have been any kind of "setting and maintaining of standards." It evolved in unregulated colloquial circumstances to fulfill a variety of non-academic functions in practical contexts, and the idea that there should be some kind of standardized variety of the *lingua franca* could hardly have arisen. (Roger Wright 8)

❊   ❊   ❊

But with *written* English around the globe, it's more tempting to see standardization on its way. Publishers and large institutions and states can often impose a standard, so the differences between the various global written Englishes are smaller than those between the spoken Englishes. Standardization is certainly a strong trend in the publication of scientific research. Still

> I'm not sure English per se, in its global circulation, is a "killer" language that leads to linguicide. I have no doubt, as Robert Phillipson makes clear, that English is involved in "linguistic imperialism," but my sense is that its circulation and uptake is complicated and typically results in "non-standard" Englishes (national varieties and other hybrid forms) beyond the control of the Anglo-American metropolis. If anything it's this kind of English beyond metropolitan control that marks the present moment. To my mind, it's more a matter of how people are taking up English inventively for their own ends.

This is from an email from John Trimbur (November 2010), who has long been engaged in work in South Africa and other non-U.S. sites. There are lots of small differences—but not too small to cause difficulties. Microsoft Word will check your spelling for something like a dozen varieties of written English. Even between close linguistic cousins, the United States and Britain, there are significant but confusing differences in spelling and punctuation (like what goes inside and outside the quotation marks). Even newspaper headlines show small but ear-catching differences in grammar: "Brazil have suffered a defeat at the hands of Camaroon."

But there are larger differences too. Most of these are born of pressure from the strongly divergent spoken versions of English. Valerie Youssef is just one of many scholars around the world who insist that "Standard English" is not owned by the British or Americans. There are other standards: "[T]here is a similar level of variation between British (BSE) and American (ASE) as between Caribbean Standard varieties and the metropolitan models" (46). It's quite common to hear people in various regions using the word "standard" for their version of English—even in the written variety. (For more on how "world

English" is not a simple, singular story, see Crystal's *English as a Global Language,* Graddol's *English Next,* and various works by Suresh Canagarajah.) There's a simple brute question lurking here: *Who owns English?* But it doesn't lurk; it is the title of numerous books and articles and of a special issue of *TESOL Quarterly* (Spring 1995).

There is a very large literature on this topic. For just three examples, see B. Kachru, Suresh Canagarajah (*The Geopolitics*), and Yamuna Kachru and Cecil L. Nelson. Kachru and Nelson call particular attention to code mixing (what Young and Canagarajah call code meshing). Here is a headline in an English language newspaper in India (*Indian Express* New Delhi, from 2002): "James Lingdoh ko gussa kyon atta hai?" (meaning "What Makes James Lingdoh angry?") (Kachru and Nelson 257). Here is a tiny ending portion of an email full of code mixing: "Love to all. I had better sleep and rest my legs as I am the only young buddhi here or my legs will jawab denge" (256). *English Today* is a useful journal that specializes in interesting and accessible articles about the various Englishes.

So the story of global English is paradoxical. From the largest perspective it's a story of massive convergence; but looking closer, we see a failure of full convergence or standardization at the center. And if I am right in what follows, the United States might help move things toward multiple written Englishes *within* a single nation.

In fact, a well-known linguist is now making a far more startling prediction. In a recent book, Nicholas Ostler argues that English will decline and no longer be the main lingua franca for the globe: "English is likely to go the way of Persian, Sanskrit and Latin and, over many hundreds of years, inevitably die out" (McCrum 6). His book is called *The Last Lingua Franca: English Until the Return of Babel.* (He is a reputable linguist whose 2005 *Empires of the Word* was critically acclaimed.) His claim is of course arguable, but he supports it with facts from linguistic/political history. He points to the decline of other dominant lingua francas like Persian, Pali, and Latin. Latin should have triumphed with the development of printing in the fifteenth century, since Latin was deemed the language for all serious writing and most literate people of *all* languages read Latin. But in fact printing led to the decline of Latin because of the growing market for novels, romances, and pamphlets in vernacular languages—fueled by a growing middle class of newly literate people.

Ostler sees the same fate for English over time. He argues that long-range technological developments will lead to machine translation that is good enough (not perfect), so that people won't need a lingua franca to get the commercial and cultural advantages they now get from using English. He sees a culture where mother tongues will flourish. He ends his book saying, "Thereafter everyone will speak and write in whatever language they choose, and the world will understand." In an interview he says:

At the moment, English-speaking groups are very much in their ascendancy, but there is only one way to go from an ascendancy. . . . The power and cheapness of computers is increasing all the time. There's no way that the little problem of the incompatibility between languages [right now] is going to stand in the way . . . for long. . . . [English dominates *only* as a *lingua franca*. [It] will be there as long as it's needed, but since it's not being picked up as a mother tongue, it's not typically being spoken by people to their children . . . [which is required] for long term survival of a language. (McCrum 6)

Divergence: Looking Forward to a New Culture of Vernacular Literacy with No Single Standard for Writing

If we narrow our perspective and look at written English in the United States (perhaps *also* in Britain, Canada, Australia, and South Africa), it seems clear to me that we're involved in a process of *divergence*. I've described various historical periods when there was no single standard for correct writing, and people wrote in their own spoken dialects of a language. It's my contention that we are moving toward this situation here—toward a new culture of *vernacular literacy*.

No one can predict the future and this is obviously a vision, but if it sounds hopelessly and idealistically impossible, notice how moderate it is when compared to the vision by Ostler—someone far more linguistically learned than I. Where he sees people all around the globe writing and speaking their mother tongues without any need for a lingua franca, my vision is mild: merely that all the various versions of English will be considered appropriate and sanctioned for serious writing; and that as readers, we'll all accept and be able to understand each other's Englishes "well enough."

I see three stages in the gradual coming to pass of this new vernacular culture. In the first stage, mainstream White spoken language will be considered acceptable for generally literate writing—but not school and academic writing. In the second stage, mainstream spoken language will be considered acceptable for school writing and academic discourse. Only in the third and final stage will nonmainstream and stigmatized versions of English be acceptable for all serious writing. There won't then be a *single* standard for good or correct or valid writing. This entire process will obviously be slow, but it's happening quickly compared to the centuries it took for the vernacular languages of Europe to become sanctioned for serious writing.

The First Stage: Mainstream Vernacular Language Is Accepted for Serious Writing

We're already immersed in the first stage of divergence—where mainstream spoken language is starting to be acceptable for generally literate serious writing. If you look at the best lively published writing, you might be tempted to say we're already there. But I'm afraid that only a minority of literate but nonprofessional writers are finally "getting" what many good professional writers have been doing—finally catching on that they too can use the kind of informal spoken language found in Krugman, Menand, and Dowd when they need to write committee reports, grant proposals, and business memos. But it won't be so long till most people realize they can use vernacular spoken language in all kinds of generally literate but serious *paper* documents. Already for a good many people, the question is no longer "Is this too informal or speechy to be acceptable?" but rather "Will this informal speech-inflected language be right for these particular readers in this genre?"

People writing business memos to unknown readers will probably not choose to be as chatty as we saw in the passage from Safire in the last chapter ("I spell it *tchotchki*. Do I need a lawyer?"), but they might well use spoken language like Krugman did in defining "Currency [as] pieces of green paper with pictures of dead presidents on them." Larry Sommers (former president of Harvard) once began a paper on finance by declaring "THERE ARE IDIOTS. Look around" . . . (MacFarquhar 48).

And of course we see even now that when people write letters to the editor, magazine articles, or committee reports to colleagues, they sometimes realize that it's rhetorically appropriate to use even Safire's chattiness. More to the point, newspapers and magazines will print that language without cleansing it. So at this first stage, the single standard for good serious writing will seem significantly relaxed.

But it's crucial to acknowledge that in a real sense we'll still have a *single* standard. The speech that has begun to "infect" writers in the *New York Times* and *The New Yorker* and other mainstream sites is mostly *mainstream* speech—a version of standardized White English. Prejudice, racism, and classism die slowly.

The Second Stage: Teachers and Academics Will Begin to Accept Mainstream White Vernacular Language

This has already started too, but it may be slower to finish. I'll look at school writing first—the writing students are asked to do.

Naturally, many teachers in the early grades have long invited young children to use the language they speak for writing. And for the last few decades or more, a substantial movement of teachers in kindergarten through second grade have been inviting children to write before they read—which is an explicit invitation to speak onto the page. In addition, many high school and college teachers of writing—especially many who identify with the field of composition—have taken a progressive stance toward language and writing for quite a while. Sometimes the stance is ideological. But more often it simply grows out of pragmatic concrete goals: trying to encourage students to *want* to write so they write a great deal; trying to help students grow to experience themselves as writers, not just students who write assignments for teachers; and hoping to elicit writing that's lively and interesting and personally invested—so it's not such a pain in the neck to read. If you really want these goals, you have to fight some rigid rules and accept or invite spoken language. I can add to this number many teachers who have conservative standards for final drafts but nevertheless invite spoken language for exploratory draft writing. So I'd guess that perhaps a majority of teachers in the United States—at least if they are writing teachers—invite spoken language on the page at least in certain ways.

There's another significant movement or mood among quite a few high school and college teachers of writing: a particular interest in "creative nonfiction." This lively but vaguely defined genre has grown prolifically in all kinds of publication sites. Teachers want to teach nonfiction but make it livelier and more interesting by inviting some of the techniques from fiction. Many teachers love this genre in itself, but there's something else: a teacher who assigns creative nonfiction is assigning exactly the kind of writing that students can see published every day of the week on op-ed pages in many newspapers around the country. Many published examples are no better than what skilled students can turn out, so teachers can help students imagine getting something published. And perhaps the most striking feature of creative nonfiction is that it opens the door to very personal writing. If you call it creative nonfiction, you don't have to apologize for allowing students to use "I" and write personally. It's an approach that often brings out some of the best student writing and helps them enjoy writing and grow as writers.

Let me turn from student writing to the writing by teachers and scholars: "academic writing." (I pass over a substantial amount of fiction and memoir and op-eds that academics now write. It's remarkable how many academics have published memoirs.) The second stage of inviting vernacular language into academic writing will take longer. Scholars and researchers have tended to be conservative about linguistic standards for writing. What could be a more perfect and trivial prohibition of speech in writing than the ban against *contractions*. We all *say* "can't" but in much academic writing we must write "cannot." This tiny prohibition can serve as a symbol of where we are in the process of change. The prohibition is gradually being loosened, and yet it still has force. In some quantitative research from 1987, Chafe and Danielewicz compare the use of contractions in various kinds of writing and discover it was near zero in published academic pieces ("Properties" 93–94).

Some academic copy editors have given up trying to remove the taint of speech in ways I illustrated in the previous chapter (correcting *"having no sense of"* into *"lacking a sense of"*). Very gradually, the rest will come along. Before too long, academics will finally learn to exploit comfortable, vernacular language to make even their academic and scholarly writing clearer, stronger, and livelier. We already see this kind of writing coming from a good number of tenured senior and respected faculty members with a secure reputation in their field. I've noticed this even in some scientific writing. It'll be slower with academics still trying to earn tenure—especially as institutions make tenure harder to get.

The flurry of academic publication in the language of deconstruction and postmodernism not so long ago had a nontrivial effect on academic language. This writing was as far from vernacular speech as possible, yet such a striking explosion of writing in a wholly new language helped break down the notion that there's only one right dialect and register for academic writing.

But in all these developments, we're still talking about a slowly growing acceptance of *mainstream* or White vernacular language.

The Third stage: Nonmainstream and stigmatized Versions of English Will Be Acceptable for All Serious Writing

This change will seem most momentous. Many people cannot imagine a culture of literacy where stigmatized versions of English are acceptable for serious writing—for example, in business writing, academic writing, and mainstream published nonfiction. But I don't think it will be *too* long till serious texts of all kinds will be written in Black English and various forms of Latino or Caribbean or West African or Indian English. Not only that; most mainstream readers will take this kind of written language for granted (despite some nostalgic regrets).

In our present culture, when people imagine such a development, many of them will see nothing but carelessness and disregarded standards. The sky is falling. It's what McWhorter laments. Lynn Truss is another disaster-monger in her *Eats, Shoots and Leaves.*

I don't want to pretend that this change is right around the corner; it'll take a good deal of time. But I'd guess that within two or three decades it will be clear that that's where we're *headed.* Let me point to signs even now that it is coming.

We are starting to see more and more respected publication of works with stigmatized versions of English: Black English, Latino/Chicano English, Spanglish, Caribbean versions of English, Hawaiian versions of English, and Australian indigenous-inflected versions of English. Lots of mainstream readers read books like *The Color Purple, Push,* and *Blu's Hanging.* And as publishers know well, mainstream readers are not the only readers and buyers. Starting as early as 1974, Geneva Smitherman wrote columns in Black English for the academic *English Journal* (see "Columns"). *Rotten English* is an anthology of published writing in mostly stigmatized versions of English (see Ahmed). In Appendix II, I have a tiny sample of published writing in nonprestige nonstandard versions of English.

As mainstream writers start to use more of *their* mainstream vernacular speech in serious writing, this will give, even now, speakers of, say, Black English a bit more linguistic wiggle room in their writing—for the interesting thing about mainstream *spoken* English is how much more plural and variable it is than "correct writing." Let me quote again the linguists on the multiplicity in what we call mainstream spoken English:

> If native speakers from Michigan, New England, and Arkansas avoid the use of socially stigmatized grammatical structures such as "double negatives" (e.g., *They didn't do nothing*), different verb agreement patterns (e.g., *They's okay*), and different irregular verb forms (e.g., *She done it*), there is a good chance they will be considered standard English speakers. . . . [I]f a person's speech is free of structures that can be identified as nonstandard, then it is considered standard. (Wolfram, Adger, and Christian 12)

There are powerful consequences in this negativity principle: if you avoid certain no-no's, you have a great deal of leeway or freedom. Remember the research by Geneva Smitherman and her colleagues on essays for NAEP tests (I mentioned it in Chapter 16). They found that writing with *styles* and *rhythms* of Black English actually raised the scores—as long as it avoided Black *grammatical* constructions.

So as we continue down the present linguistic path—as our culture loses the fear of *mainstream* speech for serious writing—more space will open up for nonmainstream speech in writing. But there will be a significant period of time during which speakers of stigmatized languages will have to know how to avoid certain racially sensitive grammatical features if they want to be read by lots of mainstream readers. In other words, we're moving fast toward a situation where speakers of mainstream English won't have to avoid their spoken vernacular for serious careful writing; and speakers of stigmatized Englishes will have *some* leeway for their spoken vernacular, but they'll still have to be careful to edit out certain taboo features of their syntax and lexicon.

Further acceptance of stigmatized vernaculars will occur as more good writers in those languages get an audience of mainstream readers. We already see plenty of this in works where stigmatized language is restricted to the mouth of a character. Then gradually, narrators or "authors" use this language. First in fiction and poetry, and then more slowly in some "literary nonfiction." It'll take a while for more serious nonfiction. Alice Walker has been a prime mover, but someone like Junot Diaz shows where things are going. There will be a gradual increase in the (presently small) number of mainstream readers who read works that are not so easy or inviting. A prime example is offered by the Jamaican poet, Louise Bennett. As you could see from her poem (p. 326—where she makes fun of taboos against vernacular language), she writes in a version of English that's difficult for mainstream U.S. and British readers. But she is committed to her language (like Dante) and her regional readers, so she forgoes some mainstream readers. Her work is good enough to make many put in the extra effort. I foresee that as this loosening process goes on; we'll find more writing by speakers of nonmainstream Englishes who have not till now written much or thought of themselves as writers. Some of what they write will be very good and will win over more readers—especially when it is published by mainstream publishing houses.

A New Wild West

But it is above all on the worldwide web that more people will gradually find writing in stigmatized versions of English that they want to read. It is on the web and in email and chat rooms that we see a new Wild West where there are no official sheriffs with badges—no institutionally sanctioned people enforcing correct written English. On the web, the line between "spoken language" and "written language" is hard to find. Of course, conventions and fashions grow up, but (except at certain sites) there are no filters to enforce a standard, single or not: no publishers, editors, copy editors, and teachers. Anyone can write any language and any version of English. Jason Epstein, an important figure in the publishing world, writes that

> [d]igitization makes possible a world in which anyone can claim to be a publisher and anyone can call him- or herself an author. In this world the traditional filters will have melted into air and only the ultimate filter—the human inability to read what is unreadable—will remain to winnow what is worth keeping in a virtual marketplace where Keats's nightingale shares space with Aunt Mary's haikus. ("Publishing: The Revolutionary Future 4)

> At a purely technical level, the internet itself has been the site of a push/pull between divergence and standardization. Early computers permitted writing only in the Roman and Cyrillic alphabets, hence excluding many of the multitude of writing systems in the world. Then in the 1980s, Unicode was introduced, and this permitted fifty-five writing systems—and yet it excluded one hundred others. Now a new version of Unicode is being developed that will permit all writers to write in their own writing systems. The technology folks are acting on the assumption that I'm arguing for: all people should be able to write in their own language.

With no one imposing any standard for correct writing—and no institutional power or teacher power—we get a *naked rhetorical open space*. It's a space where power is *rhetorically based,* the power that emerges from the confrontation between writers and readers. Of course, there are a few *favored* regions and sites and blogs on the web. If you can get yourself well placed, you have a better chance of being noticed and perhaps read. Prestige, reputation, and even friendship will still play their role. But they are not opposed to rhetoric; they are part of any rhetorical space. We like to read what is written by friends or people we admire. But these limiting factors have no damping effect on the rest of the web, which stays wide open to anything from anyone. The opportunity to write what you want and put it out there helps people become braver about working on their writing. People are putting unbelievable amounts of writing on the web. This opportunity moves people down the path toward becoming better writers.

There are other cultural practices that cooperate with the web in starting to break open literacy. Rap music and hip-hop language gain large audiences and are used in writing by more and more people. Black Planet is a social media site aimed (mostly) at African Americans and is the site of a lot of AAL. (See *Roc the Mic Right: The Language of Hip Hop Culture* by H. Samy Alim—and also Alim, Baugh, and Smitherman.) Poetry slams have become amazingly popular and they represent some interesting crossings: between text and speech; and between poetry as "high culture" and poetry as "people's culture."

But even though writers get to write whatever they want in this rhetorical open space, by the same token, *readers* get to *ignore* whatever they want. There may be no single standard for correct language, but that doesn't mean readers will read anything. In short, the absence of a *standard* doesn't mean *no standards*—no judging, no criteria, no caring about quality. People judge every time they decide to read or not read, and when they judge, they use standards or criteria—conscious or not. On the web we see plenty of blabbing—"garbage" if you prefer. But we see plenty of good writing and plenty of judging by readers of what to read.

It was just this kind of open space for naked rhetorically based power that I set up in 1973 when I laid out the guidelines for "teacherless classes" in *Writing Without Teachers*. I was troubled by the power of teachers to impose on students their institutional and unilateral criteria for good and bad writing. It seemed to me that the criteria I saw many teachers and institutions using were deeply flawed. I wanted a space where writers confront readers across a space without institutionally sanctioned criteria. And I laid out specific ways for readers to respond to writers with a kind of naked empiricism: instead of mimicking teacher responses (how good or bad? what's wrong or right? how to fix it?), to make careful accounts of what the written words *caused to happen* in their minds. The writer's job is to write; the reader's job is to give what I called "movies of the reader's mind."

As we finally get to this third stage and *the* standard falls away—mainstream correct language—the concepts of "correct" and "wrong" will lose any meaning as a standard for writing. People will stop calling language *correct, incorrect,* or *wrong.* But they will continue to call writing *good* and *bad.* Readers will look for writing that is clear, well thought out or rewarding to read—or at least that does a needed job well enough—and be annoyed at writing that lacks those and other virtues. But writing can have those virtues no matter what version of English it uses. So we will still have plenty of "*standards*"; we'll lack only *a single standard* for acceptable language.

One of the reasons teachers often comment more on incorrect language than other problems is that these comments are incontestable. When teachers tell students that a certain reason is unpersuasive or that a paragraph should be cut or moved, they cannot help but know that plenty of their smart colleagues might well disagree. An assertive student might argue with those responses. But when teachers point out mistakes in grammar and spelling, the teacher is no danger.

> I shamelessly sidestep any attempt to define "good writing." It's not necessary for this book. And I'm not hiding behind the current "rhetorical" view:
>
> > there is no Platonic standard; everything is rhetorical; "good" just means good for this occasion for this genre and for these readers.
>
> That's true. But I confess also the unrhetorical (Platonic?) belief that we still need to talk about certain kinds of "good writing" apart from the rhetorical calculus. For there is the pesky fact that some readers find that some pieces of writing are excellent even though they are *uninviting, unclear,* and *illogical* and don't do the necessary rhetorical or genre job very well. It's a fact of human reading.

When many cultured literate people contemplate what I describe, they will fear for the death of good language, good writing, and clarity. Or else they'll settle for the cynical response: "So what else is new? The world has always been going to hell." But the English language and English literature didn't suffer during the various medieval and Renaissance periods when there was no single standard for correct written language. Shakespeare did pretty well with a fairly unsettled language. We will see plenty of good writing in the new culture of vernacular literacy.

What Will It Be Like in This New Culture of Vernacular Literacy?
I want to look at what can happen when people don't have to worry about the kind of language they use. Consider LaJuane. Early in the high school year—while he was still dominated by the feeling that writing *means* correct grammar—he wrote this:

I Realy Injoy the sport. I like Hiting and running. We had a great team and great year. I would like to encourage all to play the sporth.

This is the kind of play-it-safe defensive writing that students often produce. LaJuane had doubtless been corrected over and over for wrong grammar and other mistakes.

But when his new teacher responded to this paper, she didn't make corrections; she invited him to forget about right and wrong and use whatever language came easily to mouth and mind. She just asked some questions. When he revised, here's what he came up with:

When the halmut toches my Head my body turns Like doctor Jeckel and Mr. Hide. I become a safage. And there's no one who can stop me when this happens. My blood starts racing my hart pumping. Like a great machine of power. And when the football moves that's the time for me to move and get that quarterback. And anyone who get's in my way is asking for problems. (Christensen "The Politics of Correction" 20)

Lajuane's teacher helped him realize that he could exploit speech or a speech-like process of talking onto the page—instead of trying to "write writing" or use correct language.

In her teaching, Linda Christensen didn't ignore issues of proper literacy—but she dealt with one problem at a time slowly and systematically, starting with what she decided was easiest—the rules for capitalization. And when her students made "errors" that came from Black English or African American Language ("she say . . . "), she helped them see that they are following a coherent grammar—and see the simple differences between those rules and what's needed for standardized written English.

Here's a poem that was written as a nonstop freewrite in a workshop run by Pat Schneider's organization, Amherst Writers and Artists. The author is Robert Hastings, ten years old at the time.

WEED
It is life.
It grows from the ground.
It is ground up like meat.
It gives him a sharp and good feeling,
that gives me a sharp and painful anger.
He rolls it like a red carpet
and licks it like a lollipop.
My anger gets deeper
as the smell gets worse.
As he smokes me
I get hotter and hotter. (32)

(This was published in Schneider's chapter, "Writing to Empower the Silenced" in her book, *Writing Alone and With Others*. For more about Schneider and the organization, see Chapter 7. You can find lots of other good writing by children in publications of *Teachers and Writers Collaborative,* an organization that sends writers into the schools to help children write imaginatively.)

Here is a passage from a long prose memoir written by a mature adult, Estelle Jones, who spent most of her life as a domestic servant. Having been the child of sharecroppers in South Carolina in the first decade of the twentieth century, she went to school somewhat irregularly and only to the third grade. Her fifty-six page manuscript is one long paragraph, handwritten closely, single spaced, on lined paper. It can be a little confusing to read (especially with all the dialogue), so I put a somewhat copy edited version of it in a box afterward.

> . . . . what i always want to be it was a nurst. but you had to have too years of schooling or more. now I am old I still want to be a nurst. now back to this baby which is a Boy. he is about eight. my madam one morning say Estelle I say yes. she say I deside for you to work part time with a friend of mine I say o. she say dont you think that will be good. I say yes if you say. well she say the lady could pay half and i pay half of the money I say I see my madam say I will call her now make arangement to when you start because my children are older enough now to help and i dont need a made all the time. this was a part of the job i would not have but I went alone with my madam. because i work on a job or I dont work but too people and sharing money i never would have that kind of thing too hard as it is. my madam say as she going to phone she turn back Estelle you will work for the lady morning wont you. I say no well when she say. I say afternoon my madam say no I want you to work for her morning you go to her at 9:30 to one thirty then me afternoon. but I say no I work for lady afternoon you morning. my madam say you are not being fair to me I say what is fair she say I had you first so I can say when you to work. I want you afternoon I say I go to lady afternoon my madam what about my dinner I say what about that lady dinner. now my madam want to no why I want to give lady afternoon. I say so when I finish working I can take bus like all other girls and go to Paterson. come back next morning 9:30. my madam sit down say I am no place now. You see my madam no and had it all plane. if I work for lady morning at my madam I would have made breakfast wash dishes clean House all that before I left. then go to other lady nine to about too then come back after noon clean house again cook wash iron dinner for company and no rest. again I almost left my job but the deal diden went through on both of those job it wash iron clean house cook take care children. I would leave the house to work but with all my cloth. I dont mind working on no job if I can make extra money for my self but not something some body fosting me to do. so I diden work for the lady. (Unpublished MS)

Jones's manuscript is a draft that hasn't gone through revising or copy editing. Few writers would send out a text like this, even in the culture of vernacular literacy that I predict, without giving some help to readers. And a writer with this little schooling would doubtless ask for help in copy editing—perhaps in revising too. Here's what I get when I try for minimal copy editing. I've changed mostly just spelling, punctuation, and formatting—trying to preserve her language. (She never revised it and I wouldn't dare try.)

. . . What I always want to be it was a nurse. But you had to have two years of schooling or more. Now I am old and I still want to be a nurse.

Now back to this baby, which is a boy. He is about eight. My madam one morning say "Estelle." I say "Yes." She say "I decide for you to work part time with a friend of mine." I say "Oh." She say, "don't you think that will be good?" I say "Yes if you say." "Well," she say, "the lady could pay half and I pay half of the money." I say "I see." My madam say "I will call her now and make arrangement for when you start because my children are old enough now to help and I don't need a maid all the time." This was a part of the job I would not have, but I went along with my madam. Because I work on a job or I don't work, but two people and sharing money—I never would have that kind of thing. Too hard as it is. My madam, as she going to phone, she turn back: "Estelle you will work for the lady mornings won't you." I say "No." "Well when?" she say. I say "afternoon." My madam say "No I want you to work for her mornings. You go to her 9:30 to 1:30. Then to me afternoons." But I say "No I work for the lady afternoons, you mornings." My madam say "You are not being fair to me." I say "What is fair?" She say "I had you first so I can say when you work. I want you afternoon." I say "I go to lady afternoons."

My madam, "What about my dinner?" I say "What about that lady dinner?" Now my madam want to know why I want to give lady afternoon. I say "So when I finish working I can take the bus like all the other girls and go to Paterson. Come back next morning, 9:30."

My madam sat down and say "I am no place now." You see, my madam know and had it all plan. If I work for the lady mornings, then at my madam I would have made breakfast, wash dishes, clean house—all that before I left in the morning. Then go to the other lady 9 till about 2, then come back afternoon, clean house again cook, wash, iron, dinner for company, and no rest.

Again I almost left my job but the deal didn't went through. On both of those job it wash, iron, clean house, cook, take care of children. I would leave the house to work but with all my clothes. I don't mind working on a job if I can make extra money for my self but not something somebody forcing me to do. So I didn't work for the lady.

In our present culture of proper literacy, with its single standard for correct serious writing, potential writers tend to get this message:

First you have to learn to write right. Once you learn to do that, then we'll find out if you can write anything good.

In the culture of vernacular literacy, the message will be more like this:

Write whatever you want and however you want. Use any kind of language—including your spoken language. You'll find that it's easy to put your words down. You can write just for yourself. But it's also easy to get words to readers by photocopying, emailing, or putting them on the web. Nevertheless, if you want many readers to read what you write, you might have to learn to write better than you do now. You might want to revise and perhaps get feedback. Still, there's no telling what people will like to read on the web. If you put out what I or other "experienced writers" call not good enough, some people may read it and like it and even reply—perhaps even many people. But whether or not they read or respond, the main thing is that you get to write it and put it out for others. And if you do this, you'll be learning to be a writer and getting better at it.

And teachers? What will we do in a world where there is no longer a single standard for correct written English—where it's legitimate to write in any version of spoken English? Our plight will be dire. We'll have to learn to tell the difference between writing that's *right* and writing that we judge *good* or *effective*.

There are stages in learning to do this. First we'll have to learn to ignore all issues of correctness and give feedback on the content in a piece of writing—the thinking, plot, imagery, metaphors, rhetoric—paying no attention to whether the surface conforms to the conventions of the dialect we call correct, edited "standard" written English. Some teachers have learned to do this, but many still have trouble.

In our culture teachers often feel *obliged* to "correct errors"—even though

> Here's a sad comment by an experienced teacher about a piece of writing by a speaker of AAE: "Only now can I really address the underlying thinking and understanding problems—because previously the writing was so atrocious that I couldn't see them." (I took this from a composition list-serv, but it's a common enough response—sometimes from teachers of color.) Nevertheless, it's mostly members of the larger public who get completely distracted by misspelling or "bad grammar."

that's the least satisfying or interesting part of our job. So speakers of stigmatized languages tend to get too much "error correction" and too little help with the substance of their thinking. This is sometimes a problem for mainstream students too: too much red ink leads them to be preoccupied with error and to compensate by writing oversimple wooden language.

Style. What will be trickier for most teachers will be learning to give useful feedback on the *style* in a piece of writing—once we say that anyone's vernacular spoken language is okay. But at least we'll no longer be trying to serve two masters: correctness and quality. We can put all our attention on quality. The tricky part will be helping students decide whether they want to experiment with code meshing or hybridity—and how to use it skillfully. (See the box on this topic on p. 330 in Chapter 16. Suresh Canagarajah—with his eye on World Englishes and the international scene—explores the widespread and effective use of hybridity and code meshing in general. For lots on code meshing, see Young and Martinez.)

Let's stand back and look at the main substantive criteria that most teachers use in evaluating *essays* of any sort:

> Are the ideas good or interesting? Is the thinking sound and the reasoning persuasive and more or less valid? Does it do the job required by this occasion and genre? Is the organization effective? Are the sentences clear and strong?

The important point here is that *all these goals can be achieved brilliantly in any version of English*! Teachers will learn to focus their attention on the substantive criteria and teach them, and give students feedback on how well they meet them.

Surface features. Of course these too must be faced. The surface of writing is what readers see first—especially if they don't approve of it. So even after we've attained vernacular literacy, writers will still need to copy edit for spelling, grammar, and punctuation. (This is the process I used on the passage from Estelle Jones earlier in the chapter.)

Spelling. There is a huge psychic investment in spelling in our culture, and that makes it difficult for many people to think rationally about it (see Kress). Many people get upset—even angry—at deviations from "correct" standard spelling. If I try to suggest a literacy where multiple spellings are acceptable, I find people throwing up their hands and envisioning total anarchy. They have trouble seeing the difference between *"wrong* spelling" (which will no longer be a meaningful concept) and *random, careless, variable* spelling that does in fact needlessly distract or annoy readers. For writing to work well, the spelling (like punctuation) should help readers perform the text in their minds. And most people will continue to make lots of typos that will need correcting. Think of careless emails where people don't bother to fix all the confusion sown by careless fingers.

For most nonmainstream versions of English there is no official orthography. But conventions grow up—especially with the increase of publications in alternative versions of English (like AAL and Hawaiian Creole English). I don't know how spelling decisions get worked out between copy editors and authors who write in nonmainstream versions of English. Perhaps different writers or publishing houses use somewhat different spellings. But consistent spelling *within* a text will spare readers from needless distraction. (The *Academie Fran-caise* has begun to sanction alternative spelling with a number of words.)

I first began to notice and think about writing in stigmatized speech in 1996 during a year I taught at the University of Hawaii. I learned of the remarkable flowering of literature in Hawaiian Creole English (HCE). And I learned of an interesting disagreement among Hawaiian HCE poets in the early days. Joe Hadley was an early good poet and he used a spelling that highlighted the distance between so-called "Pidgin" and mainstream English. So what he wrote was correspondingly difficult for mainstream English readers. Perhaps he wanted that. Here's the opening of his most famous poem:

Chalukyu Insai
yuno smaw kid taim
sooo mach mo pridi no
wai yofala laik skreip damounten ladet
waistaim

It's much easier to understand when read aloud, like Chaucer (not that I got every word when I had a chance to hear him in 1975 when I was there for a workshop). It could be translated like this:

> **Look You Inside**
> You know—small kid time
> So much more pretty now
> Why you fellows like to scrape the mountain like that?
> Waste of time
>
> Most later "Pidgin" poets chose an orthography easier for mainstream readers. Here's the opening from Juliet Kono's "A Scolding from My Father."
>
> **What kind Japanee you?**
> Nothing more worse in the world
> than one Japanee
> who like be something
> he not
> No matter how much you like—
> no can!
>
> This change in the written Hawaiian Creole English (and it involves more than just spelling) *may* reflect some drift of the Pidgin toward mainstream English. I doubt that Bamboo Ridge Press would have pressed for a more accessible orthography. They spearheaded the truly impressive Renaissance of writing in this version of English. (See Charlene Sato for the story of *"decreolization"* and how creole speakers sometimes push back against what may feel like the destructive magnet of the mainstream language.) Interestingly, Haitian (French) Creole does have a standard orthography. I can't resist attributing this to the influence of French culture with their preoccupation with "rational" standardization.

Grammar. Even when readers don't object to different versions of English, they can still be annoyed by grammar that is needlessly random and careless. But this is a tricky matter. For inconsistent grammar and register can be conscious and effective. Teachers will have to think about whether the student is deliberately using some hybridity or code meshing or even benefiting from unconscious but effective accidents.

Punctuation. In this coming culture of vernacular literacy, literate readers will no longer insist on calling punctuation wrong when it violates rules of our present grammatical tradition. They'll assume to start with that the punctuation represents the writer's directions for how to hear or inwardly perform the text. So if those directions lead to incoherence, readers will understandably object. In short, in this brave open new world, writers will still need to guard against carelessness or bad punctuation choices—*if* they care about getting readers, and not all writers do.

Imagining the Future

Readers have always felt free to like or dislike various writing *styles*. ("*I hate stream of consciousness novels.*") But when they say, "I *hate* that style," they don't usually think of the style as *illegal*. This is how it will be with versions of written English—most of them deriving from various spoken Englishes. Some readers will say, "I *hate* that version of English," but they won't have any feeling that it's illegal or not valid. The gradual dissipation of prejudice doesn't mean the absence of strong preferences. A few vernaculars will be hard for many mainstream readers, but in the absence of prejudice, most will be read fairly easily by most English speakers. Think of how many readers even now like to read rap—which is often not so easy to understand.

So much for readers, but what will it be like for writers? Here's a little mini-drama of a writer who wakes up in this brave new world:

> How wonderful. When I want to write something, I just open my mouth and write down whatever language comes out. I talk through my fingers. It doesn't matter what brand of talk-language I have—whether it's Texas hill country English or Hispanic/Latino inflected English; it doesn't matter how I choose to spell the words. What I put down will count as officially correct for writing. Hooray! Writing is a piece of cake!

Months pass while her excitement leads to lots and lots of writing. But then further reactions gradually emerge:

> Uh oh. There's a big problem. Writing *is* a piece of cake. But what if I want someone to *read* what I wrote. In this new world, readers see my talk-language as perfectly acceptable and comprehensible. But they usually stop reading after only a few minutes. And if I can persuade them to tell me honestly why, they say things like, "This is unclear," "This is disorganized," "This doesn't do the job that's needed." "This isn't very interesting," "This isn't carefully thought out."

> Oh dear. I can use whatever language that comes out of my mouth—but I still have to make it interesting, clear, and thoughtful? I have to make it fit the context? That's hard. I thought writing was going to be easy.

> Still, things are better than they were. I used to have to get my writing correct and get it good. My struggle to get it correct often undermined my struggle to get it good. Now I can forget about correctness and use whatever language comes easily and naturally. I can concentrate on the more important and interesting goal: making it good. I can put all my attention on how to get my writing smart, strong, clear, interesting—and pleasing—to readers.

But let me turn my focus away from the individual experiences of writers and readers. What about the *culture* as a whole? I'm writing this book because I have a vision of the democratization of literacy and especially writing. This was what pulled me to *Writing Without Teachers*, but the vision wasn't yet clear to me. Now, however, I see us already moving toward a culture of literacy where more people feel empowered to write. Many people have long experienced themselves as excluded from the networks of power that are bound up with literacy. This is changing. And as more people take up writing, we will benefit from a richer palette of writing. Shakespeare and other Elizabethans enriched the sixteenth-century palette of writing in English, and the same thing can happen again.

The Long View

I ask you to consider the possibility that we've been going through what is really a brief historical interlude during which the forces of standardization in written language have been peculiarly strong. The eighteenth century brought us a climactic frenzy of standardization and prescriptivism, and with it an unusual resistance to spoken language for correct writing. In fact, the very concept of "correctness" in language was an invention of the eighteenth century. Before then there were various ways to complain about "bad" written language—calling it incoherent, hard to understand, or too high or low in register for the occasion. But people seldom invoked the standard of "correct" and "incorrect."

When we think of how long it took for Dante's Italian and the other vernacular spoken languages to become acceptable for writing, the eighteenth century was just yesterday. And now we're entering a new period of change. Our unusually strict standard is dissipating—and much more quickly than in Dante's era. With the internet, literacy is on the road toward accepting various versions of spoken language. Globalism is somewhat loosening the grip of many nationalisms. It's tragic how English is undermining so many languages, but in the process, English is getting more multiple; people around the globe are taking more control of the version of English they need; and those Englishes are more and more inflected by the spoken language.

In most historical periods, schools have had the job of trying to hold the line against change or "*degeneration*." In multilingual and multidialectal societies, teachers have traditionally manned the front lines in this battle. But it's pretty clear that teachers don't have a prayer of stopping this remarkable process we are going through now: linguistic divergence and the dissipation of a single standard. My suggestion, on the contrary, is that we teachers now help move the process along.

I'm not asking teachers to invite or reward careless or bad writing in itself. (One exception: many people cannot actually freewrite or talk onto the page for early drafts without a little help in being careless—in stopping themselves from correcting.) The goal is good writing, and that takes enormous care. But we teachers can now create more space for more good writing by inviting more versions of English. We can empower more students to write well by opening the door to the various spoken languages they know best. For the time being, however, in our present culture of proper literacy, if we want to help our students prosper in most of the classrooms and jobs we are trying to prepare them for, we also need to help them learn to do whatever is necessary to edit out the grammatical forms that trigger mainstream readers to declare "error."

People in our present culture will continue for a while to confuse writing in spoken dialects with *bad* writing. But even though we teachers cannot legislate cultural values directly, we can do so *indirectly* by inspiring more good writing in different vernacular spoken languages—writing that people will want to read. Think of Dante.

I don't see us *so* far away from a world where *everyone* can say

> I have something I want to write. I find writing easy, but I find it very hard work to get my thoughts and words clear and strong. I'm sure I'll be frustrated trying to craft it till it's good—and even copy edit. But I'm looking forward to the work because I know that the *medium* I'll be using—the clay I'll be trying to shape into something I love—is *my own language*.

Appendix I

How Freewriting Went from Dangerous to No Big Deal in the Composition and Rhetoric Community

In the 1950s and 1960s when Ken Macrorie introduced freewriting ("Words in the Way"), it was neglected because it seemed dangerous. Now it's neglected because it seems ho hum. The story of this gradual change is interesting—especially for people in the field of composition and rhetoric.

The Initial Resistance to Freewriting

There was still a bit of resistance to freewriting when my first book came out in 1973—twenty years after Ken first introduced it. Freewriting invites students to relinquish *care,* so it produces something that scares many teachers: carelessness—in both thinking and language. In addition it often leads to personal writing that looks at things in terms of one's own experiences and feelings—even when the topic is academic. So it leads to writing that is easy to call self-indulgent.

In the first chapter, I described how people often ascribe some *magic* to the written word, and I suspect that we see here another reason why some people disapproved of freewriting. It leads to wrong writing, and I think many people at some unconscious level feel as though a wrong written word has power to infect. If that sounds silly, try the following exercise and note your reactions: quickly write down as many lies or false statements as you can think of about some topic that matters to you or that you are trying to figure out. First try for "whoppers." (*It's good if everyone cheats. Obama is stupid.*) Then try for tempting lies or seductively wrong ideas. (*It does no harm to cheat on your taxes. Obama preaches hope, but that just shows his naive lack of clear thinking.*) People often feel slightly disturbed when they write what they know is false. They often feel a certain inner twitch that says, "This could do harm." (People often feel the same unease when they deliberately write grammar that they disapprove of or hate.)

I suggest, however, that you try this kind of thing the next time you are trying to develop some thinking on a complex topic. It's a productive exercise that helps you think more clearly and it brings new insights. (See "Errors and Lies" in my *Writing With Power,* 72ff.) There used to be a nonmagical justification for this unease. It was hard to change what we wrote on vellum or parchment, wrote by hand in ink, or typed out. "Down in black and white" means *permanent.* But computers have changed this. In my early workshops, I noticed that some engineers and scientists seemed to be more open to freewriting than faculty from many other fields. This surprised me. I assumed they would be more "hard-headed," especially than my humanities tribe—more resistant to "wasting their time" with careless writing. But this was the period when computers were just beginning to be used for writing, and these engineers and scientists were using them before most other faculty. They were the first people who could see written words as mere pixels or bits of temporary electronic resistance on a screen. They had an early lens into a larger truth: written words are ephemeral. In these early days freewriting was hardest to sell to humanities faculty. Literature faculty were sometimes the most resistant—and sometimes still are. I sense they are more likely than most other faculty members to have a feeling for the magic of writing. But now pretty much everyone—even the most mandarin members of English departments—has digested the fact that written words are just pixel-dust. In a real sense, written words are more evanescent than speech (see my "Shifting Relationships between Speech and Writing").

A New Round of Resistance to Freewriting on Theoretical Grounds

After the initial resistance to freewriting died down in the 1980s, a new round flourished in the 1990s. This time, it wasn't fear of carelessness or bad magic. It was a theoretical objection growing out of the strong tide of postmodernism and anti-foundationalism in the academic world. This frame of reference helped people see (what is of course true) that there is no such thing as true freedom. Thus David Bartholomae wrote:

> [F]ree writing . . . is an expression of a desire for an institutional space free from institutional pressures, a cultural process free from the influence of culture, an historical moment outside of history, an academic setting free from academic writing. . . . As I think this argument through, I think of the pure and open space, the frontier classroom. . . . The open classroom; a free writing . . . an expression of a desire for an institutional space free from institutional pressures, a cultural process free from the influence of culture, an historical moment outside of history, an academic setting free from academic writing. (Bartholomae 64)

He rings the word "free" like a bell, speaking of "the story of an education, in a setting that is free, Edenic or Utopian" (64). He scoffs at the idea of "stepping outside of the real time and place of our writing—heading down the river, heading out to the frontier, going nowhere" (65). He links freewriting to what he calls the characteristically American dream of freedom—which he links in turn to manifest destiny, free land, and slaughtered Indians. In short, "There is no writing done in the academy that is not academic writing" (64). He wants to teach students to "see their position inside a text they did not invent and can never, at least completely, control" (65). Freewriting means cultural naivete.

An Unexamined Consensus: Why No One Fights Freewriting or Wrong Writing Any More

This objection is still on the books. But the living conviction seems to have gone out of it. No one much objects to freewriting or even fights for it (but see Bean and Elbow for a recent essay on the crucial political dimension of freewriting). In *The Bedford Bibliography for Teachers of Writing*, Bizzell and Herzberg call it "part of every writing teacher's repertoire" (8). Somehow, no one seems troubled any more about encouraging students to write fast and carelessly and to create lots of wrong words and thoughts during the early stages of writing something—even when they have to end up with something careful, good, and correct. It's not quite that so many teachers explicitly say, "Speak carelessly onto the page in your casual home vernacular," but that's what's left when people stop fighting freewriting.

Why? How did it happen that no one argues any more against all this wrongness and vernacular speech in writing? I'd love to think my brilliant advocacy did the job. But for a better explanation, I have to zoom through a quick crude history of composition studies.

Beginning in the 1960s a burgeoning number of teachers and researchers began to coalesce into a field that hadn't yet existed. In a sense, they were just looking for companionship and support as teachers of writing during a period when there were more and more first-year college writing courses. Soon there grew up a shared sense of trying to work out a theory of how writing happens and how we should teach it. By the 1970s and 1980s, a large proportion of people working in this new undefined field came together in what was eventually called the "process movement." These folks were from various fields besides English, but they shared an interest in trying to figure out the *process* that people go through or should go through when they write.

Of course there was already an ancient venerable field that had come to deal with writing, and it stretched back to pre-classical Greece: *rhetoric*. But the process movement was something new. For one thing, lots of the members (like me) had no training whatsoever in rhetoric. Many came even from the social sciences and did lots of empirical and sometimes quantitative research on people with pens in their hands—sometimes recorded on video cameras. In the long history of rhetoric, there is plenty of advice for speakers and writers, but most of that advice was about the *product*: what makes language work well or badly for an audience or how to arrange the parts of a speech or essay. There wasn't so much attention to the process of *getting* things written or on what rhetoric called "invention": the mysterious process of finding ideas you didn't have before. I'm pretty sure I read a passage (but can't find it now) from an eminent eighteenth-century rhetorician saying, in effect, that we can't investigate invention because the process is too hidden and mysterious.

But it was exactly this mysterious question that interested folks in the early process movement: where do words and ideas come from and how can we get more of them and what goes on as we try to write? In addition, the field of composition was firmly rooted in the *teaching of writing* in a way that rhetoric was not. Indeed, it could be said that the whole field grew out of the huge influx of veterans returning to college in the 1950s on the GI Bill. There came to be a vastly increased need for first-year writing courses to help these students deal with college, and this gave rise to a new generation of teachers trying to figure out how to teach writing. This inherent link to teaching marks composition apart from almost every other academic field.

By the end of the 1980s, however, there grew a hankering for composition to be a "real discipline" (ideally like physics), and not just a collection of writing teachers trying to think in various ways about writing. *Research* and *scholarship* became the watchwords and many scholars and researchers began to reject this label of "process" as something from the "old undisciplined days" and even to treat the term as tainted. Our major journal would no longer publish articles that simply described useful teaching practices: there had to be scholarship and theory. Still, others defended the process label; there were arguments about freewriting and voice and personal writing and other matters.

Nevertheless—and this is the important point in my argument here— everyone had been deeply affected by the process movement in a way that's too little acknowledged. Almost all active people in this newly contentious field had settled into a remarkable consensus. Everyone agreed—and still agrees— that a *process of drafting and revising* is central to any wise and fruitful model for how to write. In short, from the 1970s onward, there has been a widespread agreement that *most* writers, even the most talented ones, tend to produce drafts and later revise those drafts—often after getting some response from readers—and that we should try to teach our students to use this kind of process. Especially, we should try to persuade students to avoid the seductive trap of trying to write a perfect first draft: trying to get every sentence or paragraph finished and right before going on to the next sentence or paragraph.

It's a corollary that we should fight against the pervasive cultural myth that only those *born with talent* can ever write well. This myth often carries a romantic/tragic flavor: *The sign of true inborn talent is how much you suffer— and drink—and commit suicide.* Indeed, the myth sometimes implies that the suffering itself is the *source* of the talent—not just a sign of it. Teachers and theorists of writing came to realize how much harm this myth does to teaching. It makes many unskilled students give up (*I'm just not a person who could ever learn to write well*), and it leads elitist teachers to feel that their only job is to assign writing and see who turns out to be talented—and pretty much give up on the rest.

Of course people interested in writing have always known that most writers produce early drafts or versions that aren't yet right. A good handful of teachers in the "old pre-process days" found examples of messy drafts by Hemingway or Fitzgerald to show students. But somehow it took this new consensus in the academic field of composition to get most teachers to put teeth into the notion that drafting and revising are crucial even for talented students. Until this new consensus began to percolate outward, not many teachers of writing required students to turn in a draft of their essays for teacher response and even peer response—*before* revising for a final version that counts for the grade. But in the late 1970s and 1980s, many teachers learned this hugely productive teaching practice that centers on writing as a process. Requiring that students turn in drafts for feedback was an obvious sign of a teacher whose goal was to help students actually learn to *improve* their writing—not just to tell students what was strong or weak in their final drafts.

By the 1980s and 1990s, the field of composition and rhetoric had become quite divided and seriously contentious. People argued not just about "process" as a label (and whether we were "post process"), about freewriting, voice, and personal writing. Now, criticism of "old-fashioned" or out-of-date ideas and practices tended to be framed as arguments about the nature of knowledge, the self, and society. Really it was a struggle over how this increasingly powerful field should define itself: what would be our *paradigm*. With all the fighting going on, no one much noticed—and not even now—how remarkably united we all are on this nontrivial consensus about the writing process: everyone should draft and revise and try for reader response along the way.

This consensus brought with it a tacit corollary that particularly interests me: an acceptance of *writing wrong*. Most teachers and scholars wouldn't go so far as to say what fans of freewriting might say: *that it's fine to write wrong.* They'd probably say something more guarded:

> As we write, we try at every moment to write our best, but our best as we write a first draft will virtually always have problems not just in form but in content. At any early stage, we can't have enough perspective to know what's going to be right or wrong for this piece—even if we start with a careful outline. Besides, writing has a social dimension, and we can't make a good decision about how our words will work with readers till we've heard reactions and suggestions from some of them.

They might not say "wrong is fine," but they are implicitly saying "wrong is inevitable."

So here is my argument. When teachers and scholars of writing as a profession admitted the need for drafting and revising—and thus the inevitability of wrong writing—they stopped worrying about freewriting (even if there is no such thing as true freedom). They tended to neglect freewriting rather than exploit its possibilities, and many even held it in some scorn, but they no longer felt a need to fight it. And when the profession as a whole acknowledged tacitly that "it's fine to freewrite," they were also acknowledging, perhaps without realizing it, that "it's fine to speak onto the page."

I have hopes then, that when I argue in this book for speaking onto the page, people in my field will have to stop and realize that the battle has already been won while they weren't noticing. As they've stressed the importance of drafting and revising for decades, they've tacitly accepted freewriting—and in so doing, I'd say, they've tacitly accepted using the vernacular for speaking onto the page.

Autobiographical Fragment: How I Learned to Write Wrong

In 1957 I won a fellowship from Williams College to study for two years at Oxford where I found myself in the standard Oxford undergraduate situation. I was expected to write an essay each week and come to my tutor's rooms to read it aloud to him. My tutor was Jonathan Wordsworth, the grandnephew of the poet. This was his first year as a don and (as I gradually realized), he strove to be fashionably acerbic in that venerable role. (I missed out on Neville Coghill who'd gone to another college for a prestigious chair—a don who was willing to risk being genial and kind.)

During one tutorial he cleaned his rifle as I read my essay to him. On another occasion, when I read out loud the title of the famous poem by Marvell in my broad-voweled American accent: "On a Drohp of Doo." Jonathan broke in with his clipped Oxford version: "Uhn a Djrup of Djyew! Maybe *that's* why you don't understand po-try, Elbow. You don't know what it *sounds* like." By the middle of fall term I found myself knocking on his "oak" (Oxford for "door") and telling him, "I don't have an essay for you. I tried as hard as I could, but I couldn't write it." And I really *had* tried hard. I'd spent the whole week writing initial sentences, paragraphs, and pages and throwing them all away.

In my weekly diligent inability to produce an essay, I became so stuck—so unhappy, helpless, angry—that I fell into uncontrolled blurting of my feelings onto the page. I felt scared and alone in this new country and I wasn't able to pour out my frustration and "unprintable" anger to any living person. In my unhappiness I just let words fly out of my mouth-and-fingers and onto the page. It was pure venting. In retrospect, I see I was speaking onto the page and freewriting—but I didn't have either concept in 1957.

I limped along this way through the first year—occasionally producing an essay—and eventually changed tutors my second year, which enabled me to write more productively. But in fact neither the essays nor the lack of them counted for anything official; they were not graded and had no bearing on one's actual success in getting a degree. Credit and the degree depended entirely on nine three-hour exams crammed into five days at the end of two years (three years for a British undergraduate). In spite of those high-stakes exam conditions—or perhaps because of them—I *wrote*! There was no time to ago-nize. Exams have an interesting affinity to freewriting—you don't have much time and you just have to keep putting down words. If they're not good words, you simply keep going. If I'd been writing an essay at home, I'd have crossed out sentences and thrown away pages, but I had no time. This was blurting of a more pragmatic sort. I didn't do well, but I survived. The results came on a postcard from Jonathan: "Beta minus minus. About what we expected." (He forgot to say, "Congratulations. Maybe you should do more nonstop writing.")

But when I returned to this country to start a Ph.D. in English at Harvard (a stupid move for someone burned out by schooling), I soon couldn't even limp. I'd always been a diligent student, and the more trouble I had writing, the more diligent I became—and all to no avail. After a semester and a half I had to quit before I was kicked out. (I explore this story and its implications more fully in "Illiteracy at Oxford and Harvard.")

I felt like a complete failure and thought I would never again enter an insti-tution of learning. But through an accident of sudden summer openings at M.I.T. (and the "old boys network") I got a job as a humanities instructor there. I discovered that even though you can't be a student if you can't write, the disability is no impediment to teaching. I gradually overcame my fear and enjoyed teaching and decided that institutions of learning weren't so bad after all—if you were on the right side of the desk. After three years at M.I.T., I had the chance to be one of five founding faculty members at an experiment called Franconia College.

It was during these five years of teaching (1960 to 1965) that I read some-thing by Ken Macrorie. I hugely admired what I read and I sent him a pamphlet on writing that I had written for Franconia students, and he sent me a sweet reply. It follows therefore that I must have read his words about freewriting. But I don't remember it, and in my pamphlet for Franconia students, my only advice for generating ideas was to make an outline! I don't remember ever asking students to freewrite. Of course I'd already done plenty of personal nonstop venting on paper, but I didn't think of this as "freewriting" or as useful for school. I'm not sure when the word freewriting entered my own real vocabulary.

When I discovered how *good* the Franconia students were (despite terrible high school records) and also got excited at the two-year interdisciplinary co-taught core course we devised, I decided I wanted to push for change in higher education. This was the 60s, after all, and it was easy to think ambitious thoughts. But I feared that people would say, "He just doesn't like the system because he couldn't handle it" (true enough, I guess). I felt I had to remove my own stigma as a failure, so I clambered up again onto the horse that had thrown me to the ground. I began on a Ph.D. again—this time, fortunately, at Brandeis.

When I started, I was so scared that I went beyond *making* a plan; I actually stuck to it. For every essay assignment I insisted that I produce some kind of draft a *full week* before the deadline—and it had to have the required number of pages. This changed everything. When I started to try to follow my plan, my writing fell into the normal rut. I would write sentences and paragraphs and cross them out, write pages and rip them up. I was ashamed of what I wrote. I was a well-educated person with good taste. But I soon saw that if I needed twenty pages by tomorrow in order to keep my vow, I would have to stop crossing out so much and let myself write near-trash. I learned (as William Stafford famously described how he dealt with difficulty in writing) to "lower my standards."

It turned out that once I had twenty pages in my hand, no matter how bad, disorganized and off the mark they were—and a week to work on my mess—I could make an acceptable paper, sometimes a good one. In this way, I more or less prospered. But I felt scared the whole time: I tried to keep my distance and treat graduate study as a crass pragmatic job—like picking up smelly garbage for pay—rather than as part of my identity. I just wanted a degree; I didn't want to get personally invested in what I was studying.

So here's what I learned: if I try to write right, I fail; if I let myself write wrong—or when necessary force myself to write wrong—I can get it right. I can't transform the chaos in my head into coherence on paper. But if I put the chaos in my head on paper, I can transform *that* into coherence. And there's a new insight that I've only figured out now as the germ for this book: when I write without stopping, not having time to plan my words, I am relinquishing my writing gear and using my mental *speaking gear*.

Three Stages in Succumbing to Wrongness

I see three stages in my acceptance of wrong writing.

1. During my first year or so of graduate classes at Brandeis when I finally learned to produce the essays for my graduate teachers, I knew how bad some of these pages were that I forced myself to not rip up (because I needed twenty

of them by tomorrow morning). But at every moment I was still doing what most writers do: struggling to make every idea and every sentence as good as I could—and organize the parts as well as I could. In effect, I was learning the real meaning of the word *best*. I didn't formulate the idea this way, but I was saying to myself, *This may be terrible writing, but it is in fact the <u>best</u> writing I can do right now.* (By the way, I wasn't really freewriting for much of this time. As often as not I was making myself put down one word or phrase—and then painfully, almostly muscularly, eking out another word or phrase.)

2. After a year or more of this I began to trust this process more and gradually learn to relax a bit. I realized that I didn't have to strain and struggle so hard for rightness or goodness as I worked at producing twenty pages. I began to trust that even if I put down almost every thought that came to mind—knowing very well that some of them were unsatisfactory or even wrong—I could still end up with a satisfactory or even good paper. I learned I could settle for whatever words came to mind and let them go down in whatever order came to mind. In this way I could write more quickly, with less anxiety about the badness of my draft writing. This made life easier—and I *still* found I could revise this more careless writing into acceptable or even good papers. I didn't really get to this stage until after I'd written *Writing Without Teachers* (perhaps five years after my Ph.D.). Seeing the actual book in print and hearing about people using the ideas helped me be better at practicing what I had preached.

3. Finally, I have realized that I have drifted into using a process that doesn't just invite wrongness for the sake of increased ease and copiousness; it also invites *play* and *creativity*. Finally, I've learned to feel something useful about the wrongness itself. Combined with a spirit of play, wrongness can lead to new insights. When we see that something is wrong, that means it may well be a window onto something we can't see—a lens onto some blind spot in our thinking. There may well be something valuable there that our sense of rightness prevents us from seeing. Giving a second glance at what's wrong—a less condemning glance—can open the doors to new thinking and new perceptions: a different lens on the world. (This is another way of talking about a line of thinking I have pursued for my whole career, the believing game. See my essays about that topic. By the way, the cognitive force in every metaphor is a piece of wrongness; see "Metaphor as Mistake," Walker Percy.)

Appendix II

A *Sampling of Published Writing in Non-Mainstream Varieties of English*

For a wide-ranging collection of works in many different versions of English, see Dohra Ahmed's *Rotten English: A Literary Anthology*. New York: W. W. Norton, 2007.

AAL or Black English

Childress, Alice. *Like One of the Family*. Boston: Beacon, 1986. *Wedding Band: A Love/Hate Story in Black and White*. 1966.

Hurston, Zora Neale. *Their Eyes Were Watching God*. Philadelphia: J. B. Lippincott Company, 1937.

Sanchez, Sonia. *Shake Loose My Skin: New and Selected Poems*. Boston: Beacon, 1999.

Sapphire. *Push: A Novel*. New York: Knopf, 1996.

Smitherman, Geneva. See her columns in *English Journal* (collected as chapter 20 in her *Talkin That Talk*. See also parts of her *Talkin and Testifyin*. Detroit: Wayne State University Press [1986].

Walker, Alice. *The Color Purple*. New York: Harcourt Brace, 1982.

Caribbean Creole English

Bennett, Louise. *Selected Poems*. Kingston, Jamaica: Sangster's, 1982.

Clarke, Austin. *The Polished Hoe*. New York: Amistead, 2003. New York: Warner, 2000.

Hodge, Merle. *Crick-Crack Monkey*. London: Heinemann, 1981.

Hopkinson, Nalo. *The Midnight Robber*. New York: Warner, 2000.

Lovelace, Earl. *The Wine of Astonishment*. New York: Vintage, 1984.

The Penguin Book of Caribbean Verse in English (see section on oral and oral-influenced poetry). Harmondsworth, England: Penguin, 1986.

Sistren, with Honor Ford Smith, ed. *Lionheart Gal: Life Stories of Jamaican Women*. London: Women's Press, 1986.

Hawai'ian Creole English ("Pidgin")

Lum, Darrell H. Y. *Pass On, No Pass Back*. Honolulu: Bamboo Ridge Press, 1990.

Yamanaka, Lois-Ann. *Blu's Hanging*. New York: Farrar, 1997. *Saturday Night at the Pahala Theater*. Honolulu: Bamboo Ridge Press, 1993.

Hispanic/Latino/a English

Anzaldúa, Gloria. *Borderlands / La Frontera: The New Mestiza*. San Francisco: Spinters-Aunt Lute, 1987.

Cisneros, Sandra. *Woman Hollering Creek and Other Stories*. New York: Random House, 1991.

Diaz, Junot. *Drown*. New York: Riverhead, 1996. *The Brief Wondrous Life of Oscar Wao*. New York: Riverhead, 2007.

Rivera, Tomás. *. . . y no se lo trag'o la tierra/And the Earth Did Not Devour Him*. Houston: Arte P'ublico, 1992.

Trevino, Jes'us Salvador. *The Fabulous Sinkhole and Other Stories*. Houston: Arte P'ublico, 1995.

Scots

Kelman, James. *How Late It Was, How Late*. New York: Vintage, 1998.

Anthology of pieces in different versions of English

Ahmed, Dohra. *Rotten English: A Literary Anthology*. New York: W. W. Norton, 2007.

Also by Peter Elbow

Books

Writing Without Teachers. New York: Oxford University Press, 1973.

Oppositions in Chaucer. Middletown, CT: Wesleyan University Press, 1975.

(With Gerald Grant, David Riesman, and five others). *On Competence: A Critical Analysis of Competence-Based Reforms in Higher Education.* San Francisco: Jossey-Bass, 1979.

Writing With Power: Techniques for Mastering the Writing Process. New York: Oxford University Press, 1981.

Embracing Contraries: Explorations in Learning and Teaching. New York: Oxford University Press, 1986.

(With Pat Belanoff). *A Community of Writers: A Workshop Course in Writing.* New York: McGraw-Hill, 1989.

(With Pat Belanoff). *Sharing and Responding.* New York: McGraw-Hill, 1989.

What Is English? New York: Modern Language Association, 1990.

(With Pat Belanoff). *Being a Writer: A Community of Writers Revisited.* New York: McGraw-Hill, 2003.

Everyone Can Write: Essays toward a Hopeful Theory of Writing and Teaching Writing. New York: Oxford University Press, 2000.

Writing about Media: Teaching Writing, Teaching Media. Sausalito, CA: Media Education Foundation, 2008.

Edited Books or Collections

(With Pat Belanoff and Sheryl Fontaine). *Nothing Begins with N: New Explorations of Freewriting.* Carbondale: Southern Illinois University Press, 1990.

Pre/Text: An Interdisciplinary Journal of Rhetoric 11.1–2 (1990). Invited editor for a special issue devoted to personal and expressive writing that does the work of academic discourse.

Landmark Essays on Voice and Writing. Hermagoras Press (now published Mahwah, NJ: Lawrence Erlbaum), 1994.

(With Mary Deane Sorcinelli). *Writing to Learn: Strategies for Assigning and Responding to Writing in the Disciplines.* (A volume in the series, *New Directions for Teaching and Learning.*) San Francisco: Jossey-Bass, 1997.

Writing on the Edge. Spring 2000. Invited editor for a special issue devoted to stories of writing and teaching.

Essays, Articles, Reviews

"Two Boethian Speeches in *Troilus and Criseyde* and Chaucerian Irony." In *Literary Criticism and Historical Understanding.* Ed. Philip Damon. New York: Columbia University Press, 1967.

"A Method for Teaching Writing." *College English* 30.2 (November 1968). Followed by "Reply to Donald Hassler." 30.8 (May 1969).

"What Is a Conscientious Objector?" *Christian Century,* August 1968.

"The Definition of Teaching." *College English* 30.3 (December 1968).

"More Accurate Evaluation of Student Performance." *Journal of Higher Education* 40 (March 1969). (Also in *Embracing Contraries.*)

"Exploring My Teaching." *College English* 32.7 (April 1971). (A version was published in *Change Magazine,* January/February 1971, as "Teaching: My Students Tell Me." The essay is also in *Embracing Contraries.*)

"Real Learning and Nondisciplinary Courses." *Journal of General Education* 23.2 (1971). (Also in *Embracing Contraries.*)

"Shall We Teach or Give Credit? A Model for Higher Education." *Soundings* 54.3 (Fall 1971).

"Teacher Power." (Invited essay-review of *Pygmalion in the Classroom.*) *Elementary English,* June 1971.

"Concerning the Necessity of Teachers." (Invited response.) *Inter-Change: Journal of the Ontario Institute for Studies in Education* 2.4 (Winter 1971).

"Oppositions in *The Knight's Tale.*" *Chaucer Review* 7.2 (1973).

"The Pedagogy of the Bamboozled." *Soundings* 56.2 (Summer 1973). (Also in *Embracing Contraries.*)

"The Doubting Game and the Believing Game." In *Goal-Making for English Teaching.* Ed. Henry Maloney. Urbana IL: National Council of Teachers of English, 1973 (reprinted from appendix, *Writing Without Teachers*).

"Trying to Teach While Thinking about the End: Teaching in a Competence-Based Curriculum." In *On Competence: A Critical Analysis of Competence-Based Reforms in Higher Education,* Gerald Grant, David Riesman, et al. San Francisco: Jossey-Bass, 1979. (Also in *Embracing Contraries.*)

"Why Teach Writing?" and "What Is Good Writing?" *The Why's of Teaching Composition.* (no city): Washington Council of Teachers of English, 1978.

"Quick Revising." *Washington English Journal* 2.1 (Fall 1979).

"One to One Faculty Development." In *Learning about Teaching:* Volume 4 in the series *New Directions for Teaching and Learning.* Ed. Jack Noonan. San Francisco: Jossey-Bass, 1980.

"Taking the Crisis Out of the Writing Crisis." *Seattle Post-Intelligencer* 1 November 1981.

"Learning and Authentic Moments." *New Perspectives on Teaching and Learning:* Volume 7 in the series *New Directions for Teaching and Learning.* Ed. Warren Bryan Martin. San Francisco: Jossey-Bass, 1981.

"About Resistance to Freewriting and Feedback Groups." *Washington English Journal,* Winter 1982.

"Comments on Kavanaugh." (Invited response.) Little Three Symposium on "Metaphors and Representations." Wesleyan University. *Berkshire Review* 17 (1982).

"The Doubting Game and the Believing Game." *Pre/Text: An Inter-Disciplinary Journal of Rhetoric* 3.4 (Winter 1982).

"Teaching Writing by Not Paying Attention to Writing." In *Fforum: Essays on Theory and Practice in the Teaching of Writing*. Ed. Patricia Stock. Portsmouth, NH: Boynton/Cook, 1983.

"Embracing Contraries in the Teaching Process." *College English* 45 (1983). (Also in *Embracing Contraries*.) Followed by "Reply to Ronald Scheer and to Abraham Bernstein." *College English* 46.5 (September 1984).

"Spilt Milk." (Poem) *Soundings* 20, SUNY Stony Brook (Spring 1983).

"Teaching Thinking by Teaching Writing." *Change Magazine,* 15 (September 1983). (Reprinted in *Rethinking Reason: New Perspectives in Critical Thinking*. Albany: SUNY Press, 1994. Reprinted also as "Teaching Two Kinds of Thinking by Teaching Writing" in *Embracing Contraries*.)

"In the Beginning Was the Word." Review of *Before the First Word,* a videocassette published by the Encyclopaedia Brittanica Educational Foundation. *Change Magazine,* June 1984.

"The Challenge for Sentence Combining." In *Sentence Combining: A Rhetorical Perspective*. Ed. Don Daiker, Andrew Kerek, and Max Morenberg. Carbondale: Southern Illinois University Press, 1985.

"The Shifting Relationships between Speech and Writing." *College Composition and Communication* 36.2 (October 1985). (Braddock award for the best essay of the year in that journal.)

(With Pat Belanoff). "State University of New York: Portfolio-Based Evaluation Program." In *New Methods in College Writing Programs: Theory into Practice*. Ed. Paul Connolly and Teresa Vilardi. New York: Modern Language Association, 1986.

(With Pat Belanoff). "Using Portfolios to Increase Collaboration and Community in a Writing Program." *WPA: Journal of Writing Program Administration* 9.3 (Spring 1986).

(With Pat Belanoff). "Portfolios as a Substitute for Proficiency Examinations." *College Composition and Communication* 37.3 (October 1986).

"Methodological Doubting and Believing: Contraries in Inquiry." In *Embracing Contraries: Explorations in Learning and Teaching*. New York: Oxford University Press, 1986.

(With Jennifer Clarke). "Desert Island Discourse: The Benefits of Ignoring Audience." In *The Journal Book*. Ed. Toby Fulwiler. Portsmouth, NH: Boynton/ Cook 1987.

"Closing My Eyes as I Speak: An Argument for Ignoring Audience." *College English* 49.1 (January 1987).

Review of *Reclaiming the Classroom: Teacher Research as an Agency for Change*. Ed. Dixie Goswami and Peter Stillman. *ADE Bulletin* 87 (Fall 1987).

"Getting More Discussion into MLA Convention Sessions." *Modern Language Association Newsletter* 19.4 (Winter 1987).

"A Remarkable Consensus." *Massachusetts English Teacher,* March 1988.

"To the Troops in the Trenches"; "Skeleton-Making Feedback and the Teaching of Thinking"; "A Note about Collaboration"; and "A Moment from the Meeting." *Teachers and Writers* 19.4 (March–April 1988).

"My Vision for Writing and English Faculty." *Colleague* 5. Seattle WA: Rational Island Publishers, 1988.

"The Pleasures of Voices in the Literary Essay: Explorations in the Prose of Gretel Ehrlich and Richard Selzer." In *Literary Nonfiction: Theory, Criticism, Pedagogy.* Ed. Chris Anderson. Carbondale: Southern Illinois University Press, 1989.

"Foreword." Alice Brand. *The Psychology of Writing: The Affective Experience.* Westport, CT: Greenwood Press, 1989.

"Response" to David Bleich's review of my *Embracing Contraries. ADE Bulletin* 93 (Fall 1989).

"Toward a Phenomenology of Freewriting." *Journal of Basic Writing* 8.2 (Fall 1989). (Also in *Nothing Begins with N: New Investigations of Freewriting.*)

"Foreword: About Personal Expressive Academic Writing." *Pre/Text* 11.1–2 (1990).

"Reflections on Academic Discourse: How It Relates to Freshmen and Colleagues." *College English* 53.2 (February 1991).

"Some Thoughts on *Expressive Discourse:* A Review Essay." Review of *Expressive Discourse* by Jeanette Harris. *Journal of Advanced Composition* 11.1 (Winter 1991).

"Foreword." *Portfolios: Process and Product.* Ed. Pat Belanoff and Marcia Dickson. Portsmouth, NH: Heinemann-Boynton/Cook, 1991.

"Polanyian Perspectives on the Teaching of Literature and Composition." *Tradition & Discovery: The Polanyi Society Periodical* 17.1–2 (1990–91).

"Writing Assessment: Do It Less, Do It Better." *Adult Assessment Forum* 2.4 (Winter 1991).

"Making Better Use of Student Evaluations of Teachers." *ADE Bulletin* 101 (Spring 1992). (Reprinted in *Profession 92,* Modern Language Association.)

"Freewriting and the Problem of the Wheat and the Tares." In *Writing and Publishing for Academic Authors.* Ed. Joseph Moxley. University Press of America, 1992. 2nd ed., Lanham, MD: Rowman and Littlefield, 1997.

"Using Low-Stakes Writing in Judgment-Free Zones." *Writing Teacher,* May 1992.

"The Uses of Binary Thinking." *Journal of Advanced Composition* 13.1 (Winter 1993). (Reprinted in *Everyone Can Write: Essays toward a Hopeful Theory of Writing and Teaching Writing.* New York: Oxford University Press, 2000. Also, an edited version in *Taking Stock: The Writing Process Movement in the 90s.* Ed. Lad Tobin and Tom Newkirk. Portsmouth, NH: Heinemann, 1994.)

"The War between Reading and Writing—and How to End It." *Rhetoric Review* 12.1 (Fall 1993). James A. Berlin award for the best essay of the year in that journal. Reprinted in *Critical Theory and the Teaching of Literature: Politics, Curriculum Pedagogy.* Ed. James Slevin and Art Young. Urbana, IL: National Council of Teachers of English, 1996. Reprinted in *Everyone Can*

Write: Essays toward a Hopeful Theory of Writing and Teaching Writing.
New York: Oxford University Press, 2000.

"Silence: A Collage." In *Presence of Mind: Writing and the Domain Beyond the Cognitive.* Ed. Alice Brand and Richard Graves. Portsmouth, NH: Heinemann, 1993.

"Response to Glynda Hull, Mike Rose, Kay Losey Fraser, and Marisa Castellano, 'Remediation as a Social Construct.'" *College Composition and Communication* 44.4 (December 1993).

"Ranking, Evaluating, and Liking: Sorting Out Three Forms of Judgment." *College English* 55.2 (February 1993). Also a reply to four responses 56.1 (January 1994).

"Voice in Literature." *Encyclopedia of English Studies and Language Arts.* Ed. Alan Purves. Urbana, IL: National Council of Teachers of English, 1994.

"Freewriting." *Encyclopedia of English Studies and Language Arts.* Ed. Alan Purves. Urbana, IL: National Council of Teachers of English, 1994.

"Will the Virtues of Portfolios Blind Us to Their Potential Dangers?" In *New Directions in Portfolio Assessment: Reflective Practice, Critical Theory, and Large-Scale Scoring.* Ed. Laurel Black, Don Daiker, Jeffrey Sommers, and Gail Stygall. Portsmouth, NH: Heinemann, 1994.

"To Group or Not to Group: System Leads to Narrow Definition of Intelligence." *Amherst Bulletin* 25.50. (7 January 1994).

"Advanced Classes Destructive of Motivation and Curiosity." *Amherst Bulletin,* 18 November 1994.

"Group Work: Sharing and Responding." *Notes in the Margin,* Fall 1994. (Published by the Stanford University Writing Program.)

"Introduction: Voice and Writing." *Voice and Writing.* Davis, CA: Hermagoras Press (now Lawrence Erlbaum), 1994. (A shorter version is published as "What Do We Mean When We Talk about Voice in Writing?" in *Voices on Voice: Perspectives, Definitions, Inquiry.* Ed. Kathleen Blake Yancey. Urbana, IL: National Council of Teachers of English, 1994.)

"How Portfolios Show Us Problems with Holistic Scoring, but Suggest an Alternative." *Assessment Update.* 6.4 (July–August 1994). (Reprinted in *Portfolio Assessment: Uses, Cases, Scoring, and Impact.* Ed. Trudy Banta. San Francisco, CA: Jossey-Bass, 2004.)

(With Kathleen Blake Yancey). "On Holistic Scoring and the Nature of Reading: An Inquiry Composed on Email." *Assessing Writing* 1.1 (1994). (Reprinted in *Adult Assessment Forum.*)

(With Kathleen Blake Yancey). "An Annotated and Collective Bibliography of Voice: Soundings from the Voices Within." In *Voices on Voice: Perspectives, Definitions, Inquiry.* Ed. Kathleen Blake Yancey. Urbana, IL: National Council of Teachers of English, 1994.

"Group Work: Sharing and Responding." *Notes in the Margin,* Fall 1994. (Published by the Stanford University Writing Program).

"Peter Elbow on Learning" (Brief descriptions of books about learning that I consider important). In *The Reader's Companion: A Book Lover's Guide to the Most Important Books in Every Field of Knowledge as Chosen by the Experts.* Ed. Fred Bratman and Scott Lewis. New York: Hyperion Press, 1994.

"Being a Writer vs. Being an Academic: A Conflict in Goals." Also "Response to David Bartholomae." *College Composition and Communication* 46.1 (February 1995).

"Voice as a Lightning Rod for Dangerous Thinking." Eric Document: ED391171 (Paper presented at the Annual Meeting of the Conference on College Composition and Communication, Washington, DC, 1995).

"Breathing Life into the Text." In *When Writing Teachers Teach Literature: Bringing Writing to Reading*. Ed. Art Young and Toby Fulwiler. Portsmouth, NH: Heinemann-Boynton/Cook, 1995.

"Principles that Underlie My Teaching" and selected responses to student papers. In *Twelve Readers Reading*. Ed. Richard Straub and Ronald Lunsford. Kreskill, NJ: Hampton Press, 1995.

"Peter Elbow on Writing." Videotape and DVD. Northampton, MA: Media Education Foundation, 1995.

"Writing Assessment in the Twenty-first Century: A Utopian View." In *Composition in the 21st Century: Crisis and Change*. Ed. Lynn Bloom, Don Daiker, and Ed White. Carbondale, IL: Southern Illinois University Press, 1996.

"Writing Assessment: Do It Better, Do It Less." In *The Politics and Practices of Assessment in Writing*. Ed. William Lutz, Edward White, and Sandra Kamusikiri. New York: Modern Language Association, 1996.

"Speech and Writing." Essay for *Encyclopedia of Rhetoric*. Ed. Theresa Enos. New York: Garland, 1996.

(With Pat Belanoff). "Reflections on an Explosion: Portfolios in the '90s and Beyond." *Situating Portfolios: Four Perspectives*. Ed. Kathleen Blake Yancey and Irwin Weiser. Logan: Utah State University Press, 1997.

"Introductory Essay: High Stakes and Low Stakes in Assigning and Responding to Writing." In *Writing to Learn: Strategies for Assigning and Responding to Writing in the Disciplines*. Ed. Mary Deane Sorcinelli and Peter Elbow. (A volume in the series, *New Directions for Teaching and Learning*.) San Francisco CA: Jossey-Bass, 1997.

"Grading Student Writing: Make It Simpler, Fairer, Clearer." In *Writing to Learn: Strategies for Assigning and Responding to Writing in the Disciplines*. Ed. Mary Deane Sorcinelli and Peter Elbow. (A volume in the series, *New Directions for Teaching and Learning*.) San Francisco: Jossey-Bass, 1997.

"Taking Time Out from Grading and Evaluating While Working in a Conventional System." *Assessing Writing* 4.1 (Spring 1997).

"Changing Grading While Working with Grades." In *Theory and Practice of Grading Writing: Problems and Possibilities*. Ed. Chris Weaver and Fran Zak. Albany: State University of New York Press, 1998.

"Illiteracy at Oxford and Harvard: Reflections on the Inability to Write." In *Reflective Stories: Becoming Teachers of College English and English Education*. Ed. H. Thomas McCrackin and Richard L. Larson, with Judith Entes. Urbana, IL: National Council of Teachers of English, 1998.

New Introduction for the 25th anniversary edition of *Writing Without Teachers*. New York: Oxford University Press, 1998.

New Introduction for the 17th anniversary edition of *Writing With Power*. New York: Oxford University Press, 1998.

"Collage: Your Cheatin' Art." *Writing on the Edge* 9.1 (Fall/Winter 1998). (Reprinted in *Everyone Can Write: Essays toward a Hopeful Theory of Writing and Teaching Writing*. New York: Oxford University Press, 2000.)

"In Defense of Private Writing." *Written Communication* 16.2. (April 1999).

"Inviting the Mother Tongue: Beyond 'Mistakes,' 'Bad English,' and 'Wrong Language.'" *Journal of Advanced Composition* 19.2 (Spring 1999).

"Using the Collage for Collaborative Writing." *Composition Studies* 27.1 (Spring 1999).

"Individualism and the Teaching of Writing: Response to Vai Ramanathan and Dwight Atkinson." *Journal of Second Language Writing* 8.3 (1999).

Introduction. *Writing on the Edge*. Spring 2000. Invited editor for a special issue devoted to stories of writing and teaching.

Foreword. *The Original Text-Wrestling Book*. Ed. Marcia Curis et al. Dubuque, IA: Kendall/Hunt, 2001.

"Making Postmodernism and Critical Thinking Dance with Each Other." Short essay/response in *Reinventing the University: Literacies and Legitimacy in the Postmodern Academy*. Christopher L. Schroeder. Logan: Utah State UP, 2001.

(With Charles Keil and John Trimbur). "Making Choices about Voices." *Composition Studies*, 30.1 (Spring 2002).

"The Role of Publication in the Democratization of Writing." In *Publishing with Students: A Comprehensive Guide*. Ed. Chris Weber. Portsmouth, NH: Heinemann, 2002.

"The Cultures of Literature and Composition: What Could Each Learn from the Other." *College English* 64.5 (May 2002). A response and my reply are printed in the March 2003 issue of *College English*. (Reprinted in *Teaching Composition/Teaching Literature: Crossing Great Divides*. Ed. Michelle Tokarczyk and Irene Papoulis. New York: Peter Lang, 2002.)

"Vernacular Englishes in the Writing Classroom: Probing the Culture of Literacy. In *ALT DIS: Alternative Discourses and the Academy*. Ed. Christopher Schroeder, Patricia Bizzell, and Helen Fox. Portsmouth, NH: Heinemann, 2002.

"A More Spacious Model of Writing and Literacy." In *Beyond Postprocess and Postmodernism: Essays on the Spaciousness of Rhetoric*. Ed. Theresa Enos and Keith D. Miller. Mahwah, NJ: Lawrence Erlbaum, 2003.

"Should We Invite Students to Write in L1?" *Idiom*. Publication of New York State TESOL Association, Spring 2003.

"Directed Self-Placement in Relation to Assessment: Shifting the Crunch from Entrance to Exit." In *Directed Self-Placement: Principles and Practices*. Ed. Daniel J. Royer and Roger Gilles. Kresskill, NJ: Hampton Press, 2003.

Foreword. *A Way to Move: Rhetorics of Emotion and Composition Studies*. Ed. Dale Jacobs and Laura R Micciche. Portsmouth, NH: Heinemann. 2003. Also in the same volume: "Pretext—a Response."

(Co-authored with Janet Bean, Maryann Cucchiara, Robert Eddy, Rhonda Grego, Ellie Kutz, Rich Haswell, Patricia Irvine, Eileen Kennedy, Al Lehner, Paul Kei Matsuda). "Should We Invite Students to Write in Home Languages? Complicating the Yes/No Debate." *Composition Studies* 31.1 (Spring 2003).

"Three Mysteries at the Heart of Writing." In *Composition Studies in the New Millennium: Rereading the Past, Rewriting the Future*. Ed. Lynn Z. Bloom, Donald A. Daiker, and Edward M. White. Carbondale: Southern Illinois University Press, 2003.

Foreword. *Writing Alone and with Others*. Pat Schneider. New York: Oxford University Press, 2003.

Foreword. "Felt Sense and the Wrong Word." *Felt Sense: Writing with the Body*. Sondra Perl. Portsmouth, NH: Heinemann, 2004.

"Write First: Putting Writing before Reading Is an Effective Approach to Teaching and Learning." *Educational Leadership* 62.2 (October 2004). (This is a condensed version of "The War between Reading and Writing," 2003.)

"The Persistence of Voices." Foreword for *Voice as Process*. Lizbeth Bryant. Portsmouth, NH: Heinemann, 2005.

"Ken Macrorie's Commitment and the Need for What's Wild." *Writing on the Edge* 15.1 (Fall 2004).

"Bringing the Rhetoric of Assent and the Believing Game Together—and into the Classroom." *College English* 67.4 (March 2005).

"Alternative Languages: Losers Weepers, Savers Reapers." Invited, concluding essay for a special issue of the *Journal of Teaching Writing* 21.1&2 (Spring 2005). Devoted to language varieties.

(With Mary Deane Sorcinelli). "How to Enhance Learning by Using High Stakes and Low Stakes Writing." In *McKeachie's Teaching Tips: Strategies, Research, and Theory for College and University Teachers*. 12th ed. Boston: Houghton Mifflin, 2005. (Also the 13th and 14th editions).

"A Friendly Challenge to Push the Outcomes Statement Further." In *The Outcomes Book: Debate and Consensus after the WPA Outcomes Statement*. Ed. Susanmarie Harrington, Keith Rhodes, Ruth Overman Fischer, and Rita Malenczyk. Logan: Utah State University Press, 2005.

"Foreword: When the Margins Are at the Center." In *Dialects, Englishes, Creoles, and Education*. Ed. Shondel J. Nero. Mahwah, NJ: Lawrence Erlbaum, 2006.

"The Music of Form: Rethinking Organization in Writing." *College Composition and Communication* 57.4 (June 2006).

"The Believing Game and How to Make Conflicting Opinions More Fruitful." In *Nurturing the Peacemakers in Our Students: A Guide to Teaching Peace, Empathy, and Understanding*. Ed. Chris Weber. Portsmouth, NH: Heinemann, 2006.

"Do We Need a Single Standard of Value for Institutional Assessment? An Essay Response to Asao Inoue's "Community-Based Assessment Pedagogy." *Assessing Writing* (2006).

(With Mary Deane Sorcinelli). "The Faculty Writing Place: A Room of Our Own." *Change Magazine*, November/December 2006.

"Voice in Writing Again: Embracing Contraries." *College English* 70.2 (November 2007).

"Coming to See Myself as a Vernacular Intellectual: Remarks at the 2007 CCCC General Session on Receiving the Exemplar Award." *College Composition and Communication* 59.3 (February 2008).

The Believing Game or Methodological Believing. *Journal for the Assembly for Expanded Perspectives on Learning* 14 (Winter 2009).

"Reflections: Three Chances to Think Both/And." In *Renewing Rhetoric's Relation to Composition: Essays in Honor of Theresa Jarnagin Enos*. Ed. Shane Borrowman, Stuart C. Brown, and Thomas P. Miller. New York: Routledge, 2009.

(With Jane Danielewicz). "A Unilateral Grading Contract to Improve Learning and Teaching." *College Composition and Communication* 61.2 (December 2009).

(With Janet Bean). "Freewriting and Free Speech: A Pragmatic Perspective." *Journal of Teaching Writing* (Spring 2010). (Selected for *Best Writing from Independent Composition and Rhetoric Journals: 2010*. Ed. Steve Parks. West Lafayette, IN: Parlor Press).

"Why Deny to Speakers of African American Language a Choice Most of Us Offer Other Students?" In *The Elephant in the Classroom: Race and Writing*. Ed. Jane Smith. Cresskill, NJ: Hampton Press, 2010.

"What Is Real College Writing? Let the Disagreement Never End." *WPA: Writing Program Administration* 34.2 (Spring 2011).

"Good Enough Evaluation: When is it Feasible and When Is Evaluation Not Worth Having?" *Writing Assessment in the 21st Century: Essays in Honor of Edward M. White*. Eds. Norbert Elliot and Les Perelman. Hampton Press, 2011.

Interviews

"When Teachers Are Writers: Interview with Peter Elbow." *Writing Teacher*, January 1992.

"Going in Two Directions at Once: An Interview with Peter Elbow." John Boe and Eric Schroeder. *Writing on the Edge* 4.1 (Fall 1992).

"An Interview with Peter Elbow." Jeff Siegel. *Editor and Writer*, July/August 1997.

"An Interview with Peter Elbow." Kelly Peinado. *Teaching English in the Two Year College*, October 1997.

"Peter Elbow: A Quarter Century of Teaching Writing." *Williams Alumni Review*, Spring 1999, 39.

"What's the Word." Interviewed for a twenty-minute segment of the Modern Language Association radio program, Fall 1999.

On Line Interview for *Critique* Magazine: http://www.etext.org/Zines/Critique/writing/elbow.html.

(Same interview published at WOW-SCHOOLS site: http://wow-schools.net/interview-elbow.htm.)

"Freewriting, Voice, and the Virtue of Making a Mess: A Conversation with Peter Elbow." *Issues in Writing* 17.1–2. (2007–08).

Informally Published Works

"Thoughts about Writing Essays." Pamphlet handbook, Franconia College Press, 1965.

(With Bill Aldridge and Margaret Gribskov). *One-to-One Faculty Development*. Unpublished MS distributed by Evergreen State College, 1978

"A Competence-Based Management Program at Seattle Central Community College: A Case Study." In *On Competence: A Critical Analysis of Competence-Based Reforms in Higher Education*. Two-volume report put out by the Fund for the Improvement of Higher Education. Ed. Gerald Grant et al. 1979.

"Midstream Reflections." In *Moving between Practice and Research in Writing: Proceedings of the NIE-FIPSE Grantee Workshop*. Ed. Ann Humes. Los Alamitos, CA: SWRL Educational Research and Development, 1981.

"Critical Thinking Is Not Enough." *Critical Thinking/Critical Writing*. Informal publication of the 11th Annual Reninger Lecture, University of Northern Iowa, 1983.

"The Foundations of Intellectual Combat and Collaboration" and "Reply to Stanley Fish." *Proceedings of the Conference: Collaborative Learning and the Reinterpretation of Knowledge*. New York (John Jay College), 1986.

Works Cited

Adolf, Robert. *The Rise of Modern Prose Style*. New York: Cambridge University Press, 1968.

Agnihotri, R. K. "Continuing Debates over the Native Speaker: English in India." *English Today 96* 24.4 (December 2008): 51–57.

Ahmed, Dohra. *Rotten English: A Literary Anthology*. New York: W. W. Norton, 2007.

Aisenberg, Nadya and Mona Harrington. *Women of Academe*. Amherst: University of Massachusetts Press, 1988.

Akinnaso, F. Niyi. "Literacy and Individual Consciousness." In *Literate Systems and Individual Lives: Perspectives on Literacy and Schooling*. Ed. Edward M. Jennings and Alan Purves. Albany: State University of New York Press, 1991. 73–94.

Aldrich, Pearl. "Adult Writers: Some Reasons for Ineffective Writing on the Job." *College Composition and Communication* 33.3 (October 1982): 284–287.

Alim, H. Sami. *Roc the Mic Right: The Language of Hip Hop Culture*. New York: Routledge/Taylor and Francis, 2006.

Alim, H. Samy, John Baugh, and Geneva Smitherman. *Talkin Black Talk: Language, Education, and Social Change*. New York: Teachers College Press, 2006.

Anderson, Wallace L. "Recognizing Restrictive Adjective Clauses." *College English* 18.5 (February 1957): 269–271.

Anzaldúa, Gloria. *Borderlands / La Frontera: The New Mestiza*. San Francisco: Spinsters-Aunt Lute, 1987.

Aristotle. *Rhetoric*. Trans. Rhys Roberts. New York: Modern Library, 1954.

Ashbery, John. "The Virgin King." *New Yorker* 29 September 2008: 75.

Auerbach, Erich. *Mimesis: The Representation of Reality in Western Literature*. Trans. W. Traske. New York: Doubleday Anchor, 1957 (1953).

Auster, Paul. "New York Babel." *Collected Prose*. London: Faber and Faber, 2003. 325–331.

Bailey, Matthew. "Oral Composition in the Medieval Spanish Epic." *PMLA* 118.2 (March 2003): 254–269.

Baker, Nicholson. "History of Punctuation." *Size of Thoughts*. New York: Random House, 1996.

Bakhtin, Mikhail. "Discourse in Life and Discourse in Art (Concerning Sociological Poetics)." Appendix to *Freudianism: A Marxist Critique*. [V. N. Volosinov.] Tr. I. R. Titunik. Ed. Neal H. Bruss. New York: Academic Press, 1976. 93–116. (Holquist's attribution of this work to Bakhtin rather than Volosinov is generally accepted.)

Bakker, Egbert and Ahuvia Kahane. *Written Voices, Spoken Signs: Tradition, Performance, and the Epic Text*. Cambridge, MA: Harvard University Press, 1997.

Ballenger, Bruce. *The Curious Writer*. New York: Longman, 2007.

Banville, John. "Emerson: 'A Few Inches from Calamity.'" *New York Review of Books* 3 December 2009: 33–35.

Barthes, Roland. "The Grain of the Voice." *Image, Music, Text.* Trans. Stephen Heath. New York: Hill and Wang, 1977.

Bartholomae, David. "Writing with Teachers: A Conversation with Peter Elbow." *College Composition and Communication* 46.1 (February 1995): 62–71.

Barton, D., David Bloome, D. Sheridan, and Brian Street. *Ordinary People Writing: The Lancaster and Sussex Writing Research Projects.* Number 51 in the Working Paper Series, published by the Centre for Language in Social Life, Department of Linguistics and Modern English Language, Lancaster University, Lancaster, England, 1993.

Barton, D. and R. Ivanic. *Writing in the Community.* Newbury Park, CA: Sage, 1991.

Bataille, Georges. *Le Bleu du Ciel.* Paris: J. Pauvert, 1967. *Blue of Noon:* London: Penguin, 2001.

Baugh, John. *Black Street Speech: Its History, Structure, and Survival.* Austin: University of Texas Press, 1984.

Bazerman, Charles, ed. *Handbook of Research on Writing: History, Society, School, Individual, Text.* Mahwah, NJ: Erlbaum, 2007.

Bean, Janet. "The Color Line: Grammar Checker and Black Vernacular English." Presentation, National Council of Teachers of English Annual Conference, Baltimore, November 2001.

Bean, Janet and Peter Elbow. "Freewriting and Free Speech: A Pragmatic Perspective." *Journal of Teaching Writing* (Spring 2010): 1–24.

Becker, Howard. *Writing for Social Scientists: How to Start and Finish Your Thesis, Book, or Article.* Chicago: University of Chicago Press, 1986.

Behrens, Susan J. "Dialects and *The Grapes of Wrath.*" *Field Notes* 7.1 (Spring 2011): 27–29.

Belanoff, Pat. "Freewriting: An Aid to Rereading Theorists. In *Nothing Begins with N: New Investigations of Freewriting.* Ed. Pat Belanoff, Sheryl Fontaine, and Peter Elbow. Carbondale: Southern Illinois University Press, 1990. 16–31.

Belanoff, Pat, Peter Elbow, and Sheryl Fontaine. *Nothing Begins with N: New Explorations of Freewriting.* Carbondale: Southern Illinois University Press, 1990.

Bell, Anne Olivier, ed. *The Diary of Virginia Woolf.* Vol. I: 1915–1919. New York: Harcourt Brace, 1977.

Benfey, Christopher. "The Age of Teddy." *New York Review of Books* 1 April 2010: 24–26.

Bennett, Alan. *Writing Home.* London: Faber and Faber, 1994.

Bennett, Louise. *Aunty Roachy Seh.* Kingston, Jamaica: Sangster's, 1993.

Bernard, H. Russell. "Languages and Scripts in Contact: Historical Perspectives." In *Literacy: An International Handbook.* Ed. Daniel A. Wagner, Richard L. Venezky, and Brian Street. Boulder, CO: Westview Press, 1999. 22–28.

Betz, Hans Dieter. *The Greek Magical Papyri in Translation, Including the Demotic Spells.* Vol. 1, 2nd ed. Chicago: University of Chicago Press, 1993 (1986).

Biber, Douglas. *Variation across Speech and Writing.* New York: Cambridge University Press, 1988.

Biber, Douglas and Camilla Vásquez. "Writing and Speaking." In *Handbook of Research on Writing: History, Society, School, Individual, Text.* Ed. Charles Bazerman. Mahwah, NJ: Erlbaum, 2007. 535–548.

"Robert Bingham (1925–82)." *New Yorker* July 5, 1982: 100.

Bishop, Wendy. "Afterward—Colors of a Different Horse: On Learning to Like Teaching Creative Writing." In *Colors of a Different Horse: Rethinking Creative Writing Theory and Pedagogy.* Ed. Wendy Bishop and Hans Ostrom. Urbana, IL: National Council of Teachers of English, 1994. 280–295.

Bizzell, Patricia and Bruce Herzberg. *The Bedford Bibliography for Teachers of Writing.* Boston: Bedford/St. Martins, 2000.

Blau, Sheridan. "Invisible Writing: Investigating Cognitive Processes in Composition." *College Composition and Communication* 34.3 (October 1983): 297–312.

———. "Thinking and the Liberation of Attention: The Uses of Free and Invisible Writing." In *Nothing Begins with N: New Explorations of Freewriting.* Ed. Pat Belanoff, Peter Elbow, and Sheryl Fontaine. Carbondale: Southern Illinois University Press, 1990. 283–302.

Boe, John. "From the Editor: Why Can't the Americans Write English?" *Writing on the Edge* 11.2 (Spring 2000): 4–9.

Boice, Robert and Patricia E. Meyers. "Two Parallel Traditions: Automatic Writing and Freewriting." *Written Communication* 3.4 (October 1986): 471–490.

Bolinger, Dwight. *Aspects of Language*. 2nd ed. New York: Harcourt Brace Jovanovich, 1975.

———. *Intonation and Its Parts: Melody in Spoken English*. Stanford, CA: Stanford University Press, 1986.

———. *Intonation and Its Uses: Melody in Grammar and Discourse*. Stanford, CA: Stanford University Press, 1989.

Booth, Stephen. *Precious Nonsense: The Gettysburg Address, Ben Jonson's Epitaphs on His Children, and Twelfth Night*. Berkeley: University of California Press, 1998.

Bonnefoy, Y. *Du Haïku. Préface à Haïku*. Présentation et traduction de R. Munier. Paris: Fayard, 1978.

Born, Richard. "Political Cartography: The Emergence of the New Incumbent Safety in the U.S. House." *Vassar Alumni Quarterly* 100.2 (Spring 2004): 10–13.

Bourdieu, Pierre. *Distinction: A Social Critique of the Judgement of Taste*. Trans. Richard Nice. Cambridge, MA: Harvard University Press, 1984.

Boxer, Sarah. "Blogs." *New York Review of Books* 14 February 2008: 16–20.

Boyd, Richard. "'Grammatical Monstrosities' and 'Contemptible Miscreants': Sacrificial Violence in the Late Nineteenth-Century Usage Handbook." In *The Place of Grammar in Writing Instruction: Past, Present, and Future*. Ed. Susan Hunter and Ray Wallace. Portsmouth, NH: Heinemann/Boynton Cook, 1995. 54–70.

———. "Mechanical Correctness and Ritual in the Late Nineteenth-Century Composition Classroom. *Rhetoric Review* 11.2 (Spring 1993): 436–455.

Brande, Dorothea. *Becoming a Writer*. New York: Harcourt Brace, 1934.

Brandt, Deborah. *Literacy in American Lives*. Cambridge: Cambridge University Press, 2001.

Britannica 2001. "Literacy: Uses of Writing." DVD. Britannica.co.uk.

Britton, James, et al. *The Development of Writing Abilities (11–18)*. Urbana, IL: National Council of Teachers of English, 1975.

Brooks, David. "Confidence Surplus." *New York Times* 11 January 2009. Editorial page.

Brown, T. J. "Punctuation." *New Encyclopedia Britannica*. 15th ed. Vol. 29. 1985. 1006–1008.

Bryson, Bill. *The Mother Tongue: English and How It Got that Way*. New York: Harper Collins, 1991.

Buckley, William F. Jr. "With All Deliberate Speed: What's so Bad about Writing Fast?" *New York Times* 16 March 1999. Editorial page.

Bulley, Michael. "Was *That* Necessary?" *English Today* 22. 2 (April 2006): 47–49.

Burke, Kenneth. *Counter-Statement*. Berkeley: University of California Press, 1968.

———. *A Grammar of Motives*. Berkeley: University of California Press, 1969.

Butler, Samuel. "VII. On the Making of Music, Books, and the Arts." In *Note-Books of Samuel Butler*. Ed. Henry Festing Jones. BiblioLife, 2009. [no location given]

Calkins, Lucy McCormick. *The Art of Teaching Writing*. Portsmouth, NH: Heinemann Educational Books, 1986

———. *Lessons from a Child on the Teaching and Learning of Writing*. Portsmouth, NH: Heinemann Educational Books, 1983.

Campbell, Kermit E. *Gettin' Our Groove On: Rhetoric, Language, and Literacy for the Hip Hop Generation*. Detroit, MI: Wayne State University Press, 2005.

Canagarajah, A. Suresh. *The Geopolitics of Academic Writing and Knowledge Production*. Pittsburgh: University of Pittsburgh Press, 2002.

———. "The Place of World Englishes in Composition: Pluralization Continued." *College Composition and Communication* 57.4 (June 2006): 586–619.

Chafe, Wallace L. "Cognitive Constraints on Information Flow." *Coherence and Grounding in Discourse*. Ed. Russell Tomlin. Amsterdam: John Benjamins, 1987. 21–51.

———. "Differences between Colloquial and Ritual Seneca or How Oral Literature Is Literary." In *Reports from the Survey of California and Other Indian Languages*, No. 1. Ed. Alice Schlichter, Wallace L. Chafe, and Leanne Hinton. Berkeley: University of California, 1981.

———. *Discourse, Consciousness, and Time: The Flow and Displacement of Conscious Experience in Speaking and Writing.* Chicago: University of Chicago Press, 1994.

———. "The Flow of Thought and the Flow of Language." *Syntax and Semantics.* Vol. 12: *Discourse and Syntax.* Ed. Talmy Givon. New York: Academic Press, 1979. 159–181.

———. "Grammatical Subjects in Speaking and Writing." *Text* 11 (1991): 45–72.

———. "Integration and Involvement in Speaking, Writing, and Oral Literature." In *Spoken and Written Language: Exploring Orality and Literacy.* Ed. Deborah Tannen. Norwood, NJ: Ablex, 1982. 35–53.

———. "Linguistic Differences Produced by Differences between Speaking and Writing." In *Literacy, Language, and Learning: The Nature and Consequences of Reading and Writing.* Ed. D. R. Olson, Nancy Torrance, and Angela Hildyard. New York: Cambridge University Press. 1985. 105–23.

———. *The Pear Stories: Cognitive, Cultural, and Linguistic Aspects of Narrative Production.* Ed. Wallace L. Chafe. Norwood, NJ: Ablex, 1980.

———. "Punctuation and the Prosody of Written Language." *Written Communication 5* (1988): 395–426.

———. "Reading Aloud." In *Spoken English, Applied Linguistics and TESOL: Challenges for Theory and Practice.* Ed. Rebecca Hughes. London: Palgrave, 2006. 53–71.

———. "What Good Is Punctuation?" *Quarterly of the National Writing Project and the Center for the Study of Writing* 10.1 (1988): 1–8.

Chafe, Wallace and Jane Danielewicz. "How 'Normal' Speaking Leads to 'Erroneous' Punctuating." In *The Acquisition of Written Language: Response and Revision.* Ed. S. Freedman. Norwood, NJ: Ablex, 1985. 213–225.

———. "Properties of Spoken and Written Language." In *Comprehending Oral and Written Language.* Ed. Rosalind Horowitz and Jay Samuels. San Diego: Academic Press, 1987. 84–113.

Christensen, Francis. *Notes toward a New Rhetoric: Six Essays for Teachers.* New York: Harper and Row, 1967.

Christensen, Linda. "The Politics of Correction: How We Can Nurture Students in Their Writing and Help Them Learn the Language of Power." *Rethinking Schools* (Fall 2003): 20–23.

———. "Whose Standard? Teaching Standard English in Our Schools." In *Rethinking Schools: An Agenda for Change.* Ed. David Levine, Robert Lowe, Robert Peterson, and Rita Tenorio. New York: New Press, 1995. 128–135.

Clark, Romy and Roz Ivanic. *The Politics of Writing.* New York: Routledge, 1997.

Clemens, Samuel L. *Selected Mark Twain-Howells Letters: 1872–1910.* Ed. Frederick Anderson et al. Cambridge, MA: Belknap Press, 1967.

Colomb, Gregory G. and June Anne Griffin. "Coherence On and Off the Page: What Writers Can Know about Writing Coherently." *New Literary History* 35.2 (2004): 273–301.

Cook, Claire Kehrwald. *Line by Line: How to Improve Your Own Writing.* New York: MLA, 1985.

Connors, Robert J. and Andrea A. Lunsford. "Frequency of Formal Errors in Current College Writing, or Ma and Pa Kettle Do Research." *College Composition and Communication* 39.4 (December 1988): 395–409.

Cornish, Alison. "A Lady Asks: The Gender of Vulgarization in Late Medieval Italy." *PMLA* 115.2 (March 2000): 1666–1680.

Coulmas, Florian. *Writing Systems: An Introduction to Their Linguistic Analysis.* New York: Cambridge University Press, 2003.

"Cover Story." *NCIS* episode, season 4, #20, NBC.

Crain, Caleb. "Twilight of the Books." *New Yorker* (December 24 and 31, 2007): 134–139.

Crane, R. S. "The Critical Monism of Cleanth Brooks." *Critics and Criticism: Ancient and Modern.* Chicago: University of Chicago Press, 1951. 83–107.

Crawford, Lindy, Gerald Tindal, and Steve Stieber. "Using Oral Reading Rate to Predict Student Performance on Statewide Achievement Tests." *Educational Assessment* 7.4 (2001): 303–323.

Creme P. and Lea M. *Writing at University: A Guide for Students*. Buckingham, UK: Open University Press, 1997.

Crismore, Avon. *Talking with Readers: Metadiscourse as Rhetorical Act*. American University Studies Series XIV. New York: Peter Lang, 1990.

Crystal, David. *The Cambridge Encyclopedia of the English Language*. New York: Cambridge University Press, 1995.

———. *The Cambridge Encyclopedia of Language*. New York: Cambridge University Press, 1987.

———. *English as a Global Language*. New York: Cambridge University Press, 1997.

———. *The Stories of English*. New York: Overlook Press, 2004.

Csikszentmihalyi, Mihaly. *Between Boredom and Anxiety*. San Francisco: Jossey-Bass, 1975.

———. *Creativity: Flow and the Psychology of Discovery and Invention*. New York: Harper Perennial, 1996.

———. *Flow: The Psychology of Optimal Experience*. New York: Harper and Row, 1990.

Cushman, Ellen, Eugene R. Kintgen, Barry M. Kroll, and Mike Rose, eds. *Literacy: A Critical Sourcebook*. New York: Bedford/St. Martins, 2001.

Darwin, Charles. *Autobiography of Charles Darwin*. Ed. Nora Barlow. New York: W. W. Norton, 1969

Davies, Lizzy. "Words of Warning: 2,500 Languages under Threat Worldwide as Migrants Head for City." *Guardian* 27 February 1990: 7.

Dawkins, John. "The Modern Sentence and Its Punctuation." Unpublished MS, 2009. 1–20.

———. "Punctuation: Some Informing History." *Composition Forum* (Fall 1999): 52–61.

———. "Teaching Punctuation as a Rhetorical Tool." *College Composition and Communication* 46.4 (December 1995): 533–548.

De Certeau, Michel. *The Practice of Everyday Life*. Trans. Steven Rendall. Berkeley: University of California Press, 1984.

DeGraff, Michel. "Do Creole Languages Constitute an Exceptional Typological Class?" *Revue française de linguistique appliquée* 10.1 (2005): 11–24.

DeFrancis, John. *The Chinese Language: Fact and Fantasy*. Honolulu: University of Hawaii Press, 1984.

Delpit, Lisa. "What Should Teachers Do? Ebonics and Culturally Responsive Instruction." In *The Real Ebonics Debate: Power, Language, and the Education of African-American Children*. Ed. Theresa Perry and Lisa Delpit. Boston: Beacon, 1998. 17–26.

Denby, David. "Northern Lights: How Modern Life Emerged from Eighteenth-Century Edinburgh." *New Yorker* 11 October 2004: 90–98.

DeRomilly, Jacqueline. *Magic and Rhetoric in Ancient Greece*. Cambridge: Harvard University Press, 1975.

Diamond, Jared. *Guns, Germs, and Steel*. New York: W. W. Norton, 1997.

Du Bois, W. E. B. *The Souls of Black Folk*. New York: Gramercy Books, 1994.

Dyson, Freeman J. "Wise Man." Review of *Perfectly Reasonable Deviations from the Beaten Track: The Letters of Richard P. Feynman*. *New York Review of Books* 20 October 2005: 4–6.

Dyson, Michael Eric. "Textual Acts and Semiotic Gestures: Race, Writing, and Technotopia." *Open Mike: Reflections on Philosophy, Race, Sex, Culture and Religion*. New York: Basic Books, 2003. 23–41.

Edel, Leon. *The Life of Henry James: The Master (1901–1916)*. New York: Avon, 1969.

Ehri, Linnea C. "Effects of Printed Language Acquisition on Speech." In *Literacy, Language and Learning: The Nature and Consequences of Reading and Writing*. Ed. David R. Olson, Nancy Torrance, and Angela Hildyard. New York: Cambridge University Press, 1985. 368–388.

Peter Elbow. "About Resistance to Freewriting and Feedback Groups." *Washington English Journal* (Winter 1982): 24–25.

————. The Believing Game.*

————. "The Believing Game and How to Make Conflicting Opinions More Fruitful." In *Nurturing the Peacemakers in Our Students: A Guide to Teaching Peace, Empathy, and Understanding.* Ed. Chris Weber. Portsmouth, NH: Heinemann, 2006. 16–25.

————. "The Believing Game or Methodological Believing." *Journal for the Assembly for Expanded Perspectives on Learning* 14 (Winter 2009): 1–11.

————. "Bringing the Rhetoric of Assent and the Believing Game Together–and into the Classroom." *College English* 67.4 (March 2005): 388–399.

————. "The Challenge for Sentence Combining." In *Sentence Combining: A Rhetorical Perspective.* Ed. Don Daiker, Andrew Kerek, and Max Morenberg. Carbondale: Southern Illinois University Press, 1985. 232–245.

————. "Closing My Eyes as I Speak: An Argument for Ignoring Audience." *College English* 49.1 (January 1987): 50–69.

————. "Collage: Your Cheatin' Art." *Writing on the Edge* 9.1 (Fall/Winter 1998): 26–40. (Reprinted in *Everyone Can Write: Essays Toward a Hopeful Theory of Writing and Teaching Writing.* New York: Oxford University Press, 2000.)

————. "The Doubting Game and the Believing Game–An Analysis of the Intellectual Enterprise." Appendix Essay in *Writing Without Teachers.* New York: Oxford University Press, 1973. 147–191.

————. *Embracing Contraries: Explorations in Learning and Teaching.* New York: Oxford University Press, 1986.

————. "Felt Sense and the Wrong Word." Foreword to Perl, Sondra. *Felt Sense: Writing with the Body.* Portsmouth, NH: Heinemann, 2004. v–ix.

————. "Freewriting." *Encyclopedia of English Studies and Language Arts.* Ed. Alan Purves. Urbana, IL: National Council of Teachers of English, 1994. 509–510.

————. "Freewriting and the Problem of the Wheat and the Tares." In *Writing and Publishing for Academic Authors.* Ed. Joseph Moxley. New York: University Press of America, 1992. 33–47. 2nd ed. Lanham, MD: Rowman and Littlefield, 1997.

————. "Illiteracy at Oxford and Harvard: Reflections on the Inability to Write." In *Reflective Stories: Becoming Teachers of College English and English Education.* Ed. H. Thomas McCrackin and Richard L. Larson, with Judith Entes. Urbana IL: National Council of Teachers of English, 1998. 91–114.

————. "In Defense of Private Writing." *Written Communication* 16.2 (April 1999): 139–179.

————. "Methodological Doubting and Believing: Contraries in Inquiry." In *Embracing Contraries: Explorations in Learning and Teaching.* New York: Oxford University Press, 1986. 254–300.

————. "A More Spacious Model of Writing and Literacy." In *Beyond Postprocess and Postmodernism: Essays on the Spaciousness of Rhetoric.* Ed. Theresa Enos and Keith D. Miller. Mahwah, NJ: Erlbaum, 2003. 217–233.

————. "The Music of Form: Rethinking Organization in Writing." *College Composition and Communication* 57.4 (June 2006): 620–666.

————. "The Shifting Relationships between Speech and Writing." *College Composition and Communication* 36 (1985): 283–303.

————. "Silence: A Collage." In *Presence of Mind: Writing and the Domain beyond the Cognitive.* Ed. Alice Brand and Richard Graves. Portsmouth, NH: Heinemann/Boynton-Cook, 1993. 9–20.

*For those interested, I list here the various essays I've written about this topic: "The Doubting Game and the Believing Game–An Analysis of the Intellectual Enterprise," 1973. "Methodological Doubting and Believing: Contraries in Inquiry," 1986. "The Uses of Binary Thinking," 1993. "Bringing the Rhetoric of Assent and the Believing Game Together–and into the Classroom," 2005. "The Believing Game and How to Make Conflicting Opinions More Fruitful," 2006. "The Believing Game or Methodological Believing," 2009. Each is listed separately.

————. "Three Mysteries at the Heart of Writing." In *Composition Studies in the New Millennium: Rereading the Past, Rewriting the Future.* Ed. Lynn Z. Bloom, Donald A. Daiker, and Edward M. White. Carbondale: Southern Illinois University Press, 2003. 10–27.

————. "Toward a Phenomenology of Freewriting." *Journal of Basic Writing* 8.2 (Fall 1989): 44–71. (Also in *Nothing Begins with N: New Investigations of Freewriting*, Ed. Pat Belanoff, Peter Elbow, and Sheryl Fontaine.)

————. "The Uses of Binary Thinking." *Journal of Advanced Composition* 13.1 (Winter 1993): 51–78. (Reprinted in *Everyone Can Write: Essays Toward a Hopeful Theory of Writing and Teaching Writing.* New York: Oxford University Press, 2000. Also, an edited version, in *Taking Stock: The Writing Process Movement in the 90s.* Ed. Lad Tobin and Tom Newkirk. Portsmouth, NH: Heinemann Boynton/Cook, 1994.)

————. "Using the Collage for Collaborative Writing." *Composition Studies* 27.1 (Spring 1999): 7–14.

————. "Voice in Writing Again: Embracing Contraries." *College English* 70.2 (November 2007): 168–188.

————. "The War between Reading and Writing—and How to End It." *Rhetoric Review* 12.1 (Fall 1993): 5–24. (Reprinted in *Everyone Can Write: Essays Toward a Hopeful Theory of Writing and Teaching Writing.* New York: Oxford University Press, 2000.) A shorter version was published as "Write First: Putting Writing before Reading Is an Effective Approach to Teaching and Learning." *Educational Leadership* 62.2 (October 2004): 8–14.

————. "Why Deny to Speakers of African American Language a Choice Most of Us Offer Other Students?" In *The Elephant in the Classroom: Race and Writing.* Ed. Jane Smith. Cresskill, NJ: Hampton Press, 2010.

————. "Write First: Putting Writing Before Reading Is an Effective Approach to Teaching and Learning." *Educational Leadership* 62.2 (October 2004): 8–14.

————. *Writing about Media: Teaching Writing, Teaching Media.* Northampton, MA: Media Education Foundation, 2008.

————. *Writing Without Teachers.* New York: Oxford University Press, 1973.

————. *Writing With Power: Techniques for Mastering the Writing Process.* New York: Oxford University Press, 1981.

————. (With Janet Bean). "Freewriting and Free Speech: A Pragmatic Perspective." *Journal of Teaching Writing* (Spring 2010): 1–23.

————. (With Pat Belanoff). *Being a Writer: A Community of Writers Revisited.* New York: McGraw Hill, 2003.

————. (With Pat Belanoff). *A Community of Writers: A Workshop Course in Writing.* New York: McGraw Hill, 1989.

————. (With Pat Belanoff). *Sharing and Responding.* New York: McGraw-Hill, 1989.

————. (With Pat Belanoff and Sheryl Fontaine). *Nothing Begins with N: New Explorations of Freewriting.* Carbondale: Southern Illinois University Press, 1990.

————. (With Mary Deane Sorcinelli). "The Faculty Writing Place: A Room of Our Own." *Change Magazine* (November/December 2006): 17–22.

Eliot, T. S. *The Uses of Poetry and the Uses of Criticism.* Cambridge, MA: Harvard University Press, 1933.

Elsasser, Nan and Patricia Irvine. "English and Creole: The Dialectics of Choice in a College Writing Program." *Harvard Educational Review* 55 (1985): 399–415. Reprint in *Freire for the Classroom.* Ed. Ira Shor. Portsmouth, NH: Boynton/Cook, 1987. 129–149.

Emig, Janet. "Writing as a Mode of Learning." *College Composition and Communication* 28.2 (May 1977): 122–128.

Epstein, Jason. "Publishing: The Revolutionary Future." *New York Review of Books* 11 March 2010: 4–6.

————. Reply to a Response. *New York Review of Books* 25 March 2010. Letters section at end of the issue.

Fanon, Franz. *The Wretched of the Earth.* New York: Grove Weidenfeld, 1961 (1963 translation by Constance Farrington).

Farnsworth, Ward. *Farnsworth's Classical English Rhetoric.* Boston: David R. Godine, 2009.

Farrell, Thomas. "IQ and Standard English." *College Composition and Communication* 34.4 (1983): 470–484.

Figes, Orlando. "Tolstoy's Real Hero." Review of *War and Peace* newly translated by Richard Pevear and Larissa Volokhonsky. *New York Review of Books* 22 November 2007: 4–7.

Firmage, Richard A. *The Alphabet Abecedarium: Some Notes on Letters.* Boston: Godine, 1993.

Fish, Stanley. *Is There a Text in This Class? The Authority of Interpretive Communities.* Cambridge, MA: Harvard University Press, 1980.

Flower, Linda, John R. Hayes, Linda Carey, Karen Schriver, and James Stratman. "Detection, Diagnosis, and the Strategies of Revision." *College Composition and Communication* 37. 1 (February 1986): 16–55.

Fodor, Janet Dean. "Prosodic Disambiguation in Silent Reading." In *Proceedings of the North East Linguistic Society.* Ed. M. Hirotani. (2002): 113–132.

Fontaine, Sheryl I. "Recording and Transforming: The Mystery of the Ten-Minute Feewrite." In *Nothing Begins with N: New Explorations of Freewriting.* Ed. Pat Belanoff, Peter Elbow, and Sheryl Fontaine. Carbondale: Southern Illinois University Press, 1990. 3–15.

Fowler, H. W. *A Dictionary of Modern English Usage.* Broadbridge, UK: Clarendon Press, 1957 (1926).

Fox, Helen. *Listening to the World.* Urbana, IL: National Council of Teachers of English, 1994.

Garner, Bryan A. *A Dictionary of Modern American Usage.* New York: Oxford University Press, 1988.

Gates, Henry Louis Jr. *The Signifying Monkey: A Theory of African-American Literary Criticism.* New York: Oxford University Press, 1988.

Gavin, Ruth E. and William A. Sabin. *Reference Manual for Stenographers and Typists.* 4th ed. New York: Gregg/McGraw, 1970 (1951).

Gee, James Paul. "Literacy, Discourse, and Linguistics: Introduction" and "What Is Literacy." In *Literacy: A Critical Sourcebook.* Ed. Ellen Cushman, Eugene R. Kintgen, Barry M. Kroll, and Mike Rose. Boston: Bedford/St. Martins, 2001. 525–544.

———. *Social Linguistics and Literacies: Ideology in Discourses.* London: Falmer Press, 1990.

Geertz, Clifford. "Very Bad News." Review of books by Jared Diamond and Richard Posner. *New York Review of Books* 24 March 2005: 4–6.

Gendlin, Eugene T. *Focusing.* New York: Bantam Books, 2007.

———. "The Wider Role of Bodily Sense in Thought and Language." In *Giving the Body Its Due.* Ed. M. Sheets-Johnstone. Albany: State University of New York Press, 1992. 192–207.

Gibson, Sally. "Reading Aloud: A Useful Tool for Learning?" *ELT Journal* 62.1 (2008): 29–36.

Gillespie, M. K. "The Forgotten R: Why Adult Educators Should Care about Writing Instruction." In *Toward Defining and Improving Quality in Adult Basic Education: Issues and Challenges.* Ed. A. Belzer. Rutgers Invitational Symposium on Education Series. Mahwah, NJ: Erlbaum, 2007.

Gilyard, Keith. *True to the Language Game: African American Discourse, Cultural Politics, and Pedagogy.* New York: Routledge, 2011.

Godkin, E. L. "The Illiteracy of American Boys." *Educational Review* 8 (1897): 1–9.

Goldberg, Jeff. "The Quivering Bundles That Let Us Hear: The Goal: Extreme Sensitivity and Speed." *Seeing, Hearing, and Smelling in the World: A Report from the Howard Hughes Institute.* 2005. http://www.hhmi.org/senses/c120.html (accessed 9/9/05).

Goldberg, Natalie. *Writing Down the Bones.* Boston: Shambhala, 1986.

Goody, Jack and Ian Watt. "The Consequences of Literacy." *Literacy in Traditional Societies.* Cambridge: Cambridge University Press, 1968. 27–68.

Gopnik, Adam. "The Back of the World: The Troubling Genius of G. K. Chesterton." *New Yorker* 14 July 2008: 52–59.

———. "Right Again: The Passions of John Stuart Mill." *New Yorker* 6 October 2008: 85–91.

Govardhan, A. K. *A Discourse Analysis of ESL Student Writing.* Unpublished doctoral dissertation. Northern Illinois University, 1994.

Gowers, Ernest. *Plain Words: A Guide to the Use of English.* London: His Majesty's Stationery Office, 1948.

Graddol, David. "The Decline of the Native Speaker." *English in a Changing World.* Ed. David Graddol and Ulrike Meinhof. *AILA Review* 13 (1999): 57–68.

———. *English Next*. London: British Council. 2006. Available free from the website of the British Council.

Graff, Richard. "Early Views on the Integration of Speaking and Writing in Rhetorical Instruction." Conference paper, Western States Rhetoric and Literacy Conference, University of Utah, Salt Lake City, 2006.

Graves, Donald. *Writing: Teachers and Children at Work*. Portsmouth, NH: Heinemann, 1983.

Green, Lisa. *African American English: A Linguistic Introduction*. Cambridge: Cambridge University Press, 2002.

Greenblatt, Stephen. "Shakespeare in No Man's Land." Review of biography of Shakespeare by Jonathan Bate. *New York Review of Books* 17 December 2009. Accessed from *New York Review of Books* website.

Greene, Thomas M. *Poetry, Signs, and Magic*. Newark: University of Delaware Press, 2005.

Greenfield, Amy Butler. *A Perfect Red: Empire, Espionage, and the Quest for the Color of Desire*. New York: HarperCollins, 2005.

Grice, Paul. "Logic and Conversation." In *Syntax and Semantics 3: Speech Acts*. Ed. P. Cole and J. Morgan. New York: Academic Press, 1975. Reprinted in *Studies in the Way of Words*. Ed. H. P. Grice. Cambridge, MA: Harvard University Press, 1989. 22–40.

Guardian and Observer Style Guide. http://www.guardian.co.uk/styleguide/. See *"that* or *which"?* (accessed November 2008).

The Guardian Weekly 21 August 2009: 31.

Hacker, Diane. *A Writer's Reference*. 2nd ed. New York: Bedford, 1992.

Hadley, Joe. *Chalukyu Insai: An Introduction to Hawaii's Pidgin English*. Honolulu: Sandwich Island Publishing, 1972.

Halliday, M. A. K. *Complementarities in Language*. Beijing: Commercial Press, 2008.

———. "Linguistic Perspectives on Literacy: A Systemic-Functional Approach." In *Literacy in Social Processes*. Ed. F. Christie and E. Jenkins. Sidney: Literacy Technologies, 1990.

———. "Spoken and Written Modes of Meaning." In *Comprehending Oral and Written Language*. Ed. Rosalind Horowitz and S. Jay Samuels. San Diego: Academic Press, 1987. 55–82.

Halliday, M. A. K. and William S. Greaves. *Intonation in the Grammar of English*. London: Equinox, 2008.

Halliday, M. A. K. and Christian M. I. M. Matthiessen. *An Introduction to Functional Grammar*. London: Edward Arnold, 1985.

Hamer, Fannie Lou. http://www.answers.com/topic/fannie-lou-hamer (accessed 15 October 2010).

Harris, Muriel. *Teaching One-to-One: The Writing Conference*. Urbana, IL: National Council of Teachers of English, 1986.

Harris, Roy. *The Origin of Writing*. London: Duckworth, 1986.

———. *Signs of Writing*. London: Routledge, 1995.

Harris, William. V. *Ancient Literacy*. Cambridge, MA: Harvard University Press, 1989.

Harste, J., V. Woodward, and C. Burke. *Language Stories and Literacy Lessons*. Portsmouth, NH: Heinemann, 1984.

Hass, Robert. *Time and Materials: Poems, 1997–2005*. New York: Ecco/HarperCollins, 2007.

Haswell, Janis E. "Granting Authority to Multivocal Student Writing." Paper presented at the Annual Meeting of the Conference on College Composition and Communication, Milwaukee, 27–30 March 1996.

Haswell, Janis and Richard H. Haswell. "Gendership and the Miswriting of Students." *College Composition and Communication* 46.2 (1995): 223–254.

Haswell, Richard H. "Bound Forms in Freewriting: The Issue of Organization." In *Nothing Begins with N: New Explorations of Freewriting*. Ed. Pat Belanoff, Peter Elbow, and Sheryl Fontaine. Carbondale: Southern Illinois University Press, 1990. 32–69.

Havelock, Eric A. "Orality, Literacy, and Star Wars." *PRE-TEXT* 7.3–4 (Fall/Winter 1986): 123–132. Also published in *Written Communication* 3.9 (October 1986): 411–420.

———. *Preface to Plato*. Cambridge, MA: Harvard University Press, 1963.

Hayakawa, S. I. "Learning to Think and to Write: Semantics in Freshman English." *College Composition and Communication* 13 (February 1962): 5–8.

Hazlitt, William. "On Familiar Style." *Selected Writings*: Vol. II, *Table Talk: Essays on Men and Manners*. New York: Oxford University Press, 1999.

Hemingway, Ernest. *For Whom the Bell Tolls*. New York: Charles Scribner's, 1940.

Hibbert, Liesel. "English in South Africa: Parallels with African American Vernacular English." *English Today* 18.1 (January 2002): 31–36.

Hildyard, Angela and Suzanne Hidi. "Oral-Written Differences in the Production and Recall of Narratives." In *Literacy, Language and Learning: The Nature and Consequences of Reading and Writing*. Ed. David R. Olson, Nancy Torrance, and Angela Hildyard. New York: Cambridge University Press, 1985. 307–332.

Hilgers, Thomas. "Training Composition Students in the Use of Freewriting and Problem-Solving Heuristics for Rhetorical Invention." *Research in the Teaching of English* 29 (1980): 293–307.

Hirsch, E. D. Jr. *The Philosophy of Composition*. Chicago: University of Chicago Press, 1977.

Hocks, Mary E. "Understanding Visual Rhetoric in Digital Writing Environments." *College Composition and Communication* 54.4 (June 2003): 629–656.

Hollinghurst, Allan. "Passion and Henry James." *New York Review of Books* 14 February 2008: 27–29.

Honeycutt, Lee. "Literacy and the Writing Voice: The Intersection of Culture and Technology in Dictation." *Journal of Business and Technical Communication* 18.3 (July 2004): 294–327.

Hope, Jonathan. "Rats, Bats, Sparrows, and Dogs: Biology, Linguistics and the Nature of Standard English." In *The Development of Standard English 1300–1800: Theories, Descriptions, Conflicts*. Ed. Laura Wright. Cambridge: Cambridge University Press, 2000. 49–56.

Horowitz, Rosalind and S. Jay Samuels, eds. *Comprehending Oral and Written Language*. San Diego: Academic Press, 1987.

Horowitz, Rosalind and S. Jay Samuels. "Comprehending Oral and Written Language: Critical Contrasts for Literacy and Schooling." In *Comprehending Oral and Written Language*. Ed. Rosalind Horowitz and S. Jay Samuels. San Diego: Academic Press, 1987. 1–52

Huddleston, Rodney and Geoffrey Pullum. *Cambridge Grammar of the English Language*. Cambridge: Cambridge University Press, 2003.

———. "Of Grammatophobia." *Chronicle of Higher Education* 3 January 2003. 20.

Hunt, Russ. "Speech Genres, Writing Genres." http://www.stthomasu.ca/%7Ehunt/dialogic/inkshed.htm>; http://www.stthomasu.ca/~hunt/dialogic/inkshed.htm>; ttp://www.stthomasu.ca/inkshed/.

Hurston, Zora Neale. *Their Eyes Were Watching God*. Philadelphia: J. B. Lippincott, 1937.

Illich, Ivan. "Vernacular Values." *Co-Evolution Quarterly* (Summer 1980): 1–49. http://www.preservenet.com/theory/Illich/Vernacular.html#COLUMBUS. These essays were the basis of most of Illich's book *Shadow Work*. London: Marion Boyars, 1981.

Illich, Ivan and Barry Sanders. *The Alphabetization of the Popular Mind*. New York: Random House, 1989.

Irvine, Patricia and Nan Elsasser. "The Ecology of Literacy: Negotiating Writing Standards in a Caribbean Setting." In *The Social Construction of Written Communication*. Ed. B. Rafoth and D. Rubin. Norwood, NJ: Ablex, 1988.

Jacoby, Russell. *Picture Imperfect: Utopian Thought for an Anti-Utopian Age*. New York: Columbia University Press, 2005.

James, Henry. *The Golden Bowl*. New York: Grove Press, 1959 (1904).

———. "The Question of the Opportunities." In *American Essays of Henry James*. Ed. Leon Edel. Princeton, NJ: Princeton University Press, 1956. 197–203.

Janson, Tore. *Speak: A Short History of Languages*. New York: Oxford University Press, 2002.

Johnson, Mark. *The Body in the Mind: The Bodily Basis of Meaning, Imagination, and Reason*. Chicago: University of Chicago Press, 1987.

Johnstone, Barbara. *The Linguistic Individual: Self-Expression in Language and Linguistics*. New York: Oxford University Press, 1996.

Joos, Martin. *The Five Clocks: A Linguistic Excursion into the Five Styles of English Usage*. New York: Harcourt, 1961.

Kachru, Braj. *The Other Tongue: English Across Cultures*. Urbana: Illinois University Press. 1992.

Kachru, Yamuna and Cecil L. Nelson. *Asian Englishes Today: World Englishes in Asian Contexts*. Hong Kong: Hong Kong University Press, 2006.

Kalmar, Tomás Mario. *Illegal Alphabets and Adult Biliteracy: Latino Migrants Crossing the Linguistic Border*. Mahwah, NJ: Erlbaum, 2001.

Kanellos, Nicolas, ed. *Herencia: The Anthology of Hispanic Literature of the United States*. New York: Oxford University Press, 2002.

Katz, Steven B. "Letter as Essence: The Rhetorical (Im)Pulse of the Hebrew Alefbet." *Journal of Communication and Rhetoric* 26 (2003): 125–160.

Keene, Michael L. and Katherine H. Adams. *Easy Access: The Reference Handbook for Writers*. 3rd ed. New York: McGraw-Hill, 2002 (1996).

Kells, Michelle Hall. "Linguistic Contact Zones in the College Writing Classroom: An Examination of Ethnolinguistic Identity and Language Attitudes." *Written Communication* 19.1 (2002): 5–43.

Kelman, James. *How Late It Was, How Late*. New York: Vintage, 1998.

Kermode, Frank. "The Lives of Dr. Johnson." *New York Review of Books* 22 June 2006: 28–31.

Klima, E. and U. Bellugi. *The Signs of Language*. Cambridge, MA: Harvard University Press, 1979.

Kolln, Martha. *Rhetorical Grammar: Grammatical Choices, Rhetorical Effects*. New York: Macmillan, 1991.

Kono, Juliet. "A Scolding from My Father." *Tsunami Years*. Honolulu, HI: Bamboo Ridge Press, 1995.

Kress, Gunther. *Before Writing: Rethinking the Paths to Literacy*. New York: Routledge, 1997.

———. *Early Spelling: Between Convention and Creativity*. New York: Routledge, 2000.

Krugman, Paul. "Who Was Milton Friedman?" *New York Review of Books* 15 February 2007: 27–30.

Labov, William. *Language in the Inner City: Studies in the Black English Vernacular*. Philadelphia: University of Philadelphia Press, 1972.

Lakoff, Robin Tolmach. "Some of My Favorite Writers Are Literate: The Mingling of Oral and Literate Strategies in Written Communication." In *Spoken and Written Language: Exploring Orality and Literacy*. Ed. Deborah Tannen. Norwood, NJ: Ablex, 1982. 239–260.

Lakoff, George and Mark Johnson. *Metaphors We Live By*. Chicago: University of Chicago Press, 1980.

Lambert, Craig. "Poetic Patriarch." *Harvard Alumni Magazine* (November–December 2008): 36–93.

Lamott, Anne. *Bird by Bird: Some Instructions on Writing and Life*. New York: Anchor, 1994.

Lanham, Richard. *Revising Prose*. New York: MacMillan, 1987.

———. *Style: An Anti-Textbook*. New Haven: Yale University Press. 1974.

Leaf, Jonathan. "Notes on the Novel" *New Partisan: A Journal of Culture, Arts and Politics* (28 June 2004). http://www.newpartisan.com/home/notes-on-the-novel.html (accessed 25 October 2007).

Lepore, Jill. *A Is for American: Letters and Other Characters in the Newly United States*. New York: Vintage, 2002.

———. "The Creed: What Poor Richard Cost Benjamin Franklin." *New Yorker* 28 January 2008: 78–83.

Levinson, Joan Persily. *Punctuation and the Orthographic Sentence*. Dissertation. City University of New York, 1985.

Levy, Andrea. *Small Island*. New York: Picador, 2010.

Lewis and Clark. http://lewisandclarkjournals.unl.edu/index.html (accessed 22 February 2010).

Lincoln, Abraham. Speech delivered 6 March 1860. *Collected Works of Abraham Lincoln*. Ed. Roy Basler. New Brunswick: Rutgers University Press, 1953.

Lodge, David. *Author, Author*. New York: Viking, 2004.

MacFarquhar, Larissa. "The Deflationist: How Paul Krugman Found Politics." *New Yorker* 1 March 2010: 38–49.

Macrorie, Ken. "The Freewriting Relationship." In *Nothing Begins with N: New Explorations of Freewriting*. Ed. Pat Belanoff, Peter Elbow, and Sheryl Fontaine. Carbondale: Southern Illinois University Press, 1990. 173–188.

———. *Telling Writing*. 4th ed. Portsmouth, NH: Heinemann, 1985.

———. "Words in the Way." *English Journal* 40 (1951): 3–8.

———. *Writing to Be Read*. 3rd ed. Portsmouth, NH: Heinemann, 1986.

Madsen, Catherine. *The Bones Reassemble: Reconstituting Liturgical Speech*. Aurora, CO: Davies Group, 2005.

Maher, Jane. *Mina P. Shaughnessy: Her Life and Work*. Urbana, IL: National Council of Teachers of English,1997.

Mallon, Thomas. *A Book of One's Own: People and Their Diaries*. New York: Ticknor and Fields, 1984.

———. "Transfigured." *New Yorker* 5 April 2010: 68–73.

Mantel, Hilary. "Voices in the Dark." Review of *Women Writing Africa: The Southern Region*. *New York Review of Books* 10 February 2005: 28–29.

Matsushima, Tracy. "Students Document Disappearing Languages." *Malamalama: The Magazine of the University of Hawai'i*. http://www.hawaii.edu/malamalama/2010/10/documenting-disappearing-languages/ (accessed 11 October 2010).

McConnell-Ginet, Sally. "Intonation in a Man's World." *Sign* (Spring 1978): 542–559.

McCrum, Robert. "English Is Destined to Die Out, Eventually." *Guardian. Learning English* Supplement (12 November 2010): 6.

McGinn, Colin. "Looking for a Black Swan." Review of several books about Karl Popper and Ludwig Wittgenstein. *New York Review of Books* 21 November 2002: 46–50.

McWhorter, John. *Doing Our Own Thing: The Degradation of Language and Music and Why We Should, Like, Care*. New York: Gotham, 2003.

———. "Pidgins and Creoles as Models of Language Change: The State of the Art." *Annual Review of Applied Linguistics: Language Contact and Change* 23 (2003): 202–209.

Menand, Louis. "Bad Comma: Lynne Truss's Strange Grammar." *New Yorker* 28 June 2004:102–104.

———. "Breaking Away." Review of *America at the Crossroads* by Francis Fukuyama. *New Yorker* 27 March 2006: 82–84.

———. "Saved from Drowning." *New Yorker* 23 February 2009: 68–76.

Menocal, Maria Rosa. *The Ornament of the World: How Muslims, Jews and Christians Created a Culture of Tolerance in Medieval Spain*. Boston: Little, Brown, 2002.

———. *Shards of Love: Exile and the Origins of the Lyric*. Durham, NC: Duke University Press, 1994.

Micciche, Laura. "Making a Case for Rhetorical Grammar." *College Composition and Communication* 55.4 (2004): 716–737.

Michaels, Sarah and James Collins. "Oral Discourse Styles: Classroom Interaction and the Acquisition of Literacy." In *Coherence in Spoken and Written Discourse*, Vol. 12. Ed. Deborah Tannen. Norwood, NJ: Ablex, 1984. 219–243.

Miller, Thomas. *The Formation of College English: Rhetoric and Belles Lettres in the British Cultural Provinces*. Pittsburgh: University of Pittsburgh Press, 1997.

Milroy, Jim. "Historical Description and the Ideology of the Standard Language." In *The Development of Standard English 1300–1800: Theories, Descriptions, Conflicts*. Ed. Laura Wright. New York: Cambridge University Press, 2000. 11–28.

Momaday, N. Scott. "Personal Reflections." In *The American Indian and the Problem of History*. Ed. Calvin Martin. New York: Oxford University Press, 1984. 156–161.

Mullan, John. *Anonymity*. London: Faber, 2008.

National Geographic. "Beyond the Brain." March 2005: 2–31.

Nebrija. http://www.antoniodenebrija.org/indice.html.

Nero, Shondel J., ed. *Dialects, Englishes, Creoles, and Education*. Mahwah, NJ: Erlbaum, 2006. x–xv.

New London Group. "A Pedagogy of Multiliteracies: Designing Social Futures." *Harvard Educational Review* 66.1 (Spring 1996): 60–93.

Nordquist, Richard. *A Brief History of Punctuation: Where Do the Marks of Punctuation Come From and Who Made Up the Rules?* About.com Guide. http://grammar.about.com/od/punctuationandmechanics/a/PunctuationHistory.htm (accessed 20 October 2010).

Nussbaum, Martha. "Feminists and Philosophy." Review of *A Mind of One's Own: Feminist Essays on Reason and Objectivity*. *New York Review of Books* 20 October 1994: 59–63.

Ochs, Elinor. "Planned and Unplanned Discourse." In *Syntax and Semantics*. Vol. 12: *Discourse and Syntax*. Ed. Talmy Givon. New York: Academic Press, 1979. 51–80.

O'Connor. Patricia T. *Woe Is I: The Grammarphobe's Guide to Better English in Plain English*. New York: Penguin Group, 2004.

Oesterreicher, Wulf. "Types of Orality in Text." In *Written Voices, Spoken Signs: Tradition, Performance, and the Epic Text*. Ed. Egbert Bakker and Ahuvia Kahane. Harvard University Press, 1997. 190–214.

O'Hare, Frank. *Sentence Combining: Improving Student Writing without Formal Grammar Instruction*. Urbana, IL: National Council of Teachers of English,1971.

Olivo, Warren. "Phat Lines: Spelling Conventions in Rap Music." *Written Language and Literacy* 4.1 (2001): 67–85.

Ong, Walter. *Orality and Literacy: The Technologizing of the Word*. New York: Methuen, 1982.

Olson, David. "From Utterance to Text: The Bias of Language in Speech and Writing." *Harvard Educational Review* 47.3 (1977): 257–281.

———. "Orality and Literacy: A Symposium in Honor of David Olson." *Research in the Teaching of English* 41.2 (November 2006): 136–179.

———. *The World on Paper: The Conceptual and Cognitive Implications of Writing and Reading*. New York: Cambridge University Press, 1994.

Olson, David R., Nancy Torrance, and Angela Hildyard, eds. *Literacy, Language, and Learning: The Nature and Consequences of Reading and Writing*. New York: Cambridge University Press, 1985.

Ostler, Nicholas. *The Last Lingua Franca: English Until the Return of Babel*. New York: Walker, 2010.

Oxford University Press. *New Hart's Rules: The Handbook of Style for Writers and Editors*. Oxford/New York: Oxford University Press, 2005. (Adapted from the *Oxford Guide to Style*. R. M. Ritter).

Palacas, Arthur. "Liberating American Ebonics from Euro-English." *College English* 63.3 (January 2001): 326–352.

———. "Parentheticals and Personal Voice." *Written Communication* 6.4 (1989): 506–527.

———. "Saying Yes to Linguistic-Cultural Minorities in Affirmative Action and Open Enrollment Colleges and Universities: Educating the University." Presentation at the annual Conference on Composition and Communication, San Antonio, March 2004.

The Panoplist, 1.8 (January 1806): 368.

Paranto, Michelle Lynne. "Writing and Transformation in College Composition" (1 January 2005). Electronic Doctoral Dissertations for UMass Amherst. Paper AAI3179914. http://scholarworks.umass.edu/dissertations/AAI3179914.

Parkes, Malcolm B. *Pause and Effect: An Introduction to the History of Punctuation in the West*. Berkeley: University of California Press, 1993.

Percy, Walker. "Metaphor as Mistake." *Sewanee Review* 64 (Winter 1958): 79–99. Reprinted in *The Message in the Bottle*. New York: Farrar, Straus and Giroux, 1975.

Perl, Sondra. *Felt Sense: Writing with the Body*. Portsmouth, NH: Heinemann, 2004.

Perry, Theresa and Lisa Delpit. *The Real Ebonics Debate: Power, Language, and the Education of African-American Children*. Boston, MA: Beacon, 1998.

Phillipson, Robert. *Linguistic Imperialism*. New York: Oxford University Press, 1992.

Pinker, Steven. *The Language Instinct: How the Mind Creates Language*. New York: HarperCollins, 2000.

Pinker, Steven. *The Stuff of Thought: Language as a Window into Human Nature*. New York: Viking, 2007.

Plane, Sylvie. "The Materiality and Temporality of Writing: The Role of the Medium in Literary Writing." *Genre: Forms of Discourse and Culture* (2009).

Ponsot, Marie and Rosemary Deen. *Beat Not the Poor Desk: Writing: What to Teach, How to Teach It and Why*. Montclair, NJ: Boynton/Cook Press, 1982.

Poyatos, Fernando. "Punctuation as Nonverbal Communication: Toward an Interdisciplinary Approach to Writing." *Semiotica* 34. 1/2 (1981): 91–112.

Powers, Richard. *New York Times Book Review* 7 January 2007. http://www.nytimes.com/2007/01/07/books/review/Powers2.t.html?pagewanted=2&_r=1 (accessed 4 November 2010).

Pratt, Mary Louise. "Linguistic Utopias." In *The Linguistics of Writing*. Ed. Nigel Fabb et al. Manchester: Manchester University Press, 1987. 48–66.

Pritchard, William. *On Poets and Poetry*. Columbus: Swallow Press and Ohio University Press, 2009.

Ray, Katie Wood. "When Kids Make Books." *Educational Leadership* 62.2 (October 2004): 14–18.

———. *Wondrous Words: Writers and Writing in the Elementary Classroom*. Urbana, IL: National Council of Teachers of English,1999.

Ray, Katie Wood, with L. Cleaveland. *About the Authors: Writing Workshop with Our Youngest Writers*. Portsmouth, NH: Heinemann, 2004.

Redd, Teresa M. and Karen Schuster Webb. *A Teacher's Introduction to African American English: What a Writing Teacher Should Know*. Urbana, IL: National Council of Teachers of English, 2005.

Remnick, David. "The Translation Wars." *New Yorker* 7 November 2005: 98–109.

Reviewer, "Richard II with Mr. Kean." *Guardian Weekly* (archive) 3 August 2010: 22.

Richardson, Elaine. "African American Language in Online German Hip-Hop." In *Code-Meshing as World English: Pedagogy, Policy, Performance*. Ed. Vershawn Ashanti Young and Aja Y. Martinez. Urbana, IL: National Council of Teachers of English, 2011. 231–256.

Richardson, Robert D. *First We Read, Then We Write: Emerson on the Creative Process*. Ames: University of Iowa Press, 2009.

Rico, Gabriel. *Creating Re-creations: Inspiration from the Source*. 2nd ed. Spring, TX: Absey, 2002.

———. *Writing the Natural Way*. 2nd ed. New York: Penguin, 2000.

Roberts, Sam. "Big Birthday for a Powerful Little Book." *New York Times* 22 April 2009: C3.

Robinson, Andrew. *The Story of Writing: Alphabets, Hieroglyphs, and Pictograms*. London: Thames and Hudson, 1995.

Roeper, Tom. *The Prism of Grammar: How Child Language Illuminates Humanism*. Cambridge MA: MIT Press, 2007.

Rombauer, Irma S. and Marion Rombauer Becker. *The Joy of Cooking*. Indianapolis, IN: Bobbs Merrill, 1972.

Rosaldo, Renato. *Hybrid Cultures: Strategies for Entering and Leaving Modernity*. Co-author with Canclini Nestor Garcia, Silvia Lopez, Silvia L. Lopez. Trans. Christopher L. Chiappari. Minneapolis: University of Minnesota Press, 1995.

Rosen, Charles. "From the Troubadours to Frank Sinatra." Review of *The Oxford History of Western Music. New York Review of Books* 9 March 2006: 41–45.

Rosenberg, Lauren. *Rewriting Ideologies of Literacy: A Study of Writing by Newly Literate Adults*. Electronic Doctoral Dissertations for UMass Amherst. Paper AAI3242113. http://scholarworks.umass.edu/dissertations/AAI3242113.

Russell, Bertrand. "How I Write." http://www.threads.name/russell/write.html (accessed 15 October 2006).

Saarbrücken Corpus. http://www.uni-saarland.de/fak4/norrick/scose.html (accessed 9 May 2004).

Saenger, Paul. "The History of Reading." In *Literacy: An International Handbook*. Ed. Daniel A. Wagner, Richard L. Venezky, and Brian Street. Boulder, CO: Westview Press, 1999. 11–15.

———. *Space between Words: The Origins of Silent Reading*. Stanford, CA: Stanford University Press, 1997.

Safire, William. "On Language: Need Not to Know." *New York Times Magazine* February 1999: 18–19. Section 621.

Sakoda, Kent and Jeff Siegel. *Pidgin Grammar: An Introduction to the Creole Language of Hawai'i*. Honolulu: Bess Press, 2003.

Sapphire. *Push: A Novel*. New York: Knopf, 1996.

Sato, Charlene. "Language Change in a Creole Continuum: Decreolization?" In *Progression and Regression in Language: Sociocultural, Neuropsychological and Linguistic Perspectives*. Ed. Kenneth Hyltenstam and Ake Viberg. New York: Cambridge University Press. 122–143.

Scardamalia, Marlene and Carl Bereiter. "Development of Dialectical Processes in Composition." In *Literacy, Language, and Learning: The Nature and Consequences of Reading and Writing*. Ed. David R. Olson, Nancy Torrance, and Angela Hildyard. New York: Cambridge University Press, 1985. 307–331.

Schleppegrell, Mary J. "Grammar, the Sentence, and Traditions of Linguistic Analysis." In *Handbook of Research on Writing: History, Society, School, Individual, Text*. Ed. Charles Bazerman. Mahwah, NJ: Erlbaum, 2007. 549–564.

Schmandt-Besserat, Denise and Michael Erard. "Origins and Forms of Writing." In *Handbook of Research on Writing: History, Society, School, Individual, Text*. Ed. Charles Bazerman. Mahwah, NJ: Erlbaum, 2007. 7–22.

Schneider, Pat. *Writing Alone and with Others*. New York: Oxford University Press, 2003.

Schultz, John. *Writing from Start to Finish*. Montclair, NJ: Boynton/Cook, 1982.

Scholes, Robert J. and Brenda J. Willis. "Prosodic and Syntactic Functions of Punctuation: A Contribution to the Study of Orality and Literacy." *Interchange* 21.3 (Fall 1990): 13–20.

Scollon, Ron. "Language, Literacy, and Learning: An Annotated Bibliography." In *Literacy, Language and Learning: The Nature and Consequences of Reading and Writing*. Ed. David R. Olson, Nancy Torrance, and Angela Hildyard. New York: Cambridge University Press, 1985. 412–426.

Scribner, Sylvia. "Modes of Thinking and Ways of Speaking: Culture and Logic Reconsidered." In *New Directions in Discourse Processing*. Ed. Roy O. Freele. Norwood, NJ: Ablex, 1979.

Selfe, Cynthia. "The Movement of Air, the Breath of Meaning: Aurality and Multimodal Composing." *College Composition and Communication* 60:4 (June 2009): 616–663.

Severino, Carol. "English Contact Languages and Rhetorics: Implications for U.S. English Composition. Review Essay." *College Composition and Communication* 59:1 (September 2007): 128–138.

Shaughnessy, Mina. "Basic Writing." Talk at Modern Literature Conference, Michigan State University, 1977. Reprinted in Maher, Jane. *Mina P. Shaughnessy: Her Life and Work*. Urbana, IL: National Council of Teachers of English,1997. 299–310.

———. *Errors and Expectations: A Guide for the Teacher of Basic Writing*. New York: Oxford University Press, 1977.

Shell, Marc. "Hyphens: Between Deitsch and American." In *The Multilingual Anthology of American Literature: A Reader of Original Texts with English Translations*. Ed. Marc Shell and Werner Sollors. New York: New York University Press, 2000. 258–271.

Shell, Marc and Werner Sollors, eds. *The Multilingual Anthology of American Literature: A Reader of Original Texts with English Translations*. New York: New York University Press, 2000.

Sheridan, Susan Rich. "A Theory of Marks and Mind: The Effect of Notational Systems on Hominid Brain Evolution and Child Development with an Emphasis on Exchanges between Mothers and Children." 2006. http://www.marksandmind.org/scribbs.html. (accessed 10 October 2009).

Slaughter, Joseph R. "Enabling Fictions and Novel Subjects: The Bildungsroman and International Human Rights Law." *PMLA* 121.5 (October 2006): 1405–1423.

Smith, Frank. *Joining the Literacy Club: Further Essays into Education*. Portsmouth, NH: Heinemann, 1987.

Smitherman, Geneva. "'The Blacker the Berry, the Sweeter the Juice': African American Student Writers." In *The Need for Story: Cultural Diversity in the Classroom and Community*. Ed. Anne Haas Dyson and Celia Genishi. Urbana, IL: National Council of Teachers of English,1994. 80–101.

———. "Black English/Ebonics: What It Be Like?" In *The Real Ebonics Debate: Power, Language, and the Education of African-American Children*. Ed. Theresa Perry and Lisa Delpit. Boston, MA: Beacon, 1998. 29–37.

———. "Columns." *talkin that talk: Language, Culture and Education in African America*. New York: Routledge, 2000. 339–374.

———. *Talkin and Testifyin: The Language of Black America*. Detroit: Wayne State University Press, 1986.

Sollors, Werner, ed. *Multilingual America: Transnationalism, Ethnicity, and the Languages of American Literature*. New York: New York University Press, 1998.

Spenard, Corinna. "The Sun Room." *Flying Horse* 1.1 (1996): 91.

Stafford, William. *Writing the Australian Crawl: Views on the Writer's Vocation*. Ann Arbor: University of Michigan Press, 1978.

Steiner, George. *After Babel: Aspects of Language and Translation*. New York: Oxford University Press, 1975.

Street, Brian. "The Limits of the Local—'Autonomous' or 'Disembedding'?" Paper distributed at University of Massachusetts Symposium on Speech and Writing, June 2003.

———. "New Literacies, New Times: How Do We Describe and Teach the Forms of Literacy Knowledge, Skills and Values People Need for New Times?" In *55th Yearbook of the National Reading Conference*. Ed. J. Hoffman and D. Schallert. Oak Creek, WI: NRC, 2006. 21–42.

Strunk, William Jr. and E. B. White. *The Elements of Style*. New York: Macmillan, 1959.

Summers, J. Frank. *Wholly, Holey, Holy: An Adult American Spelling Book*. Houston, TX: Word Lab, 1984.

Sutherland, John. "Legacy of Lady Chatterley's Emancipation." *Guardian Weekly* 19 November 2010: 33.

Talbot, Margaret. "The Baby Lab." *New Yorker* 4 September 2006: 90–101.

Tannen, Deborah. "Oral and Literate Strategies in Spoken and Written Narratives." *Language* 58 (1982): 1–21.

———. "Relative Focus on Involvement in Oral and Written Discourse." In *Literacy, Language, and Learning: The Nature and Consequences of Reading and Writing*. Ed. David R. Olson, Nancy Torrance, and Angela Hildyard. New York: Cambridge University Press, 1985. 125–147.

———. "Spoken/Written Language and the Oral/Literate Continuum." *Proceedings of the Sixth Annual Meeting of the Berkeley Linguistic Society*. Ed. E. B. Caron et al. Berkeley: Linguistic Society, 1980. 207–818.

———. "Spoken and Written Narrative in English and Greek." In *Coherence in Spoken and Written Discourse*. Ed. Deborah Tannen. Norwood, NJ: Ablex, 1984. 21–41.

Taylor, Insup. "The Korean Writing System: An Alphabet? A Syllabary? A Logography?" *Processing of Visual Language* 2: 73. New York: Plenum Press, 1980.

Taylor, Irene and Alan Taylor. *The Assassin's Cloak: An Anthology of the World's Greatest Diarists*. Edinburgh: Canongate, 2002.

Tebeaux, E. "Keeping a Technical Writing Relevant (Or, How to Become a Dictator)." *College English* 45 (1983): 174–183.

Thomas, Rosalind. *Literacy and Orality in Ancient Greece*. London: Cambridge University Press, 1992.

Tompkins, Jane. "Me and My Shadow." *New Literary History* 19.1 (Autumn 1987): 169–178.

Tore, Jansen. *Speak: A Short History of Languages*. Oxford, UK: Oxford University Press, 2002.

Trimbur, John. *The Call to Write*. New York: Longman, 1999.

———. "Linguistic Memory and the Politics of US English." *College English* 68.6 (July 2006): 575–588.

Troyka, Lynn Quitman. *Quick Access: Reference for Writers*. 2nd ed. Upper Saddle River, NJ: Prentice Hall,1998.

Truss, Lynne. *Eats, Shoots and Leaves*. New York: Gotham Books, 2004.

Ueland, Brenda. *If You Want to Write: A Book about Art, Independence and Spirit*. St. Paul, MN: Graywolf Press, 1987 (1938).

Updike, John. "The Blessed Man of Boston, My Grandmother's Thimble, and Fanning Island." *Pigeon Feathers and Other Stories*. New York: Crest Books, Knopf, 1962. 156–167.

———. "Brother Grasshopper." *New Yorker* 14 December 1987. http://www.newyorker.com/archive/1987/12/14/1987_12_14_040_TNY_CARDS_000346684 (accessed 4 November 2006). Reprinted in *The Afterlife and Other Stories*. New York: Knopf, 1995.

Vygotsky, Lev. *Thought and Language.* Trans. Eugenia Hanfman and Gertude Vakar. Cambridge, MA: MIT Press, 1962.

Wagner, Julia Ellen. *The Letter that Gives Life: Magic, Writing, and the Teaching of Writing.* Electronic Doctoral Dissertations for UMass Amherst. Paper AAI3056285. 2002. http://scholarworks.umass.edu/dissertations/AAI3056285.

Walker, Alice. *The Color Purple.* New York: Harcourt Brace, 1982.

Weil, Simone. "Reflections on the Right Use of School Studies with a View to the Love of God." *Waiting for God.* New York: Harper, 2009 (1951).

Welty, Eudora. *One Writer's Beginnings.* Cambridge, MA: Harvard University Press, 1984.

White, Edmund. "The Panorama of Ford Madox Ford." *New York Review of Books* 24 March 2011: 29–32.

Williams, Joseph. "The Phenomenology of Error." *College Composition and Communication* 32 (1981): 152–168.

———. *Style: Ten Lessons in Clarity and Grace.* 7th ed. New York: Longman, 2003.

Williams, William Carlos. "How to Write." In *New Directions in Prose and Poetry.* Ed. James Laughlin. New York: New Directions, 1936. 45, 47. Also in William Carlos Williams. "How to Write." In *New Directions Fiftieth Anniversary Issue.* Ed. James Laughlin. New York: New Directions, 1986. 36–39.

Winnicott, D. W. *The Child, the Family, and the Outside World.* Cambridge, MA: Da Capo Press, 1992.

Wolf, Robert. *An American Mosaic.* New York: Oxford University Press, 1999.

———. *Jump Start: How to Write from Everyday Life.* New York: Oxford University Press. 2001

Wolfram, Walt, Carolyn Adger, and Donna Christian. *Dialects in Schools and Communities.* Mahwah, NJ: Erlbaum, 1999.

Wolfram, Walt and Natalie Schilling-Estes. *American English: Dialects and Variation*: Malden, MA: Blackwell, 1998.

Wood, David E. "Modeling the Relationship between Oral Reading Fluency and Performance on a Statewide Reading Test." *Educational Assessment* 11.2 (2006): 85–104.

Wood, James. "Say What?" *New Yorker* 7 April 2008: 79–81.

Wright, Laura, ed. *The Development of Standard English 1300–1800: Theories, Descriptions, Conflicts.* New York: Cambridge University Press, 2000.

Wright, Roger. "Latin and English as World Languages." *English Today: The International Review of the English Language* 20.4 (October 2004): 3–13.

The Write Place: Writing and Grammar Resources. "Example of Freewriting." http://www.alamo.edu/sac/english/lirvin/wguides/arguebrainst.htm (accessed 11 November 2010).

Young, Vershawn Ashanti. "'Nah, We Straight': An Argument against Code Switching." *JAC* 29. 1–2 (2009): 49–76.

Young, Vershawn Ashanti and Aja Y. Martinez. *Code-Meshing as World English: Pedagogy, Policy, Performance.* Urbana, IL: National Council of Teachers of English, 2011.

Youssef, Valerie. "'Is English We Speaking': Trinbagonian in the Twenty-first Century." *English Today* 20 4 (October 2004): 42–49.

Yun, Wei and Fei Jia. "Using English in China: From Chinese Pidgin English through Chinglish to Chinese English and China English." *English Today* 19.4 (October 2003): 42–47.

Zalewski, Daniel. "The Background Hum: Ian McEwan's Art of Unease." *New Yorker* 23 February 2009: 47–61.

Index

Chinese writing (character system)
  development of, 35
  difficulty mastering, 76, 337
  homophones in, 339
  illustration of, 37
  independence from spoken language, 39, 64, 320
  Korean use of, 196
  meanings of characters, 36
  pinyin, 338–39, 371
  pride in, 39, 338–39
  role of rebus in, 74
  standardization of, 371
  Vietnamese use of, 316
Chomsky, Noam, 35, 59
Christensen, Francis, 85–87, 99, 286, 292–93, 294, 314
Christensen, Linda, 352, 383
Christian, Donna, 215, 216, 330, 346, 363
Churchill, Winston, 248, 355
Cicero, 280
Clark, Romy, 259, 275
clauses, 293–94
  See also punctuation, good enough
clichés, 119
Clinton, Hillary, 65
COCA (Corpus of Contemporary American English), 26
code meshing, 253, 330–32
code switching, 330–31
coherence
  in everyday speech, 60
  in freewriting, 153
  in speech as a product, 93–98
  in spoken vs. written language, 77–78, 97–100, 115
  See also organization in writing
collage process in writing, 202–04, 207
Colomb, Gregory G., 176
commas
  hearing in speech (comma intonation), 245–46, 279–80
  in series, 291–92
  between subject and verb, 288–89
  See also punctuation, good enough
Comprehensive Grammar of the English Language, 269
Connors, Robert, 346
  "cooperative principle" in discourse, 95
  See also given-new pattern
coordinate adjectives, 292
  See also punctuation, good enough
correct speech, 27
  See also speech

correct writing
  as no one's mother tongue, 3, 4, 126, 130, 173, 345, 359
  See also culture of literacy; Edited Written English (EWE); expository writing
Coulmas, Florian, 36, 236
Crane, R.S., 174
Crawford, Lindy, 239
creative writing. *See* literary writing
creole languages, 62–63
  See also stigmatized languages
Crystal, David, 109, 117, 194, 217, 267, 330
Csikszentmihalyi, Mihaly, 72, 175, 176, 310
culture
  speaking inflected by, 21–27, 29–32
  writing inflected by, 27–29, 32–34
  See also culture of literacy; culture of vernacular literacy
culture of literacy
  as exclusionary club, 3, 6–7, 27, 128–29, 196, 232, 256, 274, 343
  and illiteracy, 27, 28
  "orality/literacy wars," 19
  overvaluation of, 344–45, 348–53
  poor writing in, 256
  and propriety anxiety in speech, 354–57
  and propriety anxiety in writing, 353–54
  rejection of spoken language in, 6–7, 359, 363
  resistance to propriety, 357–59
  standards of correctness in, 3, 5, 128–29, 363–64
  student writing in, 346–47
  See also academic writing; correct writing; culture of vernacular literacy
culture of vernacular literacy
  grammar in, 388
  idealism vs. realism in, 124–31
  Internet as Wild West, 380–82
  liberation from exclusionary standards, 128–30, 382–89
  long view, 389–90
  path toward, 7, 8, 10, 11, 131–35, 347–48, 372, 376–80
  punctuation, 388
  as real writing, 126
  spelling in, 387–88
  style, 386–87
  surface features, 387
cumulative adjectives, 292
  See also punctuation, good enough

speech vs. writing (*continued*)
  physical activities involved in, 13–14, 19, 139
  physical modalities or media for, 14, 19, 139
  privacy in, 50–52
  as social or contextual processes, 140
  temporal dimensions of, 299–302
  usefulness in unburdening oneself, 72
  vocalities of, 45–46
spelling, 321–22, 387–88
Spenard, Corinna, 158
spoken language
  attempts to standardize, 364–68, 371–72
  corpuses of, 26, 27
  general prejudice against in literate culture, 77–78
  See also specific languages; speech
Stafford, William, 81
Standard Spoken English, 215–16
Standard Written English (SWE), 135–37, 214–15
  See also correct writing
Steiner, George, 65, 368
"stereotypical writing," 16
  See also correct writing
Sterne, Laurence, 71
Stevens, Wallace, 182
Stieber, Steve, 239
stigmatized languages
  advantages of speaking onto the page, 328–36
  in new culture of vernacular literacy, 378–80
  reading aloud to revise, 336
  writing in, 328, 329, 353
  See also African American Language (AAL)
Street, Brian, 16, 28, 49–50, 344
Strunk, William, Jr., 251
student writing, 69, 133–35, 172, 346–47
  See also expository writing
stuttering, 22
  See also speech
Style: Ten Lessons in Clarity and Grace (Williams), 232, 233–35
Sumerians, 57
Summer, Frank, 322
Swift, Jonathan, 192
syllabaries
  Cherokee, 39, 235–36
  Minoan, 235
syllabic system

characteristics of, 36
  illustration, 37
  practicality of, 39
  See also Japanese language
symbols for writing
  alphabetic, 35–36
  logographic, 36
  syllabic, 36
syntax
  flexibility in freewriting, 153
  flexibility when speaking, 80–82, 153
  invention of, 56
  parataxis vs. hypotaxis, 88–90
  right- and left-branching, 85–88, 99, 314
systems for writing. *See* alphabetic system; Chinese writing (character system); syllabic system

talking. *See* speaking
Tannen, Deborah, 16, 17, 68, 78, 79, 80, 142
Taylor, Insup, 197
technology
  impact on literacy, 49–50
  See also Internet
Terkel, Studs, 133
that/which rule, 271–74, 276–77, 284
  See also punctuation, good enough
Tindal, Gerald, 239
Tolstoy, Leo, 180, 230
Tompkins, Jane, 79
Trimbur, John, 247, 350, 366, 374
Trollope, Anthony, 174, 202
Truss, Lynn, 268
  See also *Eats, Shoots & Leaves* (Truss)
Twain, Mark
  dictations by, 176–77, 178
  on Hawaiian language, 297
  use of vernacular dialects, 132
  on writing, 203
tweeting, 66, 91
typical speech, 15
  See also unplanned speech
typical writing, 15
  See also writing

Ueland, Brenda, 149
Universal Grammar, 59
unplanned speech
  coherence in, 60
  ease and informality of, 15, 18, 226
  given-new pattern in, 93–95, 225
  grammaticality of, 60, 280